Technological Innovations in Knowledge Management and Decision Support

Nilanjan Dey
Techno India College of Technology, India

A volume in the Advances in Knowledge Acquisition, Transfer, and Management (AKATM) Book Series

IGI Global
DISSEMINATOR OF KNOWLEDGE

Published in the United States of America by
IGI Global
Information Science Reference (an imprint of IGI Global)
701 E. Chocolate Avenue
Hershey PA, USA 17033
Tel: 717-533-8845
Fax: 717-533-8661
E-mail: cust@igi-global.com
Web site: http://www.igi-global.com

Library of Congress Cataloging-in-Publication Data

Names: Dey, Nilanjan, 1984- editor.
Title: Technological innovations in knowledge management and decision support / Nilanjan Dey, editor.
Description: Hershey, PA : Information Science Reference, [2019] | Includes bibliographical references.
Identifiers: LCCN 2018002492| ISBN 9781522561644 (hardcover) | ISBN 9781522561651 (ebook)
Subjects: LCSH: Decision support systems. | Knowledge management.
Classification: LCC T58.62 .T453 2019 | DDC 658.4/038--dc23 LC record available at https://lccn.loc.gov/2018002492

This book is published in the IGI Global book series Advances in Knowledge Acquisition, Transfer, and Management (AKATM) (ISSN: 2326-7607; eISSN: 2326-7615)

British Cataloguing in Publication Data
A Cataloguing in Publication record for this book is available from the British Library.

Advances in Knowledge Acquisition, Transfer, and Management (AKATM) Book Series

Murray E. Jennex
San Diego State University, USA

ISSN:2326-7607
EISSN:2326-7615

Mission

Organizations and businesses continue to utilize knowledge management practices in order to streamline processes and procedures. The emergence of web technologies has provided new methods of information usage and knowledge sharing.

The **Advances in Knowledge Acquisition, Transfer, and Management (AKATM) Book Series** brings together research on emerging technologies and their effect on information systems as well as the knowledge society.**AKATM** will provide researchers, students, practitioners, and industry leaders with research highlights surrounding the knowledge management discipline, including technology support issues and knowledge representation.

Coverage

- Cognitive Theories
- Cultural Impacts
- Information and Communication Systems
- Knowledge acquisition and transfer processes
- Knowledge management strategy
- Knowledge Sharing
- Organizational Learning
- Organizational Memory
- Small and Medium Enterprises
- Virtual communities

IGI Global is currently accepting manuscripts for publication within this series. To submit a proposal for a volume in this series, please contact our Acquisition Editors at Acquisitions@igi-global.com or visit: http://www.igi-global.com/publish/.

The Advances in Knowledge Acquisition, Transfer, and Management (AKATM) Book Series (ISSN 2326-7607) is published by IGI Global, 701 E. Chocolate Avenue, Hershey, PA 17033-1240, USA, www.igi-global.com. This series is composed of titles available for purchase individually; each title is edited to be contextually exclusive from any other title within the series. For pricing and ordering information please visit http://www.igi-global.com/book-series/advances-knowledge-acquisition-transfer-management/37159. Postmaster: Send all address changes to above address.

Titles in this Series

For a list of additional titles in this series, please visit: www.igi-global.com/book-series

Enhancing Knowledge Discovery and Innovation in the Digital Era
Miltiadis D. Lytras (The American College of Greece, Greece) Linda Daniela (University of Latvia, Latvia) and Anna Visvizi (The American College of Greece, Greece)
Information Science Reference • copyright 2018 • 363pp • H/C (ISBN: 9781522541912) • US $215.00 (our price)

N-ary Relations for Logical Analysis of Data and Knowledge
Boris Kulik (Russian Academy of Science, Russia) and Alexander Fridman (Russian Academy of Science, Russia)
Information Science Reference • copyright 2018 • 297pp • H/C (ISBN: 9781522527824) • US $225.00 (our price)

Radical Reorganization of Existing Work Structures Through Digitalization
Punita Duhan (Meera Bai Institute of Technology, India) Komal Singh (Meera Bai Institute of Technology, India) and Rahul Verma (Bhai Parmanand Institute of Business Studies, India)
Business Science Reference • copyright 2018 • 287pp • H/C (ISBN: 9781522531913) • US $235.00 (our price)

Maximizing Social Science Research Through Publicly Accessible Data Sets
S. Marshall Perry (Saint Mary's College of California, USA)
Information Science Reference • copyright 2018 • 328pp • H/C (ISBN: 9781522536161) • US $195.00 (our price)

Promoting Interdisciplinarity in Knowledge Generation and Problem Solving
Mohammed Nasser Al-Suqri (Sultan Qaboos University, Oman) Abdullah Khamis Al-Kindi (Sultan Qaboos University, Oman) Salim Said AlKindi (Sultan Qaboos University, Oman) and Naifa Eid Saleem (Sultan Qaboos University, Oman)
Information Science Reference • copyright 2018 • 324pp • H/C (ISBN: 9781522538783) • US $195.00 (our price)

Techniques for Coding Imagery and Multimedia Emerging Research and Opportunities
Shalin Hai-Jew (Kansas State University, USA)
Information Science Reference • copyright 2018 • 483pp • H/C (ISBN: 9781522526797) • US $235.00 (our price)

Cross-Disciplinary Approaches to Action Research and Action Learning
Tome Awshar Mapotse (University of South Africa, South Africa)
Information Science Reference • copyright 2018 • 339pp • H/C (ISBN: 9781522526421) • US $215.00 (our price)

Cross-Cultural Analysis of Image-Based Assessments Emerging Research and Opportunities
Lisa Keller (University of Massachusetts Amherst, USA) Robert Keller (Measured Progress, USA) and Michael Nering (Measured Progress, USA)
Information Science Reference • copyright 2018 • 166pp • H/C (ISBN: 9781522526919) • US $130.00 (our price)

IGI Global
DISSEMINATOR OF KNOWLEDGE

701 East Chocolate Avenue, Hershey, PA 17033, USA
Tel: 717-533-8845 x100 • Fax: 717-533-8661
E-Mail: cust@igi-global.com • www.igi-global.com

Table of Contents

Detailed Table of Contents

Multi-agent systems (MAS) are a powerful technology for the design and implementation of autonomous intelligent systems that can handle distributed problem solving in a complex environment. This technology has played an important role in the development of data mining systems in the last decade, the purpose of which is to promote the extraction of information and knowledge from a large database and to make these systems more scalable. In this chapter, the authors present a clustering system based on cooperative agents through a centralized and common ERP database to improve decision support in ERP systems. To achieve this, they use multi-agent system paradigm to distribute the complexity of k-means algorithm in several autonomous entities called agents, whose goal is to group records or observations on similar objects classes. This will help business decision makers to make good decisions and provide a very good response time by the use of the multi-agent system. To implement the proposed architecture, it is more convenient to use the JADE platform while providing a complete set of services and have agents comply with the specifications FIPA.

"Real-world" decision-making applications generally contain multifaceted performance requirements riddled with incongruent performance specifications. This is because decision making typically involves complex problems that are riddled with incompatible performance objectives and contain competing design requirements which are very difficult—if not impossible—to capture and quantify at the time that the supporting decision models are actually constructed. There are invariably unmodelled elements, not apparent during model construction, which can greatly impact the acceptability of the model's solutions. Consequently, it is preferable to generate several distinct alternatives that provide multiple disparate perspectives to the problem. These alternatives should possess near-optimal objective measures with respect to all known objective(s), but be maximally different from each other in terms of their decision variables. This maximally different solution creation approach is referred to as modelling-to-generate-alternatives (MGA). This chapter provides an efficient optimization algorithm that simultaneously generates multiple, maximally different alternatives by employing the metaheuristic firefly algorithm. The efficacy of this mathematical programming approach is demonstrated on a commonly tested engineering optimization benchmark problem.

A set of metaheuristics has proved its efficiency in solving rapidly NP-hard problems. Several combinatorial and continuous optimization areas drew profit from these powerful alternative techniques. This chapter intends to describe a discrete version of bat algorithm (BA) combined to generalized walk evolutionary (GEWA), also called bat algorithm with generalized fly or walk (BAG) in order to solve discrete industrial optimization. The first case of study is the well-known hybrid flow shop scheduling. The second one concerns the operating theatre that represents a critical manufacturing system, as the products delivered are patients. The last problem is the redundancy optimization (ROP) for series-parallel multi-state power system (MSS). Its resolution involves the selection of components with an appropriate level of redundancy to maximize system reliability with constrained cost. A universal moment generating function (UMGF) is used to estimate reliabilities. The modified bat algorithm on specific benchmarks was compared with the original one, and other results taken from the literature of each case study.

The supplier assessment has always been a key area to be developed for necessary advancement and evaluation by the researchers. In this chapter, the authors react upon the agile characteristics and furnish an agile supplier assessment decision support system to be utilized by the managers of the distinguish firm for assessing the agile characteristics of the partner supplier firm. The authors presented a modeling based on generalized interval-valued trapezoidal fuzzy numbers (GIVTFNs) to assess the status of partner supplier concerning agile characteristics. A multi-criterion decision-making (MCDM) appraisement module is built by the authors and a decision support system is developed by them to judge the scale of agile characteristics in the supply chain (SC) network of the supplier firm. A second-level hierarchy appraisement module is discussed by the authors to illustrate the procedural implementation of the proposed work. Here, the authors proposed a decision support model, which can grab the subjective views of the decision makers. The authors utilized GIVTFNs to clutch the uncertainty and vagueness of the measures and their metrics (sub-measures) of the discussed agile platform. In this study, a fuzzy performance important index model is presented to recognize the weak and strong agile measures and metrics of the supplier firm. The major intention of the authors in this study is to deliver a knowledge-based technical model for the sake of determining the quality of agile strategies by the supplier firm in their SC network.

The complexity of information systems leads to poor data management and therefore bad decisions. The advantage of using component-based software engineering is to divide an information system into subsystem blocks with less complexity. In fact, a component is intended to provide specific services as management of the combination and communication between the units of the system. This chapter addresses this problem by developing information systems, proposing a component identification approach and the management pattern for data management. In this work, three developed views are taken into account, which include modelization and the design to achieve the purpose of defining and building the components and how they can be assembled. A component is intended to provide specific services, as a combination and communication management between the system units, and the manager component is the important and complementary paradigm pattern and added value for the development of software systems.

Diagnosing chronic diseases is about making accurate and quick decisions based on contradictory information and constantly evolving knowledge. Hence, there has been a persistent need to help health practitioners in making correct decisions. Diabetes is a common chronic disease. It is a global healthcare threat and the eighth leading cause of death in the world. Modern artificial intelligence techniques are being used in diagnosing chronic diseases including artificial neural networks. In this chapter, a feedforward multilayer-perceptron neural network has been implemented to help health practitioners in classifying diabetes. Through the work, an algorithm was proposed in purpose of determining the number of hidden layers and neurons in a MLP. Based on the algorithm, two topologies have been introduced. Both topologies exhibited good classification accuracies with a slightly higher accuracy for the MLP with only one hidden layer. The data set was obtained from King Abdullah University Hospital in Jordan.

A web-based Decision Support System WebOptim for solving multiple objective optimization problems is presented. The system WebOptim is designed in a modular principle, extensively using XML as communication standard and web services. Its basic characteristics are: user-independent, multisolver-admissibility, method-independent, heterogeneity, web-accessibility. Core system module is an original generalized interactive scalarizing method. It incorporates a number of thirteen interactive methods. Most of the known scalarizing approaches (reference point approach, reference direction approach, classification approach etc.) are realized in this method. The Decision Maker (DM) can choose the most suitable for him/her form for setting his/her preferences: objective weights, aspiration levels, aspiration directions, aspiration intervals. This information could be changed interactively by the DM during the solution process. Depending on the DM's preferences form the suitable scalarizing method is chosen automatically. The chapter begins with an overview of Decision Support Systems (DSS). Examples of DSSs and their applications are discussed.

Influenza has been a growing concern for the public health decision makers/policy makers. Indeed, they are in need of a real geo-making tool for monitoring and surveillance. The chapter aims to introduce a novel spatiotemporal decision system based on multicriteria ranking method, information geographic system (GIS), and SEIRSW system for public health. The later was designed, implemented, and validated in previous research for influenza risk assessment. The authors highlight the use of PROMETHEE II ranking method of multi-criteria decision analysis in GIS that incorporates various factors to monitor and identify potential high-risk areas of seasonal influenza and disease mapping. Factors related to the risk of seasonal influenza are obtained from simulation system and constitute the input values of PROMETHEE II ranking method for the 26 communes of the city of Oran, Algeria. The proposed system has demonstrated analytical capabilities in targeting high-risk spots and influenza surveillance monitoring system and it can help public health policy makers prioritize in their response goals and evaluate control strategies.

Image representation and compression is one of the important fields of computer vision that contribute to the reduction of size of an image and other types of application areas such as image restoration, retrieval, etc. Image representation is important with respect to storage of image information, and it further extends to the compression, which may be lossy or lossless. Image compression can be applied to various applications which mainly include medical imaging, traffic monitoring, military, multimedia transmission, smart cell devices, and almost in all the domains that require less transmission and storage cost, specifically image retrieval processing. This chapter presents the various image representation compression and retrieval approaches. The retrieval approaches on personal computer and smart cell devices are discussed. Finally, the key issues are identified for image representation compression and retrieval on the basis of performance evaluation parameters like encoding time, decoding time, compression ratio, precision, recall, and elapsed time.

The world started to talk about optical character recognition (OCR) around 1870. Then over another 25 years OCR systems were designed for industrial applications. And now the OCR software is easily available online for free, through products like Acrobat reader, WebOCR, etc. But still the research is on. Do we need to switch direction or introduce new hypothesis are some of the key questions? The purpose of this chapter is to answer the above questions and propose new methods for character recognition.

Wireless sensor networks (WSNs) can be classified among the blazing domains of research in the recent era. WSNs have enormous day-to-day life real-time applications due their low priced, self-computing, powerful, autonomous small sensor nodes which have a small storage capacity, restricted non-removable non-rechargeable battery, and a restricted computational capacity. The applicability of WSNs are in almost all domains, like observing environmental conditions, human healthcare tracking systems, position tracking and monitoring, industry automation, process tracking and controlling, tracking and monitoring objects, mammal, human being, and control, and many more. This chapter briefly explores the basic concepts, components, network architecture, design issues, challenges, routing protocols, application domains, implemented applications, etc. in the field of WSNs. It also focuses on the performance evaluation parameters to check, analyze, diagnose, examine, and determine the performance of WSNs. At the end, the chapter concludes with the scope of research in the field of wireless sensor networks.

Preface

Decision-making support systems (DMSS) have a significant role in several real-life applications. Such systems are interactive information systems that support the decision-making process of individuals, and organizations. Treating organizational knowledge has been popularized based on management and organization theorists. Create, capture, locate, and share the knowledge to bring that knowledge to bear on opportunities and problems are the main challenges. Organizations are showing a remarkable interest in realizing knowledge management technologies and processes to adopt knowledge management as part of the overall strategy in business, healthcare, and their other activates.

Even with the current advancement in technology, few organizations are entirely capable to develop critical organizational knowledge to achieve improved performance. Numerous societies and organizations are complex as their knowledge is difficult to be shared and located, therefore inconsistent, or redundant information should be reduced. Consequently, several researchers are interested to develop algorithms based on optimization algorithms and other techniques to provide optimal solutions in the several applications where heuristics are well-known problem-solving methods having an important role in different domains, such as engineering, healthcare, social science, etc. These optimization algorithms are applied to solve cases of incomplete information and/or insufficient knowledge about the problem under concern.

OBJECTIVE OF THE BOOK

The active management of knowledge is considered a significant ingredient for organizations to ensure sustainable strategies in the different applications. This book included several studies in different knowledge management areas for organizational competitiveness, survival, and effectiveness. Consequently, effectively producing, managing, utilizing and sharing knowledge is energetic in different domains. Developing new techniques and optimization algorithms become an evolving area to support numerous engineering applications. This book provides cutting-edge research techniques in related optimization methods and other automated techniques in real-world processes. The goal of the book is to address innovative studies along the 11 studies in different applications.

ORGANIZATION OF THE BOOK

The book is organized in 11 chapters with the following brief description:

1. A Clustering Approach Based on Cooperative Agents to Improve Decision Support in ERP

This study proposed clustering system based on cooperative agents using a centralized and common ERP database for accurate decision support in ERP systems. A multi-agent system is applied to distribute the k- Means algorithm complexity to support business decision-makers.

2. Simultaneous Modelling-to-Generate-Alternatives Procedure Employing the Firefly Algorithm

An efficient optimization algorithm has been proposed in this study to simultaneously generate multiple, maximally different alternatives using the Firefly algorithm (FA). The Modelling to Generate Alternatives (MGA) procedure has been introduced to produce several problems' solutions. Since FA algorithm can be adapted to solve a wide variety of problem types.

3. Bat Algorithm With Generalized Fly for Combinatorial Production Optimization Problems Case Studies

This chapter described a Bat Algorithm with Generalized fly or walk (BAG), which combined the discrete version of Bat Algorithm (BA) to Generalized Walk Evolutionary (GEWA) to solve discrete industrial optimization. Different case studies are addressed including the well-known Hybrid Flow Shop scheduling, the operating theatre that represents a critical manufacturing system, and the Redundancy optimization (ROP) for series-parallel Multi-state power system (MSS). A Universal Moment Generating Function (UMGF) is used to estimate reliabilities.

4. Agile Supplier Assessment Using Generalized Interval-Valued Trapezoidal Fuzzy Numbers

The agile characteristics and furnish an agile supplier assessment decision support system for assessing the agile characteristics of the partner supplier firm have been introduced. A Generalized Interval-Valued Trapezoidal Fuzzy Numbers (GIVTFNs) is applied. In order to evaluate the proposed procedure, a Multi-Criterion Decision Making (MCDM) appraisement module is built. A second level hierarchy appraisement module is discussed to illustrate the procedural implementation of the proposed approach. In addition, a fuzzy performance important index model is measured for performance evaluation.

5. Approach of Modelization and Management on Software Components

This chapter developed an information system using a component identification approach with management pattern for data management. Three developed views including the monetization and the design are considered to achieve the purpose of defining and building the components and how they can be assembled.

6. Classifying Diabetes Disease Using Feedforward MLP Neural Networks

A feed-forward multilayer-perceptron neural network has been implemented to classify the diabetic cases. An algorithm has been proposed to determine the number of hidden layers and neurons in a MLP.

Two topologies have been introduced to exhibit good classification accuracies with a slightly higher accuracy for the MLP with only one hidden layer.

7. Web-Based Decision Support System for Solving Multiple-Objective Decision-Making Problems

This chapter introduced a web-based Decision Support System WebOptim to solve multiple objective optimization problems. The XML is used as communication standard and web services. The proposed system incorporated a number of thirteen interactive methods. The Decision Maker (DM) can choose the most suitable for him/her form for setting the required preferences: objective weights, aspiration levels, aspiration directions, aspiration intervals.

8. A Multicriteria Spatiotemporal System for Influenza Epidemic Surveillance

This chapter introduced a novel spatiotemporal decision system based on Multicriteria ranking method, where the Information Geographic System (GIS) and SEIRSW system for public health are used. The PROMETHEE II ranking method of Multi-Criteria Decision Analysis in GIS is applied, which incorporated various factors to monitor and identify potential high-risk areas of seasonal influenza and disease mapping.

9. Review on Image Representation Compression and Retrieval Approaches

This chapter reported various image representation compression and retrieval approaches. An extensive discussion of the different retrieval approaches on personal computer and smart cell devices is included. The key issues are identified for the image representation compression and retrieval on the basis of performance evaluation parameters, such as the encoding time, decoding time, compression ratio, precision, recall and elapsed time.

10. Possible Approaches for Character Recognition With Existing Methodologies and State-of-the-Art Techniques

This chapter analyzed different methodologies on character recognition. The commercial products and state of the art technology have been reported. The character recognition methods and recognition rates achieved by researchers have also been tabularized. The authors identified an approach for character recognition for using BBP algorithm.

11. Wireless Sensor Networks: Concepts, Analysis, Routing, and Applications

This chapter explored the main concepts, components, network architecture, design issues, challenges, routing protocols, application domains, implemented applications, etc. in the field of Wireless sensor networks (WSNs). It also focuses on the performance evaluation parameters to check, analyze, diagnose, examine, and determine the performance of WSNs.

Chapter 1
A Clustering Approach Based on Cooperative Agents to Improve Decision Support in ERP

Nadjib Mesbahi
University of Biskra, Algeria

Okba Kazar
University of Biskra, Algeria

Saber Benharzallah
University of Biskra, Algeria

Merouane Zoubeidi
University of Biskra, Algeria

Djamil Rezki
University of Biskra, Algeria

ABSTRACT

Multi-agent systems (MAS) are a powerful technology for the design and implementation of autonomous intelligent systems that can handle distributed problem solving in a complex environment. This technology has played an important role in the development of data mining systems in the last decade, the purpose of which is to promote the extraction of information and knowledge from a large database and to make these systems more scalable. In this chapter, the authors present a clustering system based on cooperative agents through a centralized and common ERP database to improve decision support in ERP systems. To achieve this, they use multi-agent system paradigm to distribute the complexity of k-means algorithm in several autonomous entities called agents, whose goal is to group records or observations on similar objects classes. This will help business decision makers to make good decisions and provide a very good response time by the use of the multi-agent system. To implement the proposed architecture, it is more convenient to use the JADE platform while providing a complete set of services and have agents comply with the specifications FIPA.

DOI: 10.4018/978-1-5225-6164-4.ch001

INTRODUCTION

Nowadays, the managers of the companies must make the right decision at the real time based on the information at hand. For this reason, most companies integrate information communication technology in their enterprise resource planning (ERP), to improve their decision-making process. An ERP is designed for very large companies; they are now implanted in SMEs Adam and O'doherty (2000). These packages constituted a set of functional modules covering the domains of finance, human resources, logistics, production, marketing and sales, integrated around a single database Philippe (2006). This software helps to manage the whole process within a company by integrating all those functions Lequeux (1998).

Moreover, ERP offers a decision module, allows more or less sophisticated processing on the ERP database to help executives make the right decisions at the right time. This decision module makes it possible to use intuitively the wealth of ERP data and meet the needs of multiple functions simultaneously: production, logistics, finance, sales, etc. It also allows all employees, regardless of their profession, to make relevant decisions based on performance indicators and to accurately track the objectives set for all departments of the company Mesbahi and Kazar (2015).

In this context and to support the decision making of the ERP, several approaches and techniques have been proposed, but they remain insufficient. For this reason, the Knowledge Discovery from Databases (KDD) and the Data Mining can bury in large databases in order to enhance the information and extraction of new decision-making knowledge and/or forecast (Nimmy et al.,2017). The KDD has become a new edge technology used to achieve the decision-making in the companies. (Karaa, Mannai, Dey, Ashour, & Olariu, 2016) It also facilitates the verification of the consistency of the data to ensure the quality of the decision. (Kausar et al., 2016) Therefore, the aim of data mining is to valorise data information in companies' information systems.

Therefore, we suggest a clustering approach based on cooperative agents to integrate the data-mining module with ERP platform, for improve decision support in ERP systems. We use the paradigm of the multi-agent system and the data mining technique k-means, which is dedicated to the task of clustering, for discover useful knowledge hidden in the ERP database and to improve the quality of response times. Moreover, in our approach, the integration of expert prior Knowledge in a data mining process is crucial for improving datasets preparation. In order to assure this integration, an ontology ERP is built by analyzing existing database ERP with the collaboration of expert users who play a central role. The design of this ontology is directed to facilitating the preparation of datasets.

In this overview, our work will be organized as follows:

A general introduction followed by a presentation of emerging technologies such as ERP systems, knowledge discovery in data and Multi-agents system. We will describe later, the related work, the proposed approach for extracting knowledge from ERP and modelling Multi-Agents of Data Mining based K-means. Then, we describe the JADE platform adapted to implement the proposed approach. Finally, a conclusion and perspectives of study will conclude this work.

BACKGROUND

Enterprise Resource Planning (ERP)

ERP is a software package integrating the main functions needed to manage flows and company procedures (accounting and finance, logistics, payroll and human resources, etc...) Benchikh and Renard (2003). According to Markess (2013) defines the solution of Enterprise Resource Planning as:

1. A software solution that can manage several functional or operational processes of an organization (HR, accounting and/or financial, purchasing, procurement, production, inventory, sales, customer relations, logistics chain, etc…).
2. Managed processes are integrated into a modular way (functional module by functional module) while sharing a single and common database.
3. The solution must cover at least two different functional domains (e.g., HR and accounting/finance, or accounting/finance and business management ...).

Moreover, One of the important characteristics of ERP is the use of what is called a WorkFlow engine which, when data is stored in the Information system, the spread in modules that have utility, according to a predefined programming Blain (2006), Ana and Dragana (2016).

KDD and Data Mining

According to those references in Piatetsky-Shapiro and Smyth (1996) and Pasquier (2000), the KDD (Knowledge Discovery in Data) is a non-trivial extraction of implicit information, previously unknown and potentially useful in data stored in databases, consisting of several steps from data preparation to the interpretation of results via the discovery process itself, the Data-Mining. In Fayyad (1996) The Data Mining is the phase of knowledge research in the more general process of knowledge discovery in data (KDD).(Bose, Mukherjee, Chakraborty, Samanta & Dey, 2013) and (Kamal, Ripon, Dey, Ashour, & Santhi, 2016) .

The process of KDD will be done in several steps, as follows in Zhang and Yang (2003):

- **Defining the Problem:** The goals of a knowledge discovery project must be identified. The goals must be verified as actionable. For example, if the goals are met, a business organization can then put the newly discovered knowledge to use. The data to be used must also be identified clearly.
- **Data Pre-Processing or Data Preparation:** Comprises those techniques concerned with analyzing raw data so as to yield quality data, mainly including data collecting, data integration, data transformation, data cleaning, data reduction, and data discretization.
- **Data Mining:** Given the cleaned data, intelligent methods are applied in order to extract data patterns. Patterns of interest are searched for, including classification rules or trees, regression, clustering, sequence modelling, dependency, and so forth.
- **Post Data Mining:** Consists of pattern evaluation, deploying the model, maintenance, and knowledge presentation.

For each step of KDD, we use specific methods to achieve it. In our work, we used the task of segmentation that aims to discover, in the database, the groups of similar objects not identified in advance, having the same characteristics, it is the clusters. (Karaa et al., 2016) This means that they should contain objects that share a high degree of similarity (maximizing the intra-cluster similarity) and that these clusters must be large enough (minimizing the inter-cluster similarity) Boris et al. (2016). The similarity of the objects is generally measured in terms of geometric distance between objects. It often uses the k-means algorithms.

Technologies Coupling Data Mining and Agent

Multi-Agent Systems (MAS) has become a new paradigm provides a very suitable architecture for a design and implementation of integrative business information systems. With agent-based technologies, a support for complex information systems development is introduced by natural decomposition, abstraction and flexibility of management for organizational structure changes Kishore (2006) and Dimple (2017). A MAS is a community of autonomous agents working together, sometimes complex ways of cooperation, coordination, competition, in order to achieve a goal: solving a complex problem (Ferber, 1995).

At the same time, the application domain of data mining (DM) and its related techniques and technologies has been greatly expanded in the last few years. Since DM systems are comprised of a number of discrete, nevertheless dependent tasks, they can be thought of as networks of collaborative, yet autonomous, units that regulate, control and organize all distributed activities involved in data cleaning, data transformation and reduction, algorithm application and result evaluation. Fayyad (1996).

The research literature on agent system architectures has proven that such kinds of problems that require the synergy of a number of distributed elements for their solution can be efficiently implemented as a multi-agent system (MAS) Ferber, J. (1999). This is why multi-agent technology has repeatedly been used as a powerful technology for developing of Data Mining systems. Zhang (2003), Mohammadiam (2004), Symeonidis and Chatzidimitriou (2007).

Clustering Algorithm by K-Means

The K-Means algorithm (K-means) is dedicated to the task of clustering, it allows dividing a given population in homogeneous K groups called clusters. The number of clusters K is determined by the user according to his expectations. The k-means algorithm has four steps Duggirala and Kishor (2016):

Step 1: Choose k objects forming k clusters which represent the average position of clusters $M_1^{(1)} \ldots\ldots M_k^{(1)}$ initial

Step 2: Assign each object O to the cluster centre of M_i such that $\text{Dist}(O, M_i)$ is minimal:

$$C_i^{(t)} = \left\{ O_j : || O_j - M_i^{(t)} || \le O_j - M_{i^*}^{(t)} || \quad \forall\ i^* = 1,2,\ldots\ldots k \right\}$$

Step 3: Recalculates each cluster (the centroid):

$$C_i^{(t+1)} = \frac{1}{C_i^{(t)}} \sum\nolimits_{Oj \in C_i^{(t)}} O_j$$

Step 4: Go to step 2 if we make an assignment.

After determining a number K of clusters we position the first K random points (we generally use the first K records). Each record is assigned to the seed from which it is closest (using the distance function). At the end of the first assignment, the average value of each cluster is calculated and the seed takes the new value. The process is repeated until stable clusters Chami and Kazar (2011) and (Kausar et al., 2016).

RELATED WORKS

Numerous approaches have been proposed in the context of integrating data mining module to ERP platform, but few of them were interested in the use of multi-agent systems. Among these works, we mention:

In the approach Al-Mudimigh and Almalaise (2012), the authors entered the field of data mining from a large ERP database. The mining method chosen in this work is the association rules; this is precisely the FP Growth algorithm to extract new rules to improve decisions in such an organization. This approach has been validated by a real case study on data of ABC organization. They applied the proposed architecture on the data related to requests and responses of clients. Therefore, they implemented the FP Growth algorithm for finding and generating new rules to meet future client requests.

The authors in Shweta and Sapna (2012) provided a comprehensive architecture for the application of data mining on the ERP platform to find answers to customer queries. The proposed architecture is composed of three layers: "CRM", "DISCOVERY OF KNOWLEDGE" and "ERP". This is primarily to extend the traditional structure layered, by adding a third layer of knowledge discovery in which the generation of association rules from the ERP database will be processed using the technique of Data Mining: Algorithm CBA distributed, which makes it better than the Apriori algorithm.

In our previous work Mesbahi and Kazar (2014) we proposed a cooperative multi-agent approach for knowledge discovery from the enterprise resource planning to extract the useful knowledge, hidden in ERP database. The proposed architecture is composed of three layers: « User Interface Layer », « ERP Layer» and «Knowledge Discovery Layer ». The principal idea that we advocate for this work based on two main dimensions: in the first, integrating a new layer of agent-based knowledge discovery in order to help leaders to make the right decisions. In the second, enriching this approach by using the multi-agent system to extract the useful knowledge through the ERP database in a very good response time.

In another previous work of Mesbahi and Kazar (2015), we proposed Multi-Agents approach for data mining based k-Means for improving the decision process in the ERP systems, to extract hidden knowledge in the ERP database. The mining method chosen for this work is the clustering, and more precisely is the k-Means algorithm. The goal of this paper is to group records or observations on similar objects classes through the ERP Database, using the k-means technique and the paradigm of the multi-agent system to distribute the complexity of several autonomous entities. This work offers a very good response time when extracting information from the ERP database by the clustering task.

In the work of Mesbahi and Kazar (2014), we proposed an approach for agent-based modelling of an Enterprise Resource Planning (ERP) capable of entering the concepts of Multi-Agent System (MAS) on the behaviour of business from the interactions of its own components with themselves and the outside world. The proposed architecture has three levels: The first is the user interface agent who acts as an interface between the system and the outside (suppliers, customers, banks ... etc.). The second level represents the domains agents such as domain agent buy / appro, domain agent of sales/commercial, domain agent of accounting/finance...etc. The third level is the service agents for each domain, it helps to achieve well-defined functions (inventory, purchasing, accounting ... etc.).

Furthermore, the authors in Brisson, Collard and Pasquier (2005) proposed the new ontology-based methodology ExCIS (Extraction using a Conceptual Information System) for integrating expert knowledge in KDD process. This methodology describes guidelines for a KDD process like CRISP-DM by the use of the ontology in order to improve datasets preparation and results in interpretation.

In all these works Shweta and Sapna (2012) and Al-Mudimigh and Almalaise (2012), the aim is to integrate the Data Mining module into an ERP platform, in order to extract hidden knowledge of ERP database. They are generally based on classical algorithms that are resource-intensive such as: (Apriori, FP Growth, CBA, K-Means), that consume longer time during its execution because of the use of ERP database, collecting and storing very large amounts of data. These last are increasing day by day. According to reference Mesbahi and Kazar (2015), the searching in very large databases of petabytes, and the extracting of the useful information, as well as the distribution of data in some cases of distributed databases, represent difficulties in the implementation of a system for data mining (Kausar, Palaniappan, Samir, Abdullah, & Dey, 2016) and (Kamal et al., 2016, 2017). The latter requires a huge volume of work and a very large execution time. To face these problems, we propose an approach to integrate the multi-agent paradigm in the data mining process. It distributes the complexity of this process on several autonomous entities called agents, who will cooperate and collaborate to achieve the reduction in execution time due to the extraction of knowledge from a large ERP database. According to Boudina and Tayeb (2007) and Jarras and Chaib-draa (2002), the use of multi-agent system is justified by the following properties: The modularity; The speed with parallelism; Reliability due to redundancy; Processing symbolic level of knowledge; The reuse and portability; The intervention of sophisticated patterns of interaction (cooperation, coordination, negotiation).

This paper presents a clustering approach based on cooperative agents to improve decision support in ERP. It implements the clustering algorithm, namely k-Means, by the multi-agent system for efficient extraction of hidden knowledge in the ERP database. The idea that we advocate is based on associated contribution with the two main dimensions: in the first, improving the KDD process by integrating an expert prior Knowledge in a data mining process in order to improve datasets preparation, then the enrichment of this approach by using the multi-agent system to improve the quality of response times. Thus, these give a powerful point of our approach compared to the approaches presented in this literature in terms of execution time improvement and of expert Knowledge integration to make the right decisions at the right time.

PROPOSED MULTI-LAYERS APPROACH OF ERP

In this section, we describe in detail our Multi-Layers approach to extract the hidden knowledge from the ERP database.

Objectives of the System

The power of our approach revolves around the use of the paradigm with the multi-agent system and the data mining technique: K-Means, which is among the best algorithms dedicated to the segmentation task to discover new knowledge (useful and unknown) hidden in the ERP database. The proposed approach is based on a multilayer architecture using agent technology, each layer has its own agents and features with specific responsibilities. Each agent has a particular skill and subset of domain knowledge that it uses to solve part of the overall problem. In our system, we choose the point-to-point mode for the transmission of information because the type of agent used is the cognitive agent. The agent sending the message must know the address (s) of the specific recipient agent.

General Architecture of System

We present a detailed description of the different layers used in our approach and the relationships between them.

In Figure 1 the proposed architecture has three layers:

- **Interface Agent DM:** This layer represents the user interface agent who acts as an interface between the system and the external (supplier, customer, bank ... etc...). Its primary role is to capture the purpose of the user to meet his needs. The user interface agent interacts with the user to help him to achieve specific tasks. This interaction results in a transformation of the user requests, which will be transformed into queries facilitate the operation of domain agents.
- **ERP Layer:** The second layer is the heart of our approach consists of a set of domain agents and a central database of ERP having a variety of data collected from any domain of the ERP. It provides communication and collaboration between domain agents such as domain agent Buy, the domain agent Sale / Commercial, domain agent of Accounting / Finance ... etc as it is used in Mesbahi and Kazar (2014-A). Thus, an ontology ERP is extracted by analyzing operational database ERP and by interacting with expert users, in order to improve datasets preparation. This ontology ERP is defined in Brisson, Collard and Pasquier (2005) as a set of concepts and relationships among them which are discovered by analyzing ERP database. It provides support both in data preparation step for building the DBOM (Data Base Oriented Mining).
- **Knowledge Discovery Layer:** Consists of a set of successive steps in order to discover new knowledge unknown and useful hidden in the ERP database. This new knowledge is collected in a knowledge base for future use, whose main purpose is to assist managers to make the right decisions at the right time. Another important point in this layer is the construction of DBOM from the data Transformation combined with the ontology ERP. The DBOM as in Brisson et al. (2005) is a relational database whose role is to store the most fine-grain data produced from the database ERP. DBOM attributes are those, which are identified as relevant for the Data Mining Agents based K-means and DBOM instances are tuples of most fine-grain values. Thus, the modelling of Data Mining Agents based K-means is described in the next section.

Figure 1. Proposed Approach Multi-Layers of ERP

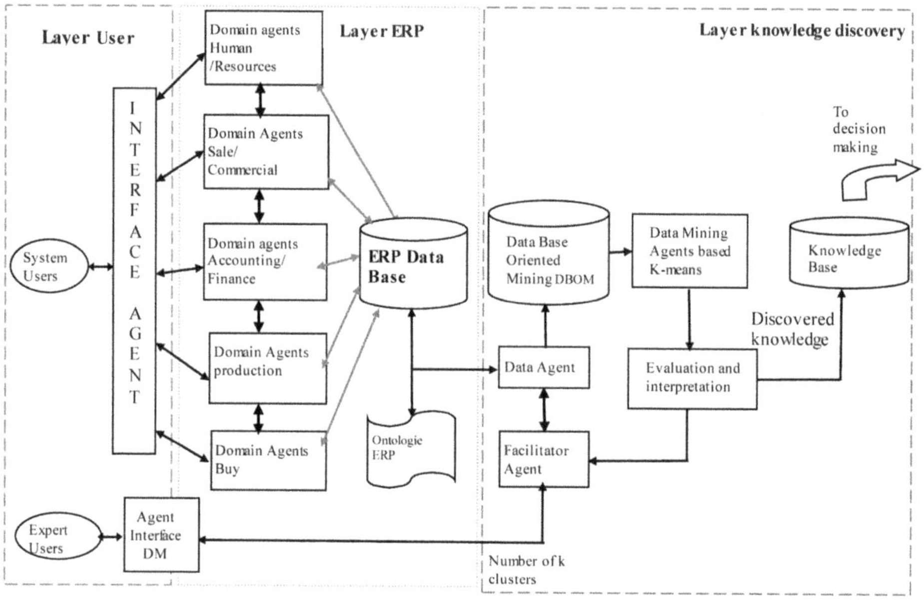

MODELING MULTI-AGENTS OF DATA MINING BASED K-MEANS

Agent Specification of Knowledge Discovery Layer

The Knowledge Discovery Layer contains several agents for Knowledge Discovery operation. In Figure 2, this layer consists of eight cognitive agents, which are: Agent Interface DM, Facilitator agent, Data Agent, Cluster Interface Agent, Init-Cluster Agent, Centroid-Calc Agent, Affect-Cluster Agent and Calc-Distance Agent.

- **Interface Agent DM:** This agent interacts with the system DM users or with the Knowledge Discovery Layer. It asks the DM user to provide his requirements and provides this user with simple results or with mined results (may be visualized). Its interface module contains methods for inter-agent communication and getting input from the user. The processing module contains methods for capturing the user input and communicating it to the facilitator agent or with the domain agents. In the knowledge module, the agent stores the history of user interaction, and user profiles with their specific preferences.
- **Facilitator Agent:** The facilitator agent is responsible for the activation and synchronization of different agents. It elaborates a work plan and is in charge of ensuring that such a work plan is fulfilled. It receives the assignments from the interface agent and may seek the services of a group of agents and synthesize the final result and present it to the interface agent. The interface module is responsible for the integrant communication; the process module contains methods for control and coordination of various tasks. The knowledge module also contains meta-knowledge about capabilities of other agents in the system.

Figure 2. Model Agent of Data Mining based K-Means

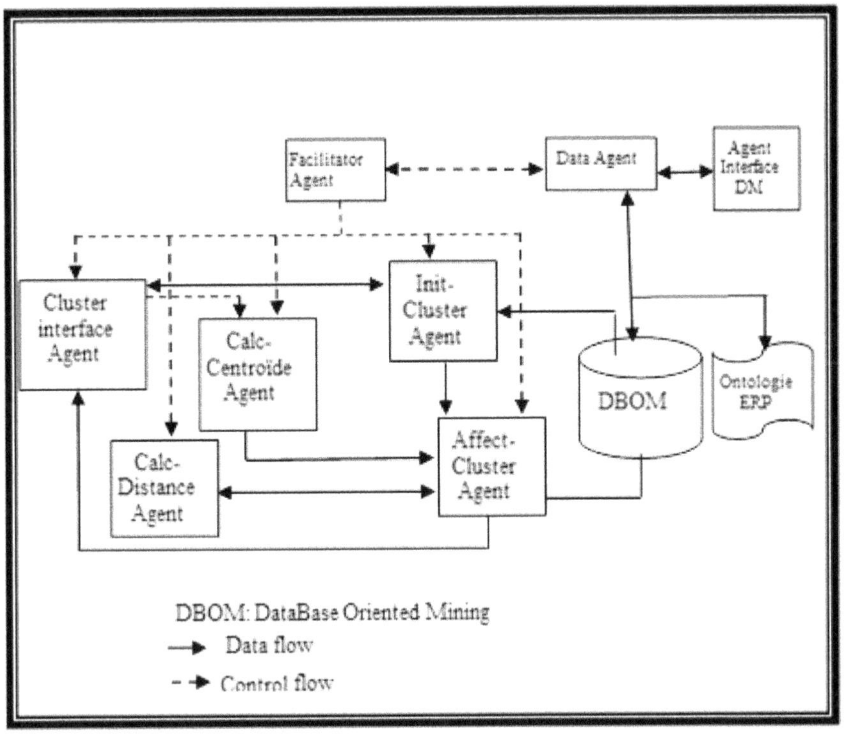

- **Data Agent:** The data agent actively maintains meta-data information about the ERP database. It is responsible for retrieving and cleansing the necessary data sets requested by the mining agent in preparation for a specific data mining operation and put it in the Data Base Oriented Mining (DBOM). It resolves conflicts in data definition and representation. Its interface module supports inter-agent communication as well as an interface to ERP database. The processing module provides facilities for predefined data retrieval. Based on the user request, appropriate queries are generated and executed against the ERP database and the results are communicated back to the facilitator agent, or other agents.
- **Cluster Interface Agent:** The responsible agent of communication with the expert users. It is considered as the interface between Layer User and knowledge discovery layer. It is responsible for providing the required number of k clusters from the expert users to start the k -means operations.
- **Init-Cluster Agent:** The initialization agent clusters activated by the Cluster interface agent, it is responsible for determining the first k records in the Data Base Oriented Mining (DBOM) committing the initial clusters, and send their information (attribute values) to Affect-Cluster agent.
- **Affect-Cluster Agent:** The affect-Cluster Agents affect the data retrieved from the DBOM in the correct cluster, its role is to create a new partition by assigning each record group whose centre of gravity is the closest based on the value of the distance provided by the Calc - Distance agent.
- **Centroid-Calc Agent:** This agent is triggered by the Affect-Cluster Agent in order to calculate the centres of the data groups.

- **Calc-Distance Agent:** This agent and the Calc-Distance agent work only with Affect-Cluster Agent, it is triggered by the latter in order to calculate the Euclidean distance between the centres of the clusters computed by the agent Centroid-Calc and segmented data.

Database oriented mining (DBOM) contains prepared data and transformed for the operation of Data Mining Agents based K-means. The control flow shown in the diagram ensures cooperation and coordination between the agents of the system and guarantees the security of the latter.

Description of Data Mining Agents Based K-Means

Cluster Interface Agent

The responsible agent of communication with the user, it is considered as the interface between the systems and the outside. It provides the clusters number k for the system to start the segmentation.

The functioning of the Cluster Interface Agent is:

1. Entering the number of clusters.
2. Sending the number entered in Init-Cluster and Cluster Affect-agents.

Init-Cluster Agent

The initialization agent clusters triggered by the interface agent, it is responsible for determining the first k records in the oriented mining database (k cluster number entered by the user and sent by the interface agent) committing the initial clusters, and send their information (attribute values) to Affect-Cluster agent.

To select the initial clusters (the records that form each a segment), the Init-Cluster agent follows the following steps:

1. Receive the message of Cluster Interface agent containing the number of clusters k.
2. Testing the received number compared to the number of records in the DBOM.
3. Access to the DBOM and selecting the first k records.
4. Extract the attribute values of these records and put them on vectors.
5. Sending vectors to the Affect-Cluster agent thus triggering the latter.

Affect-Cluster Agent

The role of the affect-Cluster Agent is to affect the data retrieved from the database in the correct cluster, extracting data previously prepared and stored in the database. In order to accomplish its role, Affect-Cluster agent do the following operations:

1. Receive the number of clusters k sent by the interface agent.
2. Extract from DBOM database, the data to be segmented.
3. Receive the message from the agent Init-Cluster containing the coordinates of the initial clusters.
4. Send the data previously extracted and initial clusters to the Calc Distance agent by triggering the latter

5. Receive calculated and sent distances by the Calc-Distance agent.
6. Affect each record to the nearest cluster (whose distance is minimal).
7. Send the new clusters to the Calc-Centroid agent in order to calculate their new centres.
8. Receive the message from the agent-Centroid Calc containing the new centroid.
9. Send to the Calc-Distance Agent a request for distance calculation compared to the new centres.
10. Return to step' and repeat all the steps that follow until the distances recovered from the Calc-Distance Agent do not change or the number of iterations is completed.

Calc-Centroïde Agent

The centroid calculation agent, triggered by the Affect-Cluster Agent in order to calculate the centres of the data groups.

To calculate the centroid, the Calc-Centroid agent works as follows:

1. Receive the Message of Affect-Cluster Agent containing the coordinates of the recently defined clusters.
2. Calculate the centroid for each cluster using the weighted average.
3. Send the calculated centroid at Affect-Cluster Agent.

Calc-Distance Agent

The Centroid-Calc Agent and the Calc-Distance agent work only with Affect-Cluster Agent, it is triggered by the latter in order to calculate the distance between the centres of the clusters computed by the agent Centroid-Calc and segmented data.

The steps below show the functioning of the Calc-Distance agent:

1. Receive the Message of Affect-Cluster Agent containing the coordinates of the cluster centres and those data to classify.
2. Calculate using the Euclidean distance, the distance of each record in relation to all the centres of the clusters.

SEQUENCE DIAGRAM OF DATA MINING AGENTS BASED K-MEANS

The following AUML sequence diagram summarizes the process of general functioning for our model agent-based Data Mining by K-means (Figure 3.).

COMMUNICATION BETWEEN AGENTS

The communication in multi-agent system allows the agents to benefit from the information and the know-how of the other agents, and consequently increases the perceptive capacities of the agents, it constitutes one of the main means ensuring the distribution of the tasks and coordination of actions (Ferber, 1995).

Figure 3. AUML sequence diagram of the proposed model

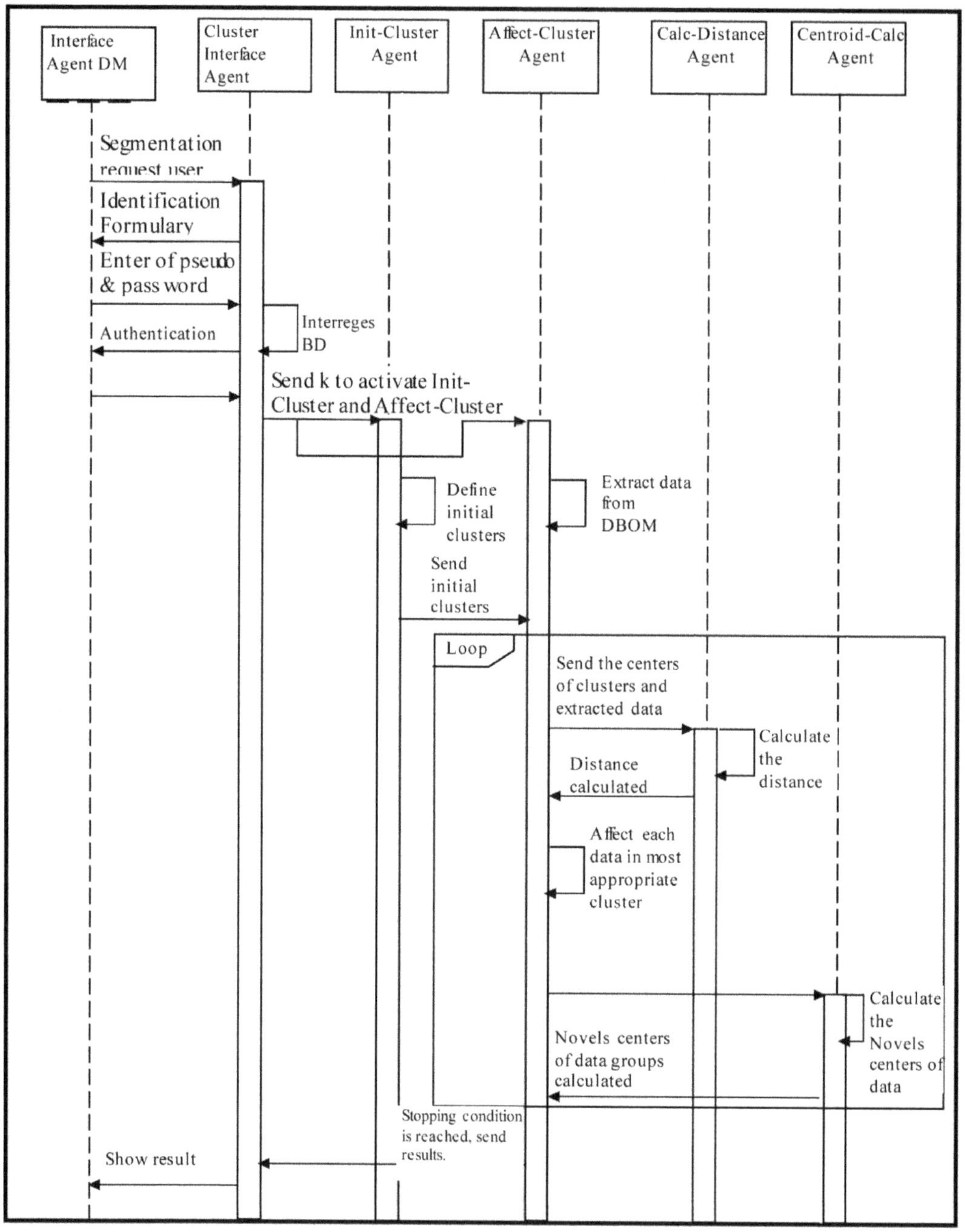

For the communication language we have chosen FIPA-ACL (Agent Communication Language) language, this language is based on sending messages between agents according to the Foundation for Intelligent Physical Agents (FIPA) specification, which provides it with maximum interoperability between agents. It allows the agents of our architecture to share the knowledge extraction problem load, subdividing it into sub-problems. Multi-agent systems based on communication by sending messages are characterized by the fact that each agent has a clean and local representation of the surrounding environment. Each agent will then interrogate other agents about this environment or send them information about their own perception of things. Communication by sending messages is in point-to-point mode or in broadcast mode. In our proposal, we chose the point-to-point mode as the mode of information transmission because the type of agent used in our architecture is the cognitive agent. The agent sending the message must know precisely the address of the agent (s) recipient (s). In Figure 4 the syntax of FIPA-ACL message is illustrated as follows:

CONCLUSION AND OUTLOOK

In this work, we have relied on the coupling of multi-agent systems and data mining. We have shown that these two domains are complementary and can evolve within the same process. Their association is able to facilitate the process of extracting knowledge from a large ERP database. In this article, we presented a clustering approach based on cooperative agents to improve decision support in ERP systems. The extraction task used in this is the clustering based on k_means method. Our architecture is based on the Multi-Agents System to minimize response time when segmenting a large amount of ERP data. In addition, integration of the ERP ontology and prior expertise in the data preparation stage improves the quality of knowledge extracted by the KDD process.

Finally, to implement the proposed approach, it is necessary to use a multi-agent system development platform. As part of this work, the JADE platform based on the JAVA language seems the most appropriate since it is compatible with cognitive agents. It also provides a complete set of services and agents that comply with FIPA specifications. Our approach is an open approach that our work does not stop at this level and the opportunities available to us. We plan to expand our work by integrating ERP ontology into other KDD steps, to improve the quality of the extracted knowledge.

Figure 4. Syntax of FIPA-ACL message

```
Request
        :sender Agent_A
               :receiver Agent_B
               :content
                       (....)
               :in-reply-to action
               :replay-with reponse
               :language FIPA-SL0)
```

REFERENCES

Adam, F., & O'doherty, P. (2000). Lessons from enterprise resource planning implementation in Ireland, toward smaller and shorter ERP projects. *Journal of Information Technology*, *15*(4), 305–316. doi:10.1080/02683960010008953

Al-Mudimigh, A. S., & Almalaise, A. (2012). Rules Generation from ERP Database: A Successful Implementation of Data Mining. *International Journal of Computer Science and Network Security*, *12*(3), 21–29.

Al-Mudimigh, A. S., Farrukh, S. F., & Zahid, U. Z. (2009). A Framework of an Automated Data Mining Systems Using ERP Model. *International Journal of Computer and Electrical Engineering*, *5*, 651–655. doi:10.7763/IJCEE.2009.V1.101

Ana, P., & Dragana, B. (2016). Metamodel of the Artifact-Centric Approach to Event Log Extraction from ERP Systems. *International Journal of Decision Support System Technology*, *8*(2), 18–28. doi:10.4018/IJDSST.2016040102

Benchikh, W., & Renard, I. (2003). *The contractual architecture of groups of contracts Enterprise Resource Planning (ERP). Memory D.E.E.S.* University of Paris Π.

Blain, F.-A. (2006). *Overview of ERP and their modular architecture*. Retrieved Mars 13, 2006, from http://fablain.developpez.com/tutoriel/presenterp.htm

Boris, D., Milan, D., & Pavlos, D. (2016). A Skiing Trace Clustering Model for Injury Risk Assessment. *International Journal of Decision Support System Technology*, *8*(1), 56–68. doi:10.4018/IJDSST.2016010104

Bose, S., Mukherjee, A., Chakraborty, S., Samanta, S., & Dey, N. (2013, December). Parallel image segmentation using multi-threading and k-means algorithm. In *Computational Intelligence and Computing Research (ICCIC), 2013 IEEE International Conference on* (pp. 1-5). IEEE. 10.1109/ICCIC.2013.6724171

Boudina, A., & Tayeb, L. (2007). *The distributed Artificial Intelligence and Multi-Agent Systems*. Retrieved Avril 13, 2007, from htttp://opera.inrialpes.fr/people/Tayeb.Lemlouma/Papers/ IAD_Presentation.pdf

Brisson, L., Collard, M., & Pasquier, N. (2005). *Improving the knowledge discovery process using ontologies*. Paper presented at the 1st international workshop on Mining Complex Data in conjunction with ICDM (5th IEEE International Conference on Data Mining) Conference, Houston, TX.

Chami, D., & Kazar, O. (2011). *A data mining agent-oriented platform*. Paper presented on the 4th International Conference on Information Systems and Economic Intelligence, Marrakech, Morocco.

Dejan, L., & Rok, R. (2009). Multi-Agent System for Decision Support in Enterprises. *Journal of JIOS*, *33*(2), 269–284.

Dimple, J., Aarti, S., Rashmi, S., & Saurabh, M. (2017). A Thorough Insight into Theoretical and Practical Developments in MultiAgent Systems. *International Journal of Ambient Computing and Intelligence*, *8*(1), 23–49. doi:10.4018/IJACI.2017010102

Duggirala, R. (2016). A Novel Hybridization of Expectation-Maximization and K-Means Algorithms for Better Clustering Performance. *International Journal of Ambient Computing and Intelligence, 7*(2), 47–74. doi:10.4018/IJACI.2016070103

Fayyad, U., Piatetsky-Shapiro, G., & Smyth, P. (1996). From Data Mining to Knowledge Discovery in Databases. American Association for Artificial Intelligence.

Ferber, J. (1995). *Multi-agent systems, towards a collective intelligence*. Paris: Inter Editions.

Ferber, J. (1999). *Multi-agent Systems - An Introduction to Distributed Artificial Intelligence*. London: Addison-Wesley.

Guttman, R. H., & Alexandros, G. (1998). *Agent-mediated Electronic Commerce: A Survey. Software Agents Group*. MIT Media Laboratory.

Haddad, M. (2002). *Extraction and Impact of knowledge on the performance of Information Retrieval Systems* (Doctoral thesis). Joseph Fourier University, Grenoble, France.

Hébrail, G., & Lechevallier, Y. (2003). *Data Mining and Data Analysis*. Academic Press.

Jarras, I., & Chaib-draa, B. (2002). *Overview of multi-agent systems, Scientific Series. Center for Inter-university Research and Analysis of Organizations (CIRANO)*. Montreal University.

Kamal, S., Dey, N., Ashour, A. S., Ripon, S., Balas, V. E., & Kaysar, M. S. (2017). FbMapping: An automated system for monitoring Facebook data. *Neural Network World, 27*(1), 27–57. doi:10.14311/NNW.2017.27.002

Kamal, S., Dey, N., Nimmy, S. F., Ripon, S. H., Ali, N. Y., Ashour, A. S., ... Shi, F. (2016). Evolutionary framework for coding area selection from cancer data. *Neural Computing & Applications*, 1–23.

Kamal, S., Ripon, S. H., Dey, N., Ashour, A. S., & Santhi, V. (2016). A MapReduce approach to diminish imbalance parameters for big deoxyribonucleic acid dataset. *Computer Methods and Programs in Biomedicine, 131*, 191–206. doi:10.1016/j.cmpb.2016.04.005 PMID:27265059

Kamal, S., Ripon, S. H., Dey, N., Ashour, A. S., & Santhi, V. (2016). A MapReduce approach to diminish imbalance parameters for big deoxyribonucleic acid dataset. *Computer Methods and Programs in Biomedicine, 131*, 191–206. doi:10.1016/j.cmpb.2016.04.005 PMID:27265059

Karaa, W. B. A., Ashour, A. S., Sassi, D. B., Roy, P., Kausar, N., & Dey, N. (2016). Medline text mining: an enhancement genetic algorithm based approach for document clustering. In *Applications of Intelligent Optimization in Biology and Medicine* (pp. 267–287). Springer International Publishing. doi:10.1007/978-3-319-21212-8_12

Karaa, W. B. A., Mannai, M., Dey, N., Ashour, A. S., & Olariu, I. (2016, August). Gene-disease-food relation extraction from biomedical database. In *International Workshop Soft Computing Applications* (pp. 394-407). Springer.

Kausar, N., Abdullah, A., Samir, B. B., Palaniappan, S., AlGhamdi, B. S., & Dey, N. (2016). Ensemble clustering algorithm with supervised classification of clinical data for early diagnosis of coronary artery disease. *Journal of Medical Imaging and Health Informatics, 6*(1), 78–87. doi:10.1166/jmihi.2016.1593

Kausar, N., Palaniappan, S., Samir, B. B., Abdullah, A., & Dey, N. (2016). Systematic analysis of applied data mining based optimization algorithms in clinical attribute extraction and classification for diagnosis of cardiac patients. In *Applications of intelligent optimization in biology and medicine* (pp. 217–231). Springer International Publishing. doi:10.1007/978-3-319-21212-8_9

Kazar, O. (1996). Design and implementation of a semantic network model. Memory Magister, 6-45.

Kishore, R., Zhang, H., & Ramesh, R. (2006). Enterprise integration using the agent paradigm: Foundations of multi-agent-based integrative business information systems. *International Journal of Decision Support Systems*, *42*(1), 48–78. doi:10.1016/j.dss.2004.09.011

Lequeux, J-L. (1998). *Manager with ERP*. Paris: Eyrolles.

Markess, I. (2013). Expectations of business for management solutions integrated ERP / PGI meet new challenges 2011-2013. Repository of Practices.

Mekroud, N. (2009). *Integration of data mining techniques in the process of knowledge management based on case-based reasoning. Memory magister*. Ferhat Abbes-Sétif University.

Mesbahi, N., & Kazar, O. (2014-A). *An agent-based modelling for an enterprise resource planning (ERP). Proceedings of the 6th Asian Conference on Intelligent Information and Database Systems ACIIDS 2014*, 551, 225-234.

Mesbahi, N., & Kazar, O. (2014b). *A cooperative multi-agent approach for knowledge discovery from the enterprise resource planning*. Paper presented in the 3rd IEEE International Workshop on Advanced Information Systems for Enterprises (IWAISE'14), Tunis, Tunisia.

Mesbahi, N., Kazar, O., Benharzallah, S., Zoubeidi, M., & Bourekkache, S. (2015). Multi-Agents approach for data mining based k-Means for improving the decision process in the ERP systems. *International Journal of Decision Support System Technology*, *7*(2), 1–14. doi:10.4018/IJDSST.2015040101

Mohammadiam, M. (2004). Intelligent Agents for Data Mining and Information Retrieval. Idea Group Inc. doi:10.4018/978-1-59140-194-0

Necir, H., & Drias, H. (2007). *Data mining approach for customer relationship management: application to customizing an e-commerce site*. Paper presented at the 4th International Conference on Sciences of Electronic, Technologies of Information and Telecommunications.

Nimmy, S. F., Kamal, M. S., Hossain, M. I., Dey, N., Ashour, A. S., & Shi, F. (2017). Neural Skyline Filtering for Imbalance Features Classification. *International Journal of Computational Intelligence and Applications*, *16*(03), 1750019. doi:10.1142/S1469026817500195

Pasquier, N. (2000). *Data Mining: Algorithms of extraction and reduction of association rules in the database* (Doctoral thesis). Clermont-Ferrand 2 University.

Philippe, P. (2006). *From information to knowledge*. Research Paper, Orléans University.

Preux P. (2011). *Notes on Data Mining*. Lille 3 University.

Shweta, T., & Sapna, C. (2012). The architecture of an Automated CBA System Using ERP Model. *International Journal of Scientific and Research Publications*, *2*(10).

Symeonidis, A., Chatzidimitriou, C., Athanasiadis, I., & Pericles, M. (2007). Data mining for agent reasoning: A synergy for training intelligent agents. *Engineering Applications of Artificial Intelligence, Elsevier*, *20*(8), 1097–1111. doi:10.1016/j.engappai.2007.02.009

Villemin, F.Y. (2010). Agent Communication Language. *Intelligent Systems NFP2012.*

Zhang, S., Zhang, C., & Yang, Q. (2003). Data preparation for data mining. *Applied Artificial Intelligence*, *17*(6), 375–381. doi:10.1080/713827180

Zhang, Z., Zhang, C., & Zhang, S. (2003). An agent-based hybrid framework for database mining. *Journal of Applied Artificial Intelligence*, *17*(5-6), 383–398. doi:10.1080/713827179

ADDITIONAL READING

Ahmed, S. S., Dey, N., Ashour, A. S., Sifaki-Pistolla, D., Bălas-Timar, D., Balas, V. E., & Tavares, J. M. R. (2017). Effect of fuzzy partitioning in Crohn's disease classification: A neuro-fuzzy-based approach. *Medical & Biological Engineering & Computing*, *55*(1), 101–115. doi:10.100711517-016-1508-7 PMID:27106754

Chatterjee, S., Chakraborty, R., Dey, N., & Hore, S. (2015). *A quality prediction method for weight lifting activity*. Michael Faraday IET International Summit. doi:10.1049/cp.2015.1691

Li, Z., Shi, K., Dey, N., Ashour, A. S., Wang, D., Balas, V. E., ... Shi, F. (2017). Rule-based back propagation neural networks for various precision rough set presented KANSEI knowledge prediction: A case study on shoe product form features extraction. *Neural Computing & Applications*, *28*(3), 613–630. doi:10.100700521-016-2707-8

Ngan, T. T., Tuan, T. M., Minh, N. H., & Dey, N. (2016). Decision Making Based on Fuzzy Aggregation Operators for Medical Diagnosis from Dental X-ray images. *Journal of Medical Systems*, *40*(12), 280. doi:10.100710916-016-0634-y PMID:27787784

Roy, P., Goswami, S., Chakraborty, S., Azar, A. T., & Dey, N. (2014). Image segmentation using rough set theory: A review. *International Journal of Rough Sets and Data Analysis*, *1*(2), 62–74. doi:10.4018/ijrsda.2014070105

Tang, R., Fong, S., Dey, N., Wong, R. K., & Mohammed, S. (2017). Cross Entropy Method Based Hybridization of Dynamic Group Optimization Algorithm. *Entropy (Basel, Switzerland)*, *19*(10), 533. doi:10.3390/e19100533

Wang, D., He, T., Li, Z., Cao, L., Dey, N., Ashour, A. S., ... Shi, F. (2016). Image feature-based affective retrieval employing improved parameter and structure identification of adaptive neuro-fuzzy inference system. *Neural Computing & Applications*, 1–16.

Wang, D., Li, Z., Cao, L., Balas, V. E., Dey, N., Ashour, A. S., ... Shi, F. (2016). Image Fusion Incorporating Parameter Estimation Optimized Gaussian Mixture Model and Fuzzy Weighted Evaluation System: A Case Study in Time-Series Plantar Pressure Data Set. *IEEE Sensors Journal*, *17*(5), 1407–1420. doi:10.1109/JSEN.2016.2641501

Wang, D., Li, Z., Dey, N., Ashour, A. S., Sherratt, R. S., & Shi, F. (2017). Case-Based Reasoning for Product Style Construction and Fuzzy Analytic Hierarchy Process Evaluation Modeling Using Consumers Linguistic Variables. *IEEE Access: Practical Innovations, Open Solutions*, *5*, 4900–4912. doi:10.1109/ACCESS.2017.2677950

KEY TERMS AND DEFINITIONS

Data Mining: The phase of knowledge research in the more general process of knowledge discovery in data.

Enterprise Resource Planning (ERP): A software package integrating the main functions needed to manage flows and company procedures.

K-Means: A data mining algorithm that dedicated to the task of clustering, it allows dividing a given population in homogeneous K groups called clusters.

Knowledge Discovery in Data (KDD): A non-trivial extraction of implicit information, previously unknown and potentially useful in data stored in databases.

Multi-Agent Systems (MAS): A community of autonomous agents working together, sometimes complex ways of cooperation, coordination, competition, in order to achieve a goal; solving a complex problem.

Chapter 2
Simultaneous Modelling-to-Generate-Alternatives Procedure Employing the Firefly Algorithm

Julian Scott Yeomans
York University, Canada

ABSTRACT

"Real-world" decision-making applications generally contain multifaceted performance requirements riddled with incongruent performance specifications. This is because decision making typically involves complex problems that are riddled with incompatible performance objectives and contain competing design requirements which are very difficult—if not impossible—to capture and quantify at the time that the supporting decision models are actually constructed. There are invariably unmodelled elements, not apparent during model construction, which can greatly impact the acceptability of the model's solutions. Consequently, it is preferable to generate several distinct alternatives that provide multiple disparate perspectives to the problem. These alternatives should possess near-optimal objective measures with respect to all known objective(s), but be maximally different from each other in terms of their decision variables. This maximally different solution creation approach is referred to as modelling-to-generate-alternatives (MGA). This chapter provides an efficient optimization algorithm that simultaneously generates multiple, maximally different alternatives by employing the metaheuristic firefly algorithm. The efficacy of this mathematical programming approach is demonstrated on a commonly tested engineering optimization benchmark problem.

DOI: 10.4018/978-1-5225-6164-4.ch002

INTRODUCTION

Typical "real world" decision-making situations involve complex problems that possess design requirements which are very difficult to incorporate into their supporting mathematical programming formulations and tend to be plagued by numerous unquantifiable components (Belarbi *et al.*, 2017; Matallah *et al.*, 2017; Brugnach *et al.*, 2007; Janssen *et al.*, 2010; Junejah *et al.*, 2017; Matthies *et al.*, 2007; Mowrer, 2000; Walker *et al.*, 2003). While mathematically optimal solutions provide the best answers to these modelled formulations, they are generally not the best solutions to the underlying real problems as there are invariably unmodelled aspects not apparent during the model construction phase (Acharjya & Anitha, 2017; Brugnach *et al.*, 2007; Janssen *et al.*, 2010; Loughlin *et al.*, 2001). Hence, it is generally considered desirable to generate a reasonable number of very different alternatives that provide multiple, contrasting perspectives to the specified problem (Matthies *et al.*, 2007; Yeomans & Gunalay, 2011). These alternatives should preferably all possess near-optimal objective measures with respect to all of the modelled objective(s), but be as fundamentally different from each other as possible in terms of the system structures characterized by their decision variables. Several approaches collectively referred to as *modelling-to-generate-alternatives* (MGA) have been developed in response to this multi-solution creation requirement (Brill *et al.*, 1982; Loughlin *et al.*, 2001; Yeomans & Gunalay, 2011).

The primary motivation behind MGA is to construct a manageably small set of alternatives that are good with respect to all measured objective(s) yet are as fundamentally different as possible from each other within the prescribed decision space. The resulting set of alternatives should provide numerous solutions that all perform somewhat similarly with respect to the modelled objectives, yet very differently with respect to the unmodelled issues (Walker *et al.*, 2003). Obviously the decision-makers must then conduct a subsequent comprehensive comparison of these alternatives to determine which options would most closely satisfy their very specific circumstances (Arrais-Castro *et al.*, 2015). Consequently, MGA approaches should necessarily be classified as a decision support processes rather than the role of explicit solution determination methods assumed, in general, for optimization (see, also: Benatia *et al.*, 2016; Sharma & Virmani, 2017; Strand *et al.*, 2017).

Previous MGA methods have employed direct, iterative processes for generating alternatives by incrementally re-running their solution algorithms whenever new alternatives must be produced (Baugh *et al.*, 1997; Brill *et al.*, 1982; Loughlin *et al.*, 2001; Yeomans & Gunalay, 2011; Zechman & Ranjithan, 2004). These iterative approaches follow the seminal MGA approach of Brill *et al.* (1982) in which, once an initial problem formulation has been optimized, the supplementary alternatives are created one-by-one. Consequently, these iterative approaches all require $n+1$ runnings of their respective algorithms to optimize the initial problem and to subsequently create their n alternatives (Imanirad & Yeomans, 2013; Imanirad *et al.*, 2012a; Yeomans & Gunalay, 2011).

For calculation and optimization purposes, Yang (2009, 2010) has demonstrated that the nature-inspired Firefly Algorithm (FA) is more computationally efficient than such commonly-used metaheuristic procedures as genetic algorithms, simulated annealing, and enhanced particle swarm optimization (Cagnina *et al.*, 2008; Gandomi *et al.*, 2011). However, what differentiates the FA from other population-based metaheuristics for functional optimization purposes, is that it has been specifically designed to simultaneously converge into a specified number of local optima (including the global ones) in highly non-linear mathematical programming problems (see, also: Arun *et al.*, 2017; Dekhici *et al.*, 2015; Dey *et al.*, 2014; Jagatheesan *et al.*, 2017; Kumar *et al.*, 2017). Imanirad & Yeomans (2013) have demonstrated how the FA's functional optimization capabilities to determine multiple local optima can be modified to produce the n maximally different alternatives required in an MGA approach after the initial optimal solution has been determined.

In this chapter, it is shown how to *simultaneously* generate sets of maximally different solution alternatives by implementing a modified version of the nature-inspired Firefly Algorithm (FA) Yang (2009, 2010) by extending previous concurrent MGA approaches of Yeomans (2018), Imanirad & Yeomans (2013) and Imanirad *et al.* (2012a, 2012b, 2013a, 2013b, 2013c). Remarkably, this new MGA procedure extends the earlier approaches of Imanirad *et al.* (2012a, 2012b, 2013a, 2013b, 2013c) to now permit the simultaneous generation of the overall best solution together with n locally optimal, maximally different alternatives in a single computational run. Namely, to generate the additional n maximally different solution alternatives, the MGA algorithm would need to run exactly the same number of times that the FA would need to be run for function optimization purposes alone (i.e. once) irrespective of the value of n Yeomans (2017a, 2017b). Therefore, this FA-directed algorithm is extremely computationally efficient for MGA purposes. Hence, this new, innovative simultaneous FA procedure is extremely computationally efficient for MGA purposes. This study illustrates the efficacy of this new approach on a commonly evaluated benchmark engineering optimization problem (Cagnina *et al.*, 2008).

FIREFLY ALGORITHM FOR FUNCTION OPTIMIZATION

While this section provides only a relatively brief synopsis of the FA procedure, more detailed explanations can be accessed in Yang (2009, 2010), Gandomi *et al.* (2011), Imanirad & Yeomans (2013) and Imanirad *et al.* (2012a). The FA is a biologically-inspired, population-based metaheuristic (Dey, 2018; Dey & Ashour, 2016; Dey & Ashour, 2017). Each firefly in the population represents one potential solution to a problem and the initial population of fireflies should be distributed uniformly and randomly throughout the solution space. The solution approach employs the following three idealized rules: (i) All fireflies within the population are considered essentially unisex, so that any one firefly could potentially be attracted to any other firefly irrespective of their sex; (ii) The relative attractiveness between any two fireflies is directly proportional to their respective brightness. This implies that for any two flashing fireflies, the less bright firefly will always be inclined to move towards the brighter one. However, attractiveness and brightness both decrease as the relative distance between the fireflies increases. If there is no brighter firefly within its visible neighborhood, then the particular firefly will move about randomly; and, (iii) The brightness of a firefly is determined by the overall landscape of the objective function. Namely, for a maximization problem, the brightness can simply be considered proportional to the value of the objective function. Based upon these three rules, the basic operational steps of the FA can be summarized within the following pseudo-code.

```
Objective Function F(X), X = (x_1, x_2,…, x_d)
Generate the initial population of n fireflies, X_i, i = 1, 2,…, n
Light intensity I_i at X_i is determined by F(X_i)
Define the light absorption coefficient γ
while (t < MaxGeneration)
    for i = 1: n, all n fireflies
        for j = 1: n, all n fireflies (inner loop)
            if (I_i < I_j), Move firefly i towards j; end if
```

```
            Vary attractiveness with distance r via e^-γr
        end for j
    end for i
    Rank the fireflies and find the current global best solution G*
end while
    Postprocess the results
```

In the FA, there are two important issues to resolve: the formulation of attractiveness and the variation of light intensity. For simplicity, it can always be assumed that the attractiveness of a firefly is determined by its brightness which in turn is associated with its encoded objective function value. In the simplest case, the brightness of a firefly at a particular location $\boldsymbol{X}$ would be its calculated objective value $F(\boldsymbol{X})$. However, the attractiveness, β, between fireflies is relative and will vary with the distance r_{ij} between firefly i and firefly j. In addition, light intensity decreases with the distance from its source, and light is also absorbed in the media, so the attractiveness needs to vary with the degree of absorption. Consequently, the overall attractiveness of a firefly can be defined as

$$\beta = \beta_0 \exp(-\gamma r^2)$$

where β_0 is the attractiveness at distance $r = 0$ and γ is the fixed light absorption coefficient for the specific medium. If the distance r_{ij} between any two fireflies i and j located at $\boldsymbol{X}_i$ and $\boldsymbol{X}_j$, respectively, is calculated using the Euclidean norm, then the movement of a firefly i that is attracted to another more attractive (i.e. brighter) firefly j is determined by

$$\boldsymbol{X}_i = \boldsymbol{X}_i + \beta_0 \exp(-\gamma(r_{ij})^2)(\boldsymbol{X}_i - \boldsymbol{X}_j) + \alpha\boldsymbol{\varepsilon}_i .$$

In this expression of movement, the second term is due to the relative attraction and the third term is a randomization component. Yang (2010) indicates that α is a randomization parameter normally selected within the range [0,1] and $\boldsymbol{\varepsilon}_i$ is a vector of random numbers drawn from either a Gaussian or uniform (generally [-0.5,0.5]) distribution. It should be explicitly noted that this expression represents a random walk biased toward brighter fireflies and if $\beta_0 = 0$, it becomes a simple random walk. The parameter γ characterizes the variation of the attractiveness and its value determines the speed of the algorithm's convergence. For most applications, γ is typically set between 0.1 to 10 (Gandomi *et al.*, 2011; Yang, 2010). In any given optimization problem, for a very large number of fireflies $n >> k$, where k is the number of local optima, the initial locations of the n fireflies should be distributed relatively uniformly throughout the entire search space. As the FA proceeds, the fireflies begin to converge into all of these local optima (including the global ones). Hence, by comparing the best solutions among all these optima, the global optima can easily be determined. Yang (2010) proves that the FA will approach the global optima when $n \to \infty$ and the number of iterations t, is set so that $t >> 1$. In reality, the FA has been found to converge extremely quickly with n set in the range 20 to 50 (Gandomi *et al.*, 2011; Yang, 2009, 2010).

Two important limiting or asymptotic cases occur when $\gamma \to 0$ and when $\gamma \to \infty$. For $\gamma \to 0$, the attractiveness is constant $\beta = \beta_0$, which is equivalent to having a light intensity that does not decrease. Thus, a firefly would be visible to every other firefly anywhere within the solution domain. Hence, a single (usually global) optima can easily be reached. If the inner loop for j in the pseudo-code is removed and X_j is replaced by the current global best G^*, then this implies that the FA reverts to a special case of the accelerated particle swarm optimization (PSO) algorithm. Subsequently, the computational efficiency of this special FA case is equivalent to that of enhanced PSO. Conversely, when $\gamma \to \infty$, the attractiveness is essentially zero along the sightline of all other fireflies. This is equivalent to the case where the fireflies randomly roam throughout a very thick foggy region with no other fireflies are visible and each firefly roams in a completely random fashion. This case corresponds to a completely random search method. As the FA operates between these two asymptotic extremes, it is possible to adjust the parameters α and γ so that the FA can outperform both a random search and the enhanced PSO algorithms (Gandomi *et al.*, 2011).

The computational efficiencies of the FA will be exploited in the subsequent MGA solution approach. As noted, within the two asymptotic extremes, the population in the FA can determine both the global optima as well as the local optima concurrently. The concurrency of population-based solution procedures holds huge computational and efficiency advantages for MGA purposes (Yeomans & Gunalay, 2011). An additional advantage of the FA for MGA implementation is that the different fireflies essentially work independently of each other, implying that FA procedures are better than genetic algorithms and PSO for MGA because the fireflies will tend to aggregate more closely around each local optimum (Gandomi *et al.*, 2011; Yang, 2010). Consequently, with a judicious selection of parameter settings, the FA will simultaneously converge extremely quickly into both local and global optima (Gandomi *et al.*, 2011; Yang, 2009, 2010).

MODELLING TO GENERATE ALTERNATIVES

Most mathematical programming approaches arising in the optimization literature have concentrated almost exclusively upon producing single optimal solutions to single-objective problem instances or, equivalently, generating noninferior solution sets to multi-objective formulations (Brill *et al.*, 1982; Janssen *et al.*, 2010; Walker *et al.*, 2003). While such algorithms may efficiently generate solutions to the derived complex mathematical models, whether these outputs actually establish "best" approaches to the underlying real problems is certainly questionable (Brill *et al.*, 1982; Brugnach *et al.*, 2007; Janssen *et al.*, 2010; Loughlin *et al.*, 2001). In most "real world" decision environments, there are innumerable system objectives and requirements that are never explicitly apparent or included in the decision formulation stage (Brugnach *et al.*, 2007; Walker *et al.*, 2003). Furthermore, it may never be possible to explicitly express all of the subjective components because there are frequently numerous incompatible, competing, design requirements and, perhaps, adversarial stakeholder groups involved. Therefore most subjective aspects of a problem necessarily must remain unquantified and unmodelled in the construction of the resultant decision models. This is a common occurrence in situations where the final decisions are constructed based not only upon clearly stated and modelled objectives, but also upon fundamentally subjective socio-political-economic goals and stakeholder preferences (Yeomans & Gunalay, 2011). Numerous "real world" examples describing these types of incongruent modelling dualities appear in Baugh *et al.* (1997), Brill *et al.* (1982), Loughlin *et al.* (2001) and Zechman & Ranjithan (2004).

When unquantified issues and unmodelled objectives exist, non-conventional approaches are required that not only search the decision space for noninferior sets of solutions, but must also explore the decision space for discernibly *inferior* alternatives to the modelled problem. In particular, any search for good alternatives to problems known or suspected to contain unmodelled objectives must focus not only on the non-inferior solution set, but also necessarily on an explicit exploration of the problem's inferior region.

To illustrate the implications of an unmodelled objective on a decision search, assume that the optimal solution for a quantified, single-objective, maximization decision problem is X^* with corresponding objective value $Z1^*$. Now suppose that there exists a second, unmodelled, maximization objective $Z2$ that subjectively reflects some unquantifiable "environmental/political acceptability" component. Let the solution X^a, belonging to the noninferior, 2-objective set, represent a potential best compromise solution if both objectives could somehow have been simultaneously evaluated by the decision-maker. While X^a might be viewed as the best compromise solution to the real problem, it would appear inferior to the solution X^* in the quantified mathematical model, since it evidently must be the case that $Z1^a \leq Z1^*$. Consequently, when unmodelled objectives are factored into the decision-making process, mathematically inferior solutions for the modelled problem can prove optimal to the underlying real problem. Therefore, when unmodelled objectives and unquantified issues might exist, different solution approachcs are needed in order to not only search the decision space for the noninferior set of solutions, but also to simultaneously explore the decision space for inferior alternative solutions to the modelled problem. Population-based methods such as the FA permit concurrent searches throughout a feasible region and thus prove to be particularly adept solution procedures for searching through such a problem's decision space.

The primary motivation behind MGA is to produce a manageably small set of alternatives that are quantifiably good with respect to modelled objectives yet are as different as possible from each other in the decision space. In doing this, the resulting alternative solution set is likely to provide truly different choices that all perform somewhat similarly with respect to the known modelled objective(s) yet very differently with respect to any unmodelled issues. By generating these good-but-different solutions, the decision-makers can explore desirable qualities within the alternatives that may prove to satisfactorily address the various unmodelled objectives to varying degrees of stakeholder acceptability.

In order to properly motivate an MGA search procedure, it is necessary to apply a more mathematically formal definition to the goals of the MGA process (Loughlin *et al.*, 2001; Yeomans & Gunalay, 2011). Suppose the optimal solution to an original mathematical model is X^* with objective value $Z^* = F(X^*)$. The following maximal difference model can then be solved to generate an alternative solution, X, that is maximally different from X^*:

Maximize $\Delta (X, X^*) = \sum_i |X_i - X_i^*|$

Subject to: $X \in D|$

$F(X) - Z^*| \leq T$

where Δ represents some difference function (for clarity, shown as an absolute difference in this instance) and T is a targeted tolerance value specified relative to the problem's original optimal objective Z^*. T is a user-supplied value that determines how much of the inferior region is to be explored in the search for acceptable alternative solutions. This difference function concept can be extended into a measure of difference between any set of alternatives by replacing X^* in the objective of the maximal difference model and calculating the overall sum (or some other function) of the differences of the pairwise comparisons between each pair of alternatives – subject to the condition that each alternative is feasible and falls within the specified tolerance constraint.

The FA-based MGA procedure to be introduced is designed to generate a pre-determined small number of close-to-optimal, but maximally different alternatives, by adjusting the value of T and using the FA to solve the corresponding maximal difference problem instance. By exploiting the population structure of the FA, the Fireflies collectively evolve toward different local optima within the solution space. The survival of solutions depends upon how well the solutions perform with respect to the problem's originally modelled objective(s) and simultaneously by how far away they are from all of the other alternatives generated in the decision space.

FA-BASED SIMULTANEOUS MGA COMPUTATIONAL ALGORITHM

The MGA method to be introduced produces a pre-determined number of close-to-optimal, but maximally different alternatives, by modifying the value of the bound T in the maximal difference model and using an FA to solve the corresponding, maximal difference problem. Each solution within the FA's population contains one potential set of p different alternatives. By exploiting the co-evolutionary solution structure within the population of the algorithm, the Fireflies collectively evolve each solution to-ward sets of different local optima within the solution space. In this process, each desired solution alternative undergoes the common search procedure of the FA. However, the survival of solutions depends both upon how well the solutions perform with respect to the modelled objective(s) and by how far away they are from all of the other alternatives generated in the decision space.

A direct process for generating alternatives with the FA would be to iteratively solve the maximum difference model by incrementally updating the target T whenever a new alternative needs to be produced and then re-running the algorithm. This iterative approach would parallel the original Hop, Skip, and Jump (HSJ) MGA algorithm of Brill *et al.* (1982) in which, once an initial problem formulation has been optimized, supplementary alternatives are systematically created one-by-one through an incremental adjustment of the target constraint to force the sequential generation of the suboptimal solutions. While this approach is straightforward, it requires a repeated execution of the optimization algorithm (Imanirad & Yeomans, 2013; Imanirad *et al.*, 2012a; Yeomans & Gunalay, 2011).

To improve upon the stepwise alternative approach of the HSJ algorithm, a concurrent MGA technique was subsequently designed based upon the concept of co-evolution Imanirad *et al.* (2012a, 2012b, 2013b). In the co-evolutionary approach, pre-specified stratified subpopulation ranges within the algorithm's overall population were established that collectively evolved the search toward the creation of the specified number of maximally different alternatives. Each desired solution alternative was represented by each respective subpopulation and each subpopulation underwent the common processing operations of the FA. The survival of solutions in each subpopulation depended simultaneously upon how well the solutions perform with respect to the modelled objective(s) and by how far away they are from all of the other alternatives. Consequently, the evolution of solutions in each subpopulation toward local optima is directly influenced by those solutions contained in all of the other subpopulations, which forces the concurrent co-evolution of each subpopulation towards good but maximally distant regions within the decision space according to the maximal difference model (Yeomans & Gunalay, 2011).

By employing this co-evolutionary concept, it becomes possible to implement an FA-based MGA procedure that concurrently produces alternatives which possess objective function bounds that are somewhat analogous to those created by the sequential, iterative HSJ-styled solution generation approach. While each alternative produced by an HSJ procedure is maximally different only from the overall optimal solution (together with its bound on the objective value which is at least x% different from the best objective (i.e. x = 1%, 2%, etc.)), a concurrent procedure is able to generate alternatives that are no more than x% different from the overall optimal solution but with each one of these solutions being as maximally different as possible from every other generated alternative that was produced. Co-evolution is also much more efficient than the sequential HSJ-style approach in that it exploits the inherent population-based searches of FA procedures to concurrently generate the entire set of maximally different solutions using only a single population (Imanirad & Yeomans, 2013; Imanirad *et al.*, 2013b).

While a concurrent approach exploits the population-based nature of the FA's solution approach, the co-evolution process occurs within each of the stratified subpopulations. The maximal differences between solutions in different subpopulations is based upon aggregate subpopulation measures. Conversely, in the following simultaneous MGA algorithm, each solution in the population contains exactly one entire set of alternatives and the maximal difference is calculated only for that particular solution (i.e. the specific alternative set contained within that solution in the population). Hence, by the evolutionary nature of the FA search procedure, in the subsequent approach, the maximal difference is simultaneously calculated for the specific set of alternatives considered within each specific solution – and the need for concurrent subpopulation aggregation measures is circumvented.

The steps in the co-evolutionary alternative generation algorithm are as follows (Yeomans 2017a, 2017b, 2018):

Initialization Step. In this preliminary step, solve the original optimization problem to determine the optimal solution, X^*. As with prior solution approaches Imanirad *et al.* (2012a, 2012b, 2013a, 2013b, 2013c) and without loss of generality, it is entirely possible to forego this step and construct the algorithm to find X^* as part of its solution processing. However, such a requirement increases the number of computational iterations of the overall procedure and the initial stages of the processing focus upon finding X^* while the other elements of each population solution remain essentially "computational overhead". Based upon the objective value $F(X^*)$, establish P target values. P represents the desired number of maximally different alternatives to be generated within prescribed target deviations from the X^*. Note: The value for P has to have been set *a priori* by the decision-maker.

Step 1: Create the initial population of size K in which each solution is divided into P equally-sized partitions. The size of each partition corresponds to the number of variables for the original optimization problem. $\mathbf{A}_p$ represents the pth alternative, p = 1,…,P, in each solution.

Step 2: In each of the K solutions, evaluate each $\mathbf{A}_p$, p = 1,…,P, with respect to the modelled objective. Alternatives meeting their target constraint and all other problem constraints are designated as feasible, while all other alternatives are designated as infeasible. A solution can only be designated as feasible if all of the alternatives contained within it are feasible.

Step 3: Apply an appropriate elitism operator to each solution to rank order the best individuals in the population. The best solution is the feasible solution containing the most distant set of alternatives in the decision space (the distance measure is defined in Step 5). Note: Because the best solution to date is always retained in the population throughout each iteration of the FA, at least one solution will always be feasible. A feasible solution for the first step can always consists of P repetitions of $\mathbf{X}^*$.

Step 4: Stop the algorithm if the termination criteria (such as maximum number of iterations or some measure of solution convergence) are met. Otherwise, proceed to Step 5.

Step 5: For each solution k = 1,…, K, calculate D_k, a distance measure between all of the alternatives contained within solution k.

As an illustrative example for determining a distance measure, calculate

$$D_k = \sum_{i=1toP} \sum_{j=1toP} \Delta\left(A_i, A_j\right)$$

This represents the total distance between all of the alternatives contained within solution *k*. Alternatively, the distance measure could be calculated by some other appropriately defined function.

Step 6: Rank the solutions according to the distance measure D_k objective – appropriately adjusted to incorporate any constraint violation penalties for infeasible solutions. The goal of maximal difference is to force alternatives to be as far apart as possible in the decision space from the alternatives of each of the partitions within each solution. This step orders the specific solutions by those solutions which contain the set of alternatives which are most distant from each other.

Step 7: Apply appropriate FA "change operations" to the each of the solutions and return to Step.

It should be apparent that the stratification approach outlined in this algorithm could be readily modified to accommodate any of the population-based solution procedures (see, for example, Tang *et al.*, 2017; Satapathy *et al.*, 2016). However, as noted in Section1, the FA is an algorithm specifically designed to simultaneously converge into numerous local optima which provides distinct computational advantages over other population-based metaheuristics. A disadvantage to the FA-based procedure in comparison to iterative MGA approaches lies in the extra computational overhead required to store the expanded population size for all of the alternatives and the additional solution time required to generate both the overall optimal solution together with the set of maximally different alternatives. Based upon preliminary testing and significant experimentation in the subsequent section, it seems that the additional storage requirements can be considered essentially negligible for all practical purposes and that the extra computational effort is virtually undetectable. However, these disadvantages could potentially become more pronounced for other problem instances that might be identified in subsequent extensions to this paper.

COMPUTATIONAL TESTING OF SIMULTANEOUS MGA ALGORITHM

As described earlier, "real world" decision-makers generally prefer to be able to select from a set of "near-optimal" alternatives that significantly differ from each other in terms of the system structures characterized by their decision variables. The effectiveness of the co-evolutionary MGA procedure to simultaneously produce such maximally different alternatives will be demonstrated using a benchmark constrained engineering optimization problem from Cagnina *et al.* (2008).

The design of a tension and compression spring has frequently been employed as a standard benchmark test problem for constrained engineering optimization algorithms (Cagnina *et al.*, 2008). The problem involves three design variables: (i) x_1, the wire diameter, (ii) x_2, the coil diameter, and (iii) x_3, the length of the coil. The aim is to essentially minimize the weight subject to constraints on deflection, stress, surge frequency and geometry.

The mathematical formulation for this test problem can be summarized as:

Minimize $F(\boldsymbol{X}) = x_1^2 x_2 \left(2 + x_3\right)$

Subject to: $g_1(\boldsymbol{X}) = 1 - \dfrac{x_2^3 x_3}{71785 x_1^4} \leq 0$

$$g_2(\boldsymbol{X}) = \frac{4x_2^2 - x_1 x_2}{12566\left(x_1^3 x_2 - x_1^4\right)} + \frac{1}{5108 x_1^2} - 1 \leq 0$$

$$g_3(\boldsymbol{X}) = 1 - \frac{140.45 x_1}{x_2^2 x_3} \leq 0$$

$$g_4(\boldsymbol{X}) = \frac{x_1 + x_2}{1.5} - 1 \leq 0$$

$0.05 \leq x_1 \leq 2.0$ $0.25 \leq x_2 \leq 1.3$ $2.0 \leq x_3 \leq 15.0$

The optimal solution for the specific design parameters employed within this formulation is $F(\boldsymbol{X}^*) = 0.0127$ with decision variable values of $\boldsymbol{X}^* = (0.051690, 0.356750, 11.287126)$ (Cagnina *et al.*, 2008). The MGA procedure was used to create the optimal solution and the 10 maximally different solutions shown in Table 1.

Table 1. Objective Values and Solutions for the 11 Maximally Different Alternatives

Increment	1.5% Increment Between Alternatives			
	$F(X)$	x_1	x_2	x_3
Optimal	0.0127	0.0517	0.3567	11.2871
Alternative 1	0.0128	0.05	0.3165	14.1598
Alternative 2	0.0128	0.0514	0.3472	12.0089
Alternative 3	0.0129	0.0529	0.3862	9.9684
Alternative 4	0.013	0.0521	0.3656	11.0667
Alternative 5	0.0131	0.0527	0.3766	10.5179
Alternative 6	0.0134	0.05	0.3157	14.978
Alternative 7	0.0137	0.052	0.3629	12.1615
Alternative 8	0.0140	0.0557	0.4307	9.5783
Alternative 9	0.0143	0.0542	0.4014	11.6481
Alternative 10	0.0146	0.0546	0.4247	10.7556

As described earlier, most "real world" optimization applications tend to be riddled with incongruent performance requirements that are exceedingly difficult to quantify. Consequently, it is preferable to create a set of quantifiably good alternatives that provide very different perspectives to the potentially unmodelled performance design issues during the policy formulation stage. The unique performance features captured within these dissimilar alternatives can result in very different system performance with respect to the unmodelled issues, hopefully thereby addressing some of the unmodelled issues into the actual solution process.

The example has demonstrated how the co-evolutionary MGA modelling perspective can be used to simultaneously generate multiple alternatives via the very computationally efficient FA that satisfy known system performance criteria according to the prespecified bounds and yet remain as maximally different from each other as possible in the decision space. In addition to its alternative generating capabilities, the FA component of the MGA approach simultaneously performs extremely well with respect to its role in function optimization. It should be explicitly noted that the overall best solution produced by the FA-based MGA procedure for the test problem is indistinguishable from the optimal one determined by Cagnina *et al.* (2008).

In summary, this section underscore several important findings with respect to the simultaneous FA-based MGA procedure: (i) The co-evolutionary capabilities within the FA can be exploited to generate more good alternatives than planners would be able to create using other MGA approaches because of the evolving nature of its population-based solution searches; (ii) By the design of the MGA algorithm, the alternatives generated are good for planning purposes since all of their structures will be maximally different from each other (i.e. these differences are not just simply different from the overall optimal solution as in an HSJ-style approach to MGA); and, (iv) The approach is computationally efficient since it need only be run a single time in order to generate its entire set of multiple, good solution alternatives (i.e. to generate n solution alternatives, the MGA algorithm needs to run exactly once irrespective of the value of n).

CONCLUSION

"Real world" decision-making problems generally possess multidimensional performance specifications compounded by incompatible performance objectives and unquantifiable requirements. These problems usually possess incongruent design requirements which are very difficult – if not impossible – to capture at the time that supporting decision models are constructed. Consequently, there are invariably unmodelled design issues, not apparent during the model construction, that can greatly impact the acceptability of the model's solutions. These uncertain and competing dimensions force decision-makers to integrate many conflicting sources into their decision process prior to final solution construction. In the face of such incongruencies, it is unlikely that any single solution could ever be constructed that simultaneously satisfies all of the ambiguous system requirements without a significant counterbalancing involving numerous tradeoffs. Therefore, any ancillary modelling techniques used to support decision formulation must somehow simultaneously account for all of these features while being flexible enough to encapsulate the impacts from the inherent planning uncertainty.

In this chapter, an MGA procedure was introduced that demonstrated how the structures of computationally efficient, population-based FA could be exploited to simultaneously generate multiple, maximally different, near-best alternatives via its co-evolutionary solution approach. In this MGA capacity, the simultaneous procedure produces numerous solutions possessing the requisite problem characteristics, with each generated alternative providing a very different perspective. Since FA techniques can be adapted to solve a wide variety of problem types, the practicality of this simultaneous MGA approach can clearly be extended into numerous disparate applications. These extensions will become the focus of future research.

ACKNOWLEDGMENT

This research was supported in part by grant OGP0155871 from the Natural Sciences and Engineering Research Council.

REFERENCES

Acharjya, D., & Anitha, A. (2017). A Comparative Study of Statistical and Rough Computing Models in Predictive Data Analysis. *International Journal of Ambient Computing and Intelligence*, *8*(2), 32–51. doi:10.4018/IJACI.2017040103

Arrais-Castro, A., Varela, M. L. R., Putnik, G. D., Ribeiro, R., & Dargram, F. C. C. (2015). Collaborative Negotiation Platform using a Dynamic Multi-Criteria Decision Model. *International Journal of Decision Support System Technology*, *7*(1), 1–14. doi:10.4018/ijdsst.2015010101

Arun, B., & Kumar, V. (2017). Materialized View Selection Using Bumble Bee Mating Optimization. *International Journal of Decision Support System Technology*, *9*(3), 1–27. doi:10.4018/IJDSST.2017070101

Baugh, J. W. Jr, Caldwell, S. C., & Brill, E. D. Jr. (1997). A Mathematical Programming Approach for Generating Alternatives in Discrete Structural Optimization. *Engineering Optimization*, *28*(1), 1–31. doi:10.1080/03052159708941125

Belarbi, M. A., Mahmoudi, S., & Belalem, G. (2017). PCA as Dimensionality Reduction for Large-Scale Image Retrieval Systems. *International Journal of Ambient Computing and Intelligence*, *8*(4), 45–58. doi:10.4018/IJACI.2017100104

Benatia, I., Laouar, M. R., Bendjenna, H., & Eom, S. (2016). Implementing a Cloud-Based Decision Support System in a Private Cloud: The Infrastructure and the Deployment Process. *International Journal of Decision Support System Technology*, *8*(1), 25–42. doi:10.4018/IJDSST.2016010102

Brill, E. D. Jr, Chang, S. Y., & Hopkins, L. D. (1982). Modelling to generate alternatives: The HSJ approach and an illustration using a problem in land use planning. *Management Science*, *28*(3), 221–235. doi:10.1287/mnsc.28.3.221

Brugnach, M., Tagg, A., Keil, F., & De Lange, W. J. (2007). Uncertainty matters: Computer models at the science-policy interface. *Water Resources Management*, *21*(7), 1075–1090. doi:10.100711269-006-9099-y

Cagnina, L. C., Esquivel, C. A., & Coello, C. A. (2008). Solving Engineering Optimization Problems with the Simple Constrained Particle Swarm Optimizer. *Informatica*, *32*, 319–326.

Dekhici, L., & Belkai, K. (2015). A Bat Algorithm with Generalized Walk for the Two-Stage Hybrid Flow Shop Problem. *International Journal of Decision Support System Technology*, *7*(3), 1–16. doi:10.4018/IJDSST.2015070101

Dey, N. (2018). *Advancements in Applied Metaheuristic Computing*. Hershey, PA: IGI Global. doi:10.4018/978-1-5225-4151-6

Dey, N., & Ashour, A. S. (2016). Antenna Design and Direction of Arrival Estimation in Meta-Heuristic Paradigm: A Review. *International Journal of Service Science, Management, Engineering, and Technology*, *7*(3), 1–18. doi:10.4018/IJSSMET.2016070101

Dey, N., & Ashour, A. S. (2017). Meta-Heuristic Algorithms in Medical Image Segmentation: A Review. *Advancements in Applied Metaheuristic Computing*, 185-203.

Dey, N., Samanta, S., Chakraborty, S., Das, A., Chaudhuri, S. S., & Suri, J. S. (2014). Firefly Algorithm for Optimization of Scaling Factors During Embedding of Manifold Medical Information: An Application in Ophthalmology Imaging. *Journal of Medical Imaging and Health Informatics*, *4*(3), 384–394. doi:10.1166/jmihi.2014.1265

Gandomi, A. H., Yang, X. S., & Alavi, A. H. (2011). Mixed Variable Structural Optimization Using Firefly Algorithm. *Computers & Structures*, *89*(23-24), 2325–2336. doi:10.1016/j.compstruc.2011.08.002

Imanirad, R., Yang, X. S., & Yeomans, J. S. (2012a). A Computationally Efficient, Biologically-Inspired Modelling-to-Generate-Alternatives Method. *Journal of Computers*, *2*(2), 43–47.

Imanirad, R., Yang, X. S., & Yeomans, J. S. (2012b). A Co-evolutionary, Nature-Inspired Algorithm for the Concurrent Generation of Alternatives. *Journal of Computers*, *2*(3), 101–106.

Imanirad, R., Yang, X. S., & Yeomans, J. S. (2013a). Modelling-to-Generate-Alternatives Via the Firefly Algorithm. *Journal of Applied Operational Research*, *5*(1), 14–21.

Imanirad, R., Yang, X. S., & Yeomans, J. S. (2013b). A Concurrent Modelling to Generate Alternatives Approach Using the Firefly Algorithm. *International Journal of Decision Support System Technology*, *5*(2), 33–45. doi:10.4018/jdsst.2013040103

Imanirad, R., Yang, X. S., & Yeomans, J. S. (2013c). A Biologically-Inspired Metaheuristic Procedure for Modelling-to-Generate-Alternatives. *International Journal of Engineering Re-search and Applications*, *3*(2), 1677–1686.

Imanirad, R., & Yeomans, J. S. (2013). Modelling to Generate Alternatives Using Biologically Inspired Algorithms. In X. S. Yang (Ed.), *Swarm Intelligence and Bio-Inspired Computation: Theory and Applications* (pp. 313–333). Amsterdam: Elsevier. doi:10.1016/B978-0-12-405163-8.00014-4

Jagatheesan, K., Anand, B., Samanta, S., Dey, N., Ashour, A. S., & Balas, V. E. (2017). Design of a Proportional-Integral-Derivative Controller for an Automatic Generation Control of Multi-Area Power Thermal Systems Using Firefly Algorithm. *IEEE/CAA Journal of Automatica Sinica*, *99*, 1-14.

Janssen, J. A. E. B., Krol, M. S., Schielen, R. M. J., & Hoekstra, A. Y. (2010). The effect of modelling quantified expert knowledge and uncertainty information on model based decision making. *Environmental Science & Policy*, *13*(3), 229–238. doi:10.1016/j.envsci.2010.03.003

Juneja, D., Singh, A., Singh, R., & Mukherjee, S. (2017). Towards a New Model of Storage and Access to Data in Big Data and Cloud Computing. *International Journal of Ambient Computing and Intelligence*, *8*(4), 31–44. doi:10.4018/IJACI.2017100103

Kumar, R., Rajan, A., Talukdar, F. A., Dey, N., Santhi, V., & Balas, V. E. (2017). Optimization of 5.5-GHz CMOS LNA Parameters Using Firefly Algorithm. *Neural Computing & Applications*, *28*(12), 3765–3779. doi:10.100700521-016-2267-y

Loughlin, D. H., Ranjithan, S. R., Brill, E. D. Jr, & Baugh, J. W. Jr. (2001). Genetic Algorithm Approaches for Addressing Unmodeled Objectives in Optimization Problems. *Engineering Optimization*, *33*(5), 549–569. doi:10.1080/03052150108940933

Matallah, H., Belalem, G., & Bouamrane, K. (2017). A Thorough Insight into Theoretical and Practical Developments in MultiAgent Systems. *International Journal of Ambient Computing and Intelligence*, *8*(1), 23–49. doi:10.4018/IJACI.2017010102

Matthies, M., Giupponi, C., & Ostendorf, B. (2007). Environmental decision support systems: Current issues, methods and tools. *Environmental Modelling & Software*, *22*(2), 123–127. doi:10.1016/j.envsoft.2005.09.005

Mowrer, H. T. (2000). Uncertainty in natural resource decision support systems: Sources, interpretation and importance. *Computers and Electronics in Agriculture*, *27*(1-3), 139–154. doi:10.1016/S0168-1699(00)00113-7

Satapathy, S. C., Raja, N. S. M., Rajinikanth, V., Ashour, A. S., & Dey, N. (2016). Multi-level Image Thresholding Using Otsu and Chaotic Bat Algorithm. *Neural Computing & Applications*, 1–23.

Sharma, K., & Virmani, J. (2017). A Decision Support System for Classification of Normal and Medical Renal Disease Using Ultrasound Images: A Decision Support System for Medical Renal Diseases. *International Journal of Ambient Computing and Intelligence*, *8*(2), 52–69. doi:10.4018/IJACI.2017040104

Strand, M., Syberfeldt, A., & Geertsen, A. (2017). A Decision Support System for Sustainable Waste Collection. *International Journal of Decision Support System Technology*, *9*(4), 49–65. doi:10.4018/IJDSST.2017100104

Tang, R., Fong, S., Dey, N., Wong, R. K., & Mohammed, S. (2017). Cross Entropy Method Based Hybridization of Dynamic Group Optimization Algorithm. *Entropy (Basel, Switzerland)*, *19*(10), 533. doi:10.3390/e19100533

Walker, W. E., Harremoes, P., Rotmans, J., Van der Sluis, J. P., Van Asselt, M. B. A., Janssen, P., & Krayer von Krauss, M. P. (2003). Defining uncertainty – a conceptual basis for uncertainty management in model-based decision support. *Integrated Assessment*, *4*(1), 5–17. doi:10.1076/iaij.4.1.5.16466

Yang, X. S. (2009). Firefly Algorithms for Multimodal Optimization. *Lecture Notes in Computer Science*, *5792*, 169–178. doi:10.1007/978-3-642-04944-6_14

Yang, X. S. (2010). *Nature-Inspired Metaheuristic Algorithms* (2nd ed.). Frome, UK: Luniver Press.

Yeomans, J. S. (2017a). Simultaneous Computing of Sets of Maximally Different Alternatives to Optimal Solutions. *International Journal of Engineering Research and Applications*, *7*(9), 21–28.

Yeomans, J. S. (2017b). An Optimization Algorithm that Simultaneously Calculates Maximally Different Alternatives. *International Journal of Computational Engineering Research*, *7*(10), 45–50.

Yeomans, J. S. (2018). An Efficient Computational Procedure for Simultaneously Generating Alternatives to an Optimal Solution Using the Firefly Algorithm. In X. S. Yang (Ed.), *Nature-Inspired Algorithms and Applied Optimization* (pp. 261–273). Cham, Switzerland: Springer. doi:10.1007/978-3-319-67669-2_12

Yeomans, J. S., & Gunalay, Y. (2011). Simulation-Optimization Techniques for Modelling to Generate Alternatives in Waste Management Planning. *Journal of Applied Operational Research*, *3*(1), 23–35.

Zechman, E. M., & Ranjithan, S. R. (2004). An Evolutionary Algorithm to Generate Alternatives (EAGA) for Engineering Optimization Problems. *Engineering Optimization*, *36*(5), 539–553. doi:10.1080/03052150410001704863

KEY TERMS AND THEIR DEFINITIONS

Biologically Inspired (Bio-Inspired) Meta-Heuristics: Meta-heuristics whose fundamental solution characteristics have been motivated by phenomena occurring in the natural environment.

Firefly Algorithm: The firefly algorithm is a computationally efficient, biologically inspired, population-based metaheuristic that derives its solution approach based upon the characteristics of fireflies.

Heuristics: Approximation schemes used in problem solving to generate good, though not necessarily optimal, solutions to mathematical programming problems.

Maximally Different Solutions: "Good" solution alternatives should possess near-optimal objective measures with respect to all of the known modelled objectives, but be fundamentally different from each other in terms of the system structures characterized by their decision variables. A difference model is employed to generate alternatives that are as far apart in the decision space as possible. The resulting alternative solution set of MGA provides disparate choices that all perform well with respect to the known modelled objectives, yet very differently with respect to any unknown, unmodeled, and/or unquantified issues. Hence, these solutions will provide entirely different perspectives to the original problem.

Meta-Heuristics: High-level, overarching heuristic approaches that have wide-ranging applicability to many different mathematical programming problems.

Modelling to Generate Alternatives (MGA): A modelling approach to systematically provide a set of "good" alternatives with respect to all of the problem's modelled objectives. The primary motivation for MGA is to produce a manageably small set of alternatives that are good with respect to the known modelled objectives yet as different as possible from each other in the decision space – namely the solution set should provide maximally different alternatives.

Unmodeled Issues: Aspects of a mathematical problem not captured during the construction and formulation of its corresponding mathematical/computer model.

Unquantified Issues: System objectives and requirements that are neither explicitly apparent nor included in the problem formulation stage – it is impossible to express these aspects quantitatively.

Chapter 3
Bat Algorithm With Generalized Fly for Combinatorial Production Optimization Problems:
Case Studies

Latifa Dekhici
University of Sciences and the Technology of Oran, Algeria

Khaled Guerraiche
National School of Electrical Engineering and Energy of Oran, Algeria

Khaled Belkadi
University of Sciences and the Technology of Oran, Algeria

ABSTRACT

A set of metaheuristics has proved its efficiency in solving rapidly NP-hard problems. Several combinatorial and continuous optimization areas drew profit from these powerful alternative techniques. This chapter intends to describe a discrete version of bat algorithm (BA) combined to generalized walk evolutionary (GEWA), also called bat algorithm with generalized fly or walk (BAG) in order to solve discrete industrial optimization. The first case of study is the well-known hybrid flow shop scheduling. The second one concerns the operating theatre that represents a critical manufacturing system, as the products delivered are patients. The last problem is the redundancy optimization (ROP) for series-parallel multi-state power system (MSS). Its resolution involves the selection of components with an appropriate level of redundancy to maximize system reliability with constrained cost. A universal moment generating function (UMGF) is used to estimate reliabilities. The modified bat algorithm on specific benchmarks was compared with the original one, and other results taken from the literature of each case study.

DOI: 10.4018/978-1-5225-6164-4.ch003

INTRODUCTION

Intelligent methods as fuzzy logic (Ahmed et al.,2017), neural network (Chatterjee et al.,2017a,b), multi agent and particularly metaheuristics (Straub, 2014, Imanirad et al. 2013) are increasingly becoming the key instrument for solving optimization problems in different decision-making levels. The problems can concern reliability and availability (Russell et al. 2009, Damerdji et Noureddine, 2017, Tyagi et al., 2017), resources planning (Filho et al.2014, Hanafizadeh et al.,2009) and tasks scheduling. They appeared in different areas either:

- Public healthcare systems and medical data (Tapia et Corchado, 2009, Walsh et al. 2011, Sharma et al., 2017,Mokeddem et al. 2014, Dey N. et al.,2014; Dey et Ashour, 2017);
- Antenna design ((dey et Ashour, 2016) ;
- Power systems as in (Altaleb et Brodsky, 2013, Kaliannan et al.,2016) and in (Jagatheesan et al., 2017 a, b, c, d) where authors used particles swarm optimization, flower pollination, firefly algorithm and other bio-inspired methods;
- Data mining (Karaa et al.,2016) or
- Manufacturing systems (Dekhici et Belkadi,2017).

Reader can refer to recent literature review of application of metaheuristic (Dey Nilanja.,2018).

Nature inspired swarm metaheuristics as Cross Entropy Dynamic Group Optimization (Tang et al.2017), ant colony, bee, firefly, and bat algorithms are ones of those intelligent methods that are widely attracting researchers. Artificial swarms became the forefront of the current studies due their efficient way to treat NP-hard combinatorial optimization.

In this chapter, a recent hybridized swarm metaheuristic based on the Bat algorithm (BA) and the Generalized Walk Evolutionary (GEWA) which is Bat Algorithm with Generalized Walk (BAG), is described. Inspired from micro-bats echolocation behavior, the Bat Algorithm has the advantage to enhance the best solutions in different ways with different probabilities whereas the Generalized Walk Evolutionary algorithm as walkers' behavior has the advantage to change the worst solution from the population with generalized walk.

Three study-cases will highlight the discretization feasibility of the main presented algorithm. First, the mono processor Hybrid Flow Shop problem is investigated. It is as many of manufacturing systems scheduling one of the NP-hard combinatorial problems that need an effective approximate method to be resolved.

A not far extension of manufacturing system optimization studied in this work is the operating theatre constrained scheduling. It concerns the assignment of patients to different operating rooms and to different recovery beds in Post Anesthesia Unit Care (PACU). The sequencing can take into account some sequencing constraints. Dedicate resources constraints can reduce the configuration to a parallel machine shop.

The third study case is the electrical structure optimization of series-parallel multi-state power production systems. The electrical system components are selected from a list of available components on the market. Electrical components are characterized by their reliability, cost and performance (capacity). An approach based on Universal Moment Generating Function (UMGF) determines the maximal reliability of series-parallel electrical topology of power system and is used under an upper cost bound.

The optimization approach could be useful for managers and engineers to better understand their system reliability and performance, and achieve better configuration.

The HFS test bed is a well know benchmark with 70 cases. The Operating theatre data sample was taken form a typical studies of operating theatres in Oran. Whereas, the redundancy power optimization sample is a common series-parallel power structure.

BAG algorithm Results on those samples are compared with the original bat algorithm, particle swarm optimization (PSO) and other methods.

BAT ALGORITHM

A Brief Review

The bat algorithm (BA) was first presented in (Yang, 2010) and it has been applied to benchmark functions. The standard bat algorithm has been applied in lot of area of optimization such as economic power dispatch problems (Ramesh et al., 2013), bloom filter optimization (Natarajan et al., 2012), and phishing website detection (Damodaram and Valarmathi, 2012). (Komarasamy and Wahi, 2012) studied K-means clustering using bat algorithm. Khan et al. (2011), (Khan and Sahari,2012a, 2012b) combined it with fuzzy logic in the context of e-learning. It is used to classify micro array data (Mishra et al., 2012). In the area of image processing, it was used to full body human pose estimation (Abdel-Rahman et al., 2012), Image matching (Du and Liu, 2012). In Other Applications, we can find its application in: optimal capacitor placement for loss reduction in distribution systems (Reddy and Manoj, 2012) and energy modelling (Lemma et al., 2011,Tamiru and Hashim, 2013). The bat algorithm was also recently used in configuring cloud (Saarker et al., 2017). In the manufacturing scheduling area, Marichelvam and al. (2013) used bat algorithm to solve multi processors flexible flow shop scheduling problems while Dekhici et Belkadi(2015) used it to mono processor hybrid flow shop. In the area of power system, Guerraiche et al. (2015a, b) used the algorithm in reliability and cost optimization in power system design. Dos Santos Coelho et al. (2016) enhanced the original bat algorithm to reduce electrical power consumption of air conditioning. Eneko Osaba et al. (2016) improved a discrete version to solve symmetric and asymmetric Traveling Salesman Problems. Satapathy et al. (2016) Otsu also used chaotic bat algorithm for Multi-level image thresholding. Chiranjeevi Karri et al. (2016) used bat algorithm to image compression. Vijay Kumaret al. (2016) modified the standard metaheuristic for Security constrained economic load dispatching with interline power flow. Elsisi et al. (2016) designed model predictive load frequency control using Bat inspired algorithm. Dehghani et al. (2017) use the bat algorithm to Copper price estimation. Gholami et al. (2017) estimated porosity from seismic attributes using a committee model with the basic algorithm. Multi-step wind speed forecasting problem was solved in (Liye Xiao et al., 2017) by improving the original version. Binary codification was given to a multi-objective technique based on bat algorithm in (Taha M. Mohamed et al.,2017). Vedik Basettiet al. (2017)also used binary coding for Optimal PMU placement for power system observability. HTTP flood attack detection in application layer was solved in (Indraneel Sreeram et al.,2017) by combining machine learning with bat algorithm. Avishek Das et al. (2017) proposed an efficient side lobe reduction technique considering mutual coupling effect in linear array antenna using the bat method. Kaced et al. (2017) maximized with bat metaheuristic the power point tracking for photovoltaic system under partial shading conditions. Most of researchers modified and enhanced the original bat algorithm to get more ability related to their application field.

Echolocation of Bats

The bat algorithm (BA) is inspired from an idealization of echolocation that can be summarized as follows:

- A virtual bat flies randomly at position (solution) x_i with a velocity v_i with a varying frequency or wavelength F_i and loudness A_i. As it searches and finds its prey, it changes frequency, pulse emission rate r and loudness.
- Search is step up by a local random walk. Selection of the best continues until certain stop criteria are met.

The algorithm, for simplicity, uses the following idealized principles:

All bats use echolocation to sense distance, and they also know the difference between prey and background barriers in some magical way;

Bats fly randomly with velocity v_i at position x_i with a fixed frequency f_{min}, varying wavelength and loudness A_0 to search for prey. They can automatically adjust the wavelength (or frequency) of their emitted pulses and adjust the rate of pulse emission r depending on the proximity of their target;

Although the loudness can vary in many ways, we assume that the loudness varies from a large (positive) A_0 to a minimum constant value A_{min}.

Bat Algorithm Parameters

Bat algorithm is based on four parameters: frequency, velocity, position and pulse rate. The bat algorithm updates all those values at each run of a certain number of iterations.

Frequency Representation. The frequency f at an iteration t is an integer or a float number depending on the selected minimum and maximum frequency.

$$f_i^t = f_{min} + (f_{max} - f_{min})\text{rand}() \tag{1}$$

rand∈[0,1]

Velocity Representation.The velocity v at an iteration t of each bat i is represented as a positive integer number. Velocity suggest show many of the bat's attributes should be changed at a certain instant. The bats will communicate with each other through the global best position gbest.

$$v_i^t = v_i^{t-1} + \left(x_i^{t-1} - gBest^{t-1}\right) \times f_i^t \tag{2}$$

Movement. The position x_i^t of a bat i at an iteration tis updated according to the best position of this bat in the last iteration x_i^{t-1}. and it actual velocity v_i^t

$$x_i^t = x_i^{t-1} + v_i^t \tag{3}$$

The next postion of a bat i can be arround the last global best position of all bats:

$$x_i^t = gBest^{t-1} + random_{-1}^{1} \times A_{avg.} \tag{4}$$

Or randomly:

$$x_i^t = x_i^{t-1} + random_{-1}^{1} \times A_{avg.} \tag{5}$$

where A_{avg} is the average sound loudness of all the bats.

Loudness Representation. A sound loudness of a bat A_i has a range between the maximum and minimum loudness. The initial loudness A_i^0 can typically be in [1, 2] (Yang, 2010). It can decrease at an iteration t using equation (6):

$$A_i^t = \alpha A_i^{t-1}, \alpha \in [0,1] \tag{6}$$

Pulse Rate Representation. Pulse rate r_i value will play a role in whether a local search procedure around the global best solution should be conducted or skipped in the iteration t

$$r_i^t = r_i^0 \times \left(1 - e^{-\gamma \times t}\right), r_i^0 \mathit{Initial\ pulse\ rates},\ \gamma > 0. \tag{7}$$

Pseudo code A bat algorithm seems to be as shown in Algorithm 1.

MODIFIED BAT ALGORITHM WITH GENERALIZED WALK (BAG)

To enhance the quality of the original bat algorithm, the bat algorithm was hybridized with the relatively recent metaheuristic which is Generalized Evolutionary Walk Algorithm (GEWA) described below.

Generalized Evolutionary Walk Algorithm (GEWA)

The Generalized Evolutionary Walk Algorithm (GEWA) is a generic metaheuristic for optimization developed by (Yang, 2010). It is based on a random global search that replace the worst solutions in a population. It is as a generalization of local search around the individual or global best position.

Three major components are in GEWA:

- Global exploration by randomization,
- Intensive local search by random walk, and
- The selection of the best solution.

The pseudo code of GEWA is shown in algorithm 2. The random walk should be carried out around the current global gbest so as to exploit the system such as the current best more effectively. We have (8) and (9).

Algorithm 1. Pseudo Code of Bat Algorithm

```
Initialize fmin=0; fmax=100; //to be adjusted
Initialize bats population xi and their velocity vi
Define impulsion frequencies fi: fi=fmin+(fmax-fmin)rand()
Initialize impulsions:ri0  [0,1]
And intensities: Ai [1,2]
aluate f(xi) and find global best position (gbest) and its fitness fGBest
Fitness(i)=f(xi), best(i)=xi
Fort=1 tomax_gendo
        Adjust frequencies (equation 1)
        update velocities (equation 2)
        generate new bats xi (equation 3)
        for i=1 to nb do //for all bats
                ifrand>ri
                        generate a new position arround the best(equation 4)
                endif
                        generate new positionby flying randomly(equation 5)
                if rand< Ai and f(X_i^t.)<fitness(i))
                        accept new solutions X_i^t
                        Increase ri and reduce Ai(equation 6,7)
                endif
        sort bats to find the best
done, done, end
```

$$w^t = \varepsilon^t d \tag{8}$$

$$x^t_{worstIndex} = gBest^{t-1} + w^t \tag{9}$$

where ε^t is drawn from a normal distribution N(0, δ^2) or Gaussian distribution. The step length is called d that is vector and should be related to the actual scales of independent variables. One can take $\delta = 1$, for simplicity.

The randomization step can be achieved by (10)

$$x^t_{worstIndex} = w_{min} + \left(w_{max} - w_{min}\right)\ \varepsilon^t . \tag{10}$$

where w_{max} and w_{min} are the upper and lower bound vectors, respectively.

There are only two algorithm dependent parameters in GEWA. The population size nb. of walkers and the randomization control parameter α. Typically, α= 0.5 is often used in most applications.

Algorithm 2. GEWA Metaheuristic

```
Procedure GEWA Meta-heuristic(Nbr_gen: max number of generations)
Begin
Wmin, wmax,δ,d,α: coefficients to be initialized
Define the objective function of f(x), x=(x1...,xnb)
nerate the initial population of walkers xi (i=1,...,nb)
Determine the global best fitness fgbest=min(fi) and its position gbest
And the worst fitness fgworst=max(fi) and  its worst_index
While (iter<Nbr_Gen*nb)
εiter=uniform(0,δ²)
If rand<α
        w=εiterd      //walk depending on step  d
        xworst_ index=gbest+w //walk around the best
else
        xworst_index=wmin+(wmax-wmin) εiter//random walk in the bounds
end if
Determine the global best  fgbest=min(fbesti) and its position gbest
Determine the global worst and its index.
iter++
End While
End procedure
```

Modified Bat Algorithm With Generalized Walk (BAG)

In the modified Bat algorithm with generalized walk a generalized fly of the worst bats as in GEWA algorithm is added to the classical bat algorithm. The worst bat flies with a probability α_g around the best bat flowing equation 9 (see the previous section). It can fly randomly if probability α_g is not reached. In addition, in the two cases, the flying distance is based on a step length d_g and a Gaussian distribution depending on δ_g^2 following formula 8. The worst bats index vector in each algorithm cycle must updated when sorting bats.

CASE STUDY 1: THE BAT ALGORITHM WITH GENARALISED FLY FOR HSF PROBLEM

Hybrid Flow Shop Problem Presentation

A Hybrid Flow Shop (HFS) also called flexible flow shop is a system composed of a set of stages, where each stage is composed of one or more parallel machines. The different jobs visit the stages in the same order. On each stage, a job is treated by one machine only. Between each stage, the jobs can wait or not in limited or unlimited buffers (Vignier et al., 1999, Billaut et al., 2000). Moreover, all jobs are assumed to be available at system entrance with release date with value 0.

Scheduling in the HFS consists to find an adequate sequence of the jobs in entrance and an assignment of the jobs on the various machines at the various stages. The objective is optimization of a criterion of performance among the criteria. One can quote the makespan or Cmax which is the completion time of the last job on the last stage, max flow time or Fmax (Srivastava 1998, Dessouky et al.,1998, Portman et al.1998, Lamica 2000, Kyparisis and Koulamas, 2006, Jin et al., 2006, Tang et al., 2006) and due date related objective (Bank et al.,2001, Kim et al., 2002, 2003, Tang et al.2002). This problem can have many constraints (Dekhici and Belkadi, 2010b).

According to Vignier et al. (1999) notation:

M: Number of stages scheduled is M

N: Number of tasks scheduled is *N.*

l_k: The number of machines in stage *k is* l_k.

The processing time of job I in stage j if machines are identical is noted t_{ij}.

General HFS studies are found in (Baker, 1974, Carlier et al.,1993). A survey is given by (Linn and Zhang, 1999). Shen and Chen (1972) were the first to tackle on a two-stage HFS with a number of machines more than two in each stage. They solved Makespan Minimization Problem Using a permutation heuristic. Buten and Shen (1973) have studied the same problem but with j precedence constraints, which they solved with a modified version of Johnson (1954) algorithm. Gupta (1988) studied the makespan problem in a two-stage HFS with l_1>=2 and l_2=1. He confirms that the makespan problem is NP-hard when one of the two stages contains more than one machine. This result is very important because it shows that any makespan minimization in a K-stage HFS is NP-hard, since the two stage HFS is been always be atypical pattern of k-stage HFS. He proposed a heuristic and lower bounds for the MMP case. Sriskandarajah and Sethi (1989) focused on the two stages HFS with parallel identical machines on the second stage and only single machine on the first stage. Other extensions can interest researchers.

Figure 1. Schema of the two stages HFS(L1=3,L2=2)| |CMAX

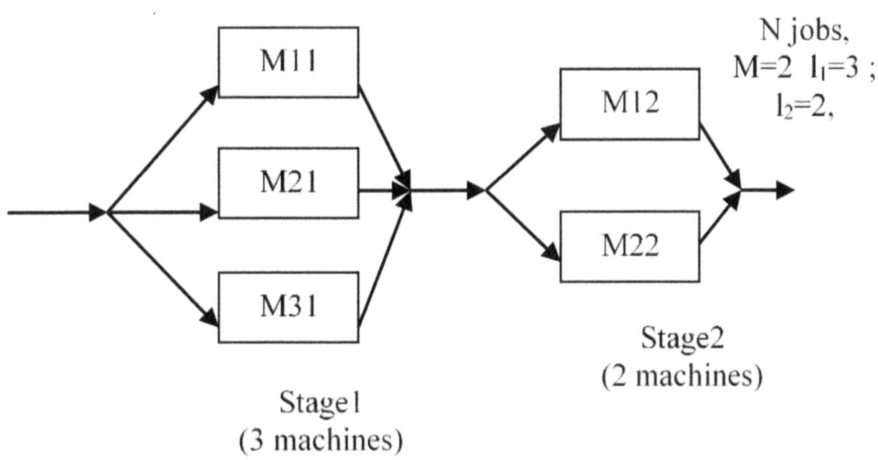

Shahvari et al. (2018) work on two stage-based hybrid algorithms for a batch scheduling using particle swarm optimization and tabu search. Dios et al. (2018) added the missing operations to the standard pattern and used heuristics. Yi-Kuei et al. (2017) studied reliability in a multi-state HFS due delays. Didem Baturetet al. (2016) applied HFS notation to a robotic cells. Recently, the firefly algorithm was applied to the mono processor HSF (Dekhici et Belkadi, 2017).

Discretization

An integer solution coding is kept in (Dekhici et Belkadi, 2015). It contains the sequence *s* and the assignments *a* as it is shown in the formula 11.

$$x = \{s_i | a_{ik}\}, 0 \le i < N, 0 \le k < M \tag{11}$$

$0 \le s_i < N$.

$0 \le a_{ik} < l_k$.

Example: Having 3 jobs and 2 stages with 5 resources in each one, an initial solution can seem to (2, 1, 0| 24, 52, 32) which means that jobs are in decrease sort, the first job 0 is assigned to the second resource in stage 1 and to the 4th resource in stage 2….etc.

When the bat flies, the position of bat *I* changes from a discrete number *x* to a real number *x'* (formula 12)

$$x' = \{s'_t | a'_{tk}\} 0 \le t < N, 0 \le k < M \tag{12}$$

$s'_t, a'_{tk} \in \mathbb{R}$

Correct sequence, authors in (Dekhici et Belkadi, 2015) proposed to sort jobs of *s* per their *s'* values. To correct assignments *a, a' is* adjusted to unsigned integers in the domain $\{0 .. l_k\text{-}1\}$. The velocity is also corrected to be in the domain of N for sequences and l_k for the assignments.

Random flying in formula 5 are replaced by a neighborhood system based on both sequence permutation and assignment change.

Parameters can be set to: $\alpha=\gamma=0.9$;fmin=0; fmax=100; $\alpha_g= 0.5$, $d_g=0.05$,$\delta_g=1$.

CASE STUDY 2: THE BAT ALGORITHM WITH GENARALIZED FLY FOR OPERATING THEATER SCHEDULING

Surgeries scheduling gives surgeries' sequences and patients' assignments to operating rooms and to revival beds in the Post anesthesia care unit (PACU). According to the different classes presented by Dekhici and Belkadi (2014), the surgeries scheduling problem can be considered as:

- A three stage hybrid flow shop (HFS)with blockage (without buffers)in presence of induction rooms;
- A two stage HFS without buffers;
- Or as a parallel machines problem if one of the stages is neglected. Usually the beds assignment can be ignored if the theater is properly sized (enough of awaking beds) and the post-anesthesia care unit is not subject to any dependency constraints.

The system has no intermediate buffer. However a job cannot leave the machine until its assigned machine in the next stage is free. That why The operating theatre scheduling purpose lies on minimizing total durations and patients blocking time on the operating room. It is also lead to minimize sequencing soft constraints as precedence, priorities and no sequencing relationship. The problem is face to a maximum constraints satisfaction. The objective function seems to be as below

$$f_x = \lambda_1 cmax_x + \lambda_2 cout\_abus_x . \tag{13}$$

where λ_1, λ_2. are coefficients of Pareto optimality, as defaults set to 1.

CASE STUDY 3: THE BAT ALGORITHM WITH GENARALISED WALK FOR POWER SYSTEM DESIGN OPTIMIZATION

Power System Redundancy Problem

Let us consider a power system containing N electrical power components connected in series-parallel. Each component I in turn contain a number of different components connected in parallel. All components

Figure 2. Schema of an operating theater with induction rooms

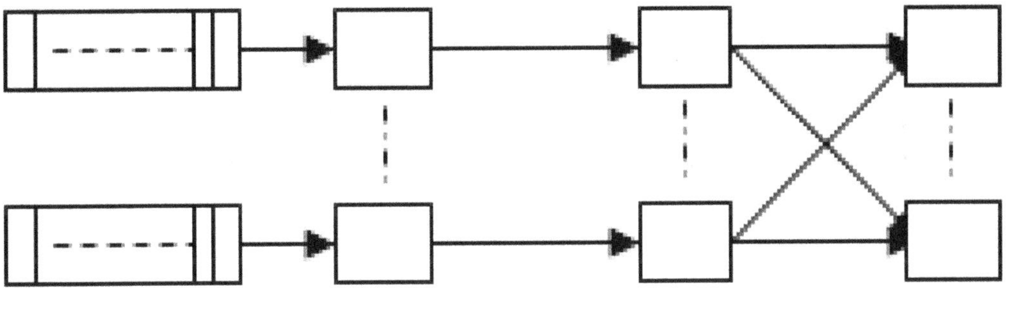

of any given subsystem belong to different versions. Components are characterized by their Reliability (A_{ij}), cost (C_{ij}) and performance (Ξ_{ij}). The structure of a subsystem i can be defined by the numbers of parallel components k_{ij} for $1 \leq j \leq V_i$, where V_i is the number of versions available for compt of type i.

The multi-state electrical power system redundancy optimization problem can be formulated as follows: find the minimal cost system configuration k_1, k_2,…k_N, such that the corresponding reliability exceeds or equal the specified reliability A_0.

$$\text{Minimize } C = \sum_{i=1}^{n} \sum_{j=1}^{V_i} k_{ij} c_{ij} \tag{14}$$

$$\text{Subject To } A\left(d,t,k_1,k_2,\ldots k_N\right) \geq A_0 \tag{15}$$

Abbreviations and Acronyms

- **i,j,l:** Respectively indices of series, versions and demand period interval.
- **N:** Number of series i
- **C_{ij}:** Cost of electrical component j of type i.
- **V_i:** Number of Available electrical components technologies of type i.
- **kij:** Number of occurrence of component j in series i.
- **Ξi:** Performance of power component i.
- **A_{ij}:** Reliability of power component j of type i.
- **A_0:** Minimum availability required.
- **M:** Number of demand period interval.
- **K_{max}**: Maximum number that can be taken from each component j.
- **P_i:** Performance probability of ith device.

Figure 3. Detailed structure of a given subsystem

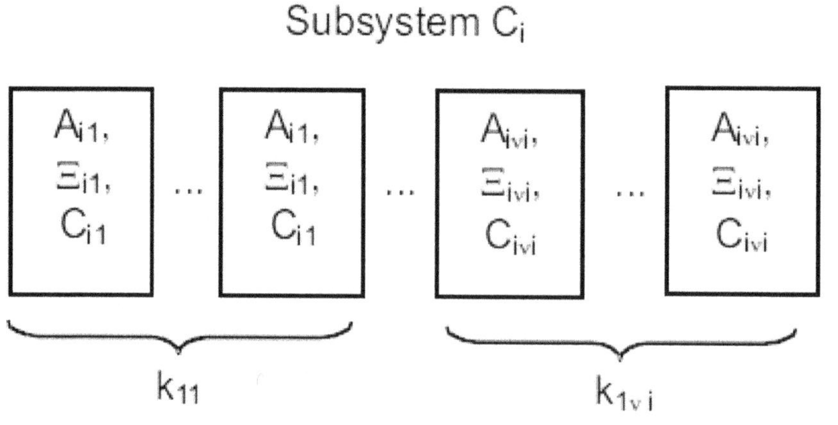

- **Q_j:** Performance probability of jth device.
- **W:** Demand levels.
- $\Im$ **:** Operator for parallel device.
- δ **:** Operator for series device.

Availability Measurement Method

The problem defined above is one of the combinatorial optimization problems, it is necessary to enumerate a huge number of possible system states. Thus, it is required to use an effective and fast procedure for structure reliability estimation. As shown above, the main problem is to evaluate the index R for arbitrary series and parallel system. The probability that the total capacity of the electrical power system is not less than a specific load demand level W must be calculated as:

$$R(W) = P\{\Xi > W\} = 1 - P\{\Xi \le W\}. \tag{16}$$

The procedure used to estimate this index is based on a modern mathematical technique: the UMGF (or u-transform) technique in. This method was first applied to real power system reliability assessment and optimization in (Levitin et al., 1989), and represent an extension of ordinary moment generating function (Guerraiche et al.,2015c). The UMGF, in our case, of a discrete variable E is defined as a polynomial

$$u(z) = \sum_{j=1}^{J} P_j z^{g_j} \tag{17}$$

Consider single devices with total failures and each device I has nominal performance ΞI and reliability Ai. The UMGF of such an device has only two terms can be defined as in (18):

$$u_i(z) = (1 - A_i)z^0 + A_i z^{Ei} = (1 - A_i) + A_i z^{\Xi_i} \tag{18}$$

To evaluate the MSS availability of a series-parallel system, two basic composition operators are introduced. These operators determine the polynomial u(z) for a group of devices.

Parallel Devices

$$\begin{aligned} \Im(u_1(z),\ u_2(z)) &= \Im\left(\sum_{i=1}^{n} P_i z^{a_i},\ \sum_{j=1}^{m} Q_j z^{b_j}\right) \\ &= \sum_{i=1}^{n}\sum_{j=1}^{m} P_i Q_j z^{a_i+b_j} \end{aligned} \tag{19}$$

Series Devices

$$\delta(u_1(z),\ u_2(z)) = \delta\left(\sum_{i=1}^{n} P_i z^{a_i},\ \sum_{j=1}^{m} Q_j z^{b_j}\right)$$

$$= \sum_{i=1}^{n}\sum_{j=1}^{m} P_i Q_j z^{\min\{a_i,\ b_j\}} \quad (20)$$

Applying composition operators $\Im$ and δ consecutively, one can obtain the UMGF of the entire series-parallel system. To do this we must first determine the individual UMGF of each device.

The discrete power redundancy problem involve that each solution provided by the bat algorithm with generalized fly (BAG) will be corrected to a discrete one representing redundancy of components.

COMPUTATIONAL RESULTS

In this section, results of the adapted BAG algorithm on the three case studies is described. Authors (Dekhici et al., 2015, Guerraiche et al., 2018) provided a part of result for this chapter.

Case Study 1: Two Stage Hybrid Flow Shop

For the experimental study, the standard mono processors two stages hybrid flow shop with related machines is chosen, which means that the processing times of a job in a stage do not depend on machine. Moreover, *N* jobs are supposed to be available at the system entrance. A buffer of infinite capacity is incorporated between stages for each machine. Three sets A, B and C of test problems are randomly generated. For the set B, the workloads at the two stages mostly to be well balanced while for the set C, the workloads incline to be unbalanced. The set A, contains a diversified mix of size and shop setting.

- **Set A:** These instances were generated in a similar way as (Haouari and M'halla, 1997). The number of jobs n is taken equal to 20, 30, 40, 50 and 100 jobs. The processing times noted 2:4, 4:2, 4:4 are drawn randomly either from the discrete uniform distribution on [1, 20] or [1,40]. The numbers of machines (l_1, l_2) are (2, 2), (2, 4) and (4, 2). We combined these problem characteristics to obtain 12 different problem classes for each fixed N. For each combination, 20 instances were generated. Hence, the Set A contains a total number of 1200 instances.
- **Set B:** It is generated in the same way in (Houari and al.,2006). The machine processing times on stage j were drawn randomly from the uniform distribution on [1, 5*l_j](j= 1, 2).The number of machines l_1 and l_2 were drawn randomly from the discrete uniform distribution on [2,6]. The number of jobs N was taken equal to 20, 30, 40, 50, 100. For each N, 50 instances were generated.
- **Set C:** This set covers250 instances that were generated in the same way as those of Set B, but the machine processing times on both stages were drawn randomly from the discrete uniform distribution on [1, 20] (Houari and al.,2006).

The number of walkers, bats or particles are 10.

The maximum CPU time is limited to 120 ms. For set A and 400 ms. for set B and C.

To compare methods, performances depend on the measures below:

Lower bound LB. LB indicates the lower bound calculated for the problem instance. The lower bounds used in this performance study were developed in (Haouari and M'halla, 1997).

$$LB = \max\left(\frac{spt(l_1)\sum_{i=1}^{N} t_{i1}}{l_1}, \frac{spt(l_2)\sum_{i=1}^{N} t_{i2}}{l_2}\right) \tag{21}$$

where spt(l_1) is the minimum sum of completion times, on stage 2, of the l_1 jobs whose processing times on stage 2 are the shortest.

Average Percentage Deviation (APD). The average Percentage deviation of a solution makespan(cmax) from the lower bound as given in (22):

$$\text{APD} = \frac{\text{cmax} \ - \text{LB}}{\text{LB}} \times 100 \tag{22}$$

Improvement rate. Improvement of the best solution as given in (23):

$$improv. = \frac{cmax_{initial} - cmax_{final}}{cmax_{initial} + cmax_{final}} \times 100 \tag{23}$$

Others. Two other analysis factors are used:

- TGB wich is the average Time to Get the global Best (optimum) when APD=0.
- NS wich is the number of instances for which optimality was proved (Number of Solved). (Ben Hamida et al.2011) used US factor (UnSolved instances) which is the number of instances-NS.

Table 1 shows average makespan and improvement rate of particle swarm optimization (PSO), bat algorithm (BA) and bat algorithm with generalized walk (BAG) when we run the program 20 times with 120ms. in each time.

The proposed discrete bat algorithm with generalized walk (BAG) reaches an improvement rate from 4.1% to more than 31.44% face to PSO which cannot reach an improvement more than 8.05%. BAG algorithm improvement on set A is better than original BA in 24 problem cases so in 40% of cases.

In Table 2 both BA and BAG are compared with other methods in literature:

1. Tabu search (TS)(Haouari and M'halla,1997).
2. Climbing bounded discrepancy search (CDDS^{L}) (Ben Hamida et al.,2007).
3. Bround and Branch(B&B) where the time limitforthe Forward (Backward) problem was set equal to 600s. (Haouari et al.,2007).

Table 1. Average CMAX and IT improvement of different methods, set A.

Problem			Cmax			Improvm.		
			PSO	BA	BAG	PSO	BA	BAG
A20	2x2	02:04	244.8	224	224	4.42	8.74	8.74
		04:02	223.55	204	204	5.71	10.16	10.16
		04:04	243.5	211	211	8.02	14.93	14.93
		02:02	158.85	127	127	5.22	16.16	16.16
	2x4	02:04	153.45	127.05	127	4.64	13.83	13.85
		04:02	174.35	158	158	8.05	12.78	12.78
		04:04	229.05	182	182	7.9	18.95	18.95
		02:02	112.3	96	96	6.44	14.05	14.05
	4x2	02:04	231.3	182	182	5.62	17.25	17.25
		04:02	154.95	92.95	92.65	7.25	31.29	31.44
		04:04	246.15	218	218	6.35	12.25	12.25
		02:02	136.75	111	111	2.63	12.81	12.81
A30	2x2	02:04	281.3	245	245	7.17	13.86	13.86
		04:02	305.35	280	280	6.65	10.87	10.87
		04:04	393.25	324.1	324.05	4.01	13.52	13.53
		02:02	205.65	165.1	165	2.72	13.54	13.57
	2x4	02:04	205.35	144.75	143.65	7.46	24.19	24.54
		04:02	322.8	315	315	6.36	7.56	7.56
		04:04	367.75	360	360	6.43	7.48	7.48
		02:02	195.55	168	168	5.11	12.53	12.53
	4x2	02:04	320.5	307	307	5.38	7.48	7.48
		04:02	221.25	173.05	173	6.51	18.39	18.41
		04:04	403.45	310.1	310.05	2.34	15.24	15.25
		02:02	161.3	137	137	3.97	11.94	11.94
A40	2x2	02:04	430.1	353.05	353	8.1	17.7	17.7
		04:02	402.75	389	389	5.19	6.91	6.91
		04:04	470.7	413.1	413	7.05	13.48	13.49
		02:02	460.85	411	411	6.27	11.83	11.83
	2x4	02:04	287.05	219.65	217.95	6.39	19.41	19.77
		04:02	440.75	419.05	419	5.29	7.77	7.78
		04:04	394.35	362	362	7.27	11.43	11.43
		02:02	224.7	210	210	6.92	10.24	10.24
	4x2	02:04	442.2	430	430	5.34	6.71	6.71
		04:02	264.3	197.3	196.65	5.4	19.54	19.7
		04:04	454.2	365.35	365.2	3.15	13.78	13.8
		02:02	218.85	197	197	4.1	9.23	9.23

continued on following page

Table 1. Continued

Problem			Cmax			Improvm.		
			PSO	BA	BAG	PSO	BA	BAG
A50	2x2	02:04	531.15	453.05	453.1	4.09	11.92	11.92
		04:02	562.15	519.05	519	5.14	9.06	9.07
		04:04	603.6	493.95	493.5	5.02	14.89	14.93
		02:02	555.2	526.1	526	5.29	7.93	7.94
	2x4	02:04	343.9	263.05	258.9	7.02	20.08	20.82
		04:02	501.15	487	487	3.94	5.35	5.35
		04:04	531.35	516	516	5.71	7.15	7.15
		02:02	286.45	261	261	4.99	9.54	9.54
	4x2	02:04	580.25	512.05	512.05	6.47	12.59	12.59
		04:02	345.4	279.05	278.7	6.03	16.46	16.52
		04:04	513.95	443.15	443	3.32	10.63	10.64
		02:02	266.7	232	232	4.94	11.77	11.77
A100	2x2	02:04	1022.55	924.65	924.6	3.43	8.41	8.41
		04:02	1077.5	1058.3	1058.35	3.21	4.1	4.1
		04:04	1180.2	1033.15	1031.6	3.54	10.14	10.21
		02:02	1110.7	1085.3	1085.15	2.96	4.1	4.11
	2x4	02:04	628.05	529.8	524.2	2.59	10.99	11.51
		04:02	1090.25	1075.2	1075.1	3.01	3.7	3.71
		04:04	1064.4	1014.3	1014.05	2.73	5.12	5.13
		02:02	534.9	514	514	3.88	5.84	5.84
	4x2	02:04	1057.65	983.6	983.55	3.36	6.95	6.96
		02:02	545.75	528	528	2.8	4.43	4.43
		04:02	673.15	537.75	535.7	2.97	14.04	14.22
		04:04	1091.55	1036.8	1036.35	2.69	5.24	5.26
AVG.			448.02	402.24	401.93	5.10	11.81	11.85

4. Climbing Depth-bounded Discrepancy Search (CDDS[2]) where Maximum CPU time Limit was 15 s and the number of instances for each case was 20. (Ben Hamida et al.,2011).

The deviation from the lower bound (APD) of BAG algorithm is less than 0.164. It is null in most cases and instances. The average APD of BAG according to all cases is 0.01 while it greater than that for PSO, TS and CDDSL. Thought the average number of solved instances of CDDS2 is more than 18 per 20 tests when it only 17.63 for BAG but APD of our modified bat algorithm is only 0.01 while it is 0.13 for CDDS2.

The average time to get the optimum makespan of BAG algorithm is in most case better than the original BA. It varies between a neglected processing time (0.00 ms) and 65 ms.

Table 2. Average criteria of different methods, Set A[1]

problem			APD %							TGB			NS				
			PSO	BA	BAG	B&B	TS	CDDS2	CDDSL	PSO	BA	BAG	PSO	BA	BAG	CDDS2	CDDSL
A20	2x2	02:04	0.472	0	0	0	NA	0.05	0.16	-	1.55	0.8	0	20	20	18	17
		04:02	0.44	0	0	0	NA	0.03	0.08	-	1.55	1.6	0	20	20	19	15
		04:04	0.663	0	0	0 .88	NA	0.39	0.48	-	7.1	4.7	0	20	20	15	9
		02:02	1.551	0	0	NA	NA	NA	NA	-	4.7	1.6	0	20	20	NA	NA
	2x4	02:04	0.715	0	0	1.71	2.9	0.95	5.79	-	9.89	1.5	0	19	20	12	20
		04:02	0.351	0	0	0	0.56	0.03	0.09	110	0.75	0	3	20	20	20	17
		04:04	1.436	0	0	0	0.92	0	0.07	-	10.1	11.7	0	20	20	20	13
		02:02	0.802	0	0	NA	NA	NA	NA	-	3.8	0	0	20	20	NA	NA
	4x2	02:04	1.521	0	0	0	0.35	0	0.12	-	7	3.8	0	20	20	20	16
		04:02	4.712	0.44	0.164	6.31	1.22	0.75	5.7	-	36.91	47.92	0	11	13	15	7
		04:04	0.942	0	0	0	0.13	0.05	0.23	-	0	0.8	0	20	20	20	17
		02:02	0.978	0	0	NA	NA	NA	NA	-	0	0	0	20	20	NA	NA
A30	2x2	02:04	0.626	0	0	0	NA	0.02	1.61	-	7.8	2.3	0	20	20	19	13
		04:02	0.661	0	0	0	NA	0	0.16	-	11.65	5.4	0	20	20	20	16
		04:04	1.158	0	0	0	NA	0.1	0.63	-	19	15.58	0	19	19	16	8
		02:02	1.352	0.03	0	NA	NA	NA	NA	-	21.67	10.2	0	18	20	NA	NA
	2x4	02:04	2.438	0.15	0	1.68	1.43	0.92	5.61	-	52.63	41	0	8	11	14	3
		04:02	0.053	0	0	0	0.27	0	0.12	90.35	0	0	2	20	20	20	17
		04:04	0.215	0	0	0	0.57	0.07	0.08	-	1.6	2.35	1	20	20	20	12
		02:02	0.676	0	0	NA	NA	NA	NA	-	8.55	3.95	0	20	20	NA	NA
	4x2	02:04	0.072	0	0	0	0.06	0	0.12	4.7	6.25	0.75	2	20	20	20	17
		04:02	2.047	0	0	6 .36	1.46	0.96	5.69	-	15.58	29.55	0	19	20	13	9
		04:04	1.057	0	0	0	0.05	0.02	0.05	-	12.21	20.53	0	19	19	19	15
		02:02	1.363	0	0	NA	NA	NA	NA	-	3.95	0.8	0	20	20	NA	NA
A40	2x2	02:04	1.546	0	0	0	NA	0	0.04	-	16.32	23.3	0	19	20	20	18
		04:02	0.296	0	0	0	NA	0	0.06	-	6.2	0.8	0	20	20	20	18
		04:04	0.742	0	0	0	NA	0.08	0.26	-	34.53	28.1	0	19	20	17	11
		02:02	0.48	0	0	NA	NA	NA	NA	17.45	22.6	6.35	1	20	20	NA	NA
	2x4	02:04	1.392	0.05	0.161	0	0.96	0.21	0.97	-	60.5	42.1	0	8	10	16	12
		04:02	0.291	0	0	0	0.34	0	0.53	-	9.35	2.47	0	19	20	20	17
		04:04	0.267	0	0	0	0.5	0.02	0.14	-	14.85	3.9	0	20	20	19	13
		02:02	0.272	0	0	NA	NA	NA	NA	-	4.65	0	0	20	20	NA	NA
	4x2	02:04	0.013	0	0	0	0.12	0	0.56	24.7	13.25	0	1	20	20	20	16
		04:02	2.861	0.03	0.003	2.14	0 .89	0.28	1.01	-	71.43	49.64	0	7	11	17	11
		04:04	1.49	0	0	0	0.12	0.01	0.17	-	26	28.72	0	15	18	19	14
		02:02	0.414	0	0	NA	NA	NA	NA	-	7	9.45	0	20	20	NA	NA

continued on following page

Table 2. Continued

problem			APD %							TGB			NS				
			PSO	BA	BAG	B&B	TS	CDDS2	CDDSL	PSO	BA	BAG	PSO	BA	BAG	CDDS2	CDDSL
A50	2x2	02:04	1.043	0	0	0	NA	0	0.07	-	27.89	22.56	0	19	18	20	17
		04:02	0.173	0	0	0	NA	0	0.56	-	26.16	13.2	0	19	20	20	17
		04:04	0.898	0.01	0	0	NA	0	0.28	-	66.25	50.93	0	8	15	20	14
		02:02	0.135	0	0	NA	NA	NA	NA	13.17	13.95	17.95	1	19	20	NA	NA
	2x4	02:04	1.81	0.03	0.021	0	0.54	0.15	0.7	-	93.5	47	0	2	2	18	14
		04:02	0.177	0	0	0	0.26	0	0.43	67.2	13.2	4.6	1	20	20	20	18
		04:04	0.165	0	0	0	NA	0	15	-	13.35	5.45	0	20	20	20	12
		02:02	0.473	0	0	NA	NA	NA	NA	42.6	11.7	17.15	1	20	20	NA	NA
	4x2	02:04	0.511	0	0	0	0.02	0	0.11	-	22.16	23.79	0	19	19	20	16
		04:02	0.915	0.018	0	0	0.04	0.37	0.69	-	51.83	54	0	6	13	12	10
		04:04	0.637	0	0.001	0	NA	0.02	0.05	-	44.6	29.47	0	20	17	18	15
		02:02	0.559	0	0	NA	NA	NA	NA	-	10.9	17.2	0	20	20	NA	NA
A100	2x2	02:04	0.724	0.01	0.005	0	0.54	0.05	0.23	-	41.92	41.14	0	13	14	19	16
		04:02	0.11	0	0	0	0.26	0	0.09	-	57.86	33.25	0	14	16	20	17
		04:04	0.607	0	0.005	0	Na	0.01	0.16	-	65.6	65.27	0	5	11	20	11
		02:02	0.087	0	0	NA	NA	NA	NA	-	32.06	22.06	0	17	17	NA	NA
	2x4	02:04	1.278	0.13	0.01	0	0.19	0.06	0.3	-	62	37.4	0	1	5	18	14
		04:02	0.029	0.01	0	0	0.07	0	0.09	-	43.39	18.5	0	16	18	20	18
		04:04	0.236	0	0	0	0.11	0	0.15	-	39.42	24.38	0	16	19	20	19
		02:02	0.508	0	0	NA	NA	NA	NA	51.9	24.2	15.6	1	20	20	NA	NA
	4x2	02:04	0.431	0	0	0	0.02	0	0.09	47.95	46.85	19.5	1	13	13	20	15
		04:02	1.394	0.06	0.004	0	0.18	0 .03	0.35	-	62.5	75	0	2	5	18	13
		04:04	0.497	0.01	0.005	0	0.01	0.01	0.09	32.4	67.2	25.93	1	10	15	18	11
		02:02	0.22	0	0	NA	NA	NA	NA	-	40.5	26.4	0	20	20	NA	NA
Avg.			0.83	0.02	0.01	0.28	0.49	0.13	1.11	45.67	25.17	18.49	0.27	16.65	17.63	18.42	14.18

Table 3. Average criteria of different methods, Set B, C.

	Cmax			Improvement%			APD%				TGB			NS			
	PSO	BA	BAG	PSO	BA	BAG	PSO	BA	BAG	B&B	PSO	BA	BAG	PSO	BA	BAG	B&B
b20	85.34	58.3	56.58	56.22	7.16	26.54	26.81	1.836	0	3.99	-	57.44	41.88	0	42	46	35
b30	119.26	84.55	81.94	81.96	4.79	22.71	22.72	0.771	0.003	3.26	-	82.1	52	0	37	30	34
b40	148.36	110.58	110.2	109.02	5	19.16	19.8	0.506	0.019	4.56	-	95.73	101.85	0	28	35	38
b50	180.56	138.68	135.25	137.42	4.16	16.93	17.35	0.598	0	2.95	-	101.27	88.55	0	32	36	37
b100	331.92	274.45	278.42	275.42	4.77	13.44	13.96	0.221	0.029	1.69	305.02	275.29	121.67	1	27	30	44
c20	106.16	82.85	78.48	78.5	6.01	21.99	21.95	0.384	0	3.78	-	25.79	33.72	0	43	44	46
c30	143.38	126.4	111.18	110.12	5.45	19.11	19.74	0.989	0.051	1.37	98.35	43.28	18.29	1	42	44	49
c40	204.38	171.84	160.9	171.82	5	14.35	14.36	0.161	0.002	0.95	-	60.74	55.17	0	39	43	49
c50	233.38	195.04	165.75	194.16	14.18	4.33	14.5	1.564	0.111	3.93	-	62.34	62.02	0	36	38	48
c100	452.46	408.06	378.45	407.94	3.67	9.25	9.25	0.035	0	0.52	-	105.31	75.31	0	36	35	49
Avg.	200.52	165.07	155.71	162.26	6.02	16.78	18.044	0.706	0.021	2.7	201.68	90.93	65.05	0.2	36.2	38.1	42.9

In the other category of computation, sets B and C, 50 instances for each case are generated. The results of sets B and C for N from 20 to 100 are represented in Table 3.

So Table 3 represents average deviations from lower bound of algorithms. We can notice that BAG algorithm yields the lower bound in most of instances that why the APD is close to zero in most of cases especially when the workloads are unbalanced (class c). While B&B and BA have relatively an important deviation in all B problems. Particle swarm optimization following the same discretization principles and within only 400ms cannot solve many instance (0.2 as an average). Though the B&B can solve about 42.9 instances per case. Its deviation in the worst instances is more than 2% while it only 0.021 for BAG and 0.706 for BA.

Case Study 2: A Neurosurgical Operating Theater Scheduling

As an operating theatre, the neurosurgical operating theater of ORAN hospital is retained (Dekhici and Belkadi, 2010a).

The well-sized theater accepts 4 planned surgeries of spins kind including two for women and 2 planned surgeries of skulls including 1 for Women on a set of 2 operating room(OR)offered to planned surgeries with 2 PACU containing 6 beds for men and 5 for women. The beds by contrast are shared with emergency surgeries. Executive times follow a triangular distribution tria. for surgeries (Table 4).

Dekhici (2016) explained many cases such as the Case with hard constrains of dedicated beds in PACU according to gender an d without sequencing constraints where the theaterproperlysizedwithl_1=2 and l_2=11 is an no wait HFS3(2,2,11)|constrains|Cmax N=6.For the case of an improperly sized system: l_1=2and l_2<11, let consider l_2=5. The system is HFS3(2,2,5)|constraints | Cmax N=6.

Figure 4 shows makespan for 20 instances for properly and improperly sized operating theatre with hard constraints of dedicated beds and without sequencing constraints. The total opening duration lie from1440 mn.=24 by BAG to 1791mn.=29,8h found by PSO.

For further analysis of the Makespan improvement, Figure 5 shows the improvement rate according to the makespan of the population. It is clear that under hard constraints, PSO improvement do not over come4 to 5,8% whereas the other swarm metaheuristics reach an improvement rate of 14% on the total opening duration.

The average deviation of the best makespans found from the lower bound are still be important while it exceeds 10%(Figure 5). This is explicable because the HFS lower bound estimation do not take into account hard assignment constraints.

As the system is hard constrained, the lower bound is never reached so the number of perfectly re-solved instance is Zero(NUS=0) for all metaheuristics.

Table 4. Duration in minutes of surgeries and awaking

Planned Surgery Class	Surgery Duration	Waking Duration
Spins/ women	Tria (163,171,266)	34
Skull/women	Tria(163,171,266)	1440
Spins/men	Tria(163,171,266)	48
Skull/men	Tria(163,171,266)	1440

Figure 4. Avg. makespan of operating theater with dedicated beds

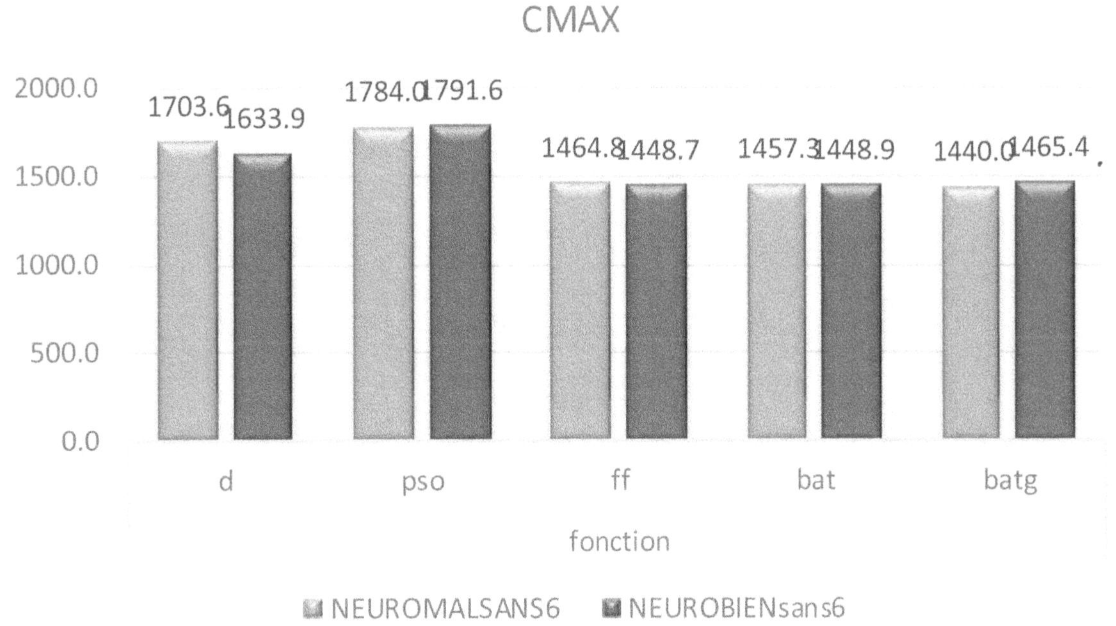

Figure 5. Makespan improvement rate of operating theater

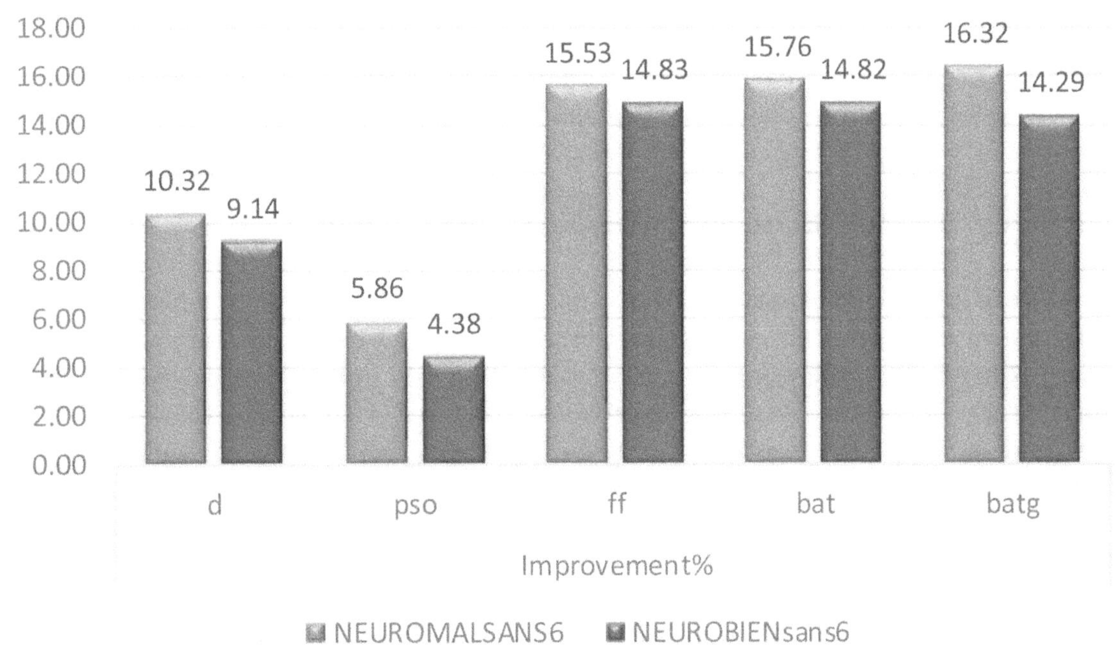

Figure 6. Average deviation from lower bound of the operating theater without sequencing constraints

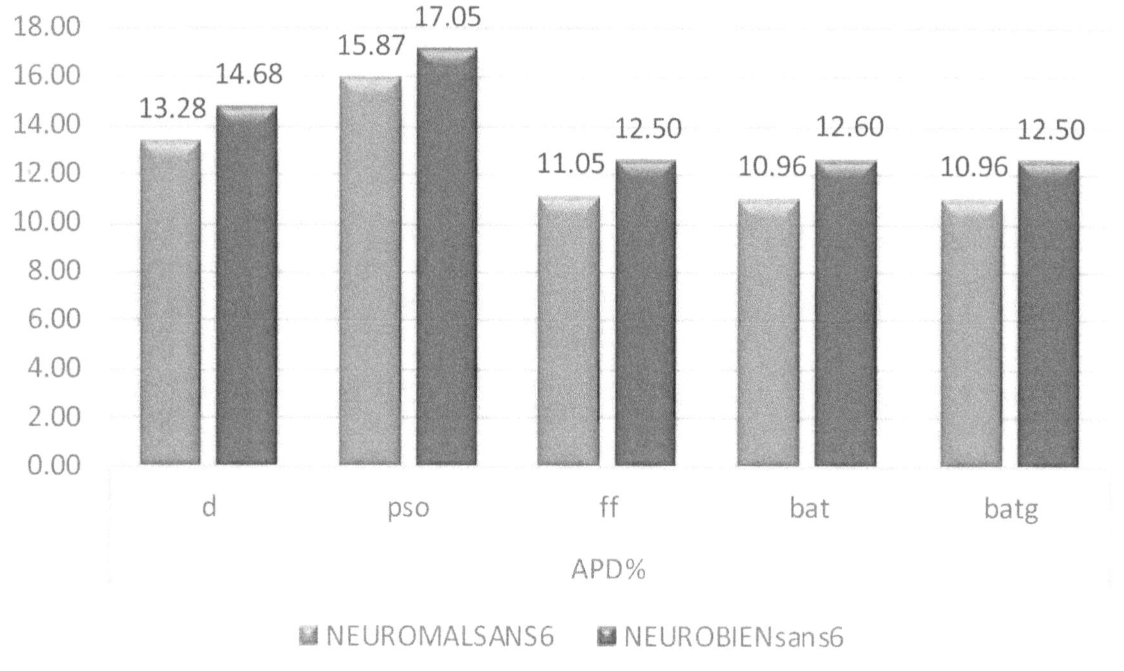

For the second Case with hard constrains of dedicated beds in PACU and with sequencing constraints, Dekhici (2016) submit the scheduling to 4 conflicting sequencing constraints (precedence, temporal location, no-sequencing and priority). Results of multi-purpose pareto function abuse cost function and total duration on properly and improperly sized neurosurgical operating theater indicate that there are not a big variance between the original bat algorithm results and the modified bat algorithm ones. This is due to the fact that conflicting constraints reduce significantly the quality of metaheuristics.

Case Study 3: A Multi State Serie-Parallel Power System

Each device in the system is considered a unit with a total failure. The data of the different versions of each subsystem are presented in Table 5. This table shows that each equipment is characterized by the reliability R in (%), the performance (nominal capacity) G in MW (Mega Watt) and the cost C in mln (Million dollar). Table 6 illustrates the cumulative annual demand of 8760 hours. The demand is 100% for an annual peak of 3504 h. Reliability is measured by the probability that its performance is greater than or equal to the demand (Wm) for a period (Tm). The electrical energy system can be described as follows:

From the raw material (fuel oil, gas and steam for a thermal power station), the electricity is produced by the first column (Subsystem 1), then the MV / HT transformation by the HV transformers, (subsystem 2).) and the transport by the HV lines (subsystem 3), a second transformation occurs by HV / MV transformers (subsystem 4), the load is fed through MV lines (subsystem 5) as shows the Figure 7.

Table 5. Characteristics of reliability system components on the market

Sub system	Version	Reliability R (%)	Cost C (mln $)	Performance G (MW)
manufacturing unit	1	0.992	7.735	6
	2	0.986	6.475	5
	3	0.994	6.698	5
	4	0.988	6.29	6
	5	0.980	6.146	6
	6	0.991	6.945	6
	7	0.992	6.984	6
	8	0.984	6.465	6
	9	0.993	6.565	5
	10	0.985	6.450	5
HT Transformer	1	0.994	2.805	18
	2	0.990	2.272	18
	3	0.997	2.594	12
	4	0.991	2.569	12
	5	0.998	1.857	8
Line HT	1	0.971	1.985	16
	2	0.997	1.983	14
	3	0.991	1.842	14
	4	0.976	1.318	12
Transformer HT/MT	1	0.978	0.842	16
	2	0.986	0.875	16
	3	0.978	0.745	14
	4	0.983	0.654	12
	5	0.981	0.625	12
	6	0.971	0.6080	12
	7	0.985	0.492	10
	8	0.973	0.415	10
Line MT	1	0.984	0.4560	14
	2	0.993	0.4320	12
	3	0.989	0.3640	10
	4	0.981	0.2830	8
	5	0.968	0.2420	8

Figure 7. Electro-energy series parallel system

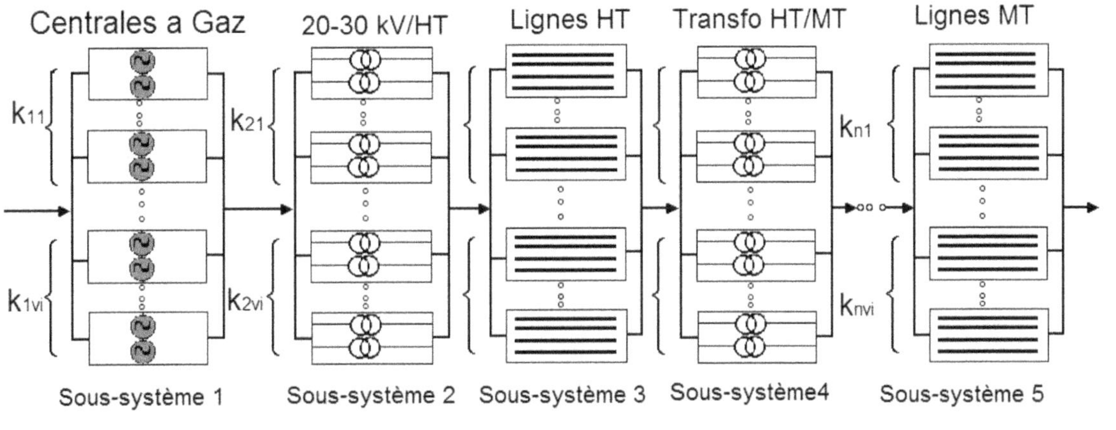

Table 6. Parameters of the cumulative demand curve

Wm (%)	40	34	26	20
Tm (h)	1752	1752	3504	1752

The objective function is to define the minimum design cost of the electric power generation and transmission system that provides the required level of availability. The set of results obtained by the hybrid algorithm BAG proposed for the different given values of $R_0$are illustrated in Table 3. The latter also shows the index of the calculated reliability R, the total cost C of the system and their corresponding structures. The reliability index R_0 has been set at three different values, namely 0.97, 0.98 and 0.99. The results of the simulation depend on largely values of the parameters of the hybrid algorithm BAT and GEWA (BAG). We define $\alpha = 0.8$, $\gamma = 0.8$ and $F_{max} = 100$ Hz. Although the combination of finely tuned parameter values leads to a better convergence of metaheuristic algorithms, choosing the best combination is very difficult and becomes a disadvantage of these algorithms.

The comparison between the solution of the BAG algorithm and the bat algorithm is given in Table 7. It can be seen that, the hybridization of the BAT and GEWA algorithms can obtain a better solution than the 'Algorithm of bats. The BAG algorithm for the redundancy optimization problem of parallel connected elements of the multi-state parallel-serial heterogeneous system (MSS) generally gives better solutions with lower cost and reasonable reliability than other algorithms.

Table 7. Comparison between the BAG algorithm and the BAT algorithm

R0	Structure	BAG	BAT
0.97	1 2 3 4 5	4, 5, 6, 7, 8, 9, 10 1, 2, 3, 4, 5 1, 2, 3, 4 3, 4, 5, 6, 7, 8 1, 2, 3, 4, 5	5(3), 7(3), 8 4(2), 5(4) 2, 3, 4(4) 6(3), 7, 8(4) 4(7)
C (mln $)		70.38	73.47
R		0.9784	0.9798
0.980	1 2 3 4 5	6, 8(4), 9, 10 5(7) 4(6) 7(2), 8(5) 3(4), 5(4)	2, 5, 6(2), 7(2), 8 2(5), 3 5 4(6) 8(6) 4(5), 5
C (mln $)		72.21	74.81
R		0.9809	0.9805
0.990	1 2 3 4 5	4, 5(2), 6, 7, 8, 9, 10 1, 2, 3, 4, 5 1, 2, 3, 4 3(2), 4, 5, 6, 7, 8 1, 2, 3, 4, 5	2, 3, 4(2), 5, 6(2), 8 2(3), 3, 4 2, 3, 4(3) 5(2), 7(3), 8 2(4), 4(3)
C (mln $)		77.27	77.73
R		0.9946	0.9989

Thus, from the point of view of the quality of the solution, the algorithms are compared with the number of iterations (900), and the number of populations (150). It should be noted that even very small improvements in reliability are essential and beneficial in the area of reliability optimization.

CONCLUSION

The goal of this Chapter was to present how some combinatorial manufacturing optimization problems issued from heterogeneous areas can be solved using both bat algorithm (BA) and a recent improved bat algorithm with generalized fly (BAG). The recent nature-inspired metaheuristic is based on the same principles as bat algorithm and a part of the generalized walk evolutionary (GEWA). While most of swarmed metaheuristic formula are interested by improving the best positions, the generalized fly formula consist on eliminating the worst positions per a generalized fly.

Three cases of combinatorial optimization problems were mentioned in this chapter. Each one involves a different discretization of BAG algorithm and needs an adequate constriction of solution provided by artificial bats movement.

The first problem is a manufacturing scheduling problem which is the flexible flow shop also called hybrid flow shop. The solution encoding kept the expressive assignment and sequencing. Authors attempted a standard two stage hybrid flow shop benchmark with 70 classes with fixed and random parameters, balanced and unbalanced workloads. Comparison criteria are the average percentage deviation from the lower bound and number of solved instances. Efficiency is compared with other method results.

The second problem is a constrained operating theater scheduling. According to the configuration established, the problem could be considered as a no wait hybrid flow shop with 2 or 3 stages or a simple parallel machines problem. The discretization of the BAG algorithm for such problem do not differ to the first case study. Experimentations concerned a neurosurgical operating theater with dedicated resources. Computational results showed that due to the number of hard assignment constraints and soft sequencing constraints, the improvement rate of metaheuristics is not consistent. Nevertheless, the bat algorithm with generalized fly (BAG) still be slightly better than the original bat algorithm.

The third case study concerns the series-parallel multi-stage power systems design or the redundancy optimization problem. The purpose is to select power components with a redundancy in each version of each subsystem in order to design a system with minimum cost respecting demand and reliability constraints. The Computational results on an example of a electrical power system with five subsystems demonstrate how the BAG algorithm outdoes the BAT algorithm by giving a better cost holding the same reliability rates.

In summary, those works seems to prove that the bat algorithm with generalized fly (BAG) keeps the advantages of GEWA and BA algorithms. It improves each bat position with different manners and in the same iteration changes the worst position of bats. This improved algorithm avoids the local optimal to yield rapidly the global best solution. The computational results show that it is better than the original bat algorithm in terms of any criterion. The method can be discretized as other metaheuristics. These findings add to a growing corpus of swarm metaheuristic a new promoting metaheuristic. They provide potential mechanisms to be implicated in continuous and combinatorial optimization.

FUTURE RESEARCH DIRECTIONS

Future investigations are necessary to validate conclusions drawn from this study. They should consider more carefully, the potential effects of moving the worst solutions while generating new population. They should explore the possibility to combine such principle to other nature-inspired swarm intelligence. Regardless, application should continue to expand to more industrial decision-makings.

ACKNOWLEDGMENT

We acknowledge Professor RAHLI M. from USTO-MB and Professor ZEBLAH A. from Sid Bel Abbes university that provide us some articles in press.

REFERENCES

Abdel-Rahman, E. M., Ahmad, A. R., & Akhtar, S. (2012). A metaheurisic bat-inspired algorithm for full body human pose estimation. *9th Conference on Computer and Robot Vision*, 369–375.

Ahmed, S. S., Dey, N., Ashour, A. S., Sifaki-Pistolla, D., Bălas-Timar, D., Balas, V. E., & Tavares, J. M. R. (2017). Effect of fuzzy partitioning in Crohn's disease classification: A neuro-fuzzy-based approach. *Medical & Biological Engineering & Computing*, *55*(1), 101–115. doi:10.100711517-016-1508-7 PMID:27106754

Altaleb, H., & Brodsky, A. (2013). A Primary Market for Optimizing Power Peak-Load Demand Limits. *International Journal of Decision Support System Technology*, *5*(2), 21–32. doi:10.4018/jdsst.2013040102

Avishek Das, D., Mandal, S.P., & Ghoshal, R. K. (2017). An efficient side lobe reduction technique considering mutual coupling effect in linear array antenna using BAT algorithm. *Swarm and Evolutionary Computation, 35*, 26-40. 10.1016/j.swevo.2017.02.004

Baker, K. R. (1974). *Introduction to Sequencing and Scheduling*. New York: Wiley.

Bank, J., & Werner, F. (2001). Heuristic algorithms for unrelated parallel machine scheduling with a common due date, release dates, and linear earliness and tardiness penalties. *Mathematical and Computer Modelling*, *33*(4–5), 363–383. doi:10.1016/S0895-7177(00)00250-8

Basetti, V., & Chandel, A. K. (2016). Optimal PMU placement for power system observability using Taguchi binary bat algorithm. *Measurement, 95*, 8-20. 10.1016/j.measurement.2016.09.031

Ben Hamida, A., Haouari, M., Huguet, M.-J., & Lopez, P. (2011). Solving two-stage hybrid flow shop using climbing depth-bounded discrepancy search. *Computers & Industrial Engineering*, *60*(2), 320–327. doi:10.1016/j.cie.2010.11.015

Ben Hamida, A., Huguet, M.-J., Lopez, P., & Haouari, M. (2007). Climbing Discrepancy Search for solving the hybrid Flow shop. *European Journal of Industrial Engineering*, *1*(2), 223–243. doi:10.1504/EJIE.2007.014110

Billaut, Proust, & Portmann. (2000). A Survey of Hybrid Flow Shop Problems. ODIP.

Buten, R. E., & Shen, V. Y. (1973, Aug.). A scheduling model for computer systems with two classes of processors. In *Proceedings of 1973 Sagamore Computer Conference Parallel Processing*. Institute of Electrical and Electronics Engineers.

Carlier, J., Chretienne, P., Erschler, J., Hanen, C., & Lopez, P. (1993). Les problemes dordonnancement. *RAIRO Operation Research.*, *7*, 77–150.

Chatterjee, S., Sarkar, S., Hore, S., Dey, N., Ashour, A. S., & Balas, V. E. (2017a). Particle swarm optimization trained neural network for structural failure prediction of multistoried RC buildings. *Neural Computing & Applications*, *28*(8), 2005–2016. doi:10.100700521-016-2190-2

Chatterjee, S., Sarkar, S., Hore, S., Dey, N., Ashour, A. S., Shi, F., & Le, D. N. (2017b). Structural failure classification for reinforced concrete buildings using trained neural network based multi-objective genetic algorithm. *Structural Engineering and Mechanics*, *63*(4), 429–438.

Damerdji, R. O., & Noureddine, M. (2017). Maintenance Decision-Making Under the Cost Criterion and the Competing Risks Approach. *International Journal of Decision Support System Technology*, *9*(1), 32–48. doi:10.4018/IJDSST.2017010103

Damodaram, R., & Valarmathi, M. L. (2012). Phishing website detection and optimization using Modified bat algorithm. *International Journal of Engineering Research and Applications*, *2*(1), 870–876.

Dehghani, H., & Bogdanovic, D. (2017). Copper price estimation using bat algorithm. *Resources Policy*. 10.1016/j.resourpol.2017.10.015

Dekhici, L. (2016). Reconfiguration et Ordonnancement des Blocs Opératoires Avec Etude de Cas. Editions universitaires européennes.

Dekhici, L., & Belkadi, K. (2010a). *Reconfiguration d'un Bloc Neurochirurgical par Simulation*. E-Medisys, Third International conference: E-Medical Systems, Fez.

Dekhici, L., & Belkadi, K. (2010b). Operating theatre scheduling under constraints. *Journal of Applied Sciences*, *10*(14), 1380–1388. doi:10.3923/jas.2010.1380.1388

Dekhici, L., & Belkadi, K. (2014). Bi-objective Operating Theater scheduling case of the paediatric hospital of Oran, In *Logistics and Operations Management (GOL), 2014 International Conference on*. IEEE. 10.1109/GOL.2014.6887438

Dekhici, L., & Belkadi, K. (2015, July). A Bat Algorithm with Generalized Walk for the Two-Stage Hybrid Flow Shop Problem. *International Journal of Decision Support System Technology*, *7*(3), 1–16. doi:10.4018/IJDSST.2015070101

Dekhici, L., & Belkadi, K. (2017). A Firefly Algorithm for the Mono-Processors Hybrid Flow Shop Problem. *International Journal of Advanced Computer Science and Applications*, *8*(12), 2017. doi:10.14569/IJACSA.2017.081256

Dessouky, M. M., Dessouky, M. I., & Verma, S. K. (1998). Flow shop scheduling with identical jobs and uniform parallel machines. *European Journal of Operational Research, 109*(3), 620–631. doi:10.1016/S0377-2217(97)00194-X

Dey, Samanta, Chakraborty, Das, Chaudhuri, & Suri. (2014). Firefly Algorithm for Optimization of Scaling Factors During Embedding of Manifold Medical Information: An Application in Ophthalmology Imaging. *Journal of Medical Imaging and Health Informatics, 4*(3), 384-394.

Dey, N. (2018). *Advancements in Applied Metaheuristic Computing*. Hershey, PA: IGI Global. doi:10.4018/978-1-5225-4151-6

Dey, N., & Ashour, A. S. (2016). Antenna Design and Direction of Arrival Estimation in Meta-Heuristic Paradigm: A Review. *International Journal of Service Science, Management, Engineering, and Technology, 7*(3), 1–18. doi:10.4018/IJSSMET.2016070101

Dey, N., & Ashour, A. S. (2017). Meta-Heuristic Algorithms in Medical Image Segmentation: A Review. *Advancements in Applied Metaheuristic Computing*, 185.

Didem Batur, Erol, & Karasan. (2016). Robot move sequence determining and multiple part-type scheduling in hybrid flexible flow shop robotic cells. *Computers & Industrial Engineering, 100*, 72-87. 10.1016/j.cie.2016.08.006

Dios, M., Fernandez-Viagas, V., & Framinan, J. M. (2018). Efficient heuristics for the hybrid flow shop scheduling problem with missing operations. *Computers & Industrial Engineering, 115*, 88-99. 10.1016/j.cie.2017.10.034

Du, Z. Y., & Liu, B. (2012). Image matching using a bat algorithm with mutation. *Applied Mechanics and Materials, 203*(1), 88–93.

Elsisi, M., Soliman, M., Aboelela, M. A. S., & Mansour, W. (2016). Bat inspired algorithm based optimal design of model predictive load frequency control. *International Journal of Electrical Power & Energy Systems, 83*, 426-433. 10.1016/j.ijepes.2016.04.036

Filho, A. T., Henriques de Gusmão, A. P., Clemente, T., Moura, J., Costa, A. P., & de Almeida, A. T. (2014). A Decision Support System for Sizing the Call Center of an Electrical Power Distributor. *International Journal of Decision Support System Technology, 6*(2), 63–76. doi:10.4018/ijdsst.2014040104

Gholami, A., & Ansari, H. R. (2017). Estimation of porosity from seismic attributes using a committee model with bat-inspired optimization algorithm. *Journal of Petroleum Science and Engineering, 152*, 238-249. 10.1016/j.petrol.2017.03.013

Guerraiche, K., Rahli, M., Dekhici, L., & Zeblah, A. (2018). (Article in Press). Conception Optimale de Redondance dans des Systemes Electriques Parallèles-Séries à l'Aide des Metaheuristiques. *Revue Roumaine des Sciences Techniques Série Électrotechnique et Energétique.*

Guerraiche, K., Rahli, M., Zeblah, A., & Dekhici, L. (2015a). Budgetary and Redundancy Optimization of Heterogeneous Series-Parallel Power Systems under Availability Constraints. *Energy Procedia Journal: ELSEVIER, 74*, 547–554. doi:10.1016/j.egypro.2015.07.748

Guerraiche, K., Rahli, M., Zeblah, A., & Dekhici, L. (2015b). Bat Algorithm to Series- Parallel Power System Design. In Multi-Conferences on Computational Engineering in Systems Applications CCCA, 3rd Communications, Computing and Control Applications, 67-71

Guerraiche, K., Rahli, M., Zeblah, A., & Dekhici, L. (2015c). Series-Parallel Power System Optimization Using Firefly Algorithm. *International Journal on Electrical Engineering and Informatics*, *1*(7), 89–101. doi:10.15676/ijeei.2015.7.1.7

Gupta, J. N. D. (1988). Two stage, hybrid flowshop scheduling problem. *The Journal of the Operational Research Society*, *3*(4), 359–364. doi:10.1057/jors.1988.63

Hanafi zadeh, P., Hashemi, A., Parvin, E. S. (2009). Robust Strategic Planning Employing Scenario Planning and Fuzzy Inference System. *International Journal of Decision Support System Technology*, *1*(3), 21-45. doi:10.4018/jdsst.2009070102

Haouari, M., Hidri, L., & Gharbi, A. (2006). Optimal scheduling of a two hybrid flow shop. *Mathematical Methods of Operations Research*, *64*(1), 107–124. doi:10.100700186-006-0066-4

Haouari, M., & M'Hallah, R. (1997). Heuristic algorithms for the two-stage hybrid flowshop problem. *Operations Research Letters*, *21*(1), 43–53. doi:10.1016/S0167-6377(97)00004-7

Imanirad, R., Yang, X., & Yeomans, J. S. (2013). A Concurrent Modelling to Generate Alternatives Approach Using the Firefly Algorithm. *International Journal of Decision Support System Technology*, *5*(2), 33–45. doi:10.4018/jdsst.2013040103

Jagatheesan, K., Anand, B., Dey, N., & Ashour, A. S. (2017a). Effect of SMES Unit in AGC of an Interconnected Multi-Area Thermal Power System With ACO-Tuned PID Controller. *Advancements in Applied Metaheuristic Computing*, 164.

Jagatheesan, K., Anand, B., Dey, N., Gaber, T., Hassanien, A. E., & Kim, T. H. (2015). A Design of PI Controller using Stochastic Particle Swarm Optimization in Load Frequency Control of Thermal Power Systems. In *Information Science and Industrial Applications (ISI), 2015 Fourth International Conference on* (pp. 25-32). IEEE. 10.1109/ISI.2015.8

Jagatheesan, K., Anand, B., Samanta, S., Dey, N., Ashour, A. S., & Balas, V. E. (2017b). Particle swarm optimisation-based parameters optimisation of PID controller for load frequency control of multi-area reheat thermal power systems. *International Journal of Advanced Intelligence Paradigms*, *9*(5-6), 464–489. doi:10.1504/IJAIP.2017.088143

Jagatheesan, K., Anand, B., Samanta, S., Dey, N., Ashour, A. S., & Balas, V. E. (2017c). Design of a proportional-integral-derivative controller for an automatic generation control of multi-area power thermal systems using firefly algorithm. *IEEE/CAA Journal of Automatica Sinica*.

Jagatheesan, K., Anand, B., Samanta, S., Dey, N., Santhi, V., Ashour, A. S., & Balas, V. E. (2017d). Application of flower pollination algorithm in load frequency control of multi-area interconnected power system with nonlinearity. *Neural Computing & Applications*, *28*(1), 475–488. doi:10.100700521-016-2361-1

Jin, Z., Yang, Z., & Ito, T. (2006). Metaheuristic algorithms for the multistage hybrid flowshop scheduling problem. *International Journal of Production Economics*, *100*(2), 322–333. doi:10.1016/j.ijpe.2004.12.025

Johnson, S. M. (1954). Optimal two- and three-stage production schedules with set-up times included. Naval Research. *Logistics Quart*, *1*(1), 61–68. doi:10.1002/nav.3800010110

Kaced, K., Larbes, C., Ramzan, N., & Bounabi, M. (2017). Bat algorithm based maximum power point tracking for photovoltaic system under partial shading conditions. *Solar Energy, 158*, 490-503. 10.1016/j.solener.2017.09.063

Kaliannan, J., Baskaran, A., Dey, N., & Ashour, A. S. (2016). Ant colony optimization algorithm based PID controller for LFC of single area power system with non-linearity and boiler dynamics. *World J. Model. Simul*, *12*(1), 3–14.

Karaa, W. B. A., Ashour, A. S., Sassi, D. B., Roy, P., Kausar, N., & Dey, N. (2016). Medline text mining: an enhancement genetic algorithm based approach for document clustering. In *Applications of Intelligent Optimization in Biology and Medicine* (pp. 267–287). Springer International Publishing. doi:10.1007/978-3-319-21212-8_12

Karri, C., & Jena, U. (2016). Fast vector quantization using a Bat algorithm for image compression. *Engineering Science and Technology, an International Journal, 29*(2), 769-781. 10.1016/j.jestch.2015.11.003

Kennedy, J., & Eberhart, R. C. (1995). Particle swarm optimization. *Proc. of IEEE International Conference on Neural Networks*, 1942–1948. 10.1109/ICNN.1995.488968

Khan, K., Nikov, A., & Sahai, A. (2011). A fuzzy bat clustering method for ergonomic screening of office workplaces, S3T 2011. *Advances in Intelligent and Soft Computing*, *101/2011*, 59–66. doi:10.1007/978-3-642-23163-6_9

Khan, K., & Sahai, A. (2012a). A comparison of BA, GA, PSO, BP and LM for training feed forward neural networks in e-learning context. *Int. J. Intelligent Systems and Applications*, *4*(7), 23–29. doi:10.5815/ijisa.2012.07.03

Khan, K., & Sahai, A. (2012b). A fuzzy c-means bi-sonar-based Metaheuristic optimization algorithm. Int. *J. of Interactive Multimedia and Artificial Intelligence*, *1*(7), 26–32. doi:10.9781/ijimai.2012.173

Kim, D. W., Kim, K. H., Jang, W., & Chen, F. F. (2002). Unrelated parallel machine scheduling with setup times using simulated annealing. *Robotics and Computer-integrated Manufacturing*, *18*(3-4), 223–231. doi:10.1016/S0736-5845(02)00013-3

Kim, D. W., Na, D. G., & Chen, F. F. (2003). Unrelated parallel machine scheduling with setup times and a total weighted tardiness objective. *Robotics and Computer-integrated Manufacturing*, *19*(1-2), 173–181. doi:10.1016/S0736-5845(02)00077-7

Komarasamy, G., & Wahi, A. (2012). An optimized K-means clustering tech- niqueusing bat algorithm. European J. *Scientific Research.*, *84*(2), 263–273.

Kyparisis, G. J., & Koulamas, C. (2006). Flexible flow shop scheduling with uniform parallel machines. *European Journal of Operational Research*, *168*(3), 985–999. doi:10.1016/j.ejor.2004.05.017

Lamica, G. (2000). Scheduling jobs with release dates and tails on two unrelated parallel machines to minimize the makespan. *European Journal of Operational Research, 120*(2), 277–288. doi:10.1016/S0377-2217(99)00156-3

Leandro dos Santos, C., & Askarzadeh, A. (2016). An enhanced bat algorithm approach for reducing electrical power consumption of air conditioning systems based on differential operator. *Applied Thermal Engineering, 99*, 834-840. 10.1016/j.applthermaleng.2016.01.155

Lemma, T. A., & Bin Mohd Hashim, F. (2011). Use of fuzzy systems and Bat algorithm for exergy modelling in a gas turbine generator. *IEEE Colloquium on Humanities, Science and Engineering (CHUSER'2011)*, 305–310.

Lin & Huang. (2017). Reliability analysis for a hybrid flow shop with due date consideration. *Reliability Engineering & System Safety*. 10.1016/j.ress.2017.07.008

Linn, R., & Zhang, W. (1999). Hybrid flow shop scheduling: A survey. *Computers & Industrial Engineering, 37*(1–2), 57–61. doi:10.1016/S0360-8352(99)00023-6

Marichelvam, M. K., Prabaharan, T., Yang, X.-S., & Geetha, M. (2013). Solving hybrid flow shop scheduling problems using bat algorithm. *International Journal of Logistics Economics and Globalisation, 5*(1), 15. doi:10.1504/IJLEG.2013.054428

Mishra, S., Shaw, K., & Mishra, D. (2012a). new meta-heuristic bat Inspired classification approach for microarray data. *Procedia Technology., 4*, 802–806. doi:10.1016/j.protcy.2012.05.131

Mohamed & Moftah. (2017). Simultaneous Ranking and Selection of Keystroke Dynamics Features Through A Novel Multi-Objective Binary Bat Algorithm. *Future Computing and Informatics Journal*. 10.1016/j.fcij.2017.11.005

Mokeddem, S., Atmani, B., & Mokaddem, M. (2014). A New Approach for Coronary Artery Diseases Diagnosis Based on Genetic Algorithm. *International Journal of Decision Support System Technology, 6*(4), 1–15. doi:10.4018/ijdsst.2014100101

Natarajan, A., Subramanian, S., & Premalatha, K. (2012). A comparative study of cuckoo search and bat algorithm for Bloom filter optimisation in spam filtering. *International Journal of Bio-inspired Computation, 4*(2), 89–99. doi:10.1504/IJBIC.2012.047179

Osaba, E., Yang, X.-S., Diaz, F., Lopez-Garcia, P., & Carballedo, R. (2016). An improved discrete bat algorithm for symmetric and asymmetric Traveling Salesman Problems. *Engineering Applications of Artificial Intelligence, 48*, 59-71. 10.1016/j.engappai.2015.10.006

Portmann, M. C., Vignier, A., Dardilhac, D., & Dezalay, D. (1998). Branch and bound crossed with GA to solve hybrid flowshops. *European Journal of Operational Research, 107*(2), 389–400. doi:10.1016/S0377-2217(97)00333-0

Ramesh, B., Mohan, V. C. J., & Reddy, V. C. V. (2013). Application of bat algorithm for combined economic load and emission dispatch.Int. *J of Electricl Engineering and Telecommunications., 2*(1), 1–9.

Reddy, V. U., & Manoj, A. (2012). Optimal capacitor placement for lossReduction in distribution systems using bat algorithm. *IOSR Journal of Engineering., 2*(10), 23–27. doi:10.9790/3021-021052327

Russell, S., & Forgionne, G. (2009). Decision Support-Related Resource Presence and Availability Awareness for DSS in Pervasive Computing Environments. *International Journal of Decision Support System Technology*, *1*(1), 15–34. doi:10.4018/jdsst.2009010102

Sarkar, M., Banerjee, S., Badr, Y., & Sangaiah, A. K. (2017). Configuring a Trusted Cloud Service Model for Smart City Exploration Using Hybrid Intelligence. *International Journal of Ambient Computing and Intelligence*, *8*(3), 1–21. doi:10.4018/IJACI.2017070101

Satapathy, S. C., Raja, N. S. M., Rajinikanth, V., Ashour, A. S., & Dey, N. (2016). Multi-level image thresholding using Otsu and chaotic bat algorithm. *Neural Computing & Applications*, 1–23.

Shahvari, O., & Logendran, R. (2018). A comparison of two stage-based hybrid algorithms for a batch scheduling problem in hybrid flow shop with learning effect. *International Journal of Production Economics, 195*, 227-248. 10.1016/j.ijpe.2017.10.015

Sharma, K., & Virmani, J. (2017). A Decision Support System for Classification of Normal and Medical Renal Disease Using Ultrasound Images: A Decision Support System for Medical Renal Diseases. *International Journal of Ambient Computing and Intelligence*, *8*(2), 52–69. doi:10.4018/IJACI.2017040104

Shen, V. Y., & Chen, Y. E. (1972). A scheduling strategy for the flow shop problem in a system with two classes of processors. *Conference on Information and Systems Science*, 45-649.

Sreeram, I., & Venkata, P. K. V. (2017). HTTP flood attack detection in application layer using machine learning metrics and bio inspired bat algorithm. *Applied Computing and Informatics*. 10.1016/j.aci.2017.10.003

Sriskandarajah, C., & Sethi, S. P. (1989). Scheduling algorithms for flexible flow shops: Worst and average performance. *European Journal of Operational Research*, *43*(2), 143–160. doi:10.1016/0377-2217(89)90208-7

Srivastava, B. (1998). An effective heuristic for minimizing makespan on unrelated parallel machines. *The Journal of the Operational Research Society*, *49*(8), 886–894. doi:10.1057/palgrave.jors.2600547

Straub, J. (2014). Evaluation of a Multi-Goal Solver for Use in a Blackboard Architecture. *International Journal of Decision Support System Technology*, *6*(1), 1–13. doi:10.4018/ijdsst.2014010101

Tamiru, A. L., & Hashim, F. M. (2013). Application of bat algorithm and Fuzzy systems to model exergy changes in a gas turbine. In Artificial Intelligence, Evolutionary Computing and Metaheuristics. Springer. doi:10.1007/978-3-642-29694-9_26

Tang, L., Luh, P. B., Liu, J., & Fang, L. (2002). Steel-making process scheduling using Lagrangian relaxation. *International Journal of Production Research*, *40*(1), 55–70. doi:10.1080/00207540110073000

Tang, L., Xuan, H., & Liu, J. (2006). Anew Lagrangian relaxation algorithm for hybrid flowshop scheduling to minimize total weighted completion time. *Computers & Operations Research*, *33*(11), 3344–3359. doi:10.1016/j.cor.2005.03.028

Tang, R., Fong, S., Dey, N., Wong, R. K., & Mohammed, S. (2017). Cross Entropy Method Based Hybridization of Dynamic Group Optimization Algorithm. *Entropy (Basel, Switzerland)*, *19*(10), 533. doi:10.3390/e19100533

Tapia, D. I., & Corchado, J. M. (2009). An Ambient Intelligence Based Multi-Agent System for Alzheimer Health Care. *International Journal of Ambient Computing and Intelligence*, *1*(1), 15–26. doi:10.4018/jaci.2009010102

Tyagi, S., Som, S., & Rana, Q. P. (2017). Trust based Dynamic Multicast Group Routing Ensuring Reliability for Ubiquitous Environment in MANETs. *International Journal of Ambient Computing and Intelligence*, *8*(1), 70–97. doi:10.4018/IJACI.2017010104

Vignier, Billaut, & Proust. (1999). Scheduling problems type hybrid flow-shop: State of the art. RAIRO. *Recherche opérationnelle, 33*(2), 117-183.

Vijay Kumar, Y. N., Sivanagaraju, S., & Chintalapudi, V. S. (2016). Security constrained economic load dispatch in the presence of interline power flow controller using modified BAT algorithm. *Ain Shams Engineering Journal, 7*(4), 1029-1043. 10.1016/j.asej.2015.07.003

Walsh, M. J., Barton, J., O'Flynn, B., Hayes, M. J., O'Mathuna, C., & Alavi, S. M. (2011). An Antiwindup Approach to Power Controller Switching in an Ambient Healthcare Network. *International Journal of Ambient Computing and Intelligence*, *3*(2), 35–55. doi:10.4018/jaci.2011040103

Xiao, L., Qian, F., & Shao, W. (2017). Multi-step wind speed forecasting based on a hybrid forecasting architecture and an improved bat algorithm. *Energy Conversion and Management, 143*, 410-430. 10.1016/j.enconman.2017.04.012

Yang, X. S. (2010). A new metaheuristic bat-inspired algorithm. In *Nature Inspired Cooperative Strategies for Optimization* (pp. 65–74). Springer. doi:10.1007/978-3-642-12538-6_6

ADDITIONAL READING

Dekhici, L., Guerraiche, K., & Belkadi, K. (2018). My choice of Metaheuristics inspired from Nature and Behavior [in French]. February 2018, *Edilivre Paris.*

KEY TERMS AND DEFINITIONS

Availability: Is a measure of the % of time the equipment is in an operable state. It is also the probability that a system is operational at a given time.

Combinatorial Optimization: Is a topic that consists of finding an optimal object from a finite set of objects. In many such problems, exhaustive search is not feasible. It operates on the domain of those optimization problems, in which the set of feasible solutions is discrete or can be reduced to discrete, and in which the goal is to find the best solution.

Hybrid Flow Shop: Also called flexible flowshop manufacturing system that contains several stages, and in each stage, there are parallel machines.

Operating Theater: Also known as operation theatre or operation suite is a facility within a hospital that contains at least operating rooms and post anesthesia care unit and where surgeries are carried out in a sterile environment.

Redundancy: In engineering, it is the duplication of critical components or functions of a system with the intention of increasing reliability of the system, usually in the form of a backup or fail-safe, or to improve actual system performance.

Reliability: The probability that a system will produce correct outputs up to some given time. There are two commonly used measures of reliability: 1) mean time between failure (MTBF), which is defined as total time in service/number of failures, and 2) Failure rate (λ), which is defined as number of failures/total time in service.

Scheduling: Is to determine the sequence of activities, and the times each one starts and finishes and to decide the assignment of resources to these activities in order to optimize a criterion.

ENDNOTE

1 NA: meansnot available.

Chapter 4
Agile Supplier Assessment Using Generalized Interval-Valued Trapezoidal Fuzzy Numbers

Atul Kumar Sahu
Guru Ghasidas Vishwavidyalaya, India

Nitin Kumar Sahu
Guru Ghasidas Vishwavidyalaya, India

Anoop Kumar Sahu
University of Johannesburg, South Africa

ABSTRACT

The supplier assessment has always been a key area to be developed for necessary advancement and evaluation by the researchers. In this chapter, the authors react upon the agile characteristics and furnish an agile supplier assessment decision support system to be utilized by the managers of the distinguish firm for assessing the agile characteristics of the partner supplier firm. The authors presented a modeling based on generalized interval-valued trapezoidal fuzzy numbers (GIVTFNs) to assess the status of partner supplier concerning agile characteristics. A multi-criterion decision-making (MCDM) appraisement module is built by the authors and a decision support system is developed by them to judge the scale of agile characteristics in the supply chain (SC) network of the supplier firm. A second-level hierarchy appraisement module is discussed by the authors to illustrate the procedural implementation of the proposed work. Here, the authors proposed a decision support model, which can grab the subjective views of the decision makers. The authors utilized GIVTFNs to clutch the uncertainty and vagueness of the measures and their metrics (sub-measures) of the discussed agile platform. In this study, a fuzzy performance important index model is presented to recognize the weak and strong agile measures and metrics of the supplier firm. The major intention of the authors in this study is to deliver a knowledge-based technical model for the sake of determining the quality of agile strategies by the supplier firm in their SC network.

DOI: 10.4018/978-1-5225-6164-4.ch004

INTRODUCTION

The value of any industrial and manufacturing firms can be increased by emphasizing on the elementary decision relating the different zones of the system. The decision accompanying the different corners and elements of the supply chain management (SCM) of the industrial and manufacturing firms is nowadays considered by the researchers to make it more effective and useful. Nowadays, Agile Supply Chain (ASC) is also drawing the attention of the researcher, which is responding towards managing flexibility, quickness, responsiveness and competency in SC network. ASC should be highly flexible and should be competent to be reconfigured quickly in responding to the changes, which occurs in an unpredictable business environment. ASC responds the thought of a dynamic network of firm, whose constituents can be structure and change frequently. ASC is the link between suppliers and customers, which impacts the planning, manufacturing and controlling of raw materials and products (Markland et al., 1995; Sahu et al., 2017b).

SC activities incorporates numerous activities i.e. product development, warehousing, production and logistics activities, information systems and medium etc. The coordination amongst these activities is must for developing and expanding SC network. SCM incorporates the business activities dealing with the flow of goods, services etc of a business firm. Successful SCM demands the effective movement & storage of raw materials, in-process and finished inventory from origin to source and vice versa. It stresses on maximizing the customer values and relations, cost, inventory etc by optimizing the associated distinguish activities, links and relations. Robust decision concerning the SCM can be taken by capturing numerous SC elements into decision arena. It is also required to develop numerous decision models, which can evaluate the incorporated elements. In this study, the authors consider agility as one of the element and presented an evaluation index to evaluate the agile status of the concerning firm for maximizing the customer relations amongst firms, which is one of the objective of SCM. Firms wants to run their SC in the most effectual and competent way. Birhanu et al. (2014) stated that the SC strategies show the companies competitiveness and their position in the market against their competitors. Hence, right SC strategy is compulsory for the companies to compete in the market. They disclosed different types of SC strategies, which are identified from literatures. Sukati et al. (2012) explored the relationship between SCM strategies and SCM practices and examined their effects on SC performance.

In recent times, business companies have started adopting the concept of ASC or agile networks; in order to react efficiently and effectively towards the increasingly dynamic and volatile markets demands (Christopher, 2000; Chong and David, 2012). ASCM can be considered as one of the most important aspects of production planning and control (Yigin et al., 2007). The successful implementation of an ASC largely depends on the firm ability to select the most significant potential partner in any given situation (Chong and David, 2010). Yang and Li (2002) emphasized that the foundation of the ASC lies in the integration of customer sensitivity, organization processes, networks and information systems. Some predictive analysis is essential to disclose the system behavior and for analyzing data and to get meaningful information (Acharjya and Anitha, 2017) and this can be done by structuring decision support systems. Sharma and Virmani (2017) proposed an efficient decision support system for detection of medical renal disease utilizing statistical features, which are computed from raw renal ultrasound images. Agility is the ability of an enterprise to meet the demands of customers in ever-shorter delivery times (Stalk and Thomas, 1990; Sharp eta l., 1999). Agility is defined as the ability of an enterprise to rapidly respond towards market changes and customers demands (Markland et al., 1995). It is sometimes represented by the agility index, which is determined by the arrangement of measured intensity levels of agility enabled attributes and measuring methods (Yusuf et al., 2001; Youssuf, 1993).

Soltan and Mostafa (2015) discussed the leanness and agility definitions, paradigms, factors, differences and combination amongst leanness and agility. They presented a hierarchic framework using MCDM methods i.e. AHP (Analytical Hierarchical Process) and ANP (Analytical Network Process), which is used to measure the leanness, agility, leagility, and overall performance of an enterprise in their work. The agility has four underlying fragments i.e. the value towards the customers, being ready for change, valuing human knowledge and skills and forming virtual partnership (Goldman et al., 1991). Patel et al., (2017) assessed the agility and identified obstacles towards agility in SC. A human perception-based framework is used for the calculation of agility in their work. They used fuzzy logic to deal with the impreciseness and vagueness and proposed the concept of a multi-grade fuzzy logic approach to determine the overall agility index. Cerruti et al. (2016) contributed towards the literature on agility and evaluated the apparent paradox, which related the specific conditions of supply relationships; needed to foster an agile strategy. They clarified these conditions to develop an Agile Supply Partnerships (ASPs) in fashion companies. Aishwarya and Balaji (2013) validated a tool named as Agile Supply Chain Transformation Matrix (ASCTM) and developed an implementation methodology by a systematic approach for attaining agility in the supplier-buyer SC. They developed the said tool by amalgamating Quality Function Deployment (QFD) and AHP techniques. Their developed tool relates the business changes and can assist the companies in creating and improving agility amongst supplier and buyer. A theoretical approach is useful in identifying key components of the big data and is useful in defining integrated decision support model, which can effectively portray a reliable visualization of the decision-related opportunities in the process of decision making (Poleto et al., 2017). Dhir et al. (2017) utilized AHP Framework for measuring, analyzing and systematically organizing the requirement parameters in requirement engineering for the agile development, which have a great impact in the agile implementation.

The supplier selection practice is principally complex, when scrutinized from a SC perspective; as it involves a series of inter-related decisions about suppliers, which impact both the formation and the performance of the SC as a whole (Chong & David, 2010). Dempsey (1978) incorporated twenty different supplier attributes into his decision-making process and developed an approach for supplier assessment, which is excessively complex and posse problems in application. Fuzzy sets theory can be employ by the researchers to deal with the problems encompassing uncertainty and incomplete information (Zadeh, 1965; Sahu et al., 2017c; Mhetre et al., 2016). Fuzziness and uncertainty plays a significant role in the affective planning and work execution. Fuzzy set is a non-classical set with a number from 0 to 1 to indicate the degree of membership for its elements (Wang et al. 2016b). The uncertainty definition leads to an improved and effective product design, when combined with fuzzy sets (Wang et al., 2017). Fuzzy theory is an important tool in the hands of the researchers, which is capable and can grip almost every decision situation. Ngan et al., (2016) proposed a novel decision making method based on fuzzy aggregation operators for medical diagnosis from dental X-Ray images and succeeded in disclosing the most potential disease using fuzzy aggregation operators. Wang, et al. (2016a) developed a fusion model for plantar pressure distribution image. A weighted fuzzy indices system for all features of the output image is developed and tested by Wang, et al. (2016a) via cross entropy, joint entropy, mutual information, mean, standard deviation, root mean square error (RMSE), deviation index, correlation coefficient, distortion index, signal to noise ratio etc.

Chong and David (2013) utilized fuzzy set theory and proposed a new fuzzy intelligent approach for partner selection in ASC in combination with radial basis functional artificial neural network. The empirical application of their developed model is presented and the data taken from 84 representative companies within the Chinese electrical components and equipment industry is utilized for illustrating its suitability and for helping organizational in making decision concerning to partner selection. Fuzzy theory can effectively grab linguistic information. Silva and Sobral (2017) worked under the arena of supplier assessment and presented a supplier selection model based on multi criteria decision making in the Brazilian dairy industry located in Serra Talhada City. Strand et al. (2017) presented a decision support system (DSS) for making the waste collection process more sustainable and disclosed that a sophisticated DSS can improve sustainability and can address the complexities in optimal waste collection process. Bidhandi and Valmohammadi (2017) identified factors affecting ASC and evaluated the effect of these factors on profitability. They determined the effects of identified factors on profitability and examined their influence on SC agility and verified the relationship amongst these factors and profitability. Malakouti et al. (2017) determined ASC Management among SMEs in manufacturing-related services sector. Structural equation modeling using partial least squares approach is employed in their study to measure the structured model. Balaji et al., (2015) worked to improve the flexibility levels of the SC of an organization by analyzing various agility criteria and calculating the agility index. Čiarnienė and Vienažindienė (2014) disclosed strategic implications and benefits of agile and their responsive in fashion SC. They stated that the fashion markets are rapidly change markets and thus commercial success or failure of these markets largely depends on the organization's flexibility and responsiveness.

In the present study, the authors consider MCDM problem for evaluating the most significant partner supplier alternatives in ASC. MCDM is concerned with configuring and solving decision problems linking with multiple criteria. MCDM replicates the involvement of more than one criterion in the process of decision making and explicitly evaluates multiple conflicting criteria in decision making. The difficulty in MCDM problem originates due to the presence of more than one criterion. MCDM or Multiple criteria decision analysis (MCDA) is a branch of operations research that is concerned with designing mathematical and computational tools to support the subjective evaluation of a finite number of decision alternatives under a finite number of performance criteria by a single decision maker or by a group (Lootsma, 1999). Decision making for assessing and evaluating a particular system usually requires quantitative as well as qualitative characteristics. The nature of these characteristics can be defined by associating them in terms of appropriateness rating as well as priority weights, which represents the performance extent and relative importance of these characteristics. It is difficult to handle a situation when dealing and defining qualitative characteristics, measures, metrics etc due to the vagueness, impreciseness and inconsistency in the obtained subjective evaluated data. The same can be managed by the exploration of the linguistic terms, which can define experts opinion, human views etc. against each of the subjective indices (Sahu et al., 2017a).

The captured subjective information needs to be transformed into a quantitative mathematic data set, which is difficult to achieve. Thus, in this study fuzzy sets theory is engaged by the authors to alter the subjective information into a quantitative mathematic data set. Fuzzy set theory and fuzzy logic is successfully applied by variety of researchers in a great variety of applications fields (Sahu et al., 2015; Klir & Yuan, 1995). Tsourveloudis and Valavanis (2002) proposed IF–THEN (Fuzzy Logic) rules to overcome the vagueness associated with the subjective assessment of expert panel. They designed novel IF-THEN rules and applied them for computing the ASC performance i.e. agility of the firms. Mandic et al. (2015) proposed a supplier selection model in telecommunications equipment that includes the dealings amongst attributes. Their model linked fuzzy logic with interpolative Boolean algebra (IBA) and TOPSIS (Technique for order preference by similarity to ideal solution). Their work concluded that $\partial m_{1.....k}$ can amalgamate their reasoning into MADM (Multi Attribute Decision Making) model using interpolative Boolean algebra. An adequate and reliable managerial decision-making support system can effectively portray the behavior of the related system (Mora et al., 2017). Rough-set theory is explored by numerous researchers in their work as it delivers an effectual analysis of data by means of constructing and synthesizing approximations of information set from acquired data (Roy et al., 2014). Rough set plays an important role in overcoming the vagueness, complexities, uncertainty, incompleteness and impreciseness in data during features analysis (Ripon et al., 2016). Li et al. (2017) developed uncertainty reason techniques including rough set, fuzzy set and neural networks to extract more accurate knowledge from normal item dataset. They applied their proposed method in shoes KANSEI evaluation system to predict the key features of it. The efficiency of the system can be improve and the best solution can be find by developing and advancing search algorithms for optimization and analysis (Tang et al., 2017). A new hybrid meta-heuristic algorithm called the cross entropy dynamic group optimization (CEDGO) algorithm is proposed by Tang et al. (2017) to overcome the local optima problem.

The ambient intelligence concept provides a vision to the society for the future and can improve the working atmosphere of the system (Bureš, 2016; Jain and Bhatnagar, 2017) and a type of intelligence can be grip into the system by developing decision support systems (Sahu et al., 2014). Sahu et al. (2016a) applied generalized interval-valued fuzzy number set along with TOPSIS methodology for evaluating supplier partner alternative firms under ASC arena. Bobar et al. (2015) projected a decision support system based on the fuzzy extent analysis method in order to make a swift decision in public procurement. A real-life case scenario of public procurement is presented by them to demonstrate the usefulness of their proposed system. Norese et al. (2015) projected an approach based on the integration of two PSM (Problem Structuring Methods). These methods are integrated to create a knowledge framework of the project context and to control uncertainties and complexities. Their proposed methodology is illustrated in relation to a public project in north-west Italy.

Performance measures acts as a tool, which can assist in knowing, managing and improving the organizations requirement in achieving a desired level of satisfaction relating specific domain. The performance evaluation of the distinguish system can be well estimated by determining and classifying the related metrics (Ahmed et al., 2017). Numerous performance measures i.e. mean absolute error (MAE), Kappa statistic, Root mean squared error (RMSE), Relative absolute error (RAE), True positive (TP) Rate, False positive (FP) Rate and F-Measure are discussed by Chatterjee et al. (2015) in their work. They assessed their presented methods by using the aforesaid different performance measures. A scientific and systematic approach is developed in this study, which can assess the firm's performance and can help in identifying the weak and strong performing areas of the associated partner firm. To declare and to compare the status of the individual firm or a group of firms, an index based on distinguishes performance measures and metrics is required. Thus, in this work; the authors react towards group of distinguish agile performance measure and related sub measures known as metrics into single arena to report an agile decision support system to the readers, practitioners. A performance index based on Generalized Interval Valued fuzzy theory is developed by the authors to understand the agile performance level of the partner supplier firm. The applications of fuzzy set theory in engineering design and planning is an important activity field to be developed for effective decision planning and execution for the today's organizations, but due to deficient development in tools, techniques, decision support systems concerning fuzzy theory in industrial and manufacturing application problems usually encountered (Zimmermann, 1996; Sahu et al., 2017d).

Thus in this study, the authors mould a decision support system based on GIVTFNs to assess the status of partner supplier pertaining to agile characteristics. They developed a MCDM appraisement module to judge the scale of agile characteristics in the SC network of the supplier firm. A second level hierarchy appraisement module is assembled by them to demonstrate the technical realization of the proposed work. Here, the authors projected a decision support system, which can grip the subjective examinations of the $\partial m_{1.....k}$.

THE GENERALIZED INTERVAL-VALUED TRAPEZOIDAL FUZZY NUMBERS (GIVTFNS)

Fuzzy sets theory is a powerful mathematical tool usually employed by the researchers for modeling uncertainty in systems (Zadeh, 1975; Sahu et al., 2017e; Chen, 2000). In this study, the authors utilized the concept of Generalized Interval-Valued Trapezoidal Fuzzy Numbers (GIVTFNs). Wang and Li (1998); Hakim et al. (2016); Secundo et al. (2017) defined IVFNs and presented their extended operational rules. Figure 1 illustrates the graphical representation of the GIVTFNs (Chen, 2006; Chen and Lai, 2011; Chen and Sanguansat 2011). This section briefly attends the concepts and properties of the GIVTFNs (Wei and Chen, 2009). The GIVTFNs is confined by two Trapezoidal Fuzzy Numbers (TFNs) termed as the lower and upper TFNs. The GIVTFNs is usually represented as

$$\tilde{\tilde{A}} = \left[\tilde{\tilde{A}}^L, \tilde{\tilde{A}}^U\right] = \left[\left(a_1^L, a_2^L, a_3^L, a_4^L; w_{\tilde{\tilde{A}}}^L\right), \left(a_1^U, a_2^U, a_3^U, a_4^U; w_{\tilde{\tilde{A}}}^U\right)\right]$$

Here $a_1^L \le a_2^L \le a_3^L \le a_4^L$, $a_1^U \le a_2^U \le a_3^U \le a_4^U$, such that $\tilde{\tilde{A}}^L$ indicates the lower IVTFNs, $\tilde{\tilde{A}}^U$ indicates the upper IVTFNs, and $\tilde{\tilde{A}}^L \subset \tilde{\tilde{A}}^U$. Let, $\tilde{\tilde{A}}$ and $\tilde{\tilde{B}}$ are two GIVTFNs, such that;

$$\tilde{\tilde{A}} = \left[\tilde{\tilde{A}}^L, \tilde{\tilde{A}}^U\right] = \left[\left(a_1^L, a_2^L, a_3^L, a_4^L; w_{\tilde{\tilde{A}}}^L\right), \left(a_1^U, a_2^U, a_3^U, a_4^U; w_{\tilde{\tilde{A}}}^U\right)\right]$$

and

$$\tilde{\tilde{B}} = \left[\tilde{\tilde{B}}^L, \tilde{\tilde{B}}^U\right] = \left[\left(b_1^L, b_2^L, b_3^L, b_4^L; w_{\tilde{\tilde{B}}}^L\right), \left(b_1^U, b_2^U, b_3^U, b_4^U; w_{\tilde{\tilde{B}}}^U\right)\right]$$

where, $0 \le w_{\tilde{\tilde{A}}}^L \le w_{\tilde{\tilde{A}}}^U \le 1$, such that $\tilde{\tilde{A}}^L \subset \tilde{\tilde{A}}^U$, and $0 \le w_{\tilde{\tilde{B}}}^L \le w_{\tilde{\tilde{B}}}^U \le 1$, such that $\tilde{\tilde{B}}^L \subset \tilde{\tilde{B}}^U$.

Here,

$$0 \le a_1^L \le a_2^L \le a_3^L \le a_4^L \le 1,\ 0 \le a_1^U \le a_2^U \le$$
$$a_3^U \le a_4^U \le 1,\ 0 \le w_{\tilde{\tilde{A}}^L} \le w_{\tilde{\tilde{A}}^U} \le 1, \tilde{\tilde{A}}^L \subset \tilde{\tilde{A}}^U$$

and

$0 \leq b_1^L \leq b_2^L \leq b_3^L \leq b_4^L \leq 1,\ 0 \leq b_1^U \leq b_2^U \leq$
$b_3^U \leq b_4^U \leq 1,\ 0 \leq w_{\tilde{\tilde{B}}^L} \leq w_{\tilde{\tilde{B}}^U} \leq 1, \tilde{\tilde{B}}^L \subset \tilde{\tilde{B}}^U$

The arithmetic operations between GIVFTNs; $\tilde{\tilde{A}}$ and $\tilde{\tilde{B}}$ are given by Chen (1995) and Wei and Chen (2009), which is reproduced as follows:

(i) The sum between two Generalized Interval-Valued Trapezoidal Fuzzy Numbers, $\tilde{\tilde{A}} \oplus \tilde{\tilde{B}}$:

$$\tilde{\tilde{A}} \oplus \tilde{\tilde{B}} = \left[\left(a_1^L, a_2^L, a_3^L, a_4^L; w_{\tilde{\tilde{A}}^L}\right), \left(a_1^U, a_2^U, a_3^U, a_4^U; w_{\tilde{\tilde{A}}^U}\right)\right] \oplus \left[\left(b_1^L, b_2^L, b_3^L, b_4^L; w_{\tilde{\tilde{B}}^L}\right), \left(b_1^U, b_2^U, b_3^U, b_4^U; w_{\tilde{\tilde{B}}^U}\right)\right]$$

$$= \begin{bmatrix} \left(a_1^L + b_1^L, a_2^L + b_2^L, a_3^L + b_3^L, a_4^L + b_4^L; \min\left(w_{\tilde{\tilde{A}}^L}, w_{\tilde{\tilde{B}}^L}\right)\right), \\ \left(a_1^U + b_1^U, a_2^U + b_2^U, a_3^U + b_3^U, a_4^U + b_4^U; \min\left(w_{\tilde{\tilde{A}}^U}, w_{\tilde{\tilde{B}}^U}\right)\right) \end{bmatrix} \quad (1)$$

(ii) The difference between two Generalized Interval-Valued Trapezoidal Fuzzy Numbers, $\tilde{\tilde{A}} - \tilde{\tilde{B}}$:

Figure 1. Representation of the Generalized Interval-Valued Trapezoidal Fuzzy Number

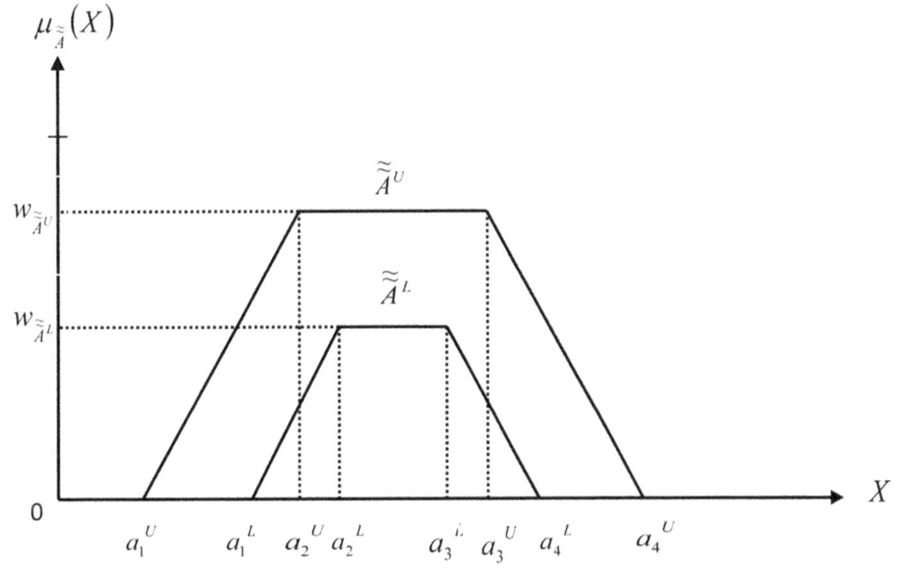

$$\tilde{\tilde{A}} - \tilde{\tilde{B}} = \left[\left(a_1^L, a_2^L, a_3^L, a_4^L; w_{\tilde{\tilde{A}}^L}\right), \left(a_1^U, a_2^U, a_3^U, a_4^U; w_{\tilde{\tilde{A}}^U}\right)\right] - \left[\left(b_1^L, b_2^L, b_3^L, b_4^L; w_{\tilde{\tilde{B}}^L}\right), \left(b_1^U, b_2^U, b_3^U, b_4^U; w_{\tilde{\tilde{B}}^U}\right)\right]$$

$$= \begin{bmatrix} \left(a_1^L - b_4^L, a_2^L - b_3^L, a_3^L - b_2^L, a_4^L - b_1^L; \min\left(w_{\tilde{\tilde{A}}^L}, w_{\tilde{\tilde{B}}^L}\right)\right), \\ \left(a_1^U - b_4^U, a_2^U - b_3^U, a_3^U - b_2^U, a_4^U - b_1^U; \min\left(w_{\tilde{\tilde{A}}^U}, w_{\tilde{\tilde{B}}^U}\right)\right) \end{bmatrix} \tag{2}$$

(iii) The product between two Generalized Interval-Valued Trapezoidal Fuzzy Numbers, $\tilde{\tilde{A}} \otimes \tilde{\tilde{B}}$ *:*

$$\tilde{\tilde{A}} \otimes \tilde{\tilde{B}} = \left[\left(a_1^L, a_2^L, a_3^L, a_4^L; w_{\tilde{\tilde{A}}^L}\right), \left(a_1^U, a_2^U, a_3^U, a_4^U; w_{\tilde{\tilde{A}}^U}\right)\right] \otimes \left[\left(b_1^L, b_2^L, b_3^L, b_4^L; w_{\tilde{\tilde{B}}^L}\right), \left(b_1^U, b_2^U, b_3^U, b_4^U; w_{\tilde{\tilde{B}}^U}\right)\right]$$

$$= \begin{bmatrix} \left(a_1^L \times b_1^L, a_2^L \times b_2^L, a_3^L \times b_3^L, a_4^L \times b_4^L; \min\left(w_{\tilde{\tilde{A}}^L}, w_{\tilde{\tilde{B}}^L}\right)\right), \\ \left(a_1^U \times b_1^U, a_2^U \times b_2^U, a_3^U \times b_3^U, a_4^U \times b_4^U; \min\left(w_{\tilde{\tilde{A}}^U}, w_{\tilde{\tilde{B}}^U}\right)\right) \end{bmatrix} \tag{3}$$

(iv) The product between a Generalized Interval-Valued Trapezoidal Fuzzy Number and a constant; $\lambda\tilde{\tilde{A}}$*:*

$$\lambda\tilde{\tilde{A}} = \lambda \times \left[\left(a_1^L, a_2^L, a_3^L, a_4^L; w_{\tilde{\tilde{A}}^L}\right), \left(a_1^U, a_2^U, a_3^U, a_4^U; w_{\tilde{\tilde{A}}^U}\right)\right]$$

$$= \left[\left(\lambda a_1^L, \lambda a_2^L, \lambda a_3^L, \lambda a_4^L; w_{\tilde{\tilde{A}}^L}\right), \left(\lambda a_1^U, \lambda a_2^U, \lambda a_3^U, \lambda a_4^U; w_{\tilde{\tilde{A}}^U}\right)\right], \quad \lambda > 0. \tag{4}$$

(v) The division between two Generalized Interval-Valued Trapezoidal Fuzzy Numbers, $\tilde{\tilde{A}} / \tilde{\tilde{B}}$ *:*

$$\tilde{\tilde{A}}/\tilde{\tilde{B}} = \left[\left(a_1^L, a_2^L, a_3^L, a_4^L; w_{\tilde{\tilde{A}}}^L\right), \left(a_1^U, a_2^U, a_3^U, a_4^U; w_{\tilde{\tilde{A}}}^U\right)\right] / \left[\left(b_1^L, b_2^L, b_3^L, b_4^L; w_{\tilde{\tilde{B}}}^L\right), \left(b_1^U, b_2^U, b_3^U, b_4^U; w_{\tilde{\tilde{B}}}^U\right)\right]$$

$$= \left[\left(\frac{a_1^L}{b_4^L}, \frac{a_2^L}{b_3^L}, \frac{a_3^L}{b_2^L}, \frac{a_4^L}{b_1^L}; \min\left(w_{\tilde{\tilde{A}}}^L, w_{\tilde{\tilde{B}}}^L\right)\right), \left(\frac{a_1^U}{b_4^U}, \frac{a_2^U}{b_3^U}, \frac{a_3^U}{b_2^U}, \frac{a_4^U}{b_1^U}; \min\left(w_{\tilde{\tilde{A}}}^U, w_{\tilde{\tilde{B}}}^U\right)\right)\right] \tag{5}$$

Here, $a_1^L, a_2^L, a_3^L, a_4^L, a_1^U, a_2^U, a_3^U, a_4^U, b_1^L, b_2^L, b_3^L, b_4^L, b_1^U, b_2^U, b_3^U, b_4^U$ are all non zero positive real numbers or all non zero negative real numbers, $0 < w_{\tilde{\tilde{A}}}^L \le w_{\tilde{\tilde{A}}}^U \le 1$ and $0 < w_{\tilde{\tilde{B}}}^L \le w_{\tilde{\tilde{B}}}^U \le 1$.

(vi) Rising the power of a constant (λ) *of a Generalized interval-valued trapezoidal fuzzy number,* $\tilde{\tilde{A}}$ *:*

$$\tilde{\tilde{A}}^{\lambda} = \left[\left(a_1^L, a_2^L, a_3^L, a_4^L; w_{\tilde{A}^L}\right), \left(a_1^U, a_2^U, a_3^U, a_4^U; w_{\tilde{A}^U}\right)\right]^{\lambda}$$

$$\left[\left((a_1^L)^{\lambda}, (a_2^L)^{\lambda}, (a_3^L)^{\lambda}, (a_4^L)^{\lambda}, w_{\tilde{A}^L}\right), \left((a_1^U)^{\lambda}, (a_2^U)^{\lambda}, (a_3^U)^{\lambda}, (a_4^U)^{\lambda}, w_{\tilde{A}^U}\right)\right] \tag{6}$$

$$\begin{cases} y_{\tilde{A}} = \begin{cases} w_{\tilde{A}}\left(\dfrac{a_3 - a_2}{a_4 - a_1} + 2\right) \Big/ 6, & a_1 \neq a_4 \\ w_{\tilde{A}} \Big/ 2, & a_1 = a_4 \end{cases} \\ x_{\tilde{A}} = \dfrac{y_{\tilde{A}}(a_2 + a_3) + (a_1 + a_4)(w_{\tilde{A}} - y_{\tilde{A}})}{2 w_{\tilde{A}}} \end{cases} \tag{7}$$

Chen and Chen (2003) introduced the center of gravity (COG) measure for GIVTFNs. The COG of a GIVTFNs, $\tilde{\tilde{A}} = \left[\tilde{\tilde{A}}^L, \tilde{\tilde{A}}^U\right] = \left[\left(a_1^L, a_2^L, a_3^L, a_4^L; w_{\tilde{A}^L}\right), \left(a_1^U, a_2^U, a_3^U, a_4^U; w_{\tilde{A}^U}\right)\right]$ can be used to define its significant impact and to compare distinguish GIVTFNs. Equation 7 can be exercise to attain the coordinates of the COG points for $\tilde{\tilde{A}}^L$ & $\tilde{\tilde{A}}^U$ of $\tilde{\tilde{A}}$ i.e. $\left(x_{\tilde{A}^L}, y_{\tilde{A}^L}\right)$ and $\left(x_{\tilde{A}^U}, y_{\tilde{A}^U}\right)$. Moreover, the COG; $x_{\tilde{\tilde{A}}}$ & $y_{\tilde{\tilde{A}}}$ of $\tilde{\tilde{A}}$ can be computed by utilizing Equation 8

$$\begin{cases} x_{\approx A} = \left(x_{\tilde{A}^L} + x_{\tilde{A}^U}\right)/2 \\ y_{\approx A} = \left(y_{\tilde{A}^L} + y_{\tilde{A}^U}\right)/2 \end{cases} \tag{8}$$

Next, the concept of Euclidean distance as discussed by Sahu et al. (2016c) can be employ to define the significant impact of the GIVTFNs. The distance between two GIVTFNs, $\tilde{\tilde{A}}$ and $\tilde{\tilde{B}}$ as suggested by Liu (2011) can also be use to define the significant impact of the GIVTFNs.

THE GROUP DECISION-MAKING PROBLEM AND THE SUCCESSIVE STEPS

Let, $\partial m_{1.....k} = \left\{\partial m_1, \partial m_1, \ldots, \partial m_k\right\}$ be the decision-makers in the process of group decision making and $\xi_i = \left\{\xi_i, \xi_2, \ldots, \xi_n\right\}$ be the set of primary indices termed as measures and $\xi_{i,j} = \left\{\xi_{1,1}, \xi_{1,2}, \ldots, \xi_{1,n}, \xi_{2,1}, \xi_{2,2}, \ldots, \xi_{m,n}\right\}$ be the set of secondary indices termed as metrics in the decision making problem. Suppose that $a_{ij,\partial m_{1.....k}} = \left(a^1_{ij,\partial m_i}, a^2_{ij,\partial m_i}, a^3_{ij,\partial m_i}, a^4_{ij,\partial m_i}; w_{ij,\partial m_i}\right)$ is the attribute value given by ∂m_i, where $\left(a^1_{ij,\partial m_i}, a^2_{ij,\partial m_i}, a^3_{ij,\partial m_i}, a^4_{ij,\partial m_i}; w_{ij,\partial m_i}\right)$ is the ratings in terms of TFNS given by ∂m_i for the indices (ij).

Let $w_{ij,,\partial m_{1.....k}} = \left(w^1_{ij,\partial m_i}, w^2_{ij,\partial m_i}, w^3_{ij,\partial m_i}, w^4_{ij,\partial m_i}; \eta_{ij}\right)$ is the ratings in terms of TFNS given by ∂m_i for the indices (ij). The aggregated fuzzy rating of the indices can be computed as:

$$\tilde{\tilde{a}}_{ij} = \left(\tilde{\tilde{a}}^1_{ij}, \tilde{\tilde{a}}^2_{ij}, \tilde{\tilde{a}}^3_{ij}, \tilde{\tilde{a}}^4_{ij}; w_{ij}\right) \tag{9}$$

where,

$$\tilde{\tilde{a}}^1_{ij} = \frac{1}{\partial m_{1.....k}} \sum_{\partial m=1}^{k} a^1_{ij};$$

$$\tilde{\tilde{a}}^2_{ij} = \frac{1}{\partial m_{1.....k}} \sum_{\partial m=1}^{k} a^2_{ij};$$

$$\tilde{\tilde{a}}^3_{ij} = \frac{1}{\partial m_{1.....k}} \sum_{\partial m=1}^{k} a^3_{ij};$$

$$\tilde{\tilde{a}}^4_{ij} = \frac{1}{\partial m_{1.....k}} \sum_{\partial m=1}^{k} a^4_{ij}$$

$$w_{ij} = \min_i \left(w_{ij}\right)$$

Then the aggregated fuzzy weight of the indices can be computed as:

$$\tilde{\tilde{w}}_{ij} = \left(\tilde{\tilde{w}}^1_{ij}, \tilde{\tilde{w}}^2_{ij}, \tilde{\tilde{w}}^3_{ij}, \tilde{\tilde{w}}^4_{ij}; \eta_{ij}\right) \tag{10}$$

where,

$$\tilde{\tilde{w}}^1_{ij} = \frac{1}{\partial m_{1.....k}} \sum_{\partial m=1}^{k} w^1_{ij};$$

$$\tilde{\tilde{w}}^2_{ij} = \frac{1}{\partial m_{1.....k}} \sum_{\partial m=1}^{k} w^2_{ij};$$

$$\tilde{w}_{ij}^{3} = \frac{1}{\partial m_{1.....k}} \sum_{\partial m=1}^{k} w_{ij}^{3} \,;$$

$$\tilde{w}_{ij}^{4} = \frac{1}{\partial m_{1.....k}} \sum_{\partial m=1}^{k} w_{ij}^{4}$$

$$\eta_{ij} = \min_{i} (\eta_{ij})$$

FPI known as Fuzzy Performance Index (Lin et al., 2006) as shown by Equation 11 can be utilize to determine the appropriateness rating for the first level evaluation index.

$$FPI = R_i = \frac{\sum R_{i,j} \otimes w_{i,j}}{\sum w_{i,j}} \tag{11}$$

where, $R_{i,j}$ represents the aggregated appropriateness fuzzy ratings of the metrics and $w_{i,j}$ is the aggregated appropriateness fuzzy weight against metrics, which is under first level indices (measures). Then fuzzy overall performance index (FOPI) as shown by Equation 12 can be utilize to compare the existing performance level with predefined performance anticipated fuzzy scale set by the management in the process of group decision making.

$$FOPI = \frac{\sum R_i \otimes w_i}{\sum w_i} \tag{12}$$

where, R_i represents the aggregated appropriateness rating and w_i is the aggregated fuzzy weight against first level indices, which is under the desired objective. Next, Fuzzy performance important index $(FPII)$ as shown by Equation 13 can be used to identify the weak and strong performing indices. $FPII$ combines the performance rating and importance weight of the indices and defines their status relating the particular firm. The higher value of $FPII$ represents the higher contribution of indices.

$$FPII = w_{i,j}^{\Lambda} \times R_{i,j} \tag{13}$$

$$FPII^{metrics} = \left\{ \left[\left\{ (1,1,1,1;1), (1,1,1,1;1) \right\} - w_{i,j} \right] \otimes R_{i,j} \right\}$$

$$w_{i,j}^{\Lambda} = \left[\left\{ (1,1,1,1;1), (1,1,1,1;1) \right\} - w_{i,j} \right] \tag{14}$$

where, $R_{i,j}$ represents the aggregated appropriateness fuzzy ratings of the metrics and $w_{i,j}$ is the aggregated appropriateness fuzzy weight against metrics, which is under first level indices (measures).

In this study, the authors utilized the conception of Liu and Jin (2012) as presented by Equation 15 to define the distance between two GIVTFNs.

$$d\left(\tilde{\tilde{A}},\tilde{\tilde{B}}\right)=\frac{1}{8}\left(\begin{array}{l}\left|w_{\tilde{\tilde{A}}^L}a_1{}^L-w_{\tilde{\tilde{B}}^L}b_1{}^L\right|+\left|w_{\tilde{\tilde{A}}^L}a_2{}^L-w_{\tilde{\tilde{B}}^L}b_2{}^L\right|+\left|w_{\tilde{\tilde{A}}^L}a_3{}^L-w_{\tilde{\tilde{B}}^L}b_3{}^L\right|\\+\left|w_{\tilde{\tilde{A}}^L}a_4{}^L-w_{\tilde{\tilde{B}}^L}b_4{}^L\right|+\left|w_{\tilde{\tilde{A}}^U}a_1{}^U-w_{\tilde{\tilde{B}}^U}b_1{}^U\right|+\left|w_{\tilde{\tilde{A}}^U}a_2{}^U-w_{\tilde{\tilde{B}}^U}b_2{}^U\right|+\\\left|w_{\tilde{\tilde{A}}^U}a_3{}^U-w_{\tilde{\tilde{B}}^U}b_3{}^U\right|+\left|w_{\tilde{\tilde{A}}^U}a_4{}^U-w_{\tilde{\tilde{B}}^U}b_4{}^U\right|\end{array}\right) \tag{15}$$

Here, if $d\left(\tilde{\tilde{A}},\tilde{\tilde{G}}\right)>d\left(\tilde{\tilde{B}},\tilde{\tilde{G}}\right)$, then $\tilde{\tilde{B}}$ is better than $\tilde{\tilde{A}}$

CASE DISCUSSIONS

To compete among rivals, it is necessary to identify the weak and the strong characteristics of rivals as well as ours. Identifying weak and the strong performing area, measures, metrics of the supplier in the network of SC is important for defining its status amongst others and are always in demand. In recent times, business companies are adopting the concept of ASC or agile networks to react efficiently and effectively towards the increasingly volatile markets demands. ASCM is one of the most important aspects for managing and controlling effective production planning. In today's age of rapid manufacturing, it is important to assess the supplier firm status under several fields. The supplier firms are nowadays; more conscious about exploring decision making tool, models, techniques for furnishing their decisions. For crafting the satisfactory consumer's response, better partner enterprises image, enhancing productivity, minimize loss, maximize profit etc, it is necessary to identify the weak and strong performance areas; accompanying measures and metrics. Thus in this study, the authors react upon the agile characteristics to furnish an agile supplier assessment framework to be utilized by the mangers of the distinguish firm for assessing the agile characteristics of the partner supplier firm. The proposed work can be utilized to define the weak and strong indices of the partner supplier firm. A second level performance appraisement hierarchical framework consisting of multiple subjective metrics in the field of ASC and agility is discussed in this study. The present research determines the FPII to determine the degree of agile supplier attitude. For the same the appropriateness linguistic ratings and appropriateness linguistic priority weights for each second level sub-measures (metrics) and appropriateness linguistic priority weights for the each first level measures is collected from the $\partial m_{1.....k}$ for assessing the FOPI, Next the FPII is determine to declare the weak and strong performing area relating the supplier firm performance. The FPII can help the managers of the alternative firm in determining its firm status via comparing it with the ideal or preset fuzzy agile assessment level by the firm. An approach escorting FPII is presented to be fruitfully implemented by the supplier firm in identifying the weak and strong measures and metrics. The GIVTFNs linguistic preference scale as discussed by Sahu et al. (2016c) is utilized in this study for collecting the subjective decision information and further the captured linguistic preferences are converted in the objective data sets by utilizing the said GIVTFNs scale.

EVALUATION PLATFORM: DATA ANALYSIS:

In this study, the authors react upon the agile characteristics to furnish an agile supplier assessment platform that can be utilized by the mangers of the distinguish firm for assessing the agile characteristics of the partner supplier firm. Thus, the performance evaluation platform as discussed by Sahu et al. (2016b) is utilized for measuring the performance of the most suitable partner supplier in ASC based on GIVTFNs. The developed agile platform is shown by Table 1, where the first level model reciprocates various measures i.e. Technology and Knowledge Capability, Industrial and Organizational Competitiveness Capability, Production and Logistics Management Capability, Marketing Capability, Human Resource Management Capability and Partnership Management Capability. For defining the procedural modeling towards recognizing the weak and strong performance indices in extent of agile SC; while evaluating the subjective information, the concepts of fuzzy theory is utilized. Next, a committee; based on group of eight experts (decision-makers) i.e. ∂m_1, ∂m_2, ∂m_3, ∂m_4, ∂m_5, ∂m_6, ∂m_7 and ∂m_8 is required to be constructed from numerous departments such as marketing, production, assembly, purchasing, environmental, complain etc. Afterwards, using GIVTFNs scale and based on several brainstorming sessions and periodical discussions, the committee has to first finalize important measures and metrics, which have to be considered for assessing the agility of SC performance extent for the candidate industry. For the same; the committee has to assign linguistic priority weight against each performance metrics. Next, the committee has to visit candidate industries and observe ongoing agile performance and based on that, the committee have to provide their judgment (evaluation information) in terms of linguistic ratings for defining the performance extent of each metrics of the ASC hierarchy. The proposed work can be utilized to define the weak and strong indices of the partner supplier firm. A second level performance appraisement hierarchical framework consisting of multiple subjective metrics in the field of ASC and agility is discussed in this study. The present research determines the FPII to determine the degree of agile supplier attitude. For the same the appropriateness linguistic ratings and appropriateness linguistic priority weights for each second level sub-measures (metrics) and appropriateness linguistic priority weights for the each first level measures is collected from the $\partial m_{1.....k}$ for assessing FOPI. The procedural steps of the proposed decision support framework for assessing the performance extent of the agile supplier is as follows:

Step 1: Collection of appropriateness ratings and priority weight for each agile evaluation measure and metrics.

A committee based on group of eight experts (decision-makers) i.e. ∂m_1, ∂m_2, ∂m_3, ∂m_4, ∂m_5, ∂m_6, ∂m_7 and ∂m_8 ; which is constructed from numerous departments is instructed to articulate their subjective preferences in linguistic terms for shaping metrics weights and appropriateness ratings of second level metrics of supplier partner industry. Next, the Linguistic preferences are transformed into GIVTFNS as discussed by Sahu et al. (2016c). The linguistic terms for assessing the priority importance weights of each second level evaluation metrics (secondary indices) is revealed in Tables 2. The appropriateness linguistic ratings against each second level evaluation metrics (secondary indices) is furnished in Tables 3. The Priority Importance of each first level evaluation metrics (primary indices) is revealed in Tables 4.

Step 2: Approximation of linguistic ratings and priority weights into GIVTFNs.

Next, the linguistic fuzzy terms are transformed into corresponding appropriateness GIVTFNs ratings and weights. Subsequently, the aggregated fuzzy rating and the aggregated fuzzy weight of the indices a shown by Equations 9 & 10 is computed. The Aggregated fuzzy appropriateness rating and aggregated fuzzy priority weight of secondary indices is shown in Table 5. The, appropriateness rating of the first level evaluation indices is computed by exploring Equation 11 where, $R_{i,j}$ represents the aggregated appropriateness fuzzy ratings of the metrics and $w_{i,j}$ is the aggregated appropriateness fuzzy weight against metrics, which falls under first level indices (measures). The computed fuzzy appropriateness rating and aggregated fuzzy priority weight of primary indices is shown in Table 6.

Step 3: Fuzzy Overall Performance Index (FOPI):

Next, the fuzzy overall performance index (FOPI) as shown by Equation.12 is computed to compare the existing performance level with predefined performance anticipated fuzzy scale set by the management. Where, R_i represents the aggregated appropriateness rating and w_i is the aggregated fuzzy weight against first level indices, which is under the desired objective. The computed FOPI in this study is found as [(0.195,0.303,0.747,1.124,0.800);(0.195,0.303,0.747,1.124,1.000)].

Step 4: Fuzzy performance important index (FPII).

Next, Fuzzy performance important index $(FPII)$ is computed in this study to identify the weak and strong performing indices. The computed values of $FPII$ are shown in Table 7.

Step 5: Performance appraisement of ASC metrics.

Next, the concept of Euclidean distance as defined by Liu and Jin (2012) is utilized in this study to evaluate and assess the weak and strong metrics of ASC. The raking order is defined in accordance with ascending order of the distance between fuzzy performance importance index of the metrics and the ideal fuzzy important index. Table 8; defines the ranking of the indices based on distance measure.

CONCLUSION

The Agile Supply Chain Management (ASCM) is the arrangement of agile thinking with SCM, which is important for increasing the ability of an enterprise for rapidly responding towards today's market changes and customer's demands. The presented work delivered the multiple subjective performance metrics for the assessment and appraising the supplier candidate industry performance in ASC environment. The exploration of Generalized Interval Valued Trapezoidal Fuzzy Numbers (GIVTFNs) in conjunction with the concept of Euclidean distance is presented in this study to evaluate and assess the weak and strong metrics of ASC. The presented fuzzy based mathematical modeling is a simple, flexible and systematic approach to quantify the industrial agile performance index. This study developed a conceptual hierarchical evaluation index platform for appraising the fuzzy performance of supplier candidate industry under the metrics of Agile SC. The presented approach can also be applied to any MCDM problems, which involves uncertainty and vagueness caused by subjectivity in the evaluation measures. The key donations of the proposed study are highlighted below:

1. MCDM problem under the arena of ASC is presented in this study for evaluating the most significant partner supplier alternatives accompanying agile characteristics.
2. Modeling based on the application of GIVTFNs is presented in this study to assess the status of partner supplier industry.
3. A decision support system based on subjective information is presented by the authors, which can be easily implemented by the mangers of the distinguish firms owing to qualitative indices.
4. A scientific and systematic approach is developed in this study, which can assess the firm's performance and can help in identifying the weak and strong performing areas of the associated partner firm.
5. An index based on distinguishes performance measures and metrics is presented to declare and to compare the status of the individual firm or a group of partner firms.

REFERENCES

Acharjya, D., & Anitha, A. (2017). A comparative study of statistical and rough computing models in predictive data analysis. *International Journal of Ambient Computing and Intelligence*, *8*(2), 32–51. doi:10.4018/IJACI.2017040103

Ahmed, S. S., Dey, N., Ashour, A. S., Sifaki-Pistolla, D., Bălas-Timar, D., Balas, V. E., & Tavares, J. M. R. (2017). Effect of fuzzy partitioning in Crohn's disease classification: A neuro-fuzzy-based approach. *Medical & Biological Engineering & Computing*, *55*(1), 101–115. doi:10.100711517-016-1508-7 PMID:27106754

Aishwarya, P., & Balaji, M. (2013). Supply Chain Transformation Matrix (ASCTM) based supplier-buyer relationships to improve supply chain agility. *International Journal of Applied Research and Studies*, *2*, 1–6.

Balaji, M., Velmurugan, V., & Subashree, C. (2015). TADS: An assessment methodology for agile supply chains. *Journal of Applied Research and Technology*, *13*(5), 504–509. doi:10.1016/j.jart.2015.10.002

Bidhandi, R. A., & Valmohammadi, C. (2017). Effects of supply chain agility on profitability. *Business Process Management Journal*, *23*(5), 1064–1082. doi:10.1108/BPMJ-05-2016-0089

Birhanu, D., Lanka, K., & Rao, A. N. (2014). A Survey of Classifications in Supply Chain Strategies. *Procedia Engineering*, *97*, 2289–2297. doi:10.1016/j.proeng.2014.12.473

Bobar, V., Mandic, K., & Suknovic, M. (2015). Bidder selection in public procurement using a fuzzy decision support system. *International Journal of Decision Support System Technology*, *7*(1), 1–19. doi:10.4018/ijdsst.2015010103

Bureš, V., Tučník, P., Mikulecký, P., Mls, K., & Blecha, P. (2016). Application of ambient intelligence in educational institutions: Visions and architectures. *International Journal of Ambient Computing and Intelligence*, *7*(1), 94–120. doi:10.4018/IJACI.2016010105

Cerruti, C., Mena, C., Skipworth, H., & Tavoletti, E. (2016). Characterizing agile supply partnerships in the fashion industry. *International Journal of Operations & Production Management*, *36*(8), 923–947. doi:10.1108/IJOPM-03-2015-0181

Chatterjee, S., Chakraborty, R., Dey, N., & Hore, S. (2015). A Quality Prediction method of Weight Lifting Activity. *Proceedings of the Michael Faraday IET International Summit - 2015 (MFIIS-2015): An IET International Conference*. 10.1049/cp.2015.1691

Chen, C. T. (2000). Extensions of the TOPSIS for group decision-making under fuzzy environment. *Fuzzy Sets and Systems*, *114*(1), 1–9. doi:10.1016/S0165-0114(97)00377-1

Chen, S. J. (2006). A new method for handling the similarity measure problems of interval-valued fuzzy numbers. *Proceedings of the second international conference on natural computation and the third international conference on fuzzy systems and knowledge discovery*, 325 - 334.

Chen, S. J., & Chen, S. M. (2003). Fuzzy risk analysis based on similarity measures of generalized fuzzy numbers. *IEEE Transactions on Fuzzy Systems*, *11*(1), 45–46. doi:10.1109/TFUZZ.2002.806316

Chen, S. M. (1995). Arithmetic operations between vague sets. *Proceeding of international joint conference of CFSA/TFIS/SOFT'95 on fuzzy theory and applications*, 206–211.

Chen, S. M., & Sanguansat, K. (2011). Analyzing fuzzy risk based on similarity measures between interval-valued fuzzy numbers. *Expert Systems with Applications*, *38*(7), 8612–8621. doi:10.1016/j.eswa.2011.01.065

Chen, T. Y., & Lai, H. L. (2011). A risk management method for enhancing patient safety based on interval-valued fuzzy numbers. *African Journal of Business Management*, *5*(30), 11925–11945.

Chong, W., & David, B. (2010). Formulating partner selection criteria for agile supply chains: A dempster–shafer belief acceptability optimization approach. *International Journal of Production Economics*, *125*(2), 284–293. doi:10.1016/j.ijpe.2010.02.010

Chong, W., & David, B. (2013). Partner selection in agile supply chains: A fuzzy intelligent approach. *Production Planning & Control: The Management of Operations*, *25*(10), 821–839.

Chong, W., & David, B. A. (2012). Dynamic feedback model for partner selection in agile supply chains. *International Journal of Operations & Production Management*, *32*(1), 79–103. doi:10.1108/01443571211195745

Christopher, M. (2000). The agile supply chain competing in volatile markets. *Industrial Marketing Management*, *29*(1), 37–44. doi:10.1016/S0019-8501(99)00110-8

Čiarnienė, R., & Vienažindienė, M. (2014). Agility and Responsiveness Managing Fashion Supply Chain. *Procedia: Social and Behavioral Sciences*, *150*, 1012–1019. doi:10.1016/j.sbspro.2014.09.113

Dempsey, W. A. (1978). Vendor selection and the buying process. *Industrial Marketing Management, 79*(4), 257–267. doi:10.1016/0019-8501(78)90044-5

Dhir, S., Kumar, D., & Singh, V. B. (2017). Requirement Paradigms to Implement the Software Projects in Agile Development Using Analytical Hierarchy Process. *International Journal of Decision Support System Technology, 9*(3), 28–41. doi:10.4018/IJDSST.2017070102

Goldman, S. L., Nagel, R. N., & Dove, P. R. (1991). *21st century manufacturing enterprise strategy*. Bethlehem, PA: Iacocca Institute.

Hakim, A., Gheitasi, M., & Soltani, F. (2016). Fuzzy model on selecting processes in Business Process Reengineering. *Business Process Management Journal, 22*(6), 1118–1138. doi:10.1108/BPMJ-05-2015-0057

Jain, A., & Bhatnagar, V. (2017). Concoction of Ambient Intelligence and Big Data for Better Patient Ministration Services. *International Journal of Ambient Computing and Intelligence, 8*(4), 19–30. doi:10.4018/IJACI.2017100102

Klir, G. J., & Yuan, B. (1995). *Fuzzy Sets and Fuzzy Logic: Theory and Applications*. Englewood Cliffs, NJ: Prentice-Hall.

Li, Z., Shi, K., Dey, N., Ashour, A. S., Wang, D., Balas, V. E., ... Shi, F. (2017). Rule-based back propagation neural networks for various precision rough set presented KANSEI knowledge prediction: A case study on shoe product form features extraction. *Neural Computing & Applications, 28*(3), 613–630. doi:10.100700521-016-2707-8

Lin, C. T., Chiu, H., & Chu, P. Y. (2006). Agility index in the supply chain. *International Journal of Production Economics, 100*(2), 285–299. doi:10.1016/j.ijpe.2004.11.013

Liu, P. (2011). A weighted aggregation operators multi-attribute group decision-making method based on interval-valued trapezoidal fuzzy numbers. *Expert Systems with Applications, 38*(1), 1053–1060. doi:10.1016/j.eswa.2010.07.144

Liu, P., & Jin, F. (2012). A multi-attribute group decision-making method based on weighted geometric aggregation operators of interval-valued trapezoidal fuzzy numbers. *Applied Mathematical Modelling, 36*(6), 2498–2509. doi:10.1016/j.apm.2011.09.006

Lootsma, F. A. (1999). *Multi-criteria decision analysis via ratio and difference judgment*. Kluwer, Academic Publishers. doi:10.1007/b102374

Malakouti, M., Rezaei, S., & Shahijan, M. K. (2017). Agile supply chain management (ASCM): A management decision-making approach. *Asia Pacific Journal of Marketing and Logistics, 29*(1), 171–182. doi:10.1108/APJML-02-2016-0031

Mandic, K., Delibasic, B., & Radojevic, D. (2015). An application of the integrated IBA-TOPSIS model in supplier selection. *International Journal of Decision Support System Technology, 7*(1), 1–16. doi:10.4018/ijdsst.2015010102

Markland, R., Vickery, S. K., & Davis, R. A. (1995). *Operation management: Concepts manufacturing and services*. New York: The West Publishing Company.

Mhetre, N. A., Deshpande, A. V., & Mahalle, P. N. (2016). Trust management model based on fuzzy approach for ubiquitous computing. *International Journal of Ambient Computing and Intelligence*, *7*(2), 33–46. doi:10.4018/IJACI.2016070102

Mora, M., Wang, F., Gómez, J. M., & Shevchenko, V. S. T. (2017). Decision-making support systems in quality management of higher education institutions: A selective review. *International Journal of Decision Support System Technology*, *9*(2), 56–79. doi:10.4018/IJDSST.2017040104

Ngan, T. T., Tuan, T. M., Minh, N. H., & Dey, N. (2016). Decision Making Based on Fuzzy Aggregation Operators for Medical Diagnosis from Dental X-ray images. *Journal of Medical Systems*, *40*(12), 280. doi:10.100710916-016-0634-y PMID:27787784

Norese, M. F., Rolando, D., & Fregonara, E. (2015). Integration of problem structuring methods: A methodological proposal for complex regional decision-making processes. *International Journal of Decision Support System Technology*, *7*(2), 1–26. doi:10.4018/IJDSST.2015040104

Patel, B. S., Samuel, C., & Sharma, S. K. (2017). Evaluation of agility in supply chains: A case study of an Indian manufacturing organization. *Journal of Manufacturing Technology Management*, *28*(2), 212–231. doi:10.1108/JMTM-09-2016-0125

Poleto, T., & Carvalho, V. (2017). The full knowledge of big data in the integration of inter-organizational information. *International Journal of Decision Support System Technology*, *9*(1), 16–31. doi:10.4018/IJDSST.2017010102

Ripon, S. H., Kamal, S., Hossain, S., & Dey, N. (2016). Theoretical Analysis of Different Classifiers under Reduction Rough Data Set: A Brief Proposal. *International Journal of Rough Sets and Data Analysis*, *3*(3), 1–20. doi:10.4018/IJRSDA.2016070101

Roy, P., Goswami, S., Chakraborty, S., Azar, A. T., & Dey, N. (2014). Image segmentation using rough set theory: A review. *International Journal of Rough Sets and Data Analysis*, *1*(2), 62–74. doi:10.4018/ijrsda.2014070105

Sahu, A. K., Sahu, A. K., & Sahu, N. K. (2017a). Appraisements of material handling system in context of fiscal and environment extent: A comparative grey statistical analysis. *International Journal of Logistics Management*, *28*(1), 2–28. doi:10.1108/IJLM-09-2015-0163

Sahu, A. K., Sahu, A. K., & Sahu, N. K. (2017d). Benchmarking of Advanced Manufacturing Machines Based on Fuzzy-TOPSIS Method. *Theoretical and Practical Advancements for Fuzzy System Integration*, 309-350.

Sahu, A. K., Sahu, N. K., & Sahu, A. (2014). Appraisal of CNC machine tool by integrated MULTI MOORA-IGVN circumstances: An empirical study. *Journal of Grey Systems: Theory and Application*, *4*(1), 104–123. doi:10.1108/GS-11-2013-0028

Sahu, A. K., Sahu, N. K., & Sahu, A. K. (2015). Benchmarking CNC machine tool using hybrid fuzzy methodology a multi indices decision making approach. *International Journal of Fuzzy System Applications*, *4*(2), 28–46. doi:10.4018/IJFSA.2015040103

Sahu, A. K., Sahu, N. K., & Sahu, A. K. (2016a). Application of Integrated TOPSIS in ASC index: Partners Benchmarking perspective. *Benchmarking: An International Journal, 23*(3), 540–563. doi:10.1108/BIJ-03-2014-0021

Sahu, A. K., Sahu, N. K., & Sahu, A. K. (2016b). Appraisal of Partner Enterprises under GTFNS Environment in Agile SC. *International Journal of Decision Support System Technology, 8*(3), 1–19. doi:10.4018/IJDSST.2016070101

Sahu, A. K., Sahu, N. K., & Sahu, A. K. (2016c). Application of Modified MULTI-MOORA for CNC Machine Tool Evaluation in IVGTFNS Environment: An Empirical Study. *International Journal of Computer Aided Engineering and Technology, 8*(3), 234–259. doi:10.1504/IJCAET.2016.077603

Sahu A. K., Sahu, N. K. & Sahu, A. K. (2017b). Performance Estimation of Firms by GLA Supply Chain under Imperfect Data. *Theoretical and Practical Advancements for Fuzzy System Integration*, 245-277.

Sahu, A. K., Sahu, N. K., & Sahu, A. K. (2017e). Fuzziness: A Mathematical Tool. *Theoretical and Practical Advancements for Fuzzy System Integration*, 1-30.

Sahu N. K., Sahu, A. K. & Sahu, A. K. (2017c). Fuzzy-AHP: A Boon in 3PL Decision Making Process. *Theoretical and Practical Advancements for Fuzzy System Integration*, 97-125.

Secundo, G., Magarielli, D., Esposito, E., & Passiante, G. (2017). Supporting decision-making in service supplier selection using a hybrid fuzzy extended AHP approach: A case study. *Business Process Management Journal, 23*(1), 196–222. doi:10.1108/BPMJ-01-2016-0013

Sharma, K., & Virmani, J. (2017). A decision support system for classification of normal and medical renal disease using ultrasound images: A decision support system for medical renal diseases. *International Journal of Ambient Computing and Intelligence, 8*(2), 52–69. doi:10.4018/IJACI.2017040104

Sharp, J. M., Irani, Z., & Desai, S. (1999). Working towards agile manufacturing in the UK Industry. *International Journal of Production Economics, 62*(1-2), 155–169. doi:10.1016/S0925-5273(98)00228-X

Silva, A. M. R., & Sobral, M. F. F. (2017). Multicriteria Model to Sort Suppliers in a Brazilian Dairy Industry. *International Journal of Decision Support System Technology, 9*(3), 42–53. doi:10.4018/IJDSST.2017070103

Soltan, H., & Mostafa, S. (2015). Lean and Agile Performance Framework for Manufacturing Enterprises. *Procedia Manufacturing, 2*, 476–484. doi:10.1016/j.promfg.2015.07.082

Stalk, G., & Thomas, H. (1990). *Competing against time*. New York: The Free Press.

Strand, M., Syberfeldt, A., & Geertsen, A. (2017). A Decision Support System for Sustainable Waste Collection. *International Journal of Decision Support System Technology, 9*(4), 49–65. doi:10.4018/IJDSST.2017100104

Sukati, I., Hamid, A. B., Baharun, R., & Yusoff, R. M. (2012). The Study of Supply Chain Management Strategy and Practices on Supply Chain Performance. *Procedia: Social and Behavioral Sciences, 40*, 225–233. doi:10.1016/j.sbspro.2012.03.185

Tang, R., Fong, S., Dey, N., Wong, R. K., & Mohammed, S. (2017). Cross Entropy Method Based Hybridization of Dynamic Group Optimization Algorithm. *Entropy (Basel, Switzerland)*, *19*(10), 533. doi:10.3390/e19100533

Tsourveloudis, N. C., & Valavanis, K. P. (2002). On the measurement of enterprise agility. *International. Journal of Intelligent & Robotic Systems*, *33*(3), 329–342. doi:10.1023/A:1015096909316

Wang, D., He, T., Li, Z., Cao, L., Dey, N., Ashour, A. S., ... Shi, F. (2016b). Image feature-based affective retrieval employing improved parameter and structure identification of adaptive neuro-fuzzy inference system. *Neural Computing & Applications*, 1–16.

Wang, D., Li, Z., Cao, L., Balas, V. E., Dey, N., Ashour, A. S., & Shi, F. (2016a). Image Fusion Incorporating Parameter Estimation Optimized Gaussian Mixture Model and Fuzzy Weighted Evaluation System: A Case Study in Time-Series Plantar Pressure Data Set. *IEEE Sensors Journal*, *17*(5), 1407–1420. doi:10.1109/JSEN.2016.2641501

Wang, D., Li, Z., Dey, N., Ashour, A. S., Sherratt, R. S., & Shi, F. (2017). Case-Based Reasoning for Product Style Construction and Fuzzy Analytic Hierarchy Process Evaluation Modeling Using Consumers Linguistic Variables. *IEEE Access : Practical Innovations, Open Solutions*, *5*, 4900–4912. doi:10.1109/ACCESS.2017.2677950

Wang, G., & Li, X. (1998). The applications of interval-valued fuzzy numbers and interval-distribution numbers. *Fuzzy Sets and Systems*, *98*(3), 331–335. doi:10.1016/S0165-0114(96)00368-5

Wei, S. H., & Chen, S. M. (2009). Fuzzy risk analysis based on interval-valued fuzzy numbers. *Expert Systems with Applications*, *36*(2), 2285–2299. doi:10.1016/j.eswa.2007.12.037

Yang, S. L., & Li, T. F. (2002). Agility evaluation of mass customization product manufacturing. *Journal of Materials Processing Technology*, *129*(1-3), 640–644. doi:10.1016/S0924-0136(02)00674-X

Yigin, I. H., Taskin, H., Cedimoglu, I. H., & Topal, B. (2007). Supplier selection: An expert system approach. *Production Planning and Control*, *18*(1), 16–24. doi:10.1080/09537280600940655

Youssuf, M. A. (1993). The impact of the intensity level of computer-based technologies on quality. *International Journal of Operations & Production Management*, *14*(4), 4–25. doi:10.1108/01443579410056010

Yusuf, Y. Y., Ren, J., & Burns, N. D. (2001). A method of evaluating enterprise agility-an empirical study. *Proceedings of the 16th International Conference on Production Research,* 168-175.

Zadeh, L. A. (1965). Fuzzy sets. *Information and Control*, *8*(3), 338–353. doi:10.1016/S0019-9958(65)90241-X

Zadeh, L. A. (1975). The concept of a linguistic variable and its application to approximate reasoning. *Information Sciences*, *8*(3), 199–249. doi:10.1016/0020-0255(75)90036-5

Zimmermann, H. J. (1996). *Fuzzy set theory and its applications*. Boston: Kluwer Academic Publishers. doi:10.1007/978-94-015-8702-0

KEY TERMS AND DEFINITIONS

Agile Supply Chain Management (ASCM): It responds towards managing flexibility, quickness, responsiveness, and competency in supply chain network. ASC should be highly flexible to be reconfigured quickly in responding to the market changes.

Decision Making: It is the mental processes resulting in the selection of a course of action amongst several alternative possibilities.

Fuzzy Logic: It is a way of representing the subjective views, opinions, thinking of the society into objective information.

Multi-Criteria Decision Making (MCDM): It is concerned with configuring and solving decision problems having multiple decision criteria.

Performance Measurement: It describes the feedback or information on actions, which are executed for accomplishing customer expectations and strategic objectives.

Subjective Information: It represents feelings, ideas, etc. of an individual, which includes words, meaningfulness, definitions, and undefined concepts.

Supply Chain Management (SCM): It deals with the business activities (i.e., flow of goods, services, etc.) of a business firm. Successful SCM demands the effective movement and storage of inventory from origin to source and vice versa.

APPENDIX

Table 1. Agile supplier valuation module

Objective (θ)	Measures	(ξ_i)	Metrics	$(\xi_{i,j})$
Agile supplier valuation module	Technology and Knowledge Capability	(ξ_1)	Information Systems and Communication	$(\xi_{1,1})$
			Knowledge of Local Business Practices	$(\xi_{1,2})$
			Special Skills and knowledge	$(\xi_{1,3})$
			Technical Capability	$(\xi_{1,4})$
	Industrial and Organizational Competitiveness Capability	(ξ_2)	Strategic Orientation	$(\xi_{2,1})$
			Bargaining flexibility	$(\xi_{2,2})$
			Industry Attractiveness	$(\xi_{2,3})$
	Production and Logistics Management Capability	(ξ_3)	Varieties of Product/Service	$(\xi_{3,1})$
			Production Volume Flexibility	$(\xi_{3,2})$
			Order Lead Time	$(\xi_{3,3})$
			Responsiveness towards customers 'needs	$(\xi_{3,4})$
			Delivery Capacity and Reliability	$(\xi_{3,5})$
	Marketing Capability	(ξ_4)	Rapid Market Entry	$(\xi_{4,1})$
			General Reputation	$(\xi_{4,2})$
			Variation in Price	$(\xi_{4,3})$
	Human Resource Management Capability	(ξ_5)	Quality of Management Team	$(\xi_{5,1})$
			Human Resource Management Skill	$(\xi_{5,2})$
			Corporate Culture	$(\xi_{5,3})$

continued on following page

Table 1. Continued

Objective (θ)	Measures	(ξ_i)	Metrics	$(\xi_{i,j})$
	Partnership Management Capability	(ξ_6)	Data Information	$(\xi_{6,1})$
			Communication level with partners	$(\xi_{6,2})$
			Foreign Experience	$(\xi_{6,3})$
			Investment in Sales Training	$(\xi_{6,4})$
			Information transparency and availability	$(\xi_{6,5})$

Table 2. Priority importance of secondary indices

Metrics	$(\xi_{i,j})$	Weight $(w_{i,j})$	Decision makers perceptions							
			∂m_1	∂m_2	∂m_3	∂m_4	∂m_5	∂m_6	∂m_7	∂m_8
Information Systems and Communication	$(\xi_{1,1})$	$(w_{1,1})$	M	H	M	MH	H	MH	ML	ML
Knowledge of Local Business Practices	$(\xi_{1,2})$	$(w_{1,2})$	H	VL	ML	L	MH	M	AH	M
Special Skills and knowledge	$(\xi_{1,3})$	$(w_{1,3})$	MH	AL	VH	AL	VL	M	VH	L
Technical Capability	$(\xi_{1,4})$	$(w_{1,4})$	VL	ML	AH	VH	VH	AH	VH	ML
Strategic Orientation	$(\xi_{2,1})$	$(w_{2,1})$	M	VL	VL	VL	MH	M	ML	VL
Bargaining flexibility	$(\xi_{2,2})$	$(w_{2,2})$	VH	ML	H	H	ML	ML	L	VH
Industry Attractiveness	$(\xi_{2,3})$	$(w_{2,3})$	ML	AL	H	M	VL	ML	VL	M
Varieties of Product/Service	$(\xi_{3,1})$	$(w_{3,1})$	M	AL	L	AL	VH	ML	VH	H
Production Volume Flexibility	$(\xi_{3,2})$	$(w_{3,2})$	MH	H	L	VH	MH	L	ML	L
Order Lead Time	$(\xi_{3,3})$	$(w_{3,3})$	M	AH	ML	AL	MH	VH	H	MH

continued on following page

Table 2. Continued

Metrics	$(\xi_{i,j})$	Weight $(w_{i,j})$	Decision makers perceptions							
			∂m_1	∂m_2	∂m_3	∂m_4	∂m_5	∂m_6	∂m_7	∂m_8
Responsiveness towards customers 'needs	$(\xi_{3,4})$	$(w_{3,4})$	MH	VL	M	ML	ML	VH	M	H
Delivery Capacity and Reliability	$(\xi_{3,5})$	$(w_{3,5})$	VL	MH	M	H	AH	VL	ML	AH
Rapid Market Entry	$(\xi_{4,1})$	$(w_{4,1})$	L	ML	AL	M	VL	M	VL	M
General Reputation	$(\xi_{4,2})$	$(w_{4,2})$	VL	ML	H	H	M	AL	ML	VL
Variation in Price	$(\xi_{4,3})$	$(w_{4,3})$	AH	VH	H	AH	M	M	AL	M
Quality of Management Team	$(\xi_{5,1})$	$(w_{5,1})$	ML	MH	VL	ML	VH	L	MH	H
Human Resource Management Skill	$(\xi_{5,2})$	$(w_{5,2})$	H	H	H	AL	VL	VL	MH	ML
Corporate Culture	$(\xi_{5,3})$	$(w_{5,3})$	L	M	MH	M	VH	VH	ML	ML
Data Information	$(\xi_{6,1})$	$(w_{6,1})$	VL	ML	MH	L	ML	VL	AL	AH
Communication level with partners	$(\xi_{6,2})$	$(w_{6,2})$	VH	M	H	MH	VL	MH	MH	H
Foreign Experience	$(\xi_{6,3})$	$(w_{6,3})$	M	AL	AH	ML	ML	AH	M	VH
Investment in Sales Training	$(\xi_{6,4})$	$(w_{6,4})$	AL	VL	H	AH	ML	H	VL	VL
Information transparency and availability	$(\xi_{6,5})$	$(w_{6,5})$	L	VH	VL	VH	MH	AL	VH	VL

Table 3. Appropriateness rating of secondary indices

Metrics	$(\xi_{i,j})$	Ratings $(R_{i,j})$	Decision makers perceptions							
			∂m_1	∂m_2	∂m_3	∂m_4	∂m_5	∂m_6	∂m_7	∂m_8
Information Systems and Communication	$(\xi_{1,1})$	$(R_{1,1})$	MP	P	M	P	AG	MP	MG	MG
Knowledge of Local Business Practices	$(\xi_{1,2})$	$(R_{1,2})$	AG	G	AP	G	M	M	G	VG
Special Skills and knowledge	$(\xi_{1,3})$	$(R_{1,3})$	AP	M	MP	M	MP	VP	AP	MP
Technical Capability	$(\xi_{1,4})$	$(R_{1,4})$	VP	M	M	VP	VG	MG	MG	AG
Strategic Orientation	$(\xi_{2,1})$	$(R_{2,1})$	MG	VG	M	AG	MP	MP	MP	VP
Bargaining flexibility	$(\xi_{2,2})$	$(R_{2,2})$	G	MP	VP	M	AP	AG	P	VG
Industry Attractiveness	$(\xi_{2,3})$	$(R_{2,3})$	MG	MG	M	M	MG	M	G	MP
Varieties of Product/Service	$(\xi_{3,1})$	$(R_{3,1})$	MP	P	MP	MG	P	MP	MP	VG
Production Volume Flexibility	$(\xi_{3,2})$	$(R_{3,2})$	AP	AG	MP	MP	AG	MG	MG	MG
Order Lead Time	$(\xi_{3,3})$	$(R_{3,3})$	P	P	M	AP	P	MP	AP	AP
Responsiveness towards customers 'needs	$(\xi_{3,4})$	$(R_{3,4})$	MG	P	VP	MG	MP	AP	G	AG
Delivery Capacity and Reliability	$(\xi_{3,5})$	$(R_{3,5})$	M	G	MG	VP	VG	MP	MP	P
Rapid Market Entry	$(\xi_{4,1})$	$(R_{4,1})$	M	AG	P	MP	MG	VP	AP	MP
General Reputation	$(\xi_{4,2})$	$(R_{4,2})$	AP	VP	AP	MP	G	M	M	P
Variation in Price	$(\xi_{4,3})$	$(R_{4,3})$	MG	MP	M	MG	VG	VP	VG	MP
Quality of Management Team	$(\xi_{5,1})$	$(R_{5,1})$	VP	MG	M	AG	M	P	AG	AP
Human Resource Management Skill	$(\xi_{5,2})$	$(R_{5,2})$	AG	MP	M	MG	MP	MP	M	M
Corporate Culture	$(\xi_{5,3})$	$(R_{5,3})$	MG	VP	VG	P	G	MG	P	VG

continued on following page

Table 3. Continued

Metrics	$(\xi_{i,j})$	Ratings $(R_{i,j})$	Decision makers perceptions							
			∂m_1	∂m_2	∂m_3	∂m_4	∂m_5	∂m_6	∂m_7	∂m_8
Data Information	$(\xi_{6,1})$	$(R_{6,1})$	M	MP	M	VP	MG	MP	M	AP
Communication level with partners	$(\xi_{6,2})$	$(R_{6,2})$	VP	MG	AP	AG	P	AG	M	M
Foreign Experience	$(\xi_{6,3})$	$(R_{6,3})$	AG	VG	AP	VP	MG	M	P	MP
Investment in Sales Training	$(\xi_{6,4})$	$(R_{6,4})$	VP	MP	MG	AP	P	MP	VG	AP
Information transparency and availability	$(\xi_{6,5})$	$(R_{6,5})$	M	G	M	G	VG	M	P	M

Table 4. Priority Importance of primary indices

Measures	(ξ_i)	Weight (w_i)	Decision makers perceptions							
			∂m_1	∂m_2	∂m_3	∂m_4	∂m_5	∂m_6	∂m_7	∂m_8
Technology and Knowledge Capability	(ξ_1)	(w_1)	ML	M	VH	MH	MH	VH	L	AH
Industrial and Organizational Competitiveness Capability	(ξ_2)	(w_2)	AH	VH	AL	VH	H	M	MH	VL
Production and Logistics Management Capability	(ξ_3)	(w_3)	M	H	H	VL	MH	VH	ML	ML
Marketing Capability	(ξ_4)	(w_4)	M	AL	AH	ML	ML	AL	L	VL
Human Resource Management Capability	(ξ_5)	(w_5)	MH	AL	VL	VH	AH	MH	H	MH
Partnership Management Capability	(ξ_6)	(w_6)	H	AH	M	H	L	M	AH	VH

Table 5. Aggregated fuzzy appropriateness rating and aggregated fuzzy priority weight of secondary indices

Metrics	Ratings $(R_{i,j})$	Aggregated fuzzy appropriateness rating	Weight $(w_{i,j})$	Aggregated fuzzy priority weight
$(\xi_{1,1})$	$(R_{1,1})$	[(0.363,0.414,0.533,0.584,0.800); (0.363,0.414,0.533,0.584,1.000)]	$(w_{1,1})$	[(0.448,0.510,0.665,0.725,0.800); (0.448,0.510,0.665,0.725,1.000)]
$(\xi_{1,2})$	$(R_{1,2})$	[(0.591,0.643,0.740,0.776,0.800); (0.591,0.643,0.740,0.776,1.000)]	$(w_{1,2})$	[(0.394,0.444,0.555,0.606,0.800); (0.394,0.444,0.555,0.606,1.000)]
$(\xi_{1,3})$	$(R_{1,3})$	[(0.144,0.185,0.283,0.329,0.800); (0.144,0.185,0.283,0.329,1.000)]	$(w_{1,3})$	[(0.350,0.388,0.448,0.476,0.800); (0.350,0.388,0.448,0.476,1.000)]
$(\xi_{1,4})$	$(R_{1,4})$	[(0.466,0.508,0.600,0.645,0.800); (0.466,0.508,0.600,0.645,1.000)]	$(w_{1,4})$	[(0.641,0.673,0.718,0.739,0.800); (0.641,0.673,0.718,0.739,1.000)]
$(\xi_{2,1})$	$(R_{2,1})$	[(0.418,0.460,0.560,0.605,0.800); (0.418,0.460,0.560,0.605,1.000)]	$(w_{2,1})$	[(0.174,0.209,0.300,0.358,0.800); (0.174,0.209,0.300,0.358,1.000)]
$(\xi_{2,2})$	$(R_{2,2})$	[(0.398,0.436,0.508,0.543,0.800); (0.398,0.436,0.508,0.543,1.000)]	$(w_{2,2})$	[(0.481,0.535,0.638,0.679,0.800); (0.481,0.535,0.638,0.679,1.000)]
$(\xi_{2,3})$	$(R_{2,3})$	[(0.449,0.515,0.678,0.740,0.800); (0.449,0.515,0.678,0.740,1.000)]	$(w_{2,3})$	[(0.213,0.255,0.355,0.406,0.800); (0.213,0.255,0.355,0.406,1.000)]
$(\xi_{3,1})$	$(R_{3,1})$	[(0.284,0.336,0.450,0.500,0.800); (0.284,0.336,0.450,0.500,1.000)]	$(w_{3,1})$	[(0.389,0.434,0.505,0.534,0.800); (0.389,0.434,0.505,0.534,1.000)]
$(\xi_{3,2})$	$(R_{3,2})$	[(0.510,0.541,0.640,0.678,0.800); (0.510,0.541,0.640,0.678,1.000)]	$(w_{3,2})$	[(0.388,0.443,0.553,0.600,0.800); (0.388,0.443,0.553,0.600,1.000)]
$(\xi_{3,3})$	$(R_{3,3})$	[(0.076,0.116,0.185,0.220,0.800); (0.076,0.116,0.185,0.220,1.000)]	$(w_{3,3})$	[(0.538,0.581,0.683,0.720,0.800); (0.538,0.581,0.683,0.720,1.000)]
$(\xi_{3,4})$	$(R_{3,4})$	[(0.386,0.420,0.510,0.551,0.800); (0.386,0.420,0.510,0.551,1.000)]	$(w_{3,4})$	[(0.401,0.456,0.578,0.630,0.800); (0.401,0.456,0.578,0.630,1.000)]
$(\xi_{3,5})$	$(R_{3,5})$	[(0.366,0.418,0.528,0.578,0.800); (0.366,0.418,0.528,0.578,1.000)]	$(w_{3,5})$	[(0.474,0.505,0.588,0.630,0.800); (0.474,0.505,0.588,0.630,1.000)]
$(\xi_{4,1})$	$(R_{4,1})$	[(0.285,0.323,0.413,0.456,0.800); (0.285,0.323,0.413,0.456,1.000)]	$(w_{4,1})$	[(0.146,0.194,0.290,0.343,0.800); (0.146,0.194,0.290,0.343,1.000)]
$(\xi_{4,2})$	$(R_{4,2})$	[(0.196,0.240,0.330,0.374,0.800); (0.196,0.240,0.330,0.374,1.000)]	$(w_{4,2})$	[(0.263,0.301,0.398,0.446,0.800); (0.263,0.301,0.398,0.446,1.000)]
$(\xi_{4,3})$	$(R_{4,3})$	[(0.460,0.509,0.615,0.660,0.800); (0.460,0.509,0.615,0.660,1.000)]	$(w_{4,3})$	[(0.576,0.624,0.708,0.740,0.800); (0.576,0.624,0.708,0.740,1.000)]
$(\xi_{5,1})$	$(R_{5,1})$	[(0.408,0.444,0.520,0.558,0.800); (0.408,0.444,0.520,0.558,1.000)]	$(w_{5,1})$	[(0.399,0.445,0.555,0.604,0.800); (0.399,0.445,0.555,0.604,1.000)]
$(\xi_{5,2})$	$(R_{5,2})$	[(0.381,0.440,0.578,0.634,0.800); (0.381,0.440,0.578,0.634,1.000)]	$(w_{5,2})$	[(0.364,0.399,0.495,0.541,0.800); (0.364,0.399,0.495,0.541,1.000)]
$(\xi_{5,3})$	$(R_{5,3})$	[(0.478,0.525,0.613,0.653,0.800); (0.478,0.525,0.613,0.653,1.000)]	$(w_{5,3})$	[(0.433,0.494,0.608,0.654,0.800); (0.433,0.494,0.608,0.654,1.000)]
$(\xi_{6,1})$	$(R_{6,1})$	[(0.235,0.288,0.410,0.465,0.800); (0.235,0.288,0.410,0.465,1.000)]	$(w_{6,1})$	[(0.245,0.271,0.343,0.384,0.800); (0.245,0.271,0.343,0.384,1.000)]

continued on following page

Table 5. Continued

Metrics	Ratings $(R_{i,j})$	Aggregated fuzzy appropriateness rating	Weight $(w_{i,j})$	Aggregated fuzzy priority weight
$(\xi_{6,2})$	$(R_{6,2})$	[(0.408,0.444,0.520,0.558,0.800); (0.408,0.444,0.520,0.558,1.000)]	$(w_{6,2})$	[(0.554,0.605,0.730,0.780,0.800); (0.554,0.605,0.730,0.780,1.000)]
$(\xi_{6,3})$	$(R_{6,3})$	[(0.380,0.418,0.493,0.529,0.800); (0.380,0.418,0.493,0.529,1.000)]	$(w_{6,3})$	[(0.489,0.530,0.610,0.643,0.800); (0.489,0.530,0.610,0.643,1.000)]
$(\xi_{6,4})$	$(R_{6,4})$	[(0.236,0.269,0.340,0.375,0.800); (0.236,0.269,0.340,0.375,1.000)]	$(w_{6,4})$	[(0.326,0.348,0.408,0.446,0.800); (0.326,0.348,0.408,0.446,1.000)]
$(\xi_{6,5})$	$(R_{6,5})$	[(0.461,0.535,0.668,0.721,0.800); (0.461,0.535,0.668,0.721,1.000)]	$(w_{6,5})$	[(0.426,0.459,0.503,0.529,0.800); (0.426,0.459,0.503,0.529,1.000)]

Table 6. Computed fuzzy appropriateness rating and aggregated fuzzy priority weight of primary indices

Measures (ξ_i)	Rating (R_i)	Computed fuzzy appropriateness rating	Weight (w_i)	Aggregated fuzzy priority weight
(ξ^1)	(R_1)	[(0.292,0.381,0.656,0.833,0.800); (0.292,0.381,0.656,0.833,1.000)]	(w_1)	[(0.569,0.619,0.715,0.753,0.800); (0.569,0.619,0.715,0.753,1.000)]
(ξ^2)	(R_2)	[(0.249,0.356,0.733,1.020,0.800); (0.249,0.356,0.733,1.020,1.000)]	(w_2)	[(0.560,0.598,0.665,0.694,0.800); (0.560,0.598,0.665,0.694,1.000)]
(ξ^3)	(R_3)	[(0.218,0.294,0.542,0.705,0.800); (0.218,0.294,0.542,0.705,1.000)]	(w_3)	[(0.451,0.503,0.620,0.670,0.800); (0.451,0.503,0.620,0.670,1.000)]
(ξ^4)	(R_4)	[(0.234,0.324,0.613,0.824,0.800); (0.234,0.324,0.613,0.824,1.000)]	(w_4)	[(0.213,0.244,0.313,0.349,0.800); (0.213,0.244,0.313,0.349,1.000)]
(ξ^5)	(R_5)	[(0.282,0.381,0.708,0.926,0.800); (0.282,0.381,0.708,0.926,1.000)]	(w_5)	[(0.549,0.581,0.668,0.703,0.800); (0.549,0.581,0.668,0.703,1.000)]
(ξ^6)	(R_6)	[(0.267,0.350,0.585,0.736,0.800); (0.267,0.350,0.585,0.736,1.000)]	(w_6)	[(0.631,0.683,0.773,0.809,0.800); (0.631,0.683,0.773,0.809,1.000)]

Table 7. Computation of Fuzzy performance importance index

Metrics	$w_{i,j}^{A} = \left[\left\{(1,1,1,1;1),(1,1,1,1;1)\right\} - w_{i,j}\right]$	$FPII^{metrics} = \left\{\left[\left\{(1,1,1,1;1),(1,1,1,1;1)\right\} - w_{i,j}\right] \otimes R_{i,j}\right\}$
$(\xi_{1,1})$	[(0.275,0.335,0.490,0.553,0.800); (0.275,0.335,0.490,0.553,1.000)]	[(0.100,0.139,0.261,0.323,0.800); (0.100,0.139,0.261,0.323,1.000)]
$(\xi_{1,2})$	[(0.394,0.445,0.556,0.606,0.800); (0.394,0.445,0.556,0.606,1.000)]	[(0.233,0.286,0.412,0.471,0.800); (0.233,0.286,0.412,0.471,1.000)]
$(\xi_{1,3})$	[(0.524,0.553,0.613,0.650,0.800); (0.524,0.553,0.613,0.650,1.000)]	[(0.075,0.102,0.173,0.214,0.800); (0.075,0.102,0.173,0.214,1.000)]
$(\xi_{1,4})$	[(0.261,0.283,0.328,0.359,0.800); (0.261,0.283,0.328,0.359,1.000)]	[(0.122,0.143,0.197,0.231,0.800); (0.122,0.143,0.197,0.231,1.000)]
$(\xi_{2,1})$	[(0.643,0.700,0.791,0.826,0.800); (0.643,0.700,0.791,0.826,1.000)]	[(0.268,0.322,0.443,0.500,0.800); (0.268,0.322,0.443,0.500,1.000)]
$(\xi_{2,2})$	[(0.321,0.363,0.465,0.519,0.800); (0.321,0.363,0.465,0.519,1.000)]	[(0.128,0.158,0.236,0.281,0.800); (0.128,0.158,0.236,0.281,1.000)]
$(\xi_{2,3})$	[(0.594,0.645,0.745,0.788,0.800); (0.594,0.645,0.745,0.788,1.000)]	[(0.266,0.332,0.505,0.583,0.800); (0.266,0.332,0.505,0.583,1.000)]
$(\xi_{3,1})$	[(0.466,0.495,0.566,0.611,0.800); (0.466,0.495,0.566,0.611,1.000)]	[(0.132,0.166,0.255,0.306,0.800); (0.132,0.166,0.255,0.306,1.000)]
$(\xi_{3,2})$	[(0.400,0.448,0.558,0.613,0.800); (0.400,0.448,0.558,0.613,1.000)]	[(0.204,0.242,0.357,0.415,0.800); (0.204,0.242,0.357,0.415,1.000)]
$(\xi_{3,3})$	[(0.280,0.318,0.419,0.463,0.800); (0.280,0.318,0.419,0.463,1.000)]	[(0.021,0.037,0.077,0.102,0.800); (0.021,0.037,0.077,0.102,1.000)]
$(\xi_{3,4})$	[(0.370,0.423,0.544,0.599,0.800); (0.370,0.423,0.544,0.599,1.000)]	[(0.143,0.177,0.277,0.330,0.800); (0.143,0.177,0.277,0.330,1.000)]
$(\xi_{3,5})$	[(0.370,0.413,0.495,0.526,0.800); (0.370,0.413,0.495,0.526,1.000)]	[(0.136,0.172,0.261,0.304,0.800); (0.136,0.172,0.261,0.304,1.000)]
$(\xi_{4,1})$	[(0.658,0.710,0.806,0.854,0.800); (0.658,0.710,0.806,0.854,1.000)]	[(0.187,0.229,0.333,0.390,0.800); (0.187,0.229,0.333,0.390,1.000)]
$(\xi_{4,2})$	[(0.554,0.603,0.699,0.738,0.800); (0.554,0.603,0.699,0.738,1.000)]	[(0.109,0.145,0.231,0.276,0.800); (0.109,0.145,0.231,0.276,1.000)]
$(\xi_{4,3})$	[(0.260,0.293,0.376,0.424,0.800); (0.260,0.293,0.376,0.424,1.000)]	[(0.120,0.149,0.231,0.280,0.800); (0.120,0.149,0.231,0.280,1.000)]
$(\xi_{5,1})$	[(0.396,0.445,0.555,0.601,0.800); (0.396,0.445,0.555,0.601,1.000)]	[(0.161,0.197,0.289,0.335,0.800); (0.161,0.197,0.289,0.335,1.000)]
$(\xi_{5,2})$	[(0.459,0.505,0.601,0.636,0.800); (0.459,0.505,0.601,0.636,1.000)]	[(0.175,0.222,0.347,0.403,0.800); (0.175,0.222,0.347,0.403,1.000)]
$(\xi_{5,3})$	[(0.346,0.393,0.506,0.568,0.800); (0.346,0.393,0.506,0.568,1.000)]	[(0.165,0.206,0.310,0.370,0.800); (0.165,0.206,0.310,0.370,1.000)]
$(\xi_{6,1})$	[(0.616,0.658,0.729,0.755,0.800); (0.616,0.658,0.729,0.755,1.000)]	[(0.145,0.189,0.299,0.351,0.800); (0.145,0.189,0.299,0.351,1.000)]

continued on following page

Table 7. Continued

Metrics	$w_{i,j}^{\Lambda} = \left[\left\{(1,1,1,1;1),(1,1,1,1;1)\right\} - w_{i,j}\right]$	$FPII^{metrics} = \left\{\left[\left\{(1,1,1,1;1),(1,1,1,1;1)\right\} - w_{i,j}\right] \otimes R_{i,j}\right\}$
$(\xi_{6,2})$	[(0.220,0.270,0.395,0.446,0.800); (0.220,0.270,0.395,0.446,1.000)]	[(0.090,0.120,0.205,0.249,0.800); (0.090,0.120,0.205,0.249,1.000)]
$(\xi_{6,3})$	[(0.358,0.390,0.470,0.511,0.800); (0.358,0.390,0.470,0.511,1.000)]	[(0.136,0.163,0.231,0.270,0.800); (0.136,0.163,0.231,0.270,1.000)]
$(\xi_{6,4})$	[(0.554,0.593,0.653,0.674,0.800); (0.554,0.593,0.653,0.674,1.000)]	[(0.131,0.159,0.222,0.253,0.800); (0.131,0.159,0.222,0.253,1.000)]
$(\xi_{6,5})$	[(0.471,0.498,0.541,0.574,0.800); (0.471,0.498,0.541,0.574,1.000)]	[(0.217,0.266,0.361,0.414,0.800); (0.217,0.266,0.361,0.414,1.000)]

Table 8. Indices ranking based on distance measure

Metrics $(\xi_{i,j})$	*Distance between fuzzy performance importance index of the metrics and the ideal fuzzy important index* $d\left(\tilde{\tilde{A}}, id\tilde{\tilde{e}}al\right)$	*Ranking*
$(\xi_{1,1})$	*0.1949*	*14*
$(\xi_{1,2})$	*0.0646*	*3*
$(\xi_{1,3})$	*0.2528*	*22*
$(\xi_{1,4})$	*0.2238*	*20*
$(\xi_{2,1})$	*0.0348*	*2*
$(\xi_{2,2})$	*0.1990*	*15*
$(\xi_{2,3})$	*0.0004*	*1*
$(\xi_{3,1})$	*0.1865*	*13*
$(\xi_{3,2})$	*0.1057*	*5*
$(\xi_{3,3})$	*0.3263*	*23*

continued on following page

Table 8. Continued

Metrics $(\xi_{i,j})$	*Distance between fuzzy performance importance index of the metrics and the ideal fuzzy important index* $d\left(\tilde{\tilde{A}}, id\tilde{\tilde{e}}al\right)$	*Ranking*
$(\xi_{3,4})$	0.1710	11
$(\xi_{3,5})$	0.1834	12
$(\xi_{4,1})$	0.1236	7
$(\xi_{4,2})$	0.2089	19
$(\xi_{4,3})$	0.2044	17
$(\xi_{5,1})$	0.1587	10
$(\xi_{5,2})$	0.1216	6
$(\xi_{5,3})$	0.1431	8
$(\xi_{6,1})$	0.1584	9
$(\xi_{6,2})$	0.2305	21
$(\xi_{6,3})$	0.1997	16
$(\xi_{6,4})$	0.2078	18
$(\xi_{6,5})$	0.0966	4

Chapter 5
Approach of Modelization and Management on Software Components

Fadoua Rehioui
University Sultan Moulay Slimane, Morocco

ABSTRACT

The complexity of information systems leads to poor data management and therefore bad decisions. The advantage of using component-based software engineering is to divide an information system into subsystem blocks with less complexity. In fact, a component is intended to provide specific services as management of the combination and communication between the units of the system. This chapter addresses this problem by developing information systems, proposing a component identification approach and the management pattern for data management. In this work, three developed views are taken into account, which include modelization and the design to achieve the purpose of defining and building the components and how they can be assembled. A component is intended to provide specific services, as a combination and communication management between the system units, and the manager component is the important and complementary paradigm pattern and added value for the development of software systems.

INTRODUCTION

Using information systems for strategic decision use many approach to meet the needs and expectations of services required, but systems with large numbers of elements, describes a complexity difficult to understand and maintain. In fact, decision making is a complex cognitive process based on criteria of choice and analysis, and the observation of the behavior can lead to the state of the decision process, as for (Chennoufi and al, 2018) with the addition of behavioral criteria of several individuals in order to arrive at decision-making strategies of a complex system, and (Wang and al, 2016) for the ANFIS generating processes included for features extraction.

DOI: 10.4018/978-1-5225-6164-4.ch005

Or appropriate for a good decision-making represented in an intelligent way towards the multidirectional analysis of the query server including the base OLAP (Selmane and al, 2015), or Aggregation Operators for Medical Diagnosis (Ngan and al, 2016). The decision process leads to chain modelization, selection, and evaluation. As a result, in the context of software consistency and quality, the software industry is moving towards component-based development and is aiming to use evolution and persistence methods, which have recently been devoted to the development orientation of component-based software.

The interest behind the use of component-based software engineering is to divide an information system with less complexity, faster development, and improved performance into reliable and efficient software components. As a result, the component paradigm provides a good representation of high-level complex systems, and can help in the decision process. The essential role of component-based development is the component model that defines how components can be built and how they can be assembled.

The resolution of the issue provides an overview of the main directions, proposing an approach. An approach is the way of approaching and treating a subject or a problematic through the use of adaptable systems such as the approach for document clustering (Karaa and al, 2016), the approach to diminish imbalance parameters for the big deoxyribonucleic acid dataset (kamal and al, 2016), and Crohn's disease classification by a neuro-fuzzy-based approach (Ahmed and al, 2017).

So the component-based software development approach is currently one of the solutions that differ from the traditional approach, in which software systems can only be implemented from scratch. Hence the idea is that software systems can be developed by the appropriate components, then to assemble them with well-defined software architecture (ACCORD project, 2002).

The idea of the component was firstly proposed in 1968 by Douglas McIlroy (McIlro, 1968). This new era of component-oriented started to grow 30 years later in: Sun EJB (Sun), OMG (OMG), CCM (CORBA), Microsoft ".NET / COM" (Microsoft. NET), etc. The design of the component-based software development approach is that software systems can be developed by appropriate components and then assembling them with a well-defined software architecture (Cai, 2000).

Software systems are developed by assembling component units that provide a set of exposed services. A component is intended to provide specific services such as combination, management, connection and communication between system units. Managing the communication between the system components requires taking into consideration the users of this system. From the principle the same world observed by several users can produce different viewpoints (Rehioui and al, 2014). Therefore, it is necessary to integrate the user in action.

The viewpoint concept is an effective means to improve the consistency of modeling and control system complexity, the main purpose of taking into account all the views and viewpoint modeling designers.

The behavior and state of an object have been reviewed by the perspectives (Bobrow, 1977), contexts (Debrauwer, 1998) and viewpoints, and therefore the viewpoint is like an advanced mechanism for object-oriented technology. The method based on viewpoint increases the participation of multiple stakeholders from different areas in the collaborative modeling process (Krumeich, 2014).

The objective of this work is to identify software components by approach representing the modelization of components, and to propose a pattern that ensures the combination and communication between software components, and offering the central element of approach of "Management Component" as a solution to facilitate the optimization of operations.

This chapter is organized as follows:

- Section 2 provides definitions and incorporates general discussions on component development and viewpoint concepts (literature review).
- Section 3 is devoted the different of issues and problems related to the topic.
- Section 4 formalizes the model of the proposed approach and its implementation on a case study.
- And it ends with a conclusion in section 5.

BACKGROUND

Generally, a component is a physical unit participating in the execution, and exposes the means and the physical reality (code, file, table ...) to implement classes presenting abstractions of the logical models. As for the component diagrams, they describe the physical elements and their relations (interface of the class, body: realization).

The development of applications by interconnection and assembly of components is old but its feasibility is recent. In fact, there is no standard for modeling a component-based system, so it is essential to propose an approach to illustrate the software system, for the identification of its components bundling the provided and required services needed to function. This chapter focuses on the abstract side (functional aspect, logical aspect) that will be represented in a component modeling aspect.

The component processes the data with a set of actions from a library and then invoking the input / output functions. Component is performed by a structure consisting of the interfaces offering or requesting some data from the rest of the application. Below a modeling of a component (see Figure 1).

A component is a part representing a feature at runtime of the system, it take their names from their abstract features of system. Typically, "Input / Output" of component are the interfaces representing a set of functional properties describing the structure, the behavior and the functionalities of the component, and a set of non-functional properties concerning the services used by the component that are not part of the application services (security, performance, etc.) that are outside that component. This work is interested in developing components with functional properties.

Figure 1. Modeling a software component

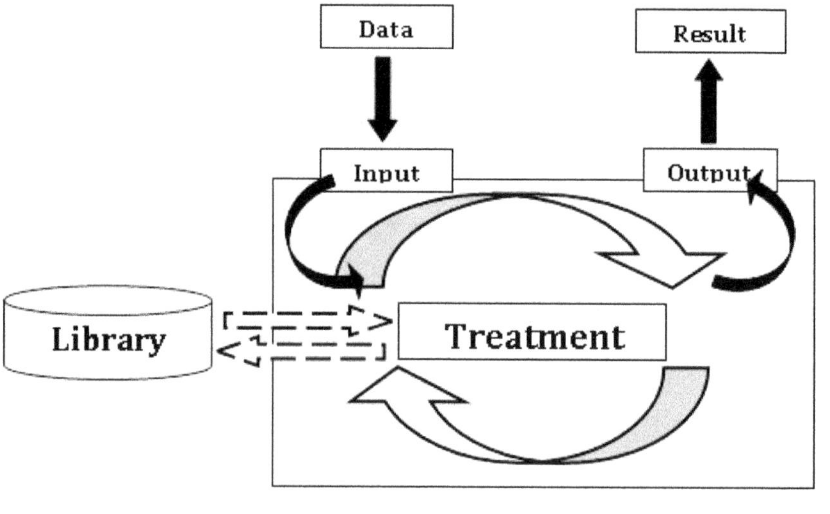

The components are divided into two types, a primitive component and / or a composite component. The composite component is an element whose internal architecture is formed of several components, exposing its contents. These internal components named subcomponents, are instantiated, interconnected and configured, represent the internal treatment and role played by a set of instances at runtime. So afterwards, it's about defining what subcomponents the component is composed of, how these components are interconnected and related to the composite component.

This work aims to present a new component development and identification of component interfaces, with the development of the notion of modeling components that ensure the consistency of the component development process and the link to the architecture of the system.

RELATED WORKS

Component-Based Software Development

The field of method development (Tang an al, 2017) deals with the definition of new methods of engineering modeling (Wang and al, 2017), design and adaptation of techniques and tools for the development of information systems. For good software quality improvement, several methods of analysis and design have been developed. This section aims to present the state of the art of engineering methods based on software components, such as:

Catalysis

Catalysis is a method of designing component-based systems from the proposed object-oriented community originally developed by Desmond D'Souza and Alan Cameron Wills in 1998 (D'Souza and Wills, 1998). Based on UML for object development, it improves and expands UML with extensions to represent components at the logical level as the physical level of the component in UML. Although this approach is complex and long to assimilate, Catalysis is based on principles of which essentially: type models, collaborations, refinement and frameworks (frameworks).

The components of the Catalysis method are abstract, and defined as a 'Type', each 'Type' is a stereotyped class. A type presents behavior in a domain, whose external behavior of each 'Type' is defined by its interfaces.

UML Component

UML Components method for the design development Objects, inspired by several methods such as Catalysis and RUP (Kruchten, 1998), proposed by J. Cheesman and J. Daniels (Cheesman, 2001). This method applies UML in the component architecture, to specify the components, their interactions, ie. focuses on component specification by enriching UML notation with stereotypes to designate the specification of system models and divide these models into components.

Indeed, UML Components contains a component identification phase, which immediately follows the needs analysis, the purpose of which is to create a preliminary definition of the system architecture and its constituents, followed during the next steps of design.

The study of the interactions between components are defined by the interfaces and thus by calls of methods and services between components.

The proposed method is limited to the design level. Indeed, it does not explain how to interpret the specification of the component in the implementation, or how to check the specifications at the compilation level.

From Object-Oriented Applications to Component-Oriented Applications via Component-Oriented Architecture

Another work of Simon Allier (Allier and al, 2011), it's to provide a semi-automatic method for identifying a component-based architecture in an object-oriented application. The method helps in understanding the original application, as well as simplifying the projection of the application into a concrete component model. The identification of a component-based architecture is done in three main steps:

- The collection of essential data for the identification process, corresponding to the dependencies between the classes and arrived at from a dynamic analysis of the application.
- Identification of the components, in three methods explored: the first one uses a lattice of Galois, the second two meta-heuristics and the last one a meta-heuristic multi-objective.
- Identification of the architecture based on application components, identifying the required / provided interfaces of each component.

The concept of projecting this component-based method into an object-oriented application; can be used as a template to perform a restructuring of an object-oriented application to a similar, component-based, operational application.

Viewpoint-Based Modeling Method

The modeling of a complex system cannot be centralized task based on unique formalism.

The first appearance of the viewpoint concept was outlined. In 1985 in a work of Wood-Harper and al (Wood-Harper, 1985) focus on the implementation of views in software engineering. Then there is often cited in Finkelstein and al in 1992 (Finkelstein, 1992).

The complex system must be able to be defined into multiple views, then access to one or more of these views are achieved according to their specific needs.

The viewpoint paradigm is an active subject of research in many areas such as software engineering collaborative design of complex systems with software (Sosnin, 2016), knowledge representation, database systems (Karaa and al, 2016), web applications, and Multi-agent system multidirectional (Juneja, 2017).

Various studies suggest a distributed development approach based on viewpoints such as:

VUML

View based Unified Modeling Language is method developed by Mahmoud Nassar (Nassar, 2003), is an extension of UML but oriented viewpoint. It provides formalism to model a software system by an approach combining objects and viewpoint from analysis to coding. The method associated with VUML allows modeling a software system according to viewpoint which represents and expresses each actor's requirements and rights. Firstly, it identifies actors of the system as in UML and associates for each actor a unique viewpoint. Then, for each viewpoint, it describes use cases, scenarios and related classes. The result is a set of viewpoint models such as class diagrams in the UML formalism (Anwar, 2010).

The viewpoint concept appears, also, to allow the models to be broken down into stakeholder-specific fragments (actor).

Viewpoint-Based Modeling to Collaborative Modeling

The concept of point of view seems to be able to decompose the models into fragments specific to the actors (actor). The collaborative modeling is defined as a "process where a number of people actively contribute to the creation of a model" (Rittgen, 2009). These people are represented by one single individual or multiple individuals working as a collective unit.

In reality, collaborative modeling is based on the creation and use of models that include multiple individuals, all of whom have collaborative work based on capabilities, shared knowledge resources, and responsibilities with different skills. To achieve point-of-view-based modeling, it is necessary to distribute the modeling of individual activities for the collaborative creation of an example of a coherent model. In order to support point-of-view modeling, additional terms must be defined:

- A point of view supports an actor by contributing to the design of the system from a specific perspective.
- A type of view provides a specific perspective of the system to stakeholders.
- A view is an instance of a view type and presents the elements of the model to an actor, the viewpoint involved and how the elements of the model can be modified.

To achieve point-of-view-based modeling, it is necessary to distribute the modeling of individual activities for the collaborative creation of an example of a coherent model.

Synthesis

Most of these proposed software component-based methods; they do not exhibit either early and clear identification of components nor a good identification and consistency of them for the rest of the system development cycle until the obtaining of the code of the system, which makes the methods unreliable and inadequate.

The data gives the key to make the decisions and methods suitable for improvement (Kamal and al, 2016). As a result of the amounts of this data generated (Nimmy and al, 2017), companies require different analyzes, supporting data-driven decision-making, for example enterprise resource planning (ERP) systems handle a huge amount of data, related to the actual execution of business processes and the work of (Pajić and al, 2016) is a detailed analysis of the concepts of approach centered on the artifact and describe its constructions by the metamodel and the capture of knowledge in data conversion. As a result, the technology revolution has brought a change in the way data is collected (Kamal and al, 2017).

Therefore, it is essential to think of a predictive analysis of the data and to obtain significant results useful for the desired task. Research has been conducted in the direction of predictive data analysis. (Acharjya and Anitha, 2017) makes a comparative analysis between statistical techniques, raw computing and hybrid techniques, carried out on a set of data on the financial bankruptcy of the Greek industrial bank ETEVA, and (Li and al, 2017) (Chatterjee and al, 2015) for prediction method. In the same way, this work proposes an approach of early identification (Kausar and al, 2016) of the software components starting from a predictive analysis, and a pattern for the management of the components of the system.

Despite specific software engineering techniques in the area of component-based software engineering, in phases such as modelization, verification or validation of applications, the components are still insufficient and require greater research efforts. Indeed, there are no prodigious results but simple principles, adaptable to identify the components.

As an indispensable element in carrying out the activities and in the specification of the needs, it is necessary to include the actor in the action. The concept of viewpoint is built from the conjunction of the actor / information. For each actor corresponds a viewpoint. This actor represents a set of users with common characteristics and expresses the same type of use of the system. The integration of the notion of viewpoint in this component-based approach and through the concept of Managing has the ability to communicate units whose accessibility and dynamic behavior change according to the viewpoint of the 'current user. To be able to support viewpoint-based modeling, additional terms have to be defined:

- A Viewpoint supports a stakeholder (actor) in contributing to system design from a specific perspective.
- A View Type offers a specific piece of system perspective to the stakeholders.
- A View is an instance of a view type and presents the model elements to a stakeholder the viewpoint concerned and how model elements can be modified.

Since the role of the components is to provide the business functionality of the system, the approach is to identify the Manager component (Rehioui and al, 2016) which represents the essential element of the communication corresponding to the views of the users.

FOCUS PRINCIPAL DU CHAPITRE

In the software industry, quality requirements play a major role in the success of projects, and are influenced by user analysis, to reduce the burden of the requirements engineering process. (Dhir and al, 2017) select only the appropriate requirements that can be associated with the final product using the analytical hierarchy process.

Essentially, the heart of the problem lies in the difficulty of making the right decisions in the identification and development of components compatible with the requirements and meeting the needs, as well as the management of communication between these components.

The objective of this work is to develop a component modelization approach and to make available a manager to take the task of the system easier due to the multitude of information to consider.

Since the role of the components is to provide the business functionality of the system, the proposed approach is to identify the different components of the system.

With the advent of UML 2.0, it has become increasingly easier to express needs and requirements such as (Karaa and al, 2016). The main addition to the UML is the new concepts.

Although originally designed as a notation for object-oriented modeling, UML has great potential for component-based systems. UML Components applies UML to the world of component architecture, demonstrating how it can be used to specify components, their interactions, and their integration into cohesive systems. The real problem in all of this is to ask these two essential questions: "What components to create?", "How to know if we have made the right choice?".

Decomposition Process of the System Into Components

In information systems modeling, it is rare to go directly to the definition of the implementation states, because in most cases, the start is describing the parts to establish the architecture, then moving to manage the dependencies between these different parts.

The multi-component treaty is usually simpler than the overall treaty of a system, as simpler each will be the subject of a separate study. Segmentation in image processing (Roy and al, 2014) (Bose and al, 2013) as decomposition process approach starts from the general, and goes to the particular, guided by the functionalities of the system, where the system is divided into components each of which must perform a function (possibly several if the component is decomposed into sub-components. with separate functions). The modeling of the components from the use cases as a type of functional model (Jacobson, 1992) considers the precision of elaboration and concrete identification of the components. These components make it possible to organize and cut the system into manageable and exchangeable pieces of software. The question of decomposition is always accompanied by certain constraints and cannot lead to a coherent answer. It then seeks to identify the components, which play a role in the operation of the system.

Functional division integrates in principle the functions of the system with its environment, in order to divide it into components taking into account all the functionalities present in these components, either to an expected work of the component, or to a desired service of an external environment. These functions defined within the component ensure the realization of the services that this component must render. So, a Component corresponds in principle to a work attached to one of the advantageous functions provided by the system.

Figure 2. Process of decomposition of the system into components

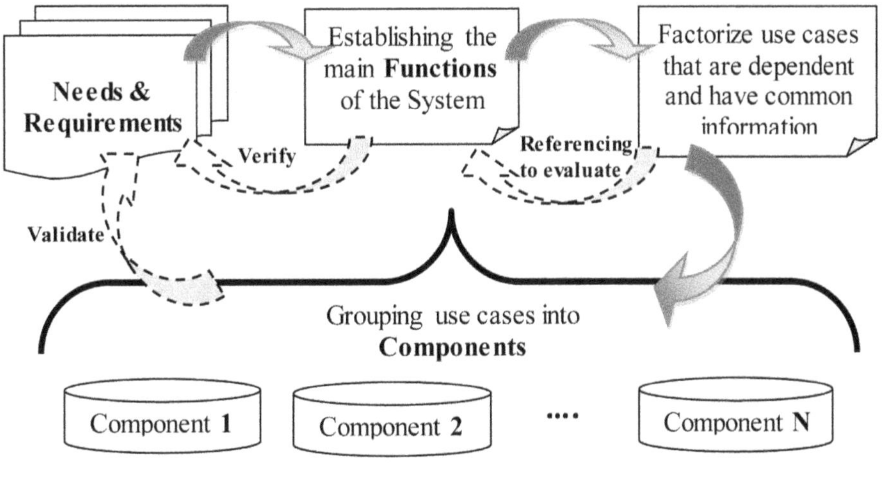

Software design is organized around functional, non-functional and architectural aspects. These aspects are focused on user needs (mostly figured in use cases). The cutting of the system is done with the help of the functionalities displaying all the main UML behavior models.

Use cases are models that ensure the consistency of the unit development process and this will be the main basis of the behavior, facilitate the early identification of system units.

All the components of the system are related by connectors that play the role of communication and connection. The design of a communication between components can be used in the control and management of connections between the units of the system.

In software architecture, components have access points defined by ports linked by connectors putting connection of the provided services to the required services. The connector is an element for assembling components by their provided and required interfaces. It has two functions: connection and communication (Ammour, 2004).

The difference between component and connector is a difference of functionality, not of kind. Indeed, a connector itself can be a component. The composite component is an element whose internal architecture is formed of several components. In UML 2.0, the components may be composites. This is to define a component exposing its contents, i.e. of which components is the composite composed, how those components are interconnected and bonded to the composite. A composite is formed of several internal components that are instantiated, configured and interconnected with the composite. The composites can also include services and other attributes (Radermacher, 2013). These components may be either primitive or composites.

Figure 3 shows the connector types, the connector above represented as a simple line, the other below represented as composite component. This composite component conforms to the same role of combination and of communication between components. The interface of the composite component exists but does not specify anything, it is a general type of interface (General) used during the definition of an architecture to attaching to the description of component model (Renaux, 2003).

Figure 3. The types of communication connectors (simple connector type, connector type as composite component)

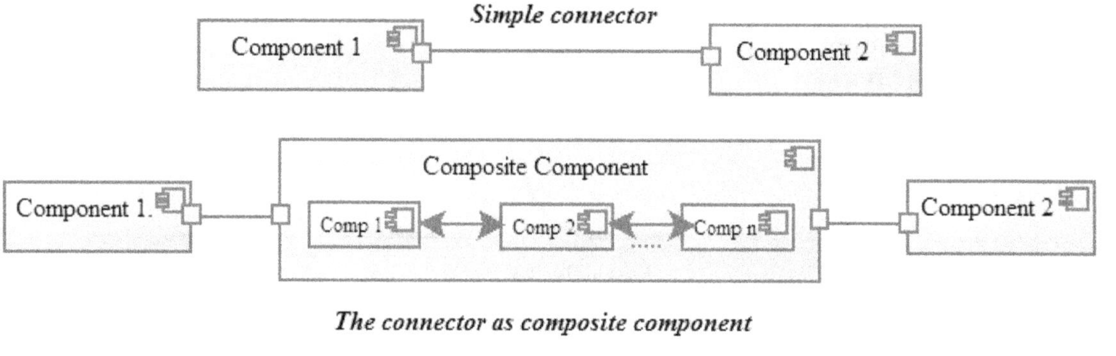

Managing Component Pattern

Integration of the point of view in the component approach is achieved by the Component Manager concept. This manager has the ability to communicate units whose accessibility and behavior dynamically change based on the current user's point of view.

The software architecture defines a system of components and the interactions between components. The focus is on composing and assembling components that are likely to have been developed separately, and even independently.

According to the fact that the connector may be a composite component, it is inspired to design a Manager Component as an intermediary to control all operations and to react and interact with other components that affect the efficiency of the software. The functionalities of Manager Component are:

- Control all call of operations, and checks the access rights of a component (enable/disable).
- Manage all connections and links existing between a base component and the other system components.
- Generalize all the functionalities of system components that allow the addition of other system components.

This component is based on three elements. Each element performs a set of tasks in order to response all the needs of system users.

Controller Component

Having control is to ensure the development and proper functioning of a process. This is indicated by all the techniques to organize and maintain the persistence of a function.

When it speaks of objects, it evokes the creation of objects. Therefore, the action to create an object with a behavior and state is performed by the allocation operation by reserving a memory space to the new object.

The code for creating and managing all these components (and specifying how they interact with the base component) is typically defined in a *Controller component*. This is not because it must be defined there, but because it's reasonable to separate all the control information from the system components.

Figure 4. The Architecture of the Manager component

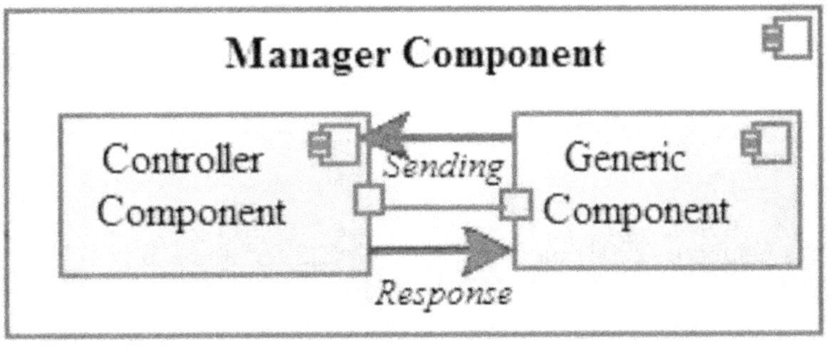

Basically declaring a field compControllerBase to hold a reference to the *Controller Component* instance. It also sets up a getter to return the instance of the Controller Component public Component-ControllerBasegetMyComponentController().

Finally, it creates a method to set the Controller Component compController by setComponent Con troller(ComponentControllerBase compController).

During work of the Controller Component, it provides the method setviewpoint() allowing to activate/ deactivate a viewpoint and the method getviewpoint() returning the active viewpoint. The active viewpoint is either an instance of the system component.

Figure 4 illustrates the Manager Component via Controller Component in interaction with Generic Component. The two arrows indicate the interaction passed through the connector, represented by the blue line and the interface presented by two intersecting circles. The green arrow represents the event of the sending, and the red arrow represents the response event.

Finally, the Controller Component set up methods of its structure to push information to the Base Component, and return them for placement in the viewpoint.

Generic Component

From the principle of generalization, the source element has all the data and the behavior of the target element; added a component, called a Generic Component, to combine all the common features and functions components.

The Generic Component also provides the method setviewpoint() allowing to activate/deactivate a viewpoint and the method getviewpoint() that returns the active viewpoint.

Another important point is that a viewpoint may evolve during the system lifetime through the addition of a new component.

The Generic Component facilitate access and select of various software components of the system, it also plays the role to link between different software components and the Base Component and to Add new components and reducing the number of connections to the Base Component. Below is a set of methods of Generic Component:

```
public void addComponent(Component comp, Object constraints) This method
changes the information about the configuration. The hierarchy must validate
thereafter to display the added component
Boolean ComponentIsSelected(Component comp) Returns the selected component
public void setEnabled(boolean b) Enable / disable a component, components are
initially disabled by default.
Class Component extends Generic {
private void addComponent(Component comp, Object constraints){ }
voidComponentIsSelected(){ }
protected void setEnabled(boolean b){ }
}
```

A composite port (Ammour, 2004) includes a set of required and / or provided ports and is used to model when a port is typed by several interfaces or when a port should facilitate bidirectional communication. The latter occurs when a composite port has both required and provided a port.

Figure 5. Generalization schema of a Generic Component

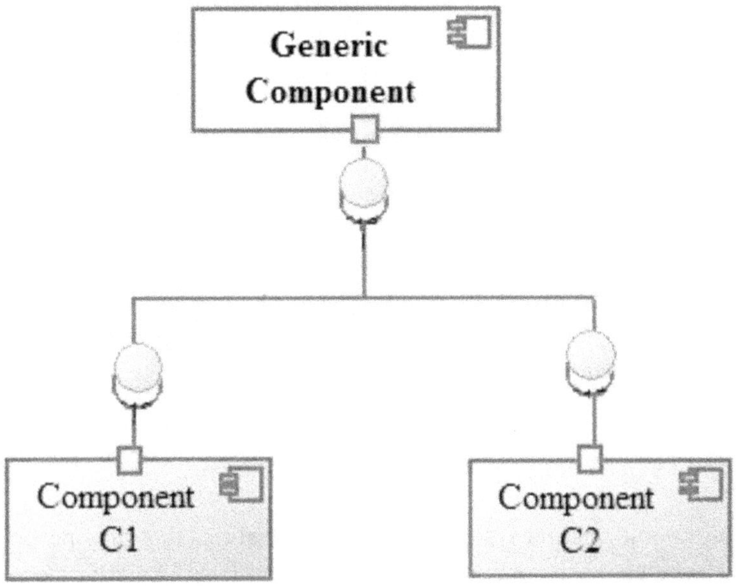

The pattern generally describes outlines of a solution, which can then be modified and adapted as needed. This pattern supports the viewpoint so if one wants to activate a component C2 knowing that the component C1 is already activated; the pattern via its component Controller disables the component C1 and then after activates the component C2.

This Figure 6 shows the combination and communication pattern with the sending of queries (green arrow) from the Generic and response to queries (red arrow) from Controller, and with the incomplete constraint that indicates that more components may be created and added.

The idea behind this pattern is as follows: Base Component joined by Manager Component-composite to system components. The incomplete constraint indicates that more components of pattern may be created and added whose number of system component is not fixed.

As for the generic component, it is generic for the direction of the building elements. In addition, this concept shares common characteristics (attributes, methods, classes, etc.) with system components and allows to see the components on the same level. These components are connected through the Generic Component by a single composite port, characterized by multiple interfaces and for performing a transmission of a multi-communications.

SOLUTIONS ET RECOMMANDATIONS

The needs analysis enables the identification of strategic and methodological options (Kausar and al, 2016) for developing the functionalities of the components. The decision to break down a system into functionalities increases the number of components, and creates elements that are by default in the initial state, estimated.

Figure 6. The Managing Pattern

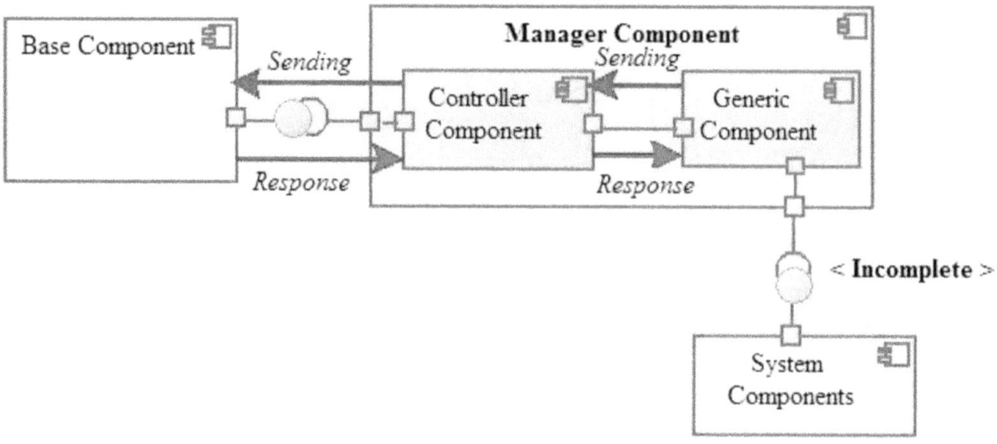

An application of the information system by the functionalities that they propose, accompanies the activity of the actors whether at the operational or decisional level. And therefore, a component is informally defined as "a data concept".

Proposed Component-Based Approach

From what precedes, development of software architecture, require to work by distinct views. The system architecture based on the use of views identifies the description of the design addressed to different concerns. This is a succinct description of the three views:

- The Analysis view formalizes the users 'needs; and their interpretations in the system specification.
- The component design view allows the identification and the visualization of the organization of the components in the development environment.
- And the Assembly view of the components represents the system in its component environment and its interactions, and elaborates the pattern of communication and combination.

The proposed approach is described according to these three system views, each of which includes a set of steps developed to meet all the needs of system users. Each of these views describes dependencies with other views and ensures overall consistency and direct system matching during the execution of the process.

This work aims to propose a new approach for identifying the system users needs using Use Cases, to elaborate system software components.

The presentation of the approach is illustrated by the case study of an *Equipment Rental Company* (Renaux, 2003), where the system manages the rental and return of equipment by customers of the company.

For this purpose, it allows to consult and to modify the information about the customers, and to modify the stock of available material, manages rental prices, as well as income. This company has several rental agencies and a head office.

Figure 7. Component based engineering approach

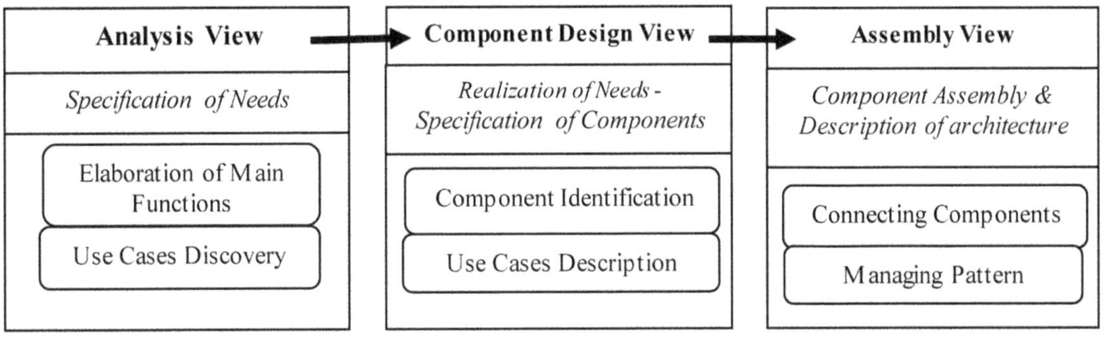

- The update of Products,
- The update of Prices,
- Research Product to Customer,
- The transmission of orders for the acquisition of Products.

Analysis View

All the specifications of system are described in the Analysis view. Before a complete elaboration of the use cases, the Analysis View represents the needs of the system bringing together all the use cases with the actor concerned in case of use cases, and the example on which the case study is *Equipment Rental Company* Management.

In the system, the Customer is assigned by a number at registration. If the customer is already registered, the Seller identifies and fills on the computer terminal application the desired Product. If the product is available, the system marks a listing that allows the customer to obtain his product at the counter. The system validates the rental and saves the return. The system provides to the Seller, every time the application is open, the list of products that have not been rented.

Now, it traces the desired functions of modeling component expressing the essential functions of each component. In this schema, it shows adequate absolute functions with the viewpoint of each component, and which responds to the needs of users.

Figure 8 shows the structure of the overall system, by providing predictive representation of functions of system. The specification of needs and the elaborating of main functions have led to: the PRICES MANAGEMENT, RECIPES MANAGEMENT, PRODUCT RENTAL, CUSTOMER MANAGEMENT, STOCK MANAGEMENT, RETURN MANAGEMENT to EQUIPMENT COMPANY system.

The goal is to find parts which combine features that are related or are part of the same "work" and that can be designed and analyzed separately.

These use cases are directly related to an actor and are designated as "main cases use". Sometimes it manages to regroup certain use cases in one or more complementary use cases that are not directly related to an actor, this is called a " internal use case". This use case will always be necessary and linked to other cases of main use case by an arrow representing the relationship called "*include*".

Figure 8. Main Functions of System schema

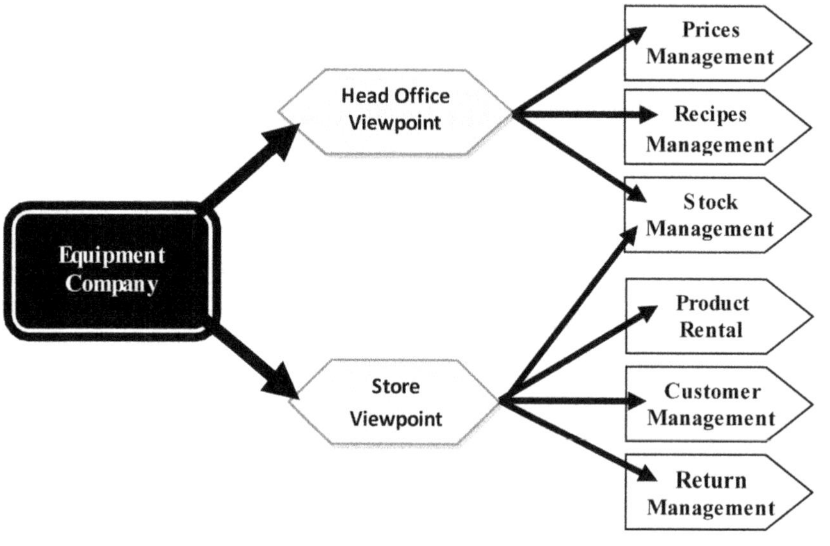

For a use case considered as an extension of another use case expressed by the relation "extends", it is used to indicate the use case source (the origin of the arrow) it is not always necessary in main use case, but it can be in certain situations (example "Rent Product " and "Consult Customer Information ").

In the case of internal main use case "Rent Procuct", it is not a necessary use case for the main use case "Consult Customer Information". Indeed, a Customer can achieve a return over the counter without the application is already validated by the Seller. Or for example, the case of using "Rent Product" not always require the use case "Edit Recipes", because in fact, the information of Recipes can be taken by a copy in case of lack of data or update.

Component Design View

This view, the component design view, describes the components architecture and their relationships. A component is informally corresponding to a list of activities specific to a given use case or result of an action interaction of a use case group. Then, the use cases are divided into a set of activities resulting from the scenarios of the system, and then the discovered actions are factored into parts. The concept of Component is done by grouping sets of related use cases, as cutting information targeted and concerned by scenarios, designating an approximate Function or functionality performed during these scenarios, and keeps this cutting across the software development lifecycle.

Such a structure of the system is composed of a Base Component (common component accessible by every actor), and system components (extending this common component) that are related to the Base Component through a connector relationship. The Base Component is also called default component because it is the unique component that is activated when no component of the system is enabled. The system component is required for each actor's needs. Each component depends on the Base Component in the sense where attributes and class of the Base Component are implicitly shared by all the viewpoints.

Figure 9. Preliminary Use Case diagram

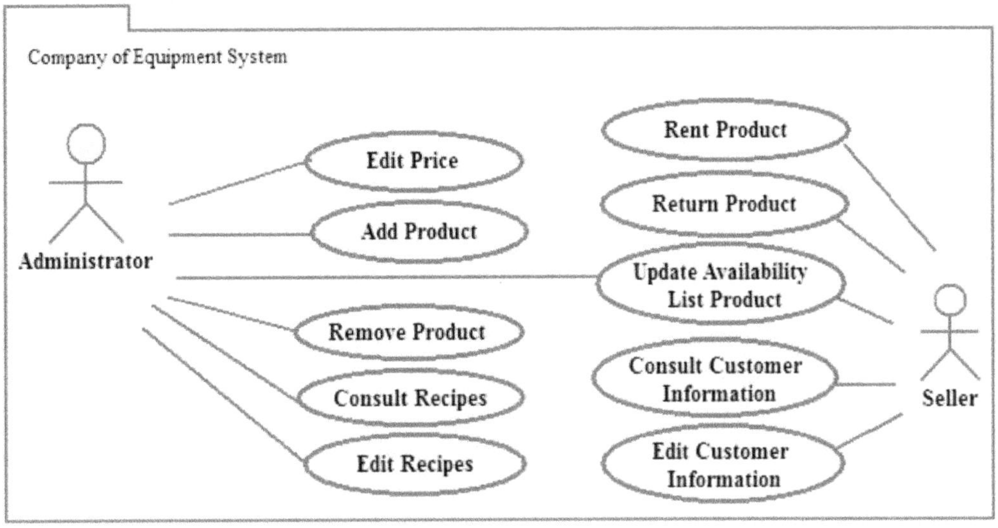

Figure 10. Description Precise use case diagram (with stereotype relationship include / extends)

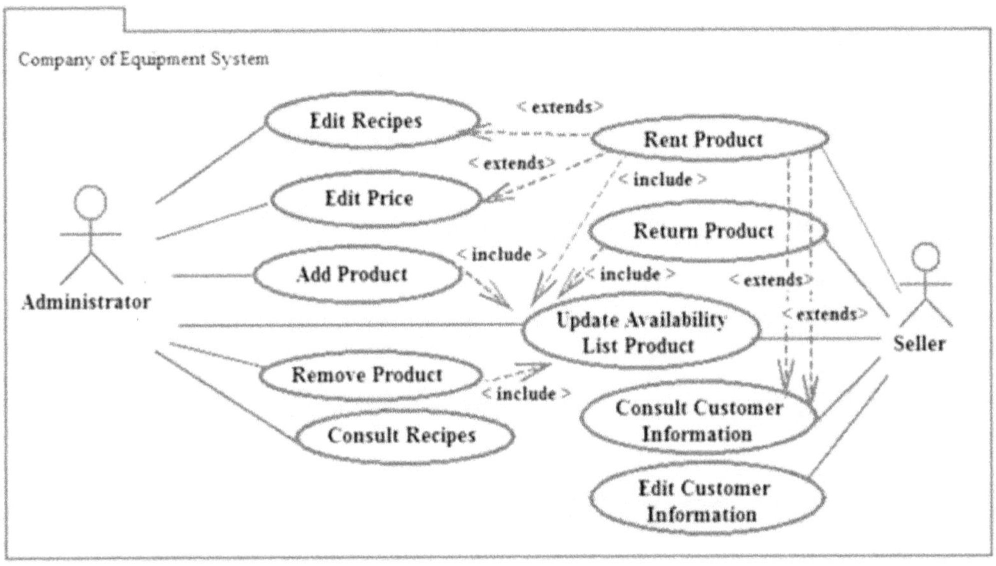

New software components were then added to the system. *Base component* is the first that includes the features and common functionalities between the different components. Components depend on the base component in the sense that the values of attributes and methods of the base are implicitly shared by the system components. A system component shapes the structural and behavioral characteristics of an actor while having the ability to redefine the characteristics of base component to which it is connected via the dependency relationship, and therefore the system component may only be applied to a single base component.

The modelization of components such as *Functions* seen at the time of analysis (those listed in the use case diagram) are not detailed enough. The next step, it establishes a table design of use cases in set of functions related to the component.

The interaction between the actors and the system also requires describing the chronology of the activities performed by the actors and by the system itself, called scenarios. The interaction is divided into several sequences and exchanges. This notion has theoretical frameworks that have guided its conceptualization and operationalization in specific research programs. This interaction can model the hidden knowledge (Wang and al, 2016) needed for effective decision-making by a selection model that includes the interaction between attributes (Mandić and al, 2015). In addition, anticipating the behavior of others is a central mechanism in interaction management, and identifying human behaviors from sensor observations is an important research problem. (Guesgen and Marsland, 2016) have described a new way of representing these data and discuss a wide variety of possible implementation strategies, by adding contextual information on past activities.

The most obvious procedure is to list all the interactions between the actors and the system in a textual way. The use case must have a clearly identified start and end. It is also necessary to specify the nominal case, the different alternative and error cases, while trying to sequentially order the descriptions, in order to improve their readability. The textual description of a set of use cases is specified by the main and alternative scenarios incoming in interactions.

Title: Product Rental.
Principal actor: Seller.
Secondary actor: Customer.

Pre-conditions:

- Internet connection established.
- The product exists and is available.

Table 1. Cutting of Modeling Components into Parts Designating Functions

Viewpoint	Part: Function	Use case
Head Office	Prices Management	Edit Price
	Recipes Management	Consult Recipes
		Edit Recipes
	Product Management	Add Product
		Remove Product
		Update Availability List Product
Store	Product Rental	Rent Product
	Customer Management	Consult Customer Information
		Edit Customer Information
	Stock Management	Update Availability List Product
	Return Management	Return Product

- The customer has been recognized by the system.

1. The Customer goes to the counter and asks for a product.
2. The Seller connects to the system.
3. The system displays the menu
4. The Seller chooses Product Rental.
5. The Seller demands the information of the Customer by his ID
6. The system displays the information of Customer
7. The Seller demands the Availability of Product.
8. The Seller enters the information on the Rental application.
9. The system verifies the validity of the data and that all mandatory fields are filled.
10. The Seller consults the price asked by Office Head
11. The Seller informs Customer of Product price
12. The Customer pays Cash or cheque receipts
13. The Seller asks to register the paid Rental and to update the state of the Stock.
14. The system informs the Seller that the Rental has been registered and the status of the stock has been updated.

Alternative Scenario:

9. The system informs the Seller that there are mandatory fields not filled in.

The Nominal Scenario resumes 8.

7. Product not available

Post-Conditions:

- The Customer takes the rented product for a given period.

A Use case Model allows to define the essential features of the system, performed by cutting the system in coherent units, it is the modeling of components. This component is a result of a set of use cases that each use case represents a feature or system actions lots. Then it passes to describe scenarios of use cases, as well as the necessary elements for the textual description of the progress of activities. Early identification of Component leads to: The Prices Management, Recipes Management, Product Management, Product Rental, Customer Management and Stock Management, Return Management system components to a Base Component Equipment Company.

Each case presents a set of activities showing the main functionality wanted, in order to define the function of each part in its intervention later to system components. The elementary activities achieved by the actor, will correspond to the scenarios contained in a use case.

Table 1 provides a description of the schema of components with the concerned activities; here it gave the example of the Loan transaction. All activities come from the already made textual description.

Figure 11. Cutting in viewpoint

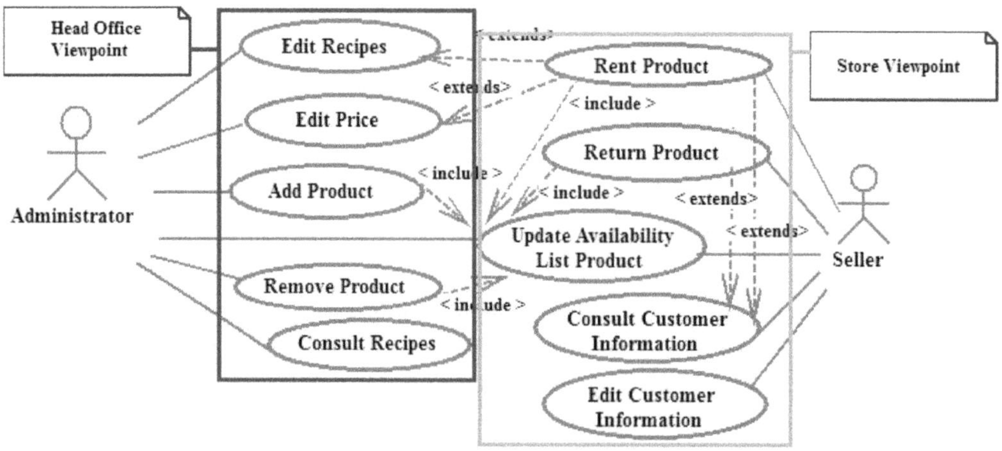

Table 2. Cutting Function in Activities; the "Product Rental" transaction

Viewpoint	Function	Activities
Head Office	Prices Management	A25: The Seller consults the price asked by Administrator
	Recipes Management	A42: Registering the paid Rental as a Recipe
Store	Product Rental	A21: The Seller chooses Product Rental. A41: The Seller fills the form of current Rental, the system verifies the validity of the data and that all mandatory fields are filled. **Alt41 (Alternative):** Invalid Data A24: The Seller enters the information on the Rental application.
	Customer Management	A11: The Customer goes to the counter and asks for a product. A22: The Seller demands the information of the Customer by hid ID A26: The Seller informs Customer of Product price A31: The Customer pays Cash or cheque receipts
	Stock Management	A23: Check Availability of Product choice - Request a list of product not yet rented **Alt23 (Alternative):** Product not available A43: The status of the stock has been updated.

It is noted from the schema (Figure 8) and from the start of scenario, interaction between the Rental Management and Prices Management. This shows the requesting of the information and that the offer, which allows a preliminary interpretation on all the services, provided and required for each part. For example, the Rental Management requests the data verification service, entered by the Seller, the "Rental Management" sends request of availability of Product to the "Stock Management", in case of success the system, demands Price of product wanted from " Price Management ". Accordingly, the Rental part offers a required service and Price Management offers provided service.

Table 1, 2 and textual description and show important information on all entities participating in the scenario and the existing dependencies between entities. The diagram in Figure 12, illustrates the message sequences induced the Product Rental by a Customer, such as the existence of the Product. Here below set of sequence diagram of set essential transactions.

Figure 12. Diagram sequences "Rental Product"

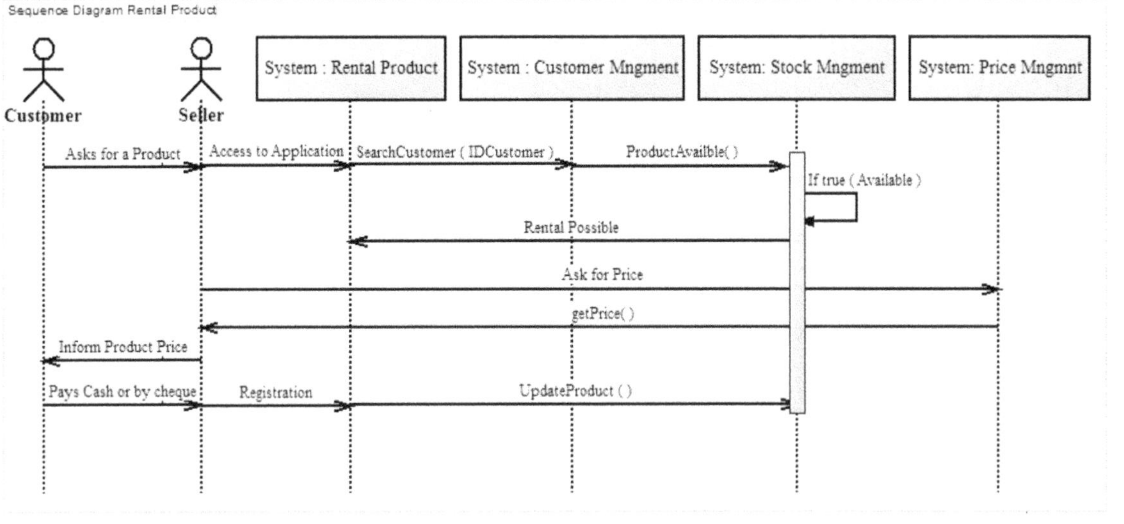

The diagram in Figure 13 is Activity Diagram of the use case "Rental Product" of the viewpoint STORE. After the needs of system with the use case diagrams, it specifies how objects and actors must participate together in a timeline through the use of sequence diagrams.

For example, this is the situation according to which the activity of the Part "Stock Management" invoked to provide access, in case of success, to the action of Consultation of Product Price posed by administrator in Head Office of Part " Price Management".

If the need arises, the decision node does a new beginning for the previous action to reenter the invalid data. These transactions of go and come at Decision node, respectfully express requests (service required) and sending (services provided) of services via the interfaces to the components. As an example of the interface "Check Product Available", and the interface "Verify validity of Rental data". Activities "Check availability of Product" and "Registering the paid Rental as Recipes" respectfully correspond to A23 and A42 already described in Table 1.

So an activity diagram is a good complement to the textual description of a use case. If a use case contains many scenarios, the activity diagram can give an overview of all possible scenarios.

Assembly View

The assembly view shows the system globally by giving a representation (Renaux, 2003) of the software components and their interactions. A component diagram describes the organization and wiring of the components in a system, it illustrates how components are together to form the structure of software system, which means that it presents an early understanding of the overall system that is being built, and offers a format to end modeling.

It allows verifying that a system's functionality is being achieved by components, thus ensuring that the final system will be acceptable.

An interface is a "use / provide" dependency relationship between the component and its environment, but the behavior of the services offered through that interface changes according to the use case

Figure 13. Activity diagram "Rental Product"

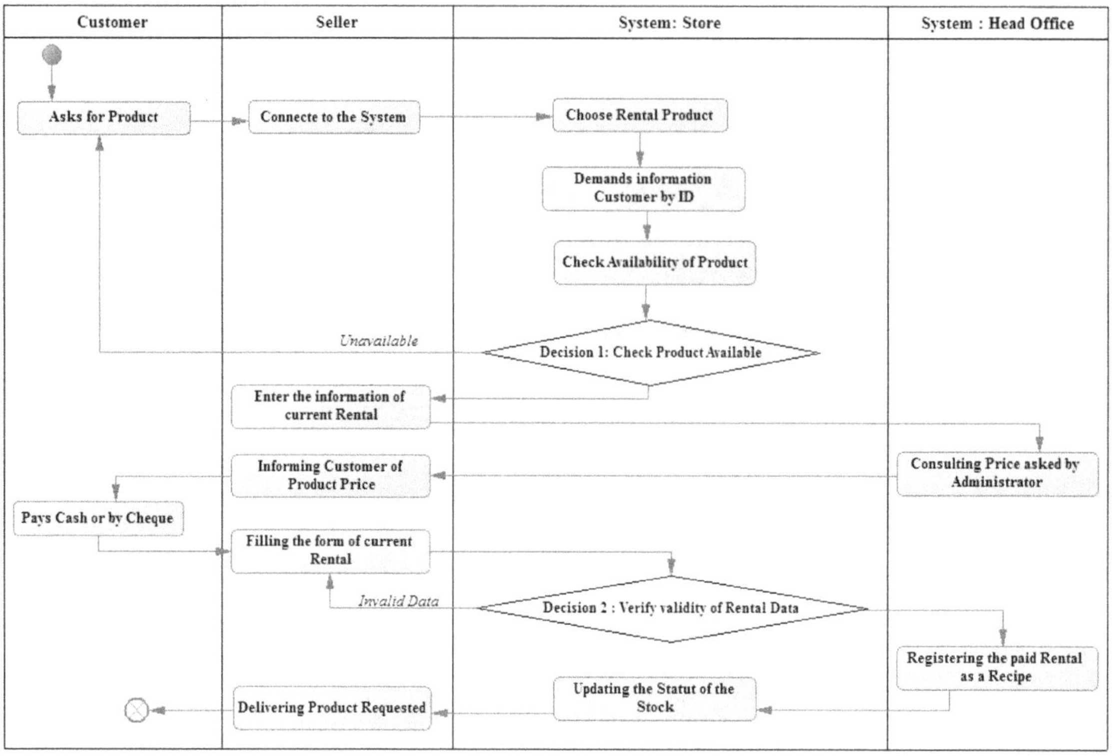

concerned with the modeling component. These interfaces are characterized by the signatures of the methods they define and by a sense of communication (provided, incoming / requested, outgoing). The interfaces view represents the component's specifications, thanks to its required / provided ports that express the interaction between components. The method proposed in the identification of the interfaces consists of the use of the appropriate actions at the sight of the use case concerned.

The purpose of assembling pre-designed software entities is to simplify the development work. The aim of assembling the components via the compositional relationship is to be able to design components called composite components. In fact, a composite component is formed by a set of subcomponents. This makes it possible to choose the best model to use as a support for the realization of this approach. Then, it goes to the stage that the objective is the association of combinations of parts obtained following of the previous step, to develop the various components, sub-components system and their services; the assembly of components.

Managing Pattern Presentation

The approach is based essentially on the fact that each viewpoint is associated to the one actor; thereby interposing between the components another component called the Manager Component.

The Manager Component is the essential element of the approach; its role is the management of existing connections between a Base Component and another system component via the viewpoint concept.

Figure 14. Controller Component in interaction with Base component

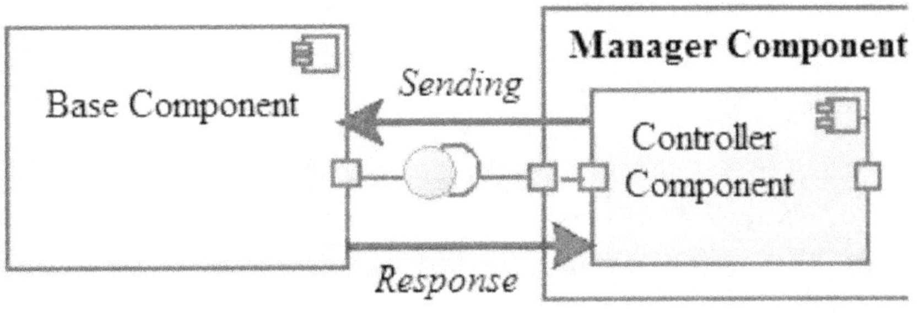

A view is a combination of functions that can be shared and reduced to software components. Figure 15 illustrates all of the components concerned by each actor and shared components between them.

Such a structure of the system is composed of a Base Component (common component accessible by every actor), and system components (extending this common component) that are related to the Base Component through a connector relationship. The system component is required for each actor's needs. Each component depends on the Base Component in the sense where attributes and class of the Base Component are implicitly shared by all the viewpoints.

Figure 16 below is the structure of the assembly showing the overall system, by providing a representation of the software components and their interactions. The system modeling has led to

PRICES, RECIPES, PRODUCT RENTAL, CUSTOMER, STOCK, RETURN system components to a Base Component EQUIPMENT COMPANY.

In order to perform management of components with the Base Component EQUIPMENT COMPANY, it's interposed between them the Manager Component for describing the interactions between the components and the Manager Component according to a given context and according to an activated viewpoint. All business rules are confined to the Manager Component in such a way that each viewpoint of system represents a component during the execution.

Components Generic/Contoller joined by Component -composite relationship to a Base Component and a list of system components corresponding to the views point.

At the Manager Component, the Generic Component selects the information source component and its corresponding viewpoints and sends the request to the Controller Component. After receiving the request, the Controller Component activates the component in question that regards the corresponding viewpoint and receives the call to check the requested service.

Figure 17 represents the overall architecture of Conference System with the Base component EQUIPMENT COMPANY and all system components. Between these components, it's integrated the composite Manager component.

After a simple step-by-step process, authors go through defining requirements, identifying components, interacting components, specifying components, and provisioning and assembling. The construction of a method must be based on the principle of the agreement of this method with the various projects; that is to say that the engineering of methods on its side poses a problem of the construction of a method quite flexible and easily adapted to the situation of each project (Ralyte, 2001).

Figure 15. Set of components concerning Administrator and Seller Actors

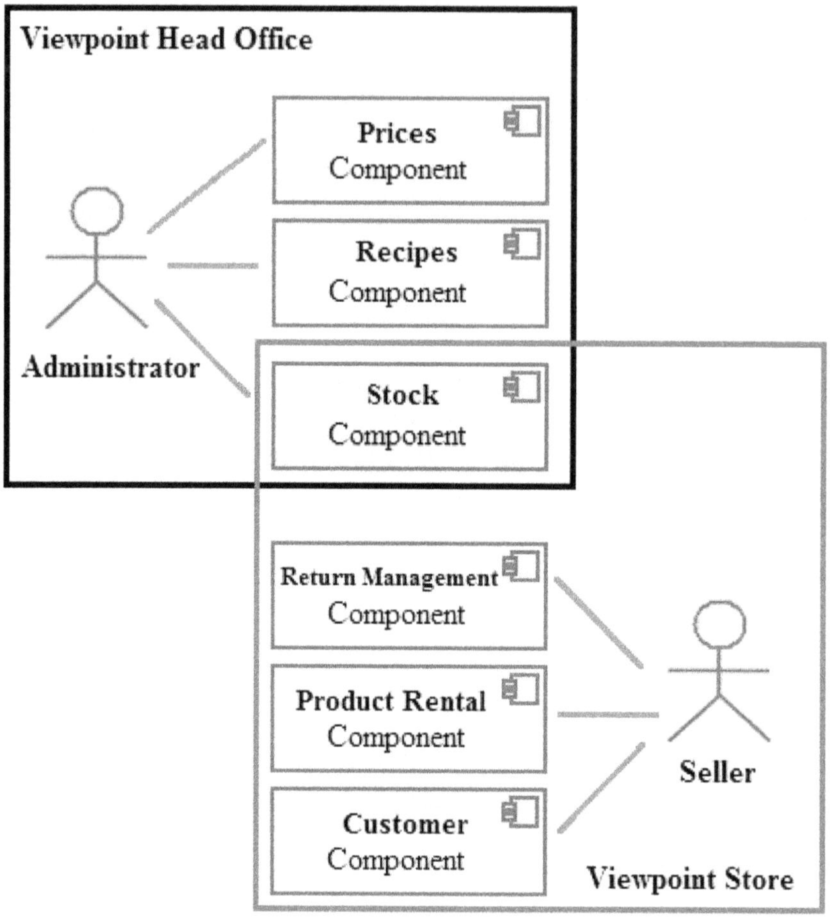

Figure 16. The assembly component

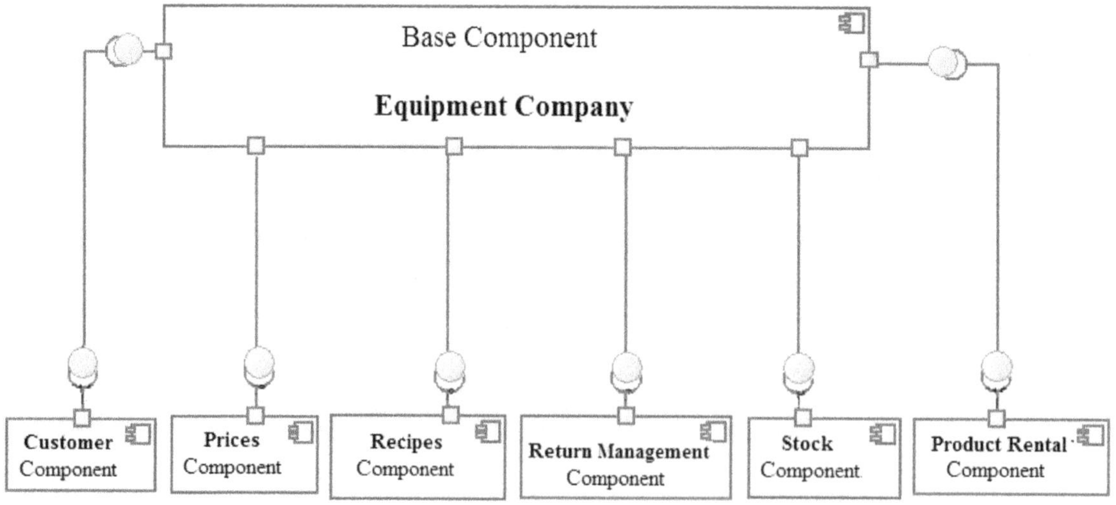

Figure 17. The Global Architecture of Conference System

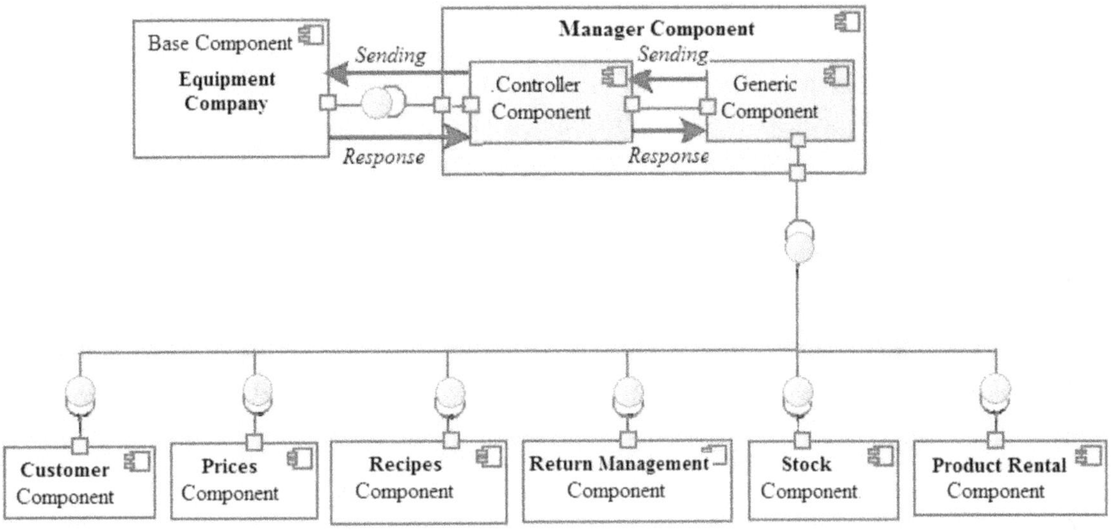

DIRECTIONS FUTURES DE RECHERCHE

The development approaches based on the component-based approach is an essential research problem whose solutions are beginning to emerge. The implementation of this approach in the industry requires a follow-up research and validates them on large scale component-based applications.

Currently, the research focuses on the complete definition of component-based information systems approach design. This type of research should lead to a real and effective method of engineering field. The goal is to define a method of component analysis / design in information systems modelization. The next goal is to represent the approach of analysis / design of components, under Model Driven Architecture MDA.

CONCLUSION

The software components are interested in problems that have not yet been solved. They have a particular vision of how to develop software, and provide measures to stimulate development, in order to arrive at a system's decision-making strategies.

It is no coincidence that the notion of component gives a great interest to the development of complex systems. This presented approach allows the early identification and the design of software components, founded on the factoring process with three views steps:

- Analysis View, based on expression of needs and functional specification leading to the elaboration of functions of system, and the use-case discovery.
- Component Design View, based on design and the early identification of the component from use cases and constituents of development activities.

- And Assembly View shows the assembly of system components, and the pattern mainly carried out.

The systems design based on components supposes that there are adequate means for modelization its communications. The concept of Manager Component is one of these means. This model offers a good adaptation to the concept of the combination and the point of view between "Manager Component" by assembling a Base Component and its system software components, because it allows the system to communicate according to its priorities.

The Pattern of Management defines elements and relationships that work together in order to facilitate communication between stakeholders by adding Manager Component. This last is constituted of two components; Controller /Generic component. The Generic Component whose function is to generalize all the characteristics of system components, and to forward requests from components to the base component. For the Controller Component, it has the role of monitor and ensures the system changes state via the corresponding viewpoints to the system's actors.

This Manager component is a complementary paradigm for the development of software systems based on view through the assemblage of systems and core components from the components to the core component (the units of the system). The features it encapsulates must be linked and consistent.

In fact, the pattern can be considered as a way to have a component-based modeling viewpoint.

REFERENCES

ACCORD project. (2002). *Component Assembly by Contracts in Open and Distributed Environment.* Technical Report, RNTL.

Acharjya, D., & Anitha, A. (2017). A Comparative Study of Statistical and Rough Computing Models in Predictive Data Analysi. *International Journal of Ambient Computing and Intelligence (IJACI).* doi:10.4018/IJACI.2017040103

Allier, S., Sadou, S., Sahraoui, H. A., & Fleurquin, R. (2011). From Object-Oriented Applications to Component-Oriented Applications via Component-Oriented Architecture. *WICSA, 2011*, 214–223.

Ammour, S., Beugnard, A., Matougui, S., & Traverson, B. (2004). Software architecture and communication abstractions: an application in the field of scientific computing. *Proceedings of RNTL ACCORD.*

Anwar, A., Ebersold, S., Coulette, B., Nassar, M., & Kriouile, A. (2010). A Rule-Driven Approach for composing Viewpoint-oriented Models. *Journal of Object Technology*, *9*(2), 89–114. doi:10.5381/jot.2010.9.2.a1

Bobrow, D. G., & Winograd, T. (1977). An Overview of KRL, a Knowledge Representation Language. *Cognitive Science, 1*(1), 3–46. doi:10.120715516709cog0101_2

Bose, S., Mukherjee, A., Chakraborty, S., Samanta, S., & Dey, N. (2013, December). Parallel image segmentation using multi-threading and k-means algorithm. In *Computational Intelligence and Computing Research (ICCIC), 2013 IEEE International Conference on* (pp. 1-5). IEEE. 10.1109/ICCIC.2013.6724171

Cai, X., Lyu, M. R., & Wong, K. F. (2000). Component-based software engineering: technologies, development frameworks, and quality assurance schemes. In *Proceedings of the Software Engineering Conference APSEC 2000* (pp. 372-379). IEEE.

Cheesman, J., & Daniels, J. (2001). *UML Components - A Simple process for specifying Compnent-Based software*. Addison-Wesley.

Chennoufi, M., Bendella, F., & Bouzid, M. (2018). Multi-Agent Simulation Collision Avoidance of Complex System: Application to Evacuation Crowd Behavior, *International Journal of Ambient Computing and Intelligence (IJACI)*. doi:10.4018/IJACI.2018010103

CORBA. (2014). Retrieved from http://www.omg.org/spec/CORBA/3.3/

D'Souza, D. F., & Wills, A. C. (1998). *Objects, Components, and Frameworks with UML - The Catalysis Approach*. Addison-Wesley.

Debrauwer, L. (1998). *Views contexts for patterning databases objects CROME* (PhD thesis). University of sciences and technologies, Lile, France.

Dhir, S., Kumar, D., & Singh, V. B. (2017). Requirement Paradigms to Implement the Software Projects in Agile Development Using Analytical Hierarchy Process, *International Journal of Decision Support System Technology (IJDSST)*. doi:10.4018/IJDSST.2017070102

Finkelstein, A., Kramer, J., Nuseibeh, B., Finkelstein, L., & Goedicke, M. (1992). Viewpoints: A Framework for Integrating Multiple Perspectives in System Development. *International Journal of Software Engineering and Knowledge Engineering*, *2*(1), 31–58. doi:10.1142/S0218194092000038

Guesgen, H. W., & Marsland, S. (2016). Using Contextual Information for Recognising Human Behaviour. *International Journal of Ambient Computing and Intelligence (IJACI)*. doi:10.4018/IJACI.2016010102

Jacobson, I. (1992). *Object-Oriented Software Engineering: A Use Case Driven Approach*. Harlow, UK: Addison - Wesley.

Juneja, D., Singh, A., Singh, R., & Mukherjee, S. (2017). A Thorough Insight into Theoretical and Practical Developments in MultiAgent System. *International Journal of Ambient Computing and Intelligence (IJACI)*. doi:10.4018/IJACI.2017010102

Kamal, S., Dey, N., Ashour, A. S., Ripon, S., Balas, V. E., & Kaysar, M. S. (2017). FbMapping: An automated system for monitoring Facebook data. *Neural Network World*, *27*(1), 27–57. doi:10.14311/NNW.2017.27.002

Kamal, S., Dey, N., Nimmy, S. F., Ripon, S. H., Ali, N. Y., Ashour, A. S., ... Shi, F. (2016). Evolutionary framework for coding area selection from cancer data. *Neural Computing & Applications*, 1–23.

Kamal, S., Ripon, S. H., Dey, N., Ashour, A. S., & Santhi, V. (2016). A MapReduce approach to diminish imbalance parameters for big deoxyribonucleic acid dataset. *Computer Methods and Programs in Biomedicine*, *131*, 191–206. doi:10.1016/j.cmpb.2016.04.005 PMID:27265059

Karaa, W. B. A., Ashour, A. S., Sassi, D. B., Roy, P., Kausar, N., & Dey, N. (2016). Medline text mining: an enhancement genetic algorithm based approach for document clustering. In *Applications of Intelligent Optimization in Biology and Medicine* (pp. 267–287). Springer International Publishing. doi:10.1007/978-3-319-21212-8_12

Karaa, W. B. A., Ben Azzouz, Z., Singh, A., Dey, N. S., Ashour, A., & Ben Ghazala, H. (2016). Automatic builder of class diagram (ABCD): An application of UML generation from functional requirements. *Software, Practice & Experience*, *46*(11), 1443–1458. doi:10.1002pe.2384

Karaa, W. B. A., Mannai, M., Dey, N., Ashour, A. S., & Olariu, I. (2016, August). Gene-disease-food relation extraction from biomedical database. In *International Workshop Soft Computing Applications* (pp. 394-407). Springer.

Kausar, N., Abdullah, A., Samir, B. B., Palaniappan, S., AlGhamdi, B. S., & Dey, N. (2016). Ensemble clustering algorithm with supervised classification of clinical data for early diagnosis of coronary artery disease. *Journal of Medical Imaging and Health Informatics*, *6*(1), 78–87. doi:10.1166/jmihi.2016.1593

Kausar, N., Palaniappan, S., Samir, B. B., Abdullah, A., & Dey, N. (2016). Systematic analysis of applied data mining based optimization algorithms in clinical attribute extraction and classification for diagnosis of cardiac patients. In *Applications of intelligent optimization in biology and medicine* (pp. 217–231). Springer International Publishing. doi:10.1007/978-3-319-21212-8_9

Krumeich, J., Werth, D., & Loos, P. (2014). Conceiving A Method For Viewpoint-Based Modeling Using Recommender Systems In A Multiple-User Environment – Conceptual Approach And Proof-Of-Concept. *Proceedings of twenty-Second European Conference on Information Systems*.

Mandić, K., Delibašić, B., & Radojević, D. (2015). An Application of the Integrated IBA-TOPSIS Model in Supplier Selection. *International Journal of Decision Support System Technology (IJDSST)*. doi:10.4018/ijdsst.2015010102

McIlro, M. D. (1968). Mass produced software components. *Proceedings NATO Conference on Software Engineering*.

Microsoft. (n.d.). *NET Framework Developer Center*. Retrieved from http://msdn.microsoft.com/fr-fr/vstudio/aa496123

Nassar, M. (2003). VUML: a Viewpoint Oriented UML extension. *Proceedings (ASE 2003) International Conference on Automated Software Engineering*, 373–376. doi:10.1109/ ASE.2003.1240341

Nimmy, S. F., Kamal, M. S., Hossain, M. I., Dey, N., Ashour, A. S., & Shi, F. (2017). Neural Skyline Filtering for Imbalance Features Classification. *International Journal of Computational Intelligence and Applications*, *16*(03), 1750019. doi:10.1142/S1469026817500195

OMG. (n.d.). *OMG Homepage*. Retrieved from http://www.omg.org

Pajić, A., & Bečejski-Vujaklija, D. (2016). Metamodel of the Artifact-Centric Approach to Event Log Extraction from ERP Systems. *International Journal of Decision Support System Technology (IJDSST)*. doi:10.4018/IJDSST.2016040102

Radermacher, A., Cuccuru, A., Gérard, S., & Hamid, B. (2013, September 24-26). Split of Composite Components for Distributed Applications (regular paper). In *Proceedings of the Forum on Specification & Design Languages FDL 2013)*. Paris, France: IEEE Computer Society.

Rehioui, F., & Hair, A. (2014). Towards a Modeling approach based on Software Components. *International Journal of Computers and Applications*, *99*(1), 10–17. doi:10.5120/17336-7178

Rehioui, F., & Hair, A. (2016). Towards a New Combination and Communication Approach of Software Components. *International Journal of Decision Support System Technology (IJDSST)*. doi:10.4018/IJDSST.2016100101

Renaux, E., Caron, O., & Geib, J. M. (2003). The Component Unified Process Project. In *Proceedings of SEA'03* (pp. 669-647). ACTA Press.

Rittgen, P. (2009). Collaborative Modeling - A Design Science Approach. In *Proceedings of the 42nd Hawaii International Conference on System Sciences (HICSS '09)*. IEEE Computer Society.

Selmane, S. A., Boussaid, O., & Bentayeb, F. (2015). Towards Collaborative Multidimensional Query Recommendation with Triadic Association Rules. *International Journal of Decision Support System Technology (IJDSST)*. doi:10.4018/ijdsst.2015070102

Sosnin, P. (2016). Precedent-Oriented Approach to Conceptually Experimental Activity in Designing the Software Intensive Systems. *International Journal of Ambient Computing and Intelligence (IJACI)*. doi:10.4018/IJACI.2016010104

Sun. (2014). *E.J.B HomePage*. Retrieved from www.oracle.com/technetwork/java/javaee/ejb/index.html

Wood-Harper, A. T., Antill, L., & Avison, D. E. (1985). *Information systems definition: The Multiview approach*. Oxford, UK: Blackwell Scientific Publications.

ADDITIONAL READING

Ahmed, S. S., Dey, N., Ashour, A. S., Sifaki-Pistolla, D., Bălas-Timar, D., Balas, V. E., & Tavares, J. M. R. (2017). Effect of fuzzy partitioning in Crohn's disease classification: A neuro-fuzzy-based approach. *Medical & Biological Engineering & Computing*, *55*(1), 101–115. doi:10.100711517-016-1508-7 PMID:27106754

Li, Z., Shi, K., Dey, N., Ashour, A. S., Wang, D., Balas, V. E., ... Shi, F. (2017). Rule-based back propagation neural networks for various precision rough set presented KANSEI knowledge prediction: A case study on shoe product form features extraction. *Neural Computing & Applications*, *28*(3), 613–630. doi:10.100700521-016-2707-8

Ngan, T. T., Tuan, T. M., Minh, N. H., & Dey, N. (2016). Decision Making Based on Fuzzy Aggregation Operators for Medical Diagnosis from Dental X-ray images. *Journal of Medical Systems*, *40*(12), 280. doi:10.100710916-016-0634-y PMID:27787784

Roy, P., Goswami, S., Chakraborty, S., Azar, A. T., & Dey, N. (2014). Image segmentation using rough set theory: A review. *International Journal of Rough Sets and Data Analysis*, *1*(2), 62–74. doi:10.4018/ijrsda.2014070105

Tang, R., Fong, S., Dey, N., Wong, R. K., & Mohammed, S. (2017). Cross Entropy Method Based Hybridization of Dynamic Group Optimization Algorithm. *Entropy (Basel, Switzerland)*, *19*(10), 533. doi:10.3390/e19100533

Wang, D., He, T., Li, Z., Cao, L., Dey, N., Ashour, A. S., ... Shi, F. (2016). Image feature-based affective retrieval employing improved parameter and structure identification of adaptive neuro-fuzzy inference system. *Neural Computing & Applications*, 1–16.

Wang, D., Li, Z., Cao, L., Balas, V. E., Dey, N., Ashour, A. S., ... Shi, F. (2016). Image Fusion Incorporating Parameter Estimation Optimized Gaussian Mixture Model and Fuzzy Weighted Evaluation System: A Case Study in Time-Series Plantar Pressure Data Set. *IEEE Sensors Journal*, *17*(5), 1407–1420. doi:10.1109/JSEN.2016.2641501

Wang, D., Li, Z., Dey, N., Ashour, A. S., Sherratt, R. S., & Shi, F. (2017). Case-Based Reasoning for Product Style Construction and Fuzzy Analytic Hierarchy Process Evaluation Modeling Using Consumers Linguistic Variables. *IEEE Access : Practical Innovations, Open Solutions*, *5*, 4900–4912. doi:10.1109/ACCESS.2017.2677950

KEY TERMS AND DEFINITIONS

Base Component: It is the first common component that includes the features and common functionalities between the different components, accessible by every user, also called default component because it is the unique component that is activated when no component of the system is enabled.

Component: It is a data concept informally corresponding to a list of activities, providing the business functionality of the system.

Controller: Component controlling all call of operations, and checks the access rights of a component (enable/disable), to ensure the development of the process to organize and maintain the persistence of a function.

Generic: Generalizes all the functionalities of system components and facilitate access, it also plays the role to link between different software components and the base component and to allow the addition of new other system components and reducing the number of connections to the base component.

Manager: Intermediary component to control all operations and to react and interact with other components that affect the efficiency of the software. Its role is the management of all connections and links existing between a base component and the other system components, the management of the ability to communicate units whose accessibility and behavior dynamically change based on the current user's point of view.

Modeling: Demonstrating appropriate behavior or activities.

Modelization: The process of modeling, constructing on the base of the function should give the functional modelization of the system, based on the conceptual function.

Chapter 6
Classifying Diabetes Disease Using Feedforward MLP Neural Networks

Ahmad Al-Khasawneh
Hashemite University, Jordan

Haneen Hijazi
Hashemite University, Jordan

ABSTRACT

Diagnosing chronic diseases is about making accurate and quick decisions based on contradictory information and constantly evolving knowledge. Hence, there has been a persistent need to help health practitioners in making correct decisions. Diabetes is a common chronic disease. It is a global health-care threat and the eighth leading cause of death in the world. Modern artificial intelligence techniques are being used in diagnosing chronic diseases including artificial neural networks. In this chapter, a feedforward multilayer-perceptron neural network has been implemented to help health practitioners in classifying diabetes. Through the work, an algorithm was proposed in purpose of determining the number of hidden layers and neurons in a MLP. Based on the algorithm, two topologies have been introduced. Both topologies exhibited good classification accuracies with a slightly higher accuracy for the MLP with only one hidden layer. The data set was obtained from King Abdullah University Hospital in Jordan.

INTRODUCTION

Healthcare is a major concern of communities and individuals. It significantly contributes in countries' economies. Information technology has spread widely in health care industry in the last few decades. Healthcare Information Technology or e-Health is the application of information processing involving both computer hardware and software that deals with the storage, retrieval, sharing, and use of health care information, data, and knowledge for communication and decision making (Brailer & Thompson, 2004). Despite the dramatic growth in the last few decades, the continuous research and the nonstopping achievements in the health care information technology industry proof that this field still in its infancy and

DOI: 10.4018/978-1-5225-6164-4.ch006

many other several research could be conducted. Health-care Information Technology systems employ several different methods. These systems can be electronic medical records (EMRS), electronic health records (EHRS), personal health record (PHR), payer-based health record, computerized physician order entry (CPOE), clinical decision support, and E-prescribing (Bray, 2010). Nowadays, Clinical Decision Support Systems (CDSSs) are mostly in demand by healthcare practitioners as they usually perform intelligently and helps in early detection of chronic diseases (Sharma & Virmani, 2017).

The medical domain is characterized by contradictory information and constantly evolving knowledge. Hence, it was of utmost important to help diagnosticians to make correct decisions (El-Sappagh & Elmogy, 2016). Generally, Decision Support Systems (DSS) enable decision makers to utilize knowledge and data to support and meet their demands for decision-making (El-Gayar, Deokar, & Tao, 2011).

CDSSs are information systems that help healthcare practitioners in making medical deci-sions about patients using relative patient and clinical data (Dinevski, Bele, Šarenac, Rajkovič, Šušteršic, 2011). The use of such systems helps in reducing medical errors, minimizing treatment cost, and improving patient's health (Golemati, Mougiakakou, Stoitsis, Valavanis, Nikita, 2005). In 2005, Garg et al. Stated that CDSSs improved practitioners' performance in 64% of the studies, and patients' outcomes in 13% of them (Garg, et al., 2005). In CDSSs, Artificial intelligence plays a vital role in the applied techniques. These techniques falls under one of two categories; knowledge-based and non-knowledge based systems (Abbasi & Kashiyarndi, 2006). Knowledge-based systems contain knowledge about very specific tasks and facts, and consist of knowledge base, infer-ence engine, and a mechanism to communicate (Abbasi & Kashiyarndi, 2006). Rule-based expert systems and Bayesian Network are examples on the knowledge-based systems. Non-knowledge-based systems employ Machine learning techniques instead, like neural Networks and genetic Algorithms. Unfortunately, there is no mutual model that can be adjusted for the diagnosis of all kinds of diseases (Mokeddem, Atmani, & Mokaddem, 2014). In health care systems, Machine learning used to learn from description of previously treated patients and help practitioners to diagnose objectively and reliably.

In sum, various intelligent techniques could be used to implement CDSS, which one to select depends on the problem domain, the probable solution, the amount of data available, the cost of the system, the required efficiency, researcher choice and purpose, and many other parameters (Abbasi & Kashiyarndi, 2006). In medicine, CDSS can help in monitoring, alerting, interpreting, assisting, diagnosing, and managing decision support (Pestotnik, 2005).

Neural networks are one of the best solutions in complex, multiple variable systems wherein applying ordinary rule-based programming and following an algorithmic solution is an improbable task. Moreover, The ANNs are suitable where traditional classification methods fail due to noisy or incomplete data. In medicine, Artificial Neural Networks (ANNs) are a hot area of concern in the fields of diagnosis, bio-medical analysis, image analysis, and drug development (Tsakona, Paschali, Tsolis, & Skapetis, 2013).

Diagnosis, in medicine, is the recognition of a disease. In traditional methods, clinical practitioners need to deal with huge amount of data of various types which cannot be handled by the human experts. Being the first step in the treatment process, diagnosis is critical and any error in this step can lead to catastrophic consequences, beside the probable delay where conventional methods may last for weeks or even months. What makes things worse is the lack of inexperienced specialists in the diagnosis of a specific disease especially in the developing countries. To summarize, incorrect diagnosis may waste time, resources, quality of health, and even human life (Wasyluk & Raś, 2010). Hence, computer-based methods are becoming inevitable in the diagnosis process due to its efficiency, accuracy, reliability, repeatability, pragmatism, and avoidance of other human being factors such as fatigue, stress, and diminished attention (Panchal & Shah, 2011). A clinical DSS that is developed mainly for diagnosing process is usually called Diagnosing Decision Support Systems (DDSS). Being such a complex real world problem, diagnosing process is best handled using ANNs.

Diabetes is a global healthcare threat and the eighth leading cause of death in the world. Indeed, it is a major health care problem that is becoming more serious over time. Its sever-ty does not reside in the disease itself solely, but also in its complex complications on the diabetic's body. According to the international diabetes federation statistics in 2017, 425 million adult have diabetes worldwide (5.6% of the population). This number is expected to rise to 629 million in 2045 (IDF, 2017). By the end 2017, 4 million deaths are expected as a result of diabetes and its complications. The vast majority of the overall cases are in the developing countries. As of 2013, Jordan ranked 37th globally and 10th in the Arab world in diabetes prevalence (IDF Diabetes Atlas, 2013). These numbers indicate a very high prevalence both locally and globally, which makes it of utmost importance to manage the disease successfully. Due to its importance and critical role in the treatment process, managing the diagnosing phase correctly and on time would reflect positively on the treatment process. In this aid developing a CDSS for the diagnosis step would help remarkably.

In this paper, a DDSS for the diabetes mellitus has been implemented using a multi-layer perceptron artificial neural network. The paper opens with an introductory section to health care, CDSS, ANNs, and diabetes. Section 2 provides a necessary theoretical background on both diabetes as an illness and ANNs as an implementation technique. Section 3 summarizes those works in literature that are relevant to this work. Section 4 explains the implementation method in details. Last but not least, the verification technique and the experimental results are discussed in section 5.

BACKGROUND

Diabetes Mellitus

A chronic disease is a long-lasting, persistent disease or a disease that comes with time. Arthritis, asthma, cancer, COPD, diabetes, hepatitis C and HIV/AIDS are common examples on chronic diseases (Ward & Black, 2016). The incidence of chronic diseases is increasing globally due to pollution and poor life habits (Woo, Yang, Lee, & Kang, 2014).

In order to produce energy, cells need to absorb sugar from blood. This is accomplished by a hormone made by the pancreas gland in the human body called insulin. For whatever reason, if sugar is not absorbed well by body cells, its percentage in blood stream will increase (hyperglycaemia) and exceed the normal level causing what is called Diabetes Mellitus (DM) or in short (Diabetes) (National Institute of Diabetes and Digestive and Kidney Disease, 2017). Diabetes is a metabolic disorder that can be classified into two main categories: type 1 and type 2 (Nichols, 2014). Type 1 and type 2 diabetes may have similar names, but they are different diseases with unique causes. Type 2 diabetes is much more common that type 1 (National Diabetes Statistics Report, 2017).

Type 1 diabetes or the "juvenile diabetes" is an insulin-dependent diabetes (IDDM), this form of diabetes results when the pancreas fails to produce enough insulin, this could happen when defence system attacks the beta cells which produces insulin in the pancreas. The reason behind this situation is still ambiguous, but viral infections such as mumps and rubella cytomegalovirus may play role (MayoClinic, 2013). This type of diabetes infects mostly children, but it can also target people at any ages. Type 1 diabetes develops rapidly; its signs and symptoms arise rapidly within weeks or months. A diabetic person may suffer from polydipsia (increased thirst), polyphagia (constant hunger), polyuria (frequent urination), extreme tiredness, sudden weight loss, slow healing wounds, recurrent infection, and blurred vision (MayoClinic, 2013). Exclusively in type 1, patient experiences diabetic ketoacidosis (a type of metabolic problems characterized by nausea, vomiting, abdominal pain, the smell of acetone on the breath, kussamul or deep breathing, and decreased level of consciousness. In order to make accurate diagnosis, several blood tests could be conducted such as A1C (although it is not recommended for type1), FPG, and OGTT (National Institute of Diabetes, Digestive and Kidney Disease, 2017). These types of tests are explained in details later. Another two types of test are conducted to differentiate type1 from type 2. The first is a blood test to check autoantibodies in the blood. The other is a urine test to check the presence of ketones. If the result of any of these tests is positive then it is type 1 diabetes. In order to control it, a patient with diabetes 1 needs insulin injection daily, healthy diet, close monitoring, and regular physical exercises (MayoClinic, 2013).

Type 2 diabetes or the (adult-onset diabetes) is a non-insulin-dependent diabetes (NIDDM), it results when body cells are unable to respond to the produced insulin. The main cause for this condition is still unknown, but primarily it might be a consequence of life style factors and genetics, it can be effected with obesity, poor diet, physical inactivity, aging, family history, ethnicity, high blood pregnancy affecting the unborn child (National Diabetes Statistics Report, 2017). Type 2 is the most common type with a percentage of 90-95% of the cases. This type can be managed with or without insulin. Thus, type 1 and type 2 are different in several aspects, Table 1 compares between these two types of diabetes.

Table 1. Comparing type 1 and Type 2 diabetes

	Type 1	Type 2
Cause	insufficient produced insulin	Insulin resistance
Genetic basis (family history)	Possible	Strongly possible
Other Risk factors	viral infection	Lifestyle factors, obesity and aging
Body size	Thin or normal	Obese
Onset	Rapidly (in weeks)	Slowly (in months or years)
Ages at onset (often)	In children	In adults
Ketoacidosis	Common	Rare
Autoantibodies	Present	Absent
Endogenous insulin	Low or absent	Normal, low or high
Concordance in identical twins	50%	90%
Gestational diabetes	---	May develop type2 later on.
Afflicted ethnics	All	African-American, Latino, Native
		American, Asian, Pacific Islander
	A1C test	A1C test
Medical tests	Random plasma glucose	Random plasma glucose
	Fasting plasma glucose	Fasting plasma glucose
	Genetic test	Oral glucose tolerance test

The condition wherein the level of glucose in blood is very high, but not high enough for a diagnosis of diabetes is called "prediabetes". A prediabetes person often suffers from diabetes type 2 later on (National Diabetes Statistics Report, 2017). Many other risk factors are considered as indicators on the presence of diabetes (National Diabetes Statistics Report, 2017):

- Waist measurement, despite the BMI value, above 40 cm for men, and above 35 cm for women
- High blood pressure: above 140/90
- High Density Lipoprotein (HDL): cholesterol—"good" cholesterol—level below 35 mg/dL, or a triglyceride Level above 250 mg/dL.
- Polycystic ovary syndrome
- History of giving birth to at least one baby weighing more than 9 pounds

Blood Tests

In order to diagnose diabetes type 1, type 2, and prediabetes accurately and early, since symptoms may arise too late especially for type 2, several blood tests could be used:

- **A1C Test:** It's called also hemoglobin A1C, HBA1C, or glycohemoglobin. It measures average blood sugar level for the past 2 or 3 months. Its result is expressed in percentages. The higher the percentage, the higher amount of sugar in blood. If this test scores 6.5% or above, then the person (National Diabetes Statistics Report, 2017). As this type of test might be not available, and as it is not recommended for diagnosing type 1 and Gestational Diabetes (although it may give correct results), and as it may cause interference and give inaccurate results for people with upnormalities like those with hemoglobin variant, or people of African, Mediterranean, or Southeast Asian descent, or people with family members with sickle cell anemia or a thalassemia, other types of tests should be conducted.
- **Fasting Plasma Glucose (FPG):** Measures sugar in a blood sample after overnight (or at least 8 hours) fasting. Blood sugar values are expressed in milligram per deciliter (mg/dl) or in millimoles per liters (mmol/L). A person with FPG equals or above 126 gm/dl is a diabetic person. This test is more convenient and less expensive than OGTT (National Diabetes Statistics Report, 2017).
- **Random Plasma Glucose (RPG):** This test is used usually for regular checkups. Blood sample is taken at a random time. If this test reports a value of sugar blood above 200 mg/dl, then the person suffers from diabetes (Nichols, 2014).
- **Oral Glucose Tolerance Test (OGTT):** This test measures blood glucose after fasting 8 hours and 2 hours after the person drinks a liquid containing 75 gm of glucose dissolved in water. If this test scored a value between 140 and 199, the person suffers from a special prediabetes called Impaired Glucose Tolerance (IGT). If the result arises to 200 gm/dl or above at two hours, then there is diabetes. The ranges of values of these tests for each of diabetic, prediabetic, and normal cases are presented in Table 2 (National Diabetes Statistics Report, 2017).

Another type of diabetes is the Gestational Diabetes. Pregnant shows resistance to insulin in week 24 and disappears after birth. Gestational Diabetes and their babies may develop type 2 diabetes on the long term. For babies, immediate risk is not as for those who had type 1 and type 2 before (National Diabetes Statistics Report, 2017). On the long term, diabetes can cause many dangerous complications which might

Table 2. Blood test levels for diagnosing diabetes

	A1C (percent)	Fasting Plasma Glucose (mg/dL)	Oral Glucose Tolerance Test (mg/dL)
Diabetes	6.5 or above	126 or above	200 or above
Prediabetes	5.7 to 6.4	100 to 125	140 to 199
Normal	About 5	99 or below	139 or below

reach to disabling and life threatening. It may cause cardiovascular disease, kidney disease, eye disease, nerve damage, diabetic foot, and pregnancy complications (National Diabetes Statistics Report, 2017).

Artificial Neural Networks (ANNs)

Artificial Neural Network is a computational model inspired by the human brain. It is a system of interconnected processing elements resemble the "neurons" that can compute values from inputs by feeding the information through the network. Figure 1 clarifies the similarity between the biological and artificial neurons. It is capable of both machine learning and pattern recognition. As mentioned before, ANNs are best suitable to resolve nonlinear problems which cannot be expressed using ordinary rule based techniques including diagnosis problems (Aleksander & Morton, 1995).

The artificial neurons are organized in layers. The structure of a typical neural network involves input layer, at least one hidden layer, and the output layer. The majority of ANNs have at least one hidden layer between the in-\put and the output layers (Fausett, 2001). The number of hidden layers will be discussed later. ANN is defined by the interconnection pattern between neurons, the learning process, and the activation function. Neurons in any ANN are fully connected; this means that each neuron in a layer is connected with each neuron in next layer through a weighted connection or synapses, these weights manipulate the data in the calculations and indicate the connection strength between the connected neurons (Fausett, 2001).

When the neural network receives data, its input layer neurons are activated. Then, the activations are transferred to the first hidden layer, processed and transferred to the next layer. This process is repeated till a neuron in the last layer is activated which resembles the output. Neural networks vary in the number of layers and directions. Several types of neural networks exist: feed forward neural network, recurrent neural network, radial basis function network, cohune self-organizing network, modular neural network, physical neural network, and learning vector quantization (Fausett, 2001).

Figure 1. Biological and artificial neurons

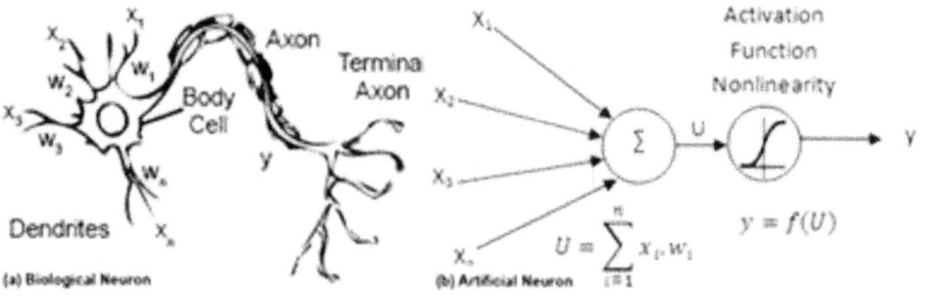

Feedforward is the simplest type of neural network which was first described by (Rumelhart & McClelland, 1986). In this neural network information is transferred in one direction from input through hidden layers to output. A feedforward network can be single layer perceptron with only one output layer, or a multilayer perceptron MLP. A MLP is a one direction feedforward neural network with multiple layers (i.e. input, hidden layers, and output). A MLP has a non-linear activation function, and is trained using backpropagation algorithm (Haykin, 1994).

Determining the number of hidden layers in a neural network is the network designer task. Indeed, it is not a trivial task, there is no precisely defined rule to follow in order to determine the number of hidden layers, but by all the odds, the number of hidden layers should increase with the increased complexity of the system (Mahesh, Suresh, & Babu, 2013). Moreover, more hidden layers are required for multi-staged model. Practically, the majority of real world problems are satisfied with only one hidden layer (Ganesan, Venkatesh, & Rama, 2010). Not only that but also, having more than one hidden layer may slow down the performance of the system. On the other hand, most studies suggest determining the number of hidden layers and nodes empirically to optimize the network performance (Wahyunggoro, Permanasari, & Chamsudin, 2013). This is usually accomplished by performing training on different topologies with different number of layers and neurons then select the topology with the highest accuracy (i.e. the minimum value of mean square error).

Determining the number of neurons in the hidden layer is also a very important issue. Using too few neurons makes it difficult to adequately detect the signals in a complicated data set, which is called "underfitting" (Heaton, 2013). On the other hand, using too many neurons makes the limited amount of information contained in the training set not enough to train all of the neurons in the hidden layers, which is called (overfitting) (Haykin, 1994). Even if the training data is sufficient, large number of hidden neurons may increase the neural network training time. Different rules-of-thumb were suggested to determine the number of neurons in hidden layers (Heaton, 2013). One suggests that it should be between the number of neurons in the input layer and the number of neurons in the output layer. Another rule suggests that the number of neurons in the hidden layer should be 2/3 the size of the input layer, plus the size of the output layer. A third rule suggests that it should be less than twice the number of neurons in the input layer (Haykin, 1994). For networks with multi-hidden layers, it was suggested that the number of neurons in each hidden layer except the first one will be the number of neurons in the previous layer divided by two (Xu & Chen, 2008).

The activation function is a function that specifies the output of the neuron to a given input. Neural networks support several forms of activation functions such as step functions, linear functions, and sigmoid (i.e. Logistic function and hyperbolic tangent function) (Karlik & Olgac, 2011). Step function is commonly used with simple network (i.e. perceptron). Using linear activation functions with multiple layers neural network would be equivalent to a single layer linear network (McClelland, 2013). Hyperbolic tangent function is a symmetric sigmoid nonlinear curve what makes it an ideal activation of MLP and in the hidden layers particularly. Its output ranges between (-1, +1) and its mathematical definition is (Karlik & Olgac, 2011):

$$\tanh(x) = \frac{e^{x} - e^{-x}}{e^{x} + e^{-x}} \quad (1)$$

Neural networks are trained via learning algorithms. To train a neural network means to allow it to learn by example. Learning algorithms could be supervised and unsupervised. In the supervised learning each vector (input) and its classification (output) in the training set is known previously. In the unsupervised learning (clustering), the output is not known before. Classification of input vectors is done automatically during the formation of the classifier (Mohri, Rostamizadeh, & Talwalkar, 2012). In this context, the authors are interested in the supervised learning process using neural networks. Large variety of supervised training algorithms exists. Backward propagation of errors or the backpropagation algorithm is the most common training algorithm to be used with multi-layer network.

Once the optimal network architecture is found, the training process starts. The training is done using pairs of predefined pairs of inputs and outputs. Herein, for each input (i.e. usually a vector or record in the training data set) the output is calculated using the weights and functions in the hidden layers (initial weights are chosen randomly). Then the resultant output is compared with the desired predefined output, the error is then propagated back to the network to adjust weights for the next input in order to hopefully get an output that is closer to the desired one. The training process performed iteratively on the same dataset until the minimum value of mean square error between the actual output and the desired output is reached (Fausett, 2001). Actually, the best performance of the system on the training dataset occurs early, thus it is not necessary to continue training until the training error stops decreasing. Thus training is usually performed for 30-45 iterations (Ganesan et al., 2010). Having finished training, the neural network needs to be verified with new examples other than those were used in the training process. If the overall accuracy of the network is acceptable, then it could be used to predict the output of any new input.

A multilayer perceptron is a feedforward neural network that utilizes a backpropagation learning algorithm and a nonlinear activation function. It is the most common neural network architecture in use today (Haykin, 1994). As its name suggests, a MLP consists of more than two layers (input, output, and one or more hidden layers), any number of neurons in each layer, any number of inputs representing the features and any number of outputs representing the classifications (Haykin, 1994). A MLP is used in complex, multivariable applications such as medical diagnosis (Abbasi & Kashiyarndi, 2006).

RELATED WORK

Applying artificial intelligent techniques in solving clinical problems has attracted many researchers especially in the diagnosis process. In this section, the authors introduce significant works wherein artificial neural networks are utilized to help in disease diagnosis process, specifically, the diabetes illness. Some of these works are listed below:

Cheruku, Edla, Kuppili, Dharavath, & Beechu (2017) Proposed an architecture for weightless neural networks (WNNs) that uses variable sized random access memories to optimise the memory usage and a modified binary TRIE data structure for reducing the test time. The results of the proposed architecture outperforms in terms of accuracy as compared to conventional neural network-based classifiers.

El-Sappagh & Elmogy (2016) introduced a systematic review that examines the current state of Case-Based Reasoning (CBR) and its limitations in the medical domain, especially for diabetes mellitus.

Ngan & Li (2015) combined the strengths of both domain-knowledge-based and machine-learning-based approaches to propose a Hypoglycemic Expert Query Parametric Estimation (H-EQPE) model and a Linear Checkpoint (L-Checkpoint) algorithm to detect hypoglycemia of diabetes patients. The paper focuses on determining the BGL monitoring threshold to prevent the patients from suffering hypoglycemic events.

Farahmand, You, Shi, & Wadhwa (2015) Compared between of two data mining techniques (i.e. Decision Tree and logistic regression modelling) for predicting diabetes. Results show that both methods present a good prediction for pre-diabetes and that Decision Tree modelling is a better indicator to predict pre-diabetes.

Fashoto, Adeyeye, Owolabi, & Odim (2015) Modelled a feedforward neural network to solve the problem associated with the medical diagnosis of acute inflammations and acute nephritises of the urinary system. The output shows that the classification accuracy of the model to be approximately 90%.

Al-Khasawneh & Hijazi (2014) developed a clinical decision support system that helps in diagnosing diabetes mellitus using a multilayer perceptron artificial neural network.

Temurtas, Yumusak, & Temurtas (2009) presented a comparative study on Pima Indian diabetes disease diagnostic by using multilayer neural network which was trained by LM algorithm and probabilistic neural network. They compared the results they obtained with other related studies conducted on the same database. (Sumathy, Mythili, Kumar, Jishnujit, & Kumar, 2010) proposed a method for diagnosing diabetes using newly designed inputs parameters and backpropagation algorithm.

Acar, Özerdem, & Akpolat (2011) trained four types of neural networks (i.e. perceptron, MLP, Elman and ART1) to forecast whether someone has diabetes or not. Finally, the best performance was observed as 82.10% in the MLP network with 8-20-1 structure. (Robert-son, Lehmann, Sandham, & Hamilton, 2011) used Elman recurrent artificial neural networks (ANNs) to make BGL predictions based on a history of Blood Glucose Level (BGLs), meal intake, and insulin injections. (Giveki, 2012) introduced an automatic approach to diagnose diabetes based on Feature Weighted Support Vector Machines (FW-SVMs) and Modified Cuckoo Search (MCS).

Karan, Bayraktar, Haluk, & Karlık (2012) presented a neural network algorithm that classifies diabetes illness data on client/server architecture. (Mahesh et al., 2013) proposed a Generalized Regression Neural Network (GRNN) based expert system to help in diagnosing the hepatitis B disease. Their system classifies each patient into infected and non-infected. If infected then how severe it is in terms of intensity rate. (Amato et al., 2013) discussed and summarized the philosophy, capabilities, and limitations of artificial neural networks in medical diagnosis through selected examples including diabetes disease.

METHOD

In this research a MLP neural network was used to diagnose diabetes and to determine its type. The system was implemented using Matlab 7.8. During the development phase the authors passed by the phases summarized in Figure 2.

Dataset

Clinical data was obtained from King Abdullah University Hospital in Jordan. The dataset contains information about 730 patients. For each patient, a set of 18 features and the diabetic diagnosis (i.e. non diabetic, prediabetes, type1 diabetes, type2 diabetes, and gestational diabetes) is stated. These pieces of information constitute the basis of the training database which will be discussed later. This sample

Figure 2. Diagnosing diabetes mellitus method

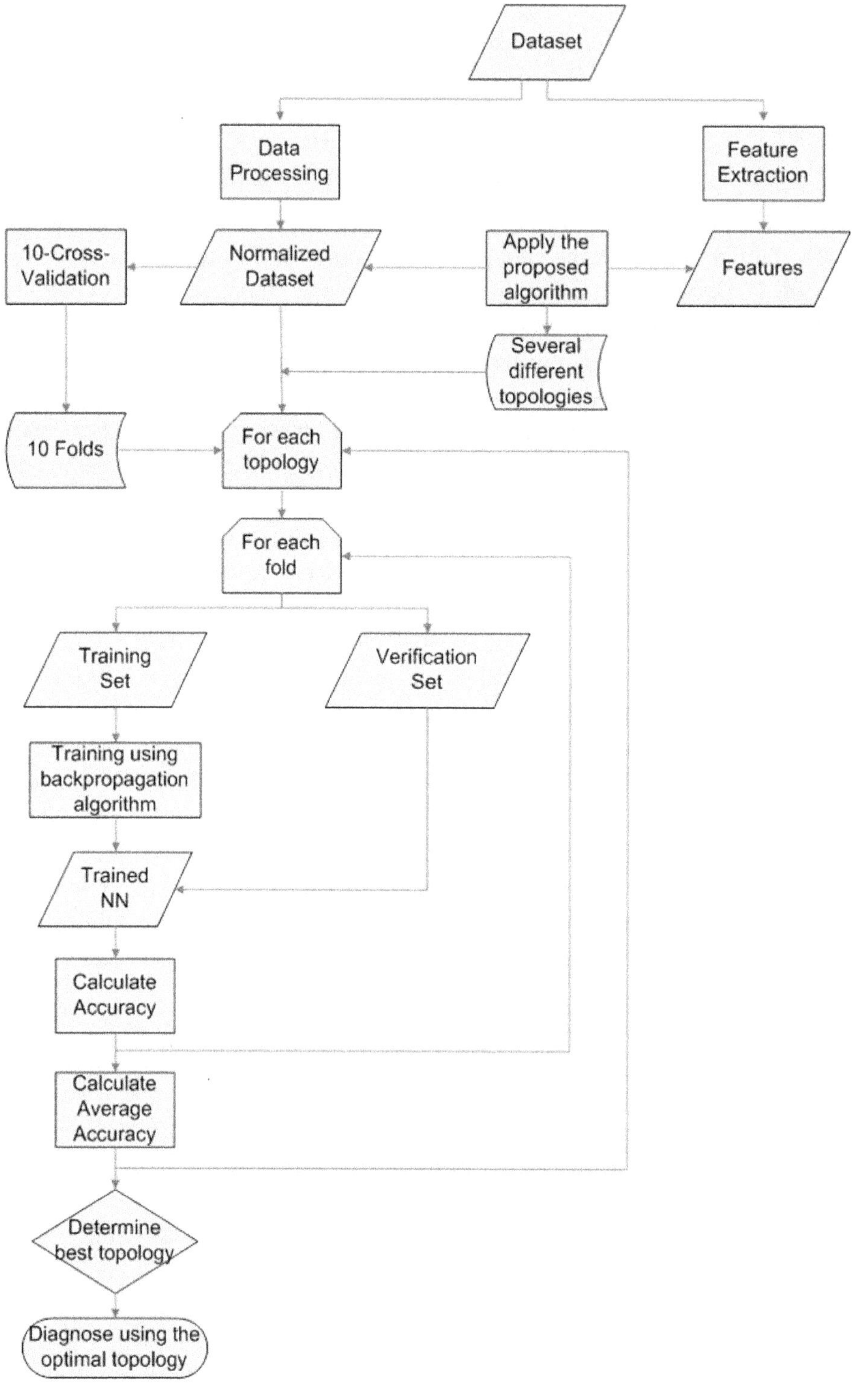

consists of 200 prediabetes, 70 type 1 diabetic, 280 type 2 diabetic, 80 gestational diabetic, and the remaining are non-diabetic.

Features Selection

Correct diagnosis depends largely on the features selected to train the network. Redundant, insufficient features should be avoided since it may make a noise affecting the output. This requires some medical experience. Herein, the features were decided upon with consultation of clinicians at King Abdullah University Hospital. The training database was built with respect to those features. A list of the selected features is displayed in Table 3.

Construct the Optimal Structure of the Neural Network

Being a MLP neural network, this network has a one input layer with 18 neurons which represent the features. Being a classification problem rather than regression, the output layer has N neurons rather than a single neuron, one for each of the N categories of the target variable. Thus this network has one output layer with 5 neurons which represent the diabetic diagnosis (i.e. non-diabetic, prediabetic, type 1 diabetic, type 2 diabetic, and gestational diabetic). A MLP should also have at least one hidden layer. As highlighted before, determining the number of hidden layers and neurons is not a trivial task. There is no way to determine the optimal number of the hidden layers and neurons. As mentioned before, many

Table 3. Diabetes features, types, and encodings

	Feature	Type	Encoding
Symptoms	Polydipsia	Boolean	Presences =1, Absence=0
	Polyphagia	Boolean	Presences =1, Absence=0
	Polyuria	Boolean	Presences =1, Absence=0
	Ketoacidosis	Boolean	Presences =1, Absence=0
	Polycystic ovary	Boolean	Presences =1, Absence=0
	A1C	Numerical	-------
	FPF	Numerical	-------
Biomedical Analysis	RPG	Numerical	-------
	OGTT	Numerical	-------
	Autoantibodies test	Boolean	Positive = 1, Negative =0
	Ketones test	Boolean	Positive = 1, Negative =0
	HDL cholesterol	Numerical	-------
	Family history	Boolean	Presences =1, Absence=0
	Age	numerical	-------
Risk Factors	Pregnancy	Boolean	Pregnancy =1, non-pregnancy=0
	BMI	Numerical	-------
	Affected twins	Boolean	Presences =1, Absence=0
	Physical activity	Boolean	Practice =0, no practice= 1

rules-of-thumb were suggested to help in this aid. In addition, a MLP with only one hidden layer is usually sufficient to solve the majority of real life problems. Nevertheless, most research recommends that determining the number of hidden layers and neurons should be determined experimentally. Therefore, in this research, neural networks of different topologies were implemented. To determine the number of topologies, the number of hidden layers in each topology, and the number of neurons in each layer, the authors proposed the algorithm 1 based on the rules-of-thumb mentioned earlier.

According to this algorithm, two topologies for the neural network were implemented, displayed in Figure 3 and Figure 4. In both topologies, each layer neuron is fully connected to the neurons in the next layer through connection weights.

Preprocessing Dataset

As any neural network input should be numerical. Non-numerical input features should be encoded so that its value is expressed using numerical data. The encoding for each feature is displayed in Table 3. Since the range of input data in a neural network may vary widely, and in order to remove any influence of the units of measure, dataset should be pre-processed and scaled. One way to this is to perform feature standardization. This makes the values for each feature have a zero-mean and a unit variance. This could be achieved by firstly calculating the mean and the standard deviation for each feature, then for each feature value the mean is subtracted and the resultant value is divided by the calculated standard deviation (Pedregosa, et al., 2011).

Preparing the Training Dataset

For subsequent 10-fold-cross-validation purposes, the dataset (760 patients) is partitioned into 10 equal size subsets (each of 76 patients). In each fold, nine of the ten partitions (i.e. 648 patients) are used as a training set and the one remaining partition is left for verification purposes (i.e. verification set or test set). This assures that all values are used for both training and validation, and each value is used for validation exactly once. Neural network learns by a series of examples called (training data-base). The structure of our training database is shown in Table 4. Our training database has 18 fields representing the features and another field represents the diagnosis. It also has 648 records; a record for each patient.

Table 4. The structure of our training database

Patient ID	Medical Data							Diagnosis
	Feature 1	Feature 2	…	Feature j	….	Feature	18	
1	Data 1,1	Data 1,2		Data 1,j		Data 1,18		Diabetes 2
2	Data 2,1	Data 2,2		Data 2,j		Data 2,18		Nondiabetes
…	…	…	…	…	…	…		…
p	Data p,1	Data p,2		Data p,j		Data p,18		Diabetes 1
P+1	Data p+1,1	Data p+1,2		Data p+1,j		Data p+1,18		Diabetes 1
…	…	…	…	…	…	…		…
648	Data 730,1	Data 730,2		Data 730,j		Data 730,18		Nondiabetes

Training the Network

For each topology, the neural network is trained 10 rounds over the 10 folds training sets. After each round, the network is verified against the verification set of that fold. For training purposes, the authors adapted a back-propagation algorithm and a sigmoid (non-linear) activation function (i.e. tangh(x)). The goal behind the training process is to adjust the weights to minimize the output error function E. In other words, to make the actual output and the target output similar as much as possible. The success of using back-propagation algorithm in training MLPs depends largely on the learning rate and the momentum value to be used. The learning rate controls the size of the weight and the bias changes during the learning process, while the momentum prevents the system from converging to a local minimum. There is no systematic way to determine the most appropriate values; overall, they are both real numbers in the range [0, 1]. Herein, a value of 0.9 was used for the momentum, 0.1 for the training rate, and 10000 for the number of iteration (epochs). Initial weights were also chosen randomly in order to break symmetry and small to avoid intermediate saturation of the activation function; usually in the range [-a, a] where $0.1<a<2$.

EXPERIMENTAL RESULTS

Verification

In order to examine how the proposed neural network model will generalize to an independent data set, cross validation technique was applied. In the cross-validation (or sometimes referred to as rotation validation) the original data set is partitioned into k partitions. One partition is used as verification set while the remaining k-1 partitions are used as a training set. The verification partition is rotated over the K partitions and thus the process is repeated K times (i.e. folds) (Poole & Mackworth, 2010).

In this system, a 10-fold cross validation was used. The original data set (760 patients) was splitted randomly into 10 equal subsets. Each topology was presented to 10 folds. At each fold, 9 of the subsets were used as training dataset, and the other remaining subset was used as verification set. Then, in the next fold, the verification subset is rotated. This guarantees that all values are used for both training and validation, and each value is used for validation exactly once. Figure 5 clarifies how the 10-fold-cross validation technique was applied in this research.

For each topology, the classification accuracy was measured at each fold using the following equation:

$$FCA = \frac{\begin{matrix} number\,of\,correct\,classifications \\ in\,the\,classification\,set \end{matrix}}{verification\,set\,size} \tag{2}$$

Then, the average of all observations for all folds was calculated. Table 5 summarizes the experimental results for topology 1 (one hidden layer) and the experimental results for topology 2 (two hidden layers). The results revealed that diagnosing diabetes using neural network models achieves a very good classification Accuracy. A comparison between the two topologies (18-15-6) and (18-15-7-5) in classification accuracy for each fold is shown in figure 6. Figure 7 shows a comparison of the general

Figure 3. Topology 1: A MLP with one hidden layer for diagnosing diabetes

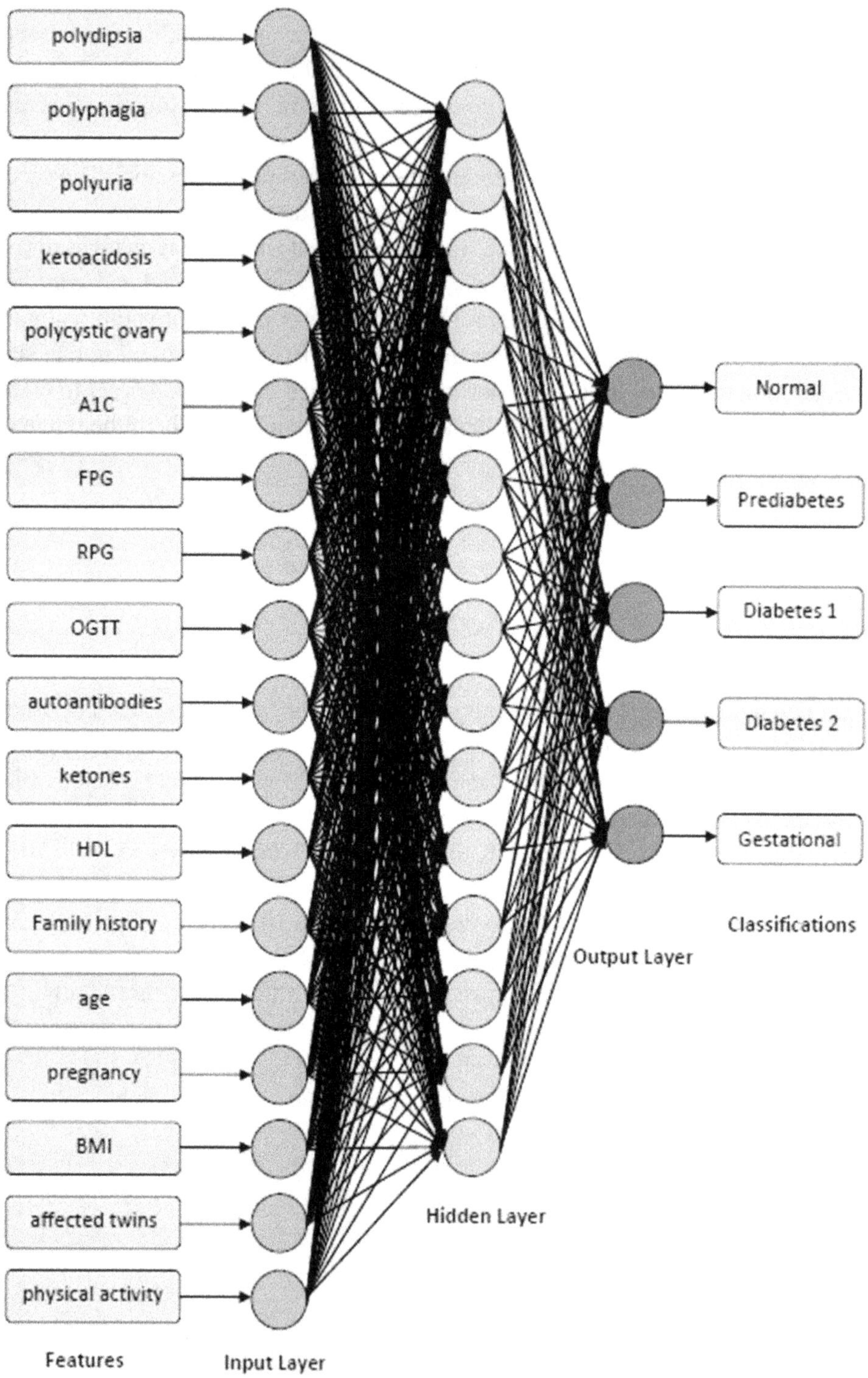

Figure 4. Topology 2: A MLP with Two Hidden Layers for Diagnosing Diabetes

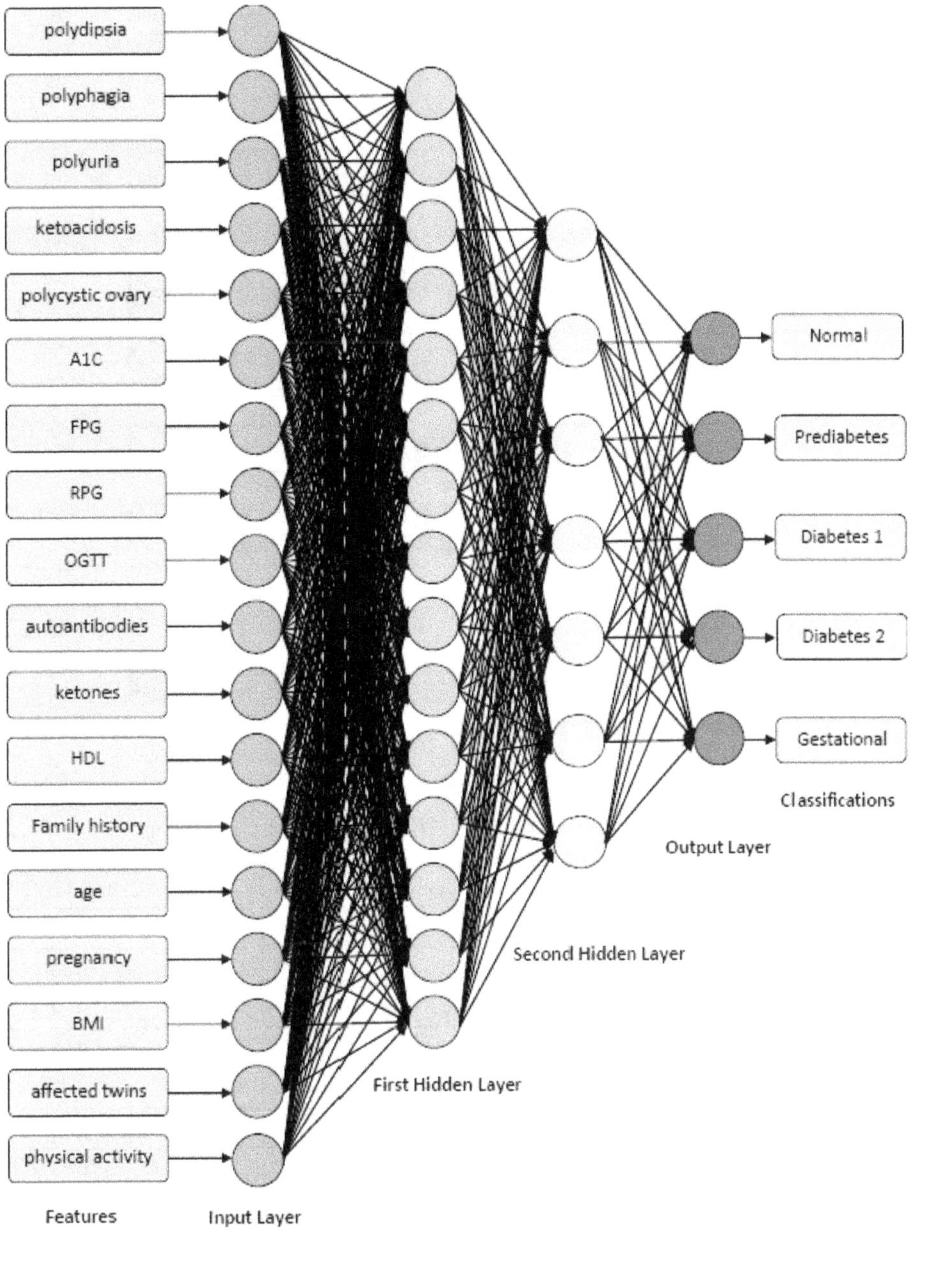

Figure 5. Applying 10-fold-cross validation on the dataset

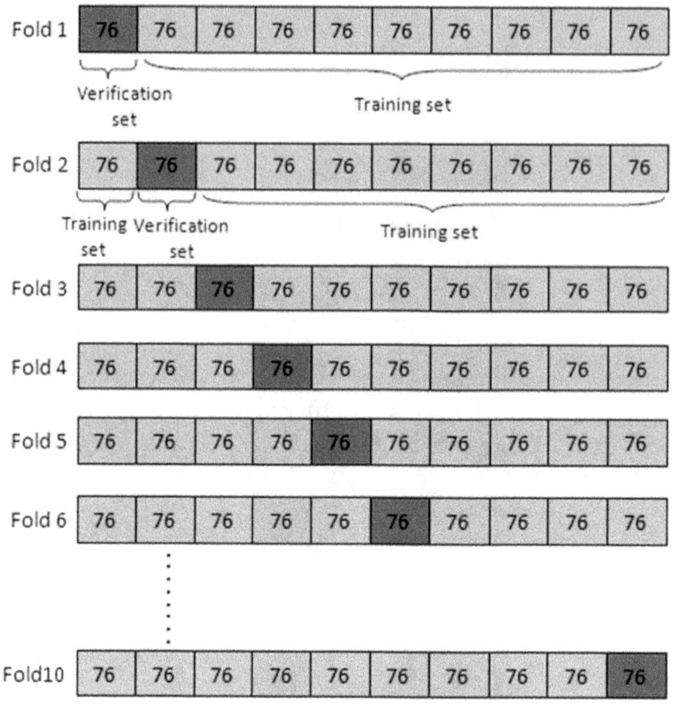

Table 5. Classification accuracy for topology 1 and topology 2

Fold	Topology 1	Topology 2
1	0.92	0.91
2	0.86	0.86
3	0.88	0.88
4	0.97	0.93
5	0.95	0.92
6	0.82	0.82
7	0.89	0.85
8	0.93	0.91
9	0.97	0.93
10	0.96	0.9
Average Accuracy	91.50%	89.10%

average classification accuracy for both topologies. The figure implies that a MLP with either a single hidden layer (topology-1) or multi-hidden layer (topology-2) gives a good classification results with a slightly higher average classification accuracy for the MLP with single hidden layer.

From these observations, it can be concluded that a neural network with one hidden layer (with a classification accuracy of (91.5%)) performs better than the network with two hidden layers (with a classification accuracy of (89.1%)). This result advocates the claims that one hidden layer is sufficient for majority of real life problems. The neural network with the highest classification accuracy (i.e. one hidden layer network) was chosen.

CONCLUSION AND FUTURE WORK

In this paper, a MLP based clinical decision support system was introduced. The system takes in 18 variables as an input. These variables represent the symptoms, biomedical analysis, and other risk factors of the diabetes illness. The output of the system classifies the diabetic status of the patient into five categories (i.e. normal, prediabetes, type1, type2, and gestational diabetes). To determine the number of hidden layers, the authors proposed an algorithm based on the already known rules of thumb. Hence, two different topologies were trained and verified using feed forward backpropagation algorithm and 10-fold cross-validation technique. The first topology (18-15-6) gave higher averaged accuracy (91.5%) than the second topology (18-15-7-5) with an averaged accuracy (89.1%). This result is consistent with the trend which says that a MLP with a single hidden layer is sufficient for the majority of real life problems.

According to these results, the implemented system seems to be a promising diabetes diagnostic tool. Practically, several barriers and obstacles to their implementation exist. One barrier is the incomplete medical knowledge base. Another barrier is the lack of electronic medical records (EMRs) in the clinical environments. Sometimes, the use of such EMRs that include computerized decision support system

Figure 6. Classification Accuracy for 10-Folds

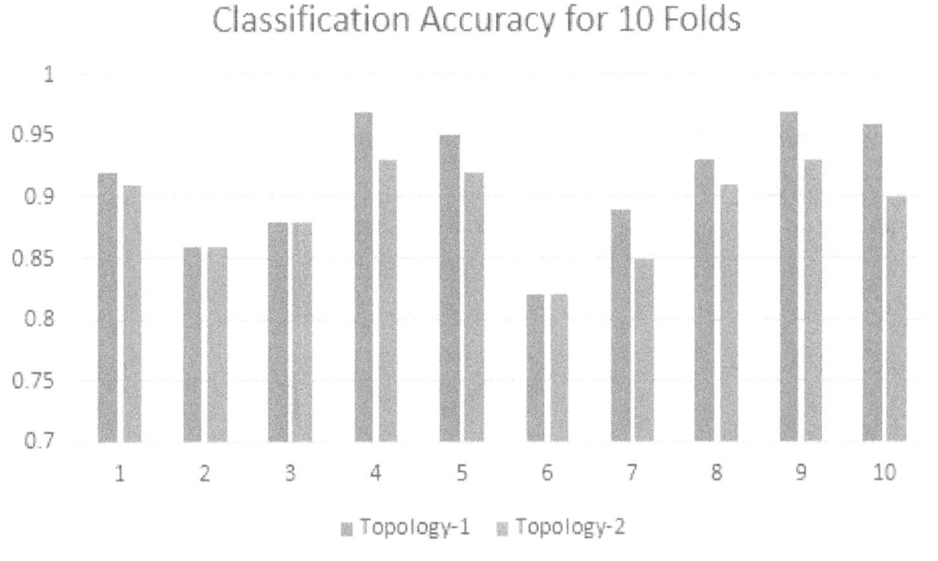

Figure 7. A Comparison between the Average Classification Accuracy between Topology-1 and Topology-2

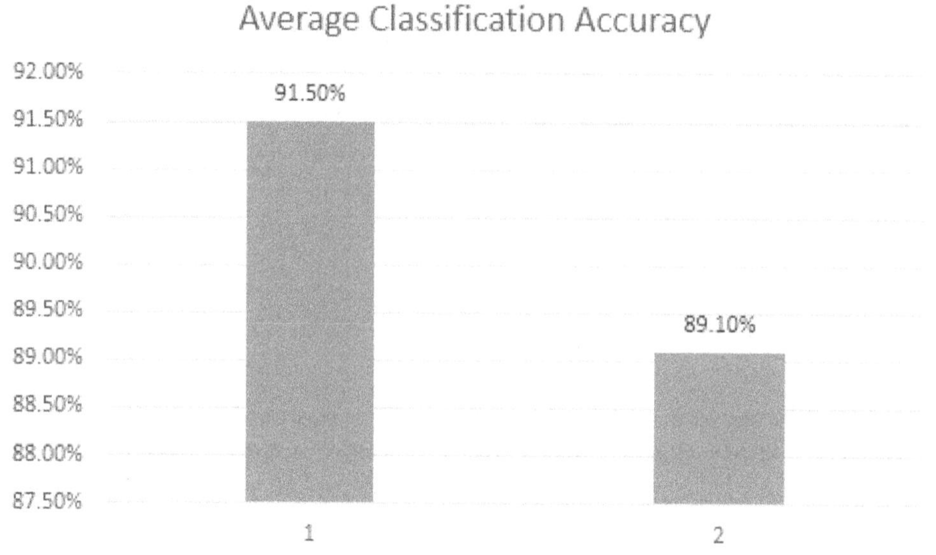

capabilities can be considered another barrier. High clinicians' resistance and low motivation to use such computerized systems is another challenging issue. On the other hand, the system is expected to give higher accuracy on larger data set. In future, the followed method could be applied on other chronic diseases like hepatitis, hypertension, and coronary. For general purposes systems, those systems could be integrated into a single general purpose diagnostic system using feature extraction techniques.

REFERENCES

Abbasi, M., & Kashiyarndi, S. (2006). *Clinical decision support systems: A discussion on different methodologies used in Health Care.* Academic Press.

Acar, E., Özerdem, M. S., & Akpolat, V. (2011). Diabetes Mellitus Forcast Using Various Types of Artificial Neural Networks. *6th International Advanced Technologies Symposium*, 196-201.

Aleksander, I., & Morton, H. (1995). *An introduc-tion to neural.* London: Int Thomson Comput Press.

Al-Khasawneh, A., & Hijazi, H. (2014). A Predictive E-Health Information System: Diagnosing Diabetes Mellitus Using Neural Network Based Decision Support System. *International Journal of Decision Support System Technology*, *6*(4), 31–48. doi:10.4018/ijdsst.2014100103

Amato, F., López, A., Peña-Méndez, E. M., Vaňhara, P., Hampl, A., & Havel, J. (2013). Artificial neural networks in medical diagnosis. *Journal of Applied Biomedicine*, *11*(2), 47–58. doi:10.2478/v10136-012-0031-x

Brailer, D., & Thompson, T. (2004). *Health IT strategic framework.* Academic Press.

Bray, O. (2010). *Health Care Information Technology: A Key to Quality and Cost Issues.* LWVUS.

Health Care Education Task Force. (2012). *Diagnosis of Diabetes and Prediabetes*. National Institute of Diabetes and Digestive and Kidney Disease.

Cheruku, R., Edla, D. R., Kuppili, V., Dharavath, R., & Beechu, N. R. (2017). Automatic disease diagnosis using optimised weightless neural networks for low-power wearable devices. *Healthcare Technology Letters*, *4*(4), 122–128. doi:10.1049/htl.2017.0003 PMID:28868148

Dinevski, D., Bele, U., Šarenac, T., Rajkovič, U., & Šušteršic, O. (2011). Telemedicine Techniques and Applications. In G. Graschew (Ed.), Clinical Decision Support Systems (pp. 185-210). InTech.

El-Gayar, O. F., Deokar, A. V., & Tao, J. (2011). DSS-CMM: A Capability Maturity Model for DSS Development Processes. *International Journal of Decision Support System Technology*, *3*(4), 14–34. doi:10.4018/jdsst.2011100102

El-Sappagh, S., & Elmogy, M. M. (2016). Medical Case Based Reasoning Frameworks: Current Developments and Future Directions. *International Journal of Decision Support System Technology*, *8*(3), 31–62. doi:10.4018/IJDSST.2016070103

Farahmand, K., You, G., Shi, J., & Wadhwa, S. S. (2015). Data Mining for Predicting Pre-diabetes: Comparing Two Approaches. *International Journal of User-Driven Healthcare*, *5*(2), 26–46. doi:10.4018/IJUDH.2015070103

Fashoto, S. G., Adeyeye, M., Owolabi, O., & Odim, M. (2015). Modelling of the Feed Forward Neural Network with its Application in Medical Diagnosis. *International Journal of Advances in Engineering and Technology*, *8*(4), 507–520.

Fausett, L. L. (2001). *Fundamentals of Neural Net-works: Architectures, Algorithms, and Applications*. New York: Addison-Wesley Inc.

Ganesan, N., Venkatesh, K., & Rama, M. A. (2010). Application of Neural Networks in Diagnosing Cancer Disease Using Demographic Data. *International Journal of Computers and Applications*, *1*(26), 76–85.

Garg, A., Adhikari, N., McDonald, H., Rosas-Arel-lano, M., Devereaux, P., Beyene, J., ... Haynes, R. B. (2005). Effects of computerized clinical decision support systems on practitioner performance and patient outcomes: A systematic review. *Journal of the American Medical Association*, *293*(10), 1223–1238. doi:10.1001/jama.293.10.1223 PMID:15755945

Giveki, D. (2012). *Automatic detection of diabetes diagnosis using feature weighted support vector machines based on mutual information and modified cuckoo search*. Academic Press.

Golemati, S., Mougiakakou, S., Stoitsis, J., Valavanis, I., & Nikita, K. S. (2005). Clinical Decision Support Systems: Basic Principles and Applications in Diagnosis and Therapy. In Clinical Decision Support Systems (pp. 250-296). Idea Group Inc.

Haykin, S. (1994). Neural Networks: A Comprehensive Foundation (2nd ed.). Pearson Education, Inc.

Heaton, J. (2013). Feedforward Backpropagation Neural Networks. In J. Heaton (Ed.), Introduction to Neural Networks for Java (2nd ed.). Heaton Research, Inc.

International Diabetes Federation. (2013). *IDF Diabetes Atlas*. Author.

International Diabetes Federation. (2017). *IDF Diabetes Atlas*. Author.

Karan, O., Bayraktar, C., Gümüşkaya, H., & Karlık, B. (2012). Diagnosing diabetes using neural net-works on small mobile devices. *Expert Systems with Applications, 39*(1), 54–60. doi:.eswa.2011.06.04610.1016/j

Karlik, B., & Olgac, A. V. (2011). Performance Analysis of Various Activation Functions in Gen-eralized MLP Architectures of Neural Networks. *International Journal of Artificial Intelligence And Expert Systems*, *1*(4), 111–122.

M. C. (2013, June 23). *Type 1 diabetes Diagnosis at Mayo Clinic*. Retrieved May 15, 2014, from Mayo Clinic: http://www.mayoclinic.org/diseases-con-ditions/type-1-diabetes/basics/tests-diagnosis/con-

Mahesh, C., Suresh, V. G., & Babu, M. (2013). Diagnosing Hepatitis B Using Artificial Neural Net-work Based Expert System. *International Journal of Engineering and Innovative Technology*, *3*(6), 139–144.

McClelland, J. L. (2013, February 6). *Explorations in parallel distributed processing: A handbook of models, programs, and exercises*. Stanford, CA: Academic Press.

Mohri, M., Rostamizadeh, A., & Talwalkar, A. (2012). *Foundations of Machine Learning*. MIT Press.

Mokeddem, S., Atmani, B., & Mokaddem, M. (2014). A New Approach for Coronary Artery Diseases Diagnosis Based on Genetic Algorithm. *International Journal of Decision Support System Technology*, *6*(4), 1–15. doi:10.4018/ijdsst.2014100101

Ngan, C.-K., & Li, L. (2015). H-EQPE Model and L-Checkpoint Algorithm: A Decision-Guidance Approach for Detecting Hypoglycemia of Diabetes Patients. *International Journal of Decision Support System Technology*, *7*(4), 20–35. doi:10.4018/IJDSST.2015100102

Nichols, H. (2014, March 3). *What is the difference between diabetes type 1 and diabetes*. Retrieved May 15, 2014, from Medical News Today: http://www. medicalnewstoday.com/articles/7504.php

Panchal, D., & Shah, S. (2011). Artificial Intelligence Based Expert System For Hepatitis B Diagnosis. *International Journal of Modeling and Optimiza-tion*, *1*(4), 362–366. doi:10.7763/IJMO.2011.V1.61

Pedregosa, F., Varoquaux, G., Gramfort, A., Michel, V., Thirion, B., Grisel, O., & … . (2011). Scikit-learn: Machine Learning in {P}ython. *Journal of Machine Learning Research, 12*, 2825–2830.

Pestotnik, S. L. (2005). Expert Clinical Decision Support Systems to Enhance Antimicrobial Steward-ship Programs. *Pharmacotherapy*, *25*(8), 1116–1125. doi:10.1592/phco.2005.25.8.1116 PMID:16207103

Poole, D., & Mackworth, A. (2010). Avoiding Overfitting. In D. Poole & A. Mackworth (Eds.), Artificial Intelligence: Foundations of Computational Agents. Cambridge University Press.

Robertson, G., Lehmann, E. D., Sandham, W., & Hamilton, D. (2011). Blood Glucose Prediction Using Artificial Neural Networks Trained with the AIDA Diabetes Simulator: A Proof-of-Concept Pilot Study. *Journal of Electrical and Computer Engineering*, *2011*, 1–11. doi:10.1155/2011/681786

Rumelhart, D. E., & McClelland, J. L. (1986). Parallel distributed processing: explorations in the mi-crostructure of cognition: Vol. 1. *Foundations*. Cambridge, MA: MIT Press.

Sharma, K., & Virmani, J. (2017). A Decision Support System for Classification of Normal and Medical Renal Disease Using Ultrasound Images: A Decision Support System for Medical Renal Diseases. *International Journal of Ambient Computing and Intelligence*, *8*(2), 52–69. doi:10.4018/IJACI.2017040104

Sumathy, M., Kumar, P., Jishnujit, T. M., & Kumar, K. R. (2010). Diagnosis of Diabetes Mel-litus based on Risk Factors. *International Journal of Computers and Applications*, *10*(4).

Temurtas, H., Yumusak, N., & Temurtas, F. (2009). A comparative study on diabetes disease diagnosis using neural networks. *Expert Systems with Applications*, *36*(4), 8610–8615. doi:10.1016/j.eswa.2008.10.032

Tsakona, A., Paschali, K., Tsolis, D., & Skapetis, G. (2013). Proposed Electronic Medical Record with Emphasis on Hepatitis Diagnosis. *International Journal of Caring Sciences*, *6*(2), 138–145.

Wahyunggoro, O., Permanasari, A. E., & Chamsudin, A. (2013). Utilization of Neural Network for Disease Forecasting. *59th ISI World Statistics Congress*, 549-554.

Ward, B. W., & Black, L. I. (2016). State and Regional Prevalence of Diagnosed Multiple Chronic Conditions Among Adults Aged ≥18 Years — United States, 2014. *Morbidity and Mortality Weekly Report*, *65*(29), 735–738. doi:10.15585/mmwr.mm6529a3 PMID:27467707

Wasyluk, H. A., & Raś, Z. W. (2010). Action Rules Approach to Solving Diagnostic Problems in Clinical Medicine. In G. Devlin (Ed.), Decision Support Systems Advances (pp. 99-106). InTech.

Woo, J.-I., Yang, J.-G., Lee, Y.-H., & Kang, U.-G. (2014). Healthcare Decision Support System for Administration of Chronic Diseases. *Healthcare Informatics Research*, *20*(3), 173–182. doi:10.4258/hir.2014.20.3.173 PMID:25152830

Xu, S., & Chen, L. (2008). A Novel Approach for Determining the Optimal Number of Hidden Layer Neurons for FNN's and Its Application in Data Mining. Proceedings of the 5th International Conference on Information Technology and Applications, 683-686.

ADDITIONAL READING

Ahmed, S. S., Dey, N., Ashour, A. S., Sifaki-Pistolla, D., Bălas-Timar, D., Balas, V. E., & Tavares, J. M. R. (2017). Effect of fuzzy partitioning in Crohn's disease classification: A neuro-fuzzy-based approach. *Medical & Biological Engineering & Computing*, *55*(1), 101–115. doi:10.100711517-016-1508-7 PMID:27106754

Ben Abdessalem Karaa, W., Ben Azzouz, Z., Singh, A., Dey, N., & Ashour, S, A., & Ben Ghazala, H. (. (2016). Automatic builder of class diagram (ABCD): An application of UML generation from functional requirements. *Software, Practice & Experience*, *46*(11), 1443–1458. doi:10.1002pe.2384

Bose, S., Mukherjee, A., Chakraborty, S., Samanta, S., & Dey, N. (2013, December). Parallel image segmentation using multi-threading and k-means algorithm. In *Computational Intelligence and Computing Research (ICCIC), 2013 IEEE International Conference on* (pp. 1-5). IEEE. 10.1109/ICCIC.2013.6724171

Chatterjee, S., Chakraborty, R., Dey, N., & Hore, S. (2015). A quality prediction method for weight lifting activity.

Kamal, S., Dey, N., Ashour, A. S., Ripon, S., Balas, V. E., & Kaysar, M. S. (2017). FbMapping: an automated system for monitoring facebook data. *Neural Network World*, *27*(1), 27–57. doi:10.14311/NNW.2017.27.002

Kamal, S., Dey, N., Nimmy, S. F., Ripon, S. H., Ali, N. Y., Ashour, A. S., ... Shi, F. (2016). Evolutionary framework for coding area selection from cancer data. *Neural Computing & Applications*, 1–23.

Kamal, S., Ripon, S. H., Dey, N., Ashour, A. S., & Santhi, V. (2016). A MapReduce approach to diminish imbalance parameters for big deoxyribonucleic acid dataset. *Computer Methods and Programs in Biomedicine*, *131*, 191–206. doi:10.1016/j.cmpb.2016.04.005 PMID:27265059

Li, Z., Shi, K., Dey, N., Ashour, A. S., Wang, D., Balas, V. E., ... Shi, F. (2017). Rule-based back propagation neural networks for various precision rough set presented KANSEI knowledge prediction: A case study on shoe product form features extraction. *Neural Computing & Applications*, *28*(3), 613–630. doi:10.100700521-016-2707-8

Karaa, W. B. A., Ashour, A. S., Sassi, D. B., Roy, P., Kausar, N., & Dey, N. (2016). Medline text mining: an enhancement genetic algorithm based approach for document clustering. In *Applications of Intelligent Optimization in Biology and Medicine* (pp. 267–287). Springer International Publishing. doi:10.1007/978-3-319-21212-8_12

Karaa, W. B. A., Mannai, M., Dey, N., Ashour, A. S., & Olariu, I. (2016, August). Gene-disease-food relation extraction from biomedical database. In *International Workshop Soft Computing Applications* (pp. 394-407). Springer, Cham.

Kausar, N., Abdullah, A., Samir, B. B., Palaniappan, S., AlGhamdi, B. S., & Dey, N. (2016). Ensemble clustering algorithm with supervised classification of clinical data for early diagnosis of coronary artery disease. *Journal of Medical Imaging and Health Informatics*, *6*(1), 78–87. doi:10.1166/jmihi.2016.1593

Kausar, N., Palaniappan, S., Samir, B. B., Abdullah, A., & Dey, N. (2016). Systematic analysis of applied data mining based optimization algorithms in clinical attribute extraction and classification for diagnosis of cardiac patients. In *Applications of intelligent optimization in biology and medicine* (pp. 217–231). Springer International Publishing. doi:10.1007/978-3-319-21212-8_9

Ngan, T. T., Tuan, T. M., Minh, N. H., & Dey, N. (2016). Decision Making Based on Fuzzy Aggregation Operators for Medical Diagnosis from Dental X-ray images. *Journal of Medical Systems*, *40*(12), 280. doi:10.100710916-016-0634-y PMID:27787784

Nimmy, S. F., Kamal, M. S., Hossain, M. I., Dey, N., Ashour, A. S., & Shi, F. (2017). Neural Skyline Filtering for Imbalance Features Classification. *International Journal of Computational Intelligence and Applications*, *16*(03), 1750019. doi:10.1142/S1469026817500195

Wang, D., He, T., Li, Z., Cao, L., Dey, N., Ashour, A. S., ... Shi, F. (2016). Image feature-based affective retrieval employing improved parameter and structure identification of adaptive neuro-fuzzy inference system. *Neural Computing & Applications*, 1–16.

Roy, P., Goswami, S., Chakraborty, S., Azar, A. T., & Dey, N. (2014). Image segmentation using rough set theory: A review. *International Journal of Rough Sets and Data Analysis*, *1*(2), 62–74. doi:10.4018/ijrsda.2014070105

Tang, R., Fong, S., Dey, N., Wong, R. K., & Mohammed, S. (2017). Cross Entropy Method Based Hybridization of Dynamic Group Optimization Algorithm. *Entropy (Basel, Switzerland)*, *19*(10), 533. doi:10.3390/e19100533

Wang, D., Li, Z., Cao, L., Balas, V. E., Dey, N., Ashour, A. S., ... Shi, F. (2016). Image Fusion Incorporating Parameter Estimation Optimized Gaussian Mixture Model and Fuzzy Weighted Evaluation System: A Case Study in Time-Series Plantar Pressure Data Set. *IEEE Sensors Journal*, *17*(5), 1407–1420. doi:10.1109/JSEN.2016.2641501

Wang, D., Li, Z., Dey, N., Ashour, A. S., Sherratt, R. S., & Shi, F. (2017). Case-Based Reasoning for Product Style Construction and Fuzzy Analytic Hierarchy Process Evaluation Modeling Using Consumers Linguistic Variables. *IEEE Access : Practical Innovations, Open Solutions*, *5*, 4900–4912. doi:10.1109/ACCESS.2017.2677950

KEY TERMS AND DEFINITIONS

Artificial Neural Network: Is a computational model inspired by the human brain that consists of interconnected processing elements resemble the "neurons" that can compute values from inputs by feeding the information through the network.

Classification Accuracy: Is the percentage of correct predictions.

Clinical Decision Support System: Is a health information system that helps health practitioners in making decisions especially in the diagnosis process.

Cross Validation: Is a technique to evaluate predictive models by partitioning the original sample into a training set to train the model, and a test set to evaluate it.

Diabetes: Is a chronic disease that results when the percentage of sugar in blood increases and exceeds the normal level.

Multilayer Perceptron: Is feedforward artificial neural network that utilizes backpropagation supervised learning for training.

Chapter 7
Web-Based Decision Support System for Solving Multiple-Objective Decision-Making Problems

Leoneed Kirilov
Bulgarian Academy of Sciences, Bulgaria

Vassil Guliashki
Bulgarian Academy of Sciences, Bulgaria

Boris Staykov
Bulgarian Academy of Sciences, Bulgaria

ABSTRACT

A web-based Decision Support System WebOptim for solving multiple objective optimization problems is presented. The system WebOptim is designed in a modular principle, extensively using XML as communication standard and web services. Its basic characteristics are: user-independent, multisolver-admissibility, method-independent, heterogeneity, web-accessibility. Core system module is an original generalized interactive scalarizing method. It incorporates a number of thirteen interactive methods. Most of the known scalarizing approaches (reference point approach, reference direction approach, classification approach etc.) are realized in this method. The Decision Maker (DM) can choose the most suitable for him/her form for setting his/her preferences: objective weights, aspiration levels, aspiration directions, aspiration intervals. This information could be changed interactively by the DM during the solution process. Depending on the DM's preferences form the suitable scalarizing method is chosen automatically. The chapter begins with an overview of Decision Support Systems (DSS). Examples of DSSs and their applications are discussed.

INTRODUCTION

DOI: 10.4018/978-1-5225-6164-4.ch007

The Decision Support Systems (DSSs) are computer assisted tools that support Decision Makers (DMs) in solving different real problems. The concepts of DSS appeared in 70s soon after introducing the concepts of Decision Making by Herbert Simon (1960) - see Scott-Morton (1962), Filip et al. (2017). During the time there are various definitions and interpretations of DSSs. They all consider three characteristics of DSS – existing of a complex decision situation, a person or group of persons authorized to make decisions (Decision Maker(s)) and computer based tool to support the DM in decision making. These characteristics define and explain the constant expansion of theoretical development and practical implementation of DSS in different areas of human knowledge – Hosack et al. (2012), Power (2008), Shim et al. (2002). Respectively, the DSS' theory development and applications is inspired by the following factors:

- The necessity of taking complex decisions in our life.
- Natural limits of people.
- The potential of contemporary Information Technology tools and Optimization and Decision Making methods in theoretical and practical aspects as well.

In particular, the development of DSS considering multiple objectives in 80's started when Multiple Criteria Decision Making (MCDM) theory takes up its own place in the science - http://www.mcdm-society.org/.

Below we present a short overview of some DSS. We divide DSS in two basic classes. The first one is DSS with general purpose. What we mean by that is that DSS is designed to solve some basic class of decision making problem having exact defined mathematical model – for example linear or nonlinear or linear integer problem possibly including multiple objectives etc. When using such DSS the user has to formulate in advance his/her decision problem in terms of corresponding decision making model and after that to solve it with the help of selected DSS.

The second class are the DSS that are designed for solving a specific real problem – for example water resources management problem, or scheduling problem (job shop, flow shop) etc. This class of DSS we call specific purpose DSS or Problem Oriented MCDSS.

The paper is organized further as follows. In the next three sections we discuss examples of DSSs and their applications. The last section concerns the proposed DSS WebOptim. The paper ends with the conclusion.

DSS WITH GENERAL PURPOSE

Ruiz et al. (2015) presented a method based on the existing NAUTILUS method and called Enhanced NAUTILUS (E-NAUTILUS). This method borrows the motivation of NAUTILUS along with the human aspects related to avoiding trading-off and anchoring bias and extends its applicability for computationally expensive multi-objective optimization problems. In the E-NAUTILUS method, a set of Pareto optimal solutions is calculated in a pre-processing stage before the decision maker is involved. When the decision maker interacts with the solution process in the interactive decision making stage, no new optimization problem is solved, thus, avoiding the waiting time for the decision maker.

A DSS for solving multi-objective Redundancy Allocation Problems (RAPs) is considered by Khalili-Damghani (2014). Initially, the technique for Order Performance by Similarity to Ideal Solution method is used to reduce the multiple objective dimensions of the problem. The authors propose an efficient ε-constraint method to generate non-dominated solutions on the Pareto front. Finally, they use a Data Envelopment Analysis model to prune the non-dominated solutions. A benchmark case is presented to assess the performance of the proposed system, demonstrate the applicability of the proposed framework, and exhibit the efficacy of the procedures and algorithms.

In Sanches et al. (2018) it is presented the use and application of the TODA (Trade-off Decision Analysis) method. TODA is based on trade-off methodology in formation of prioritization matrix. The results show that the proposed method is comparable with AHP method but it is easier to operate. The method is demonstrated in a case study about the type of car for a fleet of vehicles.

A DSS has been developed in Filatovas and Kurasova (2011) for interactive solving multiple criteria optimization problems (MOPs). The adaptive weighted-sum (AWS) approach is implemented to solve the MOPs, generating solutions on a Pareto front and Pareto-optimal solutions in non-convex areas.

A multi-criteria recommender system, STROMa (SysTem of RecOmmendation Multi-criteria) is proposed to support decisions by aggregating measures of performance contained in a performance matrix – Fomba et al. (2017). The system makes inferences about preferences using a partial order on criteria input by the decision-maker. To determine a total ordering of the alternatives, STROMa uses a multi-criteria aggregation operator, the Choquet integral of a fuzzy measure.

A general-purpose decision-support system generator, called GANetXL, for developing specific applications that require multi-objective optimization of spreadsheet-based models is presented by Savic et al. (2011). The system is developed as an Excel add-in that provides easy access to evolutionary multi-objective optimization algorithms to non-specialists by incorporating an intuitive interactive graphical user interface that allows easy creation of specific decision-support applications. GANetXL's utility is demonstrated on two examples from water engineering practice.

A concept of "objective ranking" for creation of DSS is considered by Wierzbicki (2007). The rational objective ranking can be based on reference point approach, because reference levels needed in this approach can be established objectively statistically from the given data set. Examples show that such objective ranking can be very useful in many management situations.

The main characteristics of a decision support system (DSS) dealing with multi-objective integer and mixed-integer programming problems are presented by Alves and Climaco (2004). The DSS is based on interactive reference point approaches, developed by the authors for this kind of problems. It is implemented for Windows platforms and aims at providing an open communication protocol for interaction with the decision maker(s).

A software application for solving MCDM problems based on methods DEMATEL (Decision Making Trial and Evaluation Laboratory) and MMDE (maximum mean de-entropy) is proposed in Chen (2015). The software combines the two methods in a suitable way and incorporates friendly interfaces avoiding some of their application disadvantages like finding threshold value and complicated computing.

DSS WITH SPECIFIC PURPOSE

A real-world photovoltaic (PV)-based solar powered irrigation system applying multi-objective (MO) nonlinear optimization is described by Ganesan et al (2013). The Hyp-AP method is used to construct the approximate Pareto frontier as well as to identify the best solution option.

In Lisboa et al. (2016) it is proposed a MCDM Approach to the selection of novel technologies for Innovative In-Vehicle Information Systems (IVIS). They measured candidate technologies on eight qualitative criteria that were defined by domain experts, using a group decision-making approach. The main objective is to order all alternatives by their decision score, not the selection of one or a small set of them.

A DSS for road design is considered by Brauers et al. (2008). The authors implement a methodology for multi-objective optimization of multi-alternative decisions in road construction. The methodology used is on the basis of the Ratio Analysis (MOORA) method.

An approach to support the selection of businesses in the context of collaborative-networked organizations, through a negotiation process controlled by agents is proposed in Arrais-Castro et al. (2016). It is based on a dynamic multi-criteria decision model (DMCDM). The approach combines a dynamic decision making approach - using past, current and future information - with a software agents approach, which autonomously captures business opportunities, select business partners, as well as award and process associated orders. The authors demonstrate the advantages of the method with example for evaluation and selection of business partners.

The problem of supplier selection is solved in Mandić et al. (2016). The authors use the possibilities of a multi-attribute decision making (MADM). They include in the model also a consistent fuzzy logic (interpolative Boolean algebra) to model interdependencies among attributes. The research shows that decision makers were able to integrate their reasoning into the MADM model with the help of chosen fuzzy logic.

A comprehensive model for an industrial low-density polyethylene (LDPE) tubular reactor is presented by Agrawal (2006). The model parameters are tuned using industrial data on the temperature profile, the monomer conversion and the number-average molecular weight at the end of the reactor, and estimates of the several side products from the reactor. Complete details of the model are provided. Thereafter, a two-objective optimization of this LDPE reactor is performed; the monomer conversion is maximized while the sum of the normalized concentrations of the three important side products (methyl, vinyl, and vinylidene groups) is minimized. Three variants of the binary-coded non-dominated sorting genetic algorithm namely, NSGA-II, NSGA-II-JG, and NSGA-II-aJG are used to solve the optimization problem.

A new generation intelligent transportation system (ITS) is proposed by Yang et al. (2018), implementing the new generation ITS technology. A process-oriented structured system analysis is performed on the existing intelligent transportation architecture to establish an intelligent transportation system based on the new generation wireless communication technology. The required additional capabilities of network, services and application support in the view of user, function, information, connection and communication are discussed in an in-depth analysis of the system.

A method based on embedded systems to survey the population of endangered waterbirds in natural habitat is developed by Boulmaiz et al. (2017). The identification of different waterbird species can be done from an automatic recognition of their sounds. For noise estimation in noisy water bird's sound, a tonal region detector (TRD) using a sigmoid function is introduced. Then, the features Mel Frequency Cepstral Coefficients post processed by Spectral Subtraction (MFCC-SS) are extracted for classification using Support Vector Machine classifier. A development of the Simulink analysis models of classic MFCC and MFCC-SS is described. The audio recognition system is implemented in real time.

A distributed traffic cloud data center based on SOA (Service-Oriented Architecture) fused with cloud computing is introduced in Zhang et al. (2017). In addition, network-aware energy conservation scheduling DENS (Data-center Energy-efficient Network-aware Scheduling) algorithm applied in cloud data center is put forward to realize the full utilization of all kinds of resources in the cloud data center.

Experimental results also show the effectiveness of the proposed algorithm by comparing with traditional DENS algorithms. The distributed traffic cloud data center has low utilization of IT equipment and data resources as a result of rigid IT structure, high maintenance costs and high energy consumption in system operation.

An efficient decision support system for detection of medical renal disease using small feature space consisting of only second order GLCM statistical features computed from raw renal ultrasound images is proposed by Sharma and Virmani (2017). The GLCM mean feature vector and GLCM range feature vector are computed for inter-pixel distance d varying from 1 to 10. These texture feature vectors are combined in various ways yielding GLCM ratio feature vector, GLCM additive feature vector and GLCM concatenated feature vector. This work explores the potential of five texture feature vectors computed using GLCM statistics exhaustively for differential diagnosis between normal and MRD images using SVM classifier.

A system for securing wireless sensor networks is proposed by Kumar and Nagarajan (2013).. Security scheme is designed by considering the multi cluster based topology control through a multiple intensity keying. It has low communication energy due to its multi cluster-key executive. INTK Scheme acquires results on 4.5% improved security level with lesser execution time and communication energy consumption.

A health monitoring system is designed and realized by Cinque et al. (2012). Remote and continuous monitoring of patient's vital signs is the target of an emerging business market that aims both to improve the quality of life of patients and to reduce costs of national healthcare services. Such applications, however, are particularly critical from the point of view of dependability. The design proposed by Cinque et al. (2012) is based on the results of a detailed failure modes and effects analysis (FMEA), conducted to identify the typical dependability threats of health monitoring systems. The FMEA allowed the authors to conceive a set of configurable monitoring services, enriching the system with the ability to detect failures at runtime, and enabling the realization of dependable services for future mobile health monitoring systems.

In Phoksawat, Mahmuddin (2017, 2016) an ontology-based knowledge with multi-objective optimization model framework in intercropping for crop planning is proposed. Decision models for food industry are presented in Frej et al. (2017) and Dellino et al. (2017). A DSS in the context of business decision support are presented in Abbas and Rumman (2017) and Seletos and Salmon (2017). The optimum allocation of land uses with multi-objective optimization and spatial planning is studied in Karakostas (2017). A flood risk assessment with multiple objectives is presented in Yazdani and Zarate (2017). In Labonnote et al. (2017) a DSS in construction industry is presented. A DSS with two objectives for vessel speed decision in maritime logistics is presented in Lee et al. (2017). City bus tour planning is studied in Bagloee et al. (2017).

META-HEURISTICS USED IN VARIOUS DESIGN/DECISION MAKING SYSTEMS

Dey & Ashour (2016) review antenna array design optimization as well as direction of arrival optimization problem for different antennas configurations. The authors discuss three popular population-based meta-heuristic algorithms for optimal antenna design and direction of arrival estimation. Besides hybrid methods are highlighted.

Ant Colony Optimization (ACO) techniques for tuning Proportional-Integral-Derivative (PID) controller gain values of multi-area interconnected thermal power system are considered by Jagatheesan et al. (2017a). The system response is compared with and without considering Superconducting Magnetic Energy Storage (SMES) unit in the system. The comparative results clearly established that the system response with SMES unit improve the performance of system during sudden load disturbance.

Dey and Ashour (2017) presented a survey of Meta-Heuristic Algorithms in Medical Image Segmentation. The soft computing approaches attract attention of many researchers for problems solving in medical data applications. Image segmentation is the process that partitioned an image into some groups based on similarity measures. This process is employed for abnormalities volumetric analysis in medical images to identify the disease nature. Recently, meta-heuristic algorithms ((e.g., Cellular automata, ant colony optimization, Memetic algorithms, particle swarms, Tabu search, evolutionary computation and simulated annealing) are conducted to support the segmentation techniques.

Satapathy et al. (2016) consider Multi-level image thresholding using Otsu thresholding extensive scheme and chaotic bat algorithm (CBA), used to evaluate the optimal thresholds in several image segmentation applications. Maximization of between-class variance function in Otsu technique is used as the objective function to obtain the optimal thresholds for the considered grayscale images.

Tang et al. (2017) propose a new hybridized algorithm, which combines the dynamic group optimization (DGO) algorithm with the cross entropy method. The cross entropy method takes advantage of sampling the problem space by generating candidate solutions using the distribution, then it updates the distribution based on the better candidate solution discovered. The novel algorithm avoids the decrease of the population diversity and the premature convergence, which could happen in DGO algorithm due to the two mutation operators of DGO.

Dey (2018) discusses the latest empirical research on methods and approaches that include meta-heuristics for further system improvements, applying optimization algorithms. A broad range of topics such as manufacturing, genetic programming, and medical imaging are considered.

Ahmed et al. (2017) propose a combination of a backpropagation neural network fuzzy classifier and a neuro-fuzzy model for diagnosing the Crohn's disease (CD). Factor analysis is used for data dimension reduction. The effect on the system performance has been investigated when using fuzzy partitioning and dimension reduction. Additionally, further comparison is done between the different levels of the fuzzy partition to reach the optimal performance accuracy level. The performance evaluation of the proposed system is estimated using the classification accuracy and other metrics.

Kaliannan et al. (2016) describes the application of an Artificial Intelligence (AI) optimization technique to design Proportional-Integral-Derivative (PID) controller for Load Frequency Control (LFC) of single area re-heat thermal power system. The PI-/ PID- controllers gain values are optimized using conventional method and AI optimization technique, respectively. The robustness of ACO based PID controller in the system under different loading conditions in the presence and absent of nonlinearities and boiler dynamics is proven.

Jagatheesan et al. (2017b) present an application of bio-inspired flower pollination algorithm (FPA) for tuning proportional–integral–derivative (PID) controller in load frequency control (LFC) of multi-area interconnected power system. The investigated power system comprises of three equal thermal power systems with appropriate PID controller. The controller gain (proportional, integral and derivative gain) values are tuned by using the FPA algorithm with one percent step load perturbation in area 1. The integral square error (ISE) is considered the objective function for the FPA. The supremacy performance of proposed algorithm for optimized PID controller is proved by comparing the results with genetic algorithm (GA) and particle swarm optimization (PSO)-based PID controller under the same investigated power system.

Jagatheesan et al. (2017c) consider a load frequency control (LFC) of multi-area reheat thermal power system with proportional-integral-derivative (PID) controller. The interconnected control areas are provided with a single stage reheat turbine in all areas. The proportional gain, integral gain and derivative gain values of the PID controller are simultaneously optimised using recent and powerful evolutionary computational intelligence technique, namely the particle swarm optimisation (PSO) algorithm. The superiority of the PSO-based PID controller has been proved by comparing its performance to recent modern optimisation techniques such as hill climbing (HC) algorithm and genetic algorithm (GA) tuned controllers for the same multi-area thermal power system.

Jagatheesan et al. (2017d) consider multi-area (having five areas) reheat thermal power systems are considered with Proportional-Integral-Derivative (PID) controller as a supplementary controller. Each area in the investigated power system is equipped with appropriate governor unit, turbine with reheater unit, generator and speed regulator unit. The PID controller parameters are optimized by considering nature bio-inspired Firefly Algorithm (FFA). The authors make a comparison of the proposed system performance (FFA-PID) with optimized PID controller based Genetic Algorithm (GA) (GAPID) and Particle Swarm Optimization (PSO) technique (PSOPID) for the same investigated power system. The results prove the efficiency of employing the Integral Time Absolute Error (ITAE) cost function with one percent Step Load Perturbation (1% SLP) in area 1. The proposed system based FFA achieved the least settling time compared to using the GA or the PSO algorithms, while, it attained good results with respect to the peak overshoot/undershoot.

Jagatheesan et al. (2015) design and proposed a Proportional-Integral (PI) controller for Load Frequency Control (LFC) of a single area reheat thermal power system. The controller parameters, Proportional and Integral gain values, were optimized and properly tuned using the Stochastic Particle Swarm Optimization (SPSO) technique. Three different objective functions are considered for investigation, Integral Absolute Error (IAE), Integral Square Error (ISE) and Integral Time Absolute Error (ITAE) with one percent Step Load (1% SLP). Finally, simulation results show that IAE based PI controller response settled quickly with minimum over and undershoot compared to other objective function based controller performance.

Chatterjee et al. (2017a) propose a particle swarm optimization trained neural network for structural failure prediction of multistoried RC buildings. The authors propose a particle swarm optimization-based approach to train the NN (NN-PSO). The PSO is employed to find a weight vector with minimum root-mean-square error (RMSE) for the NN. The proposed (NN-PSO) classifier is capable to tackle the problem of predicting structural failure of multistoried reinforced concrete buildings via detecting the failure possibility of the multistoried RC building structure in the future.

Karaa et al. (2016) proposed an enhancement genetic algorithm based approach for document clustering to accelerate the procedure of research and information retrieval dealing with the largest biomedical literature database MEDLINE.

Chatterjee et al. (2017b) employ a Multi-objective Genetic Algorithm (MOGA) to train a Neural Network (NN) based model for predicting the structural failure of a Reinforced Concrete (RC) structure. The NN has been trained with MOGA to minimize the Root Mean Squared Error (RMSE) and Maximum Error (ME) toward optimizing the weight vector of the NN.

BASIC CHARACTERISTICS OF DSS WEBOPTIM

DSS WebOptim is designed to solve multi-objective optimization problems.

The multi-objective optimization problem (MOP) can be defined as:

$$\text{Maximize } \left\{ f_k(x),\, k \in K \right\} \tag{1}$$

$$\text{subject to: } x \in X \tag{2}$$

where $f(x) = \left(f_1(x),\, f_2(x), \ldots.. f_k(x)\right)$ is a vector of *k* concave objective functions, which must be simultaneously maximized.

A solution $x = (x_1, x_2, \ldots\ldots, x_n)$ is a vector of *n* decision variables, belonging to non-empty feasible convex set $X \subset R^n$. The objective functions (1) constitute a *k*-dimensional subspace, called objective space $F \subset R^k,\; F = \left\{ f(x) \mid x \in X \right\}$.

It is expected that at least two among all objectives are in conflict, so that the problem (1-2) does not possess a unique optimal solution in the objective space. Instead a conception of Pareto optimality or non-domination is used - see for example (Branke et al., 2008; Miettinen, 1999; Steuer, 1986). Then a solution $x^{(1)}$ is said to be Pareto optimal if and only if there does not exist another solution x, such that $f_k(x^{(1)}) \geq f_k(x)$ for each $k \in K$ and for at least one index *k* a strict inequality holds. Sometimes a weak Pareto optimality conception is used that is a relaxation of Pareto optimality.

The Decision Maker (DM) chooses a final (best compromise) solution according his/her preferences from the set of found Pareto optimal solutions. In other words solving a MOPs is a process of decision making with participation of a human factor.

The DSS WebOptim is a successor of the general-purpose software system MKO-2 (Vassilev et al., 2008). Its main characteristics are:

- Useful to a wide variety of users from different professional backgrounds with different level of optimization competence.
- A user friendly customizable interface, reflecting the needs of different users and accessible worldwide via the Web;
- A set of solvers (unified in a generalized scalarizing method) which covers many MOP methods;
- Various solutions can be obtained applying different methods according to the same preferences;
- Designed to be easily extended by adding new solvers;
- Providing an API interface for external use by third party developers.

The system WebOptim consists of several modules, incorporated and supported by a common frame. The purpose of a frame is to ensure extensibility of the system, API interface and Web communication. The main parts of the WebOptim are the solvers. The basic solver is the generalized scalarizing interactive method (IM), called GENS-IM.

GENERALIZED SCALARIZING PROBLEM

The Interactive Scalarizing Methods (ISMs) present a significant part among the methods for solving multi-objective optimization problems - see for example (Branke et al., 2008; Hwang & Masud, 1979; Miettinen, 1999; Steuer, 1986). ISMs differ in the way the DM gives his/her aspirations (Decision Phase) and in the way the Pareto optimal solutions are generated (Computation Phase). Further each ISM has its own strategy for scanning the Pareto surface. But the common in ISMs is that each of them in practice uses some kind of scalarizing optimization problem for generating Pareto solutions. On the other hand, when trying to solve MOP - for example using methods where the DM's preferences are in terms of reference points (Korhonen & Laakso, 1986; Nakyama & Sawaragi, 1984; Wierzbicki, 1980, 1986), then in general case the computed solutions could differ for identical reference point. Therefore it is worthy of looking for ways to combine ISMs in a more general formulation. Thus the DM has the possibility to solve MOP using different strategies (methods). Another possibility is if he/she can switch the methods from iteration to iteration. The best way is the choice of a method to be hidden to the DM if possible because it is not necessary the DM to be familiar with the methodology used for solving the problem. Kaliszewski uses the term "environment" for such approach (Kaliszewski, 2004), where different methods are united and DM can be readily select the way of specifying preference information. Note that in this case the software design and interface has considerable importance also. Up to now a number of generalized algorithms and generalized scalarizing problems have been developed (Caballero et al. 2002; Gardiner & Steuer, 1994; Luque et al., 2011; Miettinen & Mäkelä, 2006; Romero 2001; Ruiz et al., 2012; Vassilev 2002; Vassileva et al. 2005).

The generalized scalarizing method for solving MOPs is based on a generalized scalarizing model GENS. This model is introduced firstly in Vassilev (2002) and an improved variant is presented in Vassileva et al. (2005).

The generalized scalarizing problem GENS is defined as:

Minimize:

$$T(x) = \max\left\{\max_{k\in K^{\geq}}\left[F_k^1 - f_k(x)\right]G_k^1\ r_1\ \max_{k\in K^{\leq}}\left[F_k^2 - f_k(x)\right]G_k^2\ r_2\ \max_{k\in K^{<}}\left[F_k^3 - f_k(x)\right]G_k^3\ r_3\ \max_{k\in K^{>}}\left[F_k^4 - f_k(x)\right]G_k^4\right\} +$$

$$+\sum_{k\in K^0}\left[F_k^5 - f_k(x)\right]G_k^5 + \rho\left\{\sum_{k\in K^{\geq}}\left[F_k^1 - f_k(x)\right]G_k^1 + \sum_{k\in K^{\leq}}\left[F_k^2 - f_k(x)\right]G_k^2 + \sum_{k\in K^{<}}\left[F_k^3 - f_k(x)\right]G_k^3 +\right.$$

$$\left. +\sum_{k\in K^{>}}\left[F_k^4 - f_k(x)\right]G_k^4 - \sum_{k\in K^{=}\cup K^{><}} f_k(x)G_k^5\right\} \tag{3}$$

subject to

$$f_k(x) \geq f_k, \quad k \in K^{>} \cup K^{=}, \tag{4}$$

$$f_k(x) \geq f_k - D_k, \quad k \in K^{\leq}, \tag{5}$$

$$f_k(x) \geq f_k - t_k^-, k \in K^{><}, \tag{6}$$

$$f_k(x) \leq f_k + t_k^+, k \in K^{><}, \tag{7}$$

$$x \in X, \tag{8}$$

where

- ρ is a small positive number;
- K is the set of all objectives' indices;
- f_k - the current objective value of $f_k(x), \quad k \in K$;
- $G_k^1, G_k^2, G_k^3, G_k^4, G_k^5$ are scalarizing coefficients for 5 classes of objectives' indices;
- $F_k^1, F_k^2, F_k^3, F_k^4, F_k^5$ are parameters, concerning aspiration, current or other levels of objectives' values;
- $r_1, r_2, r_3 \in$ {"+", ", "}
- $D_\blacklozenge$ is the amount by which the DM agrees to deteriorate the objective value f_k (0< $D_\blacklozenge < \infty$);
- $K^{\geq}$ is the set of objectives' indices for which the DM wants to improve the corresponding objective values till to the given aspiration levels F_k^1 ;
- $K^{>}$ is the set of objective' indices for which the DM wants to improve the corresponding objective values;
- $K^{\leq}$ is the set of objective' indices for which the DM agrees to deteriorate the corresponding objective values till to the given aspiration levels F_k^2 , i.e. $F_k^2 \geq f_\blacklozenge - D_k$;
- $K^{<}$ is the set of objective' indices for which the DM agrees to deteriorate the corresponding objective values;
- $K^{=}$ is the set of objective' indices for which the DM wants their current values not to be deteriorated;
- $K^{><}$ is the set of objective' indices for which the DM wants to change the corresponding objective values in some intervals;
- t_k^- and t_k^+ are the lower and upper bounds for the objective values of the objective $f_k(x)$ with index $k \in K^{><}$;
- K^0 is the set of objective' indices for which the DM does not set explicitly aspirations to change the corresponding objective values.

This scalarizing problem is correctly defined under the natural requirements $K^{\geq} \neq \emptyset$ and/or $K^{>} \neq \emptyset$ and $K^{0} \neq K$. In other words, the problem is correct if the DM wants to improve at least one objective or he/she sets his/her preferences in an implicit way.

The solutions of this problem are weak Pareto optimal or Pareto optimal in case the additive part is included (Vassileva, 2006) - see formula (3).

The following scalarizing problems can be derived from the above scalarizing problem (we use notations to make difference between them): the MinMax or Chebyshev scalarizing problem (Steuer & Choo, 1983), the weighted sum scalarizing problem WS (Gass & Saaty, 1955; Zadeh, 1963), the scalarizing problem of ε–constraint method EC (Haimes et al., 1971), STEM scalarizing problem (Benayoun et al., 1971), STOM scalarizing problem (Nakayama & Sawaragi, 1984), the scalarizing problem of the reference point RP (Wierzbicki, 1980), GUESS scalarizing problem (Buchanan, 1997), the scalarizing problem of the modified reference point MRP (Vassilev et al., 2001), the scalarizing problem of VIG method (Korhonen & Laakso, 1986; Korhonen, 1997), the scalarizing problem of reference direction method RD (Vassilev et al., 1992); Narula et al., 1992, 1994), the scalarizing problem of reference direction RD2 (Vassilev & Narula, 1993), the classification-oriented scalarizing problem NIMBUS (Miettinen, 1999; Miettinen & Mäkelä 2002; Miettinen & Mäkelä 2006) the classification-oriented scalarizing problem DALDI (Vassileva et al., 2001).

In the weighted sum scalarizing problems the DM specifies his/her preferences by the values of the criteria weights, while in the scalarizing problems of the ε-constraint method – by the selection of one function for optimization and defining the lower bounds of change of the remaining criteria. In the reference point scalarizing problem the reference point is determined by the aspiration levels of the criteria and these levels are the ones that the DM wishes or agrees to be obtained in the new solution. These aspiration levels of the criteria are parameters of the reference point scalarizing problems. In the classification-oriented scalarizing problems not only the aspiration levels could be parameters of the multicriteria problem being solved, but also the directions and intervals of alteration in the criteria values that the DM wishes or agrees to be obtained in the new solution.

Let us illustrate for example in which way the reference point method (RP) (Wierzbicki, 1980) can be derived from problem GENS.

In RP the DM defines the objective aspiration levels as reference point $\bar{z}$. After comparing the reference point $\bar{z}$ and current solution we can divide the objectives into two classes $K^{\geq}$ and $K^{\leq}$ or only members of just the first class. The formulation of RP problem is:

$$\min\ g(x)$$

$$x \in X;$$

where $g(x) = \max\left(\max_{k \in K^{\geq}} \frac{\left(\bar{z}_k - f_k(x)\right)}{\left|\bar{z}_k\right|}, \max_{k \in K^{\leq}} \frac{\left(\bar{z}_k - f_k(x)\right)}{\left|\bar{z}_k\right|} \right),$

If we use the index subsets $K^{\geq}$ and $K^{\leq}$ defined in GENS problem, and set:

1. $K^{>} = K^{<} = K^{=} = K^{><} = K^{0} = \emptyset,$

2. $R_1 = $ "," ,
3. $F_k^1 = F_k^2 = \bar{z}_k$,
4. $G_k^1 = G_k^2 = \frac{1}{|\bar{z}_k|}$,
5. $D_{\blacklozenge} = \infty$,
6. $\rho = 0$.

then the RP problem is derived.

GENERALIZED SCALARIZING INTERACTIVE METHOD

The generalized interactive method GENS - IM is developed on the basis of the scalarizing model GENS and has the following characteristics:

- The DM may set his/her preferences with the help of the criteria weights, ε - constraints, desired and acceptable levels of change of the criteria values, directions and intervals of alteration in the criteria values;
- During the multicriteria problems solving process, the DM may change the way of presenting his/her preferences;
- Starting from one and the same current solution and applying different scalarizing problems (with respective alteration of GENS parameters), the DM may obtain different new (weak) Pareto optimal solutions at a given iteration. This opportunity is especially useful in education and in comparison of different scalarizing methods.

The basic scheme of the generalized scalarizing interactive method (GENS-IM) is as follows:

- **Step 1. (Type of Preferences):** The DM sets type of preferences. The selection of an appropriate method for solving is made based on the selected type of preferences;
- **Step 2. (Preferences):** The DM sets the preference values.
- **Step 3. (Solution):** Generation of (weak) Pareto optimal solution(s);
- **Step 4. (Evaluation):** Evaluation of (weak) Pareto optimal solution(s) obtained. If the DM approves one of these solutions as the most preferred solution and he/she wishes to stop the procedure, then go to Step 5; otherwise if he/she wishes to continue the solution with the same type of preferences then go to **Step 2**, if he/she wishes to change the type of preferences then go to **Step 1.**
- **Step 5:** Stop the operation of the generalized interactive method.

In more details, the choosing the type of preferences, the setting of preferences, and the choice-defining of corresponding scalarizing problem are performed in **Step 1** as follows:.

- **Substep 1.1:** If the DM chooses to set his/her preferences by criteria weights, then:
- **1.1.1:** If he/she wishes to use a general criterion in form of weighted sum of the objectives then the problem WS is chosen; Go to **Step 2**.

- **1.1.2:** If he/she wishes to use a general criterion in form of minimization toward ideal point then the problem MinMax is chosen; Go to **Step 2**.
- **Substep 1.2:** If the DM decides to optimize one objective versus the rest of others then the problem EC is chosen; Go to **Step 2**.
- **Substep 1.3:** If the DM chooses to set his/her preferences in terms of reference point in the objective space, then:
- **1.3.1:** If the DM wants to set levels for relaxing only a part of the objectives, then the problem STEM is chosen; Go to **Step 2**.
- **1.3.2:** If the DM wants to use marginal rates of substitution, then the problem STOM is chosen; Go to **Step 2**.
- **1.3.3:** If the DM wants to search for solutions maximally remote from the nadir vector, then the problem GUESS is chosen; Go to **Step 2**.
- **1.3.4:** If the DM wants to set reference levels for all objectives without taking into account the current solution, then the problem RP is chosen; Go to **Step 2**.
- **1.3.5:** If the DM wants to set reference levels taking into account the current solution, then the problem MRP is chosen; Go to **Step 2**.
- **Substep 1.4:** If the DM decides to generate a number of solutions along a specified direction, then:
- **1.4.1:** If the DM wants to set his/her preferences in terms of reference points without taking into account the current solution, then the problem VIG is chosen; Go to **Step 2**.
- **1.4.2:** If the DM wants to divide criteria in three classes ($K^{\geq}, K^{=}, K^{\leq}$) taking into account the current solution and he/she wants to see a predefined number of solutions, then the problem RD is chosen; Go to **Step 2**.
- **1.4.3:** If the DM wants to divide criteria in three classes ($K^{\geq}, K^{=}, K^{\leq}$) according to the current solution and he/she wants to see a finite number of solutions along reference direction (from current solution to the reference point), then the problem RD2 is chosen; Go to **Step 2**.
- **Substep 1.5:** If the DM chooses to define his/her preferences in terms of classification of objectives in a number of preliminary defined sets of classes, then
- **1.5.1:** If the DM selects to set preferences for each objective using a frame of five possibilities: to be improved as much as possible, to be improved till some desired aspiration level, to either preserve or improve the current objective value, to be relaxed till some level and objectives with no limitations - then the problem NIMBUS is chosen. Go to **Step 2**.
- **1.5.2:** If the DM selects to set preferences for each objective using a frame of seven possibilities: to be improved as much as possible, to be improved by desired values or till some desired aspiration level, to preserve or improve the current value, to deteriorate, to deteriorate by desired values or till some desired aspiration level, to keep the objective values in an interval and objectives with no limitations - then the problem DALDI is chosen. Go to **Step 2**.

The proposed generalized interactive method is a method with variable scalarization and parameterization. This generalization corresponds to the classes of the problems solved, the type of defined preferences, the number and type of the scalarizing problems used, the strategies utilized in the search for new Pareto optimal solutions. Thus the generalized scalarizing method GENS-IM enables the implicit choice of different scalarizing problems.

Figure 1. Architecture of WebOptim

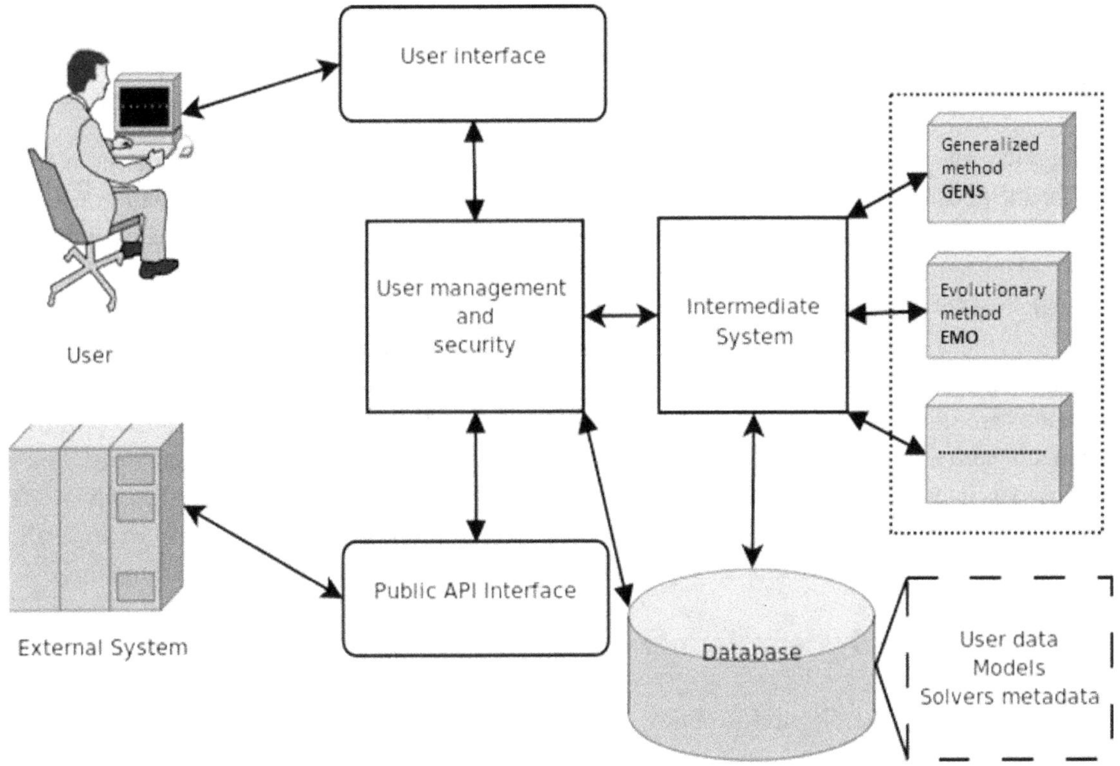

SOFTWARE DESIGN OF WEBOPTIM

The system WebOptim is designed in a modular principle. For maximum flexibility the system is composed of the following main components: user management and security, intermediate module, database and solvers - see Figure 1.

User Management and Security

This module ensures the Web-access, individual data storage and data-security, as well as suitable syntax for entering the data. In order to use the system, each user must create its own personal profile. The profile containing login credentials, user type, personal details, defined problems, their solutions and additional information about errors and specific solving details will be stored in a common database. The registration of users will be done through standard web page forms. After registering and logging in their profile, the users will be provided with interface for defining and solving problems. Those problems must be defined using the developed syntax which is very close to the LP and CPlex format. After syntax verification, each problem will be stored in the database with unique ID parameter. The user will be able to see a list of these defined problems and their status - {"Not solved", "Waiting for solution", "Solution obtained", "Solver error"} for example.

This module provides tools for the user: to preview problems and solutions; to start or to interrupt solution process for certain problem; to preview error messages received from the solvers and to obtain specific detailed debug information about the solving process (if the chosen solver provides this information).

Database

The main database stores all the data for the users, problems they have saved, solutions and metadata about the methods and solvers for use in the intermediate system. The metadata should contain at least the solver's name, description, type (integer, mixed integer, multi-criteria, etc.) and type(s) of accepted input. Because of the network environment the system will only run if the solvers need a database for temporary data during the solving process, they can use their DBMS (database management system) and databases to minimize the communication volumes and thus reduce the computation time. To overcome the lack of connection persistence between the client and the server in web-based systems all intermediate and final results are stored in the database, which is possible due to the nature of these types of optimization problems, where every intermediate result can be used as a reference point for the next (every method can be used as interactive). This also allows unbinding of the calculation process from the user interface. The user is no longer required to wait for the solution and to keep the connection alive because all the results will be stored in database and associated with his/her personal profile and problem.

Intermediate Core System Module

This module realizes the original structure of the system ensuring the intermediate communication between all other modules.

The fact that the system will be used as an educational and research tool means that it has to be as open and extensible as possible, so new methods, solvers, problem types, and basically every kind of modules can be added later. The development team is heterogeneous and not static, especially for the projected lifetime of the product, so different software libraries and components and different program languages will be used in it, which put a lot of stress on the system architectural design. To make these different parts glued together several modern technologies and principles are applied to the development process – extensive use of XML as communication standard and web services.

There is one major problem that concerns the intercommunication between the different modules in the system. The problem appears because this intercommunication needs to be done asynchronous due to its nature - mainly HTTP and SOAP protocols, which have very tight response timeouts. Depending on its size, each solving problem will take different time to be solved by a certain solver and sent back to the sender module. This makes it impossible for the communication to be done in an uninterrupted cycle of request-response.

This problem is solved by bringing in an intermediate system module, which will take care of all the communication between end user interfaces, database storage and solvers. This system will perform two main tasks – user management and solvers communication.

Solvers

All solvers implement a common XML SOAP protocol (Biron & Malhotra, 2004) for communication with the intermediate system. This allows diversity of the solvers, the machines they are running on, the language they are written in, etc. The limitation of this approach is that due the asynchronous nature of this type of communication, the control will be harder to implement, because in a simplified way the communication looks like this: intermediate system sends problem for solving and when ready, the solver gives an answer or an error message (if occurred).

By means of the Generalized interactive method GENS-IM are generated different scalarizing problems. The DM has the possibility to change his/her preferences periodically and to replace the former reference point by a new one. This step ensures the convergence of the proposed method to a desired non-dominated solution.

A solver for single objective linear and integer linear problems is included in the system. It is used internally by the method GENS-IM for solving corresponding scalarizing problems.

The DSS WebOptim up to this moment is designed for solving linear single- and multi-objective optimization problems with continuous and/or integer decision variables – (Genova et al., 2011; Staykov et al., 2011).

FUNCTIONAL FACILITIES OF THE GENERALIZED SCALARIZING METHOD GENS-IM

The multi-objective problems solving is a process of decision making, where the role of DM is crucial for the choice of the final solution. For this reason, in order one software system to be suitable for use by different groups of user – for practical, research or educational purposes, the functional facilities of the system, and particularly the system interface have essential importance.

The functional facilities of the user interface for applying the generalized scalarizing interactive method GENS-IM by the software system WebOptim can be divided in 3 groups.

The first group includes the facilities for creation, modification and storage of the input data of MOPs. The data syntax of the linear multi-objective programming problem is very close to the mathematical description. It is similar to other known formats as LP and CPlex.

The functional facilities from the second group ensure the implementation of the search process for (weak) PO solution by means of methods for multiple objective optimization. The DM has the possibility to choose the type of preferences about the search compromise solution. Here are proposed five types of preferences: by means of different criteria weights, choice of one criterion to be optimized and restricting the other criteria at the same time, input of reference values (aspiration levels) of the criteria, search for several solutions in a given direction of change for the criteria or by means of classification of the criteria according the desired change of their values. These preferences are determined according the values of the found current (weak) PO solution. For some types of preferences there is a possibility for further specifying the information entered. Further, the DM has the possibility to input by him/her-self the initial solution or this solution to be generated automatically. According to the chosen type of preferences a pop-up menu is opened for each criterion, where the DM inputs the corresponding numerical values. There is also a possibility to choose the type of searched solution - continuous one or integer one, strong or weak PO. DM can start the MOP solving from each of the solutions, found till this moment. By means of the Generalized scalarizing interactive method GENS-IM the corresponding scalarizing problem is generated implicitly. There is also a "Help" option, which gives to DM information about the current generalized scalarizing problem/method.

The third group functional facilities are connected with the visualization of information about the scalarizing problem/method being current used and about the obtained (weak) PO solutions. In order to

Figure 2. Interface of GENS-IM method

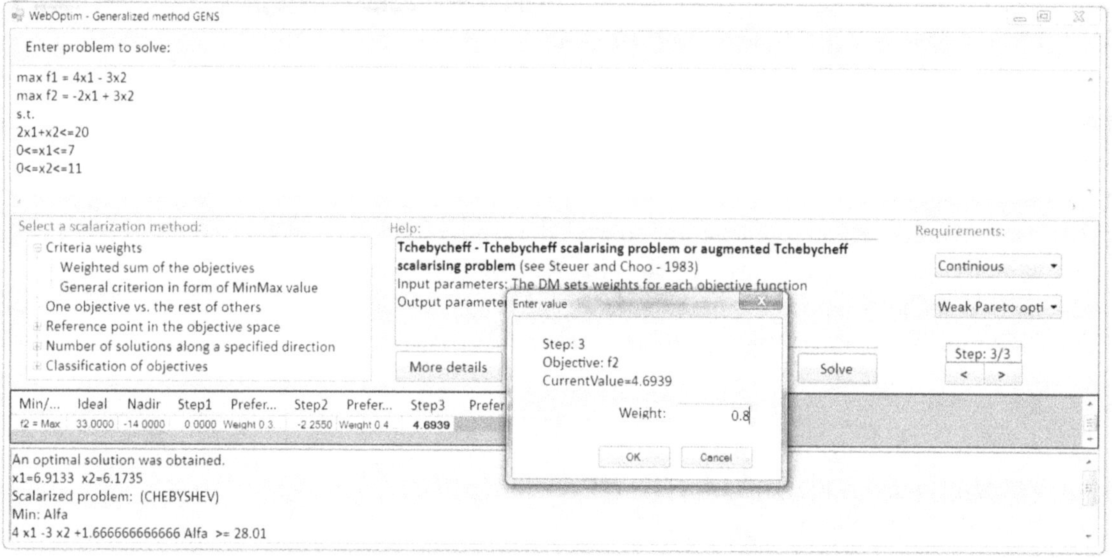

support DM in the evaluation of solutions and in the choice of his/her preferences, there are presented also the type of objective optimization (minimization / maximization) and the ideal and the nadir values.

The interface of GENS-IM is presented in Figure 2.

The DM has the possibility to store the history of the solution process in a file - computed solutions, preferences, scalarizing problems etc. This enables him/her to use this information later - for restarting from specified solution, restarting an interrupted solution process, analyzing.

THE DSS WEBOPTIM IN AN E-LEARNING CONTEXT

There are possibilities for distance/electronic education by means of WebOptim for students and post-graduate students in different areas: engineers, economists, persons making decisions (decision makers) in the management of enterprises and production processes, as well as all kinds of experts, who solve real life optimization problems in their activities (see Guliashki et al. (2013)).

The developed WebOptim system may be used as a training system for distance learning (e-learning), providing flexible high qualitative online courses in single- and multiple-objective optimization methods. The solvers engaged in WebOptim allow performance of test experiments for pure continuous, pure integer, as well as for mixed-integer optimization problems.

Because the system WebOptim is used both as an educational and as a research tool it is designed as an open and extensible system. New methods, solvers, problem types and basically every kind of modules can be added at any time. To fit different software libraries and components together the system is based on modern technologies and principles by applying extensive use of XML as communication standard and Web services.

With an Internet connection the students or postgraduate students can participate in online courses from any location in the world. The lecturer in the corresponding course has prepared series of common accessible examples with attached detailed description of the models and the methods, available for solving each example. It is suitable these series of examples to be used as training aid in the different courses. Starting by simple problems and continuing with always more and more complex problems, in this public profile the student can make steps from the fundamentals to advanced subjects. Each student has online access to the course content. The learning process is organized as follows:

Each student has to register himself into WebOptim system, creating a new account with username and password in the main menu of the system. After registering and logging in their profiles the students obtain a private status in addition to the public access. In this way after a student-lecturer communication the students obtain individual tasks. They have also individual access to concrete optimization problems and can perform exercises by means of the system.

All solvers implement a common API interface based on XML SOAP protocol for communication with the intermediate system. This allows diversity of the solvers, the machines they are running on, the language they are written in, etc. The interface is user-friendly and very convenient for mathematical presentation of different optimization problems.

There is available the possibility for choice of single-objective solvers, which can solve optimization problems with continuous and/or integer decision variables. The student obtains detailed information about the concrete solver, the implemented optimization method, as well as current results during the optimization procedure.

There is available the possibility for choose of multiple-objective solvers, which can solve the corresponding optimization problems interactively. Here can be solved already studied single-objective problems by simple addition of several new objectives into the current problem. The special features of multiple-objective problems can be studied.

In case multiple-objective problems should be solved, there are available different ways for presenting the user's preferences during the search process for a compromise non-dominated solution. The learning process includes a comparison of test results, obtained by means of different ways for submission of the user's preferences.

For tests of multiple-objective problems there are available 13 different methods, based on different type of scalarizing problems (ScPs): 1) the MinMax or Chebyshev's ScP, 2) the weighted sum ScP (WS), 3) the ScP of ε–constraint method EC, 4) STEM ScP, 5) STOM ScP, 6) the ScP of the reference point RP, 7) GUESS ScP, 8) the ScP of the modified reference point MRP, 9) the ScP of VIG method, 10) the ScP of reference direction method RD], 11) the ScP of reference direction RD2, 12) the classification-oriented ScP NIMBUS, 13) the classification-oriented ScP DALDI. The scalarizing approaches can be used by changing the method's parameters. The user can choose the most suitable for him/her form for setting his/her preferences: objective weights, aspiration levels, aspiration directions, aspiration intervals. This information could be changed interactively by the user during the solution process. Depending on the user's preferences the suitable scalarizing method is chosen automatically. In this way the demands on the user's knowledge and experience in the optimization methods area are minimized.

From the view-point of four groups of criteria for evaluation of the system quality (see Shee and Wang (2008)), WebOptim corresponds to and covers the following criteria: Group I (Learner Interface): Ease of use; User-friendliness; Ease of understanding; Operational stability; Group II (Learning Community): Ease of accessing shared data; Ease of discussion with teachers; Group III (System Content): Sufficient content; Useful content; Group IV (Personalization): Capability of controlling learning progress; Capability of recording learning performance.

CONCLUSION

The DSS WebOptim is a convenient tool for solving single and multi-objective optimization problems due to its structure and functional features. As it is pointed in Luque et al. (2011), the flexibility is the main feature of any interactive decision aid tool to be used successfully for solving real problems. This flexibility is realized in DSS WebOptim in several directions: accessibility via Internet in real time; it has user friendly interface and can be used easily by different groups of users; incorporating a large number of optimization strategies for selecting best compromise solution. The last is done due to generalized scalarizing method GENS - IM. It is a method with variable parameterization and scalarization. By changing the parameters of GENS-IM on the basis of the selected type of preferences, most known scalarizing approaches are realized.

WebOptim has an open structure and new methods could be easily incorporated.

In an e-learning context WebOptim has flexibility in several directions: 1) it is easy to be used by different group of students: for beginners and also for advanced online optimization courses; 2) it incorporates a large number of single- and multiple-objective optimization methods, as well as strategies for selecting the best compromise solution; 3) it can be easily extended by adding new solvers. In addition this system does not require any specific knowledge and experience from the students. These features make it very convenient as an e-learning application both for beginners and for advanced students or postgraduate students.

Some possibilities for future development of DSS WebOptim could be: including other exact and heuristic methods; including methods for solving some nonlinear multi-objective integer optimization problems; realization of the graphical interface.

DSS WebOptim can be found at http://weboptim.iinf.bas.bg/ .

REFERENCES

Ahmed, S. S., Dey, N., Ashour, A. S., Sifaki-Pistolla, D., Bălas-Timar, D., Balas, V. E., & Tavares, J. M. R. (2017). Effect of fuzzy partitioning in Crohn's disease classification: A neuro-fuzzy-based approach. *Medical & Biological Engineering & Computing*, *55*(1), 101–115. doi:10.100711517-016-1508-7 PMID:27106754

Alves, M. J., & Climaco, J. (2004). A note on a decision support system for multiobjective and mixed-integer programming problems. *European Journal of Operational Research*, *155*(1), 258–265. doi:10.1016/S0377-2217(02)00887-1

Arrais-Castro, A., Leonilde, M., Varela, R., Putnik, G. D., Ribeiro, R., & Dargam, F. C. (2016). Collaborative Negotiation Platform using a Dynamic Multi-Criteria Decision Model. *International Journal of Decision Support System Technology*, *7*(1), 1–14. doi:10.4018/ijdsst.2015010101

Bagloee, S. A., Tavana, M., Di Caprio, D., Asadi, M., & Heshmati, M. (2017). A multi-user decision support system for online city bus tour planning. *Journal of Modern Transportation*, *25*(2), 59–73. doi:10.100740534-017-0126-x

Benayoun, R., Montgolfier, J., Tergny, J., & Laritchev, O. (1971). Linear Programming with Multiple Objective Functions: Step Method (STEM). *Mathematical Programming*, *1*(1), 136–375. doi:10.1007/BF01584098

Biron, P., & Malhotra, A. (2004). *XML Schema Part 2: Datatypes*. Retrieved from https://www.w3.org/TR/xmlschema-2/

Boulmaiz, A., Messadeg, D., Doghmane, N., & Taleb-Ahmed, A. (2017). Design and Implementation of a Robust Acoustic Recognition System for Waterbird Species using TMS320C6713 DSK. *International Journal of Ambient Computing and Intelligence*, *8*(1), 98–118. doi:10.4018/IJACI.2017010105

Branke, J., Deb, K., Miettinen, K., & Slowinski, R. (2008). *Multiobjective Optimization: Interactive and Evolutionary Approaches*. Berlin: Springer-Verlag. doi:10.1007/978-3-540-88908-3

Brauers, W. K., Zavadskas, E. K., Peldschus, F., & Turskis, Z. (2008). Multi-objective decision-making for road design. *Transport*, *23*(3), 183–193. doi:10.3846/1648-4142.2008.23.183-193

Buchanan, J. T. (1997). A Naive Approach for Solving MCDM Problems: The GUESS Method. *The Journal of the Operational Research Society*, *48*(2), 202–206. doi:10.1057/palgrave.jors.2600349

Caballero, R., Luque, M., Molina, J., & Ruiz, F. (2002). PROMOIN: An interactive system for multi-objective programming. *International Journal of Information Theories and Decision Making*, *1*(04), 635–656. doi:10.1142/S0219622002000403

Chatterjee, S., Sarkar, S., Hore, S., Dey, N., Ashour, A. S., & Balas, V. E. (2017). Particle swarm optimization trained neural network for structural failure prediction of multistoried RC buildings. *Neural Computing & Applications*, *28*(8), 2005–2016. doi:10.100700521-016-2190-2

Chatterjee, S., Sarkar, S., Hore, S., Dey, N., Ashour, A. S., Shi, F., & Le, D. N. (2017). Structural failure classification for reinforced concrete buildings using trained neural network based multi-objective genetic algorithm. *Structural Engineering and Mechanics*, *63*(4), 429–438.

Chen, C. (2015). Construct a Multi Criteria Decision Making Tool: DEMATEL and MMDE Methods. *International Journal of Decision Support System Technology*, *7*(4), 36–50. doi:10.4018/IJDSST.2015100103

Cinque, M., Coronato, A., & Testa, A. (2012). Dependable Services for Mobile Health Monitoring Systems. *International Journal of Ambient Computing and Intelligence*, *4*(1), 1–15. doi:10.4018/jaci.2012010101

Dellino, G., Laudadio, T., Mari, R., Mastronardi, N., & Meloni, C. (2017). A reliable decision support system for fresh food supply chain management. *International Journal of Production Research*, 1–28. doi:10.1080/00207543.2017.1367106

Dey, N. (2018). Advancements in Applied Metaheuristic Computing. Hershey, PA: IGI Global. doi:10.4018/978-1-5225-4151-6

Dey, N., & Ashour, A. S. (2016). Antenna Design and Direction of Arrival Estimation in Meta-Heuristic Paradigm: A Review. *International Journal of Service Science, Management, Engineering, and Technology*, *7*(3), 1–18. doi:10.4018/IJSSMET.2016070101

Dey, N., & Ashour, A. S. (2017). Meta-Heuristic Algorithms in Medical Image Segmentation: A Review. *Advancements in Applied Metaheuristic Computing*, 185.

Filatovas, E., & Kurasova, O. (2011). A Decision Support System for Solving Multiple Criteria Optimization Problems. *Informatics in Education, 10*(2), 213–224.

Filip, F. G., Zamfirescu, B., & Ciurea, C. (2017). *Computer-Supported Collaborative Decision-Making Automation. In Collaboration & E-Services Series* (Vol. 4). Springer International Publishing AG. doi:10.1007/978-3-319-47221-8

Fomba, S., Zarate, P., Kilgour, M., Camilleri, G., Konate, J., & Tangara, F. (2017). A Recommender System Based on Multi-Criteria Aggregation. *International Journal of Decision Support System Technology*, *9*(4), 1–15. doi:10.4018/IJDSST.2017100101

Frej, E. A., Peixoto, L. R., Roselli, J. A., & Almeida, A. T. (2017). A Multicriteria Decision Model for Supplier Selection in a Food Industry Based on FITradeoff Method. *Hindawi -. Mathematical Problems in Engineering*, *2017*, 1–9. doi:10.1155/2017/4541914

Ganesan, T., Elamvazuthi, I., Shaari, K. Z., & Vasant, P. (2013). Hypervolume-Driven Analytical Programming for Solar-Powered Irrigation System Optimization. In Nostradamus 2013: Prediction, Modeling and Analysis of Complex Systems. Springer.

Gardiner, L., & Steuer, R. (1994). Unified interactive multiple objective programming: An open architecture for accommodating new procedures. *The Journal of the Operational Research Society*, *45*(12), 1456–1466. doi:10.1057/jors.1994.222

Gass, S., & Saaty, T. (1955). The Computational Algorithm for the Parametric Objective Function. *Naval Research Logistics Quarterly*, *2*(1-2), 39–45. doi:10.1002/nav.3800020106

Genova, K., Kirilov, L., Guliashki, V., Staykov, B., & Vatov, D. (2011). A Prototype of a Web-based Decision Support System for Building Models and Solving Optimization and Decision Making Problems. *Proceedings of XII Int. Conference on Computer Systems and Technologies - CompSysTech'11*, 167-172. 10.1145/2023607.2023636

Ghaleb, Y., Abbas, I. H., & Rumman, A. (2017). ERP Decision Support System Using Multi Objective Optimization – An Exploratory Study. *Proceedings of 56th IASTEM International Conference*, 57-64.

Guliashki, V., Genova, K., & Kirilov, L. (2013), The Decision Support System WebOptim in an E-Learning Context. *Proceedings of Papers of the International Conference Automatics and Informatics 2013*, 117-120.

Haimes, Y., Landson, L. S., & Wismer, D. A. (1971). On a Bicriterion Formulation of the Problems of Integrated System Identification and System Optimization. *IEEE Transactions on Systems, Man, and Cybernetics*, *1*, 296–297.

Hosack, B., Hall, D., Paradice, D., & Courtney, J. F. (2012). A look toward the future: Decision Support Systems research is alive and well. *Journal of the Association for Information Systems*, *13*(5), 315–340. doi:10.17705/1jais.00297

Hwang, C., & Masud, A. (1979). *Multiple objective decision making-methods and applications: a state of the art survey*. Berlin, Germany: Springer. doi:10.1007/978-3-642-45511-7

Jagatheesan, K., Anand, B., Dey, N., & Ashour, A. S. (2017). Effect of SMES Unit in AGC of an Interconnected Multi-Area Thermal Power System With ACO-Tuned PID Controller. *Advancements in Applied Metaheuristic Computing*, 164.

Jagatheesan, K., Anand, B., Dey, N., Gaber, T., Hassanien, A. E., & Kim, T. H. (2015, September). A Design of PI Controller using Stochastic Particle Swarm Optimization in Load Frequency Control of Thermal Power Systems. In *Information Science and Industrial Applications (ISI), 2015 Fourth International Conference on* (pp. 25-32). IEEE.

Jagatheesan, K., Anand, B., Samanta, S., Dey, N., Ashour, A. S., & Balas, V. E. (2017). Design of a proportional-integral- derivative controller for an automatic generation control of multi-area power thermal systems using firefly algorithm. *IEEE/CAA Journal of Automatica Sinica*.

Jagatheesan, K., Anand, B., Samanta, S., Dey, N., Ashour, A. S., & Balas, V. E. (2017). Particle swarm optimisation-based parameters optimisation of PID controller for load frequency control of multi-area reheat thermal power systems. *International Journal of Advanced Intelligence Paradigms*, *9*(5-6), 464–489. doi:10.1504/IJAIP.2017.088143

Jagatheesan, K., Anand, B., Samanta, S., Dey, N., Santhi, V., Ashour, A. S., & Balas, V. E. (2017). Application of flower pollination algorithm in load frequency control of multi-area interconnected power system with nonlinearity. *Neural Computing & Applications*, *28*(1), 475–488. doi:10.100700521-016-2361-1

Kaliannan, J., Baskaran, A., Dey, N., & Ashour, A. S. (2016). Ant colony optimization algorithm based PID controller for LFC of single area power system with non-linearity and boiler dynamics. *World J. Model. Simul*, *12*(1), 3–14.

Kaliszewski, I. (2004). Out of the mist—towards decision-maker-friendly multiple criteria decision making support. *European Journal of Operational Research*, *158*(2), 293–307. doi:10.1016/j.ejor.2003.06.005

Karaa, W. B. A., Ashour, A. S., Sassi, D. B., Roy, P., Kausar, N., & Dey, N. (2016). Medline text mining: an enhancement genetic algorithm based approach for document clustering. In *Applications of Intelligent Optimization in Biology and Medicine* (pp. 267–287). Springer International Publishing. doi:10.1007/978-3-319-21212-8_12

Karakostas, S. M. (2017). Bridging the gap between multi-objective optimization and spatial planning: A new post-processing methodology capturing the optimum allocation of land uses against established transportation infrastructure. *Transportation Planning and Technology*, *40*(3), 305–326. doi:10.1080/03081060.2017.1283157

Khalili-Damghani, K., Abtahi, A. R., & Tavana, M. (2014). A Decision Support System for Solving Multi-Objective Redundancy Allocation Problems. *Quality and Reliability Engineering International*, *30*(8), 1249–1262. doi:10.1002/qre.1545

Korhonen, P. (1997). Reference Direction Approach to Multiple Objective Linear Programming: Historical Overview. In Essay in Decision Making: A Volume in Honour of Stanley Zionts, (pp. 74-92). Berlin: Academic Press.

Korhonen, P., & Laakso, J. (1986). Solving Generalized Goal Programming Problems Using a Visual Interactive Approach. *European Journal of Operational Research*, *26*(3), 355–363. doi:10.1016/0377-2217(86)90137-2

Kumar, S., & Nagarajan, N. (2013). Integrated Network Topological Control and Key Management for Securing Wireless Sensor Networks. *International Journal of Ambient Computing and Intelligence*, *5*(4), 12–24. doi:10.4018/ijaci.2013100102

Labonnote, N., Skaar, C., & Rüther, P. (2017). The potential of decision support systems for more sustainable and intelligent constructions: a short overview. *Procedia Manufacturing, 12,* 33-41.

Lee, H., Aydin, N., Choi, Y., Lekhavat, S., & Irani, Z. (2017). A Decision Support System for Vessel Speed Decision in Maritime Logistics using Weather Archive Big Data. *Computers & Operations Research*. doi:10.1016/j.cor.2017.06.005

Lisboa, I. C., Vieira, J., Mouta, S., Machado, S., Ribeiro, N., Silva, E., ... Pereira, A. F. (2016). An MCDM Approach to the Selection of Novel Technologies for Innovative In-Vehicle Information Systems. *International Journal of Decision Support System Technology*, *8*(1), 43–55. doi:10.4018/IJDSST.2016010103

Luque, M., Ruiz, F., & Miettinen, K. (2011). Global formulation for interactive multiobjective optimization. *OR-Spektrum*, *33*(1), 27–48. doi:10.100700291-008-0154-3

Mandić, K., Delibašić, B., & Radojević, D. (2016). An Application of the Integrated IBA-TOPSIS Model in Supplier Selection. *International Journal of Decision Support System Technology*, *7*(1), 15–30. doi:10.4018/ijdsst.2015010102

Miettinen, K. (1999). *Nonlinear Multiobjective Optimization. Academic Publishers*. Boston: Kluwer.

Miettinen, K., & Mäkelä, M. (2002). On Scalarizing Functions in Multiobjective Optimization. *OR-Spektrum*, *24*, 193–213. doi:10.100700291-001-0092-9

Miettinen, K., & Mäkelä, M. (2006). Synchronous Approach in Interactive Multiobjective Optimization. *European Journal of Operational Research*, *170*(3), 909–922. doi:10.1016/j.ejor.2004.07.052

Nakayama, H., & Sawaragi, Y. (1984). Satisficing Trade-off Method for Multiobjective Programming. Lecture Notes in Economics and Mathematical Systems, 229, 113-122.

Narula, S., Kirilov, L., & Vassilev, V. (1992). Reference Direction Approach for Solving Multiple Objective Nonlinear Programming Problems. In *Proceedings of X-th International Conference on Multiple Criteria Decision Making* (*vol. 2*, pp. 355-362). Taipei, Taiwan: Academic Press.

Narula, S., Kirilov, L., & Vassilev, V. (1994). Reference Direction Approach for Solving Multiple Objective Nonlinear Problems. *Transactions on Systems, Man and Cybernetics*, *24*(5), 804–806. doi:10.1109/21.293497

Phoksawat, K., & Mahmuddin, M. (2016). Ontology-based knowledge and optimization model for Decision Support System to intercropping. *Proceedings of the 2016 IEEE International Computer Science and Engineering Conference (ICSEC)*. 10.1109/ICSEC.2016.7859927

Phoksawat, K., & Mahmuddin, M. (2017). Hybrid Ontology-based knowledge with multi-objective optimization model framework for Decision Support System in intercropping. *Advances in Science, Technology and Engineering Systems Journal, 2*(3), 1363–1371. doi:10.25046/aj0203172

Power, D. J. (2008). Decision support systems: a historical overview. In *Handbook on Decision Support Systems* (pp. 121–140). Springer.

Romero, C. (2001). Extended lexicographic goal programming: A unified approach. *Omega, 29*(1), 63–71. doi:10.1016/S0305-0483(00)00026-8

Ruiz, A., Sindhya, K., Miettinen, K., Ruiz, F., & Luque, M. (2015). E-NAUTILUS: A decision support system for complex multiobjective optimization problems based on the NAUTILUS method. *European Journal of Operational Research, 246*(1), 218–231. doi:10.1016/j.ejor.2015.04.027

Ruiz, F., Luque, M., & Miettinen, K. (2012). Improving the computational efficiency in global formulation (GLIDE) for interactive multi-objective optimization. *Annals of Operations Research, 197*(1), 47–70. doi:10.100710479-010-0831-x

Sanches, C., Ferreira, J. S. Jr, Santos, G., Paixão, M. R., & Meireles, M. (2018). TODA: Software for Multiple-Criteria Decisions. *International Journal of Decision Support System Technology, 10*(1), 1–20. doi:10.4018/IJDSST.2018010101

Satapathy, S. C., Raja, N. S. M., Rajinikanth, V., Ashour, A. S., & Dey, N. (2016). Multi-level image thresholding using Otsu and chaotic bat algorithm. *Neural Computing & Applications*, 1–23.

Savic, D. A., Bicik, J., & Morley, M. S. (2011). GANETXL: A DSS Generator for Multiobjective Optimisation of Spreadsheet Based Models. *Environmental Modelling & Software, 26*(5), 551–561. doi:10.1016/j.envsoft.2010.11.004

Seletos, T., & Salmon, J. (2017). Analysis of Integrating a Production Design Generator with a Business Decision Support System for System-Level Decision Making. *Systems, 5*(14).

Sharma, K., & Virmani, J. (2017). A Decision Support System for Classification of Normal and Medical Renal Disease Using Ultrasound Images: A Decision Support System for Medical Renal Diseases. *International Journal of Ambient Computing and Intelligence, 8*(2), 52–69. doi:10.4018/IJACI.2017040104

Shee, D. Y., & Wang, Y. S. (2008). Multi-criteria evaluation of the Web-based e-learning system: A methodology based on learner satisfaction and its applications. *Computers & Education, 50*(3), 894–905. doi:10.1016/j.compedu.2006.09.005

Shim, J. P., Warkentin, M., Courtney, J. F., Power, D. J., Sharda, R., & Carlsson, C. (2002). Past, present, and future of decision support technology. *Decision Support Systems, 33*(2), 111–126. doi:10.1016/S0167-9236(01)00139-7

Simon, H. (1960). *The New Science of Management Decisions*. New York: Harper Row. doi:10.1037/13978-000

Staykov, B., Andonov, F., Vatov, D., Genova, K., Kirilov, L., & Guliashki, V. (2011). Architecture of a flexible web-based framework for building models and solving decision optimization problems. In *Proceedings of XLVI Int. Scientific Conference on Information, Communication and Energy Systems and Technologies - ICEST2011* (*vol. 2*, pp. 857-860). Nis, Serbia: Academic Press.

Steuer, R. (1986). *Multiple Criteria Optimization: Theory, Computation and Applications*. New York: John Wiley & Sons, Inc.

Steuer, R., & Choo, E. (1983). An interactive weighted Tchebycheff procedure for multiple objective programming. *Mathematical Programming*, *26*(3), 326–344. doi:10.1007/BF02591870

Tang, R., Fong, S., Dey, N., Wong, R. K., & Mohammed, S. (2017). Cross Entropy Method Based Hybridization of Dynamic Group Optimization Algorithm. *Entropy (Basel, Switzerland)*, *19*(10), 533. doi:10.3390/e19100533

Vassilev, V. (2002). A generalized scalarizing problem of multicriteria optimization. *Cybernetics and Information Technologies*, *2*, 88–100.

Vassilev, V., Kirilov, L., & Atanassov, A. (1992). Reference Direction Approach for Solving Multiple Objective Programming Problems. *Problems of Engineering Cybernetics and Robotics*, *38*, 17–23.

Vassilev, V., & Narula, S. (1993). A Reference Direction Algorithm for Solving Multiple Objective Integer Linear Programming Problems. *The Journal of the Operational Research Society*, *44*(12), 1201–1209. doi:10.1057/jors.1993.199

Vassilev, V., Narula, S., & Gouljashki, V. (2001). An Interactive Reference Direction Algorithm for Solving Multi-Objective Convex Nonlinear Integer Programming Problems. *International Transactions in Operational Research*, *8*(4), 367–380. doi:10.1111/1475-3995.00271

Vassileva, M. (2006). Generalized Scalarizing Problems GENS and GENSLEX of Multicriteria Optimization. *International Journal of Information Theories and Applications*, *13*, 111–120.

Vassileva, M., Genova, K., & Vassilev, V. (2001). A Classification Based Interactive Algorithm of Multicriteria Linear Integer Programming. *Cybernetics and Information Technologies*, *1*, 5–20.

Vassileva, M., Miettinen, K., & Vassilev, V. (2005). *Generalized scalarizing problem for multicriteria optimization*. IIT Working Papers IIT/WP-205, Institute of Information Technologies, Bulgaria.

Wierzbicki, A. P. (1980). The Use of Reference Objectives in Multiobjective Optimization. *Lecture Notes in Economics and Mathematical Systems*, *177*, 468–486. doi:10.1007/978-3-642-48782-8_32

Wierzbicki, A. P. (1986). On the completeness and constructiveness of parametric characterizations to vector optimization problems. *OR-Spektrum*, *8*(2), 73–87. doi:10.1007/BF01719738

Wierzbicki, A. P. (2007). Reference Point Approaches and Objective Ranking. *Practical Approaches to Multi-Objective Optimization*. Retrieved from http://drops.dagstuhl.de/volltexte/2007/1121/pdf/06501.WierzbickiAndrzej.Paper.1121.pdf

Yang, W., Wang, X., Song, X., Yang, Y., & Patnaik, S. (2018). Design of Intelligent Transportation System Supported by New Generation Wireless Communication Technology. *International Journal of Ambient Computing and Intelligence*, *9*(1), 78–94. doi:10.4018/IJACI.2018010105

Yazdani, M., & Zarate, P. (2017). Flood Risk Assessment: A MCDM Approach. *Proceedings of the Int. Conference on DSS Technology, Data, Information and Knowledge Visualization in DSSs*, 177-183.

Zadeh, L. (1963). Optimality and Non-Scalar-valued Performance Criteria. *IEEE Transactions on Automatic Control*, *8*(1), 59–60. doi:10.1109/TAC.1963.1105511

Zhang, W., Qi, Q., & Deng, J. (2017). Building Intelligent Transportation Cloud Data Center Based on SOA. *International Journal of Ambient Computing and Intelligence*, *8*(2), 1–11. doi:10.4018/IJACI.2017040101

KEY TERMS AND DEFINITIONS

Generalized Scalarizing Method: A generalized scalarizing method is a method for solving multiple-criteria decision-making problems based on a generalized model. The generalized model incorporates a number of different scalarizing sub-models (in case of model GENS the sub-models are 13), so that different kinds of scalarizing optimization problems can be solved during the decision process.

Interactive Method: An iterative method for solving multiple-criteria decision-making problems in which the phase of computation generating pareto optimal solution(s) and the phase of dialog with the decision-maker alternate.

Pareto Optimal Solution: A solution is pareto optimal if and only if there does not exist another feasible solution that is better or equal according to all objectives simultaneously and for at least one objective a strict inequality holds. The conception for optimality in MCDM problems is connected with the orders in k-dimensional objective space. Pareto optimal solution comes from pareto order. Other used orders can be weak pareto order, lexicographic order, etc.

Preference Information: This is the information given by the decision maker (DM) in the process of solving the decision problems. The DM gives his/her preferences (or aspirations) about the desired optimal solution. Examples of preference information are: weighting coefficients for the objectives, aspiration levels for the objectives, goals, trade-offs, etc. There are four different types of MCDM methods according the way and the place of introducing the preference information: no-preference methods, a posteriori methods, a priori methods, and interactive methods.

Scalarizing Function: A real valued function constructed on the base of primary multiple-criteria decision-making problem that optimal solution is a pareto optimal solution to the primary problem.

Scalarizing Problem: A single-objective optimization problem that optimal solution is a pareto optimal solution to the initial multi-objective optimization problem.

Trade-Off: Multi-objective optimization is usually applied on real-life optimization problems. The optimal decisions need to be taken in the presence of trade-offs between two or more conflicting objectives. A trade-off between two objectives is the changing of one selected objective according to the change of one unit of other selected objective, keeping the other objectives unchanged. Note that there are different conceptions and using of trade-offs in MCDM.

Chapter 8
A Multicriteria Spatiotemporal System for Influenza Epidemic Surveillance

Fatima-Zohra Younsi
University of Oran 1, Algeria

Djamila Hamdadou
University of Oran 1, Algeria

Salem Chakhar
University of Portsmouth, UK

ABSTRACT

Influenza has been a growing concern for the public health decision makers/policy makers. Indeed, they are in need of a real geo-making tool for monitoring and surveillance. The chapter aims to introduce a novel spatiotemporal decision system based on multicriteria ranking method, information geographic system (GIS), and SEIRSW system for public health. The later was designed, implemented, and validated in previous research for influenza risk assessment. The authors highlight the use of PROMETHEE II ranking method of multi-criteria decision analysis in GIS that incorporates various factors to monitor and identify potential high-risk areas of seasonal influenza and disease mapping. Factors related to the risk of seasonal influenza are obtained from simulation system and constitute the input values of PROMETHEE II ranking method for the 26 communes of the city of Oran, Algeria. The proposed system has demonstrated analytical capabilities in targeting high-risk spots and influenza surveillance monitoring system and it can help public health policy makers prioritize in their response goals and evaluate control strategies.

INTRODUCTION

Infectious diseases are a major concern in public health, each year they are responsible for mortality and significant morbidity. Indeed, the purpose of epidemiologic surveillance is to set up methodological tools and software to define an informational environment for collect and organize data. Analysis tools are necessary to treat these data and build relevant, reliable and accurate information for the surveil-

DOI: 10.4018/978-1-5225-6164-4.ch008

lance, monitoring, and prevention. Currently, there are many approaches and tools to achieve veritable epidemiological surveillance (Stilianakis & Weber, 2008). However, each one has its advantages and disadvantages.

Mathematical and simulation models are increasingly used to study the transmission of infectious diseases to predict how they might spread in a human population in the event of an epidemic (pandemic), to evaluate different intervention strategies and to help public health decision makers with disease outbreak control and management (younsi et al, 2015b). Model can be used to represent the different state of patients in the course of the illness (S: susceptible, E: exposed, I: infective, R: removed, etc.). In this study, we used the Susceptible, Exposed, Infected, Removed (SEIR) model within SW to explore the dynamics of flu epidemic. The transmission of epidemic occurs through person to person contact, and contact between susceptible and/or infected individuals takes the form of a network. Because SEIR model cannot model this, it must be integrated with a social network model, to understand the spread of the epidemic. Moreover, the structural properties (e.g., density, diameter, clustering coefficient, etc.) of networks play an important role in affecting diffusion behavior. In previous study, we have developed SEIRSW simulation model based on Geographic Information System (GIS). The SEIRSW-GIS was implemented and validated in (Younsi et al, 2015b).

The aim of epidemiological surveillance system based on decision making concept is to bring support to epidemiologists in their monitoring task by providing appropriates indicators and helpful recommendations for making the decision. However, the traditional decision support systems are limited to simple spatiotemporal analysis of surveillance data and a visual detection of epidemic outbreaks on a geographical map. Moreover, they don't provide ways to understand and predict the dynamics of diseases spread in human populations.

The SEIRSW-GIS system generate simulation data and it cannot ranking the areas from the high level risk to low level risk, nor to identify the main factors promoting the disease spread. To fill this knowledge gap, we propose the integration of Multicriteria analysis method in SEIRSW-GIS system to monitor and identify potential high-risk areas of flu and disease mapping. To achieve this goal, we highlight the use of Preference Ranking Organization METHod for Enrichment of Evaluations (PROMETHEE II) method. Multicriteria analysis is performed on the influenza epidemic to examine the main factors influencing flu incidence number, and therefore to predict and track influenza epidemic.

The originality of our paper is to develop a new extension of spatiotemporal decision support system (SEIRSW-GIS: Susceptible- Exposed- Infected- and Removed within Small World Network using Geographic Information System). The latter is based on the development of PROMETHEE II method and its integration within a hybrid simulator (SEIRSW-GIS). The aim of the paper in one hand, to discuss SEIRSW-GIS simulation system in order to understand how epidemic spreads in human population by the coupling of the compartment epidemic model (SEIR) and the social network (SW) model. On the other hand, to assure the integration of Multicritteria analysis using PROMETHEE II in SEIRSW-GIS model in order to show the contribution of the latter in the monitoring and surveillance of influenza epidemic spread in an area, to provide a decision tool for responsible of the infection control program, to better identify risk areas and to develop methodologies to improve the relevance of information for decision making public health.

The remainder of this paper is organized as follows: Section 2, briefly overviews related work in the literature that is similar in spirit to our system. In Section 3, we describe our proposed decision-making system. We present SEIRSW-GIS model and we develop the Multicriteria ranking method (PROMETHEE

II) followed by the decision-making process adopted by the proposed system in section 4. Section 5 outlines the results of an experiment organized for this purpose. Finally, Section 6 presents our conclusions.

BACKGROUND

Simulation model and multicriteria analysis are two powerful and complementary analysis tools. The literature review shows that in most of research papers, these two tools have been used separately and there are a very few works that combine them, especially in respect to seasonal influenza surveillance. In this section, we discuss some relevant proposals:

Simulation Model within GIS

In the context of epidemiology, mathematical models are frequently used. We find simple models like Susceptible-Infective (SI), Susceptible-Infective-Recovered (SIR), Susceptible, Exposed, Infected, Removed (SEIR), and Susceptible-Infective-Susceptible (SIS), etc. Usually, the simulation of these models is governed by nonlinear ordinary differential equations. Unlike SI and SIR models, the SEIR models different health status of the host taking into account the incubation (latent) period the time interval from infection to onset of symptoms of disease. However, this model is simple while the complex topological structure of social contact network must be considered. Indeed, we are in need to combine SEIR model with complex networks, more specifically: social networks to improve its shortcomings and its features (younsi et al, 15a). In the following, we present the most famous research integration Simulation model within GIS:

In (Balcan et al, 10), the authors present the Global Epidemic and Mobility (GLEaM) model that integrates sociodemographic and population mobility data in a spatially structured stochastic disease approach to simulate the spread of epidemics at the worldwide scale. In similar research, (Wang et al, 10) designed and developed a prototype system to carry out agent-based simulation of influenza transmission and control in a geographic environment. Their results show that the model is very successfully able to generate various scenarios of an outbreak in realistic geographic urban settings by incorporating movement in the agent entities. (Mao, 2013) built a spatially-explicit network-based model to simulate influenza transmission, mitigation strategies, and their associated costs. The proposed model represents a spatio-temporal network of individuals' daily contacts, which enables the simulation of local infection and long-distance dispersion of influenza. He concluded that for a large urbanized area, the closure of affected workplaces could be an effective and cost-saving strategy to mitigate influenza outbreaks. Recently, (Haddad et al, 16) present a GIS-based spatial-temporal simulation approach and software to support public health decision making in the context of communicable diseases in urban areas. The approach fully integrates epidemiological, mobility and GIS-data models at an aggregate population level in order to support specialized interventions. In (He et al, 17), the authors aimed to analyze the geographical time-space distribution features of A/H1N1 influenza in the early pandemic phase in 2009 and evaluate the influence of international population flow and regional climate differences on the prevalence of A/H1N1 influenza. By exploring the space-time laws of prevalence of the disease, they can apply the discoveries to predict the occurrence and development of other diseases, thus to provide a scientific basis for the government to make decisions of treating and curing epidemic diseases.

Multicriteria Analysis Within GIS

Use of MCDA with and in GIS has been an active and growing topic of research since the early 1990s [Malczewski 2006]. This literature reviews also reveal use of many different combinations of methods and approaches. The Multicriteria analysis has been, also, applied to study different diseases spread. In what follow, we discuss some studies that use Multicriteria methods and GIS in the fields of public health and epidemiology:

(Tran et al, 12) developed a geographical information system (GIS)-based multicriteria evaluation (MCE) to map the suitable areas for vector-borne Rift Valley fever transmission in Italy, taking into account the three main European potential hosts (i.e. cattle, sheep and goats).

The (GIS)-based MCE served as a valuable framework and a flexible tool for mapping the areas at risk of a pathogen that is currently absent from a region. To help public health decision makers in their decisions, (Araz et al, 2013) developed an epidemiological simulation tool based on mathematical SEIR model for pandemic influenza (H1N1) which enables users to make decisions during a simulated pandemic. They designed a school closure table top exercise using their simulation model as a decision-support tool with bi-criteria analysis for evaluating the effectiveness of school closure as a community mitigation strategy for pandemic influenza. Recently, the authors in (Alimi et al, 2016) evaluated the exposure of the Northern South America to malaria risk given current access-related and environmental/climatic conditions using multi-criteria decision analysis. They produced high-resolution composite maps showing gradients of risk which were validated with geo-coded occurrence points for malaria and three dominant vector species.

The authors are interested in (Zemri and Hamdadou, 2017) to design and develop a decision support system based on multi-criteria ELECTRE TRI method and data mining techniques. The proposed system used the real data of tuberculosis generates some recommendations to decision makers in the form of epidemiological risk map. This latter cannot understand the dynamic of disease spread. In similar study, the authors in [Manogaran and Lopez, 2017] propose a big data based surveillance system that analyzes spatial climate big data and performs continuous monitoring of correlation between climate change and Dengue.

Several studies have been devoted to the study of public health problem in the modeling diseases spread context using mathematical models within social network or GIS as we have mentioned above. However, to our knowledge, no previous studies have applied a risk assessment framework to individually identify areas of high seasonal influenza risk using simulation system based on mathematical epidemic SEIR model within Small World network, Multicriteria analysis PROMETHEE II method and GIS.

SEASONAL INFLUENZA DECISIONAL SYSTEM

Control and surveillance of a health problem in an area requires having a spatiotemporal decision support system that provides rapid and reliable information giving an outbreak alert in time and space.

In this section, we introduce the architecture of the proposed decision support system. The general architecture of the proposed system is based on tree main models: the propagation model (simulation model), the multicriteria model and the territory model. Figure 1 illustrates an overview of the proposed system and the associate models are described in the following sections:

Figure 1. The proposed system

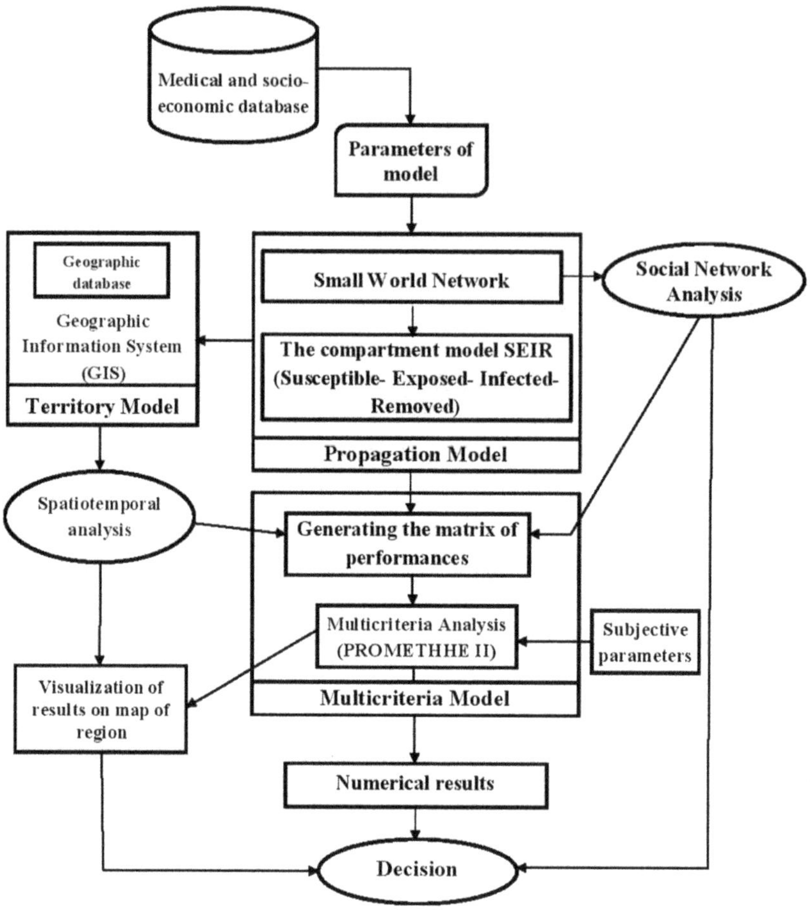

Simple SEIR

In this section, we discuss SEIR epidemic model. One of the simplest epidemiological models that divide the host population into four distinct classes: susceptible (S), Exposed (E), infectious (I), and recovered (R) and using the following coupled deterministic nonlinear ordinary differential equations:

$$\begin{cases} \dfrac{dS}{dt} = -\alpha * S(t) * I(t) \\ \dfrac{dE}{dt} = \alpha * S(t) * I(t) - \beta * E(t) \\ \dfrac{dI}{dt} = \beta * E(t) - \gamma * I(t) \\ \dfrac{dR}{dt} = \gamma * I(t) \end{cases}$$

where N= S(t)+E(t)+I(t)+R(t)

With α: is the rate of transmission or infection per unit time, β: is rate at which an infected individual becomes infectious per unit time, γ: is the rate at which an infectious individual recovers per unit time, and population size is given by N.

We prefer this model over others as it takes care of latent period i.e. exposed class which is left in SI or SIR, etc. In SEIR compartmental model illustrated in Figure 2, an infectious individual can transmit disease to susceptible individual with probability α, the susceptible enters the class of exposed individuals E and stay for a period of time $1/\beta$ (average latent period). These are the people in latent period who are infected but not yet infectious. Then, individual enters the class of infected individuals I and stay infectious for a period of time $1/\gamma$ (average infectious period). Finally, he is removed and he cannot infect nor be re-infected. For some diseases there exist specific models which describe their behaviour.

The simple SEIR model does not take care of the relationships between inividuals. However, in reality, the disease is spreading in a host population via the relationship between them. When there is an adequate contact of an infected individual (from class I) with a susceptible individual (from class S) and this individual gets infected, then he enters the class of exposed individuals E. Indeed, our propagation model combines compartment SEIR model and SW network in order to study the effect of the social network on the epidemic spread dynamics.

All symbols used by the propagation model have their usual meanings as specified in Table 1.

SEIR Model Within Small World Network Model

Mathematical epidemic models based on social network are being increasingly used as decision support tools by health officials. In contrast to aggregate differential equation based models, these network models describe diffusion of an infectious disease over a social contact network, which is constructed from individual level demographic and activity data (Xia et al, 2011). Many researches have shown that almost all realistic networks have small world and/or scale free properties (Wang & Chan, 2003)(Kim, 2014).

Various networks exist in the literature, in our research, we adopt for SW network introduced by Watts and Strogatz model (Watts & Strogatz, 1998). A SW network is an attempt to represent realistically the network of contacts between individuals, where local links predominate, but social and geographical motilities imply a fraction of random connections through which long-range transmission may occur (Verdasca et al., 2005). In the Watts-Strogatz model, the nodes of the network represent individuals. The links are then connections along which the infection spreads. Most of the individuals are connected by a shortest path through the network, and there is a clustering effect, meaning that there is a high probability that two individuals are connected directly to other individuals if they have common neighbor

Figure 2. Scheme of the simple SEIR model. Boxes represent compartments, and arrows indicate flux between the compartments

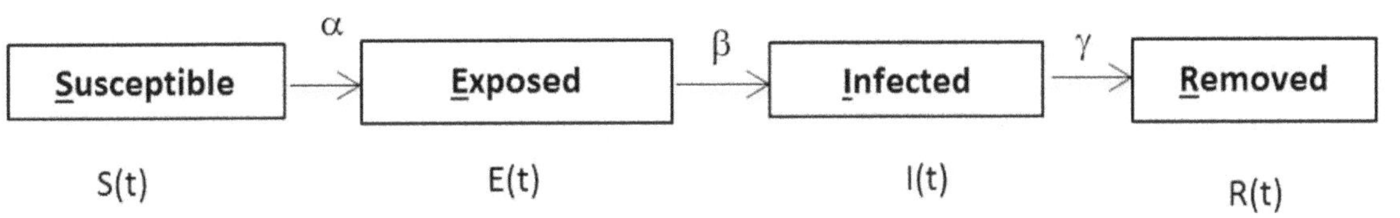

Table 1. the meaning of all parameters and state variables

State variable	Meaning
S	Number of susceptible individual
E	Number of exposed individual
I	Number of infected individual
R	Number of recovered individual
$S_0 = S(0)$	Number of susceptible individual at time t= 0
$E_0 = E(0)$	Number of exposed individual at time t= 0
$I_0 = I(0)$	Number of infected individual at time t= 0
$R_0 = R(0)$	Number of recovered individual at time t= 0
N	Total population
Parameters	**Meaning**
k	Degree of distribution
α	Transmission rate
β / β^{-1}	Latent rate / latent period
γ / γ^{-1}	Recovery rate/ infectious period

individuals. The SW model, although better suited for social networks with high clustering coefficients, it has a degree distribution and centrality measures decaying exponentially fast away from the average value (Pastor-Satorras et al, 2014). In infectious disease epidemiology, scale-free contact networks have to date been only described for sexual relationships (Duerr et al, 2007).

We construct the SW networks using Wattes & Stogatz model which is considered as the typical model of social networks model. The model starts with a ring lattice, and then a number of extra nodes are added in the middle of the lattice which are connected to a large number of sites (nodes) chosen ran-

Figure 3. Representation of the social network, from left to right: regular network, small world network with shortcuts added, and random network

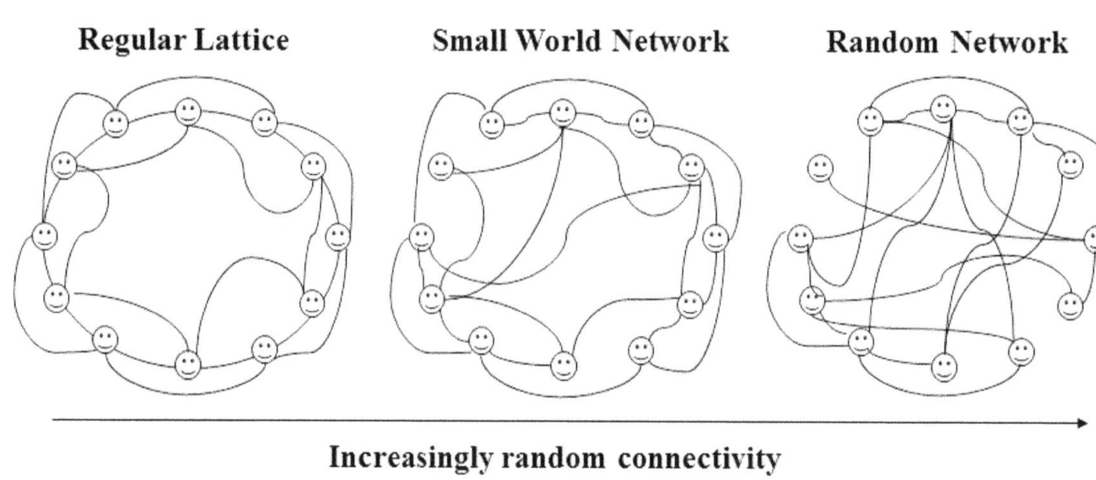

domly on the main lattice (see Figure.3). Watts and Strogatz considered that the use of a small number of random connections (Probability of rewiring: $P_w \approx 0.01$) significantly reduces the average distance between any two nodes, this property facilitates disease spread in the network. A detailed algorithm for creation of the SW social network used in this work is proposed by (younsi et al, 2014).

Generally, SW networks are characterized by three main properties: Average path length, Transitivity, Diameter. All these properties will be discussed in detail in the next section.

The SEIRSW Process

Traditionally, a network is described by a graph $G = (V, E)$ consisting of a set V of vertices (also called nodes) where $V = \{i \in \text{nodes}\}$ and a set E of edges (also called links) where $E = \{(i, j)/i, j \in V\}$. The degree of node i called also neighbors of vertex in an undirected graph, denoted as $k(i)$, is the number of edges between node i and other nodes in the graph; $k(i) = \{j\ /(i, j) \in E\}$. During the diseases, the individuals can have four states: *State*: $V = Node.S; Node.E; Node.I; Node.R$, we define a set of infected neighbors of the node $i$at the time t as $\{A_t^i\}$.

Let $Ps = Node.S \in V$ at time t and let $Pi = Node.I \in V$ be the number of infectious individuals at that instant t. If *Node.I* has a contact with *Node.S*, $(1\text{-}\alpha)^{ki}$ is the probability of transmit the infection between *Node.I* and its k neighbors *Node.S*. Accordingly, $1\text{-}(1\text{-}\alpha)^{ki}$ is the probability of infection (Stattner et al, 2011)

The process of infection is described as follows:

1. Initially, a number of infected individuals are chosen. Each simulation starts with only some initially infected nodes, all others being susceptible, and it ends when no node in the infectious state is left.
2. Disease spreads in G network with a probability of transmission $1-\left(1-\alpha\right)^{ki}$ from infectious individuals to susceptible individuals if it exists a relationship between them.
3. Then, each infected individual will be infectious after be exposed. In many papers of epidemiological models, the latent periods are typically assumed to be either exponentially distributed or fixed (Beretta and Kuang 2001). Here, we consider that the latent period and infectious period are distributed according to exponential distribution function because the latent (incubation) period and infectious period are different from one person to another.
4. Each infectious individual will be recover (becomes immune) after an infectious period. After recovery, it cannot transmit the infectious agent again. Its immunity is permanent and it cannot return to the susceptible class.
5. The network G(t) evolves to G(t+1)

The process 2, 3, 4 and 5 are repeated until no infectious individuals exist in the host population.

Usually, the majority of existing mathematical models to simulate epidemics are based on ordinary differential equations (ODE). These models have serious drawbacks, for example: They fail to simulate in a proper way the individual contact processes, the effects of individual behaviour, the spatial aspects of the epidemic spreading, and the effects of mixing patterns of the individuals (Elsayed, 2013). However, the SEIRSW model allows us to evaluate impacts of network evolution measure and compare the impact of network dynamic, by comparing the incidence curves of different regions, and understand causes and effects at global level by presenting incidence curves over time and individual level by discussing the SW properties as diameter, clustering coefficient, degree distribution and average path length.

Social Network Analysis

Social network analysis (SNA) has been used in many research disciplines to understand the structure of social communities by examining its topological properties. Many properties have been studied by researchers to understand the social structure of communities. In this section, we summarize measures to characterize structural properties of SW network used in this work:

- **Average Path Length:** Mean shortest path length over all node pairs which increases logarithmically with the number of nodes;
- **Average Coefficient of Clustering (CC):** Defined by Watts and Strogatz (1998) as the average of the local clustering coefficients of all nodes in the network: $CC = \frac{1}{N}\sum_{i=0}^{N} C\left(i\right)$ Where C(i) is clustering coefficient for a node i and: $C\left(i\right) = \frac{2.\left|\left\{\left(i,j\right) \in E \wedge \left(j,i\right) \in E\right\}\right|}{ki.\left(ki-1\right)}$;
- **Diameter:** Is the maximum distance between two vertices, denoted d(G). In the SW graph d(G) is small;
- **Degree Distribution:** The degree of a node (k) is the total number of links connected to this node. The degree distribution represents the relative frequency of each value of the node degree (k) in a given network;
- **Density:** The total number of observed relationships of an individual or subgroup divided by the total number of possible ties;
- **Modularity:** The modularity is a metric measuring the quality of partitioning the network into communities by measuring the density of cluster interiors and the scarcity of inter-cluster connections.

Territory Model

According to Rytkönen (Rytkönen, 2004), the goals of disease mapping are: 1) to describe the spatial variation in disease incidence to formulate an etiological hypothesis; 2) to identify areas of high risk in order to increase prevention; and 3) to provide a map of disease risk for a region for better risk preparedness. In the context of epidemiological analysis, GIS is known by the mechanism for organizing information on the distribution of disease within a region, storing and reporting the data in a form to display where cases have occurred, and to identify where control efforts or treatments can be focused that could be used by health decision makers. Indeed, as part of our contributions, the integration of a GIS with propagation model provides researchers with the tools to analyze the spatial and temporal distribution and variations of diseases.

The GIS is used to display disease distribution maps provided by propagation model to the user and carry out the geospatial processing. The resulting map will be examined by decision-makers concerning public health (health-care professionals, sociologist) in the study area. In the context of spatiotemporal analysis, geographically and temporally aggregated simulation data can be retrieved through GIS, which we used to obtain counts of influenza by week and commune in the study region, during a period of time. These spatiotemporal count data constitute the response Y_{it} for our illustration of the SEIRSW model.

Where Y_{it}: a count of new cases, I: number of commune, t: period of time. To calculate rates of illness, we aggregate all cases within a census block group over the time period of interest, and then divided by the total population. Moreover, cluster analysis can perform for cluster detection and spatial analysis of the distribution of disease that has been used in a variety of health outcomes, including outbreaks of infectious diseases.

Multicriteria Model

The objective of this section is to discuss in detail the Multicriteria analysis Model. The input of this model is:

- The matrix of performances obtained from the propagation model, social network analysis and spatiotemporal analysis;
- The subjective parameters given by the decision maker or generated automatically by the system.

The output is a ranking of the risk areas of influenza disease. The Multicriteria Model is based on PROMETHEE II method.

Why PROMETHEE II

Many methods have been developed for solving multiple criteria ranking problems mainly ELECTRE III (developed by Roy (1978), AHP (developed by Saaty (1980)), PROMETHEE I, II (developed by Brans & Vincke (1985)), and SMART (multi-attribute) developed by Edwards (1977).

Each of the methods is constructed around different methodological principles. For example, the ELECTRE III method of the European inspiration is based on the outranking relation, while the Analytic Hierarchy Process (AHP) method of the American inspiration is based on the multiattribute utility theory. Methods based on the total aggregation have the advantage of being simple for use, but reduce complex problems to a single scale, which is often an oversimplification.

These methods often lead to a too conservative representation of the problem. Methods of classification based on the outranking relation offer greater flexibility by introducing semi quantitative scales. Many factors influenced the specific selection of the multicriteria method PROMETHEE II to solve the ranking problem in our context. Indeed, the use of this method in ranking and classification problems, present the following advantages [Brans & Mareschal, 2002], [Hammami, 2003], [Adam, 2008], [Halouani et al, 2009], [Ayadi, 2010]:

- Mix Potential use of both quantitative and / or qualitative criteria;
- Acceptance and integration of the concept of incomparability of alternatives (useful in the case of scenarios too different to be compared), in the whole procedure of classification or ranking;
- Treatment of non-comparability, with two approximations, so as to focus on the alternatives that exhibit special characteristics;
- Simplicity of comparisons and consequentially understanding of the results;
- Exploitation of the subjective parameters (weight, indifference and preference thresholds) attributing a high level of effectively to the decision support process;

- The introduction of six different preference functions in one process; it is an extension of criteria but in a well-formalized way;
- This method succeeded in integrating the recent developments in the preferences modeling in a simple way;
- Although, PROMETHEE devoided a mathematical basis, it tried to fill this gap by proceeding and systematizing the preference function. Indeed, the decision-maker, have to choose the form of his preference among six forms, would feel rather reassured;
- The simplicity of PROMETHEE places on a good position is used if we try to rank potential actions and that the decision-maker does not find much difficulty in determining the weight of the criteria. Often this method is subjected to modifications or extensions;
- PROMETHEE method is an appropriate approach to effectively and efficiently deal with problems in which structured hierarchies of indicators are used in modeling.

Description of the Used Multicriteria Method PROMETHEE II

The PROMETHEE II method involves the basics of multi-criteria analysis, namely: a performance table (Or decision matrix), a finite set of criteria C and a finite set of actions A in which each row describes an option and each column describes the performance of the options against each criterion.

In a decision matrix A which is an $(M \times N)$ matrix, for i = {1,2,3,..., M} and j = {1,2,3,..., N}, each element a_{ij} indicates the performance of alternative Ai when it is evaluated in terms of decision criterion Cj. It is also assumed that the decision maker has determined the weights of relative performance of the decision criteria denoted as Wj, for j = {1,2,3,..., N}.

Generally, PROMETHEE family associates to each criterion a weight expressing its importance, as well as a preference function P_j defined as follows:

For every criteria j of C:

$$d_j\left(a,b\right) = g_j\left(a\right) - g_j\left(b\right)$$

$$which\, a,b \in A et \forall a \in A g_j\left(a\right) is the performance of\, a\, for\, criterion\, j$$

$$P_j : \begin{cases} P_j\left(a,b\right) = 0\left(indifference between\, a\, and\, b\right) if\, d_j\left(a,b\right) = 0 \\ P_j\left(a,b\right) \sim 0\left(Low\, preference\, of\, a\, over\, b\right) if\, d_j > 0 \\ P_j\left(a,b\right) \sim 1\left(Strong\, preference\, of\, a\, on\, b\right) if\, d_j >> 0 \\ P_j\left(a,b\right) = 1\left(Strict\, preference\, of\, a\, over\, b\right) if\, d_j >>> 0 \end{cases}$$

There is infinity of functions that satisfy this definition. PROMETHEE authors' categorized six types of these functions that appear according to the authors, cover most needs met in reality. Most of these types are defined by two parameters: (p) (Preference threshold) and (q) (Indifference threshold). The preference threshold is the threshold at which there is a difference between two actions ($i.e : d_j\left(a,b\right)$) which is perceptible and it prefers one action to another. The indifference threshold is the smallest difference that is significant. Below that threshold it is impossible to decide between two actions. The thresholds and the function preferences compose what is called the intra-criterion subjective parameters and the weight of intra-criterion subjective parameters. We mention below two examples of category (see [Hamdadou, 2016] for the other cases):

Linear functions are used when indifference and strict preference thresholds are clearly apparent in the data of multi-criteria posed problem, an indifference threshold (q) and a preference threshold (p) will be used [Hamdadou, 2016].

Function V is generally used when the data is such that the differences between them are of continuous nature, or when all intermediate values between the maximum and minimum values of these deviations are possible, only the preference threshold (p) is introduced [Hamdadou, 2016].

- The definition for each criterion of its weight, its preference function as well as the preference and indifference thresholds translates what is commonly called "the Expression of Preference." This is the initialization step of the PROMETHEE method.
- The second step is to calculate the global indices of preferences between all pairs of action. The global index of preference of an action (a) on an action (b) is given by:

$$\Pi\left(a,b\right)=\frac{\sum_{j\in F} w_j * P_j\left(a,b\right)}{\sum_{j\in F} w_j}$$

where C is the set of criteria, w_j is the weight of criteria j and P_j is the preference function for criteria j. This index represents the preference degree of (a) on (b) considering all the criteria simultaneously. By comparing all the actions with respect to each other, one obtains preferences degrees matrix E.

Figure 4. Linear preference function

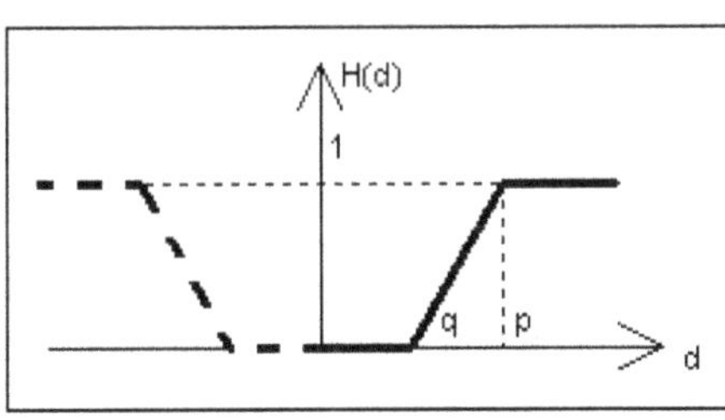

$$P(d)=\begin{cases}0 & d\leq q\\ \frac{d-q}{p-q} & q<d\leq p\\ 1 & d>p\end{cases}$$

Figure 5. The V preference function

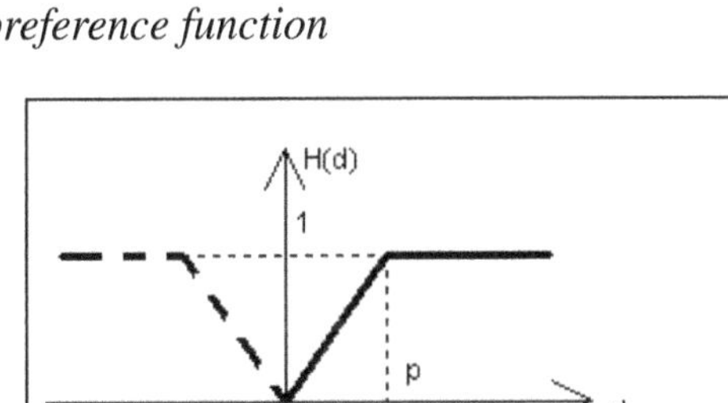

$$P(d)=\begin{cases}0 & d\leq 0\\ \frac{d}{p} & 0\leq d\leq p\\ 1 & d>p\end{cases}$$

- In the third step, we compute for each action (a) its *outgoing flow*, which represents the dominance of (a) with respect to the other actions, denoted $\Phi^{+}\left(a\right)$ as well as its *incoming flow* which represents the weakness of (a) with respect to the other actions $\Phi^{-}\left(a\right)$:

$$\Phi^{+}\left(a\right)=\frac{\sum_{b\in A}\Pi\left(a,b\right)}{n-1}$$

$$\Phi^{-}\left(a\right)=\frac{\sum_{b\in A}\Pi\left(b,a\right)}{n-1}$$

n: actions number.

- The last step consists of calculating, for each action (a), its *net flow* noted $\Phi\left(a\right)$ by the formula:

$$\Phi\left(a\right)=\Phi^{+}\left(a\right)-\Phi^{-}\left(a\right)$$

From the net flow we deduce the following relations for all pairs of actions a, b:

(a) is preferred to (b) $\Leftrightarrow \Phi\left(a\right) > \Phi\left(b\right)$

(a) is indifferent to (b) $\Leftrightarrow \Phi\left(a\right) = \Phi\left(b\right)$

The final ranking which is a complete preorder is obtained by ranking the actions on the basis of the increasing value of their aggregate net flow.

THE DECISION MAKING PROCESS ADOPTED BY SEIRSW-GIS

Decision-making in public health is a complex and dynamic process that is influenced by epidemiology, social, economic and political factors. It provides multiple and iterative analysis, and simulations. It can be summarized by the following general algorithm:

BEGIN

1. Definition of objectives;
2. Identification of spatial-temporal problem;
3. Identification of population and specification of the main characteristic of epidemic;
4. Estimation of epidemic parameters;
5. Creation of SW network, then analysis it.
6. Application of compartment model of epidemic SEIR within SW network created in (5);

7. Generating the matrix of performances from spatiotemporal analysis, propagation model and social network analysis;
8. Introducing of subjective parameters;
9. Application of Multicriteria Analysis PROMETHEE II Method ;
10. Display the numerical results on study region map by using GIS functions;
11. Solution analysis: analysis of numerical results, social network results and geo-location results;
12. Choice and decision-making: Surveillance and monitoring.

END

In Figure 6, we describe in detail, the decision-making process.

The use case diagram as shown in Figure 7 present the behavior of the proposed system. It describes the sequences of interactions between the system, scientist and decision maker.

Figure 6. Decision making process adopted by our system

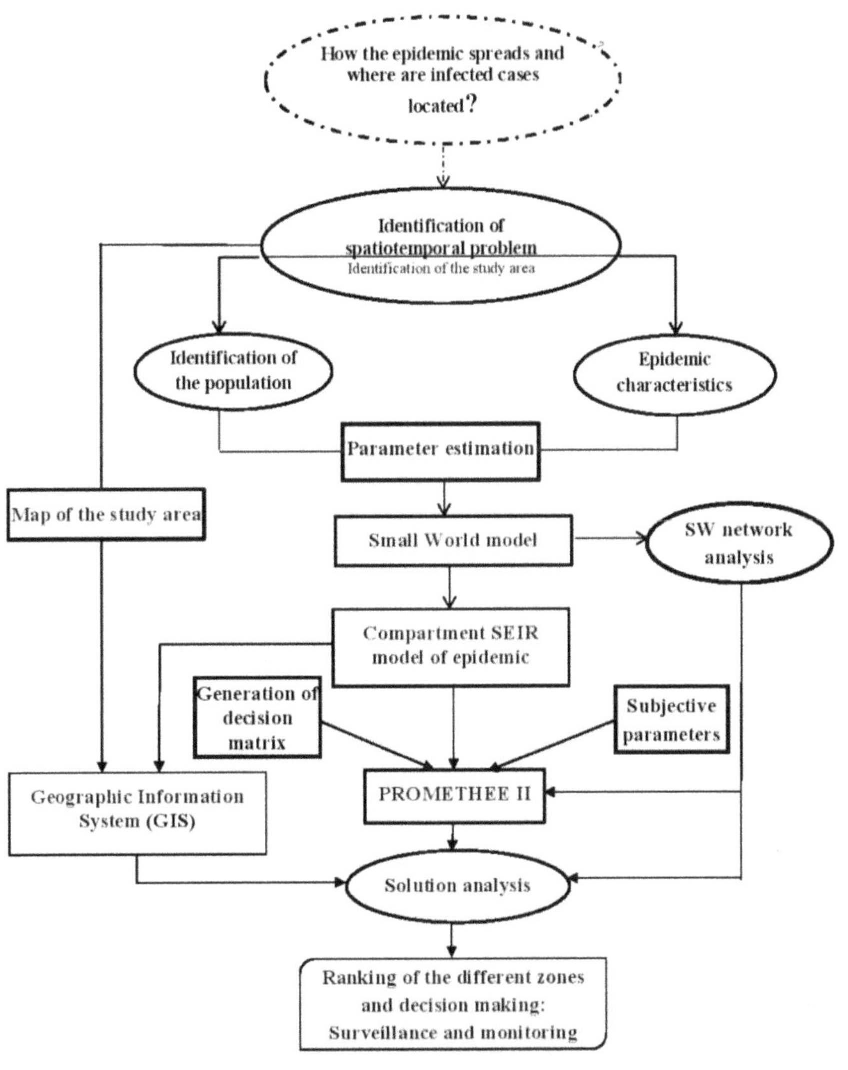

Figure 7. The use case diagram

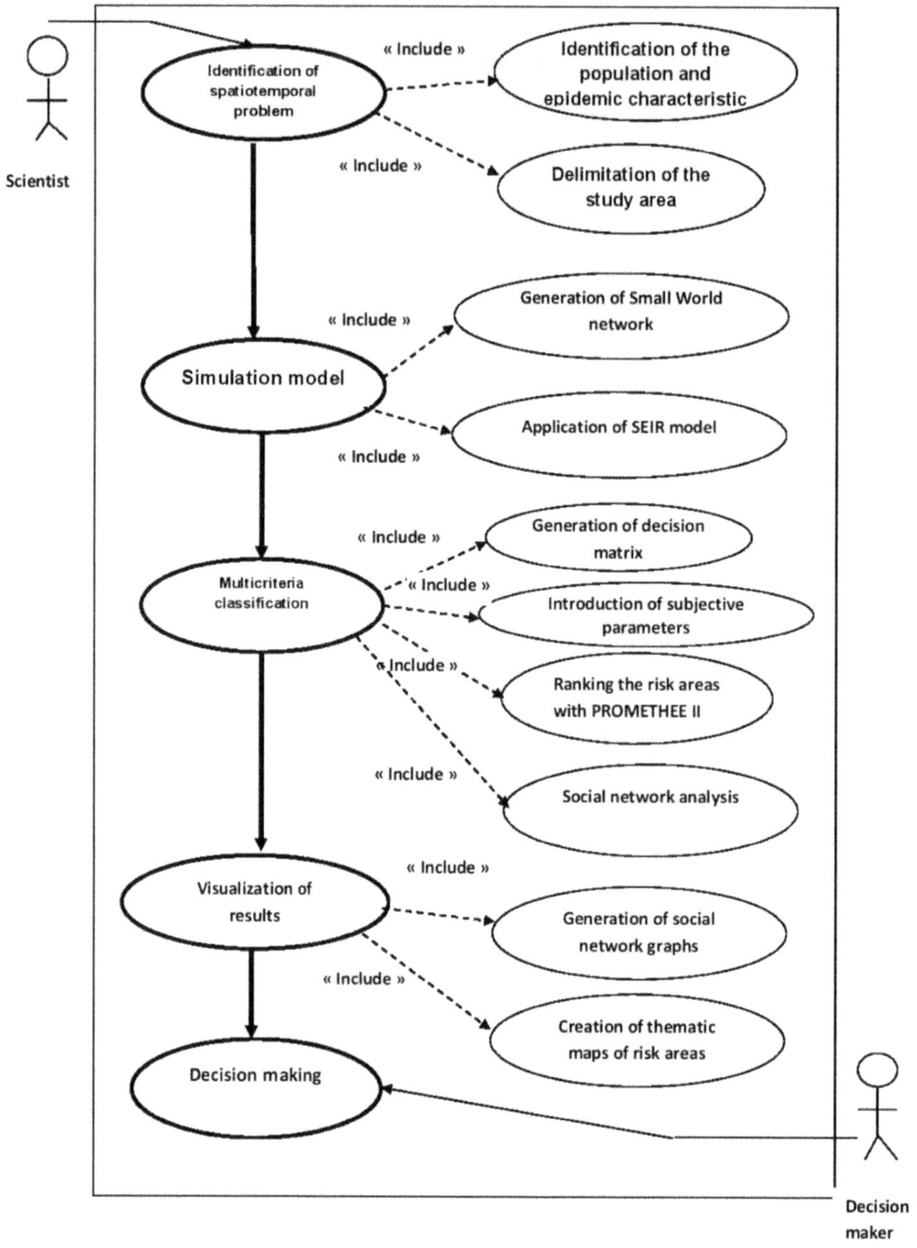

EXPERIMENTAL EVALUATION

The aim of this experiment study is to design and implement a robust and effective decision making tool for public health officials in order to assess the seasonal influence risk within the Oran region.

First, we describe the study area. Then, we present and discuss the numerical results of simulation influenza epidemic model and proprieties of SW network concerned by the current study. Finally, we discuss Multicriteria model output and we visualize potential infected communes by the virus of seasonal influenza located in Oran, Algeria, which are ranked toward levels of risks, using our integration approach.

Data

The database used in this study concerns the seasonal influenza flu (2009) in the region of Oran- Algeria. It is a medical and socio-economic database obtained from the Public Health department of Oran. It is composed of 5504 records for the 26 communes (municipalities) of Oran. The data were obtained from the Public Health Department of Oran (PHD[1]).

Our proposed model depends on the parameters represented on table .1 (section.3.1). Some parameters are determined from medical and socio-economic data (real data) and others may be obtained from the simulation model outcomes fitted to the real data.

Time series graphs of the data are shown in Figure 8 for both waves. The number of cases changed from one week to another and from one wave to another.

Description of the Study Area

The geographical area of interest for this study is the city of Oran- Algeria, this choice is due mainly to the importance of this city which is considered the second largest city in Algeria and actually has approximately 1,454,000 inhabitants in an area of 2121 km ^{2}. The population of Oran is distributed into 26 communes (municipalities). Figure 9, shows the communes of Oran.

Simulation Model

In our model, we will consider influenza flu of short duration relative to human population dynamics, we assume that the population is close i.e. with no birth and no death.

Before applying the propagation model, the decision maker must propose parameters for a propagation model which constitute the inputs of the SEIRSW model and select the area of study. He can apply

Figure 8. Time series of influenza cases (first and second waves), Oran 2009

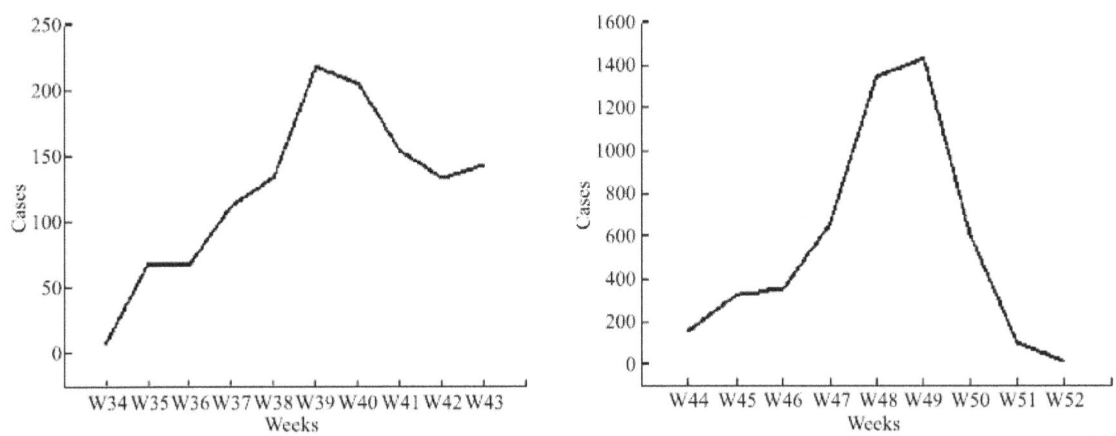

(a) First wave

(b) Second wave

Figure 9. The administrative division of the communes of Oran

the model for one commune, some communes or for all communes. The SEIRSW algorithm proposed in [Younsi el al, 2015a] is then executed.

The simulation model will run for each set of parameters and variable state, once the simulation is completed, data outputs are created. The simulation data are used to generate map outputs for a geo-location of epidemic outbreaks and other simulations statistics.

We have applied simulation model to the 26 communes of Oran, as outcomes of propagation model, we have obtained 26 results. Here, we are interested by four communes that represent a hot area of outbreak flu: commune of Oran, commune of Bethioua, commune of Boutlelis, and commune of Arzew. Estimated parameter values for simulation model and variable state are given in table 2 for the four communes of outbreak of flu with 96% confidence intervals. The fit to the real data is very good for all communes.

We present in figure 10, the trends of human population in different compartments of the principal communes which represent hot area and an outbreak of seasonal influenza.

Table 2. Estimated parameters value and variable stat for simulation model for the four communes

Commune	Alpha	1/Beta	1/Gamma	Degree K	S(0)	I(0)
Oran	0,13	2	5	10	1600	75
Bethioua	0,16	2	6	8	598	12
Boutlelis	0,13	0,2	5	7	380	7
Arzew	0,16	2	6	9	395	8

Figure 10. The evolution of SEIR within SW epidemic model over time

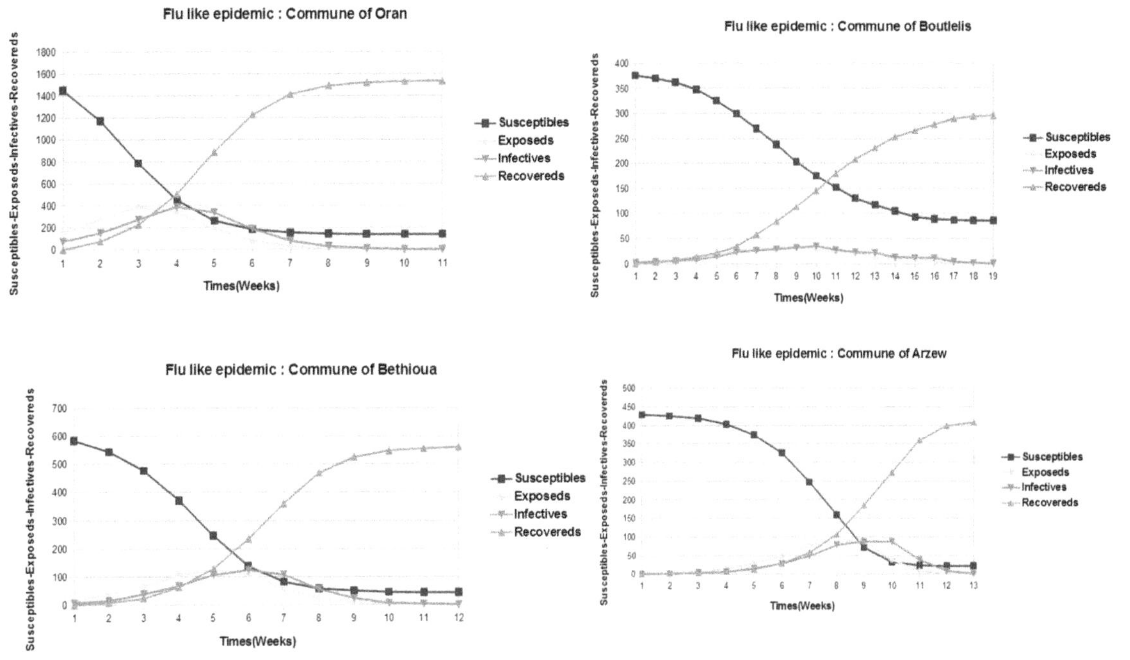

The following curves, respectively, represent the susceptible, exposed, infected and recovered cases over time of the four communes.

Discussion

In the four curves, the number of infected people will increase along with the epidemic spreading, and then it will decrease after the epidemic is brought under control. The curves of exposed individuals follow the trend of the curves of infected individuals because susceptible individuals after been infected move into the Exposed (not infectious) class after an average incubation period. At the same time, the number of susceptible will decrease. The number of recovered will be increase after a period of time where individuals begin to leave Infected class. Here, we assume an exponential distribution of incubation and infectious periods.

During the simulation and changing the parameters of model for each commune, we have observed that model factors: α, β, γ and k, are performance parameters of the epidemic diffusion system. Numerical results can be visualized also on a map of region. The curves shows also how variable state values (see Table.2) affects the number of people in the susceptible, exposed, infected, and recovered groups.

Since influenza spreads around the world in a yearly outbreak, each year and for each region, it has its new factor and parameter values. In decision making environment, decision maker or health official can imagine various scenarios for the epidemic and its evolution, by changing the initial chosen values for parameters and state variable values depending to the epidemic, then running the SEIRSW simulation tool. Moreover, SEIRSW tool is also applicable to a wide range of other infectious diseases characterized by latent period, such as tuberculosis, measles, meningococcal meningitis, to name only a few.

Multicriteria Model

The aim of Multicriteria model is the ranking of risk flu areas. PROMETHEE II method is allows one to establish a complete ranking between risks communes based on outranking relations. In that follow, we detailed the Multicriteria ranking model:

Generation of Decision Matrix

This step aims to generate the decision matrix by the formalization of the two basic elements of the decisional situation:

1. **Identification of Criteria:** To take into account the different aspects of the decision problems, the decision makers have identified a set of seven factors (criteria) that influences the risk level of each commune of the study area. A brief description of these factors is as follows:
    a. **Incidence:** This factor indicates the numbers of new cases occurring in a population during a defined period.
    b. **Density of Individual Network:** This is the proportion of relations (ties) in individual network relative to the total number of possible contact.
    c. **Presence of Industrial Area:** Air pollutants are known as the origin of many respiratory diseases and they play an important role in the transmission of seasonal influenza (Liang et al.14). Indeed, exposure to certain pollutants may contribute to chronic bronchitis. Most of these pollutants are originated in different industrial zones in the study region.
    d. **Relative Humidity (RH):** There is a relationship between the relative humidity and survival of the virus of seasonal influenza. This explains why this infection is also common in winter when it is cold and dry in the temperate zones. Several studies (e.g. Lowen et al. 2007; McDevitt et al., 2010) confirmed that low relative humidity and low temperature favour influenza survival and disease transmission.
    e. **Transmission Rate:** This factor measures the rate of disease transmission. The infection is transmitted through direct contact between an infectious person x and a susceptible person y at a rate Alpha.
    f. **Degree (k):** Each node is connected to k nearest neighbours in network, k is initial average degree of all the nodes of networks;
    g. **Clustering Coefficient (CC):** The clustering coefficient of the network is equal to the average clustering coefficient of all the nodes (Watts and Strogatz, 1998). Two critical characteristics of small world network are the shorter average path length and higher clustering coefficient.
2. **Identification of Alternatives (Actions):** The alternatives represent the possible solutions to the problem. It is important that all relevant alternatives are taken into account. In our study, it represents different communes (26 communes of Oran). Each alternative is measured by a set of criteria by one value because the performances of the alternatives are non-spatial.

The collected performances of 26 communes are provided in Table 3.

Table 3. The decision matrix

Commune	Incidence	Density	Industrial area	Rel_hum	Alpha	K	CC
AIN EL BYA	1	908	2	2	0.16	7	0.388
AIN EL KERMA	15	68	0	1	0.1	4	0.487
AIN EL TURCK	26	720	1	1	0.14	6	0.391
ARZEW	383	1722	3	1	0.16	9	0.383
BENFREHA	77	236	1	3	0.13	6	0.4
BETHIOUA	586	145	2	1	0.16	8	0.372
BIR EL DJIR	116	2351	2	2	0.11	6	0.382
BOUFATIS	1	109	1	2	0.09	4	0.404
BOUSFER	0	297	0	1	0.09	4	0.527
BOUTLELIS	248	147	1	3	0.13	7	0.389
EL ANCOR	14	129	0	1	0.1	4	0.408
EL BRAYA	2	76	0	3	0.08	4	0.695
EL KERMA	1	234	0	2	0.09	4	0.648
ES-SENIA	20	1621	1	2	0.11	6	0.424
GDYEL	245	341	1	2	0.19	6	0.385
HASSI BEN OKBA	137	291	0	3	0.1	4	0.352
HASSI BOUNIF	295	1827	1	3	0.19	8	0.393
HASSI MEFSOUKH	76	353	0	3	0.18	4	0.389
MERS EL HADJADJ	64	219	0	1	0.12	5	0.374
MERS EL KEBIR	148	1027	0	1	0.18	8	0.36
MISSERGHIN	144	51	1	3	0.12	7	0.382
ORAN	1486	10731	2	1	0.13	10	0.384
OUED TLELAT	2	171	1	4	0.1	4	0.418
SIDI BEN YEBKA	26	135	0	3	0.1	4	0.421
SIDI CHAMI	23	1249	2	2	0.11	5	0.411
TAFRAOUI	2	55	0	4	0.1	4	0.467

Generation of Subjective Parameters

The subjective parameters used are: weight, indifference, and preference. They are related to each criterion. The Table 4 illustrates the used subjective parameters.

Ranking the Risk Areas With PROMETHEE Method

The ranking obtained with the method is depicted in Figure 11. The graph shows that the commune of Oran is the high risk area of seasonal influenza epidemic. Bousfer, Boufatis, Mers El Hadjadj, Ain El Kerma, El Ancor are ranked at the very bottom. Whereas, the others communes are intermediate risk areas.

Table 4. The subjective parameters

	Incidence	Density	Industrial area	RH	Transmission rate	K	CC
weight	0.70	0.40	0.30	0.47	0.80	0.56	0.45
PREF(P)	361	2608.06	1	1	0.03	2	0.090
IND(q)	600	4016.67	2	2	0.07	4	0.164

Figure 11. The PROMETHEE graph

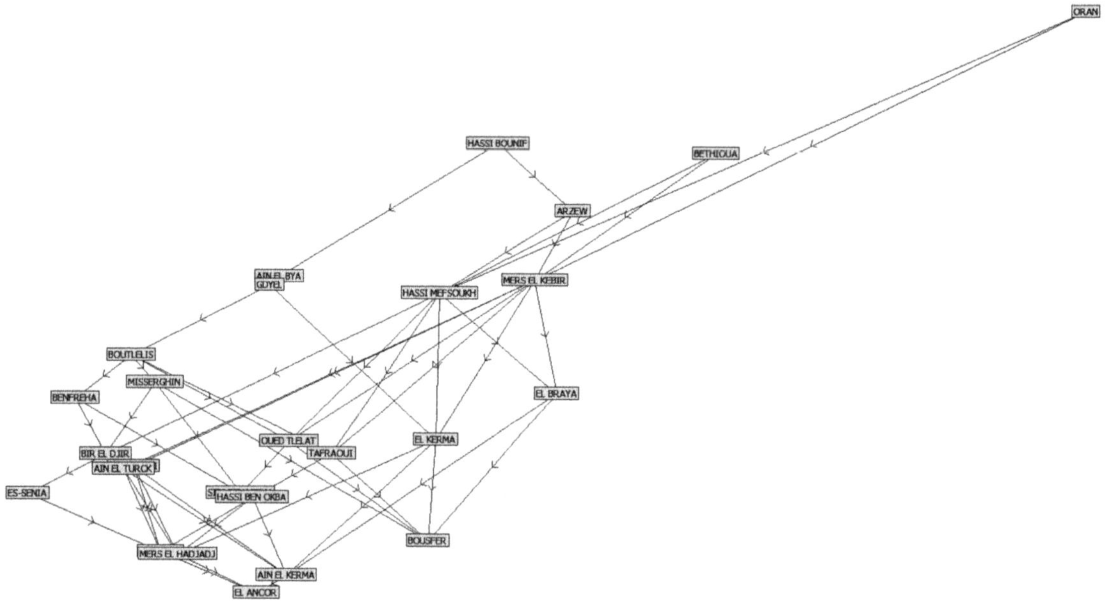

The positive, negative, and comprehensive flows with the rank of risk area (from high to low risk) obtained with PROMETHEE method are detailed in Table 5.

The Territory Model

For easy readability and clearer understanding of propagation phenomena in all communes, we propose territory model. The latter is principally based on a GIS, a geographical database of region of Oran that includes spatial reference information of the 26 municipalities and simulated data. The study area shapefile, which incorporates parameters of each commune, was created in ArcGIS 10 using geospatial data from Center for Centre for Space Technology (CTS) of Arzew (Oran). The GIS provides a real-time visualization method of spreading epidemics to enhance the visual analytics of the disease outbreak detection [Younsi et al, 2015b].

According to the simulated data and the geographical database, we can make a spatiotemporal analysis in order to control the epidemic evolution for the early detection and geo-location of an outbreak. Daily, aggregate incidence per commune was calculated by adding the number of positive cases for each commune in a given day. These visualizations make spatiotemporal trends in the data more accessible and

Table 5. Flow Values and Ranks

Rang	Action	ϕ	ϕ+	ϕ-
1	ORAN	0.3774	0.4643	0.0870
2	HASSI BOUNIF	0.2452	0.2734	0.0282
3	BETHIOUA	0.2359	0.3150	0.0791
4	ARZEW	0.1787	0.2560	0.0773
5	AIN EL BYA	0.1140	0.1607	0.0466
6	MERS EL KEBIR	0.1110	0.2143	0.1033
7	GDYEL	0.1058	0.1543	0.0486
8	HASSI MEFSOUKH	0.0980	0.1873	0.0893
9	BOUTLELIS	0.0368	0.0903	0.0535
10	MISSERGHIN	0.0094	0.0816	0.0722
11	EL BRAYA	-0.0002	0.1634	0.1636
12	BENFREHA	-0.0062	0.0568	0.0630
13	EL KERMA	-0.0465	0.1144	0.1608
14	OUED TLELAT	-0.0483	0.0817	0.1301
15	TAFRAOUI	-0.0601	0.0850	0.1451
16	BIR EL DJIR	-0.0611	0.0359	0.0970
17	SIDI CHAMI	-0.0734	0.0359	0.1092
18	AIN EL TURCK	-0.0754	0.0326	0.1080
19	SIDI BEN YEBKA	-0.0988	0.0460	0.1448
20	ES-SENIA	-0.0996	0.0000	0.0996
21	HASSI BEN OKBA	-0.1037	0.0460	0.1497
22	BOUSFER	-0.1457	0.0630	0.2087
23	BOUFATIS	-0.1565	0.0000	0.1565
24	MERS EL HADJADJ	-0.1595	0.0022	0.1617
25	AIN EL KERMA	-0.1797	0.0155	0.1952
26	EL ANCOR	-0.1974	0.0000	0.1974

interpretable for a wide variety of non-scientific readers. More illustrations of evolution of epidemic on map are in [Younsi et al, 2015b]

Figure 12, shows the outcomes of PROMETHEE II method visualized on the region map, it represents the rank of risk area of seasonal influenza epidemic.

DISCUSSION

According to the results, we observe that there are four areas of very high risk namely at Oran, Hassi Bounif, Bethioua, an Arzew. Areas of average risk were recorded in eight communes. The remaining 14 communes were designated as low risk communes. The regions of very high risk are part of the Oran

Figure 12. Risk map of influenza epidemic

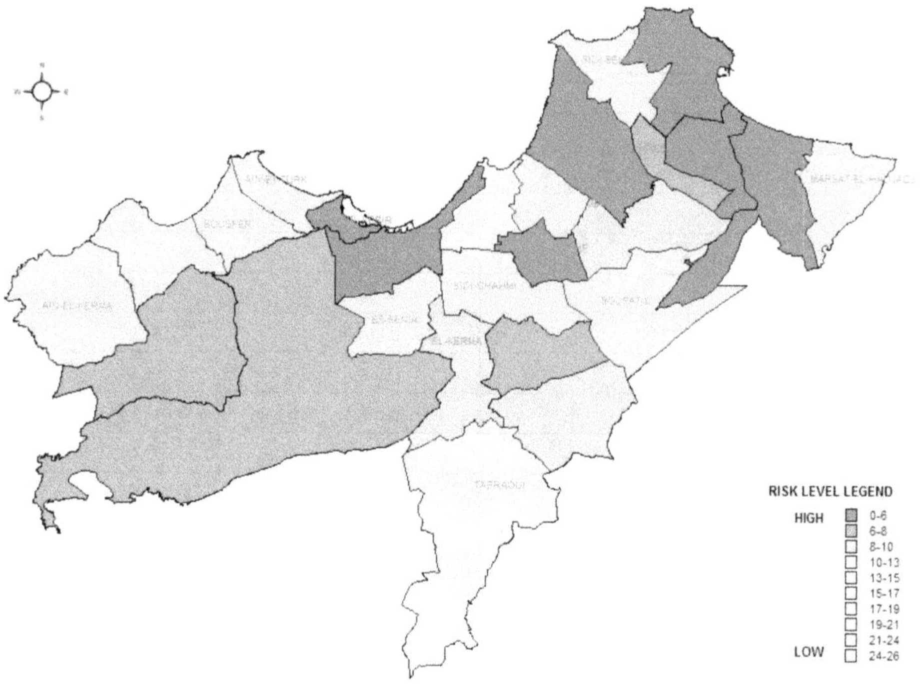

sea coast where major infrastructures are installed (hydrocarbons, ammonia production, etc.). Therefore, the air is highly polluted and promotes the transmission of respiratory diseases, especially seasonal flu. Moreover, during the winter, the region has a low temperature with low relative humidity (dry air), therefore, the seasonal influenza virus survives longer, and the transmission rate increase according to (Barreca and Shimshack, 12). Moreover, recent studies showed that influenza transmission was reduced by high humidity and high temperatures and, hence, it may be important to simultaneously use heating and ventilation, which could lead to substantial additional heating costs (Wein and Atkinson, 2009).

Although the communes with average and low risk have a large population density compared to the communes with high or very high risk. The risk of infection remains low. This confirms that the transmission of influenza is not very related to the social aspect (density) but also it is related to several factors, namely: clinical, socio-economic, climatic and environmental.

CONCLUSION

Seasonal influenza causes annual epidemics. It represents a serious public health problem that causes severe disease and death in populations at higher risk. Indeed, the surveillance and monitoring of the influenza epidemic has become a necessity to understand its evolution and occurrence.

In this research study, a novel hybrid approach is proposed for influenza epidemic surveillance. The developed method combines between advantages of GIS based on PROMETHEE II method and SEIRSW-GIS has demonstrated analytical capabilities in targeting high-risk spots and influenza epidemic surveillance monitoring system of the city of Oran. We produced risk map based on expert opinion on the spatial representation of risk of influenza transmission. The results reported in this paper show the superior capability of our hybrid model compared to others of the literature. It provides information to the public health decision maker/policy makers to give additional attention to the spatial planning of effective control measures.

In future, we will test other multi-criteria decision making methods. Indeed, in this paper, we propose to use the PROMETHEE II method, which is well-suited for our problem. However, other methods such as Dominance-based Rough Set Approach [Chakhar et al, 2016] could also be used.

REFERENCES

Adam, F. (Ed.). (2008). *Encyclopedia of decision making and decision support technologies* (Vol. 2). IGI Global. doi:10.4018/978-1-59904-843-7

Alimi, T. O., Fuller, D. O., Herrera, S. V., Arevalo-Herrera, M., Quinones, M. L., Stoler, J. B., & Beier, J. C. (2016). A multi-criteria decision analysis approach to assessing malaria risk in northern South America. *BMC Public Health, 16*(1), 221. doi:10.118612889-016-2902-7 PMID:26940004

Araz, O. M. (2013). Integrating complex system dynamics of pandemic influenza with a multi-criteria decision making model for evaluating public health strategies. *Journal of Systems Science and Systems Engineering, 22*(3), 319–339. doi:10.100711518-013-5220-y

Ayadi, D. (2010). *Optimisation multicritère de la fiabilité: application du modèle de goal programming avec les fonctions de satisfactions dans l'industrie de traitement de gaz* (Doctoral dissertation). Université d'Angers.

Balcan, D., Gonçalves, B., Hu, H., Ramasco, J. J., Colizza, V., & Vespignani, A. (2010). Modeling the spatial spread of infectious diseases: The GLobal Epidemic and Mobility computational model. *Journal of Computational Science, 1*(3), 132–145. doi:10.1016/j.jocs.2010.07.002 PMID:21415939

Brans, J. P., & Vincke, P. (1985). Note—A Preference Ranking Organisation Method: The PROMETHEE Method for Multiple Criteria Decision-Making. *Management Science, 31*(6), 647–656. doi:10.1287/mnsc.31.6.647

Brans, J. P., & Mareschal, B. (2002). *Prométhée-Gaia: une méthodologie d'aide à la décision en présence de critères multiples*. Éditions de l'Université de Bruxelles.

Barreca, A. I., & Shimshack, J. P. (2012). Absolute humidity, temperature, and influenza mortality: 30 years of county-level evidence from the United States. *American Journal of Epidemiology, 176*(suppl 7), S114–S122. doi:10.1093/aje/kws259 PMID:23035135

Beretta, E., & Kuang, Y. (2001). Modeling and analysis of a marine bacteriophage infection with latency period. In *Nonlinear Anal* (pp. 35–74). Real World. doi:10.1016/S0362-546X(99)00285-0

Chakhar, S., Ishizaka, A., Labib, A., & Saad, I. (2016). Dominance-based rough set approach for group decisions. *European Journal of Operational Research, 251*(1), 206–224. doi:10.1016/j.ejor.2015.10.060

Duerr, H. P., Schwehm, M., Leary, C. C., De Vlas, S. J., & Eichner, M. (2007). The impact of contact structure on infectious disease control: Influenza and antiviral agents. *Epidemiology and Infection, 135*(07), 1124–1132. doi:10.1017/S0950268807007959 PMID:17288643

Edwards, W. (1977). How to use multi-attribute utility measurement for social decision making. *IEEE Transactions on Systems, Man, and Cybernetics, 7*(5), 326–340. doi:10.1109/TSMC.1977.4309720

Elsayed, W. M., El-bassiouny, A. H., & Radwan, E. F. (2013). Applying Inhomogeneous Probabilistic Cellular Au-tomata Rules on Epidemic Model. *International Journal of Advanced Research in Artificial Intelligence, 2*(4).

Haddad, H., Moulin, B., & Thériault, M. (2016). A fully GIS-integrated simulation approach for analyzing the spread of epidemics in urban areas. *SIGSPATIAL Special, 8*(1), 34–41. doi:10.1145/2961028.2961034

Halouani, N., Chabchoub, H., & Martel, J. M. (2009). PROMETHEE-MD-2T method for project selection. *European Journal of Operational Research, 195*(3), 841–849. doi:10.1016/j.ejor.2007.11.016

Hamdadou, D. (2016). Méthodologie Multicritères d'Aide à la Décision, Cours et Exercices. Edition OPU 2016.

Hammami, A. (2003). *Modélisation technico-économique d'une chaîne logistique dans une entreprise réseau* (Doctoral dissertation). Ecole Nationale Supérieure des Mines de Saint-Etienne; Université Laval.

He, X., Huang, G., Liang, Z., Nong, Y., Wu, X., Luo, H., & Tang, Z. (2017). Simulation of the Spread of A/H1N1 Influenza Based on Geographic Information System Platform. *Journal of Medical Imaging and Health Informatics, 7*(3), 531–535. doi:10.1166/jmihi.2017.2067

Kim, L. Y. (2014). *Estimating network structure and propagation dynamics for an infectious disease: towards effective vaccine allocation* (Doctoral dissertation). Massachusetts Institute of Technology.

Malczewski, J. (2006). Decision Analysis for Collaborative GIS. In *Collaborative geographic information systems*. IGI Global; doi:10.4018/978-1-59140-845-1.ch010

Manogaran, G., & Lopez, D. (2017). Disease surveillance system for big climate data processing and dengue transmission. *International Journal of Ambient Computing and Intelligence, 8*(2), 88–105. doi:10.4018/IJACI.2017040106

Mao, L. (2013, November). Cost-effectiveness of workplace closure and travel restriction for mitigating influenza outbreaks: a network-based simulation. In *Proceedings of the Second ACM SIGSPATIAL International Workshop on the Use of GIS in Public Health* (pp. 77-84). ACM. 10.1145/2535708.2535709

Pastor-Satorras, R., Castellano, C., Van Mieghem, P., & Vespignani, A. (2014). *Epidemic processes in complex networks*. arXiv preprint arXiv:1408.2701.

Roy, B. (1978). ELECTRE III: Un algorithme de classement fondé sur une représentation floue des préférences en présence de critères multiples. *Cahiers du CERO, 20*(1), 3–24.

Rytkönen, M. J. (2004). Not all maps are equal: GIS and spatial analysis in epidemiology. *International Journal of Circumpolar Health, 63*(1). doi:10.3402/ijch.v63i1.17642 PMID:15139238

Saaty, T. L. (1980). *The Analytic Hierarchy Process*. New York: McGraw-Hill.

Stilianakis, N., & Weber, T. (2008). Epidemiological Modeling, Surveillance and Web-Based Information Systems. *International Disaster and Risk Conference IDRC Davos 2008, Proceedings*.

Tran, A., Ippoliti, C., Balenghien, T., Conte, A., Gely, M., Calistri, P., & Chevalier, V. (2013). A geographical information system-based multicriteria evaluation to map areas at risk for rift valley fever vector-borne transmission in Italy. *Transboundary and Emerging Diseases*, *60*(s2), 14–23. doi:10.1111/tbed.12156 PMID:24589097

Wang, X. F., & Chen, G. (2003). Complex networks: Small-world, scale-free and beyond. *Circuits and Systems Magazine*, *3*(1), 6–20. doi:10.1109/MCAS.2003.1228503

Wang, J., Xiong, J., Yang, K., Peng, S., & Xu, Q. (2010). Use of GIS and agent-based modeling to simulate the spread of influenza. In *Geoinformatics, 2010 18th International Conference on* (pp. 1-6). IEEE. 10.1109/GEOINFORMATICS.2010.5567658

Watts, D. J., & Strogatz, S. H. (1998). Collective dynamics of ‘small-world’ networks. *Nature, 393*(6684), 440-442.

Wein, L. M., & Atkinson, M. P. (2009). Assessing infection control measures for pandemic influenza. *Risk Analysis*, *29*(7), 949–962. doi:10.1111/j.1539-6924.2009.01232.x PMID:19392673

Xia, H., Chen, J., Marathe, M., & Mortveit, H. S. (2011). Synthesis and Refinement of Detailed Subnetworks in a Social Contact Network for Epidemic Simulations, Social Computing. *Behavioral-Cultural Modeling and Prediction, LNCS*, *6589*, 366–373. doi:10.1007/978-3-642-19656-0_50

Younsi, F. Z., Bounekkar, A., & Hamdadou, D. (2014, May). *SW-SEIR: un modèle de suivi de propagation d’épidémies.* Paper presented at the meeting of 8ème édition de la Conférence Avancées des Systèmes Décisionnels (ASD), Hammamet, Tunisia.

Younsi, F. Z., Bounnekar, A., Hamdadou, D., & Boussaid, O. (2015a). SEIR-SW, simulation model of influenza spread based on the Small World network. *Tsinghua Science and Technology*, *20*(5), 460–473. doi:10.1109/TST.2015.7297745

Younsi, F. Z., Hamdadoud, D., & Boussaid, O. (2015b). A surveillance and spatiotemporal visualization model for infectious diseases using social network. *International Journal of Decision Support System Technology*, *7*(4), 1–19. doi:10.4018/IJDSST.2015100101

Zemri, A., & Hamdadou, D. (2017). *Integration of Data Mining Techniques in Multi Criteria Spatial Decision Support System for Epidemiological Monitoring. International Journal of Decision Support System Technology.*

ADDITIONAL READING

Bhatt, C. M., Dey, N., & Ashour, A. (2017). *Internet of Things and Big Data Technologies for Next Generation Healthcare* (Vol. 23). Springer. doi:10.1007/978-3-319-49736-5_2

Dey, N., Hassanien, A. E., Bhatt, C., Ashour, A. S., & Satapathy, S. C. (2018). Internet of Things and Big Data Analytics Toward Next-Generation Intelligence.

Dey, N., Ashour, A. S., Shi, F., Fong, S. J., & Sherratt, S. (2017). Developing residential wireless sensor networks for ECG healthcare monitoring. *IEEE Transactions on Consumer Electronics*, *63*(4), 442–449. doi:10.1109/TCE.2017.015063

Dey, N., & Mukherjee, A. (2016). *Embedded Systems and Robotics with Open Source Tools*. CRC Press. doi:10.1201/b19730

Elhayatmy, G., Dey, N., & Ashour, A. S. (2018). Internet of Things Based Wireless Body Area Network in Healthcare. In *Internet of Things and Big Data Analytics Toward Next-Generation Intelligence* (pp. 3–20). Cham: Springer. doi:10.1007/978-3-319-60435-0_1

Kamal, S., Ripon, S. H., Dey, N., Ashour, A. S., & Santhi, V. (2016). A MapReduce approach to diminish imbalance parameters for big deoxyribonucleic acid dataset. *Computer Methods and Programs in Biomedicine*, *131*, 191–206. doi:10.1016/j.cmpb.2016.04.005 PMID:27265059

Kamal, M. S., Parvin, S., Ashour, A. S., Shi, F., & Dey, N. (2017). De-Bruijn graph with MapReduce framework towards metagenomic data classification. *International Journal of Information Technology*, *9*(1), 59–75. doi:10.100741870-017-0005-z

Kamal, M. S., Sarowar, M. G., Dey, N., Ashour, A. S., Ripon, S. H., Panigrahi, B. K., & Tavares, J. M. R. (2017). Self-organizing mapping based swarm intelligence for secondary and tertiary proteins classification. *International Journal of Machine Learning and Cybernetics*, 1–24.

Kamal, S., Dey, N., Ashour, A. S., Ripon, S., Balas, V. E., & Kaysar, M. S. (2017). FbMapping: AN AUTOMATED SYSTEM FOR MONITORING FACEBOOK DATA. *Neural Network World*, *27*(1), 27–57. doi:10.14311/NNW.2017.27.002

Yadav, P., Sharma, S., Tiwari, P., Dey, N., Ashour, A. S., & Nguyen, G. N. (2018). A Modified Hybrid Structure for Next Generation Super High Speed Communication Using TDLTE and Wi-Max. In *Internet of Things and Big Data Analytics Toward Next-Generation Intelligence* (pp. 525–549). Cham: Springer. doi:10.1007/978-3-319-60435-0_21

ENDNOTE

1 http://www.dsp-oran.dz/

Chapter 9
Review on Image Representation Compression and Retrieval Approaches

Lalit B. Damahe
Yeshwantao Chavan College of Engineering, India

Nileshsingh V. Thakur
Nagpur Institute of Technology, India

ABSTRACT

Image representation and compression is one of the important fields of computer vision that contribute to the reduction of size of an image and other types of application areas such as image restoration, retrieval, etc. Image representation is important with respect to storage of image information, and it further extends to the compression, which may be lossy or lossless. Image compression can be applied to various applications which mainly include medical imaging, traffic monitoring, military, multimedia transmission, smart cell devices, and almost in all the domains that require less transmission and storage cost, specifically image retrieval processing. This chapter presents the various image representation compression and retrieval approaches. The retrieval approaches on personal computer and smart cell devices are discussed. Finally, the key issues are identified for image representation compression and retrieval on the basis of performance evaluation parameters like encoding time, decoding time, compression ratio, precision, recall, and elapsed time.

INTRODUCTION

A two dimensional image is a finite set of digital values generally call it as pixels or picture element. The images display on the digital computing system having a unique representation and that is mostly belongs to the type of binary, gray, color or indexed color. The representation of images are related to the space and time required to store and display and depending upon the type of images space required to store may vary. For example if we consider the binary image having a resolution of 200× 200 then according to one 1 bit/pixel it will required 400 bits . For the comparable gray images it will take 3200

DOI: 10.4018/978-1-5225-6164-4.ch009

and color images it will take 9600 bits. Although True color image take lot of space to store and almost three times the gray images hence indexed images minimizes the intensity values up to 4, 16 and 256 which will ultimately leads to the memory saving but it compromises the quality. The significant role performs by the mechanism of image compression which removes the redundancies and not only reduced the space but also reduces the accessing or display time for the images or multimedia transmission. In the context of multimedia domain variety of application areas are present which specifically include the image transmission of query image and retrieval of image data from the server side stored in the repository.

But the retrieval of images takes more time to access data from the server side when images need to be displayed on Mobile devices as in Figure 1 and having a less computational power. Hence, the compression is playing important role in the multimedia domain. There are good no. of literatures are available which mainly dealing with the image processing operation like image representation, compression and retrieval which is discussed in the next section.

RELATED WORK

Various authors contributed for the image representation scheme applied on various domain of application, such as image restoration compression, retrieval etc. The following section contributes towards the image representation, compression and retrieval approaches.

Image Representation on PC

For the retrieval and image recognition, image representation using low dimensional features is important. X. He et al. (2016) proposed a image representation technique based the perspective of statistical design. The proposed algorithm called A-optimal having better representation capability and gives the

Figure 1. Query image send over wireless channel for retrieval

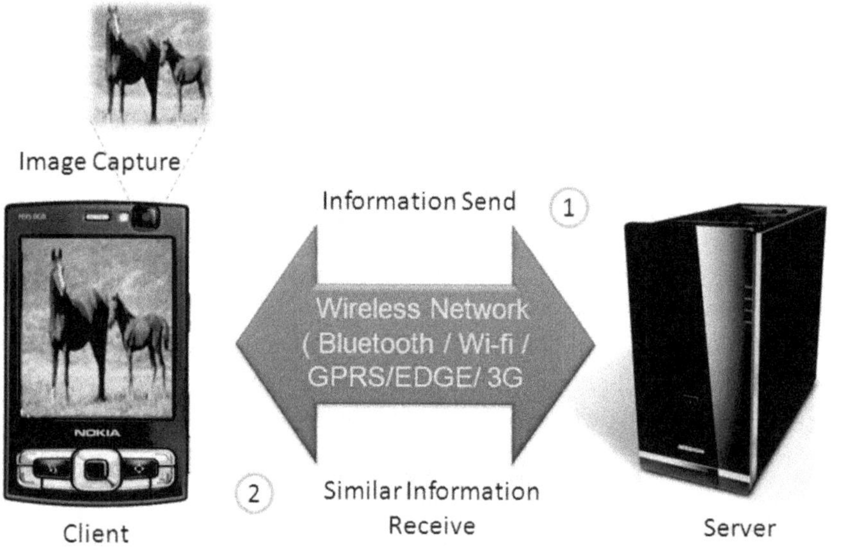

higher accuracy. Although there is a importance of image representations (K. Lenc & A. Vedaldi et al. (2015) investigate the Image representations properties (equivalence, equivariance, invariance). Equivalence gives capture and visual information, equivariance is the compression using representation, and invariance provides information regarding transformation like scaling rotation etc. A. Mahendran and A. Vedaldi (2015) carry out the analysis of visual information enclosed in representation. L. Gueguen (2016) proposed scheme is based on image patches, which encode image at a generalize level on large scale images. This scheme achieved good results in terms of error rate.

Choosing a subset of dimensions from the original feature is the good alternative than compression of feature vector. Zhang et al. (2016) proposed a approach is based on dimensionality reduction of feature vector It uses mutual information or entropy to select subset of large feature dimensions and achieved good outcome than compression methods. Machine learning based is proposed by A. Kumar et al. (2016) to detect malware for android OS. Analysis is performed for visual representation using apk file for various color spaces like grayscale, RGB, CMYK and HSL.

Person re-identification has been usually solved by single or cross-image representation. F. Wang et al. (2016) proposed a approach on ANN using convolution. The given framework shared a subset network with other two network and that capture the SIR and CIR of images. Optimization is carried out jointly to achieved better accuracy and with reasonable cost. For the large scale image retrieval hashing technique is very popular and having a better accuracy and efficiency. Learning based approach is proposed by L. Ma et al. (2017) for binary codes using unsupervised hashing and NMF. The high dimensional feature representation is obtained using NMF and then converts to hash codes. Sparse representation and multi scale transformation are well accepted techniques for fusion of image signals. F. Fakhari et al. (2017) proposed a technique, based on Fusion of MST and SR. First, the source images including five groups of multi-focus, medical, multi-modal visible-IR and visible-MMW and PMMW were decomposed to their sub-bands using MST. The group (Medical, IR, Multi-focus, MMW, Multi-modal) of images is for the given method.

S. Lee et al. proposed (2017) a approach for aggregating binary features into a unique feature vector. Histogram is created using independent aggregation of sub features and sub-features are obtained from the binary data. Training and complete quantization free approach is proposed for quick representation and it can be replace existing BoBF technique of computer vision. A. Karine et al. (2017) present a novel generic approach for radar automatic target recognition in either inverse synthetic aperture radar or synthetic aperture radar images using statistical modeling. First, a statistical dictionary is constructed using the training set. It is done by estimating the statistical parameters of the magnitude of DT-CWT coefficients using a non-Gaussian model. For the recognition task, used the weighted sparse representation based classification method that captures the linearity and locality information of image features.

For the Fruit flies identification M. Matheus et al. (2017) proposed a mid-level image representation approach for insect identification of three species of the genus *Anastrephausing* different local descriptors based on keypoints. Furthermore, we performed three robust analyses to support the development of a real-time system for fruit fly identification. The FAST detector achieved to detect many more keypoints on the image regions considered very important by specialists. The BRIEF and F-SIFT also achieved the best results of mean accuracy among all of released local descriptors and future work extend towards a mobile based system to assist the experts of this domain.

A unique framework is presented by L. Jiao et al. (2017) using Gaussian and EO. A separate treatment is given to the two (smooth and non-smooth) different categories of image patches. A combinatorial optimization is achieved in comparison with principal component. For the feature selection, subset is the good alternative than the complete vector and feature encoding. Y. Zhang (2016) proposed a method to reduce the dimension of large dimensional features such as Fisher vector or VLAD. For 1 bit representation two distance measures are developed. The proposed scheme achieved better efficiency and accuracy than feature encoding. There are a few issues need to investigate to evaluate proposed technique for large dimensions features sampled from various descriptors and also need to develop more effective feature selection methods for higher accuracy.

The proposed approach Z. Chen et al. (2017) carried out for the image and tackle problem of background-inference by the unique framework. The decomposition of complete image according to different object is carried out and separate re-ranking is performed and the future work needs to expand towards graph theoretic approach to get the semantic relation. The technique presented L. Dong (2016) is based on HVR to improve retrieval rate by finding similarity in intra-structure. It describes the global distribution of the local features of an image with respect to the entire local features set of image datasets. The local features of complete dataset are used to get the global information and achieved scaling property for big datasets. A graph theory based approach is presented by B. Chaudhuri (2016) for image retrieval of RS images. ARG is created to modeled images and archived graphs are matched with query, using inexact graph matching. Lastly, the related images are retrieved and ranked based on graph values.

Image Compression on PC

Image compression is broadly classified into two main classes i.e. prediction and transform. Following section describe the various compression mechanisms.

Various video and image processing algorithms needs FIFO and its size depends on the length and width of the filter but if affects the area and power consumptions. S. M. A. Zeinolabedin proposed (2015) an efficient approach for designing FIFO. This technique reduces the power consumption and size of the FIFO by exploiting spatial relation of adjacent pixels and data compression. Q. Yu, W. Yu (2015) proposed a efficient and adoptive approach binary coding based on probability and log domain. The designed approach achieved high encoding ratio with less complexity and does not required look up table, multiplication etc. A Laplacian model is developed using concept of probability for the DCT and its extend towards the compression (2015). The proposed system offer efficient predictive image compression and multi-resolution capability, having high coding efficiency and less complexity specifically suitable for the real time applications. The two (TCQ and CDZQ) types of quantizer is introduced coefficients is compressed using Entropy encoding (CALBIC). The optimization of CDZQ and CALCAC are further improved by SDQ algorithm. It is one of the best non-predictive compression method for image compression. The proposed technique out perform in terms of PSNR value and quality of visualization but the proposed system requires multiple passes for encoding which is not be suitable some online applications. Predictive encoding offer a flexible structure for both types of compression and lossy compression is suitable for hyperspectral and multispectral images.

M. Conoscenti et al. (2015) proposed a technique which permit lossy encoding with bounded error in reconstructed and original images. The proposed method is simple and effective, which significantly improves the performance by reducing the complexity and extended towards the compression of bit-plane entropy. A novel prediction technique, is proposed by the T. Strutz (2016) for lossless color image compression. The A prediction based, two methods namely template matching and blending is combines for lossless compression of color images. Kim and N. I. Cho (2014) proposed method is based on hierarchical prediction and adoptive arithmetic compression. The compression is performed in YCuCv color space and Y channel is encoded by the normal lossless compression technique and arithmetic coding is apply to encode chrominance layers. Image representation is important for the process of encoding of gray and color images. M. Le Pendu et al. (2016) proposes the encoding method based on YCbCr and CIE uv color space. The encoding of HDR image is represented by YCbCr format whereas a second scheme is based on the CIE uv color space. Various equations for prediction is presented for color spaces to preserve shades and method outperformed the ILP.

Transmission and storage of Images or photographs in mobile devices and platform just like cloud is the biggest challenge. H. Wu et al. (2016) proposed a unique method of lossless-compression to the reduced size of grouped JPEG images which are having correlation property. The proposed method removes the inter and intra band redundancy exists in frequency and spatial domain. The images are organized to simulate into video frames by reducing the cost required for prediction (globally). The gap between global and local cost is minimize by the spatial domain and disparity between reference and targeted images is reduced by the frequency domain. It further extended towards entropy based coding to remove intra relational redundancy. A fundamental problem with many image processing and computer vision operation like classification, segmentation, retrieval etc. includes feature compression. In reality quantization leads to loss of information or data. The technique proposed by S. Bai et al. (2016) is based on vector quantization performed in multiple stages which offer new modeling for residual vector. The concept of support vector machine is introduced to classify coarse to fine quantization level. The problem of efficient prediction is addressed by H. Shen et al. (2017) for the domain of hyperspectral lossless image compression for Region of Interest. A partial and spectral correlation of images is removed by concept of multi-stage prediction. To encode residual prediction vector, Golomb Rice encoding is introduced.

Diffusion-based compression methods accumulate only some pixels and inpaint lost regions. In spite of this binding and lack of color encoding, image colorization is integrated into transform techniques just like JPEG. The efficient color compression using diffusion based colorization is proposed by P. Peter et al. (2017) using YCbCr model. Diffusion based concept is applied on luma and croma channels to achieved reconstruction of color information. Lossless images compression remains as a great challenge for the research community even today. Medical industry, satellite imagery, remote sensing etc. make use of lossless compression schemes where the loss of information is very critical. HSV and YUV are reversible color transform which helps to increase the redundancy in images there by enhance compression. YUV transformation before encoding helps to reduce the entropy of the images and thus achieves higher compression. A lossless color image compression scheme is proposed (2016) by S. Beevi et al. using the property of YUV in Bi-level BWCA which is a variant of Burrows Wheeler Compression Algorithm (BWCA). The first level RCT reduced the number of unique symbols in the hue components of natural images, thus produce large reduction in the number of unique Y components in the second level RCT. Hence the double level RCT based bi-level BWCA provide better compression ratio for natural images.

K. J. Cheng and J. Dill proposed (2014) a scheme based on BEZW for the compression of hyperspectral images moving from lossless to lossy. Algorithm using the KL transforms and DWT to accomplished mix transforms and remove spectral and spatial correlation. The 3-D BEZW algorithm compresses hyperspectral images by implementing progressive bit plane coding. The proposed approach of lossless compression achieved a good accuracy in comparison with existing benchmark techniques. A efficient solution of depth map encoding is proposed by L. F. R. Lucas et al. (2015). A efficient depth map coding is developed to represent its characteristics which involves directions for intra-prediction and residual encoding. The optimization is performed using block partitioning method. A edge representation technique is developed, to improve the performance of conditional depth modeling mode. For the next generation multimedia application O. G. Sezer et al. (2015) proposed a new transform design method. The proposed SOT (sparse orthonormal transforms) utilize to remove the regularity of signal structures and it provides the finest representation to local regions. Sparse orthonormal transforms provides a extension to the KL transform and this extension can be achieved through Gaussian method which exploits non-Gaussian data to improve the performance and this optimize designed apply on various transform structure like lap, block etc.

For the HSI model, W. Fu et al. (2017) proposed a approach for lossy encoding by using novel technique called as SSAR. The superpixels grouping is performed to remove the different redundancy exist in HSI model and joint-sparsity is achieved through dynamic sparse representation and encoding of coefficients is performed by Huffman coding. Traditionally, intra frame compression is dual operation process which includes the block pixel predictions and then predicted block is encoded using 2D DCT coding. The application of 2D Markov processes is extended to improve the performance of prediction and transform coding. The approach proposed by F. Kamisli (2015) is based on markov process to model image blocks having minimum effects of blocking artifacts.

A generalize scheme of Set Partition Coding System (SPACS) (2016) is proposed by Q. Li et al. using degree-k SPIHT. The SPACS is constructed using this encoding scheme and aided the sub-bands which is generated by decomposition of LL band. This technique improves the coding efficiency over SPIHT and, and various bits are used to evaluate the coding efficiency of SPACS. For encoding smooth images, W. Hu et al. (2015) proposed a technique, multi-resolution graph Fourier transform. The optimization is performed on the GFT through spectral clustering and minimum graph cuts.

S. Alzahir et al. (2015) proposed a novel method of lossless compression of color images includes map, GIS etc. A fixed size codebook is used for storing 8×8 block Huffman codes and their probabilities.

Arithmetic coding is also apply on large group of color images and compression using row column reduction is apply on blocks which are not store in the codebook. Sparse representation generates the best outcome on image and signal processing operations over redundant dictionaries. But the current research moving towards the dictionary based approach using learning. Learning through boosting is presented (2016) and training is provided to the dictionaries. The proposed method outperformed the JPEG2000, and which significantly reduced the average bit-rate about 10%. S. Kim and H. J. Lee propose (2016) a unique compression algorithm for RGBW and its components increase the efficiency of BTC. Approach is implemented for LCD and OLEDs and the proposed dynamic method called LAM-BTC is employ to encode RGBW image data. The encoding is performed using 2 and 4 level BTC to improve the quality of images and achieved high PSNR over existing AM-BTC.

Image compression using fractal coding achieved a efficient compression ratio. The compression of images using Pseudo Spiral Architecture is proposed by Thakur N. V et al. (2006) and it achieved faster encoding due this architecture and conversion of 3 color plane into one. A unique compression technique is proposed by Thakur N. V. et al. (2006) for the compression of database of color images. The concept of spiral architecture is introduced with fractal coding and encoding time is reduced efficiently. For the compression of image using fractal coding N. V. Thakur & O. Kakde (2007) proposed a approach based on spiral architecture and the significant amount of encoding time is reduced for the lossy compression. The optimized version of domain block selection in fractal coding is proposed by N. V. Thakur & O. Kakde (2007) using spiral image representation and sufficient amount of encoding time is reduced in comparison with traditional method. The image is represented using WFA and this concept of finite automata is introduced by S. D. Kamble and N. V. Thakur (2018) for video compression using fractal coding. The fractal compression applied on image is presented (2009) and it extended towards the purpose of security. The compression is performed before the actual encryption and this well defined mechanism is suitable for various multimedia applications. A compression based image encryption is proposed by Razzaque A. & Thakur N. V (2012). The partial encryption technique is applied to reduced the bandwidth utilization. For the security of medical images, watermarking is one of the alternative. The approach proposed by Nilanjan Dey et al. (2012) is based on compression applied on watermark video for the Electronic patient record. Image compression using vector quantization is performed (Bose, Madhulika, Acharjee, Chowdhury, Chakraborty and Dey, 2014) and its effect on watermarking is analyzed. The DCT and DWT technique is employed for the watermarking process and performance is evaluated using different parameters like MSE, SNR, PSNR etc.

Image Retrieval on PC

Literature available for image retrieval on desktop PC is very large in comparison with that of smart cell devices. Many Researchers have worked in the field of computer vision and focused on feature extraction and similarity matching of images from the database. Various techniques are discussed by different authors for image retrieval for the desktop or standalone system. Most of discussed approaches are based on invariant transformation and fusion techniques to improve the retrieval process.

The S. Zhang et al. (2015) proposed the unsupervised fusion method to improve the retrieval precision. The method retrieves the results as rank graphs for the query image using page rank algorithm and weighted maximum density sub graph. Multiple graphs are merged and re-ranked by link analysis on fused graph. X. Liu et al. (2016) proposed multi-hash tables for fusion and ranking the images. For each query image hash table, bitwise query adaptive weights are assigned and Query specific rank fusion is calculated. The similar images are retrieved and combined in a graph using Page Rank algorithm. M. Wang et al. (2012) proposed a approach on multi-modal graph based learning and used the graph regularize framework to maintain the similarity and re-ranking. The Difference between two ranked lists is estimated using squared loss method and re-ranking is done using normalised graph laplacian and Mahalanobis distance metric is used. C. Deng et al (2013) has described Co-Regularized Multi-Graph Learning (Co-RMGL) framework for fusion of multi-graphs which consists of intra-graph concept to maximize the query to target distribution. The attribute vector Co-RMGL-AI is compared with Co-RMGL-AM

The D. Wenfei et al. (2014) proposed a fusion by applying weights for multi-features. The weights are adjusted dynamically for single features and fixed weights are assigned to the fusion based features. The L. Zheng et al. (2014) introduced Coupled Multi-index method to overcome illumination changes and improve recall. The presented model is based on packing and padding system. Packing steps consist of the fusion of descriptor as one dimension of coupled multi-index. Padding steps include techniques to increase the retrieval performance. An Inverted index is calculated which uses three parameters image ID, Term-Frequency data and metadata of each index feature. The approach proposed bu N. Bhowmik et al. (2014) is based on inverted multi-index uses the Codebook which is associated with inverted indices and merged to generate the final list. The X. Shi et al. (2015) proposed the mFFMI framework for efficient image retrieval. The mFFMI method is used for fusion and works on associating feature tuple with visual words. Extracted features are stored in the form of inverted multi-index to improve the accuracy. The mFFMI framework Multiple Assignment is used with mFFMI to enhance the recall rate. S. Bai et al. (2015) proposed the Sparse Contextual Activation (SCA) method for encoding local features of an image to improve the time efficiency, retrieval performance. Inverted index is used to store image ID and membership grade and to improve the performance of SCA by local consistency enhancement (LCE).

The L. Zheng et al. (2015) proposed a unsupervised score level Late fusion method based on L shape and to fused the graph the score value for the graph is normalized. Cumulative Match Characteristic (CMC) curve method eliminates the negative impact of worst features and handles the computational complexity by assigning global weights to features which are sensitive to change. The approach by K. Kavitha et. al. (2014), combines the local and global features. The offline phase works on feature extraction and online phase works on fusion and similarity matching. Z. XU et al. proposed (2016) a approach for online phase which retrieves local features and arranges it semantically and the offline phase is used for feature fusion and indexing. The hyper-graph method is used to obtain the relations between low-level visual features and their additional information regarding its location. The Democratic Diffusion method is proposed by Z. Gao et al. (2016), based on online and offline phase query fusion. The method used for re-ranking and effective retrieval. The main idea of the author is to reweight the feature vectors and later aggregate it to contract the image. X. Wang et al. proposed the approach (2011) that worked on online, offline stages and used re-ranking concept. The offline stage performs the task of assigning keywords to the query image and store them using semantic signature using shape and color features. The online stage performs similarity matching and re-ranking using the reference classes. Re-ranking precision is checked by assigning and comparing the global and adaptive weight for the query image.

The Fusion based approach proposed by R. Alghamdi et al. (2014) aims to extract textual and visual information of the image and used two data mining techniques association rules mining and clustering algorithm for image retrieval. This approach is based on online and offline phase. F. Yang et al. proposed (2015) the fusion of multi- feature information and re-ranking algorithm for image retrieval. Multiple features graphs are fused using Markov model and weights are assigned to images. The Vector of locally aggregated descriptor (VLAD) is used for aggregating multi-features and diffusion method is applied after fusion to minimize noise improve retrieval. The histogram of local and global features using SIFT and Upper-Lower LBP(UL-LBP) is proposed by L. Kabbai et al. (2016).A. Pancham et al. proposed (2015) a approach to overcome the computational and storage problem and reduce the dimension by using SURF-PCA. Dimentions can be reduced by PCA and SURF is used for motion tracking, object detection, image registration, and classification. Kalman filter is used for minimizing the dimension for reliable tracking and tracking for 64-D descriptor is done by projecting the matrix with lower feature space. Global NN(GNN) algorithm is used to extract the best features and track an object.

To improve the performance S. Banerji et al. (2013) proposed a approach using Local Binary Pattern (LBP) and Bag of words (BOW). LBP is combined with DCT and BoW to extract features and spatial pyramid matching (SPM) to extracted features. H. Kekre et al (2010) proposed the fusion approach for Modified Block truncation coding (MBTC) and Gabor filter. The proposed method is the modification in original block truncation coding (BTC) for content based image retrieval system and the superiority of the system is based on Gabor feature and Modified BTC. H. Yuan et al. (2011) proposed a Multiple Attribute Decision Making (MADM) approach. Fusion matrix and entropy analysis is performed and weights to the query image are assigned using correlation analysis on each feature. A feedback borda count fusion method is proposed by B. Bagheri et al. (2013). Two kinds of fusion is done using short term learning (STL) algorithms and Support Vector Machine(SVM) and the rank list is made according to the features of the query image. J. Wang et al. (2010) approach is based on feedback and multi-feature fusion for color, texture and shape. It extracts the color features of an image using the color histogram, the texture using gray co-occurrence matrix and shape using moment invariants. Precision rate of image retrieval is increased by using the weighted regulation algorithm.

The approach based on fusion of Global, Semi-global and local features is proposed by M. Rahman et al (2006). HSV color as the global feature, Region-based image retrieval (RBIR) is used as local features and semi-global features work on grid based method that divides the image into five overlapping parts. The similarity is measured by assigning weights to the query image. Y. Mistry et al (2010) approach is based on 2D complex dual tree Discrete wavelet transformation and Local binary pattern feature fusion with six and four level of decomposition. For the fusion of X-ray images H. Guan et al. (2010) proposed a technique using feature normalization. The shape of an image is extracted and images are selected according to semantic concepts and the fusion algorithm Picked-Weighted-Score (PWS) is applied. Approach is proposed by S. Sural et al. (2012) to calculate the HSV color descriptor on the basis of pixel intensity of image and color histogram and segment image. The segmentation of colors is done by using K-means clustering. For solving inappropriate segmentation P. Daga et al. proposed (2014) spectral clustering. A texture gradient is calculated for query image, its and Graylevel co-occurrence matrices (GLCM) are applied to extract features and to segregate the region. Further, the spectral clustering algorithm is applied to cluster the region. N. Khattak et al. (2007) used the concept of structure and shape representation of object for image matching. Matching is performed on corners, edges and ribbons is controlled for basic invariant operations. Multimodal features are combine by the H. Frigui et al (2008) for retrieval and it uses concept of fuzzy function for features distances. A confidence value for the retrieval ranking is generated by aggregating weights and membership Linear and nonlinear aggregation is performed through weight function and Discrete Choquet Integral.

Sparse representation through patches and SR fusion having a drawback to preserve the details and sensitive for misregistration. Yu Liu et al. (2016) approach of fusion using the sparse coding. A canovolutional sparse representation (CSR) is used and input image divided into base and detailed layer for image fusion. The SPQ based technique is proposed by Q. Ning et al. (2017) to compress high dimension vectors. Optimization is performed by reducing quantization error and codebook is generated to represent the features. Experimentation is done on Oxford dataset and performance is evaluated using Average precision rate and recall rate. Sparse Hashing with optimized anchor embedding is proposed by Y. Guo et al. (2017). The sparse hashing SH method, optimizes the integration of the anchors, to better embed and binarized. The performance is evaluated using mean average precision. L. Li et al. (2017) proposed a sparse representation using complete dictionaries to extract features of high level.

The typical patterns of edges are stored in dictionaries and block-wise representation of blurred images is stored in the dictionary and performance is evaluated through 6 standard benchmark datasets. The various CBIR approaches are discussed by N. Thakur and N. Koli (2010) for the desktop system and focusing on the existing feature extraction techniques. Belarbi M. A. et al. (2017) presented approach for the image retrieval using PCA of SIFT and SURF descriptor. The significant amount of time is reduced for the operation of retrieval. The presented chapter by Aarti Singh et al. (2017) discussed the semantics of image retrieval and further it suggests the scope of improvement to automate the existing systems. Summary of some presented literatures is given in Table 1.

Image Retrieval on Smart Cell Devices

Content based image retrieval on smart cell devices is more demanding because of inbuilt and high resolution camera capability. All the existing contribution study and examine the CS (client and server) architecture to perform retrieval on cell devices. The snap of query image is captured and transmitted to the server it acknowledged the similar images based on matching criteria. Existing contributions related

Table 1. Summary of Image Retrieval approaches on PC

Reference No, Author, Year of Publication	Concept Used	Performance Evaluation Parameter	Database Used	Claim by Authors	Our Findings
S. Zang et. al., 2015.	Unsupervised graph based precision.	N-S score, Precision, Mean Average Precision.	Holidays, Ukbench, Corel, SFlandmarks	Rank the Images. The retrieval rate is increased without compromising the Scalability	It avoids some problems like over fitting and manual annotation. Memory is consumed in storing Vocabulary tree and GIST performs poorly for Illumination.
L. Zheng et. al., 2015.	Late fusion method at score level using L-shape Curve.	Mean Average Precision.	Holidays, Ukbench, VIPeR.	To make the method query adaptive using good and bad features are normalized.	Accuracy decreases with small Change is feature weight.
L. Zheng et al., 2014.	Coupled Multi-index.	N-Score, Mean Average Precision.	UK-bench, Holi-days, DupImages, Mobile images and MIR Flickr.	To search images sharing of equal appearance is performed in real time and feature fusion is performed at Index level.	Organize through Multi-Index around the codebook to increase the accuracy.
S. Bai et al., 2016.	Sparse Contextual Acti-vation, local consistency enhancement	N-S Score, Average Re-ranking time.	PSB, YALE, MPEG-7,Uk-bench dataset.	To improve the time efficiency of re-ranking Procedure and the retrieval performance in an unsupervised manner.	It is sensitive to size of neighborhood set and local enhancement parameters. As the parameters increases the performance decreases.
[71]Jing-Yan Wang, Zhen Zhu,2010.	Feedback based feature Multi-fusion.	Precision rate	Corel	Improve the accuracy.	The fusion of multi-feature improves the accuracy and recall rate of image retrieval.
F. Yang et al., 2015.	Vector of locally Aggregated descriptor, Markov model.	N-S Score, Mean Average Precision.	Holidays, UK-bench, Oxford and Paris.	Noise is reduced and achieved better retrieval.	The VLAD performance decreases due to large view point changes in Oxford and Paris dataset.
R. Alghamdi, et al., 2014.	Multi-modal Fusion method based on Association rules mining.	Mean Average Precision.	CLEF.	Achieved best precision score amongst different query category.	It extracts both textual and visual features of the query.
C.Deng et al., 2013.	Co-Regularized Multi- Graph Learning (Co-RMGL).	Mean Average Precision.	Paris, Holidays, UKbench.	Highlight the unique strength of individual feature modality.	Weak learning is performed to remove the noise in the images. The performance decreases as the candidate image increases.
X. Shi et al., 2015.	Multiple Features Fusion Based Inverted Multi- Index (mFFM).	N-S score.	Holidays, UKbench	Improve the accuracy using inverted index.	Multiple Assignment are used with mFFMI to enhance the re-call rate.
N. Bhowmik et al., 2014.	Inverted multi-index.	Mean Average Precision.	COIL and PARIS.	Improve similarity search and efficiency.	Combining optimal configuration before similarity search can give better performance.
D. Wenfei et al., 2014.	Color histogram, correlogram, GLCM and hue moments.	Precision rate.	Corel.	Increase the accuracy and similarity search.	The weights are adjusted dynamically for single features and fixed weights are assigned to the fusion features which decreases the results
Meng Wang, Hao Li, Dacheng Tao, Ke Lu, and Xindong Wu, 2012.	Multi-modal graph	Precision Rate	1000 test images.	Introduced a re-ranking for web images search that explores concept of modality in graph-based learning.	It is robust to the sensitive parameters weights and scores.

continued on following page

Table 1. Continued

Reference No, Author, Year of Publication	Concept Used	Performance Evaluation Parameter	Database Used	Claim by Authors	Our Findings
[Leila Kabbai, Mehrez Abdellaoui, Ali Douik,2016.	HLG-SIFT method .	Precision and Recall Rate .	Corel.	Improve the accuracy it describe in the global features by a unique descriptor UL-LBP and HLG-SIFT	The novel descriptor called HLG-SIFT is presented which extract feature related to texture for each color channel, considered as a global feature and local feature extract the information of region around IPs detected using SIFT algorithm for each color channel separately
X. Liu et al., 2016	Hash Code Ranking.	Mean Average Precision, Precision and Recall Rate.	MNIST, CIFAR-10, TRECVID	Create a multiple hash tables having multiple views and generated fine-grained ranking.	For each hash table, a query-adaptive bitwise weighting is presented to alleviate the quantization loss by simultaneously exploiting the quality of hash functions and their complement for NN search and in table-wise approach, multiple hash tables are built for different data views as a joint index.
Y. Mistry et al.,2016.	Spatial Feature Level Fusion.	Precision and Recall Rate.	Corel	Improve the accuracy using Dual tree approach	Dual tree increases, the number of feature vector decreases and precision increases whereas recall decreases.
Md. Mahmudur Rahman, Bipin C. Desai, Prabir Bhattacharya,2006.	Feature level Fusion	Average Precision Rate	Corel, IAPR.	Retrieve images by combination of features (global, semi-global and local region) at different levels of abstraction.	The impact of inaccurate segmentation is decrease by fusion and improves the retrieval effectiveness.
Bahareh Bagheri, Maryam Pourmahyabadi, Hossein Nezamabadi-pour,2013.	Borda count Fussion	Average Precision Rate.	Corel	Improve the accuracy using short term algorithm.	It is sensitive to parameters and based on decision of the methods used.
Yu Liu, Xun Chen, Rabab K. Ward,and Z. Jane Wang,2016.	Convolutional sparse representation	N-S score.	Infrared Images	It overcomes the drawback of related to preservation & high sensitivity to mis-registration in SR based fusion method.	Image fusion using convolutional sparse representation (CSR) improved the performance and overcome the problem.
Qingqun Ning, Jianke Zhu, Member, Zhiyuan Zhong, Steven C.H. Hoi, and Chun Chen	Sparse product quantization.	Mean Average Precision and Recall rate.	Oxford	Improve accuracy by compression performed on the high-dimensional vectors convert to sparse representation.	Codebook generating concept is used and it is sensitive to indexed parameters.

to the image retrieval on smart cell devices is very less. Few of the available literature related to smart cell devices is studied and analyzed, and summarized as follows.

The importance of the java technology is mainly for the platform independency. The proposed (Iftikhar and Moncef, 2005) approach based on this framework use by the client to capture image using mobile device and send it to the server. Similar type of arrangement is done by the Yeh et al. (2004) that send a query image on the sever from device. After matching exists then the system performed a searching the image on google image search by the obtained keyword from the initial/ first query. To query the world wide web directly through images captured by mobile devices Jia et al (2006) designed a system. Mobile based image retrieval is analyze and proposed by Sonobe et al (2004) for retrieving fish images.

The approach is presented by the Noda et al (2002) is based on retrieving information to identify anonymous owners. The application of such type of approaches includes national park etc., where no connectivity of network is available or having limited connectivity. However both the approaches suggest a wireless network that is specifically, client-server. Because of limited amount of battery mobile devices consumed more power when it performs the retrieval using client server model. Hence Kumar et al (2008) suggests an approach for energy saving by adoptively selecting features for retrieval operation.

Most of the contribution that are existing related with cell devices with browsing the images through folder, then tags the images to classify. Image browsing can also be performed using multiple photograph albums from the various social networking sites for example Picasa, Fliker, Facebook, Instagram etc. and storage device card. Greggory's (2011), approach is based on browsing the albums from the web and the available EXIF extension not only notify about the updates of photo albums but also provides the privacy. There is no interface for searching hence difficult to find images. The application developed (Gregory, 2011) for EXIF data mainly for photos, but possibility to select photos by using this single feature is almost nil. Other alternatives to organize the collection of personal photo by using time information as a first ordering condition to interact and display (Harada, Naaman, Yee, Wang and Peapcke, 204). Information regarding the time is not only the single aspect, hence searching and browsing through facets offer more possibility. The image searching through multi-faceted browsing called as Scenique (Bartolini, 2009), facilitate the user to manage collection of photos by using tags, and visual features. This Proposed solution is designed for the desktop system and not for the mobile device and therefore it is required a display of higher resolution. In this section we describe about the existing applications that discussed the collection of images on mobile devices. The detailed overview is presented in (Mor, Rahul and Kaplun, 2008). Gareth et al (2002) discussed the various issues and scope for retrieval on mobile devices.

Wolf et al (2002) present a integration based approach to integrate Monte-Carlo localization and image retrieval and it is performed through feature exaction process which is invariant to translation, scaling and rotation. The technique presented Sarvas, Herrarte, Wilhelm, and Davis, 2004) using Metadata creation, and prototype system is designed to check metadata operations. Image retrieval on smart cell devices using java technology is discussed in (Ahmad, Abdullah, Kiranyaz and Gabouj, 2005). The concept of query progression on mobile device is presented in (Ahmad, Abdullah, Kiranyaz and Gabbouj, 2005). Guldogan and Gabbouj (2005) presented a retrieval and indexing architecture for multimedia using Symbian OS. Authors in (Iftikhar, Serkan and Moncef, 2005) aimed to minimize the different types of time or latency applicable for the query and retrieval operation. Hare and Lewis (2005) proposed a approach to performed CBIR on degraded (noise degradation) images. Gavilan (2005) presented a retrieval scheme based on the color blobs. Client-server architecture for content based image retrieval framework over connected mobile devices is proposed in (Moncef, Ifitkhar, Yasir and Serkan, 2006). Morphological color segmentation is used in (Gavilan, Takahashi, Saito and Nakajima, 2006) for mobile image retrieval, also, they used neural network to find the regions. The mobile-based image retrieval system in (Junyeong, Sanghyuk, Hacheon, Hyeran and Kyu, 2008). is based on feature extraction. The approach presented in is based on the lookup table. A multimodality based approach for mobile device is presented by Anguera et al. (2008) which permit index, annotate and search. Multimedia retrieval of audio-visual contents on mobile devices is discussed in (Ahmad and Gabbouj, 2008). Karthik (2008) presented a system of mobile phone based image retrieval and author characterizes the relation between accuracy and energy required for given operation. The work in Xavier et al, (2008) and Anguera X et al, (2008) is same as that is related to the prototype designing.

Histogram based image retrieval is proposed in (Vijay, Chen, Zhi, Gabriel, Tsai, Radek and Bernd, 2009), where vector quantization is performed through well defined tree structure scheme, stored on client and server and later it is transmitted in a tree histogram. An approach for the automatic representation of pictures on mobile devices is proposed in (La, Marco and Filippo, 2010). The authors in (Iftikhar and Moncef, 2010) present client-server architecture for image retrieval where a remote machine is running on a PC and a client on mobile device. General description about the image retrieval on mobile devices is presented in (Hub, 2010)

The study about the image retrieval for actual image is presented in (P.V.N. and Parsad, 2010). The report (Parman, 2010) is the documentation of the mobile multimodal information retrieval prototype, version four, developed for the context aware image retrieval project. A generalize structure of image retrieval using mobile device is presented in (Iftikhar and Moncef, 2011). Coarse position estimates are explored in (Samuel, Adrien, Ivan, Henning, 2011) in view of location-based image retrieval for urban environments. Mobile image retrieval for the medical image domain is proposed in (Samuel et al, 2011). Image retrieval is extended towards the application of location recognition using a mobile is discussed in (Georg, Anas, Robert, Florian and Eckehard, 2011). Summary of some discussed literatures for image retrieval on mobile devices are given in Table 2.

Table 2. Summary of Image Retrieval approaches on Mobile Devices

Ref.	Client Server Model/ Mobile device	Feature Extract	Feature Compression	Descriptor (Visual /Text)	Indexing Technique	Remarkable Contribution & Observation	Our Findings
(Ahmad et al, 2005)	Yes/ Nokia 3650, Nokia 6630, Nokia 6620	1)HSV and YUV color histogram 2)Gray level co-occurrence matrix (GLCM).	No	Image descriptor	Indexed images with corresponding features	1)Scaled down Image size [70-176] & [100-200] 2)Used Java enabled Tomcat web server & c++ 3)Support MIDP	The system having a high query latency (more than ~20000 msec).Similarly it cannot describe about the retrieval performance.
(Iftikhar et al, 2005)	Yes/ (Nokia 6630)	1)HSV and YUV color histogram 2)Gray level co-occurrence matrix (GLCM).	No	Image descriptor	Indexed images with corresponding features	1)Use PQ divide database into smaller subset(cluster) 2)PQ reduce retrieval time. It require less memory but consume lot power 3)Not having indexing on PQ 4)Generate result after fixed time interval.	Retrieve the immediate result if match of image is found otherwise the overall latency may increases. Similarly not discussed about retrieval performance.
(Iftikhar and Moncef, 2005)	Yes/ NOKIA 6620 NOKIA 6630 NOKIA 9500	1)HSV and YUV color histogram 2)Gray level co-occurrence matrix	No	Image descriptor	Indexed images with correspond-ing features	1)Resultant image compressed(QRI) 2)Image database used PNG format (1867 image) 3)Retrieve images send to client with different compression rate (different JPEQ quality)	Average client Query time achieved by WLAN (min 1684 ms),but in GPRS network it increases to 5343 msec. Similarly if quality of received image increases, time to received image will also increased
(Olcay et al, 2005)	Yes/ Nokia 6630 (on the same device client & server)	1)HSV and RGB color histogram	No	Image descriptor	Indexed images with correspond-ing features	1)DCT based down sampling during JPEG decoding. 2)This work is based on Symbian OS.	Total query time including display of results is 30 sec. further optimization may reduce the time. Not discussed about retrieval performance.

continued on following page

Table 2. Continued

Ref.	Client Server Model/ Mobile device	Feature Extract	Feature Compression	Descriptor (Visual /Text)	Indexing Technique	Remarkable Contribution & Observation	Our Findings
(Iftikhar, Serkan, Moncef, 2005)	Yes/ NOKIA 6620 NOKIA 6630 NOKIA 9500	1)HSV and YUV color histogram 2)Gray level co-occurrence matrix	No	Image descriptor	Indexed images with corresponding features	1)Used PQ (performed on subset of database) 2)used 1867 images with PNG format	Reduced time, minimize the quality of retrieved image. Matching accuracy of retrieved images not discussed.
(Moncef et al, 2006)	Yes/	1)YUV,HSV, RGB color histogram 2)GLCM	No	Image descriptor	Indexed images with corresponding features	1)Use JSP on M-MUVIS (suitable for various range of mobile devices) &Due to this java not required on client side. 2)use 476 images in database	The mean value of WLAN for client query time is 3462 msec and server query time is 2122 msec. Database size may increased the CQT and SQT due to lack in efficient indexing structure.
(Ahmadaand Gabbouj, 2008)	Yes/ (Audio visual Nokia 6630, Nokia 9500, N93 N95)	1)Visual- YUV,HSV,RGB color histogram& GLCM 2)Audio-Mel frequency cepstral coefficient (MFCC)	No	1)Audio & image descriptor For Video DB 2)Image descriptor for image DB	HCT indexing (efficient indexing technique)	1)Use M-MUVIS and JSPMUVIS both for audio & visual 2)Use IQ (Interactive query)with HCT 3)Use individual (M-MUVIS and JSPMUVIS) for AV retrieval.	Accuracy of retrieved results are not specified in terms similarity of received image. The effect of large database size, increasing the visual query time, which can be further optimized.
(Iftikhar, Moncef, 2010)	Yes/ Nokia N95 Nokia 5800	1) YUV,HSV,RGB color histogram & GLCM	No	Image descriptor	Use HCT indexing (Hierarchical cellular tree)	1)In indexed DB a query path is formed over the cluster. 2)MPEG-7 ANMRR is used to measure retrieval performance	The client unnecessarily has to wait for self defined time period. This approach is not suitable for all the domain.
(Iftikhar, Moncef, 2011)	Yes/ N5800 N95	1) YUV,HSV,RGB color histogram & GLCM	No	Image descriptor	Use HCT indexing	1)use CMD architecture (combine support for M-MUVIS & JSP MUVIS) 2)Support for NQ & IQ 3)Nokia energy profiler(NEP) is used to measure power	System provide the generic architecture but Precision and recall are the two important parameters used to find retrieval accuracy, which is not discussed here to represent the overall system effectiveness.
(Yeh et al, 2004)	Yes/ Nokia 3650	1)DFT of image 2)local texture feature based on wavelet decomposition convolving with steerable filter	No	Hybrid approach (Image descriptor & Text descriptor)	Use bottom up clustering Technique	1)applied for location recognition 2)find principal component (PC) over large no. of landmark images on web then it projected on 32 PC.	Quantitative evaluation is not performed which will give the answer of actual latency required for retrieval.
(Noda et al, 2002)	Yes/ Camera & PDA & PHS	Color and shape (color characteristics based on hue and saturation whereas shape characteristics based on circularity measure)	No	Image descriptor characteristics	Stored flowers images and characteristics of flowers	1)Experiment on normal and narrow down retrieval 2)Also experiment with deformed image.	More time is required to get the objective flower-data (within 3 minutes). Also the blurred photograph having big influence on image retrieval accuracy.

continued on following page

Table 2. Continued

Ref.	Client Server Model/ Mobile device	Feature Extract	Feature Compression	Descriptor (Visual /Text)	Indexing Technique	Remarkable Contribution & Observation	Our Findings
(Kumar et al, 2008)	No/ HP iPAQ 6945 PDA	Not specified	No	Image descriptor	Inverted index calculated offline & stored in flash	1)use large flash and small RAM 2)save energy by adoptively selecting features 3)Also used selective loading of features	This approach saves the energy but adoptive loading results in some loss of accuracy. similarly when handling the multiple queries, features may evicted from memory.
(Harada et al, 2004)	No/ HP H5500 PDA	Time	NA	Text descriptor (time)	Time based clustering	1)It is the browser for organizing photos according to timeline.	Time line is not always a better option to organise a photos. Possibility to improve performance may add
(Bartolini, 2009)	No/ Laptop	Color and texture	NA	Image and Text Descriptor (Visual, tag, visual and tag)	1)Use visual feature trees and tag trees. 2)Use hierarchical tree	1) It is a browsing interface 2)Used two DB (feature and tags) 3) Use undirected and weighted graph.	Retrieval is based on low level features. Similarly system have to maintain two databases.
(Sarvas et al, 2004)	Yes/ Nokia 3650	1)Metadata (location, time, date and username) 2)simple inferences 3)media processing(color histogram, texture,face detection or shape matching)	No	Context descriptor (location,time, date,username) and Content	All metadata including filename, cell id, time, username and annotation are stored in OO database (parent-child)	1)It uses symbian 6.1 2)Use java open source ozone 1.1 database	Efficient work in terms of metadata creation but to cope up with limited bandwidth problem sound work is not presented.
(Hare et al, 2005)	Yes/ HP h5550 iPAQ pocket PC	SIFT (use salient region)	No	Image descriptor	1)k-means clustering 2)use vector space model for indexing (inverted files)	1)first find the peaks in difference of gaussian pyramid then SIFT feature 2)visual descriptor invariant to homography, Intensity changes and degraded images 3) use 2 stage ranking.	The given system requires the two stage matching. Optimization of vocabulary generation process may further improvised which give better result.
(Gavilan et al, 2006)	Yes/ A5406CA(3G) Phone	1)color blobs(region) and its histogram i.e. extract position, shape and color feature of each blob and its histogram.	No	Image and text descriptor	1)Automatic annotation of images in four categories. 2) Also used HSI color histogram indexing of images.	1)Introduce two distance matrices a)orientation of elongated object. 1)Region histogram. 2)Quantization performed by neural network. 3)Use lookup table for mapping. 4)Image is represented by set of features and region is represented by vector of feature	The system depends upon contextual information such as GPS to improve the precision rate.

continued on following page

Table 2. Continued

Ref.	Client Server Model/ Mobile device	Feature Extract	Feature Compression	Descriptor (Visual /Text)	Indexing Technique	Remarkable Contribution & Observation	Our Findings
(Junyeong et al, 2008)	No/ Samsang SPH-m4650	Lookup table based feature extraction three histogram (one represent color and other 2 represent x, y coordinate)	No	Image descriptor (Three histogram)	Image feature (histogram) indexed with image by lookup table.	1)Experiment is performed on Corel, MSRC 1.0 and Caltech DB. 2)used Image size (160×120)	The application having the good retrieval performance but the it is suitable for small database in the range of 500 images. More number of images may reduce the performance.
(Xavier et al, 2008)	No/	1) for images: -Edge histogram 2) for audio:- 10 MFCC including CMN and excluding co-component.	No	Image and speech descriptor	Image indexing based on audio and visual feature.	1)Use MR2 algorithm. 2)Additional metadata stored automatically at the time of capturing (location, user id, date, time).	The given approach achieved good accuracy of retrieval but not specifying the retrieval time, which is important in specific domain point of view.
(Anguera et al, 2008)	No/ HTC touch smart phone	Metadata (location, date, time, user) Audio(10 MFCC including CMN & exclude C0)	No	Hybrid approach text Audio Descriptor (Speech input)	Image (photo) indexing with the collection of metadata and speech annotation	1)Use large and small database comparative study 2)Future:- fast searching in very large pictures databases, and adding image-based features	Multimodality approach may improve the result by adding image based features.
(Vijay et al, 2009)	Yes/	SURF	Yes Runlength encoding (Transmit only histogram of leaf node)	Image descriptor	1)Hierarchical k means clustering of sample image features (SVT) 2)inverted file at each node refer to database entry (images)	1)Prune a large TSVQ using the BFOS (optimization) algorithm. 2)Experiment on ZuBud and CD dataset.	The system achieve ~1000 bits/image but there is some deviation in classification(~4%).
(Iftikhar and Moncef, 2010)	No/	Face (low dimentional eigen space) background(RGB hist & gabor filter & EXIF data and time of capture	No	Image and text descriptor	Use mean shift clustering technique	1)Perform onboard image indexing	Clustering may be improved by using efficient image representation and indexing technique.
(P.V.N et al, 2010)	Yes/ PDA	1)Shape color and other texture feature(GLCM)	No	Image descriptor	Feature extracted and indexing of image	1)Matlab tool is used for Implementation. 2)translation, scale and rotation invariant.	Not mentioning the sound procedure and not suitable for fast retrieval with better precision and recall.
(Parmann, 2010)	Yes/ Nokia 5800 Xpress music	NA	No	Image descriptor	Images stored in oracle database	1)stored images search by oracle proprietary image search functionality.	Parametric evaluation is not specified and which is help to justify the suitability of application in terms of accuracy of result.
(Zhang et al, 2011)	Yes/ Cell phone and DG CAM	SIFT	No	Image (descriptor)	1)Using FLANN kd tree 2)Images geo-tag with GPS location.	1)Re-ranking based on geometric consistent rotation re-ranking. 2)used distance filter based on bayes classifier.	SIFT(Scale Invariant Feature Transform) feature having better retrieval accuracy but large query size, decreases the retrieval speed.
(Georg et al, 2011)	Yes/	BoF vector (histogram)	Yes	Image Descriptor	Inverted file indexing	1)MHVT and overlapping buffer is used. 2) Google street panorama images.	BoF(Bag of Feature) is the good option for rapid retrieval. Further optimization may improve the result

DATASET AND PERFORMANCE EVALUATION PARAMETERS

The various dataset has been created to evaluate the performance of the retrieval system. The dataset used and the evaluation parameters are discussed.

Dataset

The performance of the retrieval system depends on the parameters discussed in next section. For checking the effectiveness of the *existing* approaches most of the authors using the benchmark dataset i.e. Holidays, Corel Wang etc. details are shown in Table 3.

Image Compression Evaluation

The performance of the image compression can be measured by using following parameters.

- **Encoding Time:** It is the total time required to compressed the image
- **Decoding Time:** It is the total time required to decode the images.
- **Compression Ratio:** It is used to quantify the Image data size reduction using representation by Image compression approach or algorithm. This ratio can be measured on the basis of Average bit rate of original raw data to the average bit rate of encoded data.

Image Retrieval Evaluation

The performance of the image retrieval can be measured on the basis of following parameters.

- **Precision:** The percentage of retrieved images that are relevant to the query.
- **Recall:** The percentage of all the relevant images in the database, which are retrieved.
- **Mean Average Precision**: Average precision values at rank of relevant images.
- **Elapsed Time:** Elapsed time is simply the amount of time that passes from the beginning of query request to end of query

Table 3. List of Benchmark Datasets for Retrieval

Name of Dataset	Remark	URL
Holidays	In the given set various categories of images includes like usual scene information, manmade, effects of fire and water etc. Images is of high resolution and contains 500 groups.	Holidays Dataset [Online] Available: https://lear.inrialpes.fr/~jegou/data.php
Corel	In coral database almost 10000 images are available for 100 categories and each group contains JPEF image of 128 × 192 resolution. Dataset includes buildings, buses, people, dinosaurs, flowers, elephant, horses foods and mountains.	Corel Dataset[Online] Available: http://www.ci.gxnu.edu.cn/cbir/Dataset.aspx
Wang	It is subset of Corel dataset having 1000 images, selected manually and grouped into 10 classes. It contains group of similar images to perform query related task.	Wang dataset[online] Available: http://wang.ist.psu.edu/docs/related/

Key Issues

Depending upon the findings in the literature, following are some of the parameters on which performance of image representation, compression and retrieval mechanism can be evaluated and enhanced: Representation scheme, partitioning scheme, compression scheme, searching mechanism with aim of improving retrieval accuracy. Literatures are studied, analyzed and identify the important key issues.

- Compactness of the images needs to be investigated for better representation of image.
- Need to focus on the important properties i.e. equivariance, invariance, and equivalence of image representation for image compression and retrieval applications.
- Fusion based image retrieval improves the performance in terms of precision and recall. Optimization of fusion approaches need to be investigated.
- Compactness of image representation is not always good alternative. Selecting useful dimensions is better than compressing all dimensions. Hence need to investigate the approach to find Principal component
- Most of the retrieval approaches on desktop and mobile device are based on convolutional local features, such as SIFT but it is ineffective for representing or indexing. Hence more compact visual representations is needed.
- For the encoding and decoding of images multiple passes are required to improve the compression ratio but not suitable for real time applications. Contribution needs in the direction of reducing encoding and decoding time for real time applications such as image retrieval on smart cell devices.

CONCLUSION AND FUTURE SCOPE

The selection of Image representation and compression mechanism is exclusively depends upon the application areas and it compromises with the visual quality for the lossy compression. This chapter critically reviews and summarizes some existing methods of image representation, compression and retrieval on desktop and smart mobile devices. After study and analysis of existing literatures some of the key issues are addressed and for the future work suggested to explore in the direction of representation approach, compression scheme and searching mechanism to improve the retrieval accuracy.

REFERENCES

Ahmad, I., Abdullah, S., Kiranyaz, M. S., & Gabbouj, M. (2005). Progressive Query Technique for Image Retrieval on Mobile Devices. *Proceedings Fourth International Workshop on Content-Based Multimedia Indexing*.

Ahmad, I., Abdullah, S., Kiranyaz, S., & Gabbouj, M. (2005). Content-Based Image Retrieval on Mobile Devices. *Proceedings of SPIE (Multimedia on Mobile Devices)*, 255-264.

Ahmad & Gabbouj. (2008). Audio-Visual Multimedia Retrieval on Mobile Devices. In Multimedia Services in Intelligent Environments – Advanced Tools and Methodologies. Academic Press.

Alghamdi, R. A., Taileb, M., & Ameen, M. (2014). *A New Multimodal Fusion Method Based on Association Rules Mining for Image Retrieval. In Proceedings of Mediterranean Electrotechnical Conference* (pp. 493–499). MELECON.

Alzahir, S., & Borici, A. (2015). An Innovative Lossless Compression Method for Discrete-Color Images. *IEEE Transactions on Image Processing*, *24*(1), 44–56. doi:10.1109/TIP.2014.2363411 PMID:25330487

Anguera, X., Oliver, N., & Cherubini, M. (2008). Multimodal and Mobile Personal Image Retrieval: A User Study. *Proc. Workshop on Mobile Information Retrieval, MOBIR'08.*

Bagheri, B., Pourmahyabadi, M., & Nezamabadipour, H. (2013). A Novel Content Based Image Retrieval Approach by Fusion of Short Term Learning Methods. *Proceedings of International conference on Information and Knowledge Technology (IKT)*, 355-358. 10.1109/IKT.2013.6620093

Bai, S., & Bai, X. (2016). Sparse Contextual Activation for Efficient Vi- sual Re-Ranking. *IEEE Transactions on Image Processing*, *25*(3), 1056–1069. doi:10.1109/TIP.2016.2514498 PMID:26742133

Bai, S., Bai, X., & Liu, W. (2016). Multiple Stage Residual Model for Image Classification and Vector Compression. *IEEE Transactions on Multimedia*, *18*(7), 1351–1362. doi:10.1109/TMM.2016.2557071

Banerji, S., Sinha, A., & Liu, C. (2013). A New Bag of Words LBP(BoWL) Descriptor for Scene Image Classification. *Proceedings of International conference on Computer Analysis of Images and Patterns.* 10.1007/978-3-642-40261-6_59

Bartolini, I. (2009). A multi-faceted browsing interface for digital photo collections. *CBMI*, *7*, 237–242.

Beevi, S., Thomas, M., & Nair, M. S. & Wilscy M.(2016). Lossless color image compression using double level RCT in BBWCA. *Proceedings of 6th International Conference On Advances In Computing & Communications*, 93, 513-520. 10.1016/j.procs.2016.07.242

Belarbi, M. A., Mahmoudi, S., & Belalem, G. (2017). PCA as Dimensionality Reduction for Large-Scale Image Retrieval Systems. *International Journal of Ambient Computing and Intelligence*, *8*(4), 45–58. doi:10.4018/IJACI.2017100104

Bhowmik, N., Gonzaez, R., Gouet-Brunet, V., Pedrini, H., & Bloch, G. (2014). Efficient fusion of multidimensional descriptors for image retrieval. *Proceedings of International conference on image processing (ICIP)*, 5766-5770.

Bose, S., Madhulika, Acharjee, S., Chowdhury, S. R., Chakraborty, S., & Dey, N. (2014). Effect of watermarking in vector quantization based image compression. *Proceeding of International Conference on Control, Instrumentation, Communication and Computational Technologies (ICCICCT)*, 503-508. 10.1109/ICCICCT.2014.6993014

Chaudhuri, B., Demir, B., Bruzzone, L., & Chaudhuri, S. (2016). Region-Based Retrieval of Remote Sensing Images Using an Unsupervised Graph-Theoretic Approach. *IEEE Geoscience and Remote Sensing Letters*, *13*(7), 987-991. 10.1109/LGRS.2016.2558289

Chen, Z., Zhang, W., Hu, B., Can, X., Liu, S., & Meng, D. (2017). Retrieving Objects by Partitioning. *IEEE Transactions on Big Data*, *3*(1), 44–54. doi:10.1109/TBDATA.2016.2566664

Cheng, K., & Dill, J. (2014). Lossless to Lossy Dual-Tree BEZW Compression for Hyperspectral Images. *IEEE Transactions on Geoscience and Remote Sensing*, *52*(9), 5765–5770. doi:10.1109/TGRS.2013.2292366

Conoscenti, M., Coppola, R., & Magli, E. (2016). Constant SNR, Rate Control, and Entropy Coding for Predictive Lossy Hyperspectral Image Compression. *IEEE Transactions on Geoscience and Remote Sensing*, *54*(12), 7431–7441. doi:10.1109/TGRS.2016.2603998

Daga, P., & Dewangan, R.K. (2014). Segmentation singpectral clustering based on texture features. *International Journal of Research in Engineering and Applied Sciences, 2*(2), 37-40.

David, G. (2005). *Mobile Image Categorization and Retrieval using Color Blobs* (Masters Thesis). Tokyo institute of Technology.

Deng, C., Ji, R., Wei, L., Tao, D., & Gao, X. (2013). Visual Reranking through Weakly Supervised Multi-Graph Learning. *Proceedings of International Conference on Computer Vision*, 2600-2607. 10.1109/ICCV.2013.323

Dey N., Acharjee, S., Biswas, D., Das, A. & Chaudhuri, S. (2012). Medical Information Embedding in Compressed Watermarked Intravascular Ultrasound Video. *Scientific Bulletin of the Politehnica University of Timisoara - Transactions on Electronics and Communications, 57*(71).

Dong, L., Liang, Y., Kong, G., Zhang, Q., Cao, X., & Izquierdo, E. (2016). Holons Visual Representation for Image Retrieval. *IEEE Transactions on Multimedia*, *18*(4), 714–725. doi:10.1109/TMM.2016.2530399

Fakhari, F., Mosavi, M. R., & Lajvardi, M. M. (2017). Image fusion based on multi-scale transform and sparse representation: An image energy approach. *IET Image Processing*, *11*(11), 1041–1049. doi:10.1049/iet-ipr.2017.0104

Frigui, H., Caudill, J., & Abdallah, A. (2008). Fusion of Multi-Modal Features for Efficient Content-Based Image Retrieval. Proceedings of international conference on Fuzzy Systems, 1992-1998.

Fu, W., Li, S., Fang, L., & Benediktsson, J. A. (2017). Adaptive Spectral–Spatial Compression of Hyperspectral Image With Sparse Representation. *IEEE Transactions on Geoscience and Remote Sensing*, *55*(2), 671–682. doi:10.1109/TGRS.2016.2613848

Gao, Z., Xue, J., Zhou, W., Pnag, S., & Qi, T. (2016). Democratic Diffusion Aggregation for image retrieval. *IEEE Transactions on Multimedia*, *18*(8), 1661–1674. doi:10.1109/TMM.2016.2568748

Gavilan, D., Takahashi, H., Saito, S., & Nakajima, M. (2006). Mobile Image Retrieval using Morphological Color Segmentation. *ICMU*, *2006*, 51–58.

Georg, S. (2011). Rapid Image Retrieval for Mobile Location Recognition. *ICASSP*.

GregoryQ. (2011). *Justpictures*. Retrieved from http://code.google.com/p/justpictures

Guan, H., Antani, S., & Rodney, L. (2010). Comparative Study of Shape Retrieval using Feature Fusion Approaches. *Proceedings of IEEE International Symposium on Computer Based Medical System(CBMS)*, 226- 231. 10.1109/CBMS.2010.6042646

Gueguen, L., & Hamid, R. (2016). Toward a Generalizable Image Representation for Large-Scale Change Detection: Application to Generic Damage Analysis. *IEEE Transactions on Geoscience and Remote Sensing*, *54*(6), 3378–3387. doi:10.1109/TGRS.2016.2516402

Guo, Y., Ding, G., Li, L., Han, J., & Shao, L. (2017). Learning to Hash With Optimized Anchor Embedding for Scalable Retrieval. *IEEE Transactions on Image Processing*, *26*(3), 1344–1354. doi:10.1109/TIP.2017.2652730 PMID:28092559

Harada, S., Naaman, M., Yee, J. S., Wang, Q. Y., & Paepcke, A. (2004). Lost in memories: interacting with photo collections on pdas. *Proceedings of the 4th ACM/IEEE-CS joint conference on Digital libraries*, 325–333. 10.1145/996350.996425

Hare, J. S., & Lewis, P. H. (2005). Content-based image retrieval using a mobile device as a novel interface Storage and Retrieval Methods and Applications for Multimedia 2005, 64-75. doi:10.1117/12.588979

He, X., Zhang, C., Zhang, L., & Li, X. (2016). A-Optimal Projection for Image Representation. *IEEE Transactions on Pattern Analysis and Machine Intelligence*, *38*(5), 1009–1015. doi:10.1109/TPAMI.2015.2439252 PMID:26353361

Hu, Ortega, & Au. (2015). Multiresolution Graph Fourier Transform for Compression of Piecewise Smooth Images. *IEEE Transactions on Image Processing*, *24*(1), 419-433.

Hub. (2010). *Image Retrieval on Mobile Devices*. LWA 2010, Kassel.

Iftikhar, A., & Moncef, G. (2005). Compression and Network Effect on Content-Based Image Retrieval on Java Enabled Mobile Devices. In *Proceedings of 2005 Finnish Signal Processing Symposium, FINSIG 2005* (pp. 35-38). Kuopio, Finland: Academic Press.

Iftikhar, A., & Moncef, G. (2010). Content-based interactive image retrieval from JAVA enabled mobile devices. *Proceedings of the Fourth International Symposium on Communications, Control and Signal Processing*.

Iftikhar, A., & Moncef, G. (2011). A generic content-based image retrieval framework for mobile devices. *Multimedia Tools and Applications*, *55*(3), 423–442. doi:10.100711042-010-0556-5

Iftikhar, A., Serkan, K., & Moncef, G. (2005). An Efficient Image Retrieval Scheme on Java Enabled Mobile Devices. In *Proceedings of the 2005 IEEE Seventh Workshop on Multimedia Signal Processing, MMSP 2005* (pp. 397 – 400). Shanghai, China: IEEE.

Jerry, Z., Aaron, H., Eric, L., & Zakhor, A. (2011). Location-based image retrieval for urban environments. *ICIP, 3677-3680*, 2011.

Jia, M., Fan, X., Xie, X., Li, M., & Ma, W.-Y. (2006). Photo-to-Search: Using Camera Phones to Inquire of the Surrounding World. *Proceedings of International Conference on Mobile Data Management,* 46-46.

Jiao, L., Zhang, S., Li, L., Yang, S., Liu, F., Hao, H., & Dong, H. (2017). A Novel Image Representation Framework Based on Gaussian Model and Evolutionary Optimization. *IEEE Transactions on Evolutionary Computation, 21*(2), 265–280. doi:10.1109/TEVC.2016.2603526

Jones & Brown. (3003). Challenges and opportunities for context-aware retrieval on mobile devices. *Proc. of the SIGIR workshop on Mobile Personal Information Retrieval*, 47-56.

Junyeong, Y., Sanghyuk, P., Hacheon, S., Hyeran, B., & Kyu, L. Y. (2008). A fast image retrieval system using index lookup table on mobile device. *Proceedings of 19th International Conference on Pattern Recognition, ICPR*, 1-4. 10.1109/ICPR.2008.4761729

Kabbai, L., Abdellaoui, M., & Douik, A. (2016). Content Based Image Retrieval using Lo- cal and Global features descriptor. *Proceedings of International conference on Advanced Technologies for Signal and Image Processing (ATSIP)*, 151-154.

Kamble, S. D., Thakur, N. V., & Bajaj, P. R. (2018). Fractal Coding Based Video Compression Using Weighted Finite Automata. *International Journal of Ambient Computing and Intelligence, 9*(1), 115–133. doi:10.4018/IJACI.2018010107

Kamisli, F. (2015). Block-Based Spatial Prediction and Transforms Based on 2D Markov Processes for Image and Video Compression. *IEEE Transactions on Image Processing, 24*(4), 1247–1260. doi:10.1109/TIP.2015.2400818 PMID:25675456

Karine, A., Toumi, A., Khenchaf, A., & Hassouni, M. (2017). Target Recognition in Radar Images Using Weighted Statistical Dictionary-Based Sparse Representation. *IEEE Geoscience and Remote Sensing Letters, 14*(12), 2403-2407.

Karthik, K. (2008). *Energy Conservation for Content-based Image Retrieval on Mobile Devices* (Master Thesis).

Kavitha, K., & Sudhamani, M. V. (2014). Object based image retrieval from Database using combined features. *Proceedings International conference on Signal and image processing*, 161-165. 10.1109/ICSIP.2014.31

Kekre, H. B., Bharadi, V. A., Thepade, S. D., Mishra, B. K., Ghosalkar, S. E., & Sawant, S. M. (2010). Content Based Image Retrieval using Fusion of Gabor Magnitude and Modified Block Truncation Coding. *Proceedings of International conference on Emerging Trends in Engineering and Technology (ICETET)*, 140-145.

Khattak, N. S., & Stockman, G. (2007). Shape and structure for image matching and retrieval. *Proceedings of International Conference on Machine Vision*, 79-84. 10.1109/ICMV.2007.4469277

Kim, S., & Cho, N. I. (2014). Hierarchical Prediction and Context Adaptive Coding for Lossless Color Image Compression. *IEEE Transactions on Image Processing, 23*(1), 445–449. doi:10.1109/TIP.2013.2293428 PMID:24490231

Kim, S., & Lee, H. J. (2016). RGBW image compression by low-complexity adaptive multi-level block truncation coding. *IEEE Transactions on Consumer Electronics, 62*(4), 412–419. doi:10.1109/TCE.2016.7838094

Kumar, A., Sagar, K. P., Kuppusamy, K. S., & Aghila, G. (2016). Machine learning based malware classification for Android applications using multimodal image representations. *Proceeding of 10th International Conference on Intelligent Systems and Control (ISCO)*, 1-6. 10.1109/ISCO.2016.7726949

Kumar, K., Nimmagadda, Y., Hong, Y.-J., & Lu, Y.-H. (2008). Energy Conservation by Adaptive Feature Loading for Mobile Content-based Image Retrieval. *Proceedings of International Symposium on Low Power Electronics and Design*. 10.1145/1393921.1393963

La, C. M., Marco, M., & Filippo, V. (2010). Automatic Image Representation and Clustering on Mobile Devices. *J. Mobile Multimedia*, *6*(2), 158–169.

Le Pendu, M., Guillemot, C., & Thoreau, D. (2016). Inter-Layer Prediction of Color in High Dynamic Range Image Scalable Compression. *IEEE Transactions on Image Processing*, *25*(8), 3585–3596. doi:10.1109/TIP.2016.2571559 PMID:27244738

Lee, S., & Yang, H. S. (2017). Quantisation-free binary feature aggregation for fast image representation. Electronics Letters, 53(22), 1470-1471. doi:10.1049/el.2017.2501

Lenc, K., & Vedaldi, A. (2015). Understanding image representations by measuring their equivariance and equivalence. *Proceeding of International Conference on Computer Vision and Pattern Recognition (CVPR)*, 991-999. 10.1109/CVPR.2015.7298701

Li, L., Wu, D., Wu, J., Li, H., Lin, W., & Kot, A. C. (2016). Image Sharpness Assessment by Sparse Representation. *IEEE Transactions on Multimedia*, *18*(6), 1085–1097. doi:10.1109/TMM.2016.2545398

Li, Q., Chen, D., Jiang, W., Liu, B., & Gong, J. (2016). Generalization of SPIHT: Set Partition Coding System. *IEEE Transactions on Image Processing*, *25*(2), 713–725. doi:10.1109/TIP.2015.2509253 PMID:26730707

Liu, X., Lei, H., Cheng, D., Bo, L., & Tao, D. (2016). Query-Adaptive Hash Code Ranking for Large-Scale Multi-View Visual Search. *IEEE Transactions on Image Processing*, *25*(10), 4514–4524. doi:10.1109/TIP.2016.2593344 PMID:27448359

Liu, Y., Chen, X., Ward, R.K., & Wang, Z. (2016). Image Fusion With Convolutional Sparse Representation. *IEEE Transaction on Signal Processing Letters, 23*(12), 1882-1886.

Lucas, L. F. R., Wegner, K., Rodrigues, N. M. M., Pagliari, C. L., da Silva, E. A. B., & de Faria, S. M. M. (2015). Intra Predictive Depth Map Coding Using Flexible Block Partitioning. *IEEE Transactions on Image Processing*, *24*(11), 4055–4068. doi:10.1109/TIP.2015.2456509 PMID:26353355

Ma, L., Li, H., Meng, F., Wu, Q., & Ngan, K. N. (2017). Learning Efficient Binary Codes From High-Level Feature Representations for Multilabel Image Retrieval. *IEEE Transactions on Multimedia*, *19*(11), 2545–2560. doi:10.1109/TMM.2017.2703089

Macedo, M., Avila, S., Zucchi, R., & Faria, F. (2017). *Mid-level Image Representation for Fruit Fly Identification*. Diptera: Tephritidae. .10.1109/eScience.2017.33

Mahendran, A., & Vedaldi, A. (2015). Understanding Deep Image Representations by Inverting Them. *Proceeding of International Conference on Computer Vision and Pattern Recognition (CVPR)*, 5188-5196. 10.1109/CVPR.2015.7299155

Mahmudur, Md., Desai, B. C., & Bhattacharya, P. (2006). A Feature Level Fusion in Similarity Matching to Content-Based Image Retrieval. *Proceedings of International conference in Information Fusion*, 1-6.

Mistry, Y., Ingole, D. T., & Ingole, M. D. (2016). Efficient Content based Image Retrieval using Transform and Spatial Feature Level Fusion. *Proceedings of International conference on control, Automation and Robotics (ICCAR)*, 299-303. 10.1109/ICCAR.2016.7486744

Moncef, G., Iftikhar, A., Yasir, A. M., & Serkan, K. (2006). Content-based image retrieval for connected mobile devices. *Proceedings of the Second International Symposium on Communications, Control and Signal Processing, ISCCSP 2*, 13-15.

Mor, N., Rahul, N., & Kaplun, V. (2008). Photos on the go: a mobile application case study. In *CHI '08: Proceeding of the twenty-sixth annual SIGCHI conference on Human factors in computing systems* (pp. 1739–1748). New York: ACM.

Nejati, M., Samavi, S., Karimi, N., Soroushmehr, S. M. R., & Najarian, K. (2016). Boosted Dictionary Learning for Image Compression. *IEEE Transactions on Image Processing*, *25*(10), 4900–4915. doi:10.1109/TIP.2016.2598483

Ning, Q., Zhu, J., Zhong, Z., & Steven, C. H. (2017). Scalable Image Retrieval by Sparse Product Quantization. *IEEE Transactions on Multimedia*, *19*(3), 586–597. doi:10.1109/TMM.2016.2625260

Noda, M., & Sonobe, H. (2002). Cosmos: Convenient Image Retrieval System of Flowers for Mobile Computing Situations. *Proceedings of IASTED Conference on Information Systems and Databases*, 25-30.

Olcay, G., & Moncef, G. (2005). Content-Based Image Indexing and Retrieval Framework on Symbian Based Mobile Platform. *Proceedings of 13th European Signal Processing Conference, EUSIPCO 2005*.

Pancham, A., Withey, D., & Bright, G. (2015). Tracking Image Features with PCA-SURF Descriptors. *Proceedings of International conference on Machine Vision Applications (MVA)*, 365-368.

Parmann, E. (2010). *MMIR4 – Mobile Multimodal Image Retrieval. TR No. 11*. CAIM-UIB.

Peter, P., Kaufhold, L., & Weickert, J. (2017). Turning Diffusion-Based Image Colorization Into Efficient Color Compression. *IEEE Transactions on Image Processing*, *26*(2), 860–869. doi:10.1109/TIP.2016.2627800 PMID:27849527

Razzaque, A., & Thakur, N. V. (2012). An approach to image compression with partial encryption without sharing the secret key. *International Journal of Computer Science and Network Security*, *12*(7).

Reddy, P. V. N., & Satya Prasad, K. (2010). Image retrieval system for natural images based on local features. *Advances in Information Mining, 2*(2).

Samuel, D., Adrien, D., Ivan, E., & Henning, M. (2011). Mobile Medical Image Retrieval. In *Medical Imaging 2011: Advanced PACS-based Imaging Informatics and Therapeutic Applications* (p. 79670G). Orlando, FL: SPIE.

Sarvas, R., Herrarte, E., Wilhelm, A., & Davis, M. (2004). *Metadata Creation System for Mobile Images. MobiSys*. Boston: ACM Press.

Sezer, O. G., Guleryuz, O. G., & Altunbasak, Y. (2015). Approximation and Compression With Sparse Orthonormal Transforms. *IEEE Transactions on Image Processing*, *24*(8), 2328–2343. doi:10.1109/TIP.2015.2414879 PMID:25823033

Shen, H., Pan, W. D., & Wu, D. (2017). Predictive Lossless Compression of Regions of Interest in Hyperspectral Images With No-Data Regions. *IEEE Transactions on Geoscience and Remote Sensing*, *55*(1), 173–182. doi:10.1109/TGRS.2016.2603527

Shi, X., Guo, Z., Zhang, D., & Fang, X. (2015). Multiple Features Fusion Based Inverted Multi-Index for Image Retrieval. *Proceedings of International Conference on Virtual Reality and Visualization (ICVRV)*, 148-153. 10.1109/ICVRV.2015.39

Singh, A., Dey, N., & Ashour, A. S. (2017). *Scope of Automation in Semantics-Driven Multimedia Information Retrieval From Web*. IGI Global. doi:10.4018/978-1-5225-2483-0.ch001

Sonobe, H., Takagi, S., & Yoshimoto, F. (2004). Mobile Computing System for Fish Image Retrieval. *International Workshop on Advanced Image Technology*, 33-37.

Strutz, T. (2016). Context-Based Predictor Blending for Lossless Color Image Compression. *IEEE Transactions on Circuits and Systems for Video Technology*, *26*(4), 687–695. doi:10.1109/TCSVT.2015.2416611

Sun, C., & Yang, E. H. (2015). An Efficient DCT-Based Image Compression System Based on Laplacian Transparent Composite Model. *IEEE Transactions on Image Processing*, *24*(3), 886–900. doi:10.1109/TIP.2014.2383324 PMID:25532182

Sural, S., Qian, G., & Pramanik, S. (2012). Segmentation and histogram generation using the HSV color space for Image retrieval. *Proceedings of International conference on image processing, 2*, 589-592.

Thakur, N. V., & Kakde, O. G. (2006). Fractal Color Image Compression on a Pseudo Spiral Architecture. *Proceeding of IEEE Conference on Cybernetics and Intelligent Systems*, 1-6.

Thakur, N. V., & Kakde, O. G. (2006). A Novel Compression Technique for Color Image Database. *Proceeding of International Conference on Advanced Computing and Communications*, 240-243.

Thakur, N. V., & Kakde, O. G. (2007). Color Image Compression with Modified Fractal Coding on Spiral Architecture. *Journal of Multimedia*, *2*(4), 55–66. doi:10.4304/jmm.2.4.55-66

Thakur, N. V., & Kakde, O. G. (2007). Color Image Compression on Spiral Architecture using Optimized Domain Blocks in Fractal Coding. *Proceeding of Fourth International Conference on Information Technology,* 234-242. 10.1109/ITNG.2007.51

Thakur, N. V., & Kakde, O. G. (2009). Compression mechanism for multimedia system in consideration of information security. *Proceeding of International workshop on Machine intelligence Research*, 87-96.

Thakur, N. V., & Koli, N. A. (2010). An Overview of Feature Extraction Methods in CBIR. *International Journal of Computer Science and Applications.*, *3*(2), 71–76.

Vijay, C., Chen, D. M., Zhi, L., Gabriel, T., Tsai, S. S., Radek, G., & Bernd, G. (2009). Low-rate image retrieval with tree histogram coding. *Proceedings of the 5th International ICST Mobile Multimedia Communications Conference*.

Wang, F., Zuo, W., Lin, L., Zhang, D., & Zhang, L. (2016). Joint Learning of Single-Image and Cross-Image Representations for Person Re-identification. *Proceeding of IEEE Conference on Computer Vision and Pattern Recognition (CVPR)*, 1288-1296. 10.1109/CVPR.2016.144

Wang, J., & Zhu, Z. (2010). Image retrieval system based on multi-feature fusion and relevance feedback. *Proceedings of International Conference on Machine Learning and Cybernetics*, 4, 2053-2058. 10.1109/ICMLC.2010.5580505

Wang, M., Li, H., Tao, D., Ke, L., & Wu, X. (2012). Multimodal Graph-Based Rerank- ing for Web Image Search. *IEEE Transactions on Image Processing*, *21*(11), 4649–4661. doi:10.1109/TIP.2012.2207397 PMID:22829401

Wang, X., Ke, L., & Tang, X. (2011). Query-Specific Visual Semantic Spaces for Web Image Re-ranking. *Proceedings of International conference on Computer Vision and Pattern Recognition (CVPR)*, 857-864) 10.1109/CVPR.2011.5995399

Wenfei, D., Yu, S., Liu, S., & Zhiqiang, Z. &, Gu, W. (2014). Image retrieval based on multi-feature fusion. *Proceedings of International conference on Instrumentation and Measurement, Computer, Communications and Control*, 240-243.

Wolf, J., Burgard, W., & Burkhardt, H. (2002). Using an Image Retrieval System for Vision-Based Mobile Robot Localization. LNCS, 2383, 108–119. doi:10.1007/3-540-45479-9_12

Wu, H., Sun, X., Yang, J., Zeng, W., & Wu, F. (2016). Lossless Compression of JPEG Coded Photo Collections. *IEEE Transactions on Image Processing*, *25*(6), 2684–2696. doi:10.1109/TIP.2016.2551366 PMID:27071170

Xavier, A., Xu, J. J., & Nuria, O. (2008). Multimodal photo annotation and retrieval on a mobile phone. *Proceeding of the 1st ACM international conference on Multimedia information retrieval.*

Xu, Z., Du, J., & Ye, L. (2016). Multi-feature Indexing for image retrieval based on hyper- graph. *Proceedings of International conference on cloud computing and intelligence systems (CCIS)*, 494-500.

Yang, F., Matei, B., & Davis, L. S. (2015). Re-ranking by Multi-feature fusion with diffusion for image retrieval. *Proceedings of winter conference on Applications of Computer Vision*, 572-579. 10.1109/WACV.2015.82

Yeh, T., Tollmar, K., & Darrell, T. (2004). Searching the Web with Mobile Images for Location Recognition. *Proceedings of IEEE Computer Society Conference on Computer Vision and Pattern Recognition*, 76-81. 10.1109/CVPR.2004.1315147

Yu, Q., Yu, W., Yang, P., Zheng, J., Zheng, X., & He, Y. (2015). An Efficient Adaptive Binary Arithmetic Coder Based on Logarithmic Domain. *IEEE Transactions on Image Processing*, *24*(11), 4225–4239. doi:10.1109/TIP.2015.2462089 PMID:26241975

Yuan, H., Ye, L., & Du, L. (2011). A Novel Method for Image Feature Fusion based on MADM. *Proceedings of International conference on Multimedia Technology (ICMT)*, 2877-2879.

Zeinolabedin, S. M. A., Zhou, J., Liu, X., & Kim, T. T. H. (2015). An Area- and Energy-Efficient FIFO Design Using Error-Reduced Data Compression and Near-Threshold Operation for Image/Video Applications. *IEEE Transactions on Very Large Scale Integration (VLSI) Systems*, *23*(11), 2408–2416.

Zhang, S., Yang, M., Cour, T., Yu, K., & Metaxas, D. N. (2015). Query Specific Rank Fusion For Image Retrieval. *IEEE Transactions on Pattern Analysis and Machine Intelligence*, *37*(4), 803–815. doi:10.1109/TPAMI.2014.2346201 PMID:26353295

Zhang, Y., Wu, J., & Cai, J. (2016). Compact Representation of High-Dimensional Feature Vectors for Large-Scale Image Recognition and Retrieval. *IEEE Transactions on Image Processing*, *25*(5), 2407–2419. doi:10.1109/TIP.2016.2549360 PMID:27046897

Zhang, Y., Wu, J., & Cai, J. (2016). Compact Representation of High-Dimensional Feature Vectors for Large-Scale Image Recognition and Retrieval. *IEEE Transactions on Image Processing*, *25*(5), 2407–2419. doi:10.1109/TIP.2016.2549360 PMID:27046897

Zheng, L., Wang, S., Liu, Z., & Qi, T. (2014). Packing and Padding: Coupled Multi-index for Accurate Image Retrieval. Proceedings of International conference on computer vision and pattern recognition, 1947-1954.

Zheng, L., Wang, S., Lu, T., Fei, H., Liu, Z., & Qi, T. (2015). Query-Adaptive Late Fusion for Image Search and Person Re-identification. *Proceedings of International conference on computer vision and pattern recognition*, 1741- 1750. 10.1109/CVPR.2015.7298783

ADDITIONAL READING

Acharjee, S., Dey, N., Biswas, D., Das, P., & Chaudhuri, S. S. (2012, November). A novel Block Matching Algorithmic Approach with smaller block size for motion vector estimation in video compression. In *Intelligent Systems Design and Applications (ISDA), 2012 12th International Conference on*(pp. 668-672). IEEE. 10.1109/ISDA.2012.6416617

AlShahrani, A. M., Al-Abadi, M. A., Al-Malki, A. S., Ashour, A. S., & Dey, N. (2018). Automated system for crops recognition and classification. In Computer Vision: Concepts, Methodologies, Tools, and Applications (pp. 1208-1223). IGI Global. doi:10.4018/978-1-5225-5204-8.ch050

Bose, S., Acharjee, S., Chowdhury, S. R., Chakraborty, S., & Dey, N. (2014, July). Effect of watermarking in vector quantization based image compression. In *Control, Instrumentation, Communication and Computational Technologies (ICCICCT), 2014 International Conference on*(pp. 503-508). IEEE. 10.1109/ICCICCT.2014.6993014

Chakraborty, S., Chatterjee, S., Dey, N., Ashour, A. S., Ashour, A. S., Shi, F., & Mali, K. (2017). Modified cuckoo search algorithm in microscopic image segmentation of hippocampus. *Microscopy Research and Technique*, *80*(10), 1051–1072. doi:10.1002/jemt.22900 PMID:28557041

Chakraborty, S., Mukherjee, A., Chatterjee, D., Maji, P., Acharjee, S., & Dey, N. (2014, December). A semi-automated system for optic nerve head segmentation in digital retinal images. In *Information Technology (ICIT), 2014 International Conference on* (pp. 112-117). IEEE. 10.1109/ICIT.2014.51

Chatterjee, S., Dey, N., Shi, F., Ashour, A. S., Fong, S. J., & Sen, S. (2017). Clinical application of modified bag-of-features coupled with hybrid neural-based classifier in dengue fever classification using gene expression data. *Medical & Biological Engineering & Computing*, 1–12. PMID:28891000

Dey, N., Ashour, A. S., Chakraborty, S., Samanta, S., Sifaki-Pistolla, D., Ashour, A. S., ... Nguyen, G. N. (2016). Healthy and unhealthy rat hippocampus cells classification: A neural based automated system for Alzheimer disease classification. *Journal of Advanced Microscopy Research, 11*(1), 1–10. doi:10.1166/jamr.2016.1282

Ghosh, A., Sarkar, A., Ashour, A. S., Balas-Timar, D., Dey, N., & Balas, V. E. (2015). Grid color moment features in glaucoma classification. *Int J Adv Comput Sci Appl*, *6*(9), 1–14.

Hore, S., Chakraborty, S., Chatterjee, S., Dey, N., Ashour, A. S., Van Chung, L., & Le, D. N. (2016). An Integrated Interactive Technique for Image Segmentation using Stack based Seeded Region Growing and Thresholding. *Iranian Journal of Electrical and Computer Engineering*, *6*(6), 2773.

Kamal, M. S., Parvin, S., Ashour, A. S., Shi, F., & Dey, N. (2017). De-Bruijn graph with MapReduce framework towards metagenomic data classification. *International Journal of Information Technology*, *9*(1), 59–75. doi:10.100741870-017-0005-z

Kamble, S. D., Thakur, N. V., & Bajaj, P. R. (2018). Fractal Coding Based Video Compression Using Weighted Finite Automata. *International Journal of Ambient Computing and Intelligence*, *9*(1), 115–133. doi:10.4018/IJACI.2018010107

Kishor, D. R., & Venkateswarlu, N. B. (2016). A Novel Hybridization of Expectation-Maximization and K-Means Algorithms for Better Clustering Performance. *International Journal of Ambient Computing and Intelligence*, *7*(2), 47–74. doi:10.4018/IJACI.2016070103

Li, Z., Shi, K., Dey, N., Ashour, A. S., Wang, D., Balas, V. E., ... Shi, F. (2017). Rule-based back propagation neural networks for various precision rough set presented KANSEI knowledge prediction: A case study on shoe product form features extraction. *Neural Computing & Applications*, *28*(3), 613–630. doi:10.100700521-016-2707-8

Pal, G., Acharjee, S., Rudrapaul, D., Ashour, A. S., & Dey, N. (2015). Video segmentation using minimum ratio similarity measurement. *International journal of image mining, 1*(1), 87-110.

Saba, L., Dey, N., Ashour, A. S., Samanta, S., Nath, S. S., Chakraborty, S., ... Suri, J. S. (2016). Automated stratification of liver disease in ultrasound: An online accurate feature classification paradigm. *Computer Methods and Programs in Biomedicine*, *130*, 118–134. doi:10.1016/j.cmpb.2016.03.016 PMID:27208527

Sghaier, S., Farhat, W., & Souani, C. (2018). Novel Technique for 3D Face Recognition Using Anthropometric Methodology. *International Journal of Ambient Computing and Intelligence*, *9*(1), 60–77. doi:10.4018/IJACI.2018010104

Sharma, K., & Virmani, J. (2017). A Decision Support System for Classification of Normal and Medical Renal Disease Using Ultrasound Images: A Decision Support System for Medical Renal Diseases. *International Journal of Ambient Computing and Intelligence*, *8*(2), 52–69. doi:10.4018/IJACI.2017040104

Wang, D., He, T., Li, Z., Cao, L., Dey, N., Ashour, A. S., ... Shi, F. (2016). Image feature-based affective retrieval employing improved parameter and structure identification of adaptive neuro-fuzzy inference system. *Neural Computing & Applications*, 1–16.

Chapter 10
Possible Approaches for Character Recognition With Existing Methodologies and State-of-the-Art Techniques

Rashmi Welekar
Shri Ramdeobaba College of Engineering and Management, India

Nileshsingh V. Thakur
Nagpur Institute of Technology, India

ABSTRACT

The world started to talk about optical character recognition (OCR) around 1870. Then over another 25 years OCR systems were designed for industrial applications. And now the OCR software is easily available online for free, through products like Acrobat reader, WebOCR, etc. But still the research is on. Do we need to switch direction or introduce new hypothesis are some of the key questions? The purpose of this chapter is to answer the above questions and propose new methods for character recognition.

INTRODUCTION

Doing a comprehensive literature survey is a skillful task. We need to consider literature reviews and results of various methodologies being perceived, tried and tested by other researchers. We need to spend hours and sometime years to read all related research work and identify the key points which have scope of improvement.

After going thoroughly through all literature in detail, we can:

- Gain complete understanding of topic under consideration;
- Identify various sources of data being used by other researchers;
- Identify familiarize our self with documentation style that is required and expected to be used and followed for putting and plotting results and inferences;

DOI: 10.4018/978-1-5225-6164-4.ch010

- Identify key concepts and relationship between them;
- Identify gaps and shortcomings in literature;
- avoid the older errors and mistakes those were committed in previous work and plan more accurate and systematic approach for timely completion of proposed task;
- Develop our own strategy and verification procedure.

The well defined research proposal needs a thorough study. A detailed survey and literature review will always help to put forward a thoughtful proposal. The analysis helps us to identify key modules of our proposed research work. Once modularized, it becomes easier to sort out the issues. We may find that some of the issues pertaining to particular modules are already being addressed. Hence we can eliminate those and focus on the issues which needs more scientific analysis and the modules with scope of improvement.

Let's consider the case of optical character recognition (OCR). If we try to break the topic in key research areas then what we can conclude that the scope for research in OCR is in developing new logics instead of developing new methods of feature extraction or segmentation or improvising minimum edit distance method. It is because these areas are already flooded with lot of algorithms and logics which are producing results with accuracy more than 96% or 97%. But the most important issue is the overhead the system carries to hit that high recognition rate.

The purpose of this chapter is to present the great amount of work already being done with one mind set and then try to introduce a new approach which may reduce the performance overhead still keeping the recognition rate intact. The chapter is written with following pointes in mind:

- We need to look for the literature;
- Once we have found and retrieved all the relevant literature, we need to collate our literature - put it into groups of related themes;
- Then we need to critique them - individually and together (again within the themes);
- This is followed by summarizing the various points made by the writers of the literature, and then comparing these summarized points from paper/book, etc. to paper/book, etc. within each theme;
- Once we have done this, we can now start to write up our critiques of the various papers, research reports, books, etc. that constitute your literature.
- This process can take a long time, and if we are going to undertake any research we have to allow for this in our timetable.

REVIEW OF VARIOUS TECHNIQUES OF CHARACTER RECOGNITION

Off line handwriting character recognition system is developed to convert text available in image format into latter coding which is generally used by computer software's for text processing. The input systems present static data for the software. The software has to perform complex task of dealing with various different styles of writing as every person in the world has unique style and every handwritten text is different than the other. Most of the OCR engines focus on recognizing standard fonts or printed text.

OCR for handwritten text is a computer logic developed for electronically receiving, interpreting, and processing digital data from sources like older stationary, photos, touch screens or touch pads etc.

The chapter focuses more on these sources as we are concerned with "off line" character recognition. But there are other techniques for "on line character recognition which also need refinement for faster and efficient processing. These techniques are based on pen tip sensing where written text is being scanned on fly. The data processing is relatively easier and hence we focus only on "off line" OCR.

The handwriting recognition system is much more than just OCR. The complete system also supposed to handle preprocessing, formatting, correct segmentation of characters and identification of words, punctuation notations, numbers and other forms of information available on scanned paper.

All industries from all areas are using or in need of OCR systems. Every industry from raw material processing to packaging finished product wants to label and document every process on assembly line without human indulgence (Kressel&SchÄurmann, 1997). Hence every scanned document also needs further editing and value addition in document inform of extra data. With efficient OCR systems, the overhead of retyping same information is greatly reduced. The redundancy in data processing and editing same type of information repeatedly is a thing of past with OCR systems. This leads to accurate, efficient information processing in less time (Liu & Fujisawa, 2008).

In computer science, intelligent character recognition (ICR) is an advanced optical character recognition (OCR) or rather more specific handwriting recognition system that allows fonts and different styles of handwriting to be learned by a computer during processing to improve accuracy and recognition levels.

The key feature of efficient OCR system is its ability to learn on its own. This self learning (Franke,1997; Kohonen,1990; Liu & Nakagawa, 2001) referred to as neural network is designed to upgrade the database with every new style of handwriting. All though every other handwriting is not readable even for human beings, the structured text like text generated by printing or by fixed constrained handwriting like CAPITAL LETTERS only can produce recognition rate of 97% or better. But cursive and bad handwriting always impose challenges to even the smartest OCR systems. Smart problems need smart solutions which are suggested by us in next paper to be published as extension to this chapter. Because this process is involved in recognizing hand writing, accuracy levels may, in some circumstances, not be very good but can achieve 97%+ accuracy rates in reading handwriting in structured forms. Often to achieve these high recognition rates several read engines are used within the software and each is given elective voting rights to determine the true reading of characters (Fedorovici, 2011).

Intelligent Word Recognition (IWR)

IW can recognize and extract RIA not only printed-handwritten information, but cursive handwriting as well. ICR recognizes on the character-level, whereas IWR works with full words or phrases. Capable of capturing unstructured information from every day pages, IWR is said to be more evolved than hand print ICR.

Not meant to replace conventional ICR and OCR systems, IWR is optimized for processing real-world documents that contain mostly free-form, hard-to-recognize data fields that are inherently unsuitable for ICR. This means that the highest and best use of IWR is to eliminate a high percentage of the manual entry of handwritten data and run-on hand print fields on documents that otherwise could be keyed only by humans.

Character Search and Extraction

The documents under consideration for handwriting recognition are usually older documents which even may be century old documents. Hence every character and its writing styles will show lot of variation as per the then existing styles of writing. Hence the OCR system has to focus individually on each character separately. The problem becomes more complex when we are dealing with cursive style where multiple characters may be picked as a single character. Hence character search and recognition of every character in isolation is the biggest challenge in these OCR systems.

Character Recognition

Once the most complex task of character extraction is over, we need to deal with another time consuming task of recognition process. The recognition engines play a vital role and hence these engines are evaluated on the basis of their database, efficiency and ability of recognition of character with all sorts of writing styles.

Neural Networks

These are trained networks developed for pattern recognition. But this process itself is a reason for success or failure of the system. Each neural network trains itself differently based on samples available to for learning. However if the network trains itself with unwanted parameters which are not associated with the given task, the whole system may produce wrong results. For efficient recognition it is necessary to have properties of sample data and target data nearly similar.

Feature Extraction

Feature extraction can be considered as parallel process to network recognizers. But this has added advantages of manually determining the properties which are important.

Some example properties might be:

- Aspect Ratio of images
- Strokes and flow of image
- Average distance from image center
- Reflections in x and y axis
- Analysis of upper, lower, right and left half of pixels in image

Feature extraction offers relative ease over neural network but the cost of more development. Neural network takes less time to implement but is less reliable and less flexible than feature extraction.

Performance Evaluation Parameters for Character Recognition

Following are some of the parameters on which character recognition can be evaluated and enhanced: Recognition accuracy, Time taken for recognition, Number of features extracted, Size needed to represent a character image, Number of training samples per class, Way of representing the character images in database, and Efficiency.

General Process

There are three important general processes recommended for character recognition:

- Preprocessing of digital information.
- Feature extraction.
- Classification of processed information.

Pre processing is important because it is used to remove irrelevant information from input. Preprocessing also filters out that data which may adversely affect the recognition process. The main steps performed within pre processing are:

1. Binary conversion
2. Normalization
3. Data sampling
4. Pattern smoothing
5. De noising of image data (Chong et al.,2003).

The feature extraction analyses the pre processed data with multi dimensional vector fields and extracts higher dimension data (Lecun et al., 1998; Simard et al., 2003; Fedorovici et al., 2010). Feature extraction helps to highlight important information for the recognition model. The extracted information usually contains details like pen pressure, velocity or the changes in flow and writing direction. The classification of extracted features actually performs the character recognition. The extracted information and parameters are mapped with standard classifier definitions pertaining to different classes thereby enabling characters or words to be recognized

We have completed literature review under 2 heads.

1. Commercial products and existing technology.
2. Various new or improvised proposed logics and algorithms by researchers working in the field of character recognition

COMMERCIAL PRODUCTS AND EXISTING TECHNOLOGY

Software

Author Shelia Guberman introduced first applied pattern recognition system in 1962 in Moscow. Commercially companies like Communications Intelligence Corporation and IBM were pioneers in bringing the modules and software for handwriting recognitions in market for end users in product form. Intel software and modules were also equipped by that time to handle and understand print handwriting with separated characters.

ParaGraphInternational, and Lexicus launched handwriting recognition systems in early 1990. The systems were capable of handling cursive handwriting.

ParaGraph was a Russian company. It was founded by computer scientist StepanPachikovwhere asLexicus was founded by Ronjon Nag and Chris Kortge. All of them were students at Stanford University. The ParaGraphCalliGrapher system was deployed in the Apple Newton systems, and Lexicus Longhand system was made available commercially for the PenPoint and Windows operating system. Lexicus was acquired by Motorola in 1993 and went on to develop Chinese handwriting recognition and predictive text systems for Motorola. ParaGraph was acquired in 1997 by SGI and its handwriting recognition team formed a P&I division, later acquired from SGI by Vadem. Microsoft has acquired CalliGrapher handwriting recognition and other digital ink technologies developed by P&I from Vadem in 1999.

Research in Handwriting Recognition

SargurSrihari and Jonathan Hull developed first handwritten address interpretation system. The contextual information exploitation was the method used behind this technology. There is a big global community working on this topic. There are annual global events where all such researchers present their work on handwriting identification.

The International Conference on Frontiers in Handwriting Recognition (ICFHR), is held in even-numbered years, and the International Conference on Document Analysis and Recognition (ICDAR), is held in odd-numbered years. Both of these conferences are endorsed by the IEEE. Active areas of research in these conferences include:

- Online Recognition
- Offline Recognition
- Signature Verification
- Postal-Address Interpretation
- Bank-Check Processing

Research group of Jürgen Schmidhuber at the Swiss AI Lab IDSIA have developed several neural networks since 2009. The group has won many competitions world wide. Without any knowledge of languages like French, Arabic, and Persian, the researcher Alex Graves et. al. won three competition for the topic of cursive handwriting character recognition at 2009 International Conference on Document Analysis and Recognition (ICDAR). The authors Alex Graves et al. presented the concept of the bi-directional and multi-dimensional Long short-term memory (LSTM).

Dan Ciresan and colleagues at IDSIA won the ICDAR 2011 offline Chinese handwriting recognition contest for GPU based deep learning method for feed forward network. The popular MNIST handwritten digits problem of YannLeCun and colleagues at NYU was addressed by first artificial pattern recognizers to achieve human-competitive performance. This neural network solution was also introduced by Dan Ciresan and colleagues

The digital information generated by scanned images is translated to different readable formats using Optical Character Recognition (OCR). The formatted text can be in machine encoded text format or printed or type written format or handwritten format. OCR attempts to read every bit and piece of information like characters, words, phrases or sentences and then executes comparison and matching algorithm to identify the exact character or string of characters.

Earlier systems used to match the specific styles of writing but the advanced systems are being developed to recognize between texts or images or letters and symbols.

Online character recognition is identified by various terminologies like intelligent character recognition, dynamic character recognition, and real time character recognition. The primary performance evaluation parameter of OCR is the accuracy rate. This rate is generally affected by dynamic motion of the handwriting style and flow in cursive handwriting. The efficient OCR algorithms have successfully hit the accuracy of 99% but with constraints over speed of recognition.

The efficient OCR can provides features like machine translation, text mining, and text-to-speech which are basic expectations in advanced scanning applications. The OCR systems are of great use to various government organizations to get e-documents in editable text format. Now, it's commonly used by business houses to recognize text from scanned images of business documents like bills, memos, challans, banking documents, transaction details etc. Smart OCR's are developed to address complex problem which is done via intelligent character recognition.

Document Imaging

- **What is Imaging?:** A great description of document imaging.
- **Definition**: Defines document imaging and explains why it's not enough on its own.
- **Document Imaging**: Almost everything you want to know about document imaging.

Optical Character Recognition

- **Optical Character Recognition:** The technical paper provides an overview of OCR.
- **OCR Technology:** Provides information on the many aspects of the OCR technology.
- **Shape-free Statistical Information:** The study attempts to solve the problem of OCR in the conversion of novel glyph shades.
- **Frontiers of OCR:** The paper by George Nagy discusses the progress and possibilities of OCR.

Benefits

- **Benefits of Document Imaging:** Outlines the major benefits of imaging.
- **Imaging Benefits:** Find out why imaging is so widely used.
- **Benefits of Imaging:** A brief listing of the benefits of imaging.
- **Benefits of OCR:** An overview of the benefits of OCR.
- **Advantages of OCR:** Explains why OCR is used by thousands of corporations around the world.
- **OCR vs. Coding:** An unbiased look at the advantages and disadvantages of OCR and coding.

Software

- **Microsoft Document Imaging:** The best place to download this software.
- **OpenDocMan:** One of the top document imaging programs in the market.
- **Content Central:** Convenient all-in-one document management software.
- **OCR Software:** A comparison guide to help you find the best OCR software.
- **ABBYY FineReader 10:** Leading OCR software in the market.

- **IRISDocument Server 9:** Another accomplished OCR software.
- **OmniPage:** An award winning OCR program by Nuance.
- Popular Products
- Symbol DS6878-HC
- CN70e Mobile Computer
- BCI Cables
- **TSP 800 II Series:** TSP847 Receipt Printer

EXISTING TECHNOLOGY: VARIOUS NEW OR IMPROVISED PROPOSED LOGICS AND ALGORITHMS BY RESEARCHERS WORKING IN THE FIELD OF CHARACTER RECOGNITION

If we focus on latest research work over last 2 decades, we find more work being done on searching each and every bit and piece of information obtained from scanned paper in form of an image. Every effort has been made to identify every alphabet, symbol or character individually and the efficiency of recognition has been associated with error percentage in detecting every shape. Minimum edit distance is applied to all population and comparison is carried out on entire database of available text patterns in database. Some of research works with recognition rates are Table 1.

After going through above literature, we found that thousands of hours have been spend by group of experts together and lot many efforts have been put to make recognition process error free. The standard procedure has been followed where key steps are

- Image acquisition
- Pre-Processing
- Segmentation
- Feature extraction
- Classification
- Post processing methods
- Analysis

Various methods and algorithms are tried and successfully tested by various researchers.

One more technique is to convert image to string and use minimum edit distance for character recognition. Levenshtein distance is one of the most effective method for edit distance calculation(or edit distance). To calculate Levenshtein distance we need to count number of substitutions, deletions, or insertions required to transform source string into target string. Levenshtein distance algorithm was developed by a Russian scientist Vladimir Levenshtein, in 1965. The algorithm proved to be very usefull for many applications like spell checkers, correction systems for optical character recognition, etc.

The cost of computation in case of longer strings increases as the cost is dependent on product of lengths of two strings under consideration. This makes Levenshtein Algorithm impractical. Thus, when used to aid in fuzzy string searching in applications such as record linkage, the compared strings are usually short to help improve speed of comparisons.

There are other popular measures of edit distance, which are calculated using a different set of allowable edit operations. For instance,

Table 1. Existing Research work with recognition rates

Authors	Features	Feature extraction Techniques	Recognition rates
Andrew Senior & Robinson (Senior & Robinson, 1998)	Baseline estimation, dots, junctions, endpoints, turning points, loops	Skeletonization algorithm, connected component analysis	HMM 87%
B. Gatos, I. Pratikakis, S. J. Perantonis, (Gatos, et al., 2006)	Word image normalization, robust hybrid feature extraction	Dividing word image into set of zones & then calculate density of character pixel in each zone.	K-NN classification algorithm 81.05%
M. Blumenstein & B. Verma (Blumenstein &Verma, 1999)	Prospective segmentation points, Upper, lower word contours, vertical pixel density	Heuristic feature detection algorithm, Contour extraction algorithm, histogram analysis	Neuro-heuristic algorithm: 76.52%
Chun ki Cheng, Xin Xu Liu, M. Blumenstein, V. M. Marasamy (Cheng et al., 2004)	It analyses the surrounding of every suspicious segmentation point found by heuristic segmenter.	Modified direction feature, segmentation point validation	Using BP-MLP 67.54%
Radmilo Bozinivic, Sargur Shrihari (Bozinovic & Shrihari, 1989)	Points, countours	Event generation. Set of 16 events are used.	Letter hypothesization, Word Hypothesization 72%
Kehan & Ishwar Sethi (Hal & Sethi, 1995)	Regular features: horizontal bars, vertical bars & loops Singular Features: Singularities, end pts., branchpts,	4 connected component labeling algorithm, morphological hit or miss operation, salient curve point selection algorithm	85.07%
G. Nicchiotti and C. Scagliola (Nicchiotti & Scagliola, 2000)	Handwriting countourminima, holes, strokes	Detection of possible segmentation points, stroke generation and stroke analysis	86.9%
M. Blumenstein, X.Y. Liu & B. Verma (Blumenstein et al., 2007)	Direction feature, Modified Direction Feature	It extracts direction information from the structure of character contours. This info is integrated with a technique of detecting transitions between background & foreground pixels in character img	With MLP: Lower case:70.22% Upper case:80.33% With RBF: Lower case:71.33% Upper case:81.58%

- The Damerau–Levenshtein distance allows insertion, deletion, substitution, and the transposition of two adjacent characters;
- The longest common subsequence (LCS) distance allows only insertion and deletion, not substitution;
- The Hamming distance allows only substitution, hence, it only applies to strings of the same length.
- The jaro distance allows only transposition.

The Edit distance is matrix bounded within set of parameters and calculated with permissible set of allowed editing operations. A cost is assigned with every operation. The results are then further converted into general format using DNA sequence alignment algorithms such as the Smith–Waterman algorithm, which are application oriented and evaluate the cost on basis of applications.

Table 2. Analysis of character recognition

Authors	Survey Of Character Recognition
Pranob K Charles, V. Harish, M. Swathi CH., Deepthi *(Charles et al., 2012)*	**General Survey of techniques used for character recognition**
Radmilo M. Bozinovic & Sargur N. Shrihari (Bozinovic & Shrihari, 1989)	
V. K. Govindan and A. P. Shivaprasad (Govindan & Shivaprasad, 1990)	
C. Y. Suen, C. C. Tappert and T. Wakahara (Suen et al., 1990)	
Eugene Borovikov (Borovikov, 2014)	
Adisleven Lev and Miriam Furst (Lev & Furst, 1991)	**Studies on Japanese, Chinese, Hebrew, Indian, Cyrillic, Greek and Arabic characters and numerals in both printed and handwritten cases**
El.Sheikh and R. M. Guindi(Sheikh & Guindi, 1998)	
Shumji Mori, Kazuhiko Yamamoto and Michio Yasuda (Mori et al., 1984)	
C. C. Tappert (Tappert, 1984)	**Hand written Character Recognition Survey**
J. R. Ullmann (Ullmann, 1986)	
J. Mantas (Mantas, 1986)	
Jean R. Ward and Thedore Kuklinski (Ward & Kuklinski, 1988)	

Possible Approaches

Classification methods based on learning from examples have been widely applied to character recognition from the 1990s and have brought forth significant improvements of recognition accuracies. This class of methods includes statistical methods, artificial neural networks, support vector machines, multiple classifier combination, etc. In this paper, we discuss the characteristics of the classification methods that have been successfully applied to character recognition, and show the remaining problems that can be potentially solved by learning methods. The analysis gives the necessary direction for further research and areas where improvement is expected.

After studying the literature we can list the possible approaches for character recognition:

1. The character image can be divided into four quadrants. Each quadrant is scanned to check the possible representation of the character features. Findings of the quadrant data can be matched with characters stored in database. Pattern matching techniques can be applied to do the matching part.
2. The character can be stored as directional chaincode representation of the database image. Numbers can be encoded for the chaincode.The chaincode of the test image can be compared with the chain-code stored in database.
3. Binarize the character image and generate segments of connected 1's in image. Form segments and form the encoding of the segmenst based on their connectivity. Form the string representation of the image. The string representation of the test image can be tested with representations stored in database.
4. As we continue our literature analysis we observe that the swing in recognition techniques is in direction of making it more selective and predictive. In pursuit of making recognition process error free, many researchers have increased the size of database to a very big size which takes

time to process. At the same time too much burdon is passed on feature extraction process for the accuracy. Consider the paper by Lucian-OvidiuFedorovici where author presents the architecture of an Optical Character Recognition (OCR) technology application based on two approaches, a multilayer neural network and a Support Vector Machine (SVM) classifier using Zernike moments for feature extraction. The performance çomparison of the two approaches is based on the similar layout of most of the characters that must be recognized. The comparison shows that the improvement of the processing performance can be obtained by creating classes of blobs that use geometric similarities, and doing OCR only on the representative blob from each class. This similar concluding statements made by many authors forced us to think on selective comparison and matching techniques instead of using big datasets for 100% accuracy. . The concept of self learning and cultural evoluation with predictive logics will certainly reduce the subset of character under test thereby reducing the processing time. The character recognition is much different topic than any other image comparison and pattern matching technique. Next character in a word is very much predictive where as direction of curve on figure print is not. Hence finger print does need 100% accuracy in image recognition but spelling does not. Even if a character is wrongly interpreted it can be corrected using self learning method.

Hence we have decided to focus more on improving recognition efficiency using bounded set of population. We propose to introduce BBP algorithm with predictive optimization and elimination theory.

CONCLUSION

We have analyzed the existing methodologies on character recognition. Various techniques have been used by different researchers. We have reviewed and listed the character recognition techniques available in literature. We also have identified the general process of character recognition. The commercial products and state of the art technology is also presented. The character recognition methods and recognition rates achieved by researchers have also been tabularized. We have identified possible approaches for character recognition which will give a future direction for the budding researchers in the field of character recognition. We have also identified an approach for character recognition for our proposed system using BBP algorithm. Our contribution to the literature is different than other papers available in literature as we have listed all the existing techniques for character recognition, state of the art technologies, have given a direction for future researchers and also have identified a promising methodology for our work.

RERFERENCES

Blumenstein, M., Liu, X. Y., & Verma, B. (2007). A modified direction feature for cursive character recognition. *Pattern Recognition*, *40*(2), 376–388. doi:10.1016/j.patcog.2006.05.017

Blumenstein, M., & Verma, B. (1999).Neural Solutions for the Segmentation and Recognition of Difficult Words from a Benchmark Database. *Proceedings of the Fifth International Conference on Document Analysis and Recognition, (ICDAR '99)*, 281-284. 10.1109/ICDAR.1999.791779

Borovikov, E. (2014). *A survey of modern optical character recognition techniques,* Cornell University Library, Computer Vision and Pattern Recognition. arXiv: 1412.4183

Bozinovic, R., & Shrihari, S. (1989). Offline cursive script word recognition. *IEEE Transactions on Pattern Analysis and Machine Intelligence, 11*(1), 68–83. doi:10.1109/34.23114

Charles, P., Harish, V., Swathi, M., & Deepthi, C. H. (2012). A Review on the Various Techniques used for Optical Character Recognition. *International Journal of Engineering, Research and Applications, 2*(1), 659–662.

Cheng, C., Liu, X., Blumenstein, M., & Marasamy, V. (2004). Enhancing neural confidence based segmentation for cursive handwriting recognition. *SEAL 04 and 2004 FIRA Robot world congress.*

Chong, C. W., Mukundan, R., & Raveendran, P. (2003). An efficient algorithm for fast computation of pseudo-Zernike moment. *IJPRAI, 17,* 1011–1023.

Fedorovici, L. (2011). A Comparison between Two Character Recognition Approaches. *FACTA UNIVERSITATIS Series: Automatic Control and Robotics, 10*(2), 125–140.

Fedorovici, L. O., Voisan, E., Dragan, F., & Iercan, D. (2010). Improved neural network OCR based on preprocessed blob classes. *Proc. ICCC-CONTI 2010,* 559–564. 10.1109/ICCCYB.2010.5491211

Franke, J. (1997). Isolated handprinted digit recognition. In H. Bunke & P. S. P. Wang (Eds.), *Handbook of Character Recognition and Document Image Analysis* (pp. 103–121). World Scientific. doi:10.1142/9789812830968_0004

Gatos, B., Pratikakis, I., & Perantonis, S. J. (2006). Hybrid offline cursive handwriting word recognition. *18th International Conference on Pattern Recognition(ICPR'06),* 998-1002. 10.1109/ICPR.2006.644

Govindan, V. K., & Shivaprasad, A. P. (1990). Character recognition: A review. *Pattern Recognition J, 23*(7), 671-683.

Hal, K., & Sethi, I. (1995). Offline cursive handwriting Segmentation. *International Conference on Document Analysis and Recognition,* 894-897.

Kohonen, T. (1990). The self-organizing map. *Proceedings of the IEEE, 78*(9), 1464–1480. doi:10.1109/5.58325

Kressel, U., & SchÄurmann, J. (1997). Pattern classification techniques based on function approximation. In H. Bunke & P.S.P. Wang (Eds.), Handbook of Character Recognition and Document Image Analysis (pp. 49-78). World Scientific.

Lecun, Y., Bottou, L., Bengio, Y., & Haffner, P. (1998). Gradient-based learning applied to document recognition. *Proceedings of the IEEE, 86*(11), 2278–2324. doi:10.1109/5.726791

Lev, A., & Furst, M. (1991). Recognition of Handwritten Hebrew One-Stroke Letters by Learning Syntactic Representations of Symbols. *IEEE Transactions on System Management and Cybernetics, 19*(5), 13086–1313.

Liu, C. L., & Fujisawa, H. (2008). Classification and Learning Methods for Character Recognition: Advances and Remaining Problems. In S. Marinai & H. Fujisawa (Eds.), *Machine Learning in Document Analysis and Recognition: Studies in Computational Intelligence, 90*. Berlin: Springer. doi:10.1007/978-3-540-76280-5_6

Liu, C. L., & Nakagawa, M. (2001). Evaluation of prototype learning algorithms for nearest neighbor classifier in application to handwritten character recognition. *Pattern Recognition*, *34*(3), 601–615. doi:10.1016/S0031-3203(00)00018-2

Mantas, J. (1986). An overview of character recognition methodologies. *Pattern Recognition, 19*(6), 425-430.

Mori, S., Yamamoto, K., & Yasuda, M. (1984). Research on Machine Recognition of Handprinted Characters. *IEEE Transactions on Pattern Analysis and Machine Intelligence*, *6*(4), 386–405. doi:10.1109/TPAMI.1984.4767545 PMID:21869208

Nicchiotti, G., & Scagliola, C. (2000). A simple and effective cursive word segmentation method. *Seventh International Workshop on Frontiers in Handwriting Recognition*, 499-504.

Senior, A. W., Robinson, A. J., (1998). An Offline Cursive Handwriting Recognition System. *IEEE Transactions on Pattern Analysis and Machine Intelligence*, *20*(3), 309-321.

Sheikh, E., & Guindi, R. M. (1998). Computer Recognition of Arabic Cursive Scripts. *Pattern Recognition*, *21*(4), 216–223.

Simard, P.Y., Steinkraus, D., & Platt, J. (2003). Best practices for convolutional neural networks applied to visual document analysis. *ICDAR*, 958–962.

Suen, C. Y., Tappert, C. C., & Wakahara, T. (1990). The State of the Art in On-Line Handwriting Recognition. *IEEE Transactions on Pattern Analysis and Machine Intelligence*, *12*(8), 787–808. doi:10.1109/34.57669

Tappert, C. C. (1984). Adaptive on-line handwriting recognition. *Proc of. 7th Int. Conf. Pattern Recognition*, 1004-1007.

Ullmann, J. R. (1986). Advances character recognition in Applications of Pattern Recognition. CRC Press.

Ward, J. R., & Kuklinski, T. (1988). A Model for Variability Effects in Handwriting Character Recognition Systems. *IEEE Transactions on Systems, Man, and Cybernetics*, *18*(3), 438–451. doi:10.1109/21.7493

ADDITIONAL READING

AlShahrani, A. M., Al-Abadi, M. A., Al-Malki, A. S., Ashour, A. S., & Dey, N. (2018).Automated system for crops recognition and classification. In Computer Vision: Concepts, Methodologies, Tools, and Applications (pp. 1208-1223). IGI Global. doi:10.4018/978-1-5225-5204-8.ch050

Chakraborty, S., Chatterjee, S., Dey, N., Ashour, A. S., Ashour, A. S., Shi, F., & Mali, K. (2017). Modified cuckoo search algorithm in microscopic image segmentation of hippocampus. *Microscopy Research and Technique*, *80*(10), 1051–1072. doi:10.1002/jemt.22900 PMID:28557041

Chakraborty, S., Mukherjee, A., Chatterjee, D., Maji, P., Acharjee, S., & Dey, N. (2014, December).A semi-automated system for optic nerve head segmentation in digital retinal images.In *Information Technology (ICIT), 2014 International Conference on* (pp. 112-117).IEEE. 10.1109/ICIT.2014.51

Chatterjee, S., Dey, N., Shi, F., Ashour, A. S., Fong, S. J., & Sen, S. (2017). Clinical application of modified bag-of-features coupled with hybrid neural-based classifier in dengue fever classification using gene expression data. *Medical & Biological Engineering & Computing*, 1–12. PMID:28891000

Dey, N., Ashour, A. S., Chakraborty, S., Samanta, S., Sifaki-Pistolla, D., Ashour, A. S., ... Nguyen, G. N. (2016). Healthy and unhealthy rat hippocampus cells classification: A neural based automated system for Alzheimer disease classification. *Journal of Advanced Microscopy Research*, *11*(1), 1–10. doi:10.1166/jamr.2016.1282

Ghosh, A., Sarkar, A., Ashour, A. S., Balas-Timar, D., Dey, N., & Balas, V. E. (2015). Grid color moment features in glaucoma classification. *Int J AdvComputSciAppl*, *6*(9), 1–14.

Hore, S., Chakraborty, S., Chatterjee, S., Dey, N., Ashour, A. S., Van Chung, L., & Le, D. N. (2016). An Integrated Interactive Technique for Image Segmentation using Stack based Seeded Region Growing and Thresholding. *Iranian Journal of Electrical and Computer Engineering*, *6*(6), 2773.

Kamal, M. S., Parvin, S., Ashour, A. S., Shi, F., & Dey, N. (2017). De-Bruijn graph with MapReduce framework towards metagenomic data classification. *International Journal of Information Technology*, *9*(1), 59–75. doi:10.100741870-017-0005-z

Kamble, S. D., Thakur, N. V., & Bajaj, P. R. (2018). Fractal Coding Based Video Compression Using Weighted Finite Automata. *International Journal of Ambient Computing and Intelligence*, *9*(1), 115–133. doi:10.4018/IJACI.2018010107

Kishor, D. R., & Venkateswarlu, N. B. (2016). A Novel Hybridization of Expectation-Maximization and K-Means Algorithms for Better Clustering Performance. *International Journal of Ambient Computing and Intelligence*, *7*(2), 47–74. doi:10.4018/IJACI.2016070103

Li, Z., Shi, K., Dey, N., Ashour, A. S., Wang, D., Balas, V. E., ... Shi, F. (2017). Rule-based back propagation neural networks for various precision rough set presented KANSEI knowledge prediction: A case study on shoe product form features extraction. *Neural Computing & Applications*, *28*(3), 613–630. doi:10.100700521-016-2707-8

Pal, G., Acharjee, S., Rudrapaul, D., Ashour, A. S., &Dey, N. (2015).Video segmentation using minimum ratio similarity measurement. *International journal of image mining, 1*(1), 87-110.

Saba, L., Dey, N., Ashour, A. S., Samanta, S., Nath, S. S., Chakraborty, S., ... Suri, J. S. (2016). Automated stratification of liver disease in ultrasound: An online accurate feature classification paradigm. *Computer Methods and Programs in Biomedicine*, *130*, 118–134. doi:10.1016/j.cmpb.2016.03.016 PMID:27208527

Sghaier, S., Farhat, W., & Souani, C. (2018). Novel Technique for 3D Face Recognition Using Anthropometric Methodology. *International Journal of Ambient Computing and Intelligence*, *9*(1), 60–77. doi:10.4018/IJACI.2018010104

Sharma, K., & Virmani, J. (2017). A Decision Support System for Classification of Normal and Medical Renal Disease Using Ultrasound Images: A Decision Support System for Medical Renal Diseases. *International Journal of Ambient Computing and Intelligence*, *8*(2), 52–69. doi:10.4018/IJACI.2017040104

Wang, D., He, T., Li, Z., Cao, L., Dey, N., Ashour, A. S., ... Shi, F. (2016). Image feature-based affective retrieval employing improved parameter and structure identification of adaptive neuro-fuzzy inference system. *Neural Computing & Applications*, 1–16.

Chapter 11
Wireless Sensor Networks: Concepts, Analysis, Routing, and Applications

Sachin R. Jain
Yeshwantrao Chavan College of Engineering, India

Nileshsingh V. Thakur
Nagpur Institute of Technology, India

ABSTRACT

Wireless sensor networks (WSNs) can be classified among the blazing domains of research in the recent era. WSNs have enormous day-to-day life real-time applications due their low priced, self-computing, powerful, autonomous small sensor nodes which have a small storage capacity, restricted non-removable non-rechargeable battery, and a restricted computational capacity. The applicability of WSNs are in almost all domains, like observing environmental conditions, human healthcare tracking systems, position tracking and monitoring, industry automation, process tracking and controlling, tracking and monitoring objects, mammal, human being, and control, and many more. This chapter briefly explores the basic concepts, components, network architecture, design issues, challenges, routing protocols, application domains, implemented applications, etc. in the field of WSNs. It also focuses on the performance evaluation parameters to check, analyze, diagnose, examine, and determine the performance of WSNs. At the end, the chapter concludes with the scope of research in the field of wireless sensor networks.

INTRODUCTION

Nowadays, Wireless Sensor Networks (WSNs) (Buratti et al., 2009), (Yick et al., 2008), become more trendy, rising and one of the blazing research areas because of its broad variety of application in large areas. These types of networks (Akyildiz et al., 2007), (Puccinelli & Haenggi, 2005) are mainly composed of a very small, economical, low powered, non-rechargeable, non-removable onboard battery driven, autonomous, supportive, distributed sensor nodes that are designed for an application specific task. These types of nodes are deployed densely in big number in a region of application, as shown in

DOI: 10.4018/978-1-5225-6164-4.ch011

Figure 1, from where the important data is to be gathered and sent to the sink node or base station (BS) which is generally located away from this region (Akyildiz et al., 2002), (Akyildiz et al., 2002). The data collected from these types of sensor nodes can be further processed and analyzed. In such types of networks (Tilak, 2002), there is no fixed network infrastructure, that's why the sensor nodes must support and cooperate to accomplish communication, global control and information aggregation.

Generally, a sensor node (Akyildiz & Vuran, 2010) normally consists of four modules: a sensing unit for data acquirement from the region of interest, a small computational unit to process the sensed data, a communication unit to transmit the sensed data and a power unit consisting of a non- rechargeable, non-removable limited onboard battery. It may also have some additional components like mobilzer, a GPS system, power generator etc., which can be integrated in the basic model of sensor node depending on the type of applications. Figure 2 shows hardware structure of such type of node. The components of a sensor are described below.

- **Power Unit:** It is the main driving force of the sensor node. It usually consists of a non-removable, non-rechargeable limited energy supply battery. Other energy sources can also be used for power supply in special cases. As the power supply is limited and cannot be remove or recharge, it must be used in efficient way by the each and every component of the sensor.
- **Sensing Unit:** Depending on the type of application, this unit is designed to acquire desired information from the physical surrounding environment, such as sound, temperature, light, humidity etc. This unit is normally comprised of two sub modules: the actual sensor unit and a unit to convert analog data to digital (ADC). Generally, in most of the sensors the data produced by the sensors is in analog form, to convert these analog data into digital form an ADC unit is used. The final processed data by sensing unit is then provided as an input to the processing unit.
- **Processing Unit:** The processing unit is the controlling unit of the node which is responsible for the processing of the sensed information, like run related algorithms and handle the procedures that allow the node to perform sensing operations and work together with other nodes for wireless

Figure 1. Sample Structures of Wireless Sensor Networks

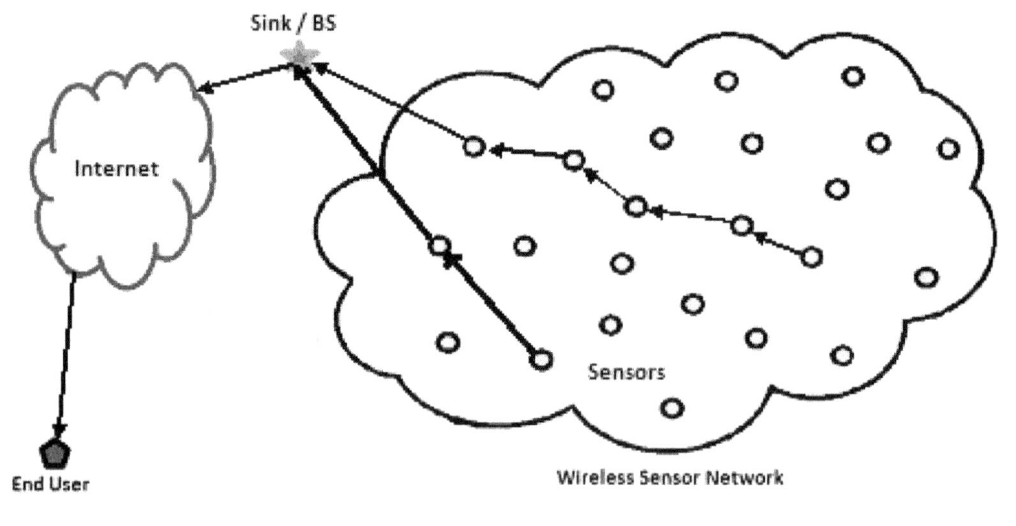

Figure 2. Hardware Architecture of a Sensor

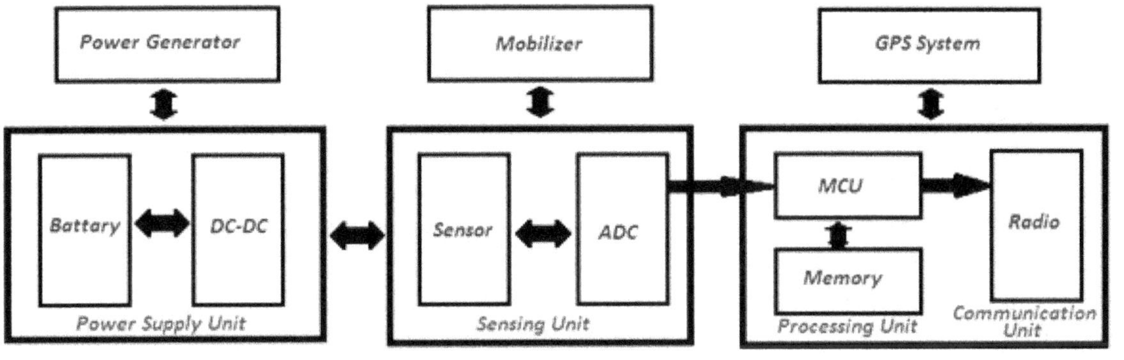

communication. It generally consists of a working memory unit and sometimes it may also have a small storage element, depending on the type of sensor and application where it is used.

- **Communication Unit:** This unit is mainly responsible for carrying out the communication between any two nodes in the network; it is done by the radio unit, i.e. the transceiver unit.
- **Power Generator:** Power supply is an essential part of the sensor node, which is fulfilled by the limited powered, non-removable battery but some applications requires a longer network lifetime, in such applications the sensors are used which are composed this optional unit. A sensor must be a tiny, small sized, light weight device, so as to maintain these characteristics; this type of optional units should be bypassed.
- **Mobilizer:** A mobilizer is also an optional unit that can be integrated in a sensor, which is used in an application that requires the mobility of the sensor nodes. The mobilizer is mainly responsible in moving the sensor node from one location to the other. Mobility of the node also requires an excessive energy to move node from one location to other, so it is necessary to handle this operation very efficiently, so as to use the power source efficiently.
- **GPS System:** It is Global Positioning System, an optional application specific system used in the wireless sensor networks, where it requires the physical location of the sensor to be processed to carry out some useful task. It is generally a hardware module; sometimes a software module is also used to implement the localization algorithms.

It is very important to have a better energy optimization technique to have a longer network lifetime, because in most of the applications the operation of wireless sensor networks is to be carried out for several days, months or years. This chapter discusses the major hardware design issue, network architecture and design issues, different routing protocols, static and mobile WSNs, applications and performance evaluation parameters for analyzing the WSNs.

MAJOR HARDWARE DESIGN ISSUES IN WSNs

There is numerous application areas of the WSNs, base on the type and place of the application, the infrastructural design of WSN may be affected by many factors (Akyildiz et al., 2002) such as: scalability, hardware constraints, power consumption, fault tolerance, production costs, environmental constraints, topology of the network, and communication medium, etc. These issues are discussed in the following sub sections.

Scalability

Scalability is one of the important characteristics that must be considered while designing a WSN, depending on the nature of the application, the count of sensor nodes used in the WSN may be very few in number or sometimes it may very large in number, like hundreds or thousands or many more than that. The network designed must be capable to occupy and handle such a variable number of sensor nodes. The network must be highly scalable in nature, so that it fits to almost every requirement of any application. The sensors must also exhibit high density characteristic of WSNs. In such networks (Cho & Chandrakasan, 2000), the density of sensor nodes can vary from a small to very large in a region of interest, which may be even less than 10 meter in diameter. The total number of sensors deployed in the area of application indicates the density of sensors in that region. Generally the node density (Bulusu et al., 2001) in such situation may be calculated using the equation 1 given below:

$$\mu\left(R\right) = \left(N\pi R^2\right) / A \tag{1}$$

where, R is the radio transmission range, N is number of sensor nodes in region A, and $\mu\left(R\right)$ indicates the total count of sensors in the transmission range of each sensor in area A.

Hardware Constraints

As shown in Figure 2, and discussed earlier, a sensor is composed up of four basic components, but depending on the nature and requirement a sensor node may also have some additional components. All of these components should be fitted into small sized module like a matchbox (Intanagonwiwat et al., 2000) or even smaller than that (Pottie & Kaiser, 2000). Apart from the size of the sensor node, there are some other rigorous constraints (Kahn et al., 1999) like, they should deplete extremely low energy, work in high density, should have low cost of production, should be robust, self-governing and flexible in nature. The power resource is also an important constraint while designing the sensor. The sensors should be designed with less complex algorithms using simpler microcontrollers and radio, so as they should be low in cost, because they are deployed in hundreds or thousands or some time more than that in number.

Power Consumption

In WSN, the sensor nodes are generally microelectronic devices, which are equipped with limited power, non-removable, non-rechargeable battery. The lifetime of the nodes and the lifetime of the whole network are ultimately depending on the actual life time of the battery of the sensors. Hence, it is important to conserve and manage the power consumption of the sensor nodes. Because of this reason the designing of power aware protocols and algorithms for WSN is catching more attention of the researchers nowadays. A formula is proposed in (Shih et al., 2001) for calculating power consumption for communication P_c and power consumption for data processing P_p. The formula for calculating P_c is given by the following formula given in equation 2:

$$P_c = N_T\left[P_T\left(T_{on} + T_{st}\right) + P_{out}\left(T_{on}\right)\right] + N_R\left[P_R\left(R_{on} + R_{st}\right)\right] \tag{2}$$

where, P_T is the power consumed by the transmitter; P_R is the receiver's power consumption; output power of transmitter is denoted by P_{out}; the total transmitter-on time is denoted by T_{on}; T_{st} is the start-up time of the transmitter; similarly, the total receiver-on time is denoted by R_{on}; receiver start-up time required is denoted by R_{st}; number of times the transmitter is switched-on per unit time is given by N_T and N_R is the number of times receiver is switched-on per unit time. The power consumption for data processing P_p can be calculated using formula given in equation 3:

$$P_p = CV_{dd}^2 f + V_{dd} I_0 e^{V_{dd}/n'V_T} \tag{3}$$

where, total switching capacitance is denoted by *C*; voltage swing is denoted by V_{dd}; the switching frequency is *f*, whereas the other part of the equation denotes the power loss because of leakage currents discussed in (Sinha et al., 2001).

The basic aim of a sensor node in a WSN is to sense the desired data from the region of deployment process it and route the same to sink node. Here, the power consumption by the nodes can be break up into three different tasks: sense data, processing it and communicate it. If periodic sensing technique is used, it might consume lesser power compared to a continuous sensing. The type application and the complexity of the sensing work are also playing important role in finding out the energy consumption.

Fault Tolerance

During the execution of the WSN, some of the sensors may fail due to drainage of the battery, due to physical damage to node or due to environmental issues, etc. This type of situation may appear frequently in the network and must be carefully handled carefully, so that the performance of the network should not get deteriorated. The concept of fault tolerance or reliability in WSNs (Hoblos et al., 2000), (Shen et al. 2001) is related to the capability of the network to keep the operations and working of network proper, fault-free, without any disturbances and interrupts due to failure of the sensors. The fault tolerance or Reliability $R_k(t)$ of a node can be given by using the Poisson distribution, discussed in (Hoblos et al., 2000). The probability that a node will not fail within the given time interval (0, t) can be calculated with the help of equation 4 given below:

$$R_k(t) = \exp(-\lambda_k t) \tag{4}$$

where, λ_k is failure rate of sensor node for the time period *t*.

Production Costs

The production cost of a sensor node may vary depending on the type and operations it carries out, which is the requirement of an application of WSN. The nodes deployed in the WSNs are sometime very large in number, it may vary from hundred to thousand or sometime more than that, so the production cost of a single node is one of the crucial parameter to calculate the overall cost of the network. If the overall cost of deploying the sensors in the network is high than deploying the traditional, older methodology and technology based sensor nodes, the sensor network will not be able justify its cost. The overall cost of the network must be maintained low and economical, to achieve this, the cost of designing of single node must be maintained lowest as much as possible. Maintaining the cost of designing and developing a sensor is considered as one of the main challenging issues in WSNs, and it must be handled carefully.

Environmental Constraints

As discussed earlier, the sensors deployed in the region of interest are very dense and they work autonomously by cooperating each other in area they are deployed. The application areas (Akyildiz et al., 2002) where these sensor nodes are deployed may be sometimes in the internal parts of a very big machine, at the base layer of a deep-sea, inside a erupting volcano, inside a big cyclone, on the surface layer of a sea during a hurricane, in a biotical affected area, a polluted field, in a battleground of enemies, in a house, in a big apartment, in a big storehouse, in big hospital, on the body part of mammals, on a fast running automobiles, on a bank or inside a river, etc. There are many constraint, conditions and scenarios, where these sensor nodes have to work efficiently and effectively. They may have to work in a very unfavorable, difficult, hostile, adverse and dangerous environment like, under high pressure, under water, under extreme heat or cold conditions. These types of environmental constraints must be considered while designing the sensors and sensor networks.

Topology of the Network

In WSNs, a huge number of sensor nodes which are autonomous, self localizing, cooperative in nature are deployed densely, the network topology to work with these huge number of nodes plays a vital role in overall performance of the network. These sensors are prone to frequent failures because of some uncertain, unexpected reasons, results in maintaining topology of the network a more challenging job (Akyildiz et al., 2002), (Shih et al. 2001). Deploying such a huge number of sensors densely in the application area requires careful approach to handle, manage and maintain the network topology. Some of the challenges regarding maintaining the topology are studied, observed and placed in different phases: Pre-deployment and deployment phase; which is related to topology of the network at the time of deployment of the sensor nodes, Post-deployment phase; which is related to the topology of network after the deployment of the sensors, and Re-deployment of additional nodes phase; which is related to the network topology while re-deployment of the addition sensors in the network.

Communication Medium

Communication is one of the basic tasks in WSNs, which deals with transmitting, receiving or forwarding a data packet in order to send the sense data to the base station or sink. In a cluster based or a multi-hop

WSNs, the communication in the network is using different sensors which are associated by each other by a wireless media to transmit or receive the data. These links are generally created and maintained by radio, infrared or optical media, whichever is feasible for the application. To facilitate universal working of the sensor network, the feasible and applicable communication media should be made available at the region of application. For such WSN, a low cost, small sized, ultralow power transceiver is required to do the predefined operations. Some of the extraordinary application specific requirements of sensors in the WSNs make the selection of communication medium more difficult and challenging.

NETWORK ARCHITECTURE AND DESIGN ISSUES

Network design and architectures are also plays important role while designing a good, efficient WSN based application. Several architectural issues and designing limitations (Akkaya & Younis, 2005) must be considered while modeling and designing a wireless sensor networks which also depends on the types of applications. The performance of a routing protocol used in the application is strongly dependent on the architecture of the network. In the following sections some of architectural issues are discussed.

Network Dynamics

The major modules of a WSN are sensors, base station and events to be monitored. It is assumed (Subramanian & Katz, 2000) that a very few network architecture are based on mobile sensor nodes, otherwise most of them have the sensor nodes stationary in nature. Routing of data packet from a mobile node is more challenging than from a stationary node, because route stability is considered as one of the important optimization factors other than bandwidth, energy etc. Depending on the application (Tilak et al., 2002), the sensed event can be either static or dynamic in nature. The networks where, the monitoring of the events are static in nature, working mode is reactive, whereas in dynamic events monitoring, the applications generally requires periodic reporting to base station that results in generating significant traffic in the network.

Node Deployment

The topological deployment of sensor node is also one of the important considerations in network. Depending on the application, generally the node deployment can be either deterministic i.e. fixed, manually placement of the sensor nodes or it can be non-deterministic, self-organizing in nature i.e. the sensors deployment is random, making an ad-hoc network structure (Tilak et al., 2002), (Akewar & Thakur, 2012). The deployment strategy of sensors in the network, definitely affects the working and operations of the routing approach used in the WSNs. In deterministic node deployment, the data packets are routed through a fixed, predefined route in the network. In non-deterministic node deployment strategy, the allocation of nodes is not homogeneous, so balanced clustering turn out to be a burning issue, resulting in affecting the energy efficiency and performance of the network (Sohrabi et al., 2000), (Younis et al., 2002).

Energy Considerations

Energy optimization is one of the key challenges in WSN, as the nodes are limited powered, non-removable, non-rechargeable battery driven devices. So, during the formation of the infrastructure, energy consumption must be considered in the process of setting up the path for routing (Wajgi & Thakur, 2012). The power required for transmission in a wireless radio is generally corresponding to square of the length; sometimes it is yet higher if more hurdles or barriers are present in the network. If the sensors are very closer to the base station, the direct communication method is preferable, otherwise multi-hop routing should be considered, as it consumes less energy than direct method (Tilak et al., 2002). If the sensors are scattered randomly in the network and far away from the base station, multi-hop routing becomes more energy aware, effective and promising than direct routing approach with the sink node.

Data Delivery Models

Data packet routing to the sink node may be done in four ways based on the nature of use of the WSN application, they may be continuous, event driven, query driven or hybrid (Akkaya & Younis, 2005), (Tilak et al., 2002). In the continuous model, each node in the network transmits data time to time to the sink. In event driven model the data packets are sent to the base station if an even is triggered in the network. In query driven models, the data packets are sent to the base station takes place in response of a query fired in the network. In the hybrid model any grouping of the three models discussed above can take place; it may use any mixture of continuous, event driven or query driven data delivery model depending on the need of the application in WSNs. The data delivery model plays a significant role in routing protocol, in consideration with energy optimization and maintaining the stability of route.

Node Capabilities

Generally the nodes in the sensor network have the similar functionality and potential in support of computing, communication and power, known as the homogeneous nodes. But based on the type of application, the nodes can be assigned with different computation, communication and power capabilities and some addition functionality too, such type of networks are known as the heterogynous network. Working on heterogeneous set of sensors nodes (Akkaya & Younis, 2003) may generate multiple technical issues in the network; such heterogeneous nodes make the network more challenging compared to homogeneous networks.

Data Aggregation

Data aggregation is also one of the important tasks in the sensor network, also known as the fusion of the data. The sensor node in the network, may generate redundant data, i.e. same data again and again, also data from different sensors may be combined together to minimize the number of occurrences of data transmissions to route the data to sink. In simple words, data aggregation is the method of processing, combining or aggregating the data collected by different sources by using some standard technique, which also eliminates duplicate data. It enhances energy optimization, reduces the traffic in the network & improving the performance of network by reducing overall overhead of more number of communications with the sink (Tilak et al., 2002), (Krishnamachari et al., 2002).

CLASSIFICATION OF ROUTING PROTOCOL

The routing protocol plays a very important role in applications of the WSNs, it is considered as one of the continuous and important process performed during the lifetime of the network, hence it also becomes a hot research area and many researchers have proposed a vast variety of routing protocols according to need of their applications which works on different principles. Some of the broad categorization of the routing protocols is data centric routing protocols, hierarchical routing protocols and location based routing protocols. All of these categories of routing protocols have their own advantages, disadvantages, limitations as well as specific application areas where they may be used. These categories are discussed in brief in the following sub section.

Data Centric Routing

Generally in WSN a large number of the nodes are randomly distributed densely in the network, where it is hard to allocate a unique identification number every sensor which results in difficulty in selecting a particular cluster of sensors to be queried for particular information. Because of this problem, every sensor node of the region transmits data to the sink directly, with significant redundant data that is not very efficient in terms of consumption of energy. To overcome this problem, the data centric routing (Akkaya & Younis, 2005) is used; in which the base station transmits queries to the specific area and keep waiting for a reply from the nodes deployed in that area. This methodology is also supports the attribute based data routing, which uses the specific properties or attributes of data that is needed from the region of interest. Some of the important data centric protocols are: DD (Directed Diffusion) (Intanagonwiwat et al., 2000), SPIN (Sensor protocols for information via negotiation) (Heinzelman et al., 1999), RR (Rumor routing) (Braginsky & Estrin, 2002), GBR (Gradient-Based Routing) by (Schurgers et al., 2001).

Hierarchical Routing

As discussed earlier in section 2.1, the scalability of the network is an important attribute of WSNs (Akkaya & Younis, 2005), in real-time scenarios, it may be needed to add some more sensor nodes in the network or sometimes there is a need to remove some of the sensor nodes from the network. The addition and deletion of sensor nodes should not affect the working, operations and performance of the network. In case of direct routing of flat routing in WSNs, if the number of sensor nodes is increased to a large number, it may cause some of the nodes which work as a gateway to transmit the data from the source node to the sink, will get overloaded. The overloading of the gateways may cause latency in communication; inadequate tracking of events and it may also cause uncertainty or unpredictable behavior in the network. In such situations, single gateway structure is not suitable, rather than it, a clustering based approach may be more useful, which is also known as hierarchical routing technique.

The primary goal of hierarchical routing is to optimize the energy consumption by involving sensor nodes in multi-hop communication, and also perform data aggregation, fusion to decrease the number of communications with the sink. In this type of routing scheme, the whole network is divided into a finite number of clusters, where each cluster composed of a finite number of sensors. In each cluster, one of the sensors elected as a cluster head (CH) and all other remaining sensors will become the member of that cluster. All the member node of each cluster transmits data to their respective cluster head using a predefined scheduling mechanism. The CH aggregates all the data transmitted by its member periodically and the collected data is transmitted to sink node using a scheduling mechanism. Custer based approach in WSNs provide much better support, functionality, advantages and better results, because of these reasons, many cluster based routing protocols have been designed and developed for WSNs. Some of the most popular and important routing protocols which supports hierarchical approach are LEACH (Low-energy adaptive clustering hierarchy) (Tilak et al., 2002), TEEN (Threshold sensitive Energy Efficient sensor Network protocol) (Manjeshwar & Agrawal, 2001), ATEEN (Adaptive Threshold sensitive Energy Efficient- sensor Network protocol) (Manjeshwar & Agrawal, 2002), (Younis et al., 2002) PEGASIS (Power-efficient GAthering in Sensor Information Systems) (Lindsey & Raghavendra, 2002), Hierarchical-PEGASIS (Lindsey et al., 2001).

Location Based Routing

Location based routing is also one of the application specific routing protocol, which uses the physical locations of the sensors to participate in routing, using a Global Positioning System (GPS) device. This type of routing uses the GPS device to find out the distance between pair of nodes or between a node and the base station. This information is further used for establishing the shortest routing paths, alternate paths to optimize the energy consumption and to improve overall performance of the network. The concept of GPS system also helps to reduce the overhead of broadcasting the same query to all sensors, though some of them are not related or involved in that task, as it uses the GPS location to multicast the query to get information from the specific sensors. This will help in reducing the total number of communications takes place during the lifetime of the network, which also optimizes the energy consumption (Finn, 1987), (Nath & Niculescu, 2002). Some of the protocols based on this approach are MECN (Minimum energy communication network) (Rodoplu & Ming, 1999), SMECN (Small minimum energy communication network) (Li & Halpern, 2001), is an extension to MECN, GAF (Geographic adaptive fidelity) (Xu et al., 2001), GEAR (Geographic and energy-aware routing) (Yu et al., 2001).

MOBILE WIRELESS SENSOR NETWORKS

The nodes that are deployed in the WSNs can be static or mobile in nature according to need of the application (Jain & Thakur, 2015). The static sensors are rigid, fixed type of sensors that cannot move from one geographic location to other, once they are deployed in the network. Mobile Wireless Sensor Networks (MWSN) (Hayes & Ali, 2016), (Velmani & Kaarthick, 2009) is more versatile than static sensor networks as the nodes have the ability to move from one location to other. The mobile nodes can be used in any scenario and should have ability to deal with dynamic changes in the topology of the network. As the nodes are mobile in nature the topology of the network changes rapidly, they produce new challenges in MWSN, which must be handled properly. Routing of sensed information from the deployed node to the base station is also one of the primary tasks of concern in MWSN (Lambrou & Panayiotou, 2009), (Aronsky & Segall 2010). All these points related to MWSN are discussed in the following section.

Challenges in MWSN

Apart from the challenges and issues in static WSNs, roughly the challenges related to MWSNs are divided in two major categories i.e., challenges related to hardware and environment. As in most of the applications, the sensors are composed of a limited energy, non-removable and non-rechargeable battery, it is considered as one of the main constraint related to the hardware. Limited energy means, it is a major point of concern for the sensors to utilize the energy efficiently so as the network lifetime should be prolonged. Designing low cost sensors is another major constraint related to the hardware. The sensors should be low in cost too, because they are deployed in hundreds or sometimes thousands in number, so they should be designed with less complex algorithms using simpler microcontrollers and radio. The major constraints related to the environmental factors are varying topology of the network, which changes continuously, and the shared channel which means that the access to the channels must be standardized. The mobility of sensor nodes are mainly responsible for the continuous change in topology of the network, which also means that the routing of data by the same sensor to the base station will not be stable, same and fixed always, it may vary with respective time.

Topology in MWSN

As discussed earlier, the routing of the data packets from the source node to the base station is decided by the topology of the network, so the selection of the network topology plays a very vital role in routing of the data. In the case of MWSNs, the nodes are mobile in nature, they move from one position to other, which results in continuous and rapid change in the network topology. Because of this reason, it is not feasible, comfortable and reliable choose any one of the topologies like, flat, chain, Unstructured, tree, or cluster based to do communication in this kind of networks. Comparatively using a hybrid topology, which comprises two or more than two topologies, instead of single topology may perform better in data collection, processing and routing of the data packets from the source to destination, which may also results in improving the overall performance of the network.

Routing in MWSN

As there is no fixed, predefined topology in MWSNs, the routing of data from a particular sensor node to the base station is considered as one of the biggest challenges in this type of networks. The routing protocols in MWSN are inspired by two major domains i.e. static WSNs and mobile ad-hoc networks (MANETs). The static WSNs are inefficient in handling the high frequency of changes in topology of the network, whereas, in MANETs, the data routing protocols are mainly developed for duplex communication which generally do not required in WSN, but the MANETs are designed to handle the mobility of the nodes. Routing protocols designed for MWSNs are generally multi-hop in nature and sometime they are inspired by the existing protocols in WSNs or MANETs. For example, the LEACH-M (Low Energy Adaptive Clustering Hierarchy for Mobile nodes) protocol for MWSNs is inspired by the simple LEACH (Low Energy Adaptive Clustering Hierarchy) protocol. Handling the mobile sensor nodes in MWSN is also one of the major issues in the hierarchical protocols, as the mobile nodes switches from one cluster to the other clusters frequently in the network. This results in large amounts of overhead in energy depletion because of mobility and re-registering themselves with different clusters again and again in the complete lifetime of the MWSN.

APPLICATION DOMAINS OF WSNS

WSNs (Buratti et al., 2009), (Akyildiz et al., 2007) were initially designed and developed for the military applications, but in the recent era, they can be modeled in lot many situations and application domains.

For example, to monitor environmental conditions like temperature, humidity, light, sound pollution, air pollution levels, pressure, wind speed, direction of wind, whether forecasts, noise pollution etc. The applications of these types of networks are not restricted to this, but they can be further extended to more complicated, huge and complex tasks like disaster management, process monitoring and control in factories, traffic monitoring, vehicular movement, health tracking and monitoring, space exploration, animal tracking and monitoring etc. (Puccinelli, & Haenggi 2005), (Akyildiz et al., 2002).

The WSN application area is very much vast; in general, it can be classified into two broad categories (Yick et al., 2008) i.e. monitoring and tracking. Brief structure of these categories is shown in Figure 3. The first category i.e. monitoring includes indoor and outdoor surrounding monitoring, monitoring of patients health, power monitoring, position monitoring, industry automation, process monitoring, and animal and human monitoring, etc. The second category is the tracking of different events and situations, which includes objects tracking, animals and humans tracking, vehicular tracking, etc. Some of the wide range of applications of WSN (Yick et al., 2008) is described in the following section.

Military Applications

A wide range of attributes of WSN like, random and distributed deployment, cooperative, automotive, self-localizing and organizing, tolerable, secure etc. make WSNs a more useful and vital for many military applications. Various attractive properties of application specific sensors also make WSN concept a stronger and better approach for battlegrounds in military. Some of the important and useful major applications of WSNs in military are battle-field surveillance, recognizing and tracking of friendly army, tools and materials; scouting of opposition army forces and their landscape; assessment of damage in battlefields; targeting etc.

Environmental Applications

This category of application of WSN includes tracking and monitoring the events based on some environmental parameters. Some of them are: whether forecasting for crops, livestock, irrigation; movements of sun, moon, earth; planetary exploration; agricultural applications; chemical and biological detection;

Figure 3. Application categories in WSN

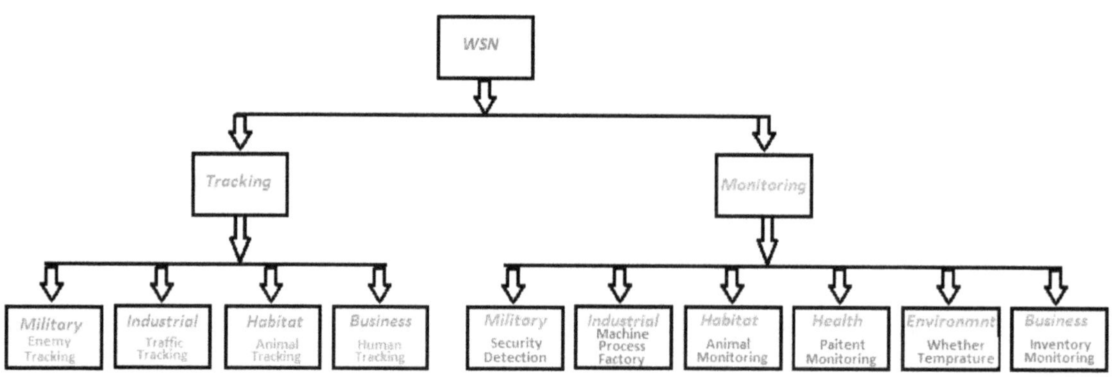

soil exploration; detection of fire in forest; flood detection; underwater monitoring, surface monitoring of sea, checking water levels in rivers, ocean, pollution tracking, monitoring, analysis, study, surrounding environmental monitoring, river water monitoring, etc.

Health Applications

WSN have a numerous applications in human health care system. Some of them are monitoring the health of a patient, monitoring the various activities in the patient's body; keep track and monitor the doctors and patients; medicine management system, providing helping aids and useful equipments for the disables; advanced tracking and monitoring of the patients; disease diagnosis expertise system; tracking and monitoring the motions and locations of animals, human or any living creature; tracking and monitoring the medical reports of human beings, etc.

Home Applications

WSNs are also useful for homes, few of the applications for home are: home automation system; designing a smart and intelligent environment. The application specific sensors can be embedded into furniture and various appliances like, television, fridge, air-conditioners, microwave oven, lights, fans, doors, lockers, etc. which have the capability to communicate with each other and sink. Here, the sink can be considered as a room server or a local server, which also communicate with other local or room servers. In this type of applications the task of sensing and computing should be consistent, reliable, continual, transparent, and accurate to have a better solution.

Other Commercial Applications

WSN can also be used in the commercial applications like inventory management, product quality monitoring; material fatigue monitoring; environmental tracking and monitoring in big apartments; robotic applications, factory automation; interactive objects; automated process tracking, monitoring control; disaster area monitoring; smart and intelligent devices; machine diagnosis; transportation management; real-time traffic monitoring, tracking; ATM monitoring, bank events tracking, monitoring and many more.

REAL-TIME APPLICATIONS OF WSN

WSN provides a great opportunity to apply the concept of computer science to observe some of the important characteristics, attributes and parameters from the real time challenging environment. It has a numerous applications which are already discussed earlier. In this section some of the major real-time implemented applications of WSN are discussed in brief, which is categorized into two sub-parts i.e. Static WSN application and Mobile WSN applications.

Applications in Static WSN

In static WSN all the sensors distributed in the application region are static or fixed in nature; here, the sensor nodes cannot move physically from one location to other by themselves. In some situations cluster heads or the sink node may be mobile in nature, according to the need of applications. These types of networks have a fixed type of network topology and have less complexity as compared to the mobile WSN. Some of the real-time applications implemented using static WSN in real-time scenarios are discussed below.

A case study of WSN "macroscope" is discussed in (Tolle et al., 2005)., that is designed to observe and record the coastal redwood trees in Sonoma, California. The sensors were deployed on around 70 meter tall redwood tree, at around every 2 meters in height, which records data around every 5 minutes in time. The data recorded by the sensors are surrounding temperature, humidity, and photo-synthetically active solar radiation from the region of interest. The system gathers the minute details of the micro-climate surrounding the coastal redwood trees, which were analyzed by the experts for the further investigations and study.

WSN have also inspired researchers to work in the area of precision agriculture. The application of WSN can help to predict crop performance more accurately and precisely by using dedicated sensors in the field. In (Lopez Riquelme et al., 2009) presented a network topology by deploying four different types of sensors in the field. The four types of sensors are soil, environmental, water and gateway sensors. The system observes and records various characteristics like, temperature, salinity and moisture level of soil. The system proposed was successfully implemented and tested on a crop of cabbage.

An application proposed in (Rahimi et al., 2005), named as Cyclops, which uses a sensor technology with CMOS imaging. It has a logical and programmable unit with a memory unit with high speed data transfer rate. To interact with outside world, a micro-controller is used in the proposed system. Cyclops is very useful in various applications, where fast processing requested or images with high quality are required for processing purpose.

Volcanic monitoring system is discussed in (Werner-Allen et al., 2006), which uses different 16 sensors, which were distributed on Volcàn Reventador in northern Ecuador to form a WSN. The sensors are deployed around 200–400 m away from each other in the region. The sensor nodes communicate to gateway node using a multi-hop routing technique and the gateway node sends the aggregated data to the sink node, which situated at distance apart. The deployed system was firstly monitored for around 19 days and approximate 230 numbers of volcano eruptions and other volcanic activities were observed in this time period, which was later studied and analyzed.

Application of Mobile WSN

It is clear that the static nodes cannot move from one location to other, but in lot many applications it is needed that a sensor node should move physically to capture some important events, values. In mobile WSN some or all the sensors deployed in the field of application are mobile by nature; the nodes can move physically from one location to other by themselves. It is not compulsory that all nodes should be mobile, some of them may be static in nature and in some situations cluster heads or the sink node may also be mobile or static in nature, according to the need of applications. These types of networks do not have a fixed type of network topology; it changes as the nodes move in the network. These types of networks have more complexity as compared to the pure static WSN. Some of the real-time applications implemented using mobile WSN in real-time scenarios are discussed below.

To monitor coral reefs and fisheries, an underwater application of MWSNs is discussed by (Vasilescu et al., 2005), which consist of both static as well as mobile application specific sensors deployed under the water, in the application area. The network has a variety of sensors for sensing temperature, pressure etc. The sensor nodes communicate with each other and base station with help of a high speed optical communication channel and a specific acoustic routing protocol. To collect the data, mobile sensor nodes generally locate and move above the static nodes, they also executes maintenance functions like, deployment, re-location, and recovery in WSNs.

A system called "TrueMobile" is discussed in (Johnson et al., 2005), is deployed for public use. They tried to build the first remotely accessible MWSN and test-bed for the sensors. In "TrueMobile" the robots are used to carry motes and single board machine with the help of a fixed field of sensor. In real-time, using "TrueMobile", the remote users can point out the location of any robot; they can manage all the single board machines, interfaces of the network, and all log data. "TrueMobile" offer simple path planning, vision based tracking system, which provides very accurate result, live maps and webcams.

(Minassians et al., 2007) discussed health observing applications with help of MWSN. These applications may increase the performance of the existing health tracking and monitoring system. The authors have discussed five different prototype designs for BP (blood pressure) measurement, observation and analysis system, infant monitoring, fire fighter vital sign monitoring, and alerting deaf peoples.

A wireless BP monitoring and observing system known as "Heart@Home" is designed. It uses a special SHIMMER mote, placed in wrist cuff which is attached to a sensor to measure the pressure. The SHIMMER mote sends the recorded reading to the sink node. Aggregated data at the sink node are processed and a graphical report of BP and heart rate (HR) are plotted periodically. For infant monitoring, SHIMMER mote is used to sense body position of the infant relative to the gravity using a three axis accelerometer. Here, SHIMMER transmits data to the sink node periodically for identifying, monitoring and analyzing the infant's position. Another system called "Baby Glove" is developed to track and observe vitals that can monitor pulse rate, temperature, and hydration of the infant.

A system known as "FireLine" is also proposed, which is a HR sensing system, which is designed to track a fire fighter's HR to detect any abnormal situation and stress in real-time. It composed of a T-mote, a HR sensor, and three re-usable electrodes, which are fixed inside a shirt used by the fire fighter. The T-mote will send the readings to the base station, which are then processed and analyze and an alert is raised if the fire fighter's HR reached to a cutoff value.

Another system known as "LISTSENse" that allows the people with hearing problems, to be informed of any perceptible information. In this system, the person using the system has to carry the T-mote with him, which is composed of LEDs and a vibrator. The transmitters composed of an omni-directional condenser microphone, which are place near objects that can be listened, e.g., alarm bell, smoke alarm, doorbell, and siren. These transmitters sample signals periodically. At any moment if the signal is more than a threshold value, it will send an alert signal to the sink node, and the sink node will activates the LEDs and vibrator to inform the person using it.

(Bychkovsky et al., 2006) discussed "CarTel" project that is a mobile distributed sensor system. In this system the sensors are placed on the auto-mobiles which cover a larger area. Here, the mobile sensors collect information from static nodes and sends them to the sink node.

A module for human-centric search for physical world, "MAX" is discussed in (Yap et al., 2005) which permit human to find out and identify physical objects at the time of their need, by providing real-time position data reference to landmarks. It uses a design that needs objects to be labeled, associated stations as landmarks, and main station to find the position of the objects. Crossbow motes were used to show the implementation of MAX, and a room of physical objects was used to take trials of the system.

"iMouse" is an integrated mobile sensor network system which is used for supervision is discussed by (Tseng et al., 2007), where mobile nodes can move to event locations, they have the ability to share data with each other and they also can record the snapshots of events. The information gathered is then transmitted to the base station.

(Zhang et al., 2004) have discussed the "ZebraNet" system, which is an application of MWSN which is used to monitor motion of the animals. In this system the sensor nodes are fixed in the color of the zebra, which is composed of a processing unit, a small storing unit, a transmitter-receiver unit (a radio device), and a location monitoring system (GPS). GPS system is used to take the zebra's location readings and send it to the sink node. The data through the sensors are gathered at base station and later process and analyzed. The system was installed at the Sweetwaters game reserve at Kenya.

Another application of mobile sensor network "Pothole Patrol" is discussed in (Eriksson et al., 2008). The system is used to check the surface conditions of the roadways. It makes use of the mobility of the participating vehicles and gathers the real-time data with the help of vibrations and GPS sensors. The real-time information is collected by the sensors and sent to the sink node. The gathered data at the sink node is process and analyze and used to make assessment of the condition of the road surfaces.

PERFORMANCE EVALUATION PARAMETERS

This section basically deals with the detail study of the various evaluation parameters, like energy dissipation at a node, packet delivery ratio (PDR), delay, jitter, throughput, mean energy dissipation at a node, mean PDR, mean delay, mean jitter, mean throughput, path loss, PSNR, spectral effects, throughput fairness and packet loss rate, that are used to check and evaluate the performance of a particular wireless sensor network which may contain static or mobile nodes (Alazzawi & Elkateeb, 2008), (Baygi & Mokhtari, 2014). These parameters are described in brief in the following sections.

Energy Dissipation

As discussed in (Tan & Korpeoglu 2003), (He et al., 2006), a simple structure for the radio hardware power dissipation is considered, whereas, the transmitter dissipates power to run the radio and the power amplifier only, and the receiver dissipates energy only to run the radio. It uses the free space model, if the distance is less than a threshold, otherwise the multi-path fading channel models can be used, which is dependent on the length in between the transmitter and receiver (Shaikh et al., 2010), (Kiri et al., 2007). The radio dissipation model in wireless sensor networks is shown in Figure 4.

Figure 4. Radio Energy Dissipation Model in WSN

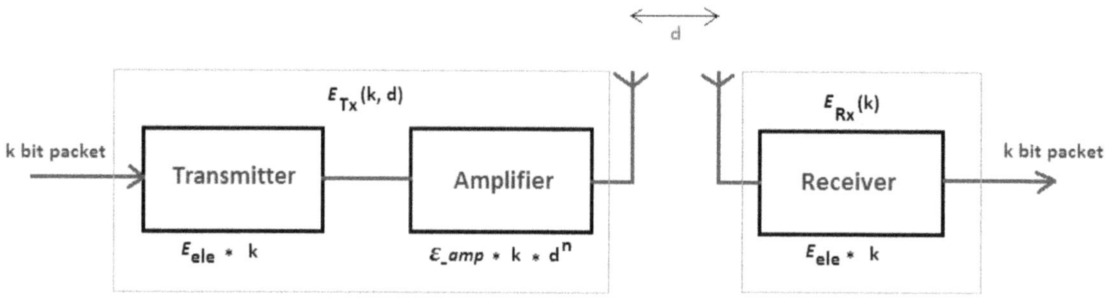

Suppose a k-bit message is to be transmitted over a distance d, the transmission energy E_{Tx} consumption at the sender node can be calculated using equations 5, which can be further simplified and formulated using equation 6, where, d_0 can be calculated by equation 7.

$$E_{Tx}\left(k,d\right)=E_{Tx_{elec}}\left(k\right)+E_{Tx_{amp}}\left(k,d\right) \quad (5)$$

$$E_{Tx}\left(k,d\right)=\begin{cases} k*E_{elec}+k*\varepsilon_{friee\_amp}*d^2 & : d<d_0 \\ k*E_{elec}+k*\varepsilon_{two\_ray\_amp}*d^4 & : d\geq d_0 \end{cases} \quad (6)$$

$$d_0=\sqrt{\frac{\varepsilon_{friss\_amp}}{\varepsilon_{two\_ray\_amp}}} \quad (7)$$

where, E_{elec} is Electronics energy, which is energy dissipation of radio to run transmitter and receiver.

ε_{friss_amp} is the transmit amplifier for free space model.

$\varepsilon_{two\_ray\_amp}$ is the transmit amplifier for multi-path fading model.

To receive this k-bit message at a particular node, the energy dissipation at the radio can be calculated using equation 8. This is further simplified in the equation 9.

$$E_{Rx}\left(k\right)=E_{Rx_{elec}}\left(k\right) \quad (8)$$

$$E_{Rx}\left(k\right)=k*E_{elec} \quad (9)$$

Packet Delivery Ratio (PDR)

Packet delivery ratio is one of the important parameter to evaluate the performance of the network. The performance of the network is considered to be better when packet delivery ratio is high in the wireless sensor networks. Packet delivery ratio (PDR) in WSNs is the ratio of data packets received successfully by the destinations to those generated by the sources, which can be simply given by the formula given in equation 10.

PDR = Rx / Tx (10)

where,

Rx: is sum of data packets successfully received by the destinations.
Tx: is sum of data packets generated by the each source.

End to End Delays (EED)

End to end delay (EED) is the time taken by the data packet to reach the destination after it has been initiated by the source. This may include the possible delay caused by queuing at the interface queue and buffering during route discovery latency. It is also considered as one of the important parameter to evaluate the performance of the wireless sensor networks. Performance of the network is considered to be better when End to End Delay is low in WSNs. It can be simply formulated by subtracting time at which the packet was sent by source node from time at which the data packet reaches to destination. It can be given by the equation 11.

$$EED = St / Nr \tag{11}$$

where,

St is the time spent to deliver number of packets to the destination.
Nr is the number of packets received by the destination.

Throughput

In general, higher PDR give higher throughput and vice versa. Throughput and PDR performance measures go hand in hand. Throughput can be defined as the number of packets delivered over a particular simulation time in the network i.e. throughput is the rate at which information is sent through the network. If a network becomes congested and there is good discipline, packets may queue up at the source and never enter the network, hence those packets are never sent, and will not contribute to throughput, but they won't affect the PDR. The performance of the network is considered to be good if throughput of the network is high. The throughput in the network can be calculated using the formula given in equation 12.

$$Throughput = BW/NRx \tag{12}$$

where,

BW is the bandwidth of the link in the network.
NRx is the number of packets received successfully by destination.

Jitter

Jitter can be considered as an undesirable effect caused by the inherent tendencies of TCP/IP networks and components. Generally, jitter is nothing but the difference in packet delay, i.e. jitter is measuring time difference in packet inter-arrival time (Ahmed & Chen, 2011), (Brun et al., 2006). In WSN, the source side transmits packets in a continuous stream and spaces them evenly apart, but because of congestion in the network, improper queuing, or configuration faults, the delay between packets may vary. As the time between two consecutive samples can vary, the packet loss may occur. Jitter can be measured by calculating the difference of time variation between two consecutive samples, which is given in equation 13.

$$\text{Jitter} = \Delta t2 - \Delta t1 \tag{13}$$

where,

$\Delta t1$, $\Delta t2$ is time of arrival of two consecutive samples at destination.

Mean Energy Dissipation

We already discussed the energy dissipation at nodes in WSNs earlier. Similarly, the mean energy dissipation for total transmissions in the network can be calculated using the equation 5 and 6, which is given in equation 14, Whereas, Mean energy dissipation for total reception in the network can be calculated using the formula given in equation 15.

$$Mean\,Energy\,Dissipation\,for\,transmission = \frac{\sum E_{Tx}}{n} \tag{14}$$

where,

E_{Tx} is total energy dissipation for transmission in the network.
n is total number of communication in the network.

$$Mean\,Energy\,Dissipation\,for\,reception = \frac{\sum E_{Rx}}{n} \tag{15}$$

where,

E_{Rx} is total energy dissipation for reception in the network.
n is total number of communication in the network.

Mean PDR

The performance of the network is considered to be better when the mean packet delivery ratio is high in the wireless sensor networks. Packet delivery ratio (PDR) in WSNs is already defined earlier, the mean PDR can also be calculated using the equation 16 given below.

$$\text{Mean PDR} = \frac{T_{Rx}}{T_{Tx}} \tag{16}$$

where,

T_{Rx} : is sum of all data packets successfully received by all destinations.
T_{Tx} : is sum of all data packets generated by all sources in the network.

Mean Delay

Mean delay is the mean of time acquired by all the data packets to reach their respective destinations after they have been initiated by the respective sources in the network. This may also include all the possible delays caused by queuing at the interface queue and buffering during route discovery latency. It can be calculated by taking the mean of subtracting time at which all the packets were sent by source from time at which the data packets reaches to destinations. The performance of the network is considered to be better when Mean Delay is low in the WSNs. It can be calculated using the following equation 17.

$$\text{Mean Delay} = \frac{T_{St}}{T_{Nr}} \tag{17}$$

where,

T_{St} is the total time spent to deliver packets to all the destinations.
T_{Nr} is the total number of packets received by all the destinations.

Mean Throughput

Mean throughput can be defined as the mean of total number of packets delivered over the total simulation time in the network. If a network becomes congested, the packets may queue up at the source and never enter the network, hence those packets are never sent, and will not contribute to mean throughput, but they won't affect the mean PDR. Mean throughput is also one of the important parameter in the evaluation of the performance of the network. The performance of the network is considered to be better if mean throughput of the network is high. The mean throughput in the network can be calculated by using following equation 18:

$$\text{Mean Throughput} = \frac{T_{BW}}{T_{NRx}} \tag{18}$$

where,

T_{BW} is the total bandwidth of all the links in the network.
T_{NRx} is total number of packets received successfully by all destinations.

Mean Jitter

Mean jitter is nothing but the mean of time differences in all packets inter-arrival time in the network. As the time between two consecutive samples can vary because of congestion in the network, improper queuing, or configuration faults, the delay between packets can vary and the packet loss may also occur. Mean jitter can be measured by calculating the mean of difference of time variations between two consecutive samples, using the equation 19.

$$\text{Mean Jitter} = \frac{\sum\left(\Delta t2 - \Delta t1\right)}{n} \tag{19}$$

where,

Δt1, Δt2 is time of arrival of consecutive samples at all destinations.
n is total number of such consecutive communications in the network.

Path Loss

Path loss is also called as path attenuation. It is the reduction in power density i.e. attenuation of an electromagnetic wave as it propagates through space. It is a main part in the analysis and design of the WSNs. Path loss generally includes propagation losses caused by the natural expansion of the radio wave front in free space (Anastassiu et al., 2014).

In WSNs, path loss can be represented by the path loss exponent, whose value varies from 2 to 4, where 2 is for free space, 4 is for relatively lossy environments. Unit to measure Path loss is dB. The simplest formula to calculate path loss can be defined using the equation 20.

{\displaystyle L=10\ n\ \log _{10}(d)+C} $L = 10 n \, log_{10}\left(d\right) + C$ (20)

where,

{\displaystyle L} L is the path loss in decibels (dB).
n {\displaystyle n}is the path loss exponent.
d {\displaystyle d}is the distance between the transmitter and the receiver.
C {\displaystyle C}is a constant which accounts for system losses.

The path loss can also be given by the following simplified formula given in equation 21, also known as the Friis transmission equation for the path loss between two isotropic antennas in free space.

{\displaystyle L=10\ n\ \log _{10}(d)+C} $L = 20 n \, log_{10}\left(\frac{4\pi d}{\lambda}\right)$ (21)

where,

{\displaystyle L} L is the path loss in decibels (dB).
λ {\displaystyle n}is the wavelength.
d {\displaystyle d}is the distance between the transmitter and the receiver.

Packet Loss Rate (PLR)

Packet loss occurs when one or more packets sent by one or more sources across the network fail to reach their destinations. It may typically causes due to network congestion. Generally, packet loss is measured as a percentage of packets lost with respect to packets sent. Transmission Control Protocol i.e. TCP, detects packet loss and performs retransmissions to ensure reliable messaging in the network. Packet loss can reduce throughput for a given sender, whether unintentionally due to network malfunction, or intentionally as a means to balance available bandwidth between multiple senders. PLR is simply calculated by counting the total number of transmitted packets minus the total number of received packets in a particular portion of time. But it must be done carefully, if there are retransmissions of same packets again. The packet loss rate can ideally be calculated using equation 22 given below.

$$PLR = (Tx - Rx)/100 \tag{22}$$

where,

Tx is total number of packet sent by all sources in the network.
Rx is total number of packets received by all receivers in the network.

OPEN ISSUES AND CHALLENGES

The wide range of application areas of WSN and many open research issues in WSN provides a strong driving force to the researcher. Most of the existing applications have application specific attributes and needs that are mixed with the existing technologies best suited for those applications. However a large variety of hardware and software platforms are designed over the last decade, still much more work is needed to upgrade these applications more robust, reliable, efficient, effective and useful to meet the expectation of today's world. So, it is must to fill the gap between the developers and researches to improve the existing technologies for better solutions to the real world's problems.

One of the main challenging tasks in most of the applications of WSNs is Energy optimization. Energy consumption is directly affecting the overall performance of the network, so one must think of energy optimization to meet one the basic aim of WSNs i.e. prolonging the lifetime of the network. The applications must be energy efficient with respect to various aspects of WSNs to achieve potential advantages of WSNs. Tto optimize the energy consumption in WSNs, the routing protocols used in the WSNs are also playing a vital role in minimizing the energy consumption, hence, resulting in maximizing the life time of network.

Many researchers have developed various types of routing protocols for WSNs as discussed earlier, among them the cluster based routing protocols is considered as more energy efficient compared to others. There are a large of applications in which the cluster based routing protocols are very effective and efficient. In cluster based routing protocols in WSNs, the cluster formation is one of the basic task.

The concept of clustering is mainly responsible for designing energy efficient, effective, robust, scalable and reliable sensor networks. Clustering aggregates the data from sensors at a specific node called as the cluster head (CH), which reduces the communication overhead and bandwidth resources, hence, lowers the energy consumption and improves the network lifetime of WSNs. Generally, the clustering mechanism is composed of two phases, i.e. the set-up and steady-state phase. Majority of clustering algorithms follow this mechanism; the major challenge in these algorithms is the selection of cluster head and cluster formation.

As discussed earlier, the WSNs can be broadly divided into two categories i.e. static WSNs (SWSNs) and Mobile WSNs (MWSNs). Most of the protocols proposed by many researchers assume that the sensor nodes are static in nature. There will be many issues that must be handled carefully if the sensors deployed in the network are mobile in nature. One of the main challenges, i.e. energy optimization becomes tougher in case of MWSNs as the topology of the network changes rapidly with respective time because of the mobility of the sensors. So, it is a greater area of focus to observe various parameters affecting the performance of WSNs, while handling the mobility of nodes in the network.

CONCLUSION

In this chapter, a brief overview about the basic concepts of Wireless sensor networks (WSNs) is discussed which includes the hardware and software structure, the issues in wireless sensor networks like, scalability, hardware constrains, power consumption, fault tolerance, environmental constraints, etc. Network architecture and design issues, like network dynamics, node deployment, energy considerations, data delivery models, communication medium, etc is also discussed in brief. It also focuses on different categories of WSNs i.e. static and mobile WSNs. Routing of data in WSN is also one of the key concept in WSNs, the classification of routing protocol which includes data centric routing, hierarchical routing and location based routing is also described in this chapter. WSNs have a wide range of application area, various application domains of WSNs, Implemented applications of static and mobile WSN is also discussed in brief. Finally, various performance evaluation parameters like energy dissipation, packet delivery ratio (PDR), end to end delays (EED), throughput, jitter, packet loss rate (PLR) etc. is discussed.

REFERENCES

Ahmed, S., & Chen, T. (2011). Minimizing the Effect of Sampling Jitters in Wireless Sensor Networks. *IEEE Signal Processing Letters, 18*(4), 219 – 222.

Akewar, M., & Thakur, N. V. (2012). A Study of Wireless Mobile Sensor Network Deployment. *International Journal of Computer Networks and Wireless Communications*, *2*(4), 533–541.

Akkaya, K., & Younis, M. (2003). An energy-aware QoS routing protocol for wireless sensor networks. *Proceedings of the IEEE Workshop on Mobile and Wireless Networks (MWN 2003)*. 10.1109/ICDCSW.2003.1203636

Akkaya, K., & Younis, M. (2005). A Survey on Routing Protocols for Wireless Sensor Networks. Elsevier Ad Hoc Network Journal, 3(3), 325-349.

Akyildiz, I., Weilian, S., Sankarasubramaniam, Y., & Cayirci, Y. (2002). A Survey on Sensor Networks. IEEE Communication Magazine, 40(8), 102-114.

Akyildiz, I. F., Melodia, T., & Chowdhury, K. R. (2007). A Survey on Wireless Multimedia Sensor Networks. *Elsevier. Computer Networks, 51*(4), 921–960. doi:10.1016/j.comnet.2006.10.002

Akyildiz, I. F., Su, W., Sankarasubramaniam, Y., & Cayirci, E. (2002). *Wireless Sensor Networks: A Survey. Computer Networks, 38*, 393–422.

Akyildiz, I. F., & Vuran, M. C. (2010). *Wireless sensor networks*. Wiley Publishing. doi:10.1002/9780470515181

Alazzawi, L., & Elkateeb, A. (2008). Performance Evaluation of the WSN Routing Protocols Scalability. *Journal of Computer Systems, Networks, and Communications*. doi:10.1155/2008/481046

Anastassiu, H. T., Vougioukas, S., Fronimos, T., Regen, C., Petrou, L., Zude, M., & Kathner, J. (2014). A Computational Model for Path Loss in Wireless Sensor Networks in Orchard Environments. *Sensors 2014*, 5118-5135.

Aronsky, A., & Segall, A. (2010). A Multipath Routing Algorithm for Mobile Wireless Sensor Networks. *3rd Joint IFIP Wireless and Mobile Networking Conference*, 1-6. 10.1109/WMNC.2010.5678765

Baygi, S. J. M., & Mokhtari, M. (2014). *Evaluation Performance of Protocols LEACH, 802.15.4 and CBRP, Using Analysis of QoS in WSNs*. Wireless Sensor Network, Scientific Research.

Braginsky, D., & Estrin, D. (2002). Rumor routing algorithm for sensor networks. In *Proceedings of the First Workshop on Sensor Networks and Applications (WSNA)*.

Brun, O., Bockstal, C., & Garcia, J. (2006). A Simple Formula for End-to-End Jitter Estimation in Packet-Switching Networks. In *Proceedings of the International Conference on Networking, International Conference on Systems and International Conference on Mobile Communications and Learning Technologies, (ICNICONSMCL'06)*. IEEE Computer Society. 10.1109/ICNICONSMCL.2006.34

Bulusu, N., Estrin, D., Girod, L., & Heidemann, J. (2001). Scalable coordination for wireless sensor networks: self-configuring localization systems. *International Symposium on Communication Theory and Applications (ISCTA 2001)*.

Buratti, C., Conti, A., Dardari, D., & Verdone, R. (2009, August). An Overview on Wireless Sensor Networks Technology and Evolution. *Sensors (Basel), 2009*(12), 6869–6896. doi:10.339090906869 PMID:22423202

Bychkovsky, V., Hull, B., Miu, A., Balakrishnan, H., & Madden, S. (2006). A measurement study of vehicular internet access using in situ Wi-Fi networks. In *Proceedings of the 12th annual international conference on Mobile computing and networking, MobiCom'06*. ACM. 10.1145/1161089.1161097

Cho, S., & Chandrakasan, A. (2000). Energy-efficient protocols for low duty cycle wireless microsensor. *Proceedings of the 33rd Annual Hawaii International Conference on System Sciences*.

Eriksson, J., Girod, L., Hull, B., Newton, R., Madden, S., & Balakrishnan, H. (2008). The pothole patrol: using a mobile sensor network for road surface monitoring. In *Proceeding of the 6th international conference on Mobile systems, applications, and services, MobiSys'08*. ACM. 10.1145/1378600.1378605

Finn, G. (1987). *Routing and addressing problems in large metropolitan-scale internetworks*. University of Southern California, Tech. Rep. ISI Research Report ISI/RR-87- 180.

Hayes, T., & Ali, F.H. (n.d.). Mobile Wireless Sensor Networks: Applications and Routing Protocols. In *Handbook of Research on Next Generation Mobile Communications Systems*. IGI Global.

He, Y., Zhang, Y., Ji, Y., & Shen, X. S. (2006). A new energy efficient approach by separating data collection and data report in wireless sensor networks. *Proceedings of the International Conference on Communications and Mobile Computing*. 10.1145/1143549.1143783

Heinzelman, W., Kulik, J., & Balakrishnan, H. (1999). Adaptive protocols for information dissemination in wireless sensor networks. *Proceedings of the 5th Annual ACM/IEEE International Conference on Mobile Computing and Networking (MobiCom_99)*. 10.1145/313451.313529

Hoblos, G., Staroswiecki, M., & Aitouche, A. (2000). Optimal design of fault tolerant sensor networks. *IEEE International Conference on Control Applications*, 467–472. 10.1109/CCA.2000.897468

Intanagonwiwat, C., Govindan, R., & Estrin, D. (2000). Directed diffusion: a scalable and robust communication paradigm for sensor networks. *Proceedings of the ACM Mobi-Com'00*, 56–67. 10.1145/345910.345920

Intanagonwiwat, C., Govindan, R., & Estrin, D. (2000). Directed iffusion: a scalable and robust communication paradigm for sensor networks. *Proceedings of the 6th Annual ACM/IEEE International Conference on Mobile Computing and Networking (MobiCom_00)*.

Jain, S. R., & Thakur, N. V. (2015). *Overview of Cluster based Routing Protocols in Static and Mobile Wireless Sensor Networks* (Vol. 339). Advances in Intelligent Systems and Computing. AISC. doi:10.1007/978-81-322-2250-7_62

Johnson, D., Stack, T., Fish, R., Flickinger, D., Ricci, R., & Lepreau, J. (2005). TrueMobile: A Mobile Robotic Wireless and Sensor Network Testbed. In *The 25th Annual Joint Conference of the IEEE Computer and Communications Societies*. IEEE Computer Society.

Kahn, J. M., Katz, R. H., & Pister, K. S. J. (1999). Next century challenges: mobile networking for smart dust. *Proceedings of the ACM MobiCom'99*, 271–278. 10.1145/313451.313558

Kiri, Y., Sugano, M., & Murata, M. (2007). On characteristics of multi-hop communication in large-scale clustered sensor networks. *IEICE Transactions on Communications E90-B*.

Krishnamachari, B., Estrin, D., & Wicker, S. (2002). Modeling data centric routing in wireless sensor networks. *Proceedings of IEEE INFOCOM*.

Lambrou, T. P., & Panayiotou, C. G. (2009). A Survey on Routing Techniques Supporting Mobility in Sensor Networks. *Proceedings of the 5th international conference on Mobile Ad Hoc and Sensor Networks (MSN'09)*, 78-85. 10.1109/MSN.2009.37

Li, L., & Halpern, J. Y. (2001). Minimum energy mobile wireless networks revisited. *Proceedings of IEEE International Conference on Communications (ICC_01).*

Lindsey, S., & Raghavendra, C. S. (2002). PEGASIS: power efficient gathering in sensor information systems. *Proceedings of the IEEE Aerospace Conference*. 10.1109/AERO.2002.1035242

Lindsey, S., Raghavendra, C. S., & Sivalingam, K. (2001). Data gathering in sensor networks using the energy delay metric. *Proceedings of the IPDPS Workshop on Issues in Wireless Networks and Mobile Computing*. 10.1109/IPDPS.2001.925196

Lopez Riquelme, J. A., Soto, F., Suardiaz, J., Sanchez, P., Iborra, A., & Vera, J. A. (2009). Wireless Sensor Networks for precision horticulture in Southern Spain. *Computers and Electronics in Agriculture*, *68*(1), 25–35. doi:10.1016/j.compag.2009.04.006

Manjeshwar, A., & Agrawal, D. P. (2001). TEEN: a protocol for enhanced efficiency in wireless sensor network. *Proceedings of the 1st International Workshop on Parallel and Distributed Computing Issues in Wireless Networks and Mobile Computing*. 10.1109/IPDPS.2001.925197

Manjeshwar, A., & Agrawal, D. P. (2002). APTEEN: a hybrid protocol for efficient routing and comprehensive information retrieval in wireless sensor networks. *Proceedings of the 2nd International Workshop on Parallel and Distributed Computing Issues in Wireless Networks and Mobile computing*. 10.1109/IPDPS.2002.1016600

Minassians, A., Dervisoglu, G., & Gutnik, L. (2007). Wireless sensor networks for home health care. AINAW.

Nath, A., & Niculescu, D. (2002). Routing on a curve. HOTNETS 1.

Pottie, G. J., & Kaiser, W. J. (2000). Wireless integrated network sensors. *Communications of the ACM*, *43*(5), 551–558. doi:10.1145/332833.332838

Puccinelli, D., & Haenggi, M. (2005). Wireless Sensor Networks: Applications and Challenges of Ubiquitous Sensing. *IEEE Circuits and Systems Magazine*, *5*(3), 19–29. doi:10.1109/MCAS.2005.1507522

Rahimi, M., Baer, R., Iroezi, O. I., Garcia, J. C., Warrior, J., Estrin, D., & Srivastava, M. (2005). Cyclops: in situ image sensing and interpretation in wireless sensor networks. *Proceedings of the Third International Conference on Embedded Networked Sensor Systems (Sensys)*. 10.1145/1098918.1098939

Rodoplu, V., & Ming, T. H. (1999). Minimum energy mobile wireless networks. *IEEE Journal on Selected Areas in Communications*, *17*(8), 1333–1344. doi:10.1109/49.779917

Schurgers, C., & Srivastava, M. B. (2001). Energy efficient routing in wireless sensor networks. *The MILCOM Proceedings on Communications for Network-Centric Operations: Creating the Information Force*. 10.1109/MILCOM.2001.985819

Shaikh, R.A., Lee, Y.K., & Lee, S. (2010). An Extended Energy Consumption Analysis of Reputation-based Trust Management Schemes of Wireless Sensor Networks. *Journal of Networks*, *5*(3), 283-291.

Shen, C., Srisathapornphat, C., & Jaikaeo, C. (2001). Sensor information networking architecture and applications. *IEEE Personal Communications*, 52–59.

Shih, E., Cho, S., Ickes, N., Min, R., Sinha, A., Wang, A., & Chandrakasan, A. (2001). Physical layer driven protocol and algorithm design for energy-efficient wireless sensor networks. *Proceedings of ACM MobiCom'01*, 272–286. 10.1145/381677.381703

Sinha, A., & Chandrakasan, A. (2001). Dynamic power management in wireless sensor networks. *IEEE Design & Test of Computers*, *18*(2), 62–74. doi:10.1109/54.914626

Sohrabi, K., Gao, J., Ailawadhi, V., & Pottie, G. J. (2000). Protocols for self-organization of a wireless sensor network. *IEEE Personal Communications*, *7*(5), 16–27. doi:10.1109/98.878532

Subramanian, L., & Katz, R. H. (Aug 2000). An architecture for building self configurable systems. *Proceedings of IEEE/ACM Workshop on Mobile Ad Hoc Networking and Computing*. 10.1109/MOBHOC.2000.869214

Tan, H.O., & Korpeoglu, I. (2003). Power efficient data gathering and aggregation in wireless sensor networks. *ACM SIGMOD Record, 32*(4), 66–71.

Tilak, S., Abu-Ghazaleh, N., & Heinzelman, W. (2002). Infrastructure tradeoffs for sensor networks. In *Proceedings of the 1st ACM international workshop on Wireless sensor networks and applications, WSNA '02*. ACM. 10.1145/570738.570746

Tilak, S., Abu-Ghazaleh, N. B., & Heinzelman, W. (2002). A taxonomy of wireless microsensor network models. *Mobile Computing and Communications Review*, *6*(2), 28–36. doi:10.1145/565702.565708

Tolle, G., Polastre, J., Szewczyk, R., Culler, D., Turner, N., Tu, K., ... Hong, W. (2005). A macroscope in the redwoods. *Proceedings of the Third International Conference on Embedded Networked Sensor Systems (Sensys)*. 10.1145/1098918.1098925

Tseng, Y., Wang, Y., Cheng, K., & Hsieh, Y. (2007). iMouse: An Integrated Mobile Surveillance and Wireless Sensor System. IEEE Computer Society, 40(6), 60-66.

Vasilescu, I., Kotay, K., Rus, D., Dunbabin, M., & Corke, P. (2005). Data collection, storage, retrieval with an underwater sensor network. *Proceedings of the Third International Conference on Embedded Networked Sensor Systems (Sensys)*. 10.1145/1098918.1098936

Velmani, R., & Kaarthick, B. (2009). An Efficient Cluster-Tree Based Data Collection Scheme for Large Mobile Wireless Sensor Networks. IEEE Sensors Journal, 15(4), 2377–2390.

Wajgi, D., & Thakur, N. V. (2012, August). Load Balancing Algorithms in Wireless Sensor Networks: A Survey. *International Journal of Computer Networks and Wireless Communications*, *2*(4), 456–460.

Werner-Allen, G., Lorincz, K., Welsh, M., Marcillo, O., Johnson, J., Ruiz, M., & Lees, J. (2006). Deploying a wireless sensor network on an active volcano. *IEEE Internet Computing*, *10*(2), 18–25. doi:10.1109/MIC.2006.26

Xu, Y., Heidemann, J., & Estrin, D. (2001). Geography-informed energy conservation for ad hoc routing. *Proceedings of the 7th Annual ACM/IEEE International Conference on Mobile Computing and Networking (MobiCom_01).* 10.1145/381677.381685

Yap, K. K., Srinivasan, V., & Motani, M. (2005). MAX: Human-centric search of the physical world. *Proceedings of the Third International Conference on Embedded Networked Sensor Systems (Sensys).* 10.1145/1098918.1098937

Yick, J., Mukherjee, B., & Ghosal, D. (2008). Wireless sensor network survey. *Elsevier. Computer Networks, 52*(12), 2292–2330. doi:10.1016/j.comnet.2008.04.002

Younis, M., Youssef, M., & Arisha, K. (2002). Energy-aware routing in cluster-based sensor networks. *Proceedings of the 10th IEEE/ACM International Symposium on Modeling, Analysis and Simulation of Computer and Telecommunication Systems (MASCOTS2002).* 10.1109/MASCOT.2002.1167069

Yu, Y., Estrin, D., & Govindan, R. (2001). *Geographical and energy aware routing: a recursive data dissemination protocol for wireless sensor networks.* UCLA Computer Science Department Technical Report. UCLA-CSD TR-01-0023.

Zhang, P., Sadler, C. M., Lyon, S. A., & Martonosi, M. (2004). Hardware design experiences in ZebraNet. *Proceedings of the SenSys'04.* 10.1145/1031495.1031522

ADDITIONAL READING

Bhatt, C. M., Dey, N., & Ashour, A. (2017). *Internet of Things and Big Data Technologies for Next Generation Healthcare* (Vol. 23). Springer. doi:10.1007/978-3-319-49736-5_2

Binh, H. T. T., Hanh, N. T., & Dey, N. (2016). Improved Cuckoo Search and Chaotic Flower Pollination optimization algorithm for maximizing area coverage in Wireless Sensor Networks. *Neural Computing & Applications*, 1–13.

Biswas, S. P., Roy, P., Patra, N., Mukherjee, A., & Dey, N. (2016). Intelligent traffic monitoring system. In *Proceedings of the Second International Conference on Computer and Communication Technologies* (pp. 535-545). Springer, New Delhi. 10.1007/978-81-322-2523-2_52

Chowdhuri, S., Chakraborty, S., Dey, N., Azar, A. T., Salem, M. A. M. M., Chaudhury, S. S., & Banerjee, P. (2014). Recent research on multi input multi output (MIMO) based mobile ad hoc network: A review. *International Journal of Service Science, Management, Engineering, and Technology, 5*(3), 54–65. doi:10.4018/ijssmet.2014070104

Chowdhuri, S., Dey, N., Chakraborty, S., & Baneerjee, P. K. (2015). Analysis of Performance of MIMO Ad Hoc Network in Terms of Information Efficiency. In *Emerging ICT for Bridging the Future-Proceedings of the 49th Annual Convention of the Computer Society of India CSI Volume 2* (pp. 43-50). Springer, Cham. 10.1007/978-3-319-13731-5_6

Dey, N., Ashour, A. S., Shi, F., Fong, S. J., & Sherratt, S. (2017). Developing residential wireless sensor networks for ECG healthcare monitoring. *IEEE Transactions on Consumer Electronics*, *63*(4), 442–449. doi:10.1109/TCE.2017.015063

Dey, N., Hassanien, A. E., Bhatt, C., Ashour, A. S., & Satapathy, S. C. (2018). Internet of Things and Big Data Analytics Toward Next-Generation Intelligence.

Elhayatmy, G., Dey, N., & Ashour, A. S. (2018). Internet of Things Based Wireless Body Area Network in Healthcare. In *Internet of Things and Big Data Analytics Toward Next-Generation Intelligence* (pp. 3–20). Cham: Springer. doi:10.1007/978-3-319-60435-0_1

Hore, S., Chatterjee, S., Dey, N., Ashour, A. S., & Balas, V. E. (2016). A Vulnerability Analysis Mechanism Utilizing Avalanche Attack Model for Dependency-Based Systems. In *Advances in Computing Applications* (pp. 243–262). Springer Singapore. doi:10.1007/978-981-10-2630-0_15

Juneja, D., Singh, A., Singh, R., & Mukherjee, S. (2017). A thorough insight into theoretical and practical developments in multiagent systems. *International Journal of Ambient Computing and Intelligence*, *8*(1), 23–49. doi:10.4018/IJACI.2017010102

Malik, S., & Khatter, K. (2018). Malicious Application Detection and Classification System for Android Mobiles. *International Journal of Ambient Computing and Intelligence*, *9*(1), 95–114. doi:10.4018/IJACI.2018010106

Mohanpurkar, A. A., & Joshi, M. S. (2016). A Traitor Identification Technique for Numeric Relational Databases with Distortion Minimization and Collusion Avoidance. *International Journal of Ambient Computing and Intelligence*, *7*(2), 114–137. doi:10.4018/IJACI.2016070106

Mukherjee, A., Dey, N., Kausar, N., Ashour, A. S., Taiar, R., & Hassanien, A. E. (2016). A disaster management specific mobility model for flying ad-hoc network. *International Journal of Rough Sets and Data Analysis*, *3*(3), 72–103. doi:10.4018/IJRSDA.2016070106

Roy, P., Patra, N., Mukherjee, A., Ashour, A. S., Dey, N., & Biswas, S. P. (2017). Intelligent Traffic Monitoring System through Auto and Manual Controlling using PC and Android Application. In *Applied Video Processing in Surveillance and Monitoring Systems* (pp. 244–262). IGI Global. doi:10.4018/978-1-5225-1022-2.ch011

Roy, S., Karjee, J., Rawat, U. S., & Dey, N. (2016). Symmetric Key Encryption Technique: A Cellular Automata based Approach in Wireless Sensor Networks. *Procedia Computer Science*, *78*, 408–414. doi:10.1016/j.procs.2016.02.082

Sosnin, P. (2016). Precedent-Oriented Approach to Conceptually Experimental Activity in Designing the Software Intensive Systems. *International Journal of Ambient Computing and Intelligence*, *7*(1), 69–93. doi:10.4018/IJACI.2016010104

Tyagi, S., Som, S., & Rana, Q. (2017). Trust based Dynamic Multicast Group Routing Ensuring Reliability for Ubiquitous Environment in MANETs. *International Journal of Ambient Computing and Intelligence*, *8*(1), 70–97. doi:10.4018/IJACI.2017010104

Yadav, P., Sharma, S., Tiwari, P., Dey, N., Ashour, A. S., & Nguyen, G. N. (2018). A Modified Hybrid Structure for Next Generation Super High Speed Communication Using TDLTE and Wi-Max. In *Internet of Things and Big Data Analytics Toward Next-Generation Intelligence* (pp. 525–549). Cham: Springer. doi:10.1007/978-3-319-60435-0_21

Yang, W., Wang, X., Song, X., Yang, Y., & Patnaik, S. (2018). Design of Intelligent Transportation System Supported by New Generation Wireless Communication Technology. *International Journal of Ambient Computing and Intelligence*, *9*(1), 78–94. doi:10.4018/IJACI.2018010105

Compilation of References

Abbasi, M., & Kashiyarndi, S. (2006). *Clinical decision support systems: A discussion on different methodologies used in Health Care.* Academic Press.

Abdel-Rahman, E. M., Ahmad, A. R., & Akhtar, S. (2012). A metaheurisic bat-inspired algorithm for full body human pose estimation. *9th Conference on Computer and Robot Vision*, 369–375.

Acar, E., Özerdem, M. S., & Akpolat, V. (2011). Diabetes Mellitus Forcast Using Various Types of Ar-tificial Neural Networks. *6th International Advanced Technologies Symposium*, 196-201.

ACCORD project. (2002). *Component Assembly by Contracts in Open and Distributed Environment.* Technical Report, RNTL.

Acharjya, D., & Anitha, A. (2017). A Comparative Study of Statistical and Rough Computing Models in Predictive Data Analysis. *International Journal of Ambient Computing and Intelligence*, *8*(2), 32–51. doi:10.4018/IJACI.2017040103

Adam, F. (Ed.). (2008). *Encyclopedia of decision making and decision support technologies* (Vol. 2). IGI Global. doi:10.4018/978-1-59904-843-7

Adam, F., & O'doherty, P. (2000). Lessons from enterprise resource planning implementation in Ireland, toward smaller and shorter ERP projects. *Journal of Information Technology*, *15*(4), 305–316. doi:10.1080/02683960010008953

Ahmad & Gabbouj. (2008). Audio-Visual Multimedia Retrieval on Mobile Devices. In Multimedia Services in Intelligent Environments – Advanced Tools and Methodologies. Academic Press.

Ahmad, I., Abdullah, S., Kiranyaz, M. S., & Gabbouj, M. (2005). Progressive Query Technique for Image Retrieval on Mobile Devices. *Proceedings Fourth International Workshop on Content-Based Multimedia Indexing.*

Ahmad, I., Abdullah, S., Kiranyaz, S., & Gabbouj, M. (2005). Content-Based Image Retrieval on Mobile Devices. *Proceedings of SPIE (Multimedia on Mobile Devices)*, 255-264.

Ahmed, S., & Chen, T. (2011). Minimizing the Effect of Sampling Jitters in Wireless Sensor Networks. *IEEE Signal Processing Letters, 18*(4), 219 – 222.

Ahmed, S. S., Dey, N., Ashour, A. S., Sifaki-Pistolla, D., Bălas-Timar, D., Balas, V. E., & Tavares, J. M. R. (2017). Effect of fuzzy partitioning in Crohn's disease classification: A neuro-fuzzy-based approach. *Medical & Biological Engineering & Computing*, *55*(1), 101–115. doi:10.100711517-016-1508-7 PMID:27106754

Aishwarya, P., & Balaji, M. (2013). Supply Chain Transformation Matrix (ASCTM) based supplier-buyer relationships to improve supply chain agility. *International Journal of Applied Research and Studies*, *2*, 1–6.

Akewar, M., & Thakur, N. V. (2012). A Study of Wireless Mobile Sensor Network Deployment. *International Journal of Computer Networks and Wireless Communications*, *2*(4), 533–541.

Akkaya, K., & Younis, M. (2005). A Survey on Routing Protocols for Wireless Sensor Networks. Elsevier Ad Hoc Network Journal, 3(3), 325-349.

Akkaya, K., & Younis, M. (2003). An energy-aware QoS routing protocol for wireless sensor networks. *Proceedings of the IEEE Workshop on Mobile and Wireless Networks (MWN 2003).* 10.1109/ICDCSW.2003.1203636

Akyildiz, I., Weilian, S., Sankarasubramaniam, Y., & Cayirci, Y. (2002). A Survey on Sensor Networks. IEEE Communication Magazine, 40(8), 102-114.

Akyildiz, I. F., Melodia, T., & Chowdhury, K. R. (2007). A Survey on Wireless Multimedia Sensor Networks. *Elsevier. Computer Networks, 51*(4), 921–960. doi:10.1016/j.comnet.2006.10.002

Akyildiz, I. F., Su, W., Sankarasubramaniam, Y., & Cayirci, E. (2002). *Wireless Sensor Networks: A Survey. Computer Networks, 38*, 393–422.

Akyildiz, I. F., & Vuran, M. C. (2010). *Wireless sensor networks.* Wiley Publishing. doi:10.1002/9780470515181

Alazzawi, L., & Elkateeb, A. (2008). Performance Evaluation of the WSN Routing Protocols Scalability. *Journal of Computer Systems, Networks, and Communications.* doi:10.1155/2008/481046

Aleksander, I., & Morton, H. (1995). *An introduc-tion to neural.* London: Int Thomson Comput Press.

Alghamdi, R. A., Taileb, M., & Ameen, M. (2014). *A New Multimodal Fusion Method Based on Association Rules Mining for Image Retrieval. In Proceedings of Mediterranean Electrotechnical Conference* (pp. 493–499). MELECON.

Alimi, T. O., Fuller, D. O., Herrera, S. V., Arevalo-Herrera, M., Quinones, M. L., Stoler, J. B., & Beier, J. C. (2016). A multi-criteria decision analysis approach to assessing malaria risk in northern South America. *BMC Public Health, 16*(1), 221. doi:10.118612889-016-2902-7 PMID:26940004

Al-Khasawneh, A., & Hijazi, H. (2014). A Predictive E-Health Information System: Diagnosing Diabetes Mellitus Using Neural Network Based Decision Support System. *International Journal of Decision Support System Technology, 6*(4), 31–48. doi:10.4018/ijdsst.2014100103

Allier, S., Sadou, S., Sahraoui, H. A., & Fleurquin, R. (2011). From Object-Oriented Applications to Component-Oriented Applications via Component-Oriented Architecture. *WICSA, 2011*, 214–223.

Al-Mudimigh, A. S., & Almalaise, A. (2012). Rules Generation from ERP Database: A Successful Implementation of Data Mining. *International Journal of Computer Science and Network Security, 12*(3), 21–29.

Al-Mudimigh, A. S., Farrukh, S. F., & Zahid, U. Z. (2009). A Framework of an Automated Data Mining Systems Using ERP Model. *International Journal of Computer and Electrical Engineering, 5*, 651–655. doi:10.7763/IJCEE.2009.V1.101

Altaleb, H., & Brodsky, A. (2013). A Primary Market for Optimizing Power Peak-Load Demand Limits. *International Journal of Decision Support System Technology, 5*(2), 21–32. doi:10.4018/jdsst.2013040102

Alves, M. J., & Climaco, J. (2004). A note on a decision support system for multiobjective and mixed-integer programming problems. *European Journal of Operational Research, 155*(1), 258–265. doi:10.1016/S0377-2217(02)00887-1

Alzahir, S., & Borici, A. (2015). An Innovative Lossless Compression Method for Discrete-Color Images. *IEEE Transactions on Image Processing, 24*(1), 44–56. doi:10.1109/TIP.2014.2363411 PMID:25330487

Amato, F., López, A., Peña-Méndez, E. M., Vaňhara, P., Hampl, A., & Havel, J. (2013). Artificial neural networks in medical diagnosis. *Journal of Applied Biomedicine, 11*(2), 47–58. doi:10.2478/v10136-012-0031-x

Ammour, S., Beugnard, A., Matougui, S., & Traverson, B. (2004). Software architecture and communication abstractions: an application in the field of scientific computing. *Proceedings of RNTL ACCORD.*

Ana, P., & Dragana, B. (2016). Metamodel of the Artifact-Centric Approach to Event Log Extraction from ERP Systems. *International Journal of Decision Support System Technology*, *8*(2), 18–28. doi:10.4018/IJDSST.2016040102

Anastassiu, H. T., Vougioukas, S., Fronimos, T., Regen, C., Petrou, L., Zude, M., & Kathner, J. (2014). A Computational Model for Path Loss in Wireless Sensor Networks in Orchard Environments. *Sensors 2014*, 5118-5135.

Anguera, X., Oliver, N., & Cherubini, M. (2008). Multimodal and Mobile Personal Image Retrieval: A User Study. *Proc. Workshop on Mobile Information Retrieval, MOBIR'08.*

Anwar, A., Ebersold, S., Coulette, B., Nassar, M., & Kriouile, A. (2010). A Rule-Driven Approach for composing Viewpoint-oriented Models. *Journal of Object Technology*, *9*(2), 89–114. doi:10.5381/jot.2010.9.2.a1

Araz, O. M. (2013). Integrating complex system dynamics of pandemic influenza with a multi-criteria decision making model for evaluating public health strategies. *Journal of Systems Science and Systems Engineering*, *22*(3), 319–339. doi:10.100711518-013-5220-y

Aronsky, A., & Segall, A. (2010). A Multipath Routing Algorithm for Mobile Wireless Sensor Networks. *3rd Joint IFIP Wireless and Mobile Networking Conference*, 1-6. 10.1109/WMNC.2010.5678765

Arrais-Castro, A., Varela, M. L. R., Putnik, G. D., Ribeiro, R., & Dargram, F. C. C. (2015). Collaborative Negotiation Platform using a Dynamic Multi-Criteria Decision Model. *International Journal of Decision Support System Technology*, *7*(1), 1–14. doi:10.4018/ijdsst.2015010101

Arun, B., & Kumar, V. (2017). Materialized View Selection Using Bumble Bee Mating Optimization. *International Journal of Decision Support System Technology*, *9*(3), 1–27. doi:10.4018/IJDSST.2017070101

Avishek Das, D., Mandal, S.P., & Ghoshal, R. K. (2017). An efficient side lobe reduction technique considering mutual coupling effect in linear array antenna using BAT algorithm. *Swarm and Evolutionary Computation, 35*, 26-40. 10.1016/j.swevo.2017.02.004

Ayadi, D. (2010). *Optimisation multicritère de la fiabilité: application du modèle de goal programming avec les fonctions de satisfactions dans l'industrie de traitement de gaz* (Doctoral dissertation). Université d'Angers.

Bagheri, B., Pourmahyabadi, M., & Nezamabadipour, H. (2013). A Novel Content Based Image Retrieval Approach by Fusion of Short Term Learning Methods. *Proceedings of International conference on Information and Knowledge Technology (IKT)*, 355-358. 10.1109/IKT.2013.6620093

Bagloee, S. A., Tavana, M., Di Caprio, D., Asadi, M., & Heshmati, M. (2017). A multi-user decision support system for online city bus tour planning. *Journal of Modern Transportation*, *25*(2), 59–73. doi:10.100740534-017-0126-x

Bai, S., & Bai, X. (2016). Sparse Contextual Activation for Efficient Vi- sual Re-Ranking. *IEEE Transactions on Image Processing*, *25*(3), 1056–1069. doi:10.1109/TIP.2016.2514498 PMID:26742133

Bai, S., Bai, X., & Liu, W. (2016). Multiple Stage Residual Model for Image Classification and Vector Compression. *IEEE Transactions on Multimedia*, *18*(7), 1351–1362. doi:10.1109/TMM.2016.2557071

Baker, K. R. (1974). *Introduction to Sequencing and Scheduling*. New York: Wiley.

Balaji, M., Velmurugan, V., & Subashree, C. (2015). TADS: An assessment methodology for agile supply chains. *Journal of Applied Research and Technology*, *13*(5), 504–509. doi:10.1016/j.jart.2015.10.002

Balcan, D., Gonçalves, B., Hu, H., Ramasco, J. J., Colizza, V., & Vespignani, A. (2010). Modeling the spatial spread of infectious diseases: The GLobal Epidemic and Mobility computational model. *Journal of Computational Science*, *1*(3), 132–145. doi:10.1016/j.jocs.2010.07.002 PMID:21415939

Banerji, S., Sinha, A., & Liu, C. (2013). A New Bag of Words LBP(BoWL) Descriptor for Scene Image Classification. *Proceedings of International conference on Computer Analysis of Images and Patterns*. 10.1007/978-3-642-40261-6_59

Bank, J., & Werner, F. (2001). Heuristic algorithms for unrelated parallel machine scheduling with a common due date, release dates, and linear earliness and tardiness penalties. *Mathematical and Computer Modelling*, *33*(4–5), 363–383. doi:10.1016/S0895-7177(00)00250-8

Barreca, A. I., & Shimshack, J. P. (2012). Absolute humidity, temperature, and influenza mortality: 30 years of county-level evidence from the United States. *American Journal of Epidemiology*, *176*(suppl 7), S114–S122. doi:10.1093/aje/kws259 PMID:23035135

Bartolini, I. (2009). A multi-faceted browsing interface for digital photo collections. *CBMI*, *7*, 237–242.

Basetti, V., & Chandel, A. K. (2016). Optimal PMU placement for power system observability using Taguchi binary bat algorithm. *Measurement, 95*, 8-20. 10.1016/j.measurement.2016.09.031

Baugh, J. W. Jr, Caldwell, S. C., & Brill, E. D. Jr. (1997). A Mathematical Programming Approach for Generating Alternatives in Discrete Structural Optimization. *Engineering Optimization*, *28*(1), 1–31. doi:10.1080/03052159708941125

Baygi, S. J. M., & Mokhtari, M. (2014). *Evaluation Performance of Protocols LEACH, 802.15.4 and CBRP, Using Analysis of QoS in WSNs*. Wireless Sensor Network, Scientific Research.

Beevi, S., Thomas, M., & Nair, M. S. & Wilscy M.(2016). Lossless color image compression using double level RCT in BBWCA. *Proceedings of 6th International Conference On Advances In Computing & Communications*, 93, 513-520. 10.1016/j.procs.2016.07.242

Belarbi, M. A., Mahmoudi, S., & Belalem, G. (2017). PCA as Dimensionality Reduction for Large-Scale Image Retrieval Systems. *International Journal of Ambient Computing and Intelligence*, *8*(4), 45–58. doi:10.4018/IJACI.2017100104

Ben Hamida, A., Haouari, M., Huguet, M.-J., & Lopez, P. (2011). Solving two-stage hybrid flow shop using climbing depth-bounded discrepancy search. *Computers & Industrial Engineering*, *60*(2), 320–327. doi:10.1016/j.cie.2010.11.015

Ben Hamida, A., Huguet, M.-J., Lopez, P., & Haouari, M. (2007). Climbing Discrepancy Search for solving the hybrid Flow shop. *European Journal of Industrial Engineering*, *1*(2), 223–243. doi:10.1504/EJIE.2007.014110

Benatia, I., Laouar, M. R., Bendjenna, H., & Eom, S. (2016). Implementing a Cloud-Based Decision Support System in a Private Cloud: The Infrastructure and the Deployment Process. *International Journal of Decision Support System Technology*, *8*(1), 25–42. doi:10.4018/IJDSST.2016010102

Benayoun, R., Montgolfier, J., Tergny, J., & Laritchev, O. (1971). Linear Programming with Multiple Objective Functions: Step Method (STEM). *Mathematical Programming*, *1*(1), 136–375. doi:10.1007/BF01584098

Benchikh, W., & Renard, I. (2003). *The contractual architecture of groups of contracts Enterprise Resource Planning (ERP). Memory D.E.E.S.* University of Paris Π.

Beretta, E., & Kuang, Y. (2001). Modeling and analysis of a marine bacteriophage infection with latency period. In *Nonlinear Anal* (pp. 35–74). Real World. doi:10.1016/S0362-546X(99)00285-0

Bhowmik, N., Gonzaez, R., Gouet-Brunet, V., Pedrini, H., & Bloch, G. (2014). Efficient fusion of multidimensional descriptors for image retrieval. *Proceedings of International conference on image processing (ICIP)*, 5766-5770.

Bidhandi, R. A., & Valmohammadi, C. (2017). Effects of supply chain agility on profitability. *Business Process Management Journal, 23*(5), 1064–1082. doi:10.1108/BPMJ-05-2016-0089

Billaut, Proust, & Portmann. (2000). A Survey of Hybrid Flow Shop Problems. ODIP.

Birhanu, D., Lanka, K., & Rao, A. N. (2014). A Survey of Classifications in Supply Chain Strategies. *Procedia Engineering, 97*, 2289–2297. doi:10.1016/j.proeng.2014.12.473

Biron, P., & Malhotra, A. (2004). *XML Schema Part 2: Datatypes*. Retrieved from https://www.w3.org/TR/xmlschema-2/

Blain, F.-A. (2006). *Overview of ERP and their modular architecture*. Retrieved Mars 13, 2006, from http://fablain.developpez.com/tutoriel/presenterp.htm

Blumenstein, M., Liu, X. Y., & Verma, B. (2007). A modified direction feature for cursive character recognition. *Pattern Recognition, 40*(2), 376–388. doi:10.1016/j.patcog.2006.05.017

Blumenstein, M., & Verma, B. (1999).Neural Solutions for the Segmentation and Recognition of Difficult Words from a Benchmark Database. *Proceedings of the Fifth International Conference on Document Analysis and Recognition, (ICDAR '99)*, 281-284. 10.1109/ICDAR.1999.791779

Bobar, V., Mandic, K., & Suknovic, M. (2015). Bidder selection in public procurement using a fuzzy decision support system. *International Journal of Decision Support System Technology, 7*(1), 1–19. doi:10.4018/ijdsst.2015010103

Bobrow, D. G., & Winograd, T. (1977). An Overview of KRL, a Knowledge Representation Language. *Cognitive Science, 1*(1), 3–46. doi:10.120715516709cog0101_2

Boris, D., Milan, D., & Pavlos, D. (2016). A Skiing Trace Clustering Model for Injury Risk Assessment. *International Journal of Decision Support System Technology, 8*(1), 56–68. doi:10.4018/IJDSST.2016010104

Borovikov, E. (2014). *A survey of modern optical character recognition techniques,* Cornell University Library, Computer Vision and Pattern Recognition. arXiv: 1412.4183

Bose, S., Madhulika, Acharjee, S., Chowdhury, S. R., Chakraborty, S., & Dey, N. (2014). Effect of watermarking in vector quantization based image compression. *Proceeding of International Conference on Control, Instrumentation, Communication and Computational Technologies (ICCICCT)*, 503-508. 10.1109/ICCICCT.2014.6993014

Bose, S., Mukherjee, A., Chakraborty, S., Samanta, S., & Dey, N. (2013, December). Parallel image segmentation using multi-threading and k-means algorithm. In *Computational Intelligence and Computing Research (ICCIC), 2013 IEEE International Conference on* (pp. 1-5). IEEE. 10.1109/ICCIC.2013.6724171

Boudina, A., & Tayeb, L. (2007). *The distributed Artificial Intelligence and Multi-Agent Systems*. Retrieved Avril 13, 2007, from htttp://opera.inrialpes.fr/people/Tayeb.Lemlouma/Papers/ IAD_Presentation.pdf

Boulmaiz, A., Messadeg, D., Doghmane, N., & Taleb-Ahmed, A. (2017). Design and Implementation of a Robust Acoustic Recognition System for Waterbird Species using TMS320C6713 DSK. *International Journal of Ambient Computing and Intelligence, 8*(1), 98–118. doi:10.4018/IJACI.2017010105

Bozinovic, R., & Shrihari, S. (1989). Offline cursive script word recognition. *IEEE Transactions on Pattern Analysis and Machine Intelligence, 11*(1), 68–83. doi:10.1109/34.23114

Braginsky, D., & Estrin, D. (2002). Rumor routing algorithm for sensor networks. In *Proceedings of the First Workshop on Sensor Networks and Applications (WSNA)*.

Brailer, D., & Thompson, T. (2004). *Health IT strategic framework*. Academic Press.

Branke, J., Deb, K., Miettinen, K., & Slowinski, R. (2008). *Multiobjective Optimization: Interactive and Evolutionary Approaches*. Berlin: Springer-Verlag. doi:10.1007/978-3-540-88908-3

Brans, J. P., & Mareschal, B. (2002). *Prométhée-Gaia: une méthodologie d'aide à la décision en présence de critères multiples*. Éditions de l'Université de Bruxelles.

Brans, J. P., & Vincke, P. (1985). Note—A Preference Ranking Organisation Method: The PROMETHEE Method for Multiple Criteria Decision-Making. *Management Science*, *31*(6), 647–656. doi:10.1287/mnsc.31.6.647

Brauers, W. K., Zavadskas, E. K., Peldschus, F., & Turskis, Z. (2008). Multi-objective decision-making for road design. *Transport*, *23*(3), 183–193. doi:10.3846/1648-4142.2008.23.183-193

Bray, O. (2010). *Health Care Information Technology: A Key to Quality and Cost Issues*. LWVUS.

Brill, E. D. Jr, Chang, S. Y., & Hopkins, L. D. (1982). Modelling to generate alternatives: The HSJ approach and an illustration using a problem in land use planning. *Management Science*, *28*(3), 221–235. doi:10.1287/mnsc.28.3.221

Brisson, L., Collard, M., & Pasquier, N. (2005). *Improving the knowledge discovery process using ontologies*. Paper presented at the 1st international workshop on Mining Complex Data in conjunction with ICDM (5th IEEE International Conference on Data Mining) Conference, Houston, TX.

Brugnach, M., Tagg, A., Keil, F., & De Lange, W. J. (2007). Uncertainty matters: Computer models at the science-policy interface. *Water Resources Management*, *21*(7), 1075–1090. doi:10.100711269-006-9099-y

Brun, O., Bockstal, C., & Garcia, J. (2006). A Simple Formula for End-to-End Jitter Estimation in Packet-Switching Networks. In *Proceedings of the International Conference on Networking, International Conference on Systems and International Conference on Mobile Communications and Learning Technologies, (ICNICONSMCL'06)*. IEEE Computer Society. 10.1109/ICNICONSMCL.2006.34

Buchanan, J. T. (1997). A Naive Approach for Solving MCDM Problems: The GUESS Method. *The Journal of the Operational Research Society*, *48*(2), 202–206. doi:10.1057/palgrave.jors.2600349

Bulusu, N., Estrin, D., Girod, L., & Heidemann, J. (2001). Scalable coordination for wireless sensor networks: self-configuring localization systems. *International Symposium on Communication Theory and Applications (ISCTA 2001)*.

Buratti, C., Conti, A., Dardari, D., & Verdone, R. (2009, August). An Overview on Wireless Sensor Networks Technology and Evolution. *Sensors (Basel)*, *2009*(12), 6869–6896. doi:10.339090906869 PMID:22423202

Bureš, V., Tučník, P., Mikulecký, P., Mls, K., & Blecha, P. (2016). Application of ambient intelligence in educational institutions: Visions and architectures. *International Journal of Ambient Computing and Intelligence*, *7*(1), 94–120. doi:10.4018/IJACI.2016010105

Buten, R. E., & Shen, V. Y. (1973, Aug.). A scheduling model for computer systems with two classes of processors. In *Proceedings of 1973 Sagamore Computer Conference Parallel Processing*. Institute of Electrical and Electronics Engineers.

Bychkovsky, V., Hull, B., Miu, A., Balakrishnan, H., & Madden, S. (2006). A measurement study of vehicular internet access using in situ Wi-Fi networks. In *Proceedings of the 12th annual international conference on Mobile computing and networking, MobiCom'06*. ACM. 10.1145/1161089.1161097

Caballero, R., Luque, M., Molina, J., & Ruiz, F. (2002). PROMOIN: An interactive system for multiobjective programming. *International Journal of Information Theories and Decision Making*, *1*(04), 635–656. doi:10.1142/S0219622002000403

Cagnina, L. C., Esquivel, C. A., & Coello, C. A. (2008). Solving Engineering Optimization Problems with the Simple Constrained Particle Swarm Optimizer. *Informatica*, *32*, 319–326.

Cai, X., Lyu, M. R., & Wong, K. F. (2000). Component-based software engineering: technologies, development frameworks, and quality assurance schemes. In *Proceedings of the Software Engineering Conference APSEC 2000* (pp. 372-379). IEEE.

Carlier, J., Chretienne, P., Erschler, J., Hanen, C., & Lopez, P. (1993). Les problemes dordonnancement. *RAIRO Operation Research.*, *7*, 77–150.

Cerruti, C., Mena, C., Skipworth, H., & Tavoletti, E. (2016). Characterizing agile supply partnerships in the fashion industry. *International Journal of Operations & Production Management*, *36*(8), 923–947. doi:10.1108/IJOPM-03-2015-0181

Chakhar, S., Ishizaka, A., Labib, A., & Saad, I. (2016). Dominance-based rough set approach for group decisions. *European Journal of Operational Research*, *251*(1), 206–224. doi:10.1016/j.ejor.2015.10.060

Chami, D., & Kazar, O. (2011). *A data mining agent-oriented platform.* Paper presented on the 4th International Conference on Information Systems and Economic Intelligence, Marrakech, Morocco.

Charles, P., Harish, V., Swathi, M., & Deepthi, C. H. (2012). A Review on the Various Techniques used for Optical Character Recognition. *International Journal of Engineering, Research and Applications*, *2*(1), 659–662.

Chatterjee, S., Chakraborty, R., Dey, N., & Hore, S. (2015). A Quality Prediction method of Weight Lifting Activity. *Proceedings of the Michael Faraday IET International Summit - 2015 (MFIIS-2015): An IET International Conference.* 10.1049/cp.2015.1691

Chatterjee, S., Sarkar, S., Hore, S., Dey, N., Ashour, A. S., & Balas, V. E. (2017a). Particle swarm optimization trained neural network for structural failure prediction of multistoried RC buildings. *Neural Computing & Applications*, *28*(8), 2005–2016. doi:10.100700521-016-2190-2

Chatterjee, S., Sarkar, S., Hore, S., Dey, N., Ashour, A. S., Shi, F., & Le, D. N. (2017b). Structural failure classification for reinforced concrete buildings using trained neural network based multi-objective genetic algorithm. *Structural Engineering and Mechanics*, *63*(4), 429–438.

Chaudhuri, B., Demir, B., Bruzzone, L., & Chaudhuri, S. (2016). Region-Based Retrieval of Remote Sensing Images Using an Unsupervised Graph-Theoretic Approach. *IEEE Geoscience and Remote Sensing Letters*, *13*(7), 987-991. 10.1109/LGRS.2016.2558289

Cheesman, J., & Daniels, J. (2001). *UML Components - A Simple process for specifying Compnent-Based software.* Addison-Wesley.

Chen, S. M. (1995). Arithmetic operations between vague sets. *Proceeding of international joint conference of CFSA/TFIS/SOFT'95 on fuzzy theory and applications*, 206–211.

Chen, C. (2015). Construct a Multi Criteria Decision Making Tool: DEMATEL and MMDE Methods. *International Journal of Decision Support System Technology*, *7*(4), 36–50. doi:10.4018/IJDSST.2015100103

Chen, C. T. (2000). Extensions of the TOPSIS for group decision-making under fuzzy environment. *Fuzzy Sets and Systems*, *114*(1), 1–9. doi:10.1016/S0165-0114(97)00377-1

Cheng, C., Liu, X., Blumenstein, M., & Marasamy, V. (2004). Enhancing neural confidence based segmentation for cursive handwriting recognition. *SEAL 04 and 2004 FIRA Robot world congress.*

Cheng, K., & Dill, J. (2014). Lossless to Lossy Dual-Tree BEZW Compression for Hyperspectral Images. *IEEE Transactions on Geoscience and Remote Sensing*, *52*(9), 5765–5770. doi:10.1109/TGRS.2013.2292366

Chennoufi, M., Bendella, F., & Bouzid, M. (2018). Multi-Agent Simulation Collision Avoidance of Complex System: Application to Evacuation Crowd Behavior, *International Journal of Ambient Computing and Intelligence (IJACI)*. doi:10.4018/IJACI.2018010103

Chen, S. J. (2006). A new method for handling the similarity measure problems of interval-valued fuzzy numbers. *Proceedings of the second international conference on natural computation and the third international conference on fuzzy systems and knowledge discovery*, 325 - 334.

Chen, S. J., & Chen, S. M. (2003). Fuzzy risk analysis based on similarity measures of generalized fuzzy numbers. *IEEE Transactions on Fuzzy Systems*, *11*(1), 45–46. doi:10.1109/TFUZZ.2002.806316

Chen, S. M., & Sanguansat, K. (2011). Analyzing fuzzy risk based on similarity measures between interval-valued fuzzy numbers. *Expert Systems with Applications*, *38*(7), 8612–8621. doi:10.1016/j.eswa.2011.01.065

Chen, T. Y., & Lai, H. L. (2011). A risk management method for enhancing patient safety based on interval-valued fuzzy numbers. *African Journal of Business Management*, *5*(30), 11925–11945.

Chen, Z., Zhang, W., Hu, B., Can, X., Liu, S., & Meng, D. (2017). Retrieving Objects by Partitioning. *IEEE Transactions on Big Data*, *3*(1), 44–54. doi:10.1109/TBDATA.2016.2566664

Cheruku, R., Edla, D. R., Kuppili, V., Dharavath, R., & Beechu, N. R. (2017). Automatic disease diagnosis using optimised weightless neural networks for low-power wearable devices. *Healthcare Technology Letters*, *4*(4), 122–128. doi:10.1049/htl.2017.0003 PMID:28868148

Chong, C. W., Mukundan, R., & Raveendran, P. (2003). An efficient algorithm for fast computation of pseudo-Zernike moment. *IJPRAI*, *17*, 1011–1023.

Chong, W., & David, B. (2010). Formulating partner selection criteria for agile supply chains: A dempster–shafer belief acceptability optimization approach. *International Journal of Production Economics*, *125*(2), 284–293. doi:10.1016/j.ijpe.2010.02.010

Chong, W., & David, B. (2013). Partner selection in agile supply chains: A fuzzy intelligent approach. *Production Planning & Control: The Management of Operations*, *25*(10), 821–839.

Chong, W., & David, B. A. (2012). Dynamic feedback model for partner selection in agile supply chains. *International Journal of Operations & Production Management*, *32*(1), 79–103. doi:10.1108/01443571211195745

Cho, S., & Chandrakasan, A. (2000). Energy-efficient protocols for low duty cycle wireless microsensor. *Proceedings of the 33rd Annual Hawaii International Conference on System Sciences*.

Christopher, M. (2000). The agile supply chain competing in volatile markets. *Industrial Marketing Management*, *29*(1), 37–44. doi:10.1016/S0019-8501(99)00110-8

Čiarnienė, R., & Vienažindienė, M. (2014). Agility and Responsiveness Managing Fashion Supply Chain. *Procedia: Social and Behavioral Sciences*, *150*, 1012–1019. doi:10.1016/j.sbspro.2014.09.113

Cinque, M., Coronato, A., & Testa, A. (2012). Dependable Services for Mobile Health Monitoring Systems. *International Journal of Ambient Computing and Intelligence*, *4*(1), 1–15. doi:10.4018/jaci.2012010101

Conoscenti, M., Coppola, R., & Magli, E. (2016). Constant SNR, Rate Control, and Entropy Coding for Predictive Lossy Hyperspectral Image Compression. *IEEE Transactions on Geoscience and Remote Sensing*, *54*(12), 7431–7441. doi:10.1109/TGRS.2016.2603998

CORBA. (2014). Retrieved from http://www.omg.org/spec/CORBA/3.3/

D'Souza, D. F., & Wills, A. C. (1998). *Objects, Components, and Frameworks with UML - The Catalysis Approach.* Addison-Wesley.

Daga, P., & Dewangan, R.K. (2014). Segmentation singpectral clustering based on texture features. *International Journal of Research in Engineering and Applied Sciences, 2*(2), 37-40.

Damerdji, R. O., & Noureddine, M. (2017). Maintenance Decision-Making Under the Cost Criterion and the Competing Risks Approach. *International Journal of Decision Support System Technology, 9*(1), 32–48. doi:10.4018/IJDSST.2017010103

Damodaram, R., & Valarmathi, M. L. (2012). Phishing website detection and optimization using Modified bat algorithm. *International Journal of Engineering Research and Applications, 2*(1), 870–876.

David, G. (2005). *Mobile Image Categorization and Retrieval using Color Blobs* (Masters Thesis). Tokyo institute of Technology.

Debrauwer, L. (1998). *Views contexts for patterning databases objects CROME* (PhD thesis). University of sciences and technologies, Lile, France.

Dehghani, H., & Bogdanovic, D. (2017). Copper price estimation using bat algorithm. *Resources Policy*. 10.1016/j.resourpol.2017.10.015

Dejan, L., & Rok, R. (2009). Multi-Agent System for Decision Support in Enterprises. *Journal of JIOS, 33*(2), 269–284.

Dekhici, L. (2016). Reconfiguration et Ordonnancement des Blocs Opératoires Avec Etude de Cas. Editions universitaires européennes.

Dekhici, L., & Belkadi, K. (2010a). *Reconfiguration d'un Bloc Neurochirurgical par Simulation.* E-Medisys, Third International conference: E-Medical Systems, Fez.

Dekhici, L., & Belkadi, K. (2014). Bi-objective Operating Theater scheduling case of the paediatric hospital of Oran, In *Logistics and Operations Management (GOL), 2014 International Conference on.* IEEE. 10.1109/GOL.2014.6887438

Dekhici, L., & Belkadi, K. (2010b). Operating theatre scheduling under constraints. *Journal of Applied Sciences, 10*(14), 1380–1388. doi:10.3923/jas.2010.1380.1388

Dekhici, L., & Belkadi, K. (2017). A Firefly Algorithm for the Mono-Processors Hybrid Flow Shop Problem. *International Journal of Advanced Computer Science and Applications, 8*(12), 2017. doi:10.14569/IJACSA.2017.081256

Dekhici, L., & Belkai, K. (2015). A Bat Algorithm with Generalized Walk for the Two-Stage Hybrid Flow Shop Problem. *International Journal of Decision Support System Technology, 7*(3), 1–16. doi:10.4018/IJDSST.2015070101

Dellino, G., Laudadio, T., Mari, R., Mastronardi, N., & Meloni, C. (2017). A reliable decision support system for fresh food supply chain management. *International Journal of Production Research*, 1–28. doi:10.1080/00207543.2017.1367106

Dempsey, W. A. (1978). Vendor selection and the buying process. *Industrial Marketing Management, 79*(4), 257–267. doi:10.1016/0019-8501(78)90044-5

Deng, C., Ji, R., Wei, L., Tao, D., & Gao, X. (2013). Visual Reranking through Weakly Supervised Multi-Graph Learning. *Proceedings of International Conference on Computer Vision*, 2600-2607. 10.1109/ICCV.2013.323

Dessouky, M. M., Dessouky, M. I., & Verma, S. K. (1998). Flow shop scheduling with identical jobs and uniform parallel machines. *European Journal of Operational Research, 109*(3), 620–631. doi:10.1016/S0377-2217(97)00194-X

Dey N., Acharjee, S., Biswas, D., Das, A. & Chaudhuri, S. (2012). Medical Information Embedding in Compressed Watermarked Intravascular Ultrasound Video. *Scientific Bulletin of the Politehnica University of Timisoara - Transactions on Electronics and Communications, 57*(71).

Dey, N., & Ashour, A. S. (2017). Meta-Heuristic Algorithms in Medical Image Segmentation: A Review. *Advancements in Applied Metaheuristic Computing*, 185.

Dey, N., & Ashour, A. S. (2017). Meta-Heuristic Algorithms in Medical Image Segmentation: A Review. *Advancements in Applied Metaheuristic Computing*, 185-203.

Dey, Samanta, Chakraborty, Das, Chaudhuri, & Suri. (2014). Firefly Algorithm for Optimization of Scaling Factors During Embedding of Manifold Medical Information: An Application in Ophthalmology Imaging. *Journal of Medical Imaging and Health Informatics, 4*(3), 384-394.

Dey, N. (2018). *Advancements in Applied Metaheuristic Computing*. Hershey, PA: IGI Global. doi:10.4018/978-1-5225-4151-6

Dey, N., & Ashour, A. S. (2016). Antenna Design and Direction of Arrival Estimation in Meta-Heuristic Paradigm: A Review. *International Journal of Service Science, Management, Engineering, and Technology*, *7*(3), 1–18. doi:10.4018/IJSSMET.2016070101

Dey, N., Samanta, S., Chakraborty, S., Das, A., Chaudhuri, S. S., & Suri, J. S. (2014). Firefly Algorithm for Optimization of Scaling Factors During Embedding of Manifold Medical Information: An Application in Ophthalmology Imaging. *Journal of Medical Imaging and Health Informatics*, *4*(3), 384–394. doi:10.1166/jmihi.2014.1265

Dhir, S., Kumar, D., & Singh, V. B. (2017). Requirement Paradigms to Implement the Software Projects in Agile Development Using Analytical Hierarchy Process. *International Journal of Decision Support System Technology*, *9*(3), 28–41. doi:10.4018/IJDSST.2017070102

Didem Batur, Erol, & Karasan. (2016). Robot move sequence determining and multiple part-type scheduling in hybrid flexible flow shop robotic cells. *Computers & Industrial Engineering, 100*, 72-87. 10.1016/j.cie.2016.08.006

Dimple, J., Aarti, S., Rashmi, S., & Saurabh, M. (2017). A Thorough Insight into Theoretical and Practical Developments in MultiAgent Systems. *International Journal of Ambient Computing and Intelligence*, *8*(1), 23–49. doi:10.4018/IJACI.2017010102

Dinevski, D., Bele, U., Šarenac, T., Rajkovič, U., & Šušteršic, O. (2011). Telemedicine Techniques and Applications. In G. Graschew (Ed.), Clinical Decision Support Systems (pp. 185-210). InTech.

Dios, M., Fernandez-Viagas, V., & Framinan, J. M. (2018). Efficient heuristics for the hybrid flow shop scheduling problem with missing operations. *Computers & Industrial Engineering, 115*, 88-99. 10.1016/j.cie.2017.10.034

Dong, L., Liang, Y., Kong, G., Zhang, Q., Cao, X., & Izquierdo, E. (2016). Holons Visual Representation for Image Retrieval. *IEEE Transactions on Multimedia*, *18*(4), 714–725. doi:10.1109/TMM.2016.2530399

Duerr, H. P., Schwehm, M., Leary, C. C., De Vlas, S. J., & Eichner, M. (2007). The impact of contact structure on infectious disease control: Influenza and antiviral agents. *Epidemiology and Infection*, *135*(07), 1124–1132. doi:10.1017/S0950268807007959 PMID:17288643

Duggirala, R. (2016). A Novel Hybridization of Expectation-Maximization and K-Means Algorithms for Better Clustering Performance. *International Journal of Ambient Computing and Intelligence*, *7*(2), 47–74. doi:10.4018/IJACI.2016070103

Du, Z. Y., & Liu, B. (2012). Image matching using a bat algorithm with mutation. *Applied Mechanics and Materials*, *203*(1), 88–93.

Edwards, W. (1977). How to use multi-attribute utility measurement for social decision making. *IEEE Transactions on Systems, Man, and Cybernetics*, *7*(5), 326–340. doi:10.1109/TSMC.1977.4309720

El-Gayar, O. F., Deokar, A. V., & Tao, J. (2011). DSS-CMM: A Capability Maturity Model for DSS Development Processes. *International Journal of Decision Support System Technology*, *3*(4), 14–34. doi:10.4018/jdsst.2011100102

El-Sappagh, S., & Elmogy, M. M. (2016). Medical Case Based Reasoning Frameworks: Current Developments and Future Directions. *International Journal of Decision Support System Technology*, *8*(3), 31–62. doi:10.4018/IJDSST.2016070103

Elsayed, W. M., El-bassiouny, A. H., & Radwan, E. F. (2013). Applying Inhomogeneous Probabilistic Cellular Au-tomata Rules on Epidemic Model. *International Journal of Advanced Research in Artificial Intelligence*, *2*(4).

Elsisi, M., Soliman, M., Aboelela, M. A. S., & Mansour, W. (2016). Bat inspired algorithm based optimal design of model predictive load frequency control. *International Journal of Electrical Power & Energy Systems, 83*, 426-433. 10.1016/j.ijepes.2016.04.036

Eriksson, J., Girod, L., Hull, B., Newton, R., Madden, S., & Balakrishnan, H. (2008). The pothole patrol: using a mobile sensor network for road surface monitoring. In *Proceeding of the 6th international conference on Mobile systems, applications, and services, MobiSys'08*. ACM. 10.1145/1378600.1378605

Fakhari, F., Mosavi, M. R., & Lajvardi, M. M. (2017). Image fusion based on multi-scale transform and sparse representation: An image energy approach. *IET Image Processing*, *11*(11), 1041–1049. doi:10.1049/iet-ipr.2017.0104

Farahmand, K., You, G., Shi, J., & Wadhwa, S. S. (2015). Data Mining for Predicting Pre-diabetes: Comparing Two Approaches. *International Journal of User-Driven Healthcare*, *5*(2), 26–46. doi:10.4018/IJUDH.2015070103

Fashoto, S. G., Adeyeye, M., Owolabi, O., & Odim, M. (2015). Modelling of the Feed Forward Neural Network with its Application in Medical Diagnosis. *International Journal of Advances in Engineering and Technology*, *8*(4), 507–520.

Fausett, L. L. (2001). *Fundamentals of Neural Net-works: Architectures, Algorithms, and Applications*. New York: Addison-Wesley Inc.

Fayyad, U., Piatetsky-Shapiro, G., & Smyth, P. (1996). From Data Mining to Knowledge Discovery in Databases. American Association for Artificial Intelligence.

Fedorovici, L. (2011). A Comparison between Two Character Recognition Approaches. *FACTA UNIVERSITATIS Series: Automatic Control and Robotics*, *10*(2), 125–140.

Fedorovici, L. O., Voisan, E., Dragan, F., & Iercan, D. (2010). Improved neural network OCR based on preprocessed blob classes. *Proc. ICCC-CONTI 2010*, 559–564. 10.1109/ICCCYB.2010.5491211

Ferber, J. (1995). *Multi-agent systems, towards a collective intelligence*. Paris: Inter Editions.

Ferber, J. (1999). *Multi-agent Systems - An Introduction to Distributed Artificial Intelligence*. London: Addison-Wesley.

Filatovas, E., & Kurasova, O. (2011). A Decision Support System for Solving Multiple Criteria Optimization Problems. *Informatics in Education*, *10*(2), 213–224.

Filho, A. T., Henriques de Gusmão, A. P., Clemente, T., Moura, J., Costa, A. P., & de Almeida, A. T. (2014). A Decision Support System for Sizing the Call Center of an Electrical Power Distributor. *International Journal of Decision Support System Technology*, *6*(2), 63–76. doi:10.4018/ijdsst.2014040104

Filip, F. G., Zamfirescu, B., & Ciurea, C. (2017). *Computer-Supported Collaborative Decision-Making Automation. In Collaboration & E-Services Series* (Vol. 4). Springer International Publishing AG. doi:10.1007/978-3-319-47221-8

Finkelstein, A., Kramer, J., Nuseibeh, B., Finkelstein, L., & Goedicke, M. (1992). Viewpoints: A Framework for Integrating Multiple Perspectives in System Development. *International Journal of Software Engineering and Knowledge Engineering*, *2*(1), 31–58. doi:10.1142/S0218194092000038

Finn, G. (1987). *Routing and addressing problems in large metropolitan-scale internetworks.* University of Southern California, Tech. Rep. ISI Research Report ISI/RR-87- 180.

Fomba, S., Zarate, P., Kilgour, M., Camilleri, G., Konate, J., & Tangara, F. (2017). A Recommender System Based on Multi-Criteria Aggregation. *International Journal of Decision Support System Technology*, *9*(4), 1–15. doi:10.4018/IJDSST.2017100101

Franke, J. (1997). Isolated handprinted digit recognition. In H. Bunke & P. S. P. Wang (Eds.), *Handbook of Character Recognition and Document Image Analysis* (pp. 103–121). World Scientific. doi:10.1142/9789812830968_0004

Frej, E. A., Peixoto, L. R., Roselli, J. A., & Almeida, A. T. (2017). A Multicriteria Decision Model for Supplier Selection in a Food Industry Based on FITradeoff Method. *Hindawi -. Mathematical Problems in Engineering*, *2017*, 1–9. doi:10.1155/2017/4541914

Frigui, H., Caudill, J., & Abdallah, A. (2008). Fusion of Multi-Modal Features for Efficient Content-Based Image Retrieval. Proceedings of international conference on Fuzzy Systems, 1992-1998.

Fu, W., Li, S., Fang, L., & Benediktsson, J. A. (2017). Adaptive Spectral–Spatial Compression of Hyperspectral Image With Sparse Representation. *IEEE Transactions on Geoscience and Remote Sensing*, *55*(2), 671–682. doi:10.1109/TGRS.2016.2613848

Gandomi, A. H., Yang, X. S., & Alavi, A. H. (2011). Mixed Variable Structural Optimization Using Firefly Algorithm. *Computers & Structures*, *89*(23-24), 2325–2336. doi:10.1016/j.compstruc.2011.08.002

Ganesan, T., Elamvazuthi, I., Shaari, K. Z., & Vasant, P. (2013). Hypervolume-Driven Analytical Programming for Solar-Powered Irrigation System Optimization. In Nostradamus 2013: Prediction, Modeling and Analysis of Complex Systems. Springer.

Ganesan, N., Venkatesh, K., & Rama, M. A. (2010). Application of Neural Networks in Diagnosing Cancer Disease Using Demographic Data. *International Journal of Computers and Applications*, *1*(26), 76–85.

Gao, Z., Xue, J., Zhou, W., Pnag, S., & Qi, T. (2016). Democratic Diffusion Aggregation for image retrieval. *IEEE Transactions on Multimedia*, *18*(8), 1661–1674. doi:10.1109/TMM.2016.2568748

Gardiner, L., & Steuer, R. (1994). Unified interactive multiple objective programming: An open architecture for accommodating new procedures. *The Journal of the Operational Research Society*, *45*(12), 1456–1466. doi:10.1057/jors.1994.222

Garg, A., Adhikari, N., McDonald, H., Rosas-Arel-lano, M., Devereaux, P., Beyene, J., ... Haynes, R. B. (2005). Effects of computerized clinical decision support systems on practitioner performance and patient outcomes: A systematic review. *Journal of the American Medical Association*, *293*(10), 1223–1238. doi:10.1001/jama.293.10.1223 PMID:15755945

Gass, S., & Saaty, T. (1955). The Computational Algorithm for the Parametric Objective Function. *Naval Research Logistics Quarterly*, *2*(1-2), 39–45. doi:10.1002/nav.3800020106

Gatos, B., Pratikakis, I., & Perantonis, S. J. (2006). Hybrid offline cursive handwriting word recognition. *18th International Conference on Pattern Recognition(ICPR'06)*, 998-1002. 10.1109/ICPR.2006.644

Gavilan, D., Takahashi, H., Saito, S., & Nakajima, M. (2006). Mobile Image Retrieval using Morphological Color Segmentation. *ICMU*, *2006*, 51–58.

Genova, K., Kirilov, L., Guliashki, V., Staykov, B., & Vatov, D. (2011). A Prototype of a Web-based Decision Support System for Building Models and Solving Optimization and Decision Making Problems. *Proceedings of XII Int. Conference on Computer Systems and Technologies - CompSysTech'11,* 167-172. 10.1145/2023607.2023636

Georg, S. (2011). Rapid Image Retrieval for Mobile Location Recognition. *ICASSP.*

Ghaleb, Y., Abbas, I. H., & Rumman, A. (2017). ERP Decision Support System Using Multi Objective Optimization – An Exploratory Study. *Proceedings of 56th IASTEM International Conference*, 57-64.

Gholami, A., & Ansari, H. R. (2017). Estimation of porosity from seismic attributes using a committee model with bat-inspired optimization algorithm. *Journal of Petroleum Science and Engineering, 152*, 238-249. 10.1016/j.petrol.2017.03.013

Giveki, D. (2012). *Automatic detection of diabetes diagnosis using feature weighted support vector machines based on mutual information and modified cuckoo search.* Academic Press.

Goldman, S. L., Nagel, R. N., & Dove, P. R. (1991). *21st century manufacturing enterprise strategy.* Bethlehem, PA: Iacocca Institute.

Golemati, S., Mougiakakou, S., Stoitsis, J., Valavanis, I., & Nikita, K. S. (2005). Clinical Decision Support Systems: Basic Principles and Applications in Diagnosis and Therapy. In Clinical Decision Support Systems (pp. 250-296). Idea Group Inc.

Govindan, V. K., & Shivaprasad, A. P. (1990). Character recognition: A review. *Pattern Recognition J, 23*(7), 671-683.

GregoryQ. (2011). *Justpictures.* Retrieved from http://code.google.com/p/justpictures

Guan, H., Antani, S., & Rodney, L. (2010). Comparative Study of Shape Retrieval using Feature Fusion Approaches. *Proceedings of IEEE International Symposium on Computer Based Medical System(CBMS)*, 226- 231. 10.1109/CBMS.2010.6042646

Gueguen, L., & Hamid, R. (2016). Toward a Generalizable Image Representation for Large-Scale Change Detection: Application to Generic Damage Analysis. *IEEE Transactions on Geoscience and Remote Sensing, 54*(6), 3378–3387. doi:10.1109/TGRS.2016.2516402

Guerraiche, K., Rahli, M., Zeblah, A., & Dekhici, L. (2015b). Bat Algorithm to Series- Parallel Power System Design. In Multi-Conferences on Computational Engineering in Systems Applications CCCA, 3rd Communications, Computing and Control Applications, 67-71

Guerraiche, K., Rahli, M., Dekhici, L., & Zeblah, A. (2018). (Article in Press). Conception Optimale de Redondance dans des Systemes Electriques Parallèles-Séries à l'Aide des Metaheuristiques. *Revue Roumaine des Sciences Techniques Série Électrotechnique et Energétique.*

Guerraiche, K., Rahli, M., Zeblah, A., & Dekhici, L. (2015a). Budgetary and Redundancy Optimization of Heterogeneous Series-Parallel Power Systems under Availability Constraints. *Energy Procedia Journal: ELSEVIER, 74*, 547–554. doi:10.1016/j.egypro.2015.07.748

Guerraiche, K., Rahli, M., Zeblah, A., & Dekhici, L. (2015c). Series-Parallel Power System Optimization Using Firefly Algorithm. *International Journal on Electrical Engineering and Informatics, 1*(7), 89–101. doi:10.15676/ijeei.2015.7.1.7

Guesgen, H. W., & Marsland, S. (2016). Using Contextual Information for Recognising Human Behaviour. *International Journal of Ambient Computing and Intelligence (IJACI).* doi:10.4018/IJACI.2016010102

Guliashki, V., Genova, K., & Kirilov, L. (2013), The Decision Support System WebOptim in an E-Learning Context. *Proceedings of Papers of the International Conference Automatics and Informatics 2013,* 117-120.

Guo, Y., Ding, G., Li, L., Han, J., & Shao, L. (2017). Learning to Hash With Optimized Anchor Embedding for Scalable Retrieval. *IEEE Transactions on Image Processing*, *26*(3), 1344–1354. doi:10.1109/TIP.2017.2652730 PMID:28092559

Gupta, J. N. D. (1988). Two stage, hybrid flowshop scheduling problem. *The Journal of the Operational Research Society*, *3*(4), 359–364. doi:10.1057/jors.1988.63

Guttman, R. H., & Alexandros, G. (1998). *Agent-mediated Electronic Commerce: A Survey. Software Agents Group*. MIT Media Laboratory.

Haddad, M. (2002). *Extraction and Impact of knowledge on the performance of Information Retrieval Systems* (Doctoral thesis). Joseph Fourier University, Grenoble, France.

Haddad, H., Moulin, B., & Thériault, M. (2016). A fully GIS-integrated simulation approach for analyzing the spread of epidemics in urban areas. *SIGSPATIAL Special*, *8*(1), 34–41. doi:10.1145/2961028.2961034

Haimes, Y., Landson, L. S., & Wismer, D. A. (1971). On a Bicriterion Formulation of the Problems of Integrated System Identification and System Optimization. *IEEE Transactions on Systems, Man, and Cybernetics*, *1*, 296–297.

Hakim, A., Gheitasi, M., & Soltani, F. (2016). Fuzzy model on selecting processes in Business Process Reengineering. *Business Process Management Journal*, *22*(6), 1118–1138. doi:10.1108/BPMJ-05-2015-0057

Hal, K., & Sethi, I. (1995). Offline cursive handwriting Segmentation. *International Conference on Document Analysis and Recognition,* 894-897.

Halouani, N., Chabchoub, H., & Martel, J. M. (2009). PROMETHEE-MD-2T method for project selection. *European Journal of Operational Research*, *195*(3), 841–849. doi:10.1016/j.ejor.2007.11.016

Hamdadou, D. (2016). Méthodologie Multicritères d'Aide à la Décision, Cours et Exercices. Edition OPU 2016.

Hammami, A. (2003). *Modélisation technico-économique d'une chaîne logistique dans une entreprise réseau* (Doctoral dissertation). Ecole Nationale Supérieure des Mines de Saint-Etienne; Université Laval.

Hanafi zadeh, P., Hashemi, A., Parvin, E. S. (2009). Robust Strategic Planning Employing Scenario Planning and Fuzzy Inference System. *International Journal of Decision Support System Technology*, *1*(3), 21-45. doi:10.4018/jdsst.2009070102

Haouari, M., Hidri, L., & Gharbi, A. (2006). Optimal scheduling of a two hybrid flow shop. *Mathematical Methods of Operations Research*, *64*(1), 107–124. doi:10.100700186-006-0066-4

Haouari, M., & M'Hallah, R. (1997). Heuristic algorithms for the two-stage hybrid flowshop problem. *Operations Research Letters*, *21*(1), 43–53. doi:10.1016/S0167-6377(97)00004-7

Harada, S., Naaman, M., Yee, J. S., Wang, Q. Y., & Paepcke, A. (2004). Lost in memories: interacting with photo collections on pdas. *Proceedings of the 4th ACM/IEEE-CS joint conference on Digital libraries*, 325–333. 10.1145/996350.996425

Hare, J. S., & Lewis, P. H. (2005). Content-based image retrieval using a mobile device as a novel interface Storage and Retrieval Methods and Applications for Multimedia 2005, 64-75. doi:10.1117/12.588979

Hayes, T., & Ali, F.H. (n.d.). Mobile Wireless Sensor Networks: Applications and Routing Protocols. In *Handbook of Research on Next Generation Mobile Communications Systems*. IGI Global.

Haykin, S. (1994). Neural Networks: A Comprehensive Foundation (2nd ed.). Pearson Education, Inc.

Health Care Education Task Force. (2012). *Diagnosis of Diabetes and Prediabetes*. National Institute of Diabetes and Digestive and Kidney Disease.

Heaton, J. (2013). Feedforward Backpropagation Neural Networks. In J. Heaton (Ed.), Introduction to Neural Networks for Java (2nd ed.). Heaton Research, Inc.

Hébrail, G., & Lechevallier, Y. (2003). *Data Mining and Data Analysis*. Academic Press.

Heinzelman, W., Kulik, J., & Balakrishnan, H. (1999). Adaptive protocols for information dissemination in wireless sensor networks. *Proceedings of the 5th Annual ACM/IEEE International Conference on Mobile Computing and Networking (MobiCom_99)*. 10.1145/313451.313529

He, X., Huang, G., Liang, Z., Nong, Y., Wu, X., Luo, H., & Tang, Z. (2017). Simulation of the Spread of A/H1N1 Influenza Based on Geographic Information System Platform. *Journal of Medical Imaging and Health Informatics*, *7*(3), 531–535. doi:10.1166/jmihi.2017.2067

He, X., Zhang, C., Zhang, L., & Li, X. (2016). A-Optimal Projection for Image Representation. *IEEE Transactions on Pattern Analysis and Machine Intelligence*, *38*(5), 1009–1015. doi:10.1109/TPAMI.2015.2439252 PMID:26353361

He, Y., Zhang, Y., Ji, Y., & Shen, X. S. (2006). A new energy efficient approach by separating data collection and data report in wireless sensor networks. *Proceedings of the International Conference on Communications and Mobile Computing*. 10.1145/1143549.1143783

Hoblos, G., Staroswiecki, M., & Aitouche, A. (2000). Optimal design of fault tolerant sensor networks. *IEEE International Conference on Control Applications*, 467–472. 10.1109/CCA.2000.897468

Hosack, B., Hall, D., Paradice, D., & Courtney, J. F. (2012). A look toward the future: Decision Support Systems research is alive and well. *Journal of the Association for Information Systems*, *13*(5), 315–340. doi:10.17705/1jais.00297

Hu, Ortega, & Au. (2015). Multiresolution Graph Fourier Transform for Compression of Piecewise Smooth Images. *IEEE Transactions on Image Processing*, *24*(1), 419-433.

Hub. (2010). *Image Retrieval on Mobile Devices*. LWA 2010, Kassel.

Hwang, C., & Masud, A. (1979). *Multiple objective decision making-methods and applications: a state of the art survey*. Berlin, Germany: Springer. doi:10.1007/978-3-642-45511-7

Iftikhar, A., & Moncef, G. (2010). Content-based interactive image retrieval from JAVA enabled mobile devices. *Proceedings of the Fourth International Symposium on Communications, Control and Signal Processing*.

Iftikhar, A., & Moncef, G. (2005). Compression and Network Effect on Content-Based Image Retrieval on Java Enabled Mobile Devices. In *Proceedings of 2005 Finnish Signal Processing Symposium, FINSIG 2005* (pp. 35-38). Kuopio, Finland: Academic Press.

Iftikhar, A., & Moncef, G. (2011). A generic content-based image retrieval framework for mobile devices. *Multimedia Tools and Applications*, *55*(3), 423–442. doi:10.100711042-010-0556-5

Iftikhar, A., Serkan, K., & Moncef, G. (2005). An Efficient Image Retrieval Scheme on Java Enabled Mobile Devices. In *Proceedings of the 2005 IEEE Seventh Workshop on Multimedia Signal Processing, MMSP 2005* (pp. 397 – 400). Shanghai, China: IEEE.

Imanirad, R., Yang, X. S., & Yeomans, J. S. (2012a). A Computationally Efficient, Biologically-Inspired Modelling-to-Generate-Alternatives Method. *Journal of Computers*, *2*(2), 43–47.

Imanirad, R., Yang, X. S., & Yeomans, J. S. (2012b). A Co-evolutionary, Nature-Inspired Algorithm for the Concurrent Generation of Alternatives. *Journal of Computers*, *2*(3), 101–106.

Imanirad, R., Yang, X. S., & Yeomans, J. S. (2013a). Modelling-to-Generate-Alternatives Via the Firefly Algorithm. *Journal of Applied Operational Research*, *5*(1), 14–21.

Imanirad, R., Yang, X. S., & Yeomans, J. S. (2013b). A Concurrent Modelling to Generate Alternatives Approach Using the Firefly Algorithm. *International Journal of Decision Support System Technology*, *5*(2), 33–45. doi:10.4018/jdsst.2013040103

Imanirad, R., Yang, X. S., & Yeomans, J. S. (2013c). A Biologically-Inspired Metaheuristic Procedure for Modelling-to-Generate-Alternatives. *International Journal of Engineering Re-search and Applications*, *3*(2), 1677–1686.

Imanirad, R., & Yeomans, J. S. (2013). Modelling to Generate Alternatives Using Biologically Inspired Algorithms. In X. S. Yang (Ed.), *Swarm Intelligence and Bio-Inspired Computation: Theory and Applications* (pp. 313–333). Amsterdam: Elsevier. doi:10.1016/B978-0-12-405163-8.00014-4

Intanagonwiwat, C., Govindan, R., & Estrin, D. (2000). Directed diffusion: a scalable and robust communication paradigm for sensor networks. *Proceedings of the ACM Mobi-Com'00*, 56–67. 10.1145/345910.345920

Intanagonwiwat, C., Govindan, R., & Estrin, D. (2000). Directed iffusion: a scalable and robust communication paradigm for sensor networks. *Proceedings of the 6th Annual ACM/IEEE International Conference on Mobile Computing and Networking (MobiCom_00).*

International Diabetes Federation. (2013). *IDF Diabetes Atlas.* Author.

International Diabetes Federation. (2017). *IDF Diabetes Atlas.* Author.

Jacobson, I. (1992). *Object-Oriented Software Engineering: A Use Case Driven Approach.* Harlow, UK: Addison - Wesley.

Jagatheesan, K., Anand, B., Dey, N., & Ashour, A. S. (2017). Effect of SMES Unit in AGC of an Interconnected Multi-Area Thermal Power System With ACO-Tuned PID Controller. *Advancements in Applied Metaheuristic Computing*, 164.

Jagatheesan, K., Anand, B., Dey, N., & Ashour, A. S. (2017a). Effect of SMES Unit in AGC of an Interconnected Multi-Area Thermal Power System With ACO-Tuned PID Controller. *Advancements in Applied Metaheuristic Computing*, 164.

Jagatheesan, K., Anand, B., Dey, N., Gaber, T., Hassanien, A. E., & Kim, T. H. (2015). A Design of PI Controller using Stochastic Particle Swarm Optimization in Load Frequency Control of Thermal Power Systems. In *Information Science and Industrial Applications (ISI), 2015 Fourth International Conference on* (pp. 25-32). IEEE. 10.1109/ISI.2015.8

Jagatheesan, K., Anand, B., Dey, N., Gaber, T., Hassanien, A. E., & Kim, T. H. (2015, September). A Design of PI Controller using Stochastic Particle Swarm Optimization in Load Frequency Control of Thermal Power Systems. In *Information Science and Industrial Applications (ISI), 2015 Fourth International Conference on* (pp. 25-32). IEEE.

Jagatheesan, K., Anand, B., Samanta, S., Dey, N., Ashour, A. S., & Balas, V. E. (2017). Design of a proportional-integral-derivative controller for an automatic generation control of multi-area power thermal systems using firefly algorithm. *IEEE/CAA Journal of Automatica Sinica.*

Jagatheesan, K., Anand, B., Samanta, S., Dey, N., Ashour, A. S., & Balas, V. E. (2017). Design of a Proportional-Integral-Derivative Controller for an Automatic Generation Control of Multi-Area Power Thermal Systems Using Firefly Algorithm. *IEEE/CAA Journal of Automatica Sinica*, *99*, 1-14.

Jagatheesan, K., Anand, B., Samanta, S., Dey, N., Ashour, A. S., & Balas, V. E. (2017c). Design of a proportional-integral-derivative controller for an automatic generation control of multi-area power thermal systems using firefly algorithm. *IEEE/CAA Journal of Automatica Sinica.*

Jagatheesan, K., Anand, B., Samanta, S., Dey, N., Ashour, A. S., & Balas, V. E. (2017b). Particle swarm optimisation-based parameters optimisation of PID controller for load frequency control of multi-area reheat thermal power systems. *International Journal of Advanced Intelligence Paradigms*, *9*(5-6), 464–489. doi:10.1504/IJAIP.2017.088143

Jagatheesan, K., Anand, B., Samanta, S., Dey, N., Santhi, V., Ashour, A. S., & Balas, V. E. (2017d). Application of flower pollination algorithm in load frequency control of multi-area interconnected power system with nonlinearity. *Neural Computing & Applications*, *28*(1), 475–488. doi:10.100700521-016-2361-1

Jain, A., & Bhatnagar, V. (2017). Concoction of Ambient Intelligence and Big Data for Better Patient Ministration Services. *International Journal of Ambient Computing and Intelligence*, *8*(4), 19–30. doi:10.4018/IJACI.2017100102

Jain, S. R., & Thakur, N. V. (2015). *Overview of Cluster based Routing Protocols in Static and Mobile Wireless Sensor Networks* (Vol. 339). Advances in Intelligent Systems and Computing. AISC. doi:10.1007/978-81-322-2250-7_62

Janssen, J. A. E. B., Krol, M. S., Schielen, R. M. J., & Hoekstra, A. Y. (2010). The effect of modelling quantified expert knowledge and uncertainty information on model based decision making. *Environmental Science & Policy*, *13*(3), 229–238. doi:10.1016/j.envsci.2010.03.003

Jarras, I., & Chaib-draa, B. (2002). *Overview of multi-agent systems, Scientific Series. Center for Interuniversity Research and Analysis of Organizations (CIRANO)*. Montreal University.

Jerry, Z., Aaron, H., Eric, L., & Zakhor, A. (2011). Location-based image retrieval for urban environments. *ICIP, 3677-3680*, 2011.

Jia, M., Fan, X., Xie, X., Li, M., & Ma, W.-Y. (2006). Photo-to-Search: Using Camera Phones to Inquire of the Surrounding World. *Proceedings of International Conference on Mobile Data Management,* 46-46.

Jiao, L., Zhang, S., Li, L., Yang, S., Liu, F., Hao, H., & Dong, H. (2017). A Novel Image Representation Framework Based on Gaussian Model and Evolutionary Optimization. *IEEE Transactions on Evolutionary Computation*, *21*(2), 265–280. doi:10.1109/TEVC.2016.2603526

Jin, Z., Yang, Z., & Ito, T. (2006). Metaheuristic algorithms for the multistage hybrid flowshop scheduling problem. *International Journal of Production Economics*, *100*(2), 322–333. doi:10.1016/j.ijpe.2004.12.025

Johnson, D., Stack, T., Fish, R., Flickinger, D., Ricci, R., & Lepreau, J. (2005). TrueMobile: A Mobile Robotic Wireless and Sensor Network Testbed. In *The 25th Annual Joint Conference of the IEEE Computer and Communications Societies.* IEEE Computer Society.

Johnson, S. M. (1954). Optimal two- and three-stage production schedules with set-up times included. Naval Research. *Logistics Quart*, *1*(1), 61–68. doi:10.1002/nav.3800010110

Jones & Brown. (3003). Challenges and opportunities for context-aware retrieval on mobile devices. *Proc. of the SIGIR workshop on Mobile Personal Information Retrieval*, 47-56.

Juneja, D., Singh, A., Singh, R., & Mukherjee, S. (2017). Towards a New Model of Storage and Access to Data in Big Data and Cloud Computing. *International Journal of Ambient Computing and Intelligence*, *8*(4), 31–44. doi:10.4018/IJACI.2017100103

Junyeong, Y., Sanghyuk, P., Hacheon, S., Hyeran, B., & Kyu, L. Y. (2008). A fast image retrieval system using index lookup table on mobile device. *Proceedings of 19th International Conference on Pattern Recognition, ICPR*, 1-4. 10.1109/ICPR.2008.4761729

Kabbai, L., Abdellaoui, M., & Douik, A. (2016). Content Based Image Retrieval using Lo- cal and Global features descriptor. *Proceedings of International conference on Advanced Technologies for Signal and Image Processing (ATSIP)*, 151-154.

Kaced, K., Larbes, C., Ramzan, N., & Bounabi, M. (2017). Bat algorithm based maximum power point tracking for photovoltaic system under partial shading conditions. *Solar Energy, 158*, 490-503. 10.1016/j.solener.2017.09.063

Kahn, J. M., Katz, R. H., & Pister, K. S. J. (1999). Next century challenges: mobile networking for smart dust. *Proceedings of the ACM MobiCom'99*, 271–278. 10.1145/313451.313558

Kaliannan, J., Baskaran, A., Dey, N., & Ashour, A. S. (2016). Ant colony optimization algorithm based PID controller for LFC of single area power system with non-linearity and boiler dynamics. *World J. Model. Simul, 12*(1), 3–14.

Kaliszewski, I. (2004). Out of the mist—towards decision-maker-friendly multiple criteria decision making support. *European Journal of Operational Research, 158*(2), 293–307. doi:10.1016/j.ejor.2003.06.005

Kamal, S., Dey, N., Ashour, A. S., Ripon, S., Balas, V. E., & Kaysar, M. S. (2017). FbMapping: An automated system for monitoring Facebook data. *Neural Network World, 27*(1), 27–57. doi:10.14311/NNW.2017.27.002

Kamal, S., Dey, N., Nimmy, S. F., Ripon, S. H., Ali, N. Y., Ashour, A. S., ... Shi, F. (2016). Evolutionary framework for coding area selection from cancer data. *Neural Computing & Applications*, 1–23.

Kamal, S., Ripon, S. H., Dey, N., Ashour, A. S., & Santhi, V. (2016). A MapReduce approach to diminish imbalance parameters for big deoxyribonucleic acid dataset. *Computer Methods and Programs in Biomedicine, 131*, 191–206. doi:10.1016/j.cmpb.2016.04.005 PMID:27265059

Kamble, S. D., Thakur, N. V., & Bajaj, P. R. (2018). Fractal Coding Based Video Compression Using Weighted Finite Automata. *International Journal of Ambient Computing and Intelligence, 9*(1), 115–133. doi:10.4018/IJACI.2018010107

Kamisli, F. (2015). Block-Based Spatial Prediction and Transforms Based on 2D Markov Processes for Image and Video Compression. *IEEE Transactions on Image Processing, 24*(4), 1247–1260. doi:10.1109/TIP.2015.2400818 PMID:25675456

Karaa, W. B. A., Ashour, A. S., Sassi, D. B., Roy, P., Kausar, N., & Dey, N. (2016). Medline text mining: an enhancement genetic algorithm based approach for document clustering. In *Applications of Intelligent Optimization in Biology and Medicine* (pp. 267–287). Springer International Publishing. doi:10.1007/978-3-319-21212-8_12

Karaa, W. B. A., Ben Azzouz, Z., Singh, A., Dey, N. S., Ashour, A., & Ben Ghazala, H. (2016). Automatic builder of class diagram (ABCD): An application of UML generation from functional requirements. *Software, Practice & Experience, 46*(11), 1443–1458. doi:10.1002pe.2384

Karaa, W. B. A., Mannai, M., Dey, N., Ashour, A. S., & Olariu, I. (2016, August). Gene-disease-food relation extraction from biomedical database. In *International Workshop Soft Computing Applications* (pp. 394-407). Springer.

Karakostas, S. M. (2017). Bridging the gap between multi-objective optimization and spatial planning: A new post-processing methodology capturing the optimum allocation of land uses against established transportation infrastructure. *Transportation Planning and Technology, 40*(3), 305–326. doi:10.1080/03081060.2017.1283157

Karan, O., Bayraktar, C., Gümüşkaya, H., & Karlık, B. (2012). Diagnosing diabetes using neural net-works on small mobile devices. *Expert Systems with Applications, 39*(1), 54–60. doi:.eswa.2011.06.04610.1016/j

Karine, A., Toumi, A., Khenchaf, A., & Hassouni, M. (2017). Target Recognition in Radar Images Using Weighted Statistical Dictionary-Based Sparse Representation. *IEEE Geoscience and Remote Sensing Letters, 14*(12), 2403-2407.

Karlik, B., & Olgac, A. V. (2011). Performance Analysis of Various Activation Functions in Gen-eralized MLP Architectures of Neural Networks. *International Journal of Artificial Intelligence And Expert Systems, 1*(4), 111–122.

Karri, C., & Jena, U. (2016). Fast vector quantization using a Bat algorithm for image compression. *Engineering Science and Technology, an International Journal, 29*(2), 769-781. 10.1016/j.jestch.2015.11.003

Karthik, K. (2008). *Energy Conservation for Content-based Image Retrieval on Mobile Devices* (Master Thesis).

Kausar, N., Abdullah, A., Samir, B. B., Palaniappan, S., AlGhamdi, B. S., & Dey, N. (2016). Ensemble clustering algorithm with supervised classification of clinical data for early diagnosis of coronary artery disease. *Journal of Medical Imaging and Health Informatics*, *6*(1), 78–87. doi:10.1166/jmihi.2016.1593

Kausar, N., Palaniappan, S., Samir, B. B., Abdullah, A., & Dey, N. (2016). Systematic analysis of applied data mining based optimization algorithms in clinical attribute extraction and classification for diagnosis of cardiac patients. In *Applications of intelligent optimization in biology and medicine* (pp. 217–231). Springer International Publishing. doi:10.1007/978-3-319-21212-8_9

Kavitha, K., & Sudhamani, M. V. (2014). Object based image retrieval from Database using combined features. *Proceedings International conference on Signal and image processing*, 161-165. 10.1109/ICSIP.2014.31

Kazar, O. (1996). Design and implementation of a semantic network model. Memory Magister, 6-45.

Kekre, H. B., Bharadi, V. A., Thepade, S. D., Mishra, B. K., Ghosalkar, S. E., & Sawant, S. M. (2010). Content Based Image Retrieval using Fusion of Gabor Magnitude and Modified Block Truncation Coding. *Proceedings of International conference on Emerging Trends in Engineering and Technology (ICETET)*, 140-145.

Kennedy, J., & Eberhart, R. C. (1995). Particle swarm optimization. *Proc. of IEEE International Conference on Neural Networks*, 1942–1948. 10.1109/ICNN.1995.488968

Khalili-Damghani, K., Abtahi, A. R., & Tavana, M. (2014). A Decision Support System for Solving Multi-Objective Redundancy Allocation Problems. *Quality and Reliability Engineering International*, *30*(8), 1249–1262. doi:10.1002/qre.1545

Khan, K., Nikov, A., & Sahai, A. (2011). A fuzzy bat clustering method for ergonomic screening of office workplaces, S3T 2011. *Advances in Intelligent and Soft Computing*, *101/2011*, 59–66. doi:10.1007/978-3-642-23163-6_9

Khan, K., & Sahai, A. (2012a). A comparison of BA, GA, PSO, BP and LM for training feed forward neural networks in e-learning context. *Int. J. Intelligent Systems and Applications*, *4*(7), 23–29. doi:10.5815/ijisa.2012.07.03

Khan, K., & Sahai, A. (2012b). A fuzzy c-means bi-sonar-based Metaheuristic optimization algorithm.Int. *J. of Interactive Multimedia and Artificial Intelligence*, *1*(7), 26–32. doi:10.9781/ijimai.2012.173

Khattak, N. S., & Stockman, G. (2007). Shape and structure for image matching and retrieval. *Proceedings of International Conference on Machine Vision*, 79-84. 10.1109/ICMV.2007.4469277

Kim, L. Y. (2014). *Estimating network structure and propagation dynamics for an infectious disease: towards effective vaccine allocation* (Doctoral dissertation). Massachusetts Institute of Technology.

Kim, D. W., Kim, K. H., Jang, W., & Chen, F. F. (2002). Unrelated parallel machine scheduling with setup times using simulated annealing. *Robotics and Computer-integrated Manufacturing*, *18*(3-4), 223–231. doi:10.1016/S0736-5845(02)00013-3

Kim, D. W., Na, D. G., & Chen, F. F. (2003). Unrelated parallel machine scheduling with setup times and a total weighted tardiness objective. *Robotics and Computer-integrated Manufacturing*, *19*(1-2), 173–181. doi:10.1016/S0736-5845(02)00077-7

Kim, S., & Cho, N. I. (2014). Hierarchical Prediction and Context Adaptive Coding for Lossless Color Image Compression. *IEEE Transactions on Image Processing*, *23*(1), 445–449. doi:10.1109/TIP.2013.2293428 PMID:24490231

Kim, S., & Lee, H. J. (2016). RGBW image compression by low-complexity adaptive multi-level block truncation coding. *IEEE Transactions on Consumer Electronics*, *62*(4), 412–419. doi:10.1109/TCE.2016.7838094

Kiri, Y., Sugano, M., & Murata, M. (2007). On characteristics of multi-hop communication in large-scale clustered sensor networks. *IEICE Transactions on Communications E90-B*.

Kishore, R., Zhang, H., & Ramesh, R. (2006). Enterprise integration using the agent paradigm: Foundations of multi-agent-based integrative business information systems. *International Journal of Decision Support Systems*, *42*(1), 48–78. doi:10.1016/j.dss.2004.09.011

Klir, G. J., & Yuan, B. (1995). *Fuzzy Sets and Fuzzy Logic: Theory and Applications*. Englewood Cliffs, NJ: Prentice-Hall.

Kohonen, T. (1990). The self-organizing map. *Proceedings of the IEEE*, *78*(9), 1464–1480. doi:10.1109/5.58325

Komarasamy, G., & Wahi, A. (2012). An optimized K-means clustering tech- niqueusing bat algorithm.European J. *Scientific Research.*, *84*(2), 263–273.

Korhonen, P. (1997). Reference Direction Approach to Multiple Objective Linear Programming: Historical Overview. In Essay in Decision Making: A Volume in Honour of Stanley Zionts, (pp. 74-92). Berlin: Academic Press.

Korhonen, P., & Laakso, J. (1986). Solving Generalized Goal Programming Problems Using a Visual Interactive Approach. *European Journal of Operational Research*, *26*(3), 355–363. doi:10.1016/0377-2217(86)90137-2

Kressel, U., & SchÄurmann, J. (1997). Pattern classification techniques based on function approximation. In H. Bunke & P.S.P. Wang (Eds.), Handbook of Character Recognition and Document Image Analysis (pp. 49-78). World Scientific.

Krishnamachari, B., Estrin, D., & Wicker, S. (2002). Modeling data centric routing in wireless sensor networks. *Proceedings of IEEE INFOCOM*.

Krumeich, J., Werth, D., & Loos, P. (2014). Conceiving A Method For Viewpoint-Based Modeling Using Recommender Systems In A Multiple-User Environment – Conceptual Approach And Proof-Of-Concept. *Proceedings of twenty-Second European Conference on Information Systems*.

Kumar, A., Sagar, K. P., Kuppusamy, K. S., & Aghila, G. (2016). Machine learning based malware classification for Android applications using multimodal image representations. *Proceeding of 10th International Conference on Intelligent Systems and Control (ISCO)*, 1-6. 10.1109/ISCO.2016.7726949

Kumar, K., Nimmagadda, Y., Hong, Y.-J., & Lu, Y.-H. (2008). Energy Conservation by Adaptive Feature Loading for Mobile Content-based Image Retrieval. *Proceedings of International Symposium on Low Power Electronics and Design*. 10.1145/1393921.1393963

Kumar, R., Rajan, A., Talukdar, F. A., Dey, N., Santhi, V., & Balas, V. E. (2017). Optimization of 5.5-GHz CMOS LNA Parameters Using Firefly Algorithm. *Neural Computing & Applications*, *28*(12), 3765–3779. doi:10.100700521-016-2267-y

Kumar, S., & Nagarajan, N. (2013). Integrated Network Topological Control and Key Management for Securing Wireless Sensor Networks. *International Journal of Ambient Computing and Intelligence*, *5*(4), 12–24. doi:10.4018/ijaci.2013100102

Kyparisis, G. J., & Koulamas, C. (2006). Flexible flow shop scheduling with uniform parallel machines. *European Journal of Operational Research*, *168*(3), 985–999. doi:10.1016/j.ejor.2004.05.017

Labonnote, N., Skaar, C., & Rüther, P. (2017). The potential of decision support systems for more sustainable and intelligent constructions: a short overview. *Procedia Manufacturing, 12,* 33-41.

La, C. M., Marco, M., & Filippo, V. (2010). Automatic Image Representation and Clustering on Mobile Devices. *J. Mobile Multimedia*, *6*(2), 158–169.

Lambrou, T. P., & Panayiotou, C. G. (2009). A Survey on Routing Techniques Supporting Mobility in Sensor Networks. *Proceedings of the 5th international conference on Mobile Ad Hoc and Sensor Networks (MSN'09)*, 78-85. 10.1109/MSN.2009.37

Lamica, G. (2000). Scheduling jobs with release dates and tails on two unrelated parallel machines to minimize the makespan. *European Journal of Operational Research, 120*(2), 277–288. doi:10.1016/S0377-2217(99)00156-3

Le Pendu, M., Guillemot, C., & Thoreau, D. (2016). Inter-Layer Prediction of Color in High Dynamic Range Image Scalable Compression. *IEEE Transactions on Image Processing, 25*(8), 3585–3596. doi:10.1109/TIP.2016.2571559 PMID:27244738

Leandro dos Santos, C., & Askarzadeh, A. (2016). An enhanced bat algorithm approach for reducing electrical power consumption of air conditioning systems based on differential operator. *Applied Thermal Engineering, 99*, 834-840. 10.1016/j.applthermaleng.2016.01.155

Lecun, Y., Bottou, L., Bengio, Y., & Haffner, P. (1998). Gradient-based learning applied to document recognition. *Proceedings of the IEEE, 86*(11), 2278–2324. doi:10.1109/5.726791

Lee, S., & Yang, H. S. (2017). Quantisation-free binary feature aggregation for fast image representation. Electronics Letters, 53(22), 1470-1471. doi:10.1049/el.2017.2501

Lee, H., Aydin, N., Choi, Y., Lekhavat, S., & Irani, Z. (2017). A Decision Support System for Vessel Speed Decision in Maritime Logistics using Weather Archive Big Data. *Computers & Operations Research*. doi:10.1016/j.cor.2017.06.005

Lemma, T. A., & Bin Mohd Hashim, F. (2011). Use of fuzzy systems and Bat algorithm for exergy modelling in a gas turbine generator. *IEEE Colloquium on Humanities, Science and Engineering (CHUSER'2011)*, 305–310.

Lenc, K., & Vedaldi, A. (2015). Understanding image representations by measuring their equivariance and equivalence. *Proceeding of International Conference on Computer Vision and Pattern Recognition (CVPR)*, 991-999. 10.1109/CVPR.2015.7298701

Lequeux, J-L. (1998). *Manager with ERP*. Paris: Eyrolles.

Lev, A., & Furst, M. (1991). Recognition of Handwritten Hebrew One-Stroke Letters by Learning Syntactic Representations of Symbols. *IEEE Transactions on System Management and Cybernetics, 19*(5), 13086–1313.

Li, L., & Halpern, J. Y. (2001). Minimum energy mobile wireless networks revisited. *Proceedings of IEEE International Conference on Communications (ICC_01)*.

Li, L., Wu, D., Wu, J., Li, H., Lin, W., & Kot, A. C. (2016). Image Sharpness Assessment by Sparse Representation. *IEEE Transactions on Multimedia, 18*(6), 1085–1097. doi:10.1109/TMM.2016.2545398

Lin & Huang. (2017). Reliability analysis for a hybrid flow shop with due date consideration. *Reliability Engineering & System Safety*. 10.1016/j.ress.2017.07.008

Lin, C. T., Chiu, H., & Chu, P. Y. (2006). Agility index in the supply chain. *International Journal of Production Economics, 100*(2), 285–299. doi:10.1016/j.ijpe.2004.11.013

Lindsey, S., & Raghavendra, C. S. (2002). PEGASIS: power efficient gathering in sensor information systems. *Proceedings of the IEEE Aerospace Conference*. 10.1109/AERO.2002.1035242

Lindsey, S., Raghavendra, C. S., & Sivalingam, K. (2001). Data gathering in sensor networks using the energy delay metric. *Proceedings of the IPDPS Workshop on Issues in Wireless Networks and Mobile Computing*. 10.1109/IPDPS.2001.925196

Linn, R., & Zhang, W. (1999). Hybrid flow shop scheduling: A survey. *Computers & Industrial Engineering*, *37*(1–2), 57–61. doi:10.1016/S0360-8352(99)00023-6

Li, Q., Chen, D., Jiang, W., Liu, B., & Gong, J. (2016). Generalization of SPIHT: Set Partition Coding System. *IEEE Transactions on Image Processing*, *25*(2), 713–725. doi:10.1109/TIP.2015.2509253 PMID:26730707

Lisboa, I. C., Vieira, J., Mouta, S., Machado, S., Ribeiro, N., Silva, E., ... Pereira, A. F. (2016). An MCDM Approach to the Selection of Novel Technologies for Innovative In-Vehicle Information Systems. *International Journal of Decision Support System Technology*, *8*(1), 43–55. doi:10.4018/IJDSST.2016010103

Liu, Y., Chen, X., Ward, R.K., & Wang, Z. (2016). Image Fusion With Convolutional Sparse Representation. *IEEE Transaction on Signal Processing Letters, 23*(12), 1882-1886.

Liu, C. L., & Fujisawa, H. (2008). Classification and Learning Methods for Character Recognition: Advances and Remaining Problems. In S. Marinai & H. Fujisawa (Eds.), *Machine Learning in Document Analysis and Recognition: Studies in Computational Intelligence, 90*. Berlin: Springer. doi:10.1007/978-3-540-76280-5_6

Liu, C. L., & Nakagawa, M. (2001). Evaluation of prototype learning algorithms for nearest neighbor classifier in application to handwritten character recognition. *Pattern Recognition*, *34*(3), 601–615. doi:10.1016/S0031-3203(00)00018-2

Liu, P. (2011). A weighted aggregation operators multi-attribute group decision-making method based on interval-valued trapezoidal fuzzy numbers. *Expert Systems with Applications*, *38*(1), 1053–1060. doi:10.1016/j.eswa.2010.07.144

Liu, P., & Jin, F. (2012). A multi-attribute group decision-making method based on weighted geometric aggregation operators of interval-valued trapezoidal fuzzy numbers. *Applied Mathematical Modelling*, *36*(6), 2498–2509. doi:10.1016/j.apm.2011.09.006

Liu, X., Lei, H., Cheng, D., Bo, L., & Tao, D. (2016). Query-Adaptive Hash Code Ranking for Large-Scale Multi-View Visual Search. *IEEE Transactions on Image Processing*, *25*(10), 4514–4524. doi:10.1109/TIP.2016.2593344 PMID:27448359

Li, Z., Shi, K., Dey, N., Ashour, A. S., Wang, D., Balas, V. E., ... Shi, F. (2017). Rule-based back propagation neural networks for various precision rough set presented KANSEI knowledge prediction: A case study on shoe product form features extraction. *Neural Computing & Applications*, *28*(3), 613–630. doi:10.100700521-016-2707-8

Lootsma, F. A. (1999). *Multi-criteria decision analysis via ratio and difference judgment*. Kluwer, Academic Publishers. doi:10.1007/b102374

Lopez Riquelme, J. A., Soto, F., Suardiaz, J., Sanchez, P., Iborra, A., & Vera, J. A. (2009). Wireless Sensor Networks for precision horticulture in Southern Spain. *Computers and Electronics in Agriculture*, *68*(1), 25–35. doi:10.1016/j.compag.2009.04.006

Loughlin, D. H., Ranjithan, S. R., Brill, E. D. Jr, & Baugh, J. W. Jr. (2001). Genetic Algorithm Approaches for Addressing Unmodeled Objectives in Optimization Problems. *Engineering Optimization*, *33*(5), 549–569. doi:10.1080/03052150108940933

Lucas, L. F. R., Wegner, K., Rodrigues, N. M. M., Pagliari, C. L., da Silva, E. A. B., & de Faria, S. M. M. (2015). Intra Predictive Depth Map Coding Using Flexible Block Partitioning. *IEEE Transactions on Image Processing*, *24*(11), 4055–4068. doi:10.1109/TIP.2015.2456509 PMID:26353355

Luque, M., Ruiz, F., & Miettinen, K. (2011). Global formulation for interactive multiobjective optimization. *OR-Spektrum*, *33*(1), 27–48. doi:10.100700291-008-0154-3

M. C. (2013, June 23). *Type 1 diabetes Diagnosis at Mayo Clinic.* Retrieved May 15, 2014, from Mayo Clinic: http://www.mayoclinic.org/diseases-con-ditions/type-1-diabetes/basics/tests-diagnosis/con-

Macedo, M., Avila, S., Zucchi, R., & Faria, F. (2017). *Mid-level Image Representation for Fruit Fly Identification.* Diptera: Tephritidae. .10.1109/eScience.2017.33

Mahendran, A., & Vedaldi, A. (2015). Understanding Deep Image Representations by Inverting Them. *Proceeding of International Conference on Computer Vision and Pattern Recognition (CVPR)*, 5188-5196. 10.1109/CVPR.2015.7299155

Mahesh, C., Suresh, V. G., & Babu, M. (2013). Diagnosing Hepatitis B Using Artificial Neural Net-work Based Expert System. *International Journal of Engineering and Innovative Technology*, *3*(6), 139–144.

Mahmudur, Md., Desai, B. C., & Bhattacharya, P. (2006). A Feature Level Fusion in Similarity Matching to Content-Based Image Retrieval. *Proceedings of International conference in Information Fusion*, 1-6.

Ma, L., Li, H., Meng, F., Wu, Q., & Ngan, K. N. (2017). Learning Efficient Binary Codes From High-Level Feature Representations for Multilabel Image Retrieval. *IEEE Transactions on Multimedia*, *19*(11), 2545–2560. doi:10.1109/TMM.2017.2703089

Malakouti, M., Rezaei, S., & Shahijan, M. K. (2017). Agile supply chain management (ASCM): A management decision-making approach. *Asia Pacific Journal of Marketing and Logistics*, *29*(1), 171–182. doi:10.1108/APJML-02-2016-0031

Malczewski, J. (2006). Decision Analysis for Collaborative GIS. In *Collaborative geographic information systems.* IGI Global; doi:10.4018/978-1-59140-845-1.ch010

Mandic, K., Delibasic, B., & Radojevic, D. (2015). An application of the integrated IBA-TOPSIS model in supplier selection. *International Journal of Decision Support System Technology*, *7*(1), 1–16. doi:10.4018/ijdsst.2015010102

Manjeshwar, A., & Agrawal, D. P. (2001). TEEN: a protocol for enhanced efficiency in wireless sensor network. *Proceedings of the 1st International Workshop on Parallel and Distributed Computing Issues in Wireless Networks and Mobile Computing.* 10.1109/IPDPS.2001.925197

Manjeshwar, A., & Agrawal, D. P. (2002). APTEEN: a hybrid protocol for efficient routing and comprehensive information retrieval in wireless sensor networks. *Proceedings of the 2nd International Workshop on Parallel and Distributed Computing Issues in Wireless Networks and Mobile computing.* 10.1109/IPDPS.2002.1016600

Manogaran, G., & Lopez, D. (2017). Disease surveillance system for big climate data processing and dengue transmission. *International Journal of Ambient Computing and Intelligence*, *8*(2), 88–105. doi:10.4018/IJACI.2017040106

Mantas, J. (1986). An overview of character recognition methodologies. *Pattern Recognition, 19*(6), 425-430.

Mao, L. (2013, November). Cost-effectiveness of workplace closure and travel restriction for mitigating influenza outbreaks: a network-based simulation. In *Proceedings of the Second ACM SIGSPATIAL International Workshop on the Use of GIS in Public Health* (pp. 77-84). ACM. 10.1145/2535708.2535709

Marichelvam, M. K., Prabaharan, T., Yang, X.-S., & Geetha, M. (2013). Solving hybrid flow shop scheduling problems using bat algorithm. *International Journal of Logistics Economics and Globalisation*, *5*(1), 15. doi:10.1504/IJLEG.2013.054428

Markess, I. (2013). Expectations of business for management solutions integrated ERP / PGI meet new challenges 2011-2013. Repository of Practices.

Markland, R., Vickery, S. K., & Davis, R. A. (1995). *Operation management: Concepts manufacturing and services.* New York: The West Publishing Company.

Matthies, M., Giupponi, C., & Ostendorf, B. (2007). Environmental decision support systems: Current issues, methods and tools. *Environmental Modelling & Software*, *22*(2), 123–127. doi:10.1016/j.envsoft.2005.09.005

McClelland, J. L. (2013, February 6). *Explorations in parallel distributed processing: A handbook of models, programs, and exercises*. Stanford, CA: Academic Press.

McIlro, M. D. (1968). Mass produced software components. *Proceedings NATO Conference on Software Engineering*.

Mekroud, N. (2009). *Integration of data mining techniques in the process of knowledge management based on case-based reasoning. Memory magister*. Ferhat Abbes-Sétif University.

Mesbahi, N., & Kazar, O. (2014-A). *An agent-based modelling for an enterprise resource planning (ERP). Proceedings of the 6th Asian Conference on Intelligent Information and Database Systems ACIIDS 2014*, 551, 225-234.

Mesbahi, N., & Kazar, O. (2014b). *A cooperative multi-agent approach for knowledge discovery from the enterprise resource planning*. Paper presented in the 3rd IEEE International Workshop on Advanced Information Systems for Enterprises (IWAISE'14), Tunis, Tunisia.

Mesbahi, N., Kazar, O., Benharzallah, S., Zoubeidi, M., & Bourekkache, S. (2015). Multi-Agents approach for data mining based k-Means for improving the decision process in the ERP systems. *International Journal of Decision Support System Technology*, *7*(2), 1–14. doi:10.4018/IJDSST.2015040101

Mhetre, N. A., Deshpande, A. V., & Mahalle, P. N. (2016). Trust management model based on fuzzy approach for ubiquitous computing. *International Journal of Ambient Computing and Intelligence*, *7*(2), 33–46. doi:10.4018/IJACI.2016070102

Microsoft. (n.d.). *NET Framework Developer Center*. Retrieved from http://msdn.microsoft.com/fr-fr/vstudio/aa496123

Miettinen, K. (1999). *Nonlinear Multiobjective Optimization. Academic Publishers*. Boston: Kluwer.

Miettinen, K., & Mäkelä, M. (2002). On Scalarizing Functions in Multiobjective Optimization. *OR-Spektrum*, *24*, 193–213. doi:10.100700291-001-0092-9

Miettinen, K., & Mäkelä, M. (2006). Synchronous Approach in Interactive Multiobjective Optimization. *European Journal of Operational Research*, *170*(3), 909–922. doi:10.1016/j.ejor.2004.07.052

Minassians, A., Dervisoglu, G., & Gutnik, L. (2007). Wireless sensor networks for home health care. AINAW.

Mishra, S., Shaw, K., & Mishra, D. (2012a). new meta-heuristic bat Inspired classification approach for microarray data. *Procedia Technology.*, *4*, 802–806. doi:10.1016/j.protcy.2012.05.131

Mistry, Y., Ingole, D. T., & Ingole, M. D. (2016). Efficient Content based Image Retrieval using Transform and Spatial Feature Level Fusion. *Proceedings of International conference on control, Automation and Robotics (ICCAR)*, 299-303. 10.1109/ICCAR.2016.7486744

Mohamed & Moftah. (2017). Simultaneous Ranking and Selection of Keystroke Dynamics Features Through A Novel Multi-Objective Binary Bat Algorithm. *Future Computing and Informatics Journal*. 10.1016/j.fcij.2017.11.005

Mohammadiam, M. (2004). Intelligent Agents for Data Mining and Information Retrieval. Idea Group Inc. doi:10.4018/978-1-59140-194-0

Mohri, M., Rostamizadeh, A., & Talwalkar, A. (2012). *Foundations of Machine Learning*. MIT Press.

Mokeddem, S., Atmani, B., & Mokaddem, M. (2014). A New Approach for Coronary Artery Diseases Diagnosis Based on Genetic Algorithm. *International Journal of Decision Support System Technology*, *6*(4), 1–15. doi:10.4018/ijdsst.2014100101

Moncef, G., Iftikhar, A., Yasir, A. M., & Serkan, K. (2006). Content-based image retrieval for connected mobile devices. *Proceedings of the Second International Symposium on Communications, Control and Signal Processing, ISCCSP 2*, 13-15.

Mora, M., Wang, F., Gómez, J. M., & Shevchenko, V. S. T. (2017). Decision-making support systems in quality management of higher education institutions: A selective review. *International Journal of Decision Support System Technology*, *9*(2), 56–79. doi:10.4018/IJDSST.2017040104

Mori, S., Yamamoto, K., & Yasuda, M. (1984). Research on Machine Recognition of Handprinted Characters. *IEEE Transactions on Pattern Analysis and Machine Intelligence*, *6*(4), 386–405. doi:10.1109/TPAMI.1984.4767545 PMID:21869208

Mor, N., Rahul, N., & Kaplun, V. (2008). Photos on the go: a mobile application case study. In *CHI '08: Proceeding of the twenty-sixth annual SIGCHI conference on Human factors in computing systems* (pp. 1739–1748). New York: ACM.

Mowrer, H. T. (2000). Uncertainty in natural resource decision support systems: Sources, interpretation and importance. *Computers and Electronics in Agriculture*, *27*(1-3), 139–154. doi:10.1016/S0168-1699(00)00113-7

Nakayama, H., & Sawaragi, Y. (1984). Satisficing Trade-off Method for Multiobjective Programming. Lecture Notes in Economics and Mathematical Systems, 229, 113-122.

Narula, S., Kirilov, L., & Vassilev, V. (1992). Reference Direction Approach for Solving Multiple Objective Nonlinear Programming Problems. In *Proceedings of X-th International Conference on Multiple Criteria Decision Making* (*vol. 2*, pp. 355-362). Taipei, Taiwan: Academic Press.

Narula, S., Kirilov, L., & Vassilev, V. (1994). Reference Direction Approach for Solving Multiple Objective Nonlinear Problems. *Transactions on Systems, Man and Cybernetics*, *24*(5), 804–806. doi:10.1109/21.293497

Nassar, M. (2003). VUML: a Viewpoint Oriented UML extension. *Proceedings (ASE 2003) International Conference on Automated Software Engineering*, 373–376. doi:10.1109/ ASE.2003.1240341

Natarajan, A., Subramanian, S., & Premalatha, K. (2012). A comparative study of cuckoo search and bat algorithm for Bloom filter optimisation in spam filtering. *International Journal of Bio-inspired Computation*, *4*(2), 89–99. doi:10.1504/IJBIC.2012.047179

Nath, A., & Niculescu, D. (2002). Routing on a curve. HOTNETS 1.

Necir, H., & Drias, H. (2007). *Data mining approach for customer relationship management: application to customizing an e-commerce site*. Paper presented at the 4th International Conference on Sciences of Electronic, Technologies of Information and Telecommunications.

Nejati, M., Samavi, S., Karimi, N., Soroushmehr, S. M. R., & Najarian, K. (2016). Boosted Dictionary Learning for Image Compression. *IEEE Transactions on Image Processing*, *25*(10), 4900–4915. doi:10.1109/TIP.2016.2598483

Ngan, C.-K., & Li, L. (2015). H-EQPE Model and L-Checkpoint Algorithm: A Decision-Guidance Approach for Detecting Hypoglycemia of Diabetes Patients. *International Journal of Decision Support System Technology*, *7*(4), 20–35. doi:10.4018/IJDSST.2015100102

Ngan, T. T., Tuan, T. M., Minh, N. H., & Dey, N. (2016). Decision Making Based on Fuzzy Aggregation Operators for Medical Diagnosis from Dental X-ray images. *Journal of Medical Systems*, *40*(12), 280. doi:10.100710916-016-0634-y PMID:27787784

Nicchiotti, G., & Scagliola, C. (2000). A simple and effective cursive word segmentation method. *Seventh International Workshop on Frontiers in Handwriting Recognition*, 499-504.

Nichols, H. (2014, March 3). *What is the difference between diabetes type 1 and diabetes.* Retrieved May 15, 2014, from Medical News Today: http://www. medicalnewstoday.com/articles/7504.php

Nimmy, S. F., Kamal, M. S., Hossain, M. I., Dey, N., Ashour, A. S., & Shi, F. (2017). Neural Skyline Filtering for Imbalance Features Classification. *International Journal of Computational Intelligence and Applications*, *16*(03), 1750019. doi:10.1142/S1469026817500195

Ning, Q., Zhu, J., Zhong, Z., & Steven, C. H. (2017). Scalable Image Retrieval by Sparse Product Quantization. *IEEE Transactions on Multimedia*, *19*(3), 586–597. doi:10.1109/TMM.2016.2625260

Noda, M., & Sonobe, H. (2002). Cosmos: Convenient Image Retrieval System of Flowers for Mobile Computing Situations. *Proceedings of IASTED Conference on Information Systems and Databases*, 25-30.

Norese, M. F., Rolando, D., & Fregonara, E. (2015). Integration of problem structuring methods: A methodological proposal for complex regional decision-making processes. *International Journal of Decision Support System Technology*, *7*(2), 1–26. doi:10.4018/IJDSST.2015040104

Olcay, G., & Moncef, G. (2005). Content-Based Image Indexing and Retrieval Framework on Symbian Based Mobile Platform. *Proceedings of 13th European Signal Processing Conference, EUSIPCO 2005.*

OMG. (n.d.). *OMG Homepage*. Retrieved from http://www.omg.org

Osaba, E., Yang, X.-S., Diaz, F., Lopez-Garcia, P., & Carballedo, R. (2016). An improved discrete bat algorithm for symmetric and asymmetric Traveling Salesman Problems. *Engineering Applications of Artificial Intelligence, 48*, 59-71. 10.1016/j.engappai.2015.10.006

Panchal, D., & Shah, S. (2011). Artificial Intelligence Based Expert System For Hepatitis B Diagnosis. *International Journal of Modeling and Optimiza-tion*, *1*(4), 362–366. doi:10.7763/IJMO.2011.V1.61

Pancham, A., Withey, D., & Bright, G. (2015). Tracking Image Features with PCA-SURF Descriptors. *Proceedings of International conference on Machine Vision Applications (MVA)*, 365-368.

Parmann, E. (2010). *MMIR4 – Mobile Multimodal Image Retrieval. TR No. 11*. CAIM-UIB.

Pasquier, N. (2000). *Data Mining: Algorithms of extraction and reduction of association rules in the database* (Doctoral thesis). Clermont-Ferrand 2 University.

Pastor-Satorras, R., Castellano, C., Van Mieghem, P., & Vespignani, A. (2014). *Epidemic processes in complex networks.* arXiv preprint arXiv:1408.2701.

Patel, B. S., Samuel, C., & Sharma, S. K. (2017). Evaluation of agility in supply chains: A case study of an Indian manufacturing organization. *Journal of Manufacturing Technology Management*, *28*(2), 212–231. doi:10.1108/JMTM-09-2016-0125

Pedregosa, F., Varoquaux, G., Gramfort, A., Michel, V., Thirion, B., Grisel, O., & ... . (2011). Scikit-learn: Machine Learning in {P}ython. *Journal of Machine Learning Research*, *12*, 2825–2830.

Pestotnik, S. L. (2005). Expert Clinical Decision Support Systems to Enhance Antimicrobial Steward-ship Programs. *Pharmacotherapy*, *25*(8), 1116–1125. doi:10.1592/phco.2005.25.8.1116 PMID:16207103

Peter, P., Kaufhold, L., & Weickert, J. (2017). Turning Diffusion-Based Image Colorization Into Efficient Color Compression. *IEEE Transactions on Image Processing*, *26*(2), 860–869. doi:10.1109/TIP.2016.2627800 PMID:27849527

Philippe, P. (2006). *From information to knowledge*. Research Paper, Orléans University.

Phoksawat, K., & Mahmuddin, M. (2016). Ontology-based knowledge and optimization model for Decision Support System to intercropping. *Proceedings of the 2016 IEEE International Computer Science and Engineering Conference (ICSEC)*. 10.1109/ICSEC.2016.7859927

Phoksawat, K., & Mahmuddin, M. (2017). Hybrid Ontology-based knowledge with multi-objective optimization model framework for Decision Support System in intercropping. *Advances in Science, Technology and Engineering Systems Journal*, *2*(3), 1363–1371. doi:10.25046/aj0203172

Poleto, T., & Carvalho, V. (2017). The full knowledge of big data in the integration of inter-organizational information. *International Journal of Decision Support System Technology*, *9*(1), 16–31. doi:10.4018/IJDSST.2017010102

Poole, D., & Mackworth, A. (2010). Avoiding Overfitting. In D. Poole & A. Mackworth (Eds.), Artificial Intelligence: Foundations of Computational Agents. Cambridge University Press.

Portmann, M. C., Vignier, A., Dardilhac, D., & Dezalay, D. (1998). Branch and bound crossed with GA to solve hybrid flowshops. *European Journal of Operational Research*, *107*(2), 389–400. doi:10.1016/S0377-2217(97)00333-0

Pottie, G. J., & Kaiser, W. J. (2000). Wireless integrated network sensors. *Communications of the ACM*, *43*(5), 551–558. doi:10.1145/332833.332838

Power, D. J. (2008). Decision support systems: a historical overview. In *Handbook on Decision Support Systems* (pp. 121–140). Springer.

Preux P. (2011). *Notes on Data Mining*. Lille 3 University.

Puccinelli, D., & Haenggi, M. (2005). Wireless Sensor Networks: Applications and Challenges of Ubiquitous Sensing. *IEEE Circuits and Systems Magazine*, *5*(3), 19–29. doi:10.1109/MCAS.2005.1507522

Radermacher, A., Cuccuru, A., Gérard, S., & Hamid, B. (2013, September 24-26). Split of Composite Components for Distributed Applications (regular paper). In *Proceedings of the Forum on Specification & Design Languages FDL 2013)*. Paris, France: IEEE Computer Society.

Rahimi, M., Baer, R., Iroezi, O. I., Garcia, J. C., Warrior, J., Estrin, D., & Srivastava, M. (2005). Cyclops: in situ image sensing and interpretation in wireless sensor networks. *Proceedings of the Third International Conference on Embedded Networked Sensor Systems (Sensys)*. 10.1145/1098918.1098939

Ramesh, B., Mohan, V. C. J., & Reddy, V. C. V. (2013). Application of bat algorithm for combined economic load and emission dispatch.Int. *J of Electricl Engineering and Telecommunications.*, *2*(1), 1–9.

Razzaque, A., & Thakur, N. V. (2012). An approach to image compression with partial encryption without sharing the secret key. *International Journal of Computer Science and Network Security*, *12*(7).

Reddy, P. V. N., & Satya Prasad, K. (2010). Image retrieval system for natural images based on local features. *Advances in Information Mining, 2*(2).

Reddy, V. U., & Manoj, A. (2012). Optimal capacitor placement for lossReduction in distribution systems using bat algorithm. *IOSR Journal of Engineering.*, *2*(10), 23–27. doi:10.9790/3021-021052327

Rehioui, F., & Hair, A. (2014). Towards a Modeling approach based on Software Components. *International Journal of Computers and Applications*, *99*(1), 10–17. doi:10.5120/17336-7178

Rehioui, F., & Hair, A. (2016). Towards a New Combination and Communication Approach of Software Components. *International Journal of Decision Support System Technology (IJDSST)*. doi:10.4018/IJDSST.2016100101

Renaux, E., Caron, O., & Geib, J. M. (2003). The Component Unified Process Project. In *Proceedings of SEA'03* (pp. 669-647). ACTA Press.

Ripon, S. H., Kamal, S., Hossain, S., & Dey, N. (2016). Theoretical Analysis of Different Classifiers under Reduction Rough Data Set: A Brief Proposal. *International Journal of Rough Sets and Data Analysis*, *3*(3), 1–20. doi:10.4018/IJRSDA.2016070101

Rittgen, P. (2009). Collaborative Modeling - A Design Science Approach. In *Proceedings of the 42nd Hawaii International Conference on System Sciences (HICSS '09)*. IEEE Computer Society.

Robertson, G., Lehmann, E. D., Sandham, W., & Hamilton, D. (2011). Blood Glucose Prediction Using Artificial Neural Networks Trained with the AIDA Diabetes Simulator: A Proof-of-Concept Pilot Study. *Journal of Electrical and Computer Engineering*, *2011*, 1–11. doi:10.1155/2011/681786

Rodoplu, V., & Ming, T. H. (1999). Minimum energy mobile wireless networks. *IEEE Journal on Selected Areas in Communications*, *17*(8), 1333–1344. doi:10.1109/49.779917

Romero, C. (2001). Extended lexicographic goal programming: A unified approach. *Omega*, *29*(1), 63–71. doi:10.1016/S0305-0483(00)00026-8

Roy, B. (1978). ELECTRE III: Un algorithme de classement fondé sur une représentation floue des préférences en présence de critères multiples. *Cahiers du CERO*, *20*(1), 3–24.

Roy, P., Goswami, S., Chakraborty, S., Azar, A. T., & Dey, N. (2014). Image segmentation using rough set theory: A review. *International Journal of Rough Sets and Data Analysis*, *1*(2), 62–74. doi:10.4018/ijrsda.2014070105

Ruiz, A., Sindhya, K., Miettinen, K., Ruiz, F., & Luque, M. (2015). E-NAUTILUS: A decision support system for complex multiobjective optimization problems based on the NAUTILUS method. *European Journal of Operational Research*, *246*(1), 218–231. doi:10.1016/j.ejor.2015.04.027

Ruiz, F., Luque, M., & Miettinen, K. (2012). Improving the computational efficiency in global formulation (GLIDE) for interactive multi-objective optimization. *Annals of Operations Research*, *197*(1), 47–70. doi:10.100710479-010-0831-x

Rumelhart, D. E., & McClelland, J. L. (1986). Parallel distributed processing: explorations in the microstructure of cognition: Vol. 1. *Foundations*. Cambridge, MA: MIT Press.

Russell, S., & Forgionne, G. (2009). Decision Support-Related Resource Presence and Availability Awareness for DSS in Pervasive Computing Environments. *International Journal of Decision Support System Technology*, *1*(1), 15–34. doi:10.4018/jdsst.2009010102

Rytkönen, M. J. (2004). Not all maps are equal: GIS and spatial analysis in epidemiology. *International Journal of Circumpolar Health*, *63*(1). doi:10.3402/ijch.v63i1.17642 PMID:15139238

Saaty, T. L. (1980). *The Analytic Hierarchy Process*. New York: McGraw-Hill.

Sahu A. K., Sahu, N. K. & Sahu, A. K. (2017b). Performance Estimation of Firms by GLA Supply Chain under Imperfect Data. *Theoretical and Practical Advancements for Fuzzy System Integration*, 245-277.

Sahu N. K., Sahu, A. K. & Sahu, A. K. (2017c). Fuzzy-AHP: A Boon in 3PL Decision Making Process. *Theoretical and Practical Advancements for Fuzzy System Integration*, 97-125.

Sahu, A. K., Sahu, A. K., & Sahu, N. K. (2017d). Benchmarking of Advanced Manufacturing Machines Based on Fuzzy-TOPSIS Method. *Theoretical and Practical Advancements for Fuzzy System Integration*, 309-350.

Sahu, A. K., Sahu, N. K., & Sahu, A. K. (2017e). Fuzziness: A Mathematical Tool. *Theoretical and Practical Advancements for Fuzzy System Integration*, 1-30.

Sahu, A. K., Sahu, A. K., & Sahu, N. K. (2017a). Appraisements of material handling system in context of fiscal and environment extent: A comparative grey statistical analysis. *International Journal of Logistics Management*, *28*(1), 2–28. doi:10.1108/IJLM-09-2015-0163

Sahu, A. K., Sahu, N. K., & Sahu, A. (2014). Appraisal of CNC machine tool by integrated MULTI MOORA-IGVN circumstances: An empirical study. *Journal of Grey Systems: Theory and Application*, *4*(1), 104–123. doi:10.1108/GS-11-2013-0028

Sahu, A. K., Sahu, N. K., & Sahu, A. K. (2015). Benchmarking CNC machine tool using hybrid fuzzy methodology a multi indices decision making approach. *International Journal of Fuzzy System Applications*, *4*(2), 28–46. doi:10.4018/IJFSA.2015040103

Sahu, A. K., Sahu, N. K., & Sahu, A. K. (2016a). Application of Integrated TOPSIS in ASC index: Partners Benchmarking perspective. *Benchmarking: An International Journal*, *23*(3), 540–563. doi:10.1108/BIJ-03-2014-0021

Sahu, A. K., Sahu, N. K., & Sahu, A. K. (2016b). Appraisal of Partner Enterprises under GTFNS Environment in Agile SC. *International Journal of Decision Support System Technology*, *8*(3), 1–19. doi:10.4018/IJDSST.2016070101

Sahu, A. K., Sahu, N. K., & Sahu, A. K. (2016c). Application of Modified MULTI-MOORA for CNC Machine Tool Evaluation in IVGTFNS Environment: An Empirical Study. *International Journal of Computer Aided Engineering and Technology*, *8*(3), 234–259. doi:10.1504/IJCAET.2016.077603

Samuel, D., Adrien, D., Ivan, E., & Henning, M. (2011). Mobile Medical Image Retrieval. In *Medical Imaging 2011: Advanced PACS-based Imaging Informatics and Therapeutic Applications* (p. 79670G). Orlando, FL: SPIE.

Sanches, C., Ferreira, J. S. Jr, Santos, G., Paixão, M. R., & Meireles, M. (2018). TODA: Software for Multiple-Criteria Decisions. *International Journal of Decision Support System Technology*, *10*(1), 1–20. doi:10.4018/IJDSST.2018010101

Sarkar, M., Banerjee, S., Badr, Y., & Sangaiah, A. K. (2017). Configuring a Trusted Cloud Service Model for Smart City Exploration Using Hybrid Intelligence. *International Journal of Ambient Computing and Intelligence*, *8*(3), 1–21. doi:10.4018/IJACI.2017070101

Sarvas, R., Herrarte, E., Wilhelm, A., & Davis, M. (2004). *Metadata Creation System for Mobile Images. MobiSys.* Boston: ACM Press.

Satapathy, S. C., Raja, N. S. M., Rajinikanth, V., Ashour, A. S., & Dey, N. (2016). Multi-level image thresholding using Otsu and chaotic bat algorithm. *Neural Computing & Applications*, 1–23.

Satapathy, S. C., Raja, N. S. M., Rajinikanth, V., Ashour, A. S., & Dey, N. (2016). Multi-level Image Thresholding Using Otsu and Chaotic Bat Algorithm. *Neural Computing & Applications*, 1–23.

Savic, D. A., Bicik, J., & Morley, M. S. (2011). GANETXL: A DSS Generator for Multiobjective Optimisation of Spreadsheet Based Models. *Environmental Modelling & Software*, *26*(5), 551–561. doi:10.1016/j.envsoft.2010.11.004

Schurgers, C., & Srivastava, M. B. (2001). Energy efficient routing in wireless sensor networks. *The MILCOM Proceedings on Communications for Network-Centric Operations: Creating the Information Force.* 10.1109/MILCOM.2001.985819

Secundo, G., Magarielli, D., Esposito, E., & Passiante, G. (2017). Supporting decision-making in service supplier selection using a hybrid fuzzy extended AHP approach: A case study. *Business Process Management Journal*, *23*(1), 196–222. doi:10.1108/BPMJ-01-2016-0013

Seletos, T., & Salmon, J. (2017). Analysis of Integrating a Production Design Generator with a Business Decision Support System for System-Level Decision Making. *Systems, 5*(14).

Selmane, S. A., Boussaid, O., & Bentayeb, F. (2015). Towards Collaborative Multidimensional Query Recommendation with Triadic Association Rules. *International Journal of Decision Support System Technology (IJDSST)*. doi:10.4018/ijdsst.2015070102

Senior, A. W., Robinson, A. J., (1998). An Offline Cursive Handwriting Recognition System. *IEEE Transactions on Pattern Analysis and Machine Intelligence*, *20*(3), 309-321.

Sezer, O. G., Guleryuz, O. G., & Altunbasak, Y. (2015). Approximation and Compression With Sparse Orthonormal Transforms. *IEEE Transactions on Image Processing*, *24*(8), 2328–2343. doi:10.1109/TIP.2015.2414879 PMID:25823033

Shahvari, O., & Logendran, R. (2018). A comparison of two stage-based hybrid algorithms for a batch scheduling problem in hybrid flow shop with learning effect. *International Journal of Production Economics, 195*, 227-248. 10.1016/j.ijpe.2017.10.015

Shaikh, R.A., Lee, Y.K., & Lee, S. (2010). An Extended Energy Consumption Analysis of Reputation-based Trust Management Schemes of Wireless Sensor Networks. *Journal of Networks, 5*(3), 283-291.

Sharma, K., & Virmani, J. (2017). A Decision Support System for Classification of Normal and Medical Renal Disease Using Ultrasound Images: A Decision Support System for Medical Renal Diseases. *International Journal of Ambient Computing and Intelligence*, *8*(2), 52–69. doi:10.4018/IJACI.2017040104

Sharp, J. M., Irani, Z., & Desai, S. (1999). Working towards agile manufacturing in the UK Industry. *International Journal of Production Economics*, *62*(1-2), 155–169. doi:10.1016/S0925-5273(98)00228-X

Shee, D. Y., & Wang, Y. S. (2008). Multi-criteria evaluation of the Web-based e-learning system: A methodology based on learner satisfaction and its applications. *Computers & Education*, *50*(3), 894–905. doi:10.1016/j.compedu.2006.09.005

Sheikh, E., & Guindi, R. M. (1998). Computer Recognition of Arabic Cursive Scripts. *Pattern Recognition*, *21*(4), 216–223.

Shen, C., Srisathapornphat, C., & Jaikaeo, C. (2001). Sensor information networking architecture and applications. *IEEE Personal Communications*, 52–59.

Shen, H., Pan, W. D., & Wu, D. (2017). Predictive Lossless Compression of Regions of Interest in Hyperspectral Images With No-Data Regions. *IEEE Transactions on Geoscience and Remote Sensing*, *55*(1), 173–182. doi:10.1109/TGRS.2016.2603527

Shen, V. Y., & Chen, Y. E. (1972). A scheduling strategy for the flow shop problem in a system with two classes of processors. *Conference on Information and Systems Science*, 45-649.

Shih, E., Cho, S., Ickes, N., Min, R., Sinha, A., Wang, A., & Chandrakasan, A. (2001). Physical layer driven protocol and algorithm design for energy-efficient wireless sensor networks. *Proceedings of ACM MobiCom'01*, 272–286. 10.1145/381677.381703

Shim, J. P., Warkentin, M., Courtney, J. F., Power, D. J., Sharda, R., & Carlsson, C. (2002). Past, present, and future of decision support technology. *Decision Support Systems*, *33*(2), 111–126. doi:10.1016/S0167-9236(01)00139-7

Shi, X., Guo, Z., Zhang, D., & Fang, X. (2015). Multiple Features Fusion Based Inverted Multi-Index for Image Retrieval. *Proceedings of International Conference on Virtual Reality and Visualization (ICVRV)*, 148-153. 10.1109/ICVRV.2015.39

Shweta, T., & Sapna, C. (2012). The architecture of an Automated CBA System Using ERP Model. *International Journal of Scientific and Research Publications*, *2*(10).

Silva, A. M. R., & Sobral, M. F. F. (2017). Multicriteria Model to Sort Suppliers in a Brazilian Dairy Industry. *International Journal of Decision Support System Technology*, *9*(3), 42–53. doi:10.4018/IJDSST.2017070103

Simard, P.Y., Steinkraus, D., & Platt, J. (2003). Best practices for convolutional neural networks applied to visual document analysis. *ICDAR*, 958–962.

Simon, H. (1960). *The New Science of Management Decisions*. New York: Harper Row. doi:10.1037/13978-000

Singh, A., Dey, N., & Ashour, A. S. (2017). *Scope of Automation in Semantics-Driven Multimedia Information Retrieval From Web*. IGI Global. doi:10.4018/978-1-5225-2483-0.ch001

Sinha, A., & Chandrakasan, A. (2001). Dynamic power management in wireless sensor networks. *IEEE Design & Test of Computers*, *18*(2), 62–74. doi:10.1109/54.914626

Sohrabi, K., Gao, J., Ailawadhi, V., & Pottie, G. J. (2000). Protocols for self-organization of a wireless sensor network. *IEEE Personal Communications*, *7*(5), 16–27. doi:10.1109/98.878532

Soltan, H., & Mostafa, S. (2015). Lean and Agile Performance Framework for Manufacturing Enterprises. *Procedia Manufacturing*, *2*, 476–484. doi:10.1016/j.promfg.2015.07.082

Sonobe, H., Takagi, S., & Yoshimoto, F. (2004). Mobile Computing System for Fish Image Retrieval. *International Workshop on Advanced Image Technology*, 33-37.

Sosnin, P. (2016). Precedent-Oriented Approach to Conceptually Experimental Activity in Designing the Software Intensive Systems. *International Journal of Ambient Computing and Intelligence (IJACI)*. doi:10.4018/IJACI.2016010104

Sreeram, I., & Venkata, P. K. V. (2017). HTTP flood attack detection in application layer using machine learning metrics and bio inspired bat algorithm. *Applied Computing and Informatics*. 10.1016/j.aci.2017.10.003

Sriskandarajah, C., & Sethi, S. P. (1989). Scheduling algorithms for flexible flow shops: Worst and average performance. *European Journal of Operational Research*, *43*(2), 143–160. doi:10.1016/0377-2217(89)90208-7

Srivastava, B. (1998). An effective heuristic for minimizing makespan on unrelated parallel machines. *The Journal of the Operational Research Society*, *49*(8), 886–894. doi:10.1057/palgrave.jors.2600547

Stalk, G., & Thomas, H. (1990). *Competing against time*. New York: The Free Press.

Staykov, B., Andonov, F., Vatov, D., Genova, K., Kirilov, L., & Guliashki, V. (2011). Architecture of a flexible web-based framework for building models and solving decision optimization problems. In *Proceedings of XLVI Int. Scientific Conference on Information, Communication and Energy Systems and Technologies - ICEST2011* (*vol. 2*, pp. 857-860). Nis, Serbia: Academic Press.

Steuer, R. (1986). *Multiple Criteria Optimization: Theory, Computation and Applications*. New York: John Wiley & Sons, Inc.

Steuer, R., & Choo, E. (1983). An interactive weighted Tchebycheff procedure for multiple objective programming. *Mathematical Programming*, *26*(3), 326–344. doi:10.1007/BF02591870

Stilianakis, N., & Weber, T. (2008). Epidemiological Modeling, Surveillance and Web-Based Information Systems. *International Disaster and Risk Conference IDRC Davos 2008, Proceedings*.

Strand, M., Syberfeldt, A., & Geertsen, A. (2017). A Decision Support System for Sustainable Waste Collection. *International Journal of Decision Support System Technology*, *9*(4), 49–65. doi:10.4018/IJDSST.2017100104

Straub, J. (2014). Evaluation of a Multi-Goal Solver for Use in a Blackboard Architecture. *International Journal of Decision Support System Technology*, *6*(1), 1–13. doi:10.4018/ijdsst.2014010101

Strutz, T. (2016). Context-Based Predictor Blending for Lossless Color Image Compression. *IEEE Transactions on Circuits and Systems for Video Technology*, *26*(4), 687–695. doi:10.1109/TCSVT.2015.2416611

Subramanian, L., & Katz, R. H. (Aug 2000). An architecture for building self configurable systems. *Proceedings of IEEE/ACM Workshop on Mobile Ad Hoc Networking and Computing*. 10.1109/MOBHOC.2000.869214

Suen, C. Y., Tappert, C. C., & Wakahara, T. (1990). The State of the Art in On-Line Handwriting Recognition. *IEEE Transactions on Pattern Analysis and Machine Intelligence*, *12*(8), 787–808. doi:10.1109/34.57669

Sukati, I., Hamid, A. B., Baharun, R., & Yusoff, R. M. (2012). The Study of Supply Chain Management Strategy and Practices on Supply Chain Performance. *Procedia: Social and Behavioral Sciences*, *40*, 225–233. doi:10.1016/j.sbspro.2012.03.185

Sumathy, M., Kumar, P., Jishnujit, T. M., & Kumar, K. R. (2010). Diagnosis of Diabetes Mel-litus based on Risk Factors. *International Journal of Computers and Applications*, *10*(4).

Sun. (2014). *E.J.B HomePage*. Retrieved from www.oracle.com/technetwork/java/javaee/ejb/index.html

Sun, C., & Yang, E. H. (2015). An Efficient DCT-Based Image Compression System Based on Laplacian Transparent Composite Model. *IEEE Transactions on Image Processing*, *24*(3), 886–900. doi:10.1109/TIP.2014.2383324 PMID:25532182

Sural, S., Qian, G., & Pramanik, S. (2012). Segmentation and histogram generation using the HSV color space for Image retrieval. *Proceedings of International conference on image processing, 2*, 589-592.

Symeonidis, A., Chatzidimitriou, C., Athanasiadis, I., & Pericles, M. (2007). Data mining for agent reasoning: A synergy for training intelligent agents. *Engineering Applications of Artificial Intelligence, Elsevier*, *20*(8), 1097–1111. doi:10.1016/j.engappai.2007.02.009

Tamiru, A. L., & Hashim, F. M. (2013). Application of bat algorithm and Fuzzy systems to model exergy changes in a gas turbine. In Artificial Intelligence, Evolutionary Computing and Metaheuristics. Springer. doi:10.1007/978-3-642-29694-9_26

Tan, H.O., & Korpeoglu, I. (2003). Power efficient data gathering and aggregation in wireless sensor networks. *ACM SIGMOD Record, 32*(4), 66–71.

Tang, L., Luh, P. B., Liu, J., & Fang, L. (2002). Steel-making process scheduling using Lagrangian relaxation. *International Journal of Production Research*, *40*(1), 55–70. doi:10.1080/00207540110073000

Tang, L., Xuan, H., & Liu, J. (2006). Anew Lagrangian relaxation algorithm for hybrid flowshop scheduling to minimize total weighted completion time. *Computers & Operations Research*, *33*(11), 3344–3359. doi:10.1016/j.cor.2005.03.028

Tang, R., Fong, S., Dey, N., Wong, R. K., & Mohammed, S. (2017). Cross Entropy Method Based Hybridization of Dynamic Group Optimization Algorithm. *Entropy (Basel, Switzerland)*, *19*(10), 533. doi:10.3390/e19100533

Tapia, D. I., & Corchado, J. M. (2009). An Ambient Intelligence Based Multi-Agent System for Alzheimer Health Care. *International Journal of Ambient Computing and Intelligence*, *1*(1), 15–26. doi:10.4018/jaci.2009010102

Tappert, C. C. (1984). Adaptive on-line handwriting recognition. *Proc of. 7th Int. Conf. Pattern Recognition*, 1004-1007.

Temurtas, H., Yumusak, N., & Temurtas, F. (2009). A comparative study on diabetes disease diagnosis using neural networks. *Expert Systems with Applications*, *36*(4), 8610–8615. doi:10.1016/j.eswa.2008.10.032

Thakur, N. V., & Kakde, O. G. (2006). A Novel Compression Technique for Color Image Database. *Proceeding of International Conference on Advanced Computing and Communications*, 240-243.

Thakur, N. V., & Kakde, O. G. (2007). Color Image Compression on Spiral Architecture using Optimized Domain Blocks in Fractal Coding. *Proceeding of Fourth International Conference on Information Technology,* 234-242. 10.1109/ITNG.2007.51

Thakur, N. V., & Kakde, O. G. (2006). Fractal Color Image Compression on a Pseudo Spiral Architecture. *Proceeding of IEEE Conference on Cybernetics and Intelligent Systems*, 1-6.

Thakur, N. V., & Kakde, O. G. (2007). Color Image Compression with Modified Fractal Coding on Spiral Architecture. *Journal of Multimedia, 2*(4), 55–66. doi:10.4304/jmm.2.4.55-66

Thakur, N. V., & Kakde, O. G. (2009). Compression mechanism for multimedia system in consideration of information security. *Proceeding of International workshop on Machine intelligence Research*, 87-96.

Thakur, N. V., & Koli, N. A. (2010). An Overview of Feature Extraction Methods in CBIR. *International Journal of Computer Science and Applications., 3*(2), 71–76.

Tilak, S., Abu-Ghazaleh, N. B., & Heinzelman, W. (2002). A taxonomy of wireless microsensor network models. *Mobile Computing and Communications Review, 6*(2), 28–36. doi:10.1145/565702.565708

Tilak, S., Abu-Ghazaleh, N., & Heinzelman, W. (2002). Infrastructure tradeoffs for sensor networks. In *Proceedings of the 1st ACM international workshop on Wireless sensor networks and applications, WSNA '02*. ACM. 10.1145/570738.570746

Tolle, G., Polastre, J., Szewczyk, R., Culler, D., Turner, N., Tu, K., ... Hong, W. (2005). A macroscope in the redwoods. *Proceedings of the Third International Conference on Embedded Networked Sensor Systems (Sensys)*. 10.1145/1098918.1098925

Tran, A., Ippoliti, C., Balenghien, T., Conte, A., Gely, M., Calistri, P., & Chevalier, V. (2013). A geographical information system-based multicriteria evaluation to map areas at risk for rift valley fever vector-borne transmission in Italy. *Transboundary and Emerging Diseases, 60*(s2), 14–23. doi:10.1111/tbed.12156 PMID:24589097

Tsakona, A., Paschali, K., Tsolis, D., & Skapetis, G. (2013). Proposed Electronic Medical Record with Emphasis on Hepatitis Diagnosis. *International Journal of Caring Sciences, 6*(2), 138–145.

Tseng, Y., Wang, Y., Cheng, K., & Hsieh, Y. (2007). iMouse: An Integrated Mobile Surveillance and Wireless Sensor System. IEEE Computer Society, 40(6), 60-66.

Tsourveloudis, N. C., & Valavanis, K. P. (2002). On the measurement of enterprise agility. *International. Journal of Intelligent & Robotic Systems, 33*(3), 329–342. doi:10.1023/A:1015096909316

Tyagi, S., Som, S., & Rana, Q. P. (2017). Trust based Dynamic Multicast Group Routing Ensuring Reliability for Ubiquitous Environment in MANETs. *International Journal of Ambient Computing and Intelligence, 8*(1), 70–97. doi:10.4018/IJACI.2017010104

Ullmann, J. R. (1986). Advances character recognition in Applications of Pattern Recognition. CRC Press.

Vasilescu, I., Kotay, K., Rus, D., Dunbabin, M., & Corke, P. (2005). Data collection, storage, retrieval with an underwater sensor network. *Proceedings of the Third International Conference on Embedded Networked Sensor Systems (Sensys)*. 10.1145/1098918.1098936

Vassileva, M., Miettinen, K., & Vassilev, V. (2005). *Generalized scalarizing problem for multicriteria optimization*. IIT Working Papers IIT/WP-205, Institute of Information Technologies, Bulgaria.

Vassileva, M. (2006). Generalized Scalarizing Problems GENS and GENSLEX of Multicriteria Optimization. *International Journal of Information Theories and Applications, 13*, 111–120.

Vassileva, M., Genova, K., & Vassilev, V. (2001). A Classification Based Interactive Algorithm of Multicriteria Linear Integer Programming. *Cybernetics and Information Technologies*, *1*, 5–20.

Vassilev, V. (2002). A generalized scalarizing problem of multicriteria optimization. *Cybernetics and Information Technologies*, *2*, 88–100.

Vassilev, V., Kirilov, L., & Atanassov, A. (1992). Reference Direction Approach for Solving Multiple Objective Programming Problems. *Problems of Engineering Cybernetics and Robotics*, *38*, 17–23.

Vassilev, V., & Narula, S. (1993). A Reference Direction Algorithm for Solving Multiple Objective Integer Linear Programming Problems. *The Journal of the Operational Research Society*, *44*(12), 1201–1209. doi:10.1057/jors.1993.199

Vassilev, V., Narula, S., & Gouljashki, V. (2001). An Interactive Reference Direction Algorithm for Solving Multi-Objective Convex Nonlinear Integer Programming Problems. *International Transactions in Operational Research*, *8*(4), 367–380. doi:10.1111/1475-3995.00271

Velmani, R., & Kaarthick, B. (2009). An Efficient Cluster-Tree Based Data Collection Scheme for Large Mobile Wireless Sensor Networks. IEEE Sensors Journal, 15(4), 2377–2390.

Vignier, Billaut, & Proust. (1999). Scheduling problems type hybrid flow-shop: State of the art. RAIRO. *Recherche opérationnelle, 33*(2), 117-183.

Vijay Kumar, Y. N., Sivanagaraju, S., & Chintalapudi, V. S. (2016). Security constrained economic load dispatch in the presence of interline power flow controller using modified BAT algorithm. *Ain Shams Engineering Journal, 7*(4), 1029-1043. 10.1016/j.asej.2015.07.003

Vijay, C., Chen, D. M., Zhi, L., Gabriel, T., Tsai, S. S., Radek, G., & Bernd, G. (2009). Low-rate image retrieval with tree histogram coding. *Proceedings of the 5th International ICST Mobile Multimedia Communications Conference.*

Villemin, F.Y. (2010). Agent Communication Language. *Intelligent Systems NFP2012.*

Wahyunggoro, O., Permanasari, A. E., & Chamsudin, A. (2013). Utilization of Neural Network for Disease Forecasting. *59th ISI World Statistics Congress*, 549-554.

Wajgi, D., & Thakur, N. V. (2012, August). Load Balancing Algorithms in Wireless Sensor Networks: A Survey. *International Journal of Computer Networks and Wireless Communications*, *2*(4), 456–460.

Walker, W. E., Harremoes, P., Rotmans, J., Van der Sluis, J. P., Van Asselt, M. B. A., Janssen, P., & Krayer von Krauss, M. P. (2003). Defining uncertainty – a conceptual basis for uncertainty management in model-based decision support. *Integrated Assessment*, *4*(1), 5–17. doi:10.1076/iaij.4.1.5.16466

Walsh, M. J., Barton, J., O'Flynn, B., Hayes, M. J., O'Mathuna, C., & Alavi, S. M. (2011). An Antiwindup Approach to Power Controller Switching in an Ambient Healthcare Network. *International Journal of Ambient Computing and Intelligence*, *3*(2), 35–55. doi:10.4018/jaci.2011040103

Wang, J., Xiong, J., Yang, K., Peng, S., & Xu, Q. (2010). Use of GIS and agent-based modeling to simulate the spread of influenza. In *Geoinformatics, 2010 18th International Conference on* (pp. 1-6). IEEE. 10.1109/GEOINFORMATICS.2010.5567658

Wang, D., He, T., Li, Z., Cao, L., Dey, N., Ashour, A. S., ... Shi, F. (2016b). Image feature-based affective retrieval employing improved parameter and structure identification of adaptive neuro-fuzzy inference system. *Neural Computing & Applications*, 1–16.

Wang, D., Li, Z., Cao, L., Balas, V. E., Dey, N., Ashour, A. S., & Shi, F. (2016a). Image Fusion Incorporating Parameter Estimation Optimized Gaussian Mixture Model and Fuzzy Weighted Evaluation System: A Case Study in Time-Series Plantar Pressure Data Set. *IEEE Sensors Journal*, *17*(5), 1407–1420. doi:10.1109/JSEN.2016.2641501

Wang, D., Li, Z., Dey, N., Ashour, A. S., Sherratt, R. S., & Shi, F. (2017). Case-Based Reasoning for Product Style Construction and Fuzzy Analytic Hierarchy Process Evaluation Modeling Using Consumers Linguistic Variables. *IEEE Access : Practical Innovations, Open Solutions*, *5*, 4900–4912. doi:10.1109/ACCESS.2017.2677950

Wang, F., Zuo, W., Lin, L., Zhang, D., & Zhang, L. (2016). Joint Learning of Single-Image and Cross-Image Representations for Person Re-identification. *Proceeding of IEEE Conference on Computer Vision and Pattern Recognition (CVPR)*, 1288-1296. 10.1109/CVPR.2016.144

Wang, G., & Li, X. (1998). The applications of interval-valued fuzzy numbers and interval-distribution numbers. *Fuzzy Sets and Systems*, *98*(3), 331–335. doi:10.1016/S0165-0114(96)00368-5

Wang, J., & Zhu, Z. (2010). Image retrieval system based on multi-feature fusion and relevance feedback. *Proceedings of International Conference on Machine Learning and Cybernetics*, 4, 2053-2058. 10.1109/ICMLC.2010.5580505

Wang, M., Li, H., Tao, D., Ke, L., & Wu, X. (2012). Multimodal Graph-Based Rerank- ing for Web Image Search. *IEEE Transactions on Image Processing*, *21*(11), 4649–4661. doi:10.1109/TIP.2012.2207397 PMID:22829401

Wang, X. F., & Chen, G. (2003). Complex networks: Small-world, scale-free and beyond. *Circuits and Systems Magazine*, *3*(1), 6–20. doi:10.1109/MCAS.2003.1228503

Wang, X., Ke, L., & Tang, X. (2011). Query-Specific Visual Semantic Spaces for Web Image Re-ranking. *Proceedings of International conference on Computer Vision and Pattern Recognition (CVPR)*, 857-864) 10.1109/CVPR.2011.5995399

Ward, B. W., & Black, L. I. (2016). State and Regional Prevalence of Diagnosed Multiple Chronic Conditions Among Adults Aged ≥18 Years — United States, 2014. *Morbidity and Mortality Weekly Report*, *65*(29), 735–738. doi:10.15585/mmwr.mm6529a3 PMID:27467707

Ward, J. R., & Kuklinski, T. (1988). A Model for Variability Effects in Handwriting Character Recognition Systems. *IEEE Transactions on Systems, Man, and Cybernetics*, *18*(3), 438–451. doi:10.1109/21.7493

Wasyluk, H. A., & Raś, Z. W. (2010). Action Rules Approach to Solving Diagnostic Problems in Clinical Medicine. In G. Devlin (Ed.), Decision Support Systems Advances (pp. 99-106). InTech.

Watts, D. J., & Strogatz, S. H. (1998). Collective dynamics of 'small-world' networks. *Nature, 393*(6684), 440-442.

Wein, L. M., & Atkinson, M. P. (2009). Assessing infection control measures for pandemic influenza. *Risk Analysis*, *29*(7), 949–962. doi:10.1111/j.1539-6924.2009.01232.x PMID:19392673

Wei, S. H., & Chen, S. M. (2009). Fuzzy risk analysis based on interval-valued fuzzy numbers. *Expert Systems with Applications*, *36*(2), 2285–2299. doi:10.1016/j.eswa.2007.12.037

Wenfei, D., Yu, S., Liu, S., & Zhiqiang, Z. &, Gu, W. (2014). Image retrieval based on multi-feature fusion. *Proceedings of International conference on Instrumentation and Measurement, Computer, Communications and Control*, 240-243.

Werner-Allen, G., Lorincz, K., Welsh, M., Marcillo, O., Johnson, J., Ruiz, M., & Lees, J. (2006). Deploying a wireless sensor network on an active volcano. *IEEE Internet Computing*, *10*(2), 18–25. doi:10.1109/MIC.2006.26

Wierzbicki, A. P. (2007). Reference Point Approaches and Objective Ranking. *Practical Approaches to Multi-Objective Optimization.* Retrieved from http://drops.dagstuhl.de/volltexte/2007/1121/pdf/06501.WierzbickiAndrzej.Paper.1121.pdf

Wierzbicki, A. P. (1980). The Use of Reference Objectives in Multiobjective Optimization. *Lecture Notes in Economics and Mathematical Systems, 177*, 468–486. doi:10.1007/978-3-642-48782-8_32

Wierzbicki, A. P. (1986). On the completeness and constructiveness of parametric characterizations to vector optimization problems. *OR-Spektrum, 8*(2), 73–87. doi:10.1007/BF01719738

Wolf, J., Burgard, W., & Burkhardt, H. (2002). Using an Image Retrieval System for Vision-Based Mobile Robot Localization. LNCS, 2383, 108–119. doi:10.1007/3-540-45479-9_12

Wood-Harper, A. T., Antill, L., & Avison, D. E. (1985). *Information systems definition: The Multiview approach*. Oxford, UK: Blackwell Scientific Publications.

Woo, J.-I., Yang, J.-G., Lee, Y.-H., & Kang, U.-G. (2014). Healthcare Decision Support System for Administration of Chronic Diseases. *Healthcare Informatics Research, 20*(3), 173–182. doi:10.4258/hir.2014.20.3.173 PMID:25152830

Wu, H., Sun, X., Yang, J., Zeng, W., & Wu, F. (2016). Lossless Compression of JPEG Coded Photo Collections. *IEEE Transactions on Image Processing, 25*(6), 2684–2696. doi:10.1109/TIP.2016.2551366 PMID:27071170

Xavier, A., Xu, J. J., & Nuria, O. (2008). Multimodal photo annotation and retrieval on a mobile phone. *Proceeding of the 1st ACM international conference on Multimedia information retrieval.*

Xia, H., Chen, J., Marathe, M., & Mortveit, H. S. (2011). Synthesis and Refinement of Detailed Subnetworks in a Social Contact Network for Epidemic Simulations, Social Computing. *Behavioral-Cultural Modeling and Prediction, LNCS, 6589*, 366–373. doi:10.1007/978-3-642-19656-0_50

Xiao, L., Qian, F., & Shao, W. (2017). Multi-step wind speed forecasting based on a hybrid forecasting architecture and an improved bat algorithm. *Energy Conversion and Management, 143*, 410-430. 10.1016/j.enconman.2017.04.012

Xu, S., & Chen, L. (2008). A Novel Approach for Determining the Optimal Number of Hidden Layer Neurons for FNN's and Its Application in Data Mining. Proceedings of the 5th International Conference on Information Technology and Applications, 683-686.

Xu, Z., Du, J., & Ye, L. (2016). Multi-feature Indexing for image retrieval based on hyper- graph. *Proceedings of International conference on cloud computing and intelligence systems (CCIS)*, 494-500.

Xu, Y., Heidemann, J., & Estrin, D. (2001). Geography-informed energy conservation for ad hoc routing. *Proceedings of the 7th Annual ACM/IEEE International Conference on Mobile Computing and Networking (MobiCom_01).* 10.1145/381677.381685

Yang, F., Matei, B., & Davis, L. S. (2015). Re-ranking by Multi-feature fusion with diffusion for image retrieval. *Proceedings of winter conference on Applications of Computer Vision*, 572-579. 10.1109/WACV.2015.82

Yang, S. L., & Li, T. F. (2002). Agility evaluation of mass customization product manufacturing. *Journal of Materials Processing Technology, 129*(1-3), 640–644. doi:10.1016/S0924-0136(02)00674-X

Yang, W., Wang, X., Song, X., Yang, Y., & Patnaik, S. (2018). Design of Intelligent Transportation System Supported by New Generation Wireless Communication Technology. *International Journal of Ambient Computing and Intelligence, 9*(1), 78–94. doi:10.4018/IJACI.2018010105

Yang, X. S. (2009). Firefly Algorithms for Multimodal Optimization. *Lecture Notes in Computer Science, 5792*, 169–178. doi:10.1007/978-3-642-04944-6_14

Yang, X. S. (2010). A new metaheuristic bat-inspired algorithm. In *Nature Inspired Cooperative Strategies for Optimization* (pp. 65–74). Springer. doi:10.1007/978-3-642-12538-6_6

Yang, X. S. (2010). *Nature-Inspired Metaheuristic Algorithms* (2nd ed.). Frome, UK: Luniver Press.

Yap, K. K., Srinivasan, V., & Motani, M. (2005). MAX: Human-centric search of the physical world. *Proceedings of the Third International Conference on Embedded Networked Sensor Systems (Sensys)*. 10.1145/1098918.1098937

Yazdani, M., & Zarate, P. (2017). Flood Risk Assessment: A MCDM Approach. *Proceedings of the Int. Conference on DSS Technology, Data, Information and Knowledge Visualization in DSSs*, 177-183.

Yeh, T., Tollmar, K., & Darrell, T. (2004). Searching the Web with Mobile Images for Location Recognition. *Proceedings of IEEE Computer Society Conference on Computer Vision and Pattern Recognition*, 76-81. 10.1109/CVPR.2004.1315147

Yeomans, J. S. (2017a). Simultaneous Computing of Sets of Maximally Different Alternatives to Optimal Solutions. *International Journal of Engineering Research and Applications*, *7*(9), 21–28.

Yeomans, J. S. (2017b). An Optimization Algorithm that Simultaneously Calculates Maximally Different Alternatives. *International Journal of Computational Engineering Research*, *7*(10), 45–50.

Yeomans, J. S. (2018). An Efficient Computational Procedure for Simultaneously Generating Alternatives to an Optimal Solution Using the Firefly Algorithm. In X. S. Yang (Ed.), *Nature-Inspired Algorithms and Applied Optimization* (pp. 261–273). Cham, Switzerland: Springer. doi:10.1007/978-3-319-67669-2_12

Yeomans, J. S., & Gunalay, Y. (2011). Simulation-Optimization Techniques for Modelling to Generate Alternatives in Waste Management Planning. *Journal of Applied Operational Research*, *3*(1), 23–35.

Yick, J., Mukherjee, B., & Ghosal, D. (2008). Wireless sensor network survey. *Elsevier. Computer Networks*, *52*(12), 2292–2330. doi:10.1016/j.comnet.2008.04.002

Yigin, I. H., Taskin, H., Cedimoglu, I. H., & Topal, B. (2007). Supplier selection: An expert system approach. *Production Planning and Control*, *18*(1), 16–24. doi:10.1080/09537280600940655

Younis, M., Youssef, M., & Arisha, K. (2002). Energy-aware routing in cluster-based sensor networks. *Proceedings of the 10th IEEE/ACM International Symposium on Modeling, Analysis and Simulation of Computer and Telecommunication Systems (MASCOTS2002)*. 10.1109/MASCOT.2002.1167069

Younsi, F. Z., Bounekkar, A., & Hamdadou, D. (2014, May). *SW-SEIR: un modèle de suivi de propagation d'épidémies.* Paper presented at the meeting of 8ème édition de la Conférence Avancées des Systèmes Décisionnels (ASD), Hammamet, Tunisia.

Younsi, F. Z., Bounnekar, A., Hamdadou, D., & Boussaid, O. (2015a). SEIR-SW, simulation model of influenza spread based on the Small World network. *Tsinghua Science and Technology*, *20*(5), 460–473. doi:10.1109/TST.2015.7297745

Younsi, F. Z., Hamdadoud, D., & Boussaid, O. (2015b). A surveillance and spatiotemporal visualization model for infectious diseases using social network. *International Journal of Decision Support System Technology*, *7*(4), 1–19. doi:10.4018/IJDSST.2015100101

Youssuf, M. A. (1993). The impact of the intensity level of computer-based technologies on quality. *International Journal of Operations & Production Management*, *14*(4), 4–25. doi:10.1108/01443579410056010

Yu, Y., Estrin, D., & Govindan, R. (2001). *Geographical and energy aware routing: a recursive data dissemination protocol for wireless sensor networks.* UCLA Computer Science Department Technical Report. UCLA-CSD TR-01-0023.

Yuan, H., Ye, L., & Du, L. (2011). A Novel Method for Image Feature Fusion based on MADM. *Proceedings of International conference on Multimedia Technology (ICMT)*, 2877-2879.

Yu, Q., Yu, W., Yang, P., Zheng, J., Zheng, X., & He, Y. (2015). An Efficient Adaptive Binary Arithmetic Coder Based on Logarithmic Domain. *IEEE Transactions on Image Processing*, *24*(11), 4225–4239. doi:10.1109/TIP.2015.2462089 PMID:26241975

Yusuf, Y. Y., Ren, J., & Burns, N. D. (2001). A method of evaluating enterprise agility-an empirical study. *Proceedings of the 16th International Conference on Production Research,* 168-175.

Zadeh, L. (1963). Optimality and Non-Scalar-valued Performance Criteria. *IEEE Transactions on Automatic Control*, *8*(1), 59–60. doi:10.1109/TAC.1963.1105511

Zadeh, L. A. (1965). Fuzzy sets. *Information and Control*, *8*(3), 338–353. doi:10.1016/S0019-9958(65)90241-X

Zadeh, L. A. (1975). The concept of a linguistic variable and its application to approximate reasoning. *Information Sciences*, *8*(3), 199–249. doi:10.1016/0020-0255(75)90036-5

Zechman, E. M., & Ranjithan, S. R. (2004). An Evolutionary Algorithm to Generate Alternatives (EAGA) for Engineering Optimization Problems. *Engineering Optimization*, *36*(5), 539–553. doi:10.1080/03052150410001704863

Zeinolabedin, S. M. A., Zhou, J., Liu, X., & Kim, T. T. H. (2015). An Area- and Energy-Efficient FIFO Design Using Error-Reduced Data Compression and Near-Threshold Operation for Image/Video Applications. *IEEE Transactions on Very Large Scale Integration (VLSI) Systems*, *23*(11), 2408–2416.

Zemri, A., & Hamdadou, D. (2017). *Integration of Data Mining Techniques in Multi Criteria Spatial Decision Support System for Epidemiological Monitoring. International Journal of Decision Support System Technology.*

Zhang, P., Sadler, C. M., Lyon, S. A., & Martonosi, M. (2004). Hardware design experiences in ZebraNet. *Proceedings of the SenSys'04*. 10.1145/1031495.1031522

Zhang, S., Yang, M., Cour, T., Yu, K., & Metaxas, D. N. (2015). Query Specific Rank Fusion For Image Retrieval. *IEEE Transactions on Pattern Analysis and Machine Intelligence*, *37*(4), 803–815. doi:10.1109/TPAMI.2014.2346201 PMID:26353295

Zhang, S., Zhang, C., & Yang, Q. (2003). Data preparation for data mining. *Applied Artificial Intelligence*, *17*(6), 375–381. doi:10.1080/713827180

Zhang, W., Qi, Q., & Deng, J. (2017). Building Intelligent Transportation Cloud Data Center Based on SOA. *International Journal of Ambient Computing and Intelligence*, *8*(2), 1–11. doi:10.4018/IJACI.2017040101

Zhang, Y., Wu, J., & Cai, J. (2016). Compact Representation of High-Dimensional Feature Vectors for Large-Scale Image Recognition and Retrieval. *IEEE Transactions on Image Processing*, *25*(5), 2407–2419. doi:10.1109/TIP.2016.2549360 PMID:27046897

Zhang, Z., Zhang, C., & Zhang, S. (2003). An agent-based hybrid framework for database mining. *Journal of Applied Artificial Intelligence*, *17*(5-6), 383–398. doi:10.1080/713827179

Zheng, L., Wang, S., Liu, Z., & Qi, T. (2014). Packing and Padding: Coupled Multi-index for Accurate Image Retrieval. Proceedings of International conference on computer vision and pattern recognition, 1947-1954.

Zheng, L., Wang, S., Lu, T., Fei, H., Liu, Z., & Qi, T. (2015). Query-Adaptive Late Fusion for Image Search and Person Re-identification. *Proceedings of International conference on computer vision and pattern recognition*, 1741- 1750. 10.1109/CVPR.2015.7298783

Zimmermann, H. J. (1996). *Fuzzy set theory and its applications*. Boston: Kluwer Academic Publishers. doi:10.1007/978-94-015-8702-0

About the Contributors

Ahmad Al-Khasawneh is a professor of computer information systems. He holds the PhD and M.Sc. of information and software systems and technology from Newcastle University, Australia and B.S in computer and automatic control engineering. Dr. Khasawneh has 22 years of experience in ICT field and in ICT applications and acts as technical advisor to the Royal Jordanian Airlines (NDC Jordan) director on issues related to the development of travel industry and ICT strategy. Prior to joining the Hashemite University of Jordan, he held several key positions with major international ICT consultancy and solutions firms and lecturer in IT related topics at Newcastle University, Australia. One of his key positions is the founder and director of eLearning center and, he is the former dean of the Prince Hussein Bin Abdullah II for Information Technology at Hashemite University. Currently, he is the director of center of information and communication technology and eLearning. He is the contact person (at HU) for two Tempus projects; and three erasmus+ project, and a head and member of the many committees of another Tempus and Erasmus+ project.

Khaled Belkadi has been a Research-professor at the USTO-MB (University of Sciences and Technology of Oran, Mohamed Boudiaf) since September 6, 1987. He has a PhD in computer science in July 1986 in Clermont Ferrand (France). He obtained a Doctorate in computer science in December 2006 in Oran (Algeria). K. Belkadi works in modelling, simulation, optimization and performance evaluation of manufacturing systems and hospital systems.

Saber Benharzallah is an associate professor in the computer science department of Batna 2 University (Algeria). Dr. Benharzallah is currently the team leader of semantic interoperability and their applications in information systems and web services, in LINFI laboratory (Biskra University). His current research interests include knowledge management, internet of things, semantic interoperability, and context management.

Salem Chakhar joined the Portsmouth Business School in August 2013 as a Research Fellow in the Operations & Systems Management subject group. He has a PhD in Computer Science from the University of Paris-Dauphine (Paris, France), an MPhil degree in Computer Science and Modelling from the High School of Management of Tunis (Tunis, Tunisia), and a degree in Computer Science from the Faculty of Economics and Management, University of Sfax (Sfax, Tunisia). He worked at the Centre for Research in Regional Planning and Development, University Laval (Québec, QC, Canada), the University of Paris-Dauphine (Paris, France), the High School of Economic and Commercial Sciences (University of Tunis, Tunisia), the Institute of Higher Commercial Studies (University of Carthage, Tunisia), and Regional Institute in Computer Sciences and Telecommunications (Tunis, Tunisia). He is a member of the International Cartographic Association (ICA) commission on geospatial analysis and modelling.

Lalit B. Damahe has received Diploma in Electrical Engineering from BTE, Mumbai, India, in 1998, B.E. Degree in Computer Technology from Rashtrasant Tukdoji Maharaj Nagpur University, Nagpur, India, in 2003, M. Tech. Degree in CSE from Rashtrasant Tukdoji Maharaj Nagpur University, Nagpur, India, in 2010. Presently, he is pursuing PhD in Computer Science and Engineering from Sant Gadge Baba Amravati University, Amravati, India. He has more than 12 years of experience in teaching. Currently, he is working as Assistant Professor in Computer Technology at Yeshwantrao Chavan College of Engineering, Nagpur, India. His areas of interest are Image Processing and Computer Graphics, Computer Networks and Computer vision. He is the member of ACM and IACSIT professional society and he has more than 10 papers in National/International Conferences/Journals to his credit.

Latifa Dekhici is a lecturer at the department of computers sciences, mathematics and computing faculty, university of sciences and the technology of Oran, Mohamed Boudiaf (USTO-MB). In her PhD thesis, she worked in modeling, discrete simulation and scheduling of the operating theatres of Oran. She is actually working in the field of home heathcare routing, hospital systems optimization as well as bi-objective optimization of the power systems design and dispatch using metaheuristics. L. Dekhici is attached to LAMOSI (Laboratory of Simulation of Systems of Industries).

Khaled Guerraiche received his BS degree in electrical engineering from the Electrical Engineering Institute of The University of Sciences and Technology of Oran (USTOMB) in 2004, the MS degree from the Electrical Engineering Institute of The University of Sciences and Technology of Oran (USTO) in 2008, and the PhD degree from the same Institute in 2016. He is currently a lecturer at The Higher School of Electrical Engineering and Energy, Oran, Algeria. K. Guerraiche research interests include operations, planning and economics of electric energy systems, as well as optimization theory and its applications.

Vassil G. Guliashki is currently an Associate Professor at the Institute of Information and Communication Technologies – Bulgarian Academy of Sciences (IICT - BAS), department "Information Processes and Decision Support Systems". He earned his Master of Science (Automation and System-Technique) at Technical University – Sofia, Bulgaria, in 1988 and his PhD in Technical Cybernetics from the Institute of Information Technologies – BAS (IIT – BAS since 1992) in 1994, with scientific advisors Prof. Vassil Vassilev and Prof. Vassil Sgurev. In his thesis work entitled "Algorithms for Solving Convex Nonlinear Integer Programming Problems" he created a Tabu Search heuristic algorithm for single objective problems and an interactive reference direction algorithm for multiple objective integer problems.

Djamila Hamdadou received her engineering degree in computer science and her MSc degree from the Computer Science Institute in 1993 and 2000, respectively. She also obtained her PhD degree in 2008. She received her HDR in 2012 from the Computer Science Department of the Faculty of Science. Her research interests include multicriteria decision support system, spatiotemporal modeling, geographic information system, and negotiation models.

Haneen Hijazi is an assistant tutor at Prince Al-Hussein bin Abdullah II Faculty of Information Technology at Hashemite University, Jordan. She is pursuing research on the fundamental principles of Software Engineering with an emphasis on projects and risk management, quality assurance, e-learning, neural networks, decision support systems and natural language processing. She holds a M.Sc. Degree in Computer Science with a concentration in Software Engineering from Al-balqa Applied University and B.Sc. degree in Software Engineering from the Hashemite University, Jordan, in 2006.

Sachin R. Jain has received Degree in Computer Technology from Rashtrasant Tukdoji Maharaj Nagpur University, Nagpur, India in 2002, M.Tech. in Computer Science & Engineering from Rashtrasant Tukdoji Maharaj Nagpur University, Nagpur, India in 2010. He is pursuing his PhD from Sant Gadge Baba Amravati University, Amrawati, India. He has more than 14 years of teaching experience. He is currently working in Information Technology Department, Yeshwantrao Chanvan College of Engineering, Nagpur, Maharashtra, India. His areas of interest are Wireless Sensor Networks, Internet of Things, Artificial Intelligence and Object Oriented Methodology. He is member of IAENG professional society and he has more than 20 papers in National/International Conferences/Journals to his credit.

Pr. Okba Kazar is an associate professor at computer science department of Biskra university. He is actually the chief of Smart Computing Laboratory. Pr. Kazar is interested to the multi-agents systems and their applications, advanced information systems, Web services, semantic Web. He is member of editorial board of the SJI Journal. He is an author of some publication in international journals and session chair in international conferences.

Leoneed M. Kirilov is currently an Associate Professor at the Institute of Information and Communication Technologies – Bulgarian Academy of Sciences (IICT - BAS), department "Information Processes and Decision Support Systems". He earned his Master of Science (Mathematics – Operations Research) at Sofia University in Sofia, Bulgaria, in 1984 and his PhD in Technical Cybernetics in 1992 from the Institute of Technical Cybernetics and Robotics – BAS (Inst. of Information Technologies (IIT) – BAS since 1992), working with Prof. Vassil Vassilev. In his thesis work entitled "Interactive Methods for Solving Multiple Objective Mathematical Programming Problems" he introduces new methods for solving linear and nonlinear Multiple Objective Programming Problems – MOPPs. One of them is the Reference Direction Approach for Solving Multiple Objective Programming Problems – MOPPs (RD method). It was applied to solve nonlinear MOPPs. His main research areas are Multiple Criteria Decision Making (MCDM) and Decision Support Systems (DSS).

Nadjib Mesbahi works as an executive in the Algerian Oil Company (Sonatrach Group), where he studied and developed several information systems. He finalizes his thesis at the LINFI Laboratory in the University of Biskra. His current research interests include enterprise resource planning (ERP), multi-agent systems, data mining and ontology.

Arvind R. Bhagat Patil has received B.E. degree in Computer Engineering from BNCOE, Pusad, India, in 1992, M. Tech. degree in Computer Science and Engineering from Nagpur University in 2009. Presently, he is pursuing PhD in Computer Science and Engineering from Rashtrasant Tukdoji Maharaj Nagpur University, Nagpur, India. He has more than 26 years of teaching and administration experience.

Currently, he is working as the Associate Professor in Department of Computer Technology is currently working as Dean (Planning and Development) at Yeshwantrao Chavan College of Engineering Nagpur, India. His areas of interest are Computer Network, Network Security, Cyber Science and Security. He is the member of ACM, ISTE and IE professional society and he has more than 35 papers in National/ International Conferences/Journals to his credit.

Fadoua Rehioui is Ph. D. student in Laboratory of Modeling and Computation, University Sultan Moulay Slimane, Morocco. She interests include integration of viewpoints and Object-Oriented Analysis /Design, Component Based System Engineering, etc. Her research topic is Software Engineering, Data mining, and Computer Sciences etc. She has 2 research articles in peer-reviewed journals.

Djamil Rezki obtained his Engineering degree in Computer Science from the University of Constantine, Algeria. He prepares his Doctorate thesis in Industrial Engineering Department, University of Batna, Algeria. He is interested in software engineering, artificial intelligence and manufacturing system.

Anoop Kumar Sahu is Post Doctoral Research Fellow (PDRF) in the department of Engineering & the Built Environment, Postgraduate School of Engineering Management, University of Johannesburg, South Africa. He obtained his Ph.D degree from National Institute of Technology, Rourkela, India.

Atul Kumar Sahu is Assistant Professor in the department of Industrial & Production Engineering, Guru Ghasidas Vishwavidyalaya (Central), Bilaspur, India and obtained his master degree in Production Engineering from National Institute of Technology, Rourkela, India

Nitin Kumar Sahu is Assistant Professor in the department of Industrial & Production Engineering, Guru Ghasidas Vishwavidyalaya (Central), Bilaspur, India and obtained his master degree in Production Engineering from Delhi College of Engineering, India.

Boris Staykov is a Research Associate at the Institute of Information and Communication Technologies – Bulgarian Academy of Sciences (IICT - BAS), department "Modelling and optimization" since 2004. He earned his Master of Science (Informatics and Information Technologies) at Technologies at New Bulgarian University in 2002. His main scientific interests are decision support systems – methods, algorithms and their software implementation.

Nileshsingh V. Thakur received Bachelor of Engineering degree in Computer Science Engineering from Government College of Engineering, Amravati, India and Master of Engineering degree from College of Engineering, Badnera under Amravati University and Sant Gadge Baba Amravati University in 1992 and 2005 respectively. He received Ph.D. degree in Computer Science Engineering under Department of Computer Science Engineering from Visvesvaraya National Institute of Technology, Nagpur, India on 1st February, 2010. His research interest includes image and video processing, sensor network, computer vision, pattern recognition, network security, artificial neural network, bio-inspired and evolutionary approaches. He is having over 25 years of teaching and research experience. Presently, he is Principal at Nagpur Institute of Technology, Nagpur, Maharashtra, India. He is the author or co-author of more than

90 scientific publications in refereed International Journal, International Conferences, National Journal, and National Conferences. He is a member of editorial board of over eight International journals; also, he is the life member of ISTE, India, IAENG and IAEME. He also worked as the reviewer for refereed international journals and conferences.

Rashmi R. Welekar has received B.E. Degree in Computer Science and Engineering from COE, Badnera, India, in 1999, M. Tech. Degree in Computer Science and Engineering from Nagpur University in 2007. Presently, she is pursuing PhD in Computer Science and Engineering from Rashtrasant Tukdoji Maharaj Nagpur University, Nagpur, India. She has more than 17 years of teaching and industry experience. Currently, she is working as the Assistant Professor in Computer Science and Engineering at Shri Ramdeobaba College of Engineering and Management, Nagpur, India. Her areas of interest are Bio-inspired Computing, Evolutionary Computing, Pattern Recognition and Image Processing. She is the member of ISTE professional society and she has more than 30 papers in National/International Conferences/Journals to her credit.

Julian Scott Yeomans is a Professor of Operations Management and Information Systems at York University's Schulich School of Business in Toronto. He holds degrees in mathematics, environmental engineering, and management science and information systems, and teaches courses on spreadsheet-based decision support systems and VBA programming. His current research interests include simulation-optimization, modelling-to-generate-alternatives, environmental informatics, solid/hazardous waste management, remanufacturing and reverse logistics, and the optimal dehydration of fruits, vegetables and fungi.

Fatima-Zohra Younsi is Senior lecturer in computer science at department of Science and Technic in University of Abdelhamid Ibn Badis, Algeria, where she has been since 2009. She received her engineer degree in computer science from the University of Oran Es-Senia, Algeria in 2004. She also obtained her PhD degree in 2016 from the University of Oran1, Algeria and the University of Lyon 2, France. Her current research interests span both data analysis and epidemic surveillance. Much of her work has been on improving the understanding, design, and performance of decisional information systems, mainly through the application of Geographic Information System (GIS), social network analysis, Business intelligence (BI), Artificial Neural Network and mathematical modeling.

Merouane Zoubeidi is a director strategic pilotage in the Algerian Oil Company (Sonatrach Group). He finalizes his thesis at the LINFI Laboratory in the University of Biskra. His current research interests include semantic interoperability, ontology, multi-agent systems and web techniques.

Index

I

J

K

M

O

P

R

S

T

U

V

W

www.ingramcontent.com/pod-product-compliance
Lightning Source LLC
LaVergne TN
LVHW060421300926
849162LV00006B/1494